SOUTHEAST ASIA

FODOR'S TRAVEL GUIDES

are compiled, researched and edited by an international team of travel writers, field correspondents and editors. The series, which now almost covers the globe, was founded by Eugene Fodor in 1936.

OFFICES

New York & London

Fodor's Southeast Asia:

Editor: Debra Bernardi

Principal Area Editor: Robin J. Danhorn

Area Editors: Larry Francia, Don Shapiro

Contributing Editor: Lee Buenaventura

Drawings: Frances Hedges, Kaminura Kyoichi, Michael Kaplan

Cartography: Leslie S. Haywood, Pictograph

FODOR'S®

SOUTHEAST ASIA 1986

FODOR'S TRAVEL GUIDES
New York & London

ISBN 0-679-01275-3 (Traveltex)
ISBN 0-340-38384-4 (Hodder & Stoughton edition)

All the following Guides are current (most of them also in the Hodder and Stoughton British edition).

FODOR'S COUNTRY AND AREA TITLES:

AUSTRALIA, NEW ZEALAND AND SOUTH PACIFIC
AUSTRIA
BELGIUM AND LUXEMBOURG
BERMUDA
BRAZIL
CANADA
CANADA'S MARITIME PROVINCES
CARIBBEAN AND BAHAMAS
CENTRAL AMERICA
EASTERN EUROPE
EGYPT
EUROPE
FRANCE
GERMANY
GREAT BRITAIN
GREECE
HOLLAND
INDIA, NEPAL, AND SRI LANKA
IRELAND
ISRAEL
ITALY
JAPAN
JORDAN AND HOLY LAND
KOREA
MEXICO
NORTH AFRICA
PEOPLE'S REPUBLIC OF CHINA
PORTUGAL
SCANDINAVIA
SCOTLAND
SOUTH AMERICA
SOUTHEAST ASIA
SOVIET UNION
SPAIN
SWITZERLAND
TURKEY
YUGOSLAVIA

CITY GUIDES:

AMSTERDAM
BEIJING, GUANGZHOU, SHANGHAI
BOSTON
CHICAGO
DALLAS AND FORT WORTH
GREATER MIAMI
HONG KONG
HOUSTON
LISBON
LONDON
LOS ANGELES
MADRID
MEXICO CITY AND ACAPULCO
MUNICH
NEW ORLEANS
NEW YORK CITY
PARIS
ROME
SAN DIEGO
SAN FRANCISCO
STOCKHOLM, COPENHAGEN, OSLO, HELSINKI, AND REYKJAVIK
TOKYO
TORONTO
VIENNA
WASHINGTON, D.C.

FODOR'S BUDGET SERIES:

BUDGET BRITAIN
BUDGET CANADA
BUDGET CARIBBEAN
BUDGET EUROPE
BUDGET FRANCE
BUDGET GERMANY
BUDGET HAWAII
BUDGET ITALY
BUDGET JAPAN
BUDGET LONDON
BUDGET MEXICO
BUDGET SCANDINAVIA
BUDGET SPAIN
BUDGET TRAVEL IN AMERICA

USA GUIDES:

ALASKA
CALIFORNIA
CAPE COD
COLORADO
FAR WEST
FLORIDA
HAWAII
NEW ENGLAND
PACIFIC NORTH COAST
PENNSYLVANIA
SOUTH
TEXAS
USA (in one volume)

GOOD TIME TRAVEL GUIDES:

ACAPULCO
MONTREAL
OAHU
SAN FRANCISCO

MANUFACTURED IN THE UNITED STATES OF AMERICA
10 9 8 7 6 5 4 3 2 1

CONTENTS

FOREWORD

Traveling in the East is an exceptional experience for any Westerner. The Orient is ancient and mystical and even its most modern cities seem to have few similarities to their Occidental counterparts.

Southeast Asia is a diverse area steeped in tradition and religion and *Fodor's Southeast Asia* has been written to help you understand and appreciate this remarkable land. We have attempted to describe and explain each country to you and to help you decide where you want to go and what you want to do once you get there. Since there are a chaos of possibilities tempting travelers to Southeast Asia, we have concentrated on giving you the broadest range of choices within each country and presented selections that will be safe, solid, and of value to you. The descriptions we provide are just enough for you to make your own choices from among our selections based on your own tastes and pocketbook—but you'll find your money goes far in most places in Southeast Asia. We have also provided essays to introduce you to the Southeast Asian way of life, history, culture, and religion. In addition, we have provided tourist phrases in a number of different Oriental languages to help you get along.

The selections and comments in *Fodor's Southeast Asia* are based on the editor's personal experiences. We feel that our first responsibility is to inform and protect you, the reader.

Errors are bound to creep into any travel guide, however. We go to press in the summer of the year and much change can and will occur in Southeast Asia even while we are on press and during the succeeding 12 months or so when this edition is on sale. We cannot, therefore, be responsible for the sudden closing of a restaurant or hotel or price changes that may occur. We sincerely welcome letters from readers on these changes, or from those whose opinions differ from ours. Send your letters to the editors at:

In the United States: Fodor's Travel Guides, 2 Park Ave., New York, New York 10016.

In Great Britian: Fodor's Travel Guides, 9–10 Market Place, London W1N 7AG, England.

FACTS AT YOUR FINGERTIPS

FACTS AT YOUR FINGERTIPS

PLANNING YOUR TRIP. First-time travelers to a new destination area usually fall into the trap of trying to cram too much into their available schedule. This is particularly true in Asia, which is so packed with touristic temptations. If one has only two weeks available, then three major destinations are about the most that can be handled comfortably, with stopovers in perhaps two other smaller attractions. To attempt more will result in fatigue, frustration at not being able to see everything and, probably, complete mental indigestion. A two-week itinerary might thus cover Taipei, Hong Kong, and Bangkok, with side trips to Sun Moon Lake in Taiwan and Pattaya Beach in Thailand.

A three-week itinerary could include up to five major touring centers, say the above three, plus Singapore and Bali; but even this would probably seem tiring.

Touring Asia can be an exhausting business, partly because of the hot tropical climate, partly because one is likely to be leading a much more active life than usual due to all the sightseeing and partly due to the strangeness and unfamiliarity of the whole experience, which will make this a drain on one's mental and well as physical energies.

Traveling between destinations is also likely to be something of a strain, with each major journey taking up to a full day, from checking out of the hotel in one place, to being fully installed in the next. So a five-destination trip involves up to five days of travel and adjustment to new places—a major portion of the total three-week period available. With each major Oriental city or sightseeing destination demanding such a lot of energy it is advisable to include at least one complete day of rest, free of major sightseeing or shopping commitments, for every week "on the road."

From studying the various country chapters of this book you will be able to plan your own itineraries around the attractions and destinations you find most appealing, allowing, perhaps, a day or two in small or limited-interest places, up to a week in major sightseeing centers.

There are daily air services, at least, between most neighboring destinations in the Southeast Asia region, so there are not likely to be many serious time limitations dictated by travel or flight delays, this allows you to spend any number of days in each place. The following outline of sample itineraries gives you a range of varied touristic experiences, combining some relaxation breaks with sightseeing and shopping opportunities, cities and countryside, and a not-too-strenuous travel itinerary. They could all cover either point-to-point "trans-Asian" itineraries between two major aviation gateways to the region, or be operated on a "circle" plan back to a single gateway point.

Another possibility to get the most from an Asian holiday is to select one major center, say Bangkok, and then take trips radiating out to other tour destinations, such as Burma, Malaysia, Singapore, and Hong Kong/Macau.

Three sample Two-Week Itineraries:

1) Tokyo (gateway)–Taipei/Taiwan–Hong Kong–Bangkok/Pattaya Beach (departing point, Bangkok).
2) Hong Kong (gateway)–Macau–Manila–Singapore–Jakarta/Bali–Singapore (departure point).
3) Bangkok–Malaysia/Penang/Kuala Lumpur and Malacca–Singapore and/or Hong Kong (departure point).

Three sample Three-Week Itineraries

1) Bangkok–Malaysia–Singapore–Bali–Hong Kong–Taipei.
2) Hong Kong–Macau–Philippines–Singapore–Bali.
3) Bangkok–Burma–Singapore–Hong Kong.

Three sample Four-Week Itineraries

1) Taipei–Hong Kong–Macau–Bangkok–North or South Thailand–Burma–Singapore–Jakarta–Bali.
2) Hong Kong–Manila–North and South Philippines–Brunei–Singapore–Penang–Sumatra–Bangkok.
3) Bangkok–Pattaya–overland through Malaysia to Singapore–Jakarta–Java–Bali–Hong Kong–Macau–Tokyo.

A sample Two-Month Itinerary

Tokyo–Taipei/Taiwan–Hong Kong/Macau–Bangkok/Chiang Mai/Pattaya–Burma–Bangkok–Malaysia (overland), Penang/Kuala Lumpur–Singapore–Jakarta–overland through Java–Bali–Singapore–Sarawak–Brunei–Sabah–Manila/Cebu/Zamboanga–Hong Kong.

WHAT WILL IT COST? "What to say, lah?" is one answer—"Mai pen rai" is another. No, we're not being obscure or facetious. The question of budgeting for costs can only be answered honestly using these two Asian phrases. Singaporenas, when asked a question to which there is no definite answer, simply shrug their shoulders and smilingly reply, "What to say, lah?"—"lah" being a suffix which implies friendliness without commitment. "Mai pen rai" means in Thai: "never mind it'll all work out."

We realize that these very Asian answers do not help as you sit working out a budget amid a welter of confusing and conflicting information. But it might be a good idea to keep them in mind because prices in Southeast Asia (as in the rest of the world) are rising fast, with little indication of stopping.

Two factors should be kept in mind as you plan your trip: *First,* the area has a relatively high rate of inflation and travel costs within the region, and domestically within each country may seem quite high compared to Europe and the USA. Hotel and restaurant cost levels vary considerably, however, and it pays to shop around. *The second factor,* which modifies the first, is that for the last few years, Asian countries have been preparing for a massive tourist influx and are making great efforts to keep new facilities occupied. Indeed, some places, have overbuilt so much that the careful traveler should be able to get more for his money.

Southeast Asia generally has never provided much for the middle-income tourist. Travelers to this region find excellent first-class and deluxe hotels, restaurants, and transport where their dollars will buy more luxury and better service than they would in Europe or the United States. On the other hand, those who are on a very tight budget and are willing to travel third class (which means staying in small local hotels, eating at street stalls, or in neighborhood restaurants, and traveling by bus or third-class train) will also discover a network of available facilities. In between, one possible means is group travel, where you will be able to take advantage of discount rates and still enjoy the better facilities.

If you are traveling on an individual basis you should divide your costs into four main categories: air travel, which includes your return fare home as well as some of your travel within the region; local transport and touring; accommodation and food; and shopping.

Transportation will take the biggest bite of your budget. Air fares are high, but remember, you will be coming halfway around the world—some will even be circumnavigating the globe. A number of companies based mainly in Britain and Germany run very inexpensive charter flights between Europe and Southeast Asia. These flights originate in Europe and usually must be booked there. They are in no way substandard but offer regular, scheduled service and provide meals, drinks and attendants. The term "charter" merely means that there is a fixed destination with no stopovers, and that you must make prepaid, confirmed bookings well in advance. Hong Kong and Bangkok are the principal destinations, but there are flights to other centers as well.

The most comprehensive source of information on charters for students, teachers and younger travelers is the Council on International Educational Exchange, 205 E. 42nd St., New York, N.Y. 10017, 212–661–1414; 312 Sutter St., San Francisco, CA. 94108. Their *Whole World Handbook,* revised annually, is full of detailed, practical information on special situations available to students and young people, such as charter flights, Youth Hostels and hitchhiking.

Once you are there, you will be dismayed to find air travel within the region as expensive per mile as similar distances in Europe. This is a case where time equals money. Usually given a limited amount of time and an unlimited desire to see everything, most travelers prefer to fly, trimming the budget on other items such as forgoing a few sumptuous dinners. In any case, several airlines offer regional excursion rates which mean that the traveler must spend a minimum time on the journey, but with as many stops as he likes. A favorite excursion route is Hong Kong–Manila–Bangkok–Singapore–Hong Kong. Another is Singapore–Java–Bali–Singapore. Your travel agent will have the most up-to-date information on excursion rates. Do, not, however, confuse the latter with "group fares," which is another matter altogether. Most regional airlines do offer "advance purchase" (APEX) fare concessions, fixed—period excursion rates, and special prices for students.

Getting around constitutes one of the heaviest items in your budget. The quickest and best way to become familiar with a new place is to take a city tour. Despite the cattle-like handling which most tour guides seem to employ, you will learn more in a short time at a minimum cost than you would on your own. After that you will know which places you wish to see again and which to avoid. Prices for city tours, most of which last about four hours, range from $10 to $15.

After taking a city tour you will want to explore on your own. Since most Asians don't own cars, public transport is more available there than in the West. It may be slow and it will probably be crowded, but it is an excellent way to sightsee, less systematic but far more vivid and immediate than a tour-for-foreigners. And infinitely cheaper. Get on any bus or tram, observe the system, pay the few pennies required, ride to the end of the line, get off, stroll around for a while, then take the same line back to where you started. Walking short distances is pleasant in the early morning or evening, but remember Noel Coward's dictum about "mad dogs and Englishmen" and don't plan on extensive promenading in the noonday sun! In most cities, hiring a car either with or without a driver can be done, through your hotel. In major cities you can consult the *Yellow Pages* or local newspapers for bargain car rental agencies.

If you have had experience driving in Asia, you should be comfortable driving in any of the major cities and on most country roads except in Indonesia. Bear in mind, however, that in the last few years, traffic has multiplied at an enormous rate. Traffic jams are daily occurrences in every major city.

If you have never driven in Asia, we recommend that you do NOT drive yourself in the following cities: Bangkok, Manila, Jakarta, or Hong Kong.

Pedestrians, cyclists, and small children have a tendency to approach a street crossing much as they would a river—moving across slowly with the current. Pedestrians, who seemingly dart in front of your car, are assuming that you will continue at your present speed and therefore will not run over them, as they carefully proceed through the traffic.

Other drivers rarely accept one fundamental law of nature—two separate bodies cannot occupy the same space at the same time. Thus, be on the lookout for other cars, trucks, and buses that change lanes suddenly.

In an effort to regulate the increased flow of traffic, most Asian cities have introduced complicated one-way street systems. Another problem is that the street signs are often in the local scripts, or not present at all.

Car rental prices vary from country to country but throughout the region wages are lower than in the West, so employing a driver with your car is not a very expensive luxury.

Taxis are still the best means of short-distance travel, but insist on meters (except in Bangkok, where every single one has been broken for years).

Accommodations. Most people traveling in Southeast Asia spend about three nights at each stop. You will find that accommodation costs are highest in Hong Kong, Singapore, and big cities. In major cities, international hotel chains such as Inter-Continental, Holiday Inn, Hyatt or Hilton provide comfortable modern hostelries which include several restaurants, a swimming pool, tour services, shopping arcades, and helpful staff. Costs range from about $140 a night for high quality to $60 for average. (All prices quoted refer to a standard double room.) The difference between "high quality" and "average" depends on such subjective items as the thickness of the carpet, the grandeur of the lobby, the elegance of the restaurants. There is no need to pay top prices to get good service or comfortable accommodations.

In addition to visiting capital cities and commercial centers, you will almost certainly be staying at one or more resort areas, such as Penang, Pattaya, or Bali. Here hotel costs are as high (and service a bit less reliable, although much more eager) as in cities. More remote resorts such as Phuket in Thailand seem to charge less, but beware of hidden costs in transport. Once you are in an isolated resort hotel, you are at the mercy of the management, so in your planning inquire about the price of meals, etc., as well as the room rate. Generally, however, in small beach resorts, the food tends to be quite cheap, especially in restaurants outside hotels.

You might find yourself in areas where there are few recognized international hotels—such as Brunei, upcountry Indonesia, Malaysia, Thailand, or the Philippines—but where there are locally styled and managed establishments. Quality varies here, as does price, and you can sometimes find excellent bargains, accommodations that are simple but clean and comfortable for surprisingly little. In every place it pays to shop around, and don't be afraid to ask for a discount in places where you suspect hotels are less than full.

Restaurant meals, which were once Asia's best bargain, have increased in price as well as in range of styles available. Nevertheless, careful planning will allow you to try some excellent Oriental cuisine as well as superb Western cooking. Your hotel will probably have several restaurants. In the coffee shop the quality of à la carte menus tends to be mixed. Most coffee shops, however, feature set lunch and dinner menus, or buffet meals that are tasty, varied, and of good value. Cost runs upwards from $15 for three courses and beverage. Dinner in the hotel will be expensive, but everyone enjoys splurging at one of the posh European places because the food, service and ambience are uniformly good. Most international hotels employ a European chef and one or two imported cooks, so the discriminating gourmet can eat happily and, perhaps, at less cost than he would in the United States or Europe. A Western-style dinner with appetizer, entrée, salad, and dessert with coffee plus a drink or two will cost from $50 for two. On the other end of the scale, in the open-air markets of Singapore you can get a large meal for under $10. Obviously you will have to judge these local, ad hoc situations for yourself individually. We merely point out that they are there for you to try out.

Warning: Wine in Southeast Asia is expensive and selection is often limited. Because wine does not travel well to the tropics, we recommend that, unless you are a confirmed wine drinker, you order one of the many respectable Australian wines or stick to beer. Bars in hotels also tend to be very pricey in Asia by comparison to outside establishments.

Most cities have excellent restaurants outside the hotels in almost every price range. Local variations on Italian and Mexican cooking can be quite tasty and are usually in the middle price range. Consult our country-by-country listings, especially for excellent native, Chinese, and Indian restaurants.

Shopping Bargains. Asia is still a shopper's delight: bargains abound, especially such goods as local handicrafts, batik, ceramics, embroidery, basketware, gems, and jewelry, all of which make wonderful presents. Watches, cameras, pocket calculators, and transistor radios have gone up substantially over the last few years but are still cheaper in Singapore and Hong Kong than in Europe or the United States. Fine jewelry has, of course, followed the price of gold, but the workmanship of Asian jewelers remains superb, especially in Hong Kong. Nearly every country has become sensitive about the illegal export of antiques (especially Chinese export porcelain, carvings, and Thai bronzes), check with your dealer about export licenses and permission. Some countries prohibit the export of religious items or ethnic artifacts. Folk art is an area in which you may still find good buys if you distinguish between what Asians make to use themselves and the "souvenirs" displayed in the shops of most tourist hotels; and it requires no permits.

Budget Traveling

There can be a very exact inverse relationship between time and money when you travel. The more time you can spend, the less money you need spend. And vice versa. If you are short of time you will have to spend more money—to ensure precise connections, guaranteed reservations, tours exactly when you need them, no looking around, etc. Pinch-penny travel in Asia is best if you have an open schedule, can do plenty of comparison shopping for hotels and meals, can enjoy the picturesque but sometimes erratic aspects of local transportation, and do not always require luxury-international standards in everything you touch or use. If you are on a limited time budget, you must fly, otherwise you can travel extensively by bus or train and save substantial sums.

In Malaysia, Thailand, and to some extent in the Philippines and Indonesia, you may take advantage of local tours and excursions. The best selection is available from Bangkok. A welter of tour agencies run bus tours which include adequate accommodations and meals. Booking them in advance from Europe may lead to disappointment; therefore we suggest you remain flexible and on your arrival check with local agents as to what is available. From Singapore or Bangkok, for example, you can take a 10-day tour by coach and train all the way to Chiang Mai in Northern Thailand.

In most parts of Southeast Asia, you will find small, local hotels and restaurants run by the Overseas Chinese. These vary enormously in quality. Some of them are dubious at best. But many of them are very adequate, clean, quiet, and well-run, however modest in décor. They cater to middle-class business and professional people in those countries, and single rooms in them run $10–20 and up. In Penang, for example, some of them are converted mansions and have a very charming air of slightly faded prewar elegance. In Malaysia and parts of Indonesia, there are also cheap government rest houses; and some larger cities have YMCA's. Rooms in the Chinese hotels usually have double beds, and the price is the same for one person or for two. Bear this in mind, for if you assume that you must pay more for double occupancy, the extra money will be blandly accepted. The announced rates are often subject to bargaining.

In Bangkok, most of these Chinese-owned hotels are clustered around the Hualampong railway station. In Hong Kong, they are mostly on the Kowloon side of the harbor; and in Taipei, they are in the older part of the city, near the Yuan Huan Circle. In Kuala Lumpur, they are in Jalan Tuanku Abdul Rahman; and in Manila, in the Ermita and Quiapo sections. In Singapore, Bencoolen Street and Beach Road are good areas for cheap accommodations.

After you have been in any country for two or three days, you can form a good idea of the range of local conditions, and, having inquired and compared, choose what suits you. And when you arrive in a given country, remember that even though you may not stay in a large, expensive hotel, such hotels are more and more becoming self-contained little cities in themselves and you can use them very conveniently for shops, agencies, and sources of information and arrangements of all kinds.

Many budget travelers look like "hippies" with their long hair, casual clothes, and backpacks. This is misleading. Although many may have spent months traveling, few are genuine drop-outs. Most are students, or professional people —doctors, engineers, teachers—who are taking a year off for "The Grand Tour" in the modern manner. These people will be your best source of information about cheap accommodations ($15 a night and less) and meals ($8 a day). Don't be shy about stopping a hairy pale-face to ask for advice; in most cases the genuine traveler is friendly and eager to be helpful. As mentioned above, the *Council on International Educational Exchange,* 205 E. 42nd St., New York, N.Y. 10017, is the most important source of leads for budget travel, and their *Whole World Handbook* contains a wealth of information useful not only to students and travelers under 25.

The Youth Hostel movement is spreading in Asia; Hong Kong, Indonesia, Malaysia, the Philippines, and Thailand all have hostels now, but facilities tend to be primitive. In larger cities, YMCAs are also available (Hong Kong and Bangkok, for example).

Moderate-Cost Traveling

The middle-class traveler will do well to check on the many Group Tours originating from Europe or the United States. These are all-inclusive tours which will provide your airfare, accommodations, sightseeing tours, and some meals. The advantages are obvious: lower costs, arranged tours, and knowledgeable guides who will handle all the nuisances of baggage, transport, and airport procedures. The disadvantage is also obvious. Throughout your trip, you will be with the same group of people, and much of your travel time will be devoted to interpersonal relationships. You will make some lifelong friends . . . and, maybe, at least one enemy. *Thai International Airway's* "Royal Orchid Holidays" cover the region and are very good value; they allow for people to travel as individuals, rather than in a group.

Scores of agencies offer comprehensive tours of Asia. Among the experienced ones are *Sovereign* and *Speedbird (British Airways), Kuoni Houlders, Thomas Cook, Maupintour,* and *Travcoa.* Specialty tours such as *Quester Nature Tours* and the *Lindblad Safaris* are well known for their exciting and unique itineraries. There are many other agencies, most of them reliable, experienced, and friendly. Our advice is to shop around, and if possible consult with friends (or friends of friends) for advice.

Summing up, then, Asia is likely to cost more than Europe because it has less of the highly developed middle range of accommodations that have made Europe such a tempting target. Western ways of living—space, furniture, food, sanitation, services, privacy, quiet, and the like—are largely imported ways, foreign ways, in Asia, so you must pay accordingly. How much of these you require depends on you individually—your age, health, habits, temperament, interests, and flexibility. And very much on how much time you have, for if your visit to Asia must be tightly scheduled you will need reservations, and these can be made only on a relatively expensive level. Standardized, "international" (i.e., Americanized Western) style comfort and luxury are now available in every major center in Asia, and many minor ones as well. And because these hotels are mostly new, they are often far superior to most of the accommodations available in, say, Paris. Hotels of this kind are standardized, reliable, familiar, comfortable, and convenient. But they are also uniform, artificial, and expensive. They are *in,* but not *of,* Asia. For first-class accommodations, three reasonable Western meals, and city sightseeing by scheduled coach tours, figure up to U.S. $130 per person per day. For moderate accommodations and meals figure on about $90.

Specific luxuries that you may be used to, such as cigarettes, magazines, liquor, etc., are likely to cost more (up to twice as much) in Asia. Asian beers are excellent. But Asian traditional drinks may well be an acquired taste. English-language newspapers and magazines are published in almost every country in Asia, and you would do much better to read this local press than to seek your own. However, *Newsweek* and *Time* have Asian editions which are up to the minute and which carry international news. Asian tobaccos are not always to Western taste, even though the Philippines export to Western manufacturers. Philippine cigars are good, and Asian cigarettes come in a choice of price ranges (which is not the case in America). Most requirements can be purchased in Asia, but they may not be the brands to which you are used.

The most important single factor will always be your own personal demands and expectations in the way of accustomed comfort and consumption patterns. If you insist on living exactly as you would at home (or better!) you can certainly do so; but if you can try other people's ways of doing things, it can be much cheaper. International-style hotels are available all over Asia. Really cheap accommodations are for the young and adventurous. Travel in the middle range will require some adjustment on your part, but it can be done.

The vital factor is time, for, paradoxically, the more time you can spend in Asia, the more money you can save doing it. The point is quite simple.

SOURCES OF INFORMATION. Every Asian country has a national tourist promotion organization that supplies free information. Some of this is available through embassies. Or, write to the following:

Entire Pacific Area, *Pacific Area Travel Association* 228 Grant Ave., San Francisco, Ca. 94108.

Hong Kong. There are 7 *Hong Kong Tourist Ass'n* offices in the U.S.A.: 421 Powell St., Suite 200, San Francisco, Ca. 94102; 548 Fifth Ave., N.Y. 10036; 333 North Michigan Ave., Chicago, Ill. 60601; 1411 4th Ave., Room 1327, Seattle, Wa. 98101; 5757 W. Century Blvd., Suite 330, Los Angeles, Ca., 90045;

1000 Connecticut Ave., N.W., Washington, D.C. 20036; 777 Brickell Ave., Miami, FL. 33131.

In England, HKTA is at 125 Pall Mall, London SW1Y 5EA. The HKTA also has offices in Frankfurt, Paris, Rome, Sydney, Auckland, Tokyo, and other cities within Southeast Asia.

Macau. It is easy to get information about Macau in Hong Kong at *Macau Tourist Information* Bureau, 1729 Star House, Kowloon. In the U.S., MTIB, P.O. Box 1860, 3133 Lake Hollywood Dr., Los Angeles, Ca. 90078; 608 Fifth Ave., Suite 309, New York, NY 10020; and Box 37157, Honolulu, HI 96837. In Britain, *Macau Information,* 13 Dover St., London W1. In Canada, 150 Dundes St. W., Toronto, Ontario M5G 1Z6. The MTIB also has offices in Frankfurt, Tokyo, and major Southeast Asian cities.

Taiwan. Write directly to *Taiwan Visitors Association,* 1 World Trade Center, Suite 8855, New York, N.Y. 10048; 166 Geary St., Suite 1605, San Francisco, Ca. 94108; 3325 Wilshire Blvd., Suite 515, Los Angeles, Ca. 90010.

Thailand. Information available at any of these *Tourism Authority of Thailand* offices: *U.S.:* 5 World Trade Center, Suite 2449, New York, N.Y. 10048; 3440 Wilshire Blvd., Los Angeles, Ca. 90010. *London:* 9 Stafford St., W1. The TAT also has offices in Frankfurt, Paris, Tokyo, Singapore, and Kuala Lumpur.

Burma. You will need no more information than this book. For visas, apply to the Embassy of Burma, 2300 S St., N.W. Washington, D.C., 20008; or to the Consulate General of Burma, 10 E. 77 St., New York, N.Y. 10021. The simplest way is to buy your airline ticket from Union of Burma Airways or Thai International in Bangkok and have a local agent handle the visa work for you, or work through a local tour agency. In Britain: Burmese Embassy, 19a Charles St., London W1.

Malaysia. Write directly to the *Malaysia Tourist Information Center,* Transamerica Building, 600 Montgomery St., 5th Floor, San Francisco, Ca. 94111. In Britain: *Tourist Development Corporation of Malaysia,* 17 Curzon St., London W1. The MTC also has offices in Frankfurt, Tokyo, Hong Kong, Bangkok, Singapore, and Sydney.

Singapore. You can write directly to or visit *Tourist Promotion Board,* 342 Madison Ave., New York, N.Y. 10017; 251 Post St., San Francisco, Ca. 94108. In Britain: 33 Heddon St., London W1. The STPB also has offices in Frankfurt, Paris, Perth, Hong Kong, Tokyo, Zurich, and Auckland, and in New York at 342 Madison Ave. 10173.

Indonesia. A Tourist Promotion Board is maintained at 3457 Wilshire Blvd., Los Angeles, Ca. 90010. In Europe, tourism promotion is handled from Frankfurt, Germany, Wiessenhutlenplatz 26, D-6000.

Philippines. The Philippine *Ministry of Tourism* maintains overseas offices at the Philippine Center, 556 Fifth Ave., New York, N.Y. 10036; 3460 Wilshire Blvd., Suite 1212, Los Angeles, Ca. 90010; 30 N. Michigan Ave., Suite 1111, Chicago, Ill. 60602; and in Canada at 60 Bloor St. W., Suite 1204, Toronto, Ontario M4W 3B8. In Australia: at Philippine Center Bldg., 27–33 Wentworth Ave., Sydney, N.S.W., 2010. In Britain: *Philippine Tourist Office,* 199 Piccadilly, London W1.

HOW TO GET TO SOUTHEAST ASIA. The four ways are obviously land, sea, air, and a combination of these. **From North America,** you can go by air or sea, or a combination of these. There are four possibilities to look into when you plan your trip. They are: 1) the maximum use of stopover privileges and side trips at little or no extra cost on your airline ticket; 2) including many more places for relatively little extra, and going around the

Pacific Basin rather than retracing the same route when you head back; 3) various combinations of plane and ship that will give you greater variety, and chances to rest in between countries and bouts of sightseeing; 4) side trips by local airlines and road or rail companies within Southeast Asia, if you have time and can go with an open schedule.

From Europe there is one main land route—by express bus from major northern cities, via Istanbul, Erzerum, Tabriz, to Teheran, then Meshed, Herat, Kandahar, Kabul, Peshawar, Lahore, and Delhi to Nepal; after that, travelers usually reach Southeast Asia by air. However, during recent years, political conditions in Turkey, Iran, and Afghanistan made travel along this formerly popular route impossible. At press time (mid-1985), it is still impossible to pass safely through Iran or Afghanistan.

From Europe by air is either the "great circle" route, over Russia, or by the southern route with a variety of interesting stopovers as time permits. Shortest flying time from Europe is over Russia; from London or Paris to Bangkok is 12¾ hours. Chartered flights from Europe and North America to Hong Kong and Bangkok are frequent. From Europe, England and Germany are the main centers. From the U.S. West Coast the quickest route is the long flight over the Pacific, with the usual gateways in Asia being Tokyo or Hong Kong.

GETTING THERE BY AIR. Southeast Asia is well served by air from Europe, North America, Australia, and New Zealand. While few people who fly these days are seduced by glossy advertisements that imply that long plane journeys are as exciting as the destination they are bound for, it must be admitted that some of the world's best airlines are based in the Pacific area. There are exceptions, but the carriers of the East usually maintain a level of operating efficiency equal to that of most Western airlines while tending to offer more attentive cabin staff and better food and drink.

As we go into print, *Thai International* and *S.I.A.* rank highest among passengers in the popularity stakes. On long-haul flights, they are noted for superior in-flight service. Both airlines operate the latest B-747s and offer links from America with the Orient as well as Europe and Australia.

Several trans-Pacific airlines have arrangements with steamship companies for those who wish to fly across in one direction and return by ship. These arrangements vary from year to year and are often part of specific cruise packages so it is best to check with a travel agent or shipping company such as *Holland American Cruises, Princess Cruises,* or *Royal Viking Line.*

From North America

Apart from *Pan Am's* regular non-stop 747SP service between New York and Tokyo, Hong Kong and Singapore, the fastest flights to the East depart from the West Coast and Hawaii. Tokyo is well served from Vancouver, Seattle, San Francisco, Los Angeles, and Honolulu by *Japan Airlines, Pan Am, Northwest Orient, S.I.A., Korean* and *Thai International,* but if you do not wish to visit Japan en route to Southeast Asia or leave it until you are on your way home, other possibilities are: San Francisco-Manila *(Philippine Airlines);* San Francisco-Taipei *(China Airlines* 747SP nonstop); San Francisco-Hong Kong *(Pan Am* 747SP nonstop).

Bonus Stopovers: If you have flown out direct, why not return home via the South Seas and Australia? For an extra charge it may be possible to substantially broaden the ticket to include Sydney, Fiji, and Tahiti.

While the extra charge is substantial, it is still a long way from what you would be charged to make a separate trip to the South Seas and Australia. Please check with your travel agent for "excursion" fares from America's west coast, and return, and other special fares.

The special Circle Pacific fare is known by most large tour operators and is growing increasingly popular. However, few persons outside the travel business are as yet aware of this outstanding travel offer. You may have to specifically request it when making a booking because it is little publicized, and travel agency personnel are still learning about it. Kuoni Travel is one reputable tour operator that has featured Circle Pacific tours in the past. Since offerings and conditions change frequently, we cannot emphasize enough the importance of consulting a travel agent with experience in booking passage to this corner of the world.

Supposing you have decided on a trip through Southeast Asia ending at Singapore, a Circle Pacific routing will allow you optional stopovers at Honolulu and Taipei, and then to Hong Kong, a short 501 miles farther. There are direct flights from Hong Kong to Bangkok, from where you then turn south to Malaysia. Between Bangkok and Singapore a stop may be made at Phuket, Kuala Lumpur or Penang.

What about the return trip to Los Angeles and side trips in the area? If you wish to visit Manila, a routing can be set up for you. For visits to Burma and Bali which may be reached through Bangkok and Jakarta, there is usually a surcharge depending on the complete routing.

Routing via the South Pacific. Returning to the U.S., you may fly from Singapore to Sydney, Australia. After visiting Australia, a stop may be made at Noumea, New Caledonia, or Auckland, New Zealand. Then comes Fiji, an island group that has been gaining increasing attention.

Next follows Papeete, Tahiti, your final stopover point before returning to Los Angeles. Not only will you have covered Southeast Asia but you also will have broadened the scope of your trip to take in a widely contrasting area of the Pacific, Australia, and the South Seas.

In Australia, Sydney may, of course, be used as a base for optional side trips to Melbourne, Queensland, and the Outback. There is also direct service between Southeast Asian cities and Darwin, Perth, Brisbane, and Melbourne.

Circling the North Pacific. Supposing you are not going as far as Singapore, what stopovers may be made on a New York/Hong Kong ticket via the Pacific? Leaving New York you can fly first to San Francisco or Los Angeles and then cross to Honolulu. After a stopover in Hawaii, you have a choice of onward routings. You may fly first to Manila and then into Hong Kong or wing west from Honolulu to Tokyo and then into Hong Kong. On a more northerly routing, Anchorage may be included. This takes you from New York to the Alaska city, then via Tokyo into Hong Kong. Circle trips can be constructed to give you Hawaii going to the Orient, and Alaska returning from it.

Tokyo, Seoul, Taipei, and Manila may be included between New York and Hong Kong.

From Britain and the Continent

Over recent years point-to-point flight times have been substantially reduced between Europe and Asia by the reduction of the number of intermediate stops. Overall flying time is now usually 12–14 hours. London, Zurich, and Frankfurt are among the best European departure points. *British Airways* and *Singapore Airlines* maintain daily jumbo jet flights between London and Singapore. The route to Bangkok from London is shared by *British Airways* and *Thai International* three times a week; to Kuala Lumpur, *British Airways* with the four times a week services and *Malaysian Airline System (MAS);* Hong Kong is reached daily by *British Airways* or by *Cathay Pacific.* Other countries in this guide can be reached from London by making connections in Europe and/or Asia. From the Continent all the major European airlines fly to various destinations in Southeast Asia, often with non- or one-stop services.

Stopovers en route to Southeast Asia are not as enticing for travelers from Britain and the Continent as they once were because of the wide range of low-cost promotional APEX and point-to-point fares now available. The Advance Purchase Excursion Fares (APEX) can be booked only one month in advance. Charter flights (without advance-purchase restrictions), either one-way or round-trip, are available from the United Kingdom, Germany, and Scandinavia, though it is quite common for "charter" passengers to find themselves on scheduled flights.

There is little doubt that nowhere else in the world are the airfare regulations broken more readily by certain travel agents than between Europe and Southeast Asia. The advertisements of the national press in Britain and the London weekly entertainment magazine, *Time Out,* will tell you all about cheap flights; elsewhere watch the local press. Having said all that, if you are prepared to pay much more than an APEX fare you will find that the ordinary first- or economy-class fare between Europe and Bali is nearly as much as a round-the-world ticket and free stopovers could be taken almost everywhere in a circumnavigation of the globe providing you kept moving in roughly the same direction. For those who like the extra comfort of first class, but can only afford the economy class fare, a good compromise is the business class services available on most carriers in Asia.

From Australia

Australians know that Sydney, Melbourne, and Perth, and to a lesser extent Brisbane and Darwin, are gateway cities to Southeast Asia whose capitals are linked by Qantas Australian Airways and Singapore Airlines, Cathay Pacific (Hong Kong), Thai International (Bangkok), Garuda (Jakarta), and Royal Brunei. Some stopovers are available on full first- or economy-class tickets but again there are cheaper excursion fares that do not always permit them so check with your travel agent or airline.

AIR TRAVEL TIPS

International air travel is in a constant state of flux, although the fluctuations in prices to the Orient are not quite as drastic as those on North American/European routes. Nonetheless, it behooves you to check with a travel agent or with several airlines before booking passage—even typical economy fares between Los Angeles and Hong Kong, for example, can vary by several hundred dollars depending on how long in advance the reservation is made (and paid for), how long a stay is involved, whether any land arrangements are tied in, how many stopovers are included and other factors.

The former distinction between charter or "supplemental" carriers and regularly scheduled airlines is a blurry one, with some alleged "charter" tour packagers simply block-booking seats on major airlines at reduced prices, and with major airlines offering special charter-like prices in order to boost travel on certain routes during certain periods. Regardless of formal status, *all* flights must meet the same U.S. federal government standards of aircraft maintenance and safety, crew qualifications, and reliability. Thus, though there will be minor variations in meals and frills of service, you are just as safe on a charter flight as on the most expensive scheduled flight.

Southeast Asia is best served from such West Coast cities as Vancouver, Seattle, San Francisco, and Los Angeles and by such airlines as *Japan, Northwest Orient, Philippine, Singapore, Pan Am,* and others. Generally speaking, the cheapest fares are going to be those available on charters or through package tour operators. Frequently, you may do well booking an entire package even if you don't plan to do any sightseeing with the tour or plan to use only a few of the hotels en route. Adding some of your own stops will probably still work out cheaper than booking the entire trip independently. The next best group of fares are known as APEX. Basic requirements are round-trip advance booking and a prescribed minimum stay. Certain changes are allowed on standard APEX bookings, usually for a service charge.

There are a host of other fare groupings, ranging from full-fare economy (generally used by business travelers) right up to first class. All of these fares, and the restrictions that govern them, are constantly changing depending on the time of year (summer peak, winter low, fall, and spring "shoulder" periods), how heavy competition is at any given moment and how well-traveled a particular route is.

An unusually lucid and systematic survey of the whole situation, with candid appraisals of the advantages and disadvantages of the various alternatives, is *How to Fly For Less, A Consumer's Guide to Low Cost Air Charters and Other Travel Bargains,* by Jens Jurgen, published by Travel Information Bureau, 44 County Line Rd., Farmingdale, N.Y. 11735. In addition to a detailed discussion of the ins and outs of the charter-flight business, it contains listings of charter-flight programs by destination and a directory of charter and tour operators. And good for initial "comparison shopping" are the travel sections of most major Sunday newspapers, which are invariably overflowing with enticing charter and package-tour offerings.

Bumping. A confirmed reservation does not necessarily guarantee a seat—check the wording of your ticket agreement. Airlines tend to overbook to ensure against cancellations and sometimes someone gets left behind or "bumped." Make sure your ticket's in order, comply with instructions, check-in at the right place and the right time, and if you're bumped it is their responsibility. *Stay put and protest,* often and firmly. Don't leave the check-in areas so you don't go out of sight and mind. The airline should cover all extra costs, meals and accommodation, incurred by the delay and they may even give you compensation relative to the time delayed and the distance of the flight. *Always reconfirm your onward reservation within 72 hours of departure.*

Baggage Handling.

Don't pack valuables—jewelry, important papers, money and travelers' checks. They should be close to you at all times. And don't leave them unattended at your seat if you leave the aircraft during transit stops.

Lock each item and put name and address labels both inside and outside.

Ensure that the check-in clerk puts the correct destination on the baggage tag and fixes it on properly.

Check that he puts the correct destination on the baggage claim tag attached to your passenger ticket.

Keep your baggage within the free allowance—excess baggage charges can prove very expensive.

If, by unlikely chance, your baggage doesn't appear on arrival, tell the airline representative immediately, so they have the details necessary to start their tracing system straightaway. Nowadays this tracing system is usually very quick and efficient, but if you do lose everything, even for a short while, the airline should compensate you financially.

Cameras and Film. Don't leave already exposed film in your pockets or in any hand luggage while passing through airport X-ray machines. The process can sometimes fog the film and you may find a whole trip's photographs ruined. It is worth investing in a product called *Filmashield,* a lead-laminated pouch. It stores flat when not in use and holds quite a lot of film—or, indeed, your camera with half-used film in it. It is available in many countries: SIMA Products Corp., 4001 W. Devon Ave., Chicago, IL 60646; 312–286–2333.

One final important point to remember. You may not use either portable radios or television sets on board aircraft, since they interfere with the plane's communications system. Calculators, portable tape recorders, and hearing aids are no problem.

GETTING THERE BY SEA. Most areas of Southeast Asia are accessible via sea, with a few cruise liners including major Far East ports on their schedules. Accommodations usually have to be booked well in advance. Cruise ships provide a variety of entertainment programs en route.

Special cruises to Southeast Asia, frequently as part of round-the-world itineraries, are operated by leading travel agents and the smartest shipping lines. The ships may call at Singapore, Pattaya (for Bangkok), Hong Kong, Bali, Colombo, Penang, Yokohama, or Hawaii. They sometimes visit the South Seas, and less well known ports in Asia, too; itineraries vary considerably.

Exact schedules not available at press time, so check with a travel agent or the shipline. Most departures of world cruises are from New York, most arrivals on the West Coast. From Britain, departures and arrivals are at Southampton.

From North America

American President Lines, 1950 Franklin St., Oakland, Ca. 94612. Trans-Pacific service, now limited to freighters, still has limited passenger accommodation of 12 per ship. Voyages start from Oakland or Seattle; prices and duration of voyage vary according to route taken.

The simplest way to book freighter accommodations is through a specialist in freighter travel. But you may also write directly to the shipping company for schedules, space and rates.

From Europe

There are very few companies plying from Europe to Southeast Asia these days. Cruise operators, sometimes round-the-world ones, still run quite intriguing forays to the area. A big highlight of world trips is a visit to China, which in this case means Shanghai and Canton. Ask your travel agent for the latest possibilities available in this area; they change every year, but the trend is toward more and more.

TRAVEL AGENTS. The critical issues in choosing a travel agent are how knowledgeable that person is about travel and how reliable his or her bookings are, regardless of whether you are looking for a package tour or planning to go it independently. The cost will be substantially the same whether you go to a major tour operator such as *Maupintour, American Express, Thos. Cook & Son,* and *Olson's,* or to the small agency around the corner: most commissions are paid by airlines, hotels, and tour operators.

With trips as costly and often with as many stopovers as those to Southeast Asia, the importance of a travel agent is not merely for the making of reservations, however. In such situations, a good travel agent familiar with the variety of routing possibilities within the area can help tailor a trip to your specific needs, interests, and budget. In the case of package tours, you want to be sure that the tour operator can deliver the package being offered. Here again, a local travel agent can be helpful by advising you on the reliability of a tour packager and how realistic a given tour prospectus is in terms of how much time you want to spend in transit and how much you want to be able to explore on your own.

Certainly the organizations named above have established their reputations based on reliability—the inevitable occasional foulup notwithstanding. If there is any doubt, ask whether the agent is a member of the American Society of Travel Agents (ASTA), 4400 MacArthur Blvd., N.W. Washington D.C., 20007, (202) 965–7520, or the Pacific Area Travel Association (PATA), 228 Grant Ave., San Francisco, Ca. 94108; membership in either is generally a good sign of reliability. In the United Kingdom, contact ABTA (Association of British Travel Agents), 55 Newman St., London W1P 4AH.

PACKAGE TOURS. In the United States: Package tours to the whole area are many and varied. Often they begin with Japan, then proceed by way of different routings and combinations of countries, events, culture, and scenery—and via land, sea, and air travel. Typically comprehensive is Four Winds' "Complete Orient," a 23-day tour giving a good overview of the region. The itinerary includes Japan (five days), Taiwan, China, Hong Kong, Thailand, Malaysia, Singapore and Bali. Land costs alone are $3000, including all meals; airfare will be approximately another $2000. You may need a vacation after such extensive globe-trotting!

Maupintour runs a 28-day "Grand Orient" tour that costs in the vicinity of $4,800, stopping in Japan for 7 days before moving on to Taiwan, Manila, Singapore, Bangkok, and Hong Kong. A separate 25-day "South Pacific" jaunt focuses on Tahiti, New Zealand, and Fiji, and costs in the range of $4,128.

Less extravagant but equally notable for consistency in services are packages put together by *American Express* and *Percival.* The former's 14-day "Asian Highlights" stops in Tokyo, Hakone, Kyoto, Taipei, and Hong Kong, with the 20-day "Grand Asia" tour adding Bangkok and Singapore. Prices run approximately $800 and $1,250, respectively, plus airfare. Percival tours are similarly laid out and priced. All of the above can be arranged by most travel agents.

Other tour operators worth investigating include the following airlines: *Singapore,* which incidentally is frequently the airline used by other tour packagers, *Pan Am, Japan, Northwest Orient,* and *Phillippine.* Check the White Pages for telephone numbers or consult a travel agent for specific details. *Kouni,* 11 East 44 St., New York, N.Y. 10017, has a wide selection of tours that tend to be a little more budget-minded than most, as per a 15-day "Eastern Delights" covering Hong Kong, Bangkok, and Taipei for about $900 including airfare from London.

In the United Kingdom: *Bales Tours,* Bales House, Barrington Road, Dorking, Surrey, offers a number of Southeast Asia holidays, including a 14-day package taking in Hong Kong, Bangkok, and Singapore; 1985 prices start at £899.

Thomas Cook, 45 Berkeley St., London W1, has several packages of interest. The 18-day "Oriental Journey" covers Singapore, Hong Kong, Bangkok, China, and Pattaya, from £995, fully escorted; the "Eastern Experience" lasts 15 days, visiting Bangkok, Pattaya, Hong Kong, with an option to Bali, for around £749. For the more adventurous, they offer a "Thailand Golden Triangle" tour, which involves hiking, visits to the Hill Tribes, and some sleeping in the open. This tour lasts 18 days and costs around £785.

Kuoni Travel, 33 Maddox St., London W1, covers all the main centers. A week at a Sri Lankan beach resort costs around £600 in 1985. Or combine a coastal stay with an inland tour; 2 weeks in 1985 cost £800. Asian tours. For example, to Hong Kong, Bali, and Bangkok: 11 nights from £796. Their "Oriental Panorama" holiday lasts 14 nights and includes Singapore, Bali, Hong Kong, and Bangkok; from £942 with an optional extension at a Thai beach resort from only £42 for seven nights.

Sovereign Worldwide, West London Air Terminal, Cromwell Rd., London SW7 4ED, offers Hong Kong packages at £653–872 for 7 nights.

Swan Hellenic Tours, Ltd., Canberra House, 47 Middlesex St., London E1, has a 21-day tour covering south Thailand, Malaysia, and Singapore. From £2085 in 1985.

Speedbird, Alta House, 152 King St., London W6, offers "Orientations," multicenter tours from £765 for 17 days, and a "Golden Triangle" tour from £785, also for 17 days.

Silk Cut Travel, Meon House, Petersfield, Hampshire GU32, has an "Escape East" tour through Bangkok, Pattaya, Hong Kong, and Singapore for 18 days at around £1149.

TRAVEL DOCUMENTS. The essentials are: passport, visas, tickets (and money, credit cards, etc.). You cannot leave your own country without a passport issued by your government. Visas (permission from foreign governments to enter their countries) are granted, where required, by foreign consulates and embassies. Requirements vary, so check under *Practical Information* for each country separately. Few Asian countries still require cholera, or yellow fever immunizations, but be sure to check before you leave home. Smallpox, happy to report, has been eradicated.

CUSTOMS ENTERING SOUTHEAST ASIA. These vary greatly, so check *Practical Information* section for each country you visit. In general, however: firearms, pornography, and narcotics other than alcohol and tobacco are always forbidden. Gem-producing countries like Burma control their removal, while in Bangkok they are bargain souvenir items. Most control export of artifacts over 100 years old. In fact, taking out antiques, works of art, old religious images and the like is another touchy area. Thailand protects its national heritage strictly, whereas Singapore and Hong Kong, having none of their own, are markets for everything.

Limited to "reasonable amounts of personal use," are liquor, tobacco, watches, radios, tape recorders, cameras and film, appliances, etc. On the whole, Customs inspections are less difficult than you may think, but attitudes differ. The Philippines and Burma may be suspicious of what you bring in. (Americans often find that their most unpleasant customs experience comes upon reentering the U.S.) Customs in the U.S. and U.K. are increasingly strict on imports of any articles made from endangered animal species. This now includes such things as elephant ivory, some snake and reptile skins, furs, etc. Check at home before your trip if you're considering buying such items.

WHAT TO TAKE—PACKING. In many instances, you will be going through several different types of climate so a wardrobe will have to reflect this. The new synthetic materials are highly recommended provided they are *wash-and-wear* variety. Good cotton dresswear is excellent for any place in Southeast Asia, particularly if it is *drip-dry.* Do not bring any exotic fabrics with you as there might be some difficulty in having them laundered. It may be wise to bring your favorite toilet articles (in plastic containers to avoid breakage and reduce the weight of luggage). Make sure that bottles containing liquid are tightly capped to prevent leakage. If you are visiting Hong Kong, leave your perfume behind since this item is cheaper in the colony than in Paris. Facial tissues, American toothpaste, and other such articles can be purchased with ease in such cities as Hong Kong, Singapore, and Bangkok. The paths leading to temples in Southeast Asia can be rough, so a good pair of walking shoes is in order for sightseeing. Don't plan to buy shoes here (except in the international shopping centers of Singapore and Hong Kong): Asian feet are smaller and differently proportioned than Western ones. Pack all you will need, preferably unlaced ones for easy removal in temples, etc.

In general, for sightseeing in Asia, dress for comfort and allow for the tropic sun, by bringing along a hat and sun screen. Mosquito repellant is a good idea, too. Toilet paper is not always supplied in public places. A sweater or shawl, or in the gentleman's case, a lightweight linen jacket, will be quite sufficient for dining and evening wear in the hot Southeast Asian countries—the accent is on the casual look.

CLIMATE. Hong Kong and Macau are semitropical with three basic seasons, best September through March, though it can be cold and wet during this period. April through June is rainy, June to September is hot and humid.

Taiwan is a subtropical island, quite hot in summer, which lasts from May through October, with the occasional typhoon. During winter southern Taiwan is cool and dry while the north is often overcast and showery. The best weather is in October, November, March, and April.

Thailand is never cool, but November through February is best; the days are moderately hot, and the nights are a little cooler. March, April, and May are hot and humid. June through October is the rainy season. Bangkok temperatures are in the 80's year-round; comfort, or otherwise, depends on the humidity.

Burma, too, is semitropical, hot from March to May, rainy from June to October, cooler from November to February.

Malaysia has hot, sunny days throughout the year. Nights are generally cool. October to January is the rainiest season, temperatures year-round are in the 70's to mid-80's.

Singapore is only 90 miles from the Equator, but sea breezes and air conditioning make it fairly comfortable. Temperatures vary little the year round: 86°F. (30°C.) by day, 73°F. (23°C.) at night. Heaviest rainfall is November through January.

Indonesia is tropical year-round. Heaviest rain is December through March, but sudden showers occur anytime. January and February in Bali can be too wet to be enjoyable.

The Philippines are warm the year-round, typically tropical and full of sunshine, except the rainy days in June to October. Rest of the year is dry, with December to February the most pleasant months.

AVERAGE MONTHLY TEMPERATURES (Farenheit)

		Jan.	*Feb.*	*Mar.*	*Apr.*	*May*	*Jun.*	*Jul.*	*Aug.*	*Sep.*	*Oct.*	*Nov.*	*Dec.*
Bali:	Max.	92	94	93	92	93	93	93	94	93	95	96	95
	Min.	70	70	68	65	61	60	58	61	62	64	67	68
Bangkok:	Max.	89	91	93	95	93	91	90	90	89	88	87	87
	Min.	68	72	75	77	77	76	76	76	76	75	72	68
Hong	Max.	64	63	67	75	82	85	87	87	85	81	74	68
Kong:	Min.	56	55	60	67	74	78	78	78	77	73	65	59
Kuala	Max.	90	92	92	91	91	91	90	90	90	89	89	89
Lumpur:	Min.	72	72	73	74	74	73	72	73	73	73	73	72
Manila:	Max.	86	88	91	93	93	91	88	87	88	88	87	86
	Min.	69	69	71	73	75	75	75	75	75	74	72	70
Rangoon:	Max.	89	92	96	97	92	86	85	85	86	88	88	88
	Min.	65	67	71	76	77	76	76	76	76	76	73	67
Singapore:	Max.	86	88	88	88	89	88	88	87	87	87	87	87
	Min.	73	73	75	75	75	75	75	75	75	74	74	74
Taipei:	Max.	65	65	70	77	83	89	92	91	88	81	75	69
	Min.	54	53	57	63	69	73	76	75	73	67	62	57

TIME ZONES. To know what time it is in an Asian country add the number of hours shown to U.S. EST. Japan, 14; Hong Kong, 13; Singapore, 12½; Indonesia, 12; Philippines, 13; Malaysia, 12½; Burma, 11½; Thailand, 12; Taiwan, 13. Thus 8 A.M. in New York is 9 P.M. in Hong Kong. If you are in Asia and want to phone home without getting your family out of bed reverse the procedure; 9 P.M. in Hong Kong is breakfast time in New York.

SECURITY. Standards of personal safety and security have declined in Asia over the past decade, as in most other places. Although the visitor is generally safer traveling the Orient than in many other parts of the world, it does pay to be cautious in the common sense sort of way. Do not display ostentatious wealth, gold or jewelry, in remote places or big cities. Do not leave valuables in an unoccupied hotel room, nor take them on the beach while you are swimming. Make use of hotel safety deposit boxes, which are usually free. Lock all bags being checked on air trips, and carry valuable belongings in a hand bag. Take these with you during any transit stops when you leave the aircraft. Take travelers' checks rather than cash and record the numbers in a different place than the checks. Insure all cameras, watches, etc. Ladies should use a shoulder bag with a strong strap and carry it tucked under an arm when in crowded places. If you are robbed, don't attempt to resist, and report the matter to the local police as soon as possible to get a report notice for the insurance company. Do not expect police in most Asian countries to be of much help, nor are they likely to be able to speak English. The work in all matters of security is "common sense." Use this and there are likely to be no ugly incidents to mar a happy holiday.

$P£

MONEY. Money fluctuates in Asia just as everywhere. Hong Kong, Singapore, and Bangkok are free money markets where you can buy and sell any currency at the going rate. Make sure you know what that is before you deal; Chinese moneychangers are not Santa Claus. Rates are published every week in the Asian edition of *Newsweek,* and daily in English-language newspapers throughout the region.

We suggest that you check for the current rates of exchange both during the planning stages of your trip and during the trip itself, to be sure that you have a regularly updated concept of general values for each country you will be visiting. In the economic climate of today, this is a sensible precaution for all travelers abroad. Hotels usually give a lower exchange rate than banks or moneychangers. In some places the difference is considerable, so check first.

More and more places in Asia honor the credit cards of organizations such as American Express, The Diners Club, Visa, Carte Blanche, etc. If you belong to any of these, consult their directories, of course. Travelers' checks are a good way to protect your money. They are sold by banks and agencies for major currencies, especially: American, British, Canadian, German, Japanese, and French. Those of First National City Bank and Bank of America are very convenient in Asia. Bank of Tokyo, Cook's and American Express are also widely used. Avoid the checks issued by smaller banks, as you may have trouble changing them in some areas. Also, always keep a written record of the travelers' check numbers in a place other than that where you carry the checks or give the numbers to a companion or friend. In the event they are lost or stolen this will greatly facilitate obtaining replacement checks.

Always carry a few single dollar bills, they will save you changing small travelers' checks, as well as coming in handy for last-minute airport shopping. All Asian airports have moneychanging desks, so get into the habit of changing some local money immediately upon arrival to cover taxis to the hotel, baggage porters, etc. Any balance should be changed back into U.S.$ or £s on departure from the airport, as some currencies cannot be exchanged when one gets home.

HOTEL RESERVATIONS. Every Asian capital (except Rangoon), major city, and important resort now has at least one and probably several luxurious, new, international-style hotels. Many of these belong to the big international chains such as Sheraton, Oberoi, Hyatt, Hilton, Mandarin, Holiday Inn, and Inter-Continental; and many of the others have representatives in the United States. If you visit Asia on either a tour or a cruise, you have no problem. If you travel independently, however, your hotel reservations should be made well in advance in order to avoid any disappointment with a room which you have had to take on short notice. This is particularly true in the Dec.–Jan. high season. The same crowded situation exists in autumn, at Chinese New Year, and usually over Easter. A good rule is to request your hotel space at least two months prior to arrival. If you reserve later than that, you will be able to get a room, but it may be less desirable. If you do arrive in an Asian capital without a hotel reservation you will generally find a hotel desk at the airport, through which you can make an immediate booking. This service is generally efficient, and free.

You will find the service in all luxury and first-class hotels excellent, and accommodations good in all major cities covered in this guide. Only Burma has *no* good hotels at present. In most Asian countries, hotel facilities are definitely comparable to standards of those considered first-class superior in Western Europe and in North America.

GETTING AROUND SOUTHEAST ASIA. By Air. A large number of airlines operate international services within the region. As in Europe, almost every nation has its own flag carrier with a domestic network as well as services between its base and the other major capitals. Equipment ranges from the latest wide-body jets, such as the Airbus, to twin engine turboprop planes linking towns and villages in the vast sprinkling of islands that make up such nations as Indonesia and the Philippines.

As we said earlier, the leading Asian carriers are very good indeed and this applies to their regional flights just as much as to their long-haul ones. On many routes, all airlines are permitted to serve alcoholic drinks free to economy-class passengers; generally, meals and snacks are more substantial than on similarly short flights within the U.S. or Europe. Among lines that we have always had good experience with are *S.I.A., Thai International,* and *Cathay Pacific.*

You may also have the choice of European or American airlines which fly between various Southeast Asian cities to and from their respective countries. While Americans flying across the Pacific will usually be able to make free stopovers and utilize any airline's services, Britons and other Europeans using the cheaper single-destination fares such as APEX or charter flights may want to buy tickets from their base in Asia in order to explore another country. Within the region, excursion fares do exist, but not to the same extent as in Europe. Bangkok is generally reckoned to be the best source of low-cost air tickets within the Asian region.

By Car. The cost of transporting an automobile to and around Southeast Asia is prohibitive, and the involved and lengthy application forms and the expensive bonds one must post to prevent resale will certainly dampen any desire remaining. The roads, to be sure, are good in some places, as those from Singapore up through the scenic Malay Peninsula to Thailand. Hiring a car with driver is usually less expensive than one realizes in Asia, and can be arranged by your travel agent through his correspondent, or upon your arrival. Less expensive and perhaps preferable are organized tours or day trips with car and guide which will give you a chance to see the countryside and still enjoy the convenience of city facilities (including airconditioning) on your return at night. Generally, self-drive car hire is not to be recommended, except in Malaysia.

By Train. Some countries have excellent rail systems, but others are not as well equipped. International rail travel is presently limited to the Singapore-Bangkok express. This two-day trip is quite romantic, especially if you like to speculate about your fellow passengers' possible missions and intrigues, and there is always at least one air-conditioned coach. Be sure to take along enough reading matter, however, and do not expect gourmet food.

Public Transport. Most Asians don't own cars, so public transport is actually far more developed in Asia than in America, but it is, of course, crowded. In Hong Kong it is excellent everywhere. The main problem is language; in many countries signs are not in Roman letters. City buses can be very confusing, so, if you have a precise destination get written instructions from your hotel clerk. But in your free time they can give you very cheap and realistic sightseeing tours. Get on, pay a few pennies, ride to the end of the line observing everything you can, get out, walk around for a while, then get on again and ride back to your hotel. The real Asia that you have been looking for is all about you. Remember that if the natives of a given country can get about, so can you, and it can be interesting that way. See under *Practical Information* for each country.

LAUNDRY AND DRY CLEANING. In most hotels in Southeast Asia, you can get your laundry the same day or your dry cleaning in a few hours if you pay extra surcharges. The ordinary time for both services is about twenty-four hours. However, in smaller destinations or resorts you must expect that dry cleaning will take up to four or five days. Laundry in Southeast Asia is often done with harsh soaps and water that is not quite hot enough, so that your clothes may take a beating. Similarly, dry cleaning is most commonly effected with harsh chemicals, so you should not entrust delicate fabrics to the ordinary establishment. At the higher priced hotels, of course, you can expect the standards of both services to be up to the European or American levels of performance. This high quality means prices nearly identical to European costs but slightly less than what you would have to pay in America. Laundry is usually cheaper than in the United States or Europe.

COSMETICS. Except in Hong Kong and Singapore, where European and American cosmetics may be purchased tax-free, imported toilet articles are usually much more expensive than back home. You would be well prepared if you come to Southeast Asia with enough of your favorite brands.

SHOPPING. There are a few things about shopping abroad that knowledgeable shoppers will always take into account!

Wherever possible carry your purchases home with you, especially if they are valuable or fragile. Postal services are not always reliable, especially from Burma and Indonesia.

Find out all about customs regulations. You could be stung for a small fortune and turn a bargain into a very expensive commodity indeed.

If you are shipping goods home, be very sure you have understood the terms, how the shipment will be made, when it should arrive . . . and get it all in writing. It is generally better to ship the item yourself, from the local Post Office, than to entrust the job to the shopkeeper. Certain parts of Asia, and the smaller shops and dealers are notoriously unreliable in this matter.

This is the time to warn you about those duty free, tax free shops. While they *can* offer bargains, especially in liquor, cigarettes and perfume—because of the huge taxes these attract in the normal shops—the "DUTY FREE" signs can often be unpleasant hoaxes. Some airport shops charge higher prices than those charged for exactly the same local manufactured goods sold in town. Cameras, radios, calculators are among the goods which fall into the "Think Twice" category.

DYNASTIES AND ERAS. For the shopper who can't remember whether a *Ming* vase is older or newer than a *T'ang* piece, and for the amateur historian, we give an abbreviated list of the major dynasties of China.

The Mongol-based dynasties are shown in italics.

Dynasty	Era
Hsia	c. 2200–1766 B.C.
Shang (Yin)	1766–1122 B.C.
Chou	1122–249 B.C.
West Chou	1122–771 B.C.

Spring and Autumn Period	722–481 B.C.
Warring States	453–221 B.C.
Chin	221–207 B.C.
Former Han	202 B.C.–A.D. 8
Later Han	c. A.D. 25–220
Three Kingdoms	220–280
Chin	265–420
Northern and Southern Dynasties	420–587
Sui	581–618
Dynasty	**Era**
T'ang	618–907
Ten Kingdoms, Five Dynasties	907–979
Northern Sung	960–1126
Southern Sung	1127–1279
Yuan	1279–1368
Ming	1368–1644
Ch'ing	1644-1912
Republic	1912–

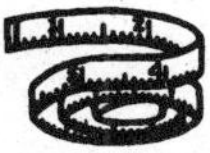

MEASUREMENTS. Except for British-influenced areas and the Philippines, the metric system is most widely used throughout this area. In this book we have given all distances in miles, yards, and feet, but in such countries as Thailand and Taiwan, for example, you will constantly be faced with the kilometer, meter and centimeter. The kilometer is .62 mile, and an easy rule of thumb is that 8 kilometers equals 5 miles. There are, of course, 1,000 meters in a kilometer, and 100 centimeters in a meter. A meter is just over 3 feet in length and a centimeter is about four-tenths of a inch.

Temperature in many Asian countries is measured by the Centigrade system. Water boils at 100 degrees Centigrade, which is 212 degrees Fahrenheit. Water freezes at 0 degrees C. and at 32 degrees F. To convert to Fahrenheit, multiply Centigrade by nine-fifths (9/5) and add 32. To convert to Centrigrade, subtract 32 and multiply Fahrenheit by five-ninths (5/9). There are 2.2 pounds in every kilogram, but we doubt that you will be buying anything in terms of weight out here. If you have rented a car, and are buying gasoline, you should remember that four liters is slightly over one gallon (U.S.), and just under one imperial gallon.

If you order clothes custom-made, insist on several fittings. If you buy ready-made clothes, not only the sizes but the body proportions will be different. Thus, a man buying a shirt in Thailand will find that if the neck fits properly, the chest will be too narrow and the sleeves too short. Asians are built differently. Also, they are generally smaller, so Westerners needing large sizes will have much trouble in Asia. Women find that dresses labeled "American size 12" are really about size 10. Whenever possible, try on ready-made clothes before buying.

Rubber elastic in Asian clothes, especially underwear, often does not withstand laundering.

In Hong Kong, Singapore, and other British-influenced areas, the old British measurements are sometime used. An American woman's 34 dress is a British C-2, a Junior miss size 10 in the U.S. is an A-1, and so forth. American and English, shoes, stockings, and hats use the same size system, though ladies' stockings in England have longer tops. Men's glove sizes are the same, also. The Philippines use the American size system and adhere to it rather accurately. Malaysia is converting to the metric system.

CONVERTING METRIC TO U.S. MEASUREMENTS

Multiply:	by:	to find:
Length		
millimeters (mm)	.039	inches (in)
meters (m)	3.28	feet (ft)
Multiply:	**by:**	**to find:**
meters	1.09	yards (yd)
kilometers (km)	.62	miles (mi)
Area		
hectare (ha)	2.47	acres
Capacity		
liters (L)	1.06	quarts (qt)
liters	.26	gallons (gal)
liters	2.11	pints (pt)
Weight		
gram (g)	.04	ounce (oz)
kilogram (kg)	2.20	pounds (lb)
metric ton (MT)	.98	tons (t)
Power		
kilowatt (kw)	1.34	horsepower (hp)
Temperature		
degrees Celsius	9/5 (then add 32)	degrees Fahrenheit

CONVERTING U.S. TO METRIC MEASUREMENTS

Multiply:	by:	to find:
Length		
inches (in)	25.40	millimeters (mm)
feet (ft)	.30	meters (m)
yards (yd)	.91	meters
miles (mi)	1.61	kilometers (km)
Area		
acres	.40	hectares (ha)
Capacity		
pints (pt)	.47	liters (L)
quarts (qt)	.95	liters
gallons (gal)	3.79	liters
Weight		

ounces (oz)	28.35	grams (g)
pounds (lb)	.45	kilograms (kg)
tons (t)	1.11	metric tons (MT)
Power		
horsepower (hp)	.75	kilowatts
Temperature		
degrees Fahrenheit	5/9 (after subtracting 32)	degrees Celsius

LANGUAGE. Erratic English is our term for the often incomprehensible English spoken by taxi drivers, pedicab operators, and others dealing with tourists in Southeast Asia. While influenced heavily by the recent influx of foreign visitors and Western TV and movies, Erratic English is basically derived from Pidgin English, that fine old form of communication dating back to the days of the Opium Wars and the Yankee Clippers. Especially in Hong Kong and Singapore, but also prevalent wherever Chinese influence is felt, Pidgin English and its modern form remain a valid means of getting one's thoughts across. If facing a communications problem, stay cool, speak slowly and quietly, concentrating on the simplest of messages. If you still have problems ask passersby if they speak English—they will usually produce a helpful, if not always efficient, translator.

Communication with your driver. In former British and American colonies, you can expect your driver to understand your directions. In all other countries in this area, it is recommended that you have your hotel front desk write down, in the local language, the name and address of your destination. Also carry with you a card from your hotel so that you can get back without tears. Remember that in certain cities, such as Bangkok, taxi fares must always be bargained for in advance.

CUSTOMS RETURNING HOME. For those traveling to Southeast Asia, where the market for cameras, audio and video equipment, watches and electronic gear is great, it is especially important to remember to register any such items you may be taking with you from home with local Customs agents before leaving. This is a quick, simple procedure that can save you much time (and money, if a conflict arises) upon returning home. You may also carry the original receipts for such items as proof of purchase in the U.S.

Protected Species. A number of countries now place restrictions on the import or export of products and souvenirs made from protected wildlife species. Both the USA and England ban the importation of new ivory, tiger or other skins from endangered animals. The tourist traveler is asked, most sincerely, not to encourage the further slaughter of endangered species by purchasing souvenirs made from their dead bodies.

U.S. residents may bring in $400 worth of foreign merchandise as gifts or for personal use without having to pay duty, provided they have been out of the country more than 48 hours and provided they have not claimed a similar exemption within the previous 30 days. Every member of a family is entitled to the same exemption, regardless of age, and the exemptions can be pooled.

The $400 figure is based on the fair retail value of the goods in the country where acquired. Included for travelers over the age of 21 are one liter of alcohol, 100 cigars (non-Cuban), and 200 cigarettes. Any amount in excess of those limits will be taxed at the port of entry, and may additionally be taxed in the traveler's home state. Only one bottle of perfume trademarked in the U.S. may be brought in. However, there is no duty on antiques or art over 100 years old—though you may be called upon to provide verification of the item's age.

Under a program known as the General System of Preferences (GSP), an unlimited amount of some goods can be brought into the United States, duty free, from a number of specially designated "developing nations." As it turns out, many Southeast Asian countries fall into this category. Those covered in this book currently include: Taiwan, Thailand, Burma, Malaysia, Singapore, Indonesia and the Philippines. The countries covered by this program change frequently, however, according to the idiosyncracies of the Customs Bureau, so it is advisable to write for their pamphlet "GSP and the Traveler," Department of the Treasury, U.S. Customs Service, Washington, D.C. 20229, before departing. Write to the same address for information regarding importation of automobiles and/or motorcycles. You may not bring home meats, fruits, plants, soil, or other agricultural items.

Gifts valued at under $50 may be mailed to friends or relatives at home, but not more than one per day (of receipt) to any one addressee. These gifts must not include perfumes costing more than $5, tobacco, or liquor.

Military personnel returning from abroad should check with the nearest American Embassy for special regulations pertaining to them.

British subjects may bring into the U.K. the following goods duty-free: 200 cigarettes, or 100 cigarillos, or 50 cigars, or 250 grams tobacco; plus one liter of alcohol of more than 38.8% proof, or 2 liters of alcohol not more than 38.8% proof, or 2 liters of fortified or sparkling wine and 2 liters of still table wine; plus 50 grams of perfume and ¼ liter of toilet water; plus other goods to the value of £28.

Canadian residents may, after 7 days out of the country, and upon written declaration, claim a duty exemption of $300 a year, which will include the value of 40 ounces of liquor, 50 cigars, 200 cigarettes, and 2 pounds of tobacco. Personal gifts should be mailed as "unsolicited gift"—value under $40 in Canadian funds. For details, request the Canada Customs brochure, *I Declare.*

Women Traveling Alone. Women can and do travel alone in Southeast Asia, but those who do are invariably Western women. The sort of independence that permits a woman to pack her bags and go off on a world tour by herself is unheard of in the traditional societies of Southeast Asia. Women there are viewed as creatures in need of protection that only a male or a group of companions can provide.

This doesn't mean that the Western woman should unpack her bags. In most major cities of Southeastern Asia, the steady flow of tourists has inured the residents to the peculiarities of Western culture. It does mean, though, that a woman alone should be sensitive to the local viewpoint. When undecided about appropriate behavior or dress, it's best to err on the side of conservatism to avoid cultural misunderstandings.

If you plan to visit small towns or villages off the beaten path, expect some curious stares and maybe even some verbal probing to confirm that you really are traveling on your own. Don't be put off by the whispered asides and gapes that may follow this revelation—it's not disapproval but astonishment that is being registered. The friendly curiosity you are accorded can even be an advantage in opening the door to interesting conversations with local people, a welcome diversion when you have no companion.

You can expect to feel perfectly at ease during daylight hours in the large cities, particularly in the tourist areas. Of course, every city has its rough areas that are not recommended for any lone traveler, male or female. If your wanderings take you to a part of the city where groups of loitering young males display a greater than usual interest in your movements, trust your instincts and leave promptly.

Going out in the evening, as might be expected, requires a bit more circumspection. Walking alone is reasonably safe, provided you stick to well-lit areas with plenty of other people around. Dark, deserted streets are as hazardous in Southeast Asia as in the United States, perhaps even more so, since the foreign tourist looks temptingly affluent to the criminal elements in underdeveloped countries. If you plan to go far afield from your hotel, either on foot or by taxi, then you really would be better off with a companion.

Hotel dining rooms are obvious choices for dinner, but they are not the only option. Your presence will not raise eyebrows in any restaurant that is part of the tourist circuit, or is primarily a restaurant (and not a bar). In some cities, open-air restaurants appear miraculously in parking lots and along streets during the evening. Here you will be comfortably lost in the crowd that jockeys for position around the aromatic food stalls, and it is more than likely that you will share your small, wooden table with an assortment of fellow diners.

For entertainment, check out the many hotels and restaurants that offer floor shows, which are often cultural presentations, along with dinner. Don't overlook the cheerful excitement of the night markets found in most cities—noisy, crowded, brightly lit, and crammed with stalls full of cheap goods. (Haggle—and keep a firm grip on your handbag.)

What if you feel like going out to have a drink at night? In many major tourist hotels, the lobby encompasses a comfortable bar and lounge area where you can sit, sip a martini, and enjoy the passing scene. It may be that this is too tame for you, and what you really want is conversation. You can probably find it, and still retain your respectability, in the main bar of the hotel.

In deciding whether to go to bars outside the hotel, proceed with caution. The singles bar of the United States is largely unknown in this part of the world. In the crossroads cities of Hong Kong and Singapore, there are few places where young, single people meet and mingle. But locations shift according to which establishment is currently popular, so check with the concierge or information desk to find out what's "in."

In general, you will probably not feel comfortable by yourself in the local watering holes. "Hostesses" are standard fixtures in bars in Southeast Asia. These women earn their living by providing companionship to lone males, and they will not look kindly upon those they view as interlopers. Local males will almost surely assign an interpretation to your presence that you may not have intended.

Southeast Asian males, incidentally, are apt to find you a fascinating enigma. Expect to be approached almost anywhere by the local swains, who are as unsure of the rules of the encounter as you are.

At any rate, traveling alone needn't be lonely. Hotels and local travel agents offer group tours to local attractions. Fellow tourists might look like a flock of milling sheep, but you may discover some wonderfully interesting people in that flock.

If you belong to any clubs or professional associations, check to see if they have sister organizations in the region. This may lead to contact with resident expatriates, who are good sources of useful information on where to find the best dinner or the greatest bargains. And don't miss the opportunity to look up any friend-of-a-friend.

Should you find yourself a guest in a local home, a small gift to your hostess will be considered a mark of fine manners. Asians generally don't touch one another unless they are very good friends. The airy kisses or friendly pats on the back that are a standard component of greetings and farewells in some segments of American society are unacceptable in most of Southeast Asia. The Philippines is an exception, but even here the custom is confined to the upper classes.

When introduced to a Muslim man, don't even offer your hand. To do so would cause confusion and embarrassment, as Islam forbids a man to touch a woman who is not his wife. There are a few other rules of polite behavior in Muslim societies that you might want to be aware of, although you as a foreigner will be excused for not following them: always offer or accept objects with the right hand, not the left, and avoid crossing your legs in such a way that the sole of your foot points toward another person.

Don't worry unduly about the local customs. Common sense is your best guide, and, provided your manner is pleasant, any unintentional gaffes will be overlooked.

THE SOUTHEAST ASIAN SCENE

INTRODUCTION

Why Go East?

The East has always woven a spell to enchant the West. Asia is vast and teeming and infinitely complex, an inexhaustible source of riches and wonder, and from Marco Polo to Somerset Maugham, Westerners have fired their imaginations with its color and strangeness, its size and diversity, its violent extremes and brilliant contrasts, its challenge and reward. Vasco da Gama, Conrad, Prokosch, Fleming, Malraux, Whitman, Hesse, Burton, Loti, Jules Verne, Hilton, Raffles, David-Neel, Gordon, Gurdjieff, Francis Xavier, are but a few of the writers, travelers who have made the journey to the East, some only in inspired imagination, but all in search of something they missed at home—another part of themselves. And the tales they have brought back have become a part of our lives, too; for the East is a region of the mind.

Alexander of Macedon was one of the first, and though he found death in the Sind rather than the gardens and palaces of Scheherazade, the trail he blazed is traveled today more than ever. The gold of Rome was drained to pay for the silks of China, and the artistic influence of Greece passed through Persia and India till it came to rest in far Japan. The tale of the West's involvement with the East is one of the oldest and most absorbing adventures in human history.

Today it is all so easy. Machines can carry you in a few hours where once it took men months and even years to go, on foot, and in the face of appalling hardships. Yet Asia still holds, for the mind of the West, the lure, the challenge, the spell, and the rewards that have drawn generation after generation of Westerners from their snug, familiar lives into a world utterly different from everything they have known, thought, and believed. For Asia is half the world, the other half. And while no one volume could possibly encompass all of its vastness, complexity, depth and wonder, we have tried, in this book, to give you an introduction to one very specific part of it, an introduction practical enough so that you can go there yourself and not only look at the glittering surface that you see in the travel but have some idea of what it's all about. No man in a lifetime could understand all of Asia; scholars and specialists have failed at that. But it is quite possible to have a clear, overall idea of the different regions and countries of Asia, to visit some of them, and to appreciate something of the meaning, value, and relevance of what you see. The East may well be strange, but it doesn't have to be frustrating. Once you have actually been there you may still find it mysterious, but that's what will make it *really* interesting.

Why Southeast Asia?

If Asia is half a world, this book covers about half of Asia. *Southeast* Asia to be precise. Every currently accessible country from Taiwan through Burma and down to Indonesia, over 5 million square kilometers containing 13 states (including Indo-China which is at present not easily accessible as a tourist destination)—kingdom, republic, colony, province—and over 400 million people in several major nationalities and countless ethnic and religious groups. A rich and fascinating mixture of races, colors, languages, cultures, religions, governments, and ways of life, spanning centuries, from the Stone Age tribes of New Guinea to the factories of Hong Kong. Here are some of the world's oldest continuous civilizations, and some of its newest nation-states, democratic socialism and the ruins of empires. An area where every generalization you can make is true *and* false, where everything you have thought can be contradicted, and where everything you see may be contradicted, too.

Southeast Asia can be defined as that vast area which, in varying degrees, has come under the influence of China. Every nation in Southeast Asia has had to orient itself in relation to the Middle Kingdom and that great tradition, to adopt it, absorb it, or adapt to it. Throughout Southeast Asia you will see its traces, feel its presence, and see how it has blended with other cultures, Indian, Islamic, indigenous. The spectrum changes gradually from Hong Kong and Singapore across the six countries of the Indo-China and Malay Peninsula, into Burma and to the borders of India, where another great civilization begins. It is a fantastic spectacle, yet understandable, for all its complexity.

A Few Constants

Amidst all this diversity (which is, after all, Southeast Asia's greatest advantage to you as a tourist) there are constant factors that tie together this immense grab bag of peoples and customs. One, as we have made quite clear, is the influence of China. Southeast Asia is the Chinese cultural sphere, a creation of the greatest single continuous tradition in human history.

English, you will find, ironically enough, and to your great relief, is the lingua franca of Southeast Asia today, as of the whole world. Except for small pockets of French (in Cambodia and Laos), English is increasingly used everywhere in Asia. In centuries past, educated men could converse through the medium of the Chinese written character (as with Latin in Europe until 400 years ago); but today, Asia's elite read Asia's own English-language newspapers and magazines to learn what is going on in their part of the world. Almost every country in this book has at least one, and usually several, English-language newspapers and magazines published locally. This Asian English press, if you read it observantly, can be one of your best sources of useful information, and of often unexpected and valuable insights. World news, of course; local festivals, cultural events, exhibitions, restaurants, shops, tour possibilities, too; and, more than that, a glimpse of how other people think, what they consider important, what they take for granted, values very different from your own. The spoken variety of English has undergone some odd changes in its travels, and in speaking with people you must adjust (see "Language" in *Facts at Your Fingertips*); but with patience, flexibility, and a sense of humor, you can get a lot further than you might think.

Religion is another common denominator. Much of your sightseeing will be in temples, and after a while they may all begin to blur together in your mind. And while Buddhism asserts that there is no god, Hinduism worships many, all of them different aspects of the One. If you do some background reading on Taoism, Buddhism (two main types), Islam, and Hinduism before you set out, it will enrich your tour immensely. Christian ways of thinking don't apply here; these religions are not only older and vaster than Christianity, but their ways of thinking are becoming increasingly influential in the West. Relativity, coexistence of opposites, the many faces of truth, the indescribability of God, timelessness—there is much to be learned from Asian ideas about such things.

Food need be no problem at all. Your trip through Southeast Asia can be a gastronomic adventure if you want it to be. Or it can be fearful, cramped and monotonous. You have to be willing to drop many of your old ideas about what is edible and what is not. Never forget that in the West, frogs' legs, rattlesnake stew, snails, eels, and raw oysters are delicacies. Every country of Southeast Asia has its own distinctive style of cooking, and you will be missing a lot if you do not try them all. However you may *think* that many Asian dishes *sound* unpleasant, you cannot decide until you have tried them for yourself. Standardized Western food is available in all Southeast Asian cities, of course, but it is rarely of interesting quality, and the tremendous diversity of Asian cooking is one of this region's great attractions. And beyond all the variety of local styles is the universality of Chinese cooking, one of the two great international gastronomical languages (along with French). Enjoy it to the fullest, everywhere. Chopsticks, incidentally, are simple, convenient, and quite easy to use. Spend a couple of hours practicing up beforehand; it's worth it.

Nationalism is another strong factor in Asia today, and you must try to see things from Asian points of view. In Hong Kong you may sense the last pleasant echoes of that snug world of colonial privilege that vanished for ever in 1942; but elsewhere throughout Asia you will find peoples proud of their independence and determined to build their own futures. From the Asian point of view, however noble its intentions and its rationalizations, the West has brought humiliation and exploitation to much of Asia; and more recent Western involvement has brought division, ruin, misery, and death to hundreds of thousands of Asians (in Korea and Vietnam). This idea may be uncongenial to Westerners; but whether they do it well or badly, Asians want to settle their own affairs in their own way. They know that their traditions are enduring and valuable, so they can distinguish between a national culture and its values on the one hand and its most recent governmental clique on the other. From the political vacuum left behind by the departure of the various colonial powers—Dutch, French, British, and American—a sense of regionalism is emerging very gradually, which has never really been present in Asia before. Such groupings as ASEAN (the Association of South East Asian Nations—comprising Indonesia, Brunei, Singapore, Thailand, Malaysia, and the Philippines) are starting to produce a feeling of interrelationship and interdependence which is fascinating to study as it is such a novel concept within the region. This is currently the fastest growing region of the world, economically, and it is now struggling to reconcile the many factors, some opposing, that are found within its borders. This new awareness that the countries of the region have to understand each other better could lead to some major commonality of policies towards the "developed" nations, and will probably enable the region to have a much greater say than ever before in the affairs of the world.

Face to Face Etiquette and Personal Relations

"Face" is another very important factor in Southeast Asian life, and knowing how to deal with people is essential to the success of your tour. In Southeast Asian society, every person has a place, and that place must be respected. Another person's place should never be trespassed on, nor his personal dignity directly affronted. There is always a middle way of compromise that can be satisfactory to both sides. The Chinese say that because the bamboo bends, it does not break. If you are flexible and sympathetic, your trip can be packed with unexpected but enriching experiences. If you are rigid, fussy, overbearing, and noisy, you are asking for trouble. Get the other man on your side. Tell him, courteously, what you would like, and then ask what *he* would *suggest.* Then listen. If there are delays, take advantage of them to look about you. Examine seeming inefficiency; there is usually some reason for it. Asians know more about Asia than you do, and, if you are sympathetic, they will gladly teach you. There is no need to be cheated or abused; you can be quiet and courteous and still be firm. Never raise your voice or lose your temper; you degrade only yourself. Westerners enjoy clear decisions and clear-cut personal victories, but this doesn't work in Asia. Anger, criticism, ridicule, and argument are deeply offensive to Southeast Asians. They value harmony, and that is something worth getting to know, too.

Asians may not express openly how they feel. You must learn to sense what an Asian is thinking, and, far more important, how he *feels.* This is not always easy, but it can develop your awareness amazingly. Asians use language to express feelings and attitudes as much as to convey information. Degrees of probability are more important to them than seemingly clear-cut certainty. Learn to use these terms: "maybe," "more or less," "it depends." In Southeast Asia *everything* "depends." And it depends on people more often than not. Asia is crowded, and people have learned how to get along together through sheer necessity. You will find that there is far more genuine personal privacy in Asia than in the West, because Asians have had to invent "public privacy." You may often see surprisingly intimate, uninhibited, or undignified behavior in public. But where else? In Asia there often is no other place to do things. So, you just don't see it. For as long as a person does not too grossly inconvenience others, he is left alone to do or feel as he likes, and you pay no attention to what he is doing. The kind of immediate, easy familiarity which Americans are accustomed to seems vulgar and intrusive to Asians. Back-slapping is out. There is plenty of physical contact between Asians; they are actually far less neurotic about that than many Westerners. But not on first acquaintance. Getting to know an Asian is a long, delicate process of give and take, during which the two parties feel one another out gradually and very carefully. Don't expect too much too soon. Asians value and protect their personal privacy and their personal relations. In the East, the bonds of family remain strong and the extended family group, with its mutual responsibilities, is still the keystone of society.

The position of women in Asia is different from that in the West. Though at first glance this may not seem to be so, women's place is still at home and in the family; business, entertaining, and public activities are between men. If the group is mixed, it is the men who take the initiative and do the talking, while women show their femininity and their good manners by taking a retiring role. Behind the scenes, however, Asian women do exert a great deal of influence—some believe even more than do Western women. Asian women are notable for their grace and delicacy; and in Asia, overtalkativeness, assertiveness and loud clothes are all signs of low class and vulgarity in women. Westerners are often unfortunately insensitive to this point. In fact, all over Asia, loud clothes and loud voices are in bad taste in men and women alike, no matter what you may think of the behavior of the local people.

Ungeneralizations

Of course all these generalities do not hold uniformly true all over Southeast Asia. Some points of behavior have to be checked separately for each country. One of these is attitudes about being photographed. Chinese usually get very angry about having their photographs taken, and you must be very careful how you point your camera here. In some countries you take your shoes off indoors, a custom that has much to recommend it. In other countries you do not. Wear shoes without laces and be ready for both. Temple etiquette must be observed carefully. Muslim mosques and Hindu temples are open to non-believers in some countries, but not in others. It is often well to go with some local person; always inquire carefully about picture-taking in religious places. The Chinese consider bargaining to be one of life's most fascinating sports; in dealing with them always expect to match wits. Always do so courteously and good-naturedly. If you lose your temper you lose your face and your money as well. It's marvelous training in self-discipline, if you can do it. (In America it's called "horsetrading.") Concepts of personal honesty vary widely too. In some parts of Southeast Asia, you are expected to have your wits about you, and are a fool if you don't.

All this may seem confusing at first. But the more alert you are, the more you will get out of your Asian tour. Asian ways of doing things have been worked out over many centuries. These traditions are old and viable. They have lasted because they make sense in their own way and in their own context. Try to understand what those are. Reality, in Southeast Asia, is preeminently social, a matter of what people think and how they act and interact. It is the study of people, rather than noble piles of brick and stone, that can make your trip to Southeast Asia an exciting and revealing experience.

Ancient Is as Ancient Does

One of the most unmercifully abused words in the tourist lexicon today is "ancient." Everywhere you go you will be told that the temple, palace, statue, painting, monastery, or whatnot that you are looking at is "ancient." The Pyramids were built about 2500–1500 B.C. They are ancient. And the Parthenon was built in 432 B.C. But Borobudur was built about A.D. 850; Bangkok was not even founded until 1782. And the Marble Temple in Bangkok, which is wonderfully colorful, was built in 1911—in traditional style. The civilization of Southeast Asia is very old indeed; but Asians have never had that awe for material remains that Westerners now have. Continuity, yes. Permanence, no. It is the form that continues, though the pieces change, and what you will see in Southeast Asia is a civilization, a cultural tradition, long-enduring *forms* of art, architecture, religion, family, and society, rather than individual monuments that are in themselves particularly "ancient" or otherwise.

Southeast Asians have generally built in brick and wood, and these materials perish. In the case of the Malays, for example, a rich, sensitive artistic tradition depends entirely on wood, cloth, and leather, as the museums of Singapore and Kuala Lumpur will show. Not unless you travel to India and Sri Lanka will you find major achievements in stone (except at Angkor and Borobudur). So do not seek mere "ancient-ness" for you will not find it. And it does not really matter. Look rather for the meaning and forms of the traditions—political, religious, social, artistic—that are carried in what you see. For much of this is still alive. In art museums you may see people offer rice, money, flowers, and prayers in front of statues of the Buddha, because it is a sacred object rather than a work of art. The Western tourist will ask: Is this old? Is this artistic? To many Asians, that is not important. The Buddha-nature is timeless, and the concept of "museum" is a very late, and foreign, invention. Some Asian museums are still temples because they contain sacred objects. And some Asian temples have been turned into sideshows because they contain works of art.

Fabled Cities and (Modern) Chaos

One result of this Asian attitude is the ugliness of Asian cities. Colorful they are, but beautiful most of them definitely are not. The architectural harmony and unity that make Amsterdam, Vienna, Prague, Cracow, Avila, Siena, or Venice truly beautiful cities hardly exists in Southeast Asia. Broad, symmetrical, planned, and orderly public spaces—parks, squares, boulevards, circles, terraces—are almost nonexistent in Southeast Asian cities, except in temples and palaces. For the ordinary citizenry there are few, as was the case in Europe, too, until a hundred years ago. Bangkok is chaotic and hideous. Hong Kong is an outpost of the oldest continuous civilization on earth, yet as a city it is neither old nor beautiful, though it is tremendously colorful and exciting. The treasures you have come to see are tucked away amidst the mishmash. You must know how to look for them. And you must be willing to look at the mishmash for what it is, a piling up of traditional and modern that is the reality of Southeast Asia today.

We mentioned earlier that most of the generalizations that one can make about this area are open to contradiction. So no apology is offered here if that has been done. If this chapter has contradicted itself, then it has succeeded as an introduction to Southeast Asia as it really is, a complex, vivid, variegated, ever-continuing, ever-changing world of its own—one which you are about to go and see for yourself. With that well in mind, we come to the practical side of your trip, the background for choosing, and the details for planning, that will tell you where and get you there, conveniently and efficiently. First, the background for choosing, a general and introductory survey of the tourist attractions and touring conditions of each of the countries in this book, before you study them in detail, chapter by chapter, in the main text.

Note: Due to the political instability currently existing in Indo-China, we have chosen not to include Vietnam, Kampuchea (formerly known as Cambodia), and Laos in this edition of *Fodor's Southeast Asia* as conditions in that region are too unpredictable for tourism. The names Kampuchea and Cambodia are used interchangeably in this book.

Editorial Acknowledgments

Scores of personalities in the region have aided and advised our editors and contributors in their effort to produce a most complete and up-to-date *Guide to Southeast Asia.*

To name them all would constitute an impossible challenge. All we can do is attempt to express our gratitude to a number of people and organizations whose cooperation was of utmost importance in the realization of this project.

We are especially indebted to the following:

Hong Kong—The efficient and helpful Hong Kong Tourist Association.

Malaysia—Mr. Leong Kum Fatt.

Brunei—Mr. George Capps.

Burma—Mr. Julian Geisinger and Mr. Adul Sattar.

Thailand—Ms. Maren Carl-Fricke and Luzi Matzig.

Macau—Brian Cuthbertson of the Macau Tourist Information Bureau.

Taiwan—Don Shapiro.

The Philippines—We wish to thank Director Salvador Pena of the Ministry of Tourism; Ms. M. L. Farolan, of American Express, Manila; and, as always, Hilario Francia, who updated this entire section.

Singapore—Our thanks are due Mr. Dan Thygisen and to the efficient staff of the Singapore Tourist Promotion Board's Tanglin Road head office.

Lee Buenaventura wrote the section on "Women Traveling Alone" for *Facts at Your Fingertips.*

This year's revisions have again been under the general supervision of Robin Dannhorn, who has put his deep knowledge and love of the area at our disposal.

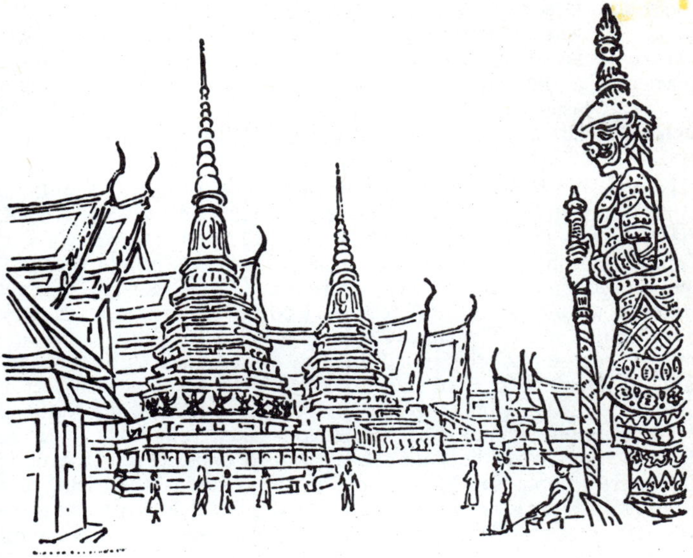

SOUTHEAST ASIA AT A GLANCE

Capsule Comments

Hong Kong is compact, well organized, well equipped, and convenient. The British Crown Colony encompasses 405 square miles on 235 islands and with a population of around 5.5 million is one of the most exciting places in the world. Your first impression will be the magnificent natural setting; your second will be the swarming, tingling, vibrantly colorful life and energy of the Chinese who make up 98 percent of the population. Then you can enjoy the food, night life, shopping, and cosmopolitan atmosphere of the colony, its sophisticated, internationalized upper crust, and the daily life of its Chinese masses in both the crowded cities and the farming and fishing villages of the countryside. You can see Hong Kong in about a week; the only question is to know what you want. The colony is brilliantly organized for tourism of all kinds, especially for people who want lots of good eating and shopping, plus recreation and some exotic sightseeing in wonderfully colorful surroundings. If this is your goal, Hong Kong is the place for you. If you want to see an amazing economic achievement, Hong Kong is also the place for you.

Macau, six square miles, population 400,000, Portuguese-administered, once was a quiet European, rather than Oriental, town. Recent construction is increasingly disrupting this antique atmosphere. Three-quarters of an hour or so by jetfoil from Hong Kong, Macau's highlights can easily be seen on foot in one day. Or, since the night life includes legalized gambling, you might want to stay over for two days.

Taiwan, 13,893 square miles, population just over 19.5 million, capital Taipei (pop. 3 million). Once underpopulated and undeveloped, the island was taken over in 1949 by the millions of refugees who fled Communism in Mainland China. These industrious people have created an economic miracle, a modernized and industrial state that yet preserves an antique cultural heritage. Tourism in Taiwan tends to be stopover-in-Taipei. The city itself is, at first sight, colorless, and you have to look more closely to find the bazaars, temples, shrines, restaurants, theaters, shops, and side streets where you can get the feel of Chinese life. Highlights of the city are, on the one hand, the National Palace Museum, with its superb collections taken from Peking; and, on the other, a night life that caters to notoriously opposite tastes. Around Taipei are resorts; Sun-Moon Lake, in the center of the island, is a pleasant place for a quiet interlude; otherwise the chief attraction is the mountain scenery. Taroko Gorge, at the east end of the East–West Highway, Mount Ali, and the beaches at Oluanpi all offer quiet refuges from harried urban living. Transportation is good; conditions in general are clean, modern, orderly, and efficient; and Taipei itself has many new hotels. From four to six days is quite adequate.

Indo-China. The three Indo-Chinese countries, Vietnam, Cambodia (now generally known as Kampuchea), and Laos, are not included as chapters in this book as they are currently too unstable, politically, socially, and practically to be predictable from the touristic point of view. One sad trend in this book from its earliest years was the gradually reduced coverage given to the Indo-Chinese nations as they became less suitable as travel destinations. They were finally eliminated altogether after 1975, when the Communist takeover was completed. The three countries have among them a population of some 68 million and offer potentially diverse and richly rewarding touristic experiences. It is to be hoped, from humanitarian and social reasons more than touristic ones, that the tragedy of Indo-China will be resolved soon in the future. Once the nations welcome, and are able to provide properly for, foreign travelers, we shall once again give them the coverage they deserve.

Thailand, 198,455 square miles, population 52 million, capital Bangkok (pop. 6 million). Tourism in Thailand is concentrated on Bangkok, which has a number of fantastically ornate and glittering temples, the overrated floating market, and a highly organized apparatus of expensive, ultra-modern, international-style hotels, exotic restaurants, flashy nightclubs, elegant luxury and souvenir shops, banks, offices, agencies and big-city facilities of every kind. The temples really are spectacular, and the facilities are very convenient. But this air-conditioned little world is misleading. Much of Bangkok is chaotic and hideous, like Tokyo, a monument to the horrors of sudden, unplanned growth, Westernization and commercialization. And, like Taipei, it has a night life which caters to all tastes. The tourists' Bangkok, like the tourists' Hong Kong, is glittering, glamorous and exotic. Outside the capital, chief excursions are to important temples and ruins, in smaller towns in the Bangkok basin, a hot, flat, wet, rice-growing plain, the epitome of sub-tropical Asia. The eastern and northeastern parts of the country are arid and poor, with little of touristic interest. In the north, Chiang Mai, the second city, is a pleasant provincial town in a cool mountain plateau, with a few good hotels, tranquil atmosphere, nice scenery and native crafts. Outside the central plain, Thailand offers several beach resorts which are gradually being opened up for tourism. Pattaya is the leading one, 85 miles south of Bangkok and Asia's largest integrated resort. There are increasingly good opportunities for touring down to the south toward the Malaysian border—miles of sand beaches and fishing villages, and into jungle areas such as the River Kwai. At least a week is needed to see even the superficial attractions. Plan on two weeks if including upcountry travel.

Burma, 261,217 square miles, population about 39 million, capital Rangoon (pop. about 800,000). As of this writing the best you can hope for in Burma is a one-week visa for a stopover. The Burmese bureaucracy is sullen and inefficient, and Rangoon itself is shabby and falling apart, but the stopover is worth the trouble if only for just one thing, the incredible sight of the Shwe Dagon Pagoda by night. Entirely sheathed in gold, a towering 320 feet into the air, floodlighted against the deep blue-black of a tropical night sky, this is one of the most deeply moving and truly awe-inspiring sights in all of Asia, and is one of the great holy places of this earth. It should not be missed. Other tourist goals in Burma, if you can get there, are the old royal capital of Mandalay, the pagoda-studded ruins of Pagan, and the resort of Inle Lake. Of more than passing interest is the experience of an economy in almost total stagnation.

Malaysia, 127,316 square miles, population 15 million, capital Kuala Lumpur (pop. 850,000) is divided into two parts, Peninsular Malaysia, the western part (with 83 percent of the population), contains the chief cities, sightseeing, and resorts. The racial balance is delicate, 54 percent Malay, 35 percent Chinese, 10 percent Indian. In the past this has created social and political problems, but with a new-found economic prosperity tolerance and interracial relationships are improving. English is common everywhere, the country is prosperous, and its facilities—hotels, restaurants, shops, transportation, etc.—are clean, modern, up-to-date and not expensive. The scenery is spectacular, with jungles and rugged hills in the interior, plantations and superb beaches around the coasts. Main towns are along the west coast, and are heavily Chinese. The less traveled east coast is entirely Malay. Kuala Lumpur is a clean, comfortable city with a collection of rather disconcerting Victorian-Moorish architecture, a strikingly beautiful National Mosque and a good National Museum. Within easy reach of the two main tourist centers, Kuala Lumpur and Penang, are cool hill stations such as Fraser's Hill and the Genting and Cameron highlands. Eastern Malaysia is the states of Sarawak and Sabah in northern Borneo. For tourists, this is frontier country and with only limited facilities, but interesting for its wild scenery—jungles and mountains—and for its tribal life. Major highlights can be seen in 7 to 10 days.

Brunei is primarily a stopover between Sabah and Sarawak in East Malaysia. It is a small Malay Sultanate with rich oil revenues, but still limited tourist facilities. Population around 200,000, mostly found in the sleepy little tropical capital, Bandar Seri Begawan.

Singapore, 225 square miles, population 2.5 million is a city-state; it is also an independent country, a tight, efficient economy, a highly disciplined welfare state and a remarkable multi-racial social achievement. The mystery and romance of the literary "exotic East" are largely gone. What you will find is a bright, clean, attractive, modern tropical city that has neither the excitement and glamour of Hong Kong, nor, mercifully, its brutal contrasts of wealth and squalor. But where Hong Kong is an overwhelmingly Chinese society, Singapore is truly multi-racial; and its human geography, the wonderful variety of faces and human types that you see just walking down any street, is one of its greatest attractions. It is a major port and shopping center; and hotel and tourist facilities are excellent. Sightseeing takes only 2 or 3 days, but shopping temptations can keep the visitor busy for longer.

Indonesia, four large islands and about 13,000 small ones totaling 581,655 square miles, population 155.6 million, capital Jakarta, a city of over 7 million. Tourist goals in Indonesia are mostly in Java and Bali. Java, smallest of the main islands, contains the capital, 70 percent of the population, the chief monuments and the best range of Muslim cultural centers. Jakarta shows clearly the successive influences that have made this country; the native markets for the ordinary life of the people; the Jakarta Museum for the historical heritage of the former kingdoms; the presence of the Chinese; the passage of the Dutch; and finally the pompous prestige projects of the Sukarno era. In central Java is Borobudur, the greatest Buddhist monument in the world. And in Yogyakarta and Surabaya are the palaces of the sultans. Bali is only 90 miles long but has over 3 million people, and (possibly) over 10,000 temples. Since the destruction of Tibet, this is the only remaining example in the world today of a complete traditional society, one in which all facets of the whole of life—agriculture, economics, politics, technics, manners, art, music, dance, and drama—are all welded by religion (in this case Hinduism) into a unified and total way of life. Balinese life is passionate, beautiful, deeply meaningful, and satisfying. In Bali, magic is part of everyday life, and artistic creation is the common right of the humblest farmer. The construction of a jet airport and international-style hotels bodes well for the tourist, if not for the tradition. Although conditions in Indonesia are improving, it is best to work through a travel agency; outside of that, conditions can be highly unpredictable, making independent tour planning difficult. Sumatra to the north, with its exciting ethnic minorities and charming hill station, Lake Toba, is just opening for tourism. Minimum travel time should be a week, more if one wants to tour Java and the other main islands in addition to Bali and Jakarta, which continue to be the main attractions.

The Philippines, seven major and 7,100 minor islands totaling 115,831 square miles, population 54 million, capital Quezon City, with Manila still the center of economic, political, cultural and commercial life of the nation. Tourism in the Philippines is concentrated in the Metro Manila area (pop. around 8 million), where there are plenty of modern international hotels, good restaurants, night clubs, shops selling luxury and souvenir items, etc. Elsewhere on the main island of Luzon, hill resorts, beaches and subtropical scenery and climate plus the warm, friendly people are the attractions. The Philippines contain about 55 ethnic groups, all with distinctive dialects, customs, and traditions. The five major groups are the Ilocanos, the Tagalogs, the Visayans, the Bicolanos, and the Muslims in the South. The diverse character of the people is a direct reflection of their constantly changing history. First were the Malays, mostly Muslims, and the various indigenous groups; then came the Spanish, Dutch, the British, and the Americans, all of whom ruled for varying periods as colonial powers. Freedom and independence have produced periods of political instability and social upheaval, but there are now signs that the community is stabilizing with a strong sense of national identity. Problems still exist, especially in the South, where Muslim factions are still opposed to central government. If one sees only Manila, then a couple of days will suffice, but to see the upcountry areas and the exotic southern islands like Cebu, as one properly should, will give travel opportunities for up to ten days or more.

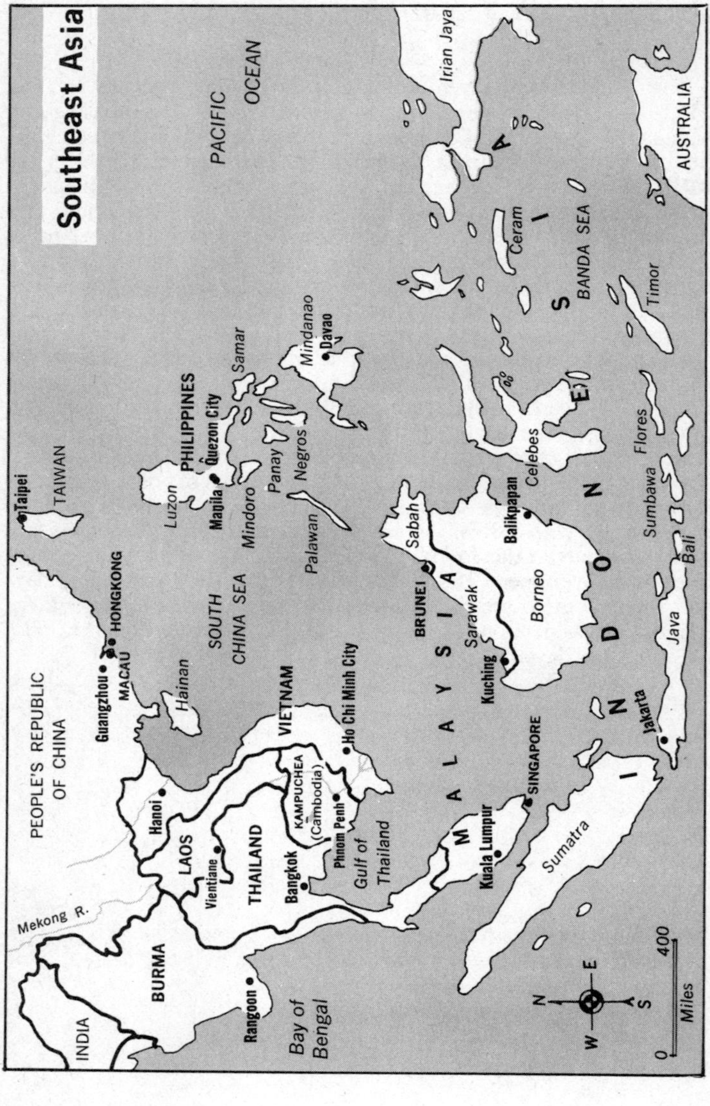
Southeast Asia
PEOPLE'S REPUBLIC OF CHINA
PACIFIC OCEAN
TAIWAN
Taipei
Guangzhou
MACAU
HONGKONG
Hainan
SOUTH CHINA SEA
PHILIPPINES
Luzon
Quezon City
Manila
Mindoro
Panay
Negros
Samar
Mindanao
Davao
Palawan
INDIA
BURMA
Mekong R.
Rangoon
Bay of Bengal
LAOS
Hanoi
Vientiane
THAILAND
Bangkok
VIETNAM
KAMPUCHEA (Cambodia)
Phnom Penh
Ho Chi Minh City
Gulf of Thailand
MALAYSIA
Kuala Lumpur
SINGAPORE
BRUNEI
Sabah
Sarawak
Kuching
Borneo
Balikpapan
Celebes
INDONESIA
Sumatra
Jakarta
Java
Bali
Sumbawa
Flores
Timor
BANDA SEA
Ceram
Irian Jaya
AUSTRALIA
N
S
E
W
0
400
Miles

THE ASIAN WAYS OF LIFE

Two Different Worlds—Urban and Peasant

Throughout its long history, this area, which European travelers call Southeast Asia, has been a busy crossroads of diverse cultures, religions, and ethnic groups. From the Arabs who sailed across the ocean during the Middle Ages to the Americans who arrived by air just the day before yesterday, adventurous peoples have come and brought with them their religions, customs, and values. Sharp religious and ethnic differences, which discouraged intermarriage among the major groups such as the Chinese, Malays, Europeans, and Indians, hindered cultural amalgamation. However, the tropical climate served to blur the militancy of Islam, the ascetic idealism of Buddhism, and the intellectual strictures of Confucianism. Thus, the various communal groups developed their separate and individual lifestyles with little accompanying warfare and strife.

City-Led but Agricultural Majority

In the 20th century mass media, especially television, and easy transport have lured many people, especially the young, to cities and towns. There, they mingle freely with those of other communities as they sample the delights of the cinema and the shopping center. The rigid rules of the village vanish in factories and on crowded buses and restaurants. The watchful eyes of disapproving elders do not penetrate the walls of high-rise apartment buildings, nor does the village busybody frequent the cinema or discothèque. Thus, communal barriers are gradually loosening. A new way of life, incorporating customs from all communities, is emerging in the region, especially in the cities.

City life has come to dominate national psyches only in recent years with the advent of independence for most nations in the region. During the days of colonial rule, with the British in Malaya, Singapore, and Burma; the Dutch in Indonesia; and the Americans in the Philippines, cities were the realm of white administrators and of all kinds of foreign entrepreneurs, including the Chinese. The Chinese came to cities and towns, often on the edge of starvation, and by thrift and a single-minded pursuit of capital, became the leading traders and entrepreneurs of the entire region.

Thus, Asian cities became a blend of European and Chinese customs. Take, for example, the Dinner Party. Chinese have always been fond of food—Chinese cuisine rivals the French in its variety and richness. Inventive cooks have worked miracles with bears' paws, sea slugs, and chrysanthemums, which makes the French garlic snail seem pedestrian indeed. Eating food is a serious business, as you might well imagine. Once the last course has been served, the evening is at an end and departure of the guests is swift. For most Europeans, however, the last course of a dinner is only the prelude to several hours of brandy, cigars, and lively conversation. If you blend the two traditions, a heavy dinner plus the usual Western overload of cocktails, hors d'oeuvres and food with wine, you find yourself in a situation where you desperately fight to stay awake as your Chinese host beams blandly over his bountiful table. One Chinese magnate, not wishing to lose face by serving less than is expected both by Eastern and by Western standards, has neatly solved the problem by showing a film after dinner so that gastronomical weaklings may snooze in the anonymous comfort of the darkened theater.

The sumptuous consumption of food in opulent surroundings is enjoyed by only the privileged few. The majority of Southeast Asia's population still lives outside the central urban areas on a simple monotonous diet of rice with a bit of fish and vegetable. In the less industrialized Asian countries, up to 80 percent of the people live in villages and their livelihood depends on agriculture. Although in many countries improved roads have opened villages to the 20th century, traditional customs dictate the life of the people in most rural areas.

In addition to the urban and village people, a third group is usually lumped together under the catchall title: Tribal Minorities. This grouping includes such sophisticated peoples as the Kachin, Yao, and Karen hill tribes of Northern Thailand and Burma, down to the recently discovered Tasaday people of the Philippines, who dwell in a Stone Age limbo. The ethnic backgrounds of the people vary from the round-eyed Negritos in Malaya to the fair-skinned Rukai of Taiwan. Despite the differences in appearance, all these people share (just as American Indians) a deep regard for the land, which they believe is theirs on loan from the gods and belongs to no single individual. To the uninitiated Western eye the hill tribes' slash-and-burn system of agriculture is wanton waste. However, if the Western agricultural expert were to stay around 12 or 20 years and study their ways more closely, he would soon realize that the seemingly haphazard farming systems of these so-called primitive people are based on an understanding of the need for crop rotation.

Traditionally tied to a nomadic life, many of the tribal people are harassed by the intricacies of national boundaries (instituted by remote central governments) that have little meaning for them. Future generations will, no doubt, learn to adapt to new ways. Many countries, such as Thailand, are taking great pains in their efforts to involve the tribal peoples in the national picture through education, trade, and increased communication facilities.

Southeast Asian Cities

The cities of Southeast Asia can be categorized into five groupings. First are those port cities that were established to serve the British Empire and are now predominantly Chinese in character. These include: Hong Kong, Singapore, and Penang. Other port cities—Bangkok, Manila, Jakarta—share only the similarity that they are *not* ex-British and that the Chinese, although they play an important economic role, participate little in the political and cultural vitality of urban life. Two capital cities, Taipei and Kuala Lumpur, are inland towns penned in by hills and mountains. One city remains in a class by itself as a result of its government's Closed Door policy—and that is Rangoon.

How do most Asian city dwellers live and in what circumstances? Until recent years, class (as well as income) delineated and circumscribed the quality of urban life. The rich lived in spacious residences with ample quarters for squads of servants; the poor huddled in cramped tenements, often so crowded that the members of a family would sleep in shifts. Nowadays, an emerging middle class has created blocks of luxury apartments and spreading neighborhoods of semi-detached units fronted by postage-stamp gardens.

Extremes remain, however, and every Southeast Asian city retains enclaves of the wealthy, who live in a style available only to mega-millionaires in the West. These luxurious homes are in sharp contrast to the areas where any place to sleep under shelter is considered home to thousands.

Nevertheless, a visitor should remember that contrasting living standards in cities where the rich boast gold-plated bathroom fixtures and the poor brush their teeth in canals that serve as communal toilet and tub, are now leavened by the emergence of an expanding middle class who demand modern housing and facilities. Indoor plumbing, for example, with all the ease and comfort that this implies, is a recent novelty to the average city dweller. Even today, especially in outlying areas, the "honey wagon," a tasteless foreign euphemism for a human waste collection cart, is a familiar sight on many streets.

Urban Kampongs

The "honey wagon" calls most often in rural communities such as the ones that nestle along the highways leading to international airports. The houses are frequently screened from the tourist's view (and his camera) by huge billboards advertising airlines, cigarettes, and soft drinks. These *kampongs* or *barrios* or squatter villages also dot the entire urban area, near railway lines, market centers, or wherever spare space might be available. The houses are often substantially built, with yard space for a few domestic animals, chickens, goats and perhaps a pig (in non-Muslim neighborhoods). Nearby is a center for communal activities such as laundry, barbering, marketing, and a stop for minibus, taxi, or rickshaw. In these neighborhoods most individual dwellings do not connect with civic services such as running water, paved roads, or sewage lines.

Here, communal attitudes, carried over from rural living patterns, persist. Weddings, funerals, coming-of-age parties all present an opportunity for a festive turnout. Families save for these occasions and spend lavishly on food, decorations, and entertainment. A band—often two: one traditional and one "pop"—is hired along with perhaps a theatrical troupe to provide entertainment for the entire community. At hired tables, festooned with bottles, the men sit, accompanied by their wives clad in laces and their best batiks or silk. Children, their faces sticky from too many sweets and their eyes shining with excitement, dart between the tables and under the platform where the bands play their deafening music.

The squatter village maintains this communal cohesiveness in times of calamity as well. Disasters arrive with dismaying regularity, most often in the form of flood or fire, and, in Manila or Hong Kong, devastating typhoons. Then the community works together to rebuild, sharing materials and labor and personal comfort.

A visitor to Southeast Asia who takes time to wander through these *kampong* neighborhoods will be richly rewarded if he refrains from using his camera. Here, away from the crush and noise of the city, he will find a warm, if sometimes reserved, welcome (except, of course, during the time of political uneasiness when a prudent traveler stays close to his hotel). If a visitor minds his manners and behaves in a decorous way he will easily make friends whether in the *mubaans* near Klong Toey in Bangkok, the shanty-town *barrios* in Manila, or the *kampongs* that flourish all over Malaysia and Indonesia.

"Chinatown"

Many Western visitors are astonished to find that "Chinatowns" exist in most Southeast Asian cities. Even Singapore, where 75 percent of the population is Chinese, has the remains of a once flourishing "Chinatown," which attracts tourists and travelers from all over the world.

A bit of historical background quickly clears up this seeming paradox: with the exception of Taipei every urban area includes a special section that housed the original emigrants from China. Flophouses and tenements took in these newcomers and as their number increased, traditional service organizations (both legal and illegal) developed. Clan associations, a sort of immigrants' insurance agency for burial fees, collected dues that were then used for loans for medical and educational emergencies. As the Chinese prospered, the clans acquired properties and built special *kongsi* temples that served both as meeting places and repositories for clan records. The *kongsi* or clans came to specialize in giving scholarship aid, for the Chinese have an almost religious veneration for education.

An illegal aspect of this sort of association were the *tongs* or secret societies, criminal groups that lent money at exorbitant rates and operated extortion, prostitution, and smuggling rackets. They became so powerful that whenever there was a *tong* war, such as the famous riots in Penang in 1867, the entire community suffered. Even today, these secret societies flourish despite vigorous government efforts to stamp them out. It comes as no surprise that the film *The Godfather* was a spectacular success in Southeast Asian cities.

At the same time, shopkeepers in these Chinese sections quickly established businesses to cater to special needs, customs, and habits. Herbal medicine shops fascinate foreigners with their bottles of strangely colored liquids and jars with peculiar objects floating in a murky liquid. Powders and bones, grasses and dried flowers are arranged in neat little glass-fronted drawers. Hanging on the walls of these shops are anatomical charts painted in garish colors. Another familiar sight in Chinatown are small shops that fabricate elaborate paper-and-tinsel houses, motor cars, TV sets, and fake money, which are burnt at funerals so the deceased may enter the next world handsomely endowed with the goods of this.

Visiting a Chinatown in Southeast Asia is like stepping back to pre-Revolutionary China. Here one finds the heady atmosphere of hustling and huckstering that has largely disappeared in the People's Republic of China. Pushcarts jam the narrow, traffic-choked streets, which are filled wall to wall with masses of people. One can buy almost anything: plastic shoes, fresh fruit (oranges, rambutans, starfruit), wind-up metal toys that emit strange quacks and roars, and textile goods of all description.

Chinatown residents live in three- or four-storied apartments over shophouses and warehouses. Often, the shop-owning family occupies one floor, renting out extra apartments and rooms to laboring families. Creaky, narrow stairs lead up to the living quarters where a minimum of furnishing accommodates a great number of people of all ages. Toilet facilities, meager at best, are often located in an area behind the building. Cooking is done over a clay charcoal brazier or a two-burner hot plate. Poor families, who cannot afford capital investment for fuel, utensils and cooking staples, frequent the food stalls and local cookhouses. Yet, no matter how sparse the accommodations, each living unit has a family shrine where a deity (often Kuan Yin, the goddess of mercy) flanked by portraits of honored ancestors, presides over offerings of incense and flowers.

Hanging near the altar or on the walls in appropriate places are mottos from Confucius or the Bible, inscribed in gold ink on red paper. Usually a single low-wattage bulb hanging from the ceiling on a long cord provides the only illumination for the room . . . except in some homes, where the ghostly glare of a television set flickers in the darkened room.

The Chinese, although not a deeply spiritual people as a whole, do pay attention to religious matters. No matter which city one visits in Southeast Asia, the oldest and most interesting temples are usually in Chinatown. For those unfamiliar with Chinese patterns of worship, however, a building which at first sight looks like a temple, often turns out to be a *kongsi* compound, complete with a richly decorated temple and annexes that contain ancestral portraits, records and meeting rooms that are decorated with pictures illustrating Confucian virtues. (Filial piety seems to be a favorite theme: a good example is a vividly drawn story of a son who, dismayed by the clouds of mosquitoes disturbing his father's slumber, stripped himself naked in order to attract the bloodthirsty creatures away from his revered parent.)

Sanitary conditions being poor in these areas, a visitor should nevertheless not be deterred by the presence of unpleasant odors or the sight of cockroaches, flies, or rats. He should also be prepared to see exhibitions (both alive and slaughtered) of culinary exotica such as turtle, snake, and occasionally dog. The faint-hearted might use their imaginations to project what a Chinatown resident might feel in the streets of our homelands with their heavy odors of fish and chips, pizzas and hamburgers, the pervading atmosphere of smog and automobile exhausts, the sight of littered paper wrappers and tin cans, and the disturbing presence of young and old vagrants, prostitutes, and dope addicts wandering along the pavements.

Togetherness in the High-Rise

More and more Southeast Asian city dwellers are moving to high-rise apartment buildings. Many of the governments—particularly Singapore, and to a less successful degree Hong Kong and Bangkok—provide low-cost housing for the working classes. In Singapore, tens of thousands of new public housing units have been built, while in Hong Kong more thousands of low-cost developments have been built to accommodate the flow of emigrants from China.

Many families discover that the transition from the social cohesion of a street-oriented community to the isolation of an anonymous apartment is difficult. Despite the fact that many organizations provide community services, the suicide rate is alarmingly high. In Singapore, for example, the suicide rate has almost doubled in recent years. Leaping from these multi-storied fortresses of future shock is a favorite method of self-destruction.

Probably the two most serious afflictions annoying high-rise dwellers are noise and vandalism. The balmy tropical climate means that windows are always open, and a cacophony of TV programs, cries of colicky infants, shouts during marital altercations, flow right through every apartment. Vandalism, stemming from ignorance, carelessness, or frustration, causes frequent breakdown in essential services such as the elevators and rubbish disposal units. These modern housing developments have also contributed to the breakdown of the large and traditionally close-knit family unit—a problem growing throughout Asia. Nevertheless, despite these problems, most families are grateful for the increased privacy and conveniences offered by the new housing.

Suburbia

In Southeast Asia, as elsewhere, those who can afford it flee to the suburbs in search of fresh air, quiet, and space. Formerly, these areas were reserved mainly for wealthy foreigners and colonial officers. Now, as living patterns change, young executives and professional men forsake ethnic neighborhoods for the status and comfort of suburbia.

For a glimpse of suburban life, let's look at the house of Dr. Chin Ho Meng and his family, who live in Kuala Lumpur, where, as in most Asian cities, the Chinese dominate the professional and financial worlds. In all probability, our Dr. Chin is a member of a family network of businesses, shops, plantations, and transport that spreads to several neighboring countries. If you visit any non-European home in Southeast Asia, this is likely to be the kind to which you will be invited, as the rich will be happy to show it off to you—less wealthy friends may well be living in cramped or unattractive quarters and simply be unable to entertain you in the manner they imagine you require.

Dr. Chin lives in quiet comfort on Kenny Hill in a spacious modern house, where the mechanics of family life are managed by a squad of servants. A Malay chauffeur drives the air-conditioned Mercedes; a Tamil gardener manicures and lovingly prunes the flowering shrubs and trees; while a Chinese couple does the shopping, cooking, and cleaning. A washerwoman comes daily to do the laundry.

In the circular driveway, lined with stately travelers' palms, sits a snappy sports car for the family youngsters to use. Two are attending school in Kuala Lumpur, preparing to go to England for their higher education. Like affluent teenagers everywhere, they wear the contemporary international youth costume: patched jeans and T-shirts emblazoned with slogans from American TV.

As a unit, the family is not as tightly knit as other generations were in former (and not as affluent) times. The eldest son spends too much time going out late to the local discos, with friends of whom his parents disapprove. Constant friction exists between him and his father, who cannot understand why the boy is frustrated working in his uncle's office. The eldest daughter arouses family consternation, for she has not married although she returned from overseas study four years ago. She holds a challenging position as a public relations officer for an international hotel. Her mother suspects she has a European boyfriend but does not dare mention it to her husband, who has plans for the girl to marry a distant cousin in the family banking business.

In the house itself, the furnishings are a curious mishmash of heavy blackwood traditional Chinese furniture, inlaid with mother-of-pearl, and curved, elegantly upholstered Western sofas. Scattered on tables are knickknacks and souvenirs from the family's travels in Europe. In one corner of the room a six-foot-long bar, padded in black leather, stands before mirrored glass shelves on which are displayed bottles of expensive whisky and liquors of every description. Slowly revolving ceiling fans cool the living and dining areas, while air-conditioners maintain a chill atmosphere in the bedrooms.

Getting Around, Asian Style

In the last few years the automobile has been slowly strangling the flow of transport in Southeast Asian cities. The concept of individual mobility has become a popular goal as well as a recognized status symbol. In urban areas, the motor car population has increased almost as rapidly as the birth-rate in rural areas, and now no major urban center is without daily traffic jams. In Singapore, for example, one survey estimates one automobile for every 19 people. Several governments are taking active steps to curb the explosion, either by controlling imports of cars, especially luxury models, or imposing new restrictions on entering and parking in city centers.

This increase in numbers of automobiles, trucks, and motorbikes has driven traditional modes of transport from most major thoroughfares. In Hong Kong, for example, where no new licenses for hand-drawn rickshaws are issued, their number has dwindled to under 50, manned by illiterate, older immigrants from the mainland. Their customers are mostly tourists who spend most of their time snapping photos of themselves in this unique carriage.

Vanishing at a slower rate is the cycle-driven rickshaw in all its variations, from the *bejak* in Indonesia, where the passengers sit in front of the driver, to the *tri-shaw* in northern Thailand, where the passengers squeeze onto a narrow seat behind the driver. In Jakarta the *bejak* has undergone some modernizing revision, with passengers now enclosed in a sort of bubble-shaped sidecar. The procedure for payment, however, remains the same: bargain the price *before* you embark in order to avoid unpleasant scenes at your destination.

Most Westerners find the idea of being hauled along by human muscle-power on bicycle-rickshaw somewhat distasteful. Therefore, visitors who wish to forsake the comfortable isolation of tour bus or hired car—and the traveler on a tight budget—can use local mini-buses, which ply the back roads and side streets. In this category, the most colorful are Manila's *jeepneys,* formerly converted jeeps, now mostly Toyota vehicles, decorated with fanciful, highly colored paintings. Less brilliant, but just as serviceable, are Indonesian *bimos,* which can be hailed by a gentle waving of your hand, palm downward. The most exhilarating ride of all is careening through Bangkok streets in *tuktuks,* whose drivers spin their vehicles around corners, dangerously balanced on two of its three wheels.

Several Southeast Asian cities offer unique rides. In both Penang and Hong Kong, hillside railways take visitors up to the highest peak for a spectacular view. The funicular railway in Penang ascends through jungle vegetation up to well-manicured estates where British-style gardening produces fine roses and lawns. Bangkok, of course, is famous for its *klongs,* where long-tailed sampans ferry passengers to the famous floating markets. Singapore has a cable-car system that, in a 17-minute ride, takes a passenger away from the teeming city out over the harbor and onto peaceful Sentosa Island. Kuala Lumpur also has a cable car.

Urban Fun and Games

Chinese films featuring masters of martial arts, which are popular in the West, have long been entertainment king in Southeast Asia. The story line in each movie follows a single familiar pattern with minor variations. The theme is almost always a vengeance fight where the hero utilizes some special technique, whether with sword, knife or fists, to defeat a host of villains. Blood flows copiously, bones snap and crack in an orgy of violence. Most of the films are produced by a small group of studios based primarily in Hong Kong and Taiwan. The biggest is the famous Shaw Brothers Studio, under the management of Run Run Shaw in Hong Kong and Runme Shaw in Singapore. The late Bruce Lee, with productions such as *Sword of the Dragon,* won international fame until his untimely death in 1973. Even today his films draw record-breaking crowds all over the area.

Also popular are "spaghetti Westerns" and gangster films from Italy and America. Obviously the pressures of urban living create a pressing need for emotional release in violent terms, as anyone who attends one of these films in Southeast Asia can tell you. The audience reacts vociferously to the scenes of violence, gasping with admiration as the hero bludgeons a bloody path through a horde of enemies.

Romance, especially tinged with sorrow, and perhaps a soupçon of the supernatural, is another popular film topic. Indian films lead the list of this type of tear-jerker, but Indonesia, Malaysia, and Thailand produce some fine examples of the soggy-Kleenex picture. Many of these center on familiar ghost-story themes set in villages where the ghost of a jilted lover, a ghastly spectacle of ghoulish makeup and horrendous shrieks, upsets the entire community—as well as the audience, which loves every spooky moment.

Family outings involve picnics, a stroll through a park or a visit to a zoo, amusement park, and, of course, holiday festivals. Singapore, which is the most advanced city and also the urban center with the least amount of country space for weekend escape offers the most varied entertainments: two zoos (one with a spectacular Bird Park), a cable car ride, a new waxworks museum and an aquarium, plus several spacious parks that feature Sunday band concerts, as well as a few crowded and admittedly polluted beaches. Manila's waterfront park provides spectacular sunsets as well as a modernistic playground. Bangkok also has several parks and a zoo, as does Kuala Lumpur. Near Taipei, the countryside features several spectacular parks designed in traditional Chinese fashion with waterfalls, moon-bridges, and secluded nooks for lovers.

In each city are clubs established for specialized entertainment. Racing is a favorite pastime, and the racetracks in Singapore, Bangkok, and Hong Kong have elegant clubhouses where proud owners of winning horses dispense champagne with a liberal hand. The oil industry has established lavish entertainment centers in Singapore and Jakarta. Art associations, amateur theater groups and film associations draw budding intellectuals together with rising young executives on the prowl for culture.

Less publicized, but certainly as well organized, is entertainment for men only. Bangkok's massage parlors are internationally famous and areas such as Patpong Road offer varied and "unique" entertainments. In Taipei, the Poh Tek district (Peitou) is renowned among Asian businessmen as offering great opportunities for relaxation in opulent surroundings. On a more proletarian level are the Wanchai district in Hong Kong, Bugis Street in Singapore, and the cemeteries in Jakarta.

Sport in Southeast Asia, as all over the world, centers more and more on organized competitions, Rugby, soccer, and swimming are favorites and draw large crowds. The Asian Games, held every five years, capture the interest of the entire region. Badminton and table tennis are also popular and not just as spectator sports. Just as in America, backyards have a hoop for young basketball hopefuls and badminton nets festoon suburban yards everywhere.

Traditional Asian pastimes such as kite flying remain popular. In Bangkok, especially, kite flying has developed into a graceful warring dance between male and female kites. And let's not forget the popularity—prompted by the flood of Chinese boxer movies of the martial arts—of *judo, Kung fu, tae kweando,* and *tai chi.*

Future Shock for the Peasant

Urban dwellers in Southeast Asia face the jolts and jerks of future shock more intensely than city-folk in industrialized countries. Escalators, traffic jams, air, noise and water pollution, instant communication through music, TV, radio, and the movies have only recently become a way of life here. Although the impact of modernization has caused confusion and divisions, the entire region finds excitement in the challenges offered by the future. Disillusionment and alienation, which pervade the mood of the West, do not find a home among the majority of the rising middle class in Southeast Asia. Doubts, however, do exist among intellectuals and economic planners who view the growing gap between rich and poor and particularly the widening gulf separating the rural peoples, who by and large are not sharing in the rising prosperity, as a potential disaster. The rural people have little opportunity to enjoy exciting new entertainments and material goods. Thus, while change is progressing at a geometric rate in Southeast Asian cities, the villages and towns remain tied to the rhythms of agriculture and maintain a way of life that has basically changed little throughout the centuries.

The Peasants' Way of Life

The Spanish chronicler who described Filipino houses in 1609 might have been writing about almost any rural home in Southeast Asia today: "The houses are of the same design, generally built on poles or posts high from the ground, with narrow rooms and low ceilings made of interwoven strips of wood or bamboo and covered with palm-leaf roofing, each house standing by itself and not joined to any other."

As the 20th-century traveler can see, neither rural housing styles nor the way of life have changed much in the past 375 years. Where roads have opened up once isolated communities, a few outward changes may be noticeable: zinc or asbestos sheet roofing sometimes replaces palm-leaf, the simple *sarong* might be exchanged for shorts or trousers, and in town pop music or movies probably draw bigger crowds than a puppet show. However, the basic way of life in rural Southeast Asia follows its timeless pattern.

The tropical climate that exists throughout Southeast Asia and shared historical influences (Chinese and Indian) result in striking similarities. With minor regional differences, the Filipino *barrio,* Thai *bang,* Malaysian *kampong,* and Javanese *desa* are all variations on the same theme.

What does the traveler see in a typical rural village? Bamboo or wood and thatch cottages made from materials that grow everywhere and are quickly constructed. A yard where chickens, ducks, dogs, and pigs mix with children under the coconut and banana palms. In bigger villages or towns, there will be a temple, pagoda, mosque, or church, while all around are never-ending *padi* fields where the essence of life, rice, is grown. There might be miles of rubber, tea, or oil palm plantations, fields of sugarcane, corn, or tapioca, vast teak forests or tin mines.

There will certainly be clumps of bamboo that bend gracefully with the seasonal winds and provide inspiration to artists as well as fulfilling a hundred and one more practical purposes. When split, bamboo can be woven into walls, fences, mats, and baskets; segments of a wide stem carry water or make a disposable cooking pot; leaves can be woven, while the stems are used for simple furniture, hunting implements, traps, musical instruments, and alarms. Even the young shoots are prized as a delicious vegetable.

Tall, slender coconut palms are about as versatile as the bamboo. The leaves are used for thatch, mats, baskets, and hats, while the tough ribs of the leaves make skewers, and the husk becomes a doormat. The shell of the coconut is used for ladles or bowls, and also makes excellent charcoal. The dried flesh, copra, is pressed to extract the oil that is used in the manufacture of margarine, lard, and soap. The grated flesh provides rich creamy milk that is the basis of many fragrant meat and vegetable dishes, while the thin watery liquid makes a refreshing drink. Another ever-present plant is the fast-growing banana, with nourishing fruit and leaves that are used for wrapping food before roasting or steaming, or even as plates.

The rhythm of life in the country is tied to the all-important crops and therefore the changing seasons. The fisherman works daily until the heavy monsoon storms make it unsafe for him to set out to sea in his fragile boat. The next couple of months will be spent repairing boats and nets and perhaps making a few items for sale to bring in a little money during this lean period. Inland fishermen who drag the rivers with large nets or use fishtraps are not, of course, restricted by the seasons and their produce forms an essential part of the diet of most people.

Where crops such as rice, sugar, tobacco, and corn are grown, the harvesting season is a period of great activity. The "green revolution" has brought improved strains of rice and in some areas double cropping has quickened the tempo of rural life. In districts with a marked dry season that is unsuitable for rice growing, alternative crops such as peanuts are planted.

The Agricultural Industries

Vast rubber plantations dominate the countryside in Malaysia and can also be seen in parts of Indonesia, Thailand, and Burma. The thin blotchy trunk and small, dull green leaves of the rubber tree give it an insignificant appearance that belies its value. Since the first rubber seedling was brought from South America to Asia less than 100 years ago, rubber has earned many millions of dollars.

When a rubber tree is about six years old, it is slashed diagonally around the trunk in the early hours of the morning so that the maximum amount of milky white latex is able to drip into the small cup tied to the tree. The latex is collected around noon each day the tree is cut (ideally twenty days per month, though some trees are still tapped daily), then mixed with formic acid and pressed into sheets of crude rubber, which harden and turn reddish-brown.

The threat of synthetic rubber and the increasing demand for palm oil has led to many old rubber trees being replaced with the oil palm. Large bunches of orange-to-black berries that release valuable oil when crushed can be seen at the base of the luxuriant green fronds growing out from the trunk of this attractive, medium-sized palm.

The rice cycle dominates the lives of millions of Asians. The amazing terraced *padi* fields that climb like emerald steps up and down steep hills are thought to have been in existence 3,000 years ago in the Philippines and Java. The earth dikes of the terraced *padi* fields, as well as those of those of the *padi* fields that stretch across the great flat plains of countries like Thailand, are constructed so that water can pass from one field to the next. Irrigation is vital, for without water rice cannot grow.

Before rice can be planted, a field must be cleaned of all weeds and thoroughly dug, generally by a water buffalo pulling a simple wooden plough. Rice seeds are scattered in a small bed of earth and kept covered with water until they shoot up to about 10 inches. Then the soft green shoots are planted out, one by one, about 6 inches apart, into the wet fields. This is the toughest job of all, bending over at the waist in the burning sun, up to the knees in mud, pushing rice shoots into the water-covered earth hour after hour.

While the rice is growing, little needs to be done apart from keeping the fields free from weeds and tending the dikes. But when the green shoots have turned to rich gold and the heads of grain hang heavily, every pair of hands is needed for harvesting. Men, women, and children descend like a plague of locusts, tiny semicircular knives held in the palm of the hand, to cut the rice. The stalks are then bunched into sheaves, which are dried before threshing, cleaning, and husking.

Rice is so vital to life that it's not surprising that a rice goddess is worshipped in many areas. This is particularly noticeable in Bali, where tiny shrines with offerings to *Dewi Sri* adorn every *padi* field.

Tea is another prime industry in some countries of the region. It grows in hill country at altitudes between 2,000 and 7,000 feet. It is grown on terraces in the hillsides, and the bushes, which can live for fifty years, are severely pruned to waist height. Women pluck the pale-green top growth, which consists of the top leaf and two lower leaves only, and place it in the wicker basket which is fastened to their backs by means of forehead straps. The loads are tipped into scales at collecting points, weighed, and taken by lorries to the processing plants. There rollers twist and curl the leaves, evaporating the moisture and crushing the pieces to liberate the aromatic juice. Then humidifiers oxidize the green tea, through copper color to the familiar black that we recognize, and the tea is graded and packed for shipment.

A number of other agricultural products are important to the domestic and exporting economies of the Asian countries. Tobacco, grown traditionally in the Philippines, in Burma, Java, and Sumatra, and increasingly in northern Thailand, supplies high-grade leaf for local and export consumption. Plantations are usually seen at medium elevations, usually inland, in places where extremes in climate, heat and cold, will not harm the delicate growing plants. When fully grown, the leaves are carefully harvested and dried, either naturally, or in kiln-sheds and sent to factories for further processing. As other traditional sources, such as Africa, have become less reliable over recent years, the value of tobacco as a major industry in Asia has become increasingly important. Both Indonesia and the Philippines produce good cigars, and the Burmese cheroots appeal to those liking a really strong smoke.

Timber, especially the valuable tropical hardwoods such as teak and mahogany, has become depleted over recent years. Although overcutting and the lack of planned reforestation have produced a growing problem throughout the region, timber is still a major industry in a number of Asian countries, particularly Indonesia, Borneo, Malaysia, and Thailand.

Sugar production has grown very rapidly over recent years within Asia as worldwide prices and demand have increased. Major producers are the Philippines and Thailand.

Coffee; tapioca (used extensively in the West as animal feed and in commercial, processed food production); spices; coconut products; tropical fruit, either fresh or tinned; and even fresh orchids all play important roles in the economies of various Asian nations.

The most valuable crop of Asia is an illegal one—opium. The notorious "Golden Triangle," in the border area where Thailand, Laos, and Burma join, is one of the world's largest sources of opium and its processed derivative, heroin. The illegal harvest is the one cash crop available to many of the tribal peoples in the remote hill areas, who are not aware of the damage their crop is having on countries far away. Their products are smuggled out, usually through Thailand, to the world's markets and, in spite of governmental efforts and international cooperation by drug-control agencies, continues at a high level. It has become a multi-billion-dollar industry and the profit margins are so staggering, with the temptations for financial gain so irresistible, both to the farmers and officials who are supposed to be fighting the trade, that its suppression within Asia is unlikely. But any foreigner who might be tempted to join in the traffic should take notice that the penalties are terrible indeed for those who are caught. Traffickers arrested in Thailand are often given jail sentences of twenty years or more and in Singapore and Malaysia the death sentence is sometimes carried out. However tempting the apparent availability of drugs may seem to be in parts of Asia, foreigners must be made aware of the very grave risks they are taking, even in buying for their own consumption.

Markets and Medicine Men

Very few rural people are entirely self-sufficient, so this means trips to a market. To many travelers, an Asian market is one of the world's most fascinating free shows. Markets usually operate daily in the towns, but in small villages market day comes every three to five days. Stalls are set up in a square or line the dirt roads. A bewildering assortment delights the eye and sometimes assaults the nose: piles of luscious fruit, deep purple eggplants, vivid red chilies, and vegetables in every shade of green. Stacks of pungent dried fish, jostle with sacks of rice, dried peas and lentils, while bundles of noodles provide a creamy white contrast to piles of red onions. Mountains of exotic tropical fruits, some of them almost unknown outside the region provide a colorful display in every market. Another attraction in any Asian market is the itinerant medicine man, the Orient's ubiquitous and most popular traveling salesman, stands in the center of a fascinated circle who hang on every word regarding the latest virility potion or miraculous snake cure. A snake is pulled from a bag, obligingly bites the salesman, who quickly rubs in his medicine and behold! He's still alive. Markets also often feature performances of local music, fortune tellers, and other irresistible sights and camera subjects.

Simple Routines

The routine of daily life in the countryside follows a pattern that is altered only during the busy harvest season or when festivals occur. Usually, everyone is up at dawn and after a snack (perhaps some cold rice or a banana and a hot drink) sets to work. The men leave for the fields or rivers, while the women and younger children stay to clean the home, wash the clothes, tend the animals and prepare the daily food.

A substantial meal is eaten around noon, then it's back to work until late afternoon, when it's time for the daily bath at the nearest stream or well, and for fetching water for the household. After the evening meal (generally the same food as that served at mid-day, with perhaps another dish) there is time for relaxation as night falls.

The interior of most houses is simple, with little furniture. There may be a slightly raised sleeping platform where mats, pillows and bolsters are spread each evening, with a cupboard or chest for storing clothing, but solid chairs and tables seldom replace the woven mat.

Leisure time is spent chatting with friends, tending songbirds or fighting cocks, telling and retelling stories or riddles, playing games with boards and stones, or chewing betel (which stains the mouth a vivid red and is supposed to strengthen the teeth as well as give a slight "kick"). Modernity sometimes appears in the shape of a transistor radio, or, increasingly, TV sets, which quickly follow the arrival of electricity in the more remote villages. More strenuous activities include ball games involving a light rattan ball that is kicked across a net (popular right across Southeast Asia from Burma to the Philippines), while badminton is another firm favorite.

Religious or harvest festivals provide an excuse for all kinds of excitement, and are times for kite flying, top spinning, buffalo or bull races, cockfights (and furious gambling), processions, visiting relatives, and going on picnics.

The staple food of almost all of Southeast Asia is rice. Its importance is stressed by the fact that the words for "rice" and "meal" are the same in many countries. Where peasants produce all their own rice, but do not have access to a machine mill, women must perform the daily task of pounding the rice in a huge stone or wooden mortar to break the tough husk that is then shaken away. Rice is eaten at least twice daily, together with side dishes that vary depending upon availability and the prosperity of the peasants. Vegetables, fresh and dried fish, eggs, meat, poultry, clear soups and soya bean curd (introduced by the Chinese and widely used as a valuable source of protein) are the main foods. Fish is important owing to the Muslim and Hindu taboos on pork and beef and the absence of lamb and for many poor people is the only available source of animal protein.

Mealtimes are informal, with the entire family rarely sitting down together. Each person helps himself to a bowl of rice and the four or five other dishes on the table. Hot chili-based sauces and fermented fish sauce add piquancy to dishes that have probably already been cooked with freshly ground spices, fragrant roots, grasses, and leaves or tiny acidic fruits.

The Family

Families in rural Southeast Asia are very closely knit, and larger than those usually found in Western countries, much to the despair of family-planning organizations. The extended family system of old China, where sons bring their wives to live in the family compound, is still found in some Asian countries, but is gradually breaking down everywhere. Ideally, a newly married couple will set up their own home after marriage or after the birth of the first child, though aged parents are always welcome to live with them and visiting relatives are immediately accepted into the home.

The women of Southeast Asia are a beautiful blend of silk and steel, usually petite and graceful with a gentle manner that belies their strength and influence. Although men are respected and pampered, in all but conservative Muslim societies, it is the women who hold the purse strings and have a say in major decisions. Their strong social role is no doubt partly due to their economic importance. These wives, like their Western counterparts, clean and maintain their homes and bring up their children. They also look after the domestic animals, work in the *padi* fields, tap rubber trees, plant corn and sugar, make baskets and mats, decorate oiled paper umbrellas, shape crude clay cooking pots, weave cloth, sell produce in the markets, make daily offerings to the gods, and tend the family shrines. In the cities they occupy an increasingly important place in administration, industry, commerce, and the professions.

Their clothing, except during ceremonial occasions, is simple and practical. Traditionally, in most areas an ankle-length cloth is wrapped around the waist and hips (known as a *panyung* in Thailand, a *longyi* in Burma, and a *sarong* or *kain* in Malaysia and Indonesia). This is topped by a shirt or blouse. Jewelry is not only a lovely adornment regarded as an essential item all over Southeast Asia but a form of investment, since women buy pieces of jewelry (usually gold or silver) with their savings rather than banking them.

Men working in the fields may change the traditional *sarong* for a pair of loose shorts and jacket that bear a similarity to the clothing once worn by Chinese coolies—a resemblance reinforced by the conical bamboo hats worn in many areas. It is a sad part of change in Asia that the traditional, and colorful, forms of local dress are relentlessly giving way to modern Western forms—particularly the ubiquitous jeans and T-shirt.

The children of Southeast Asia are remarkable; they rarely fight among themselves, are seldom disciplined by their elders, yet are generally well behaved and responsible at an early age. They are an inseparable part of the family and are taken everywhere; they join in games, visits, meals, all-night performances, and special ceremonies. They are expected to help as soon as they are able. By the time they're five or six, little girls will be carrying a younger brother or sister on their hips and helping their mothers in the home. The young boys feed the chickens, watch the ducks paddle around the *padi* fields, gather fruit, help at harvest time, and tend the water buffalos (a much envied task that allows the boys to frolic in the water with the huge but docile beasts).

An increasing percentage of rural children attend village schools where a very elementary education can be gained. Many of them leave school by the time they are 12 or 13 years of age, and in areas where books or newspapers are scarce or too expensive, reading skills are regrettably forgotten. The religious schools of Burma and Thailand still educate some young boys, though their importance and influence has decreased considerably in recent years. School hours are brief (generally half a day) and frequently suspended when children are needed at harvest time.

Old people still have an important part to play in rural life. The grandmothers help with the children or manage the household when the mother is busy elsewhere, while grandfathers teach their grandsons all they learned from their fathers, such as how to catch fish in the *padi* fields and how to trap birds.

The strong bonds of love, respect, and interdependence found in an Asian family undoubtedly contribute to its enviable sense of security and serenity. Another stabilizing factor is the very real presence of religious faith, an integral part of daily life. The major faiths of Buddhism (in Thailand, Burma, Hong Kong, Macau, and parts of Taiwan), Islam (throughout Malaysia, most of Indonesia and the southern Philippines), Christianity (90 percent of the Filipinos), and Hinduism (in Bali) all have a strong influence on the way people think, feel, and act.

Despite this strong religious faith, animism, or belief in spirits, persists and does not appear to be regarded as inconsistent with religion. Offerings to placate spirits can be found along roadsides in Taiwan, under trees in Thailand and Malaysia, near houses in Burma, or tucked under the windscreen wiper of a bus in Bali.

To most people living in rural Southeast Asia, a central government is a dimly (if at all) perceived entity. Respect for traditional laws that were made to ensure harmonious communal living is still strong. Almost all communities have some sort of headman or leader who mediates in minor disputes and acts as a representative of the faraway government.

Life Cycles, Life Styles

A pervading simplicity and lack of materialism is evident in most rural areas. This is particularly so in Buddhist countries, where the accumulation of religious merit (which can be taken on to the next life) is seen as more important than the accumulation of material wealth. Islam, with its doctrine of accepting the will of Allah, also tends to discourage driving ambition. An element of fatalism, of accepting one's *karma* (fate) is a factor that makes many rural people averse to change and modernization. And, of course, the hot tropical climate has the predictable effect of slowing people down.

The important stages in the cycle of life—birth, coming-of-age, marriage, and death—are marked with special ceremonies. Most of these are occasions for performances of traditional arts such as dance music and are invariably accompanied by feasts to which everyone (even the passing traveler) is invited.

The birth of a child is a cause for celebration, especially in the case of a son, for Asians adore their children. By the time a child reaches puberty, a coming-of-age ceremony is held. In Muslim societies this will be a circumcision, while young Buddhist boys shave their heads and enter the monkhood for a brief period. In Bali, young girls undergo a tooth-filing ceremony, while in other parts of Southeast Asia different forms of celebrations are held to mark the time when a girl reaches physical maturity.

It is unthinkable to an Asian that he or she should not become married; rural society in particular has no place for a single person. In many parts of Southeast Asia, marriage is a relatively simple affair, with elopement widely accepted in Bali, Burma, and Thailand. For the Malays and most Indonesians, as well as the Taiwanese, a wedding is an occasion for great display and ceremony. Elaborate finery is used for the bride and groom who, in Malaysia and Indonesia, become "king and queen for a day."

Death, the closing chapter, is treated quickly and silently by Muslims. The soul is given a very noisy send-off in Chinese communities, with much clashing of cymbals and music to keep away evil spirits. Bali's famous cremations, where the soul is freed from the body and able to return to heaven, are stunning occasions when a huge cremation tower with decorations that have taken a full month to create literally goes up in smoke.

For all its seeming simplicity and tranquility, life—and death—in rural Southeast Asia is not without its moments of grandeur.

The Tribal Peoples

To the sophisticated Western eye, perhaps the most tranquil and simple life is that led by the tribal people who exist in the natural habitats created by forest and river. In a general introduction to such a wide geographical area as Southeast Asia, the minorities—tribal and aboriginal—cannot be dealt with adequately because their ways of life remain so diversified, depending on local conditions. Scattered along the hills and in remote river valleys, they cling to simple, yet highly complex, ways of life despite incursions of war and peaceful intrusions in the form of economic development by the national majority.

Nevertheless, the enterprising visitor has opportunities to sample and observe the life styles of a few of the tribal minorities who live near cities such as Chiang Mai in Thailand and Kuching in Sarawak, Malaysia. The introduction of roads has made hill-tribe villages accessible also in Thailand and Sumatra and motorized sampans travel quickly up placid jungle rivers to the longhouses of the Dayaks in East Malaysia.

The Yao, a highly developed tribe in Northern Thailand and Laos, have a legend that gives the following explanation for the distribution of people: "Then the man did as he was told and cut the fruit into small pieces. But he got mixed up and threw the seeds out on the plain and the meat of the fruit up onto the mountains. Therefore, there are many people on the plain and few in the hills and mountains . . . but as the saying goes 'hill people are better' (referring to them as the nourishing meat of the fruit)."

Certainly the hill tribes are a minority, although in recent years immigration—plus a lowered death rate—has caused a population increase. Striking variations in costume, language, and marriage traditions distinguish the various tribes from one another. Most groups are basically animist in religion, although Buddhism and Christianity are widespread. Indeed, Christian missionary work has been a major influence in introducing literacy to many groups. Government aid, as well as programs initiated by international aid groups have helped bring the tribal people into the 20th century. In Chiang Mai, special centers market tribal craft such as silver and exquisite embroidery.

Aside from dry rice farming and supplementary vegetable growing, the major crop in the Thai area is still opium. In recent years this area, called the Golden Triangle, has been the scene of great international intrigue, with elements of the old Nationalist Chinese Army (KMT), Burmese rebels, Communist factions, foreign adventurers trafficking in opium, and at least three governments trying, with helicopters, police units, and narcotics suppression advisers, to suppress the evil trade. Several agencies in cooperation with the Thai government have introduced alternative crops such as red beans, peaches and potatoes.

The people themselves use drugs sparingly. Opium is used mostly by old people and the sick. Opium derivatives such as morphine and heroin were not known here until the last few years and now are used by alienated youth in search of excitement and rebellion.

No such problems exist among the tribal people in East Malaysia. Here the Dayaks, land and sea, are becoming integrated slowly into the mainstream of Malaysian life. Excavation at prehistoric sites at Niah Cave has shown that these people have been here for a long time, the earliest evidence showing modern man present 35,000 years ago. Ancient, yet complex societies have also been found in Thailand, where, at a tiny northeastern village, Ban Chiang, traces of an advanced Bronze Age culture, 4,000–6,000 years old, have been unearthed.

In the Philippines, tribal minorities are scattered all over the islands. The largest minority is the Muslim population in the Southern islands, who still live in a semi-feudal, family- or tribe-orientated society. Controversy and division have troubled these areas for years with some Muslim political activists urging for secession and supported by local Communists and foreign-based interests. However, negotiations are being conducted between the secessionists and the government for a peaceful settlement of the controversy.

Aboriginal peoples exist in the back of the beyond in most countries. Probably the most famous are the Sakai, who inhabit the deep jungle between Malaysia and Thailand. The Thais call these people "nok" after the hairy *rambutan* fruit, which resembles the aborigines' curly hair. Except for their small stature, they look very much like light-skinned Blacks, with curly hair, flat noses, and round eyes. Most live a nomadic existence—the men hunting and the women looking after sparse crops and the children. After each harvest the tribes pack up, leaving the straw and bamboo huts, and go off to their next dwelling place in the forest. Their chief hunting weapon is a long bamboo blowpipe, through which they fire a poisoned dart. Their accuracy in aim is amazing, especially considering the poor visibility in the gloom of the deep jungle.

From Taiwan to Burma, the visitor will see a wide variety of life styles: food eaten with chopsticks, with fork and spoon or with the right hand from a banana leaf; dress ranging from a few strategically placed leaves to elaborate robes in silk and gold thread. Right now is the best time to travel in Southeast Asia, because the lifestyle of most people is still firmly rooted in traditions—traditions that go back hundreds and even thousands of years. It's hoped that television, the automobile and a plastic way of living won't exterminate these traditions too quickly, but these influences are certainly producing great changes, not all of them for the better.

SOUTHEAST ASIAN HISTORY

400,000 Years in a Nutshell

The beginnings of the history of Southeast Asia coincide with what may well be the beginning of the history of human life. In 1891, the oldest human remains ever found were unearthed in Trinil, Central Java. Known as Pitheocanthropus Erectus (or more popularly, Java Man) he dates back an almost unbelievable 400,000 years.

Similar, though slightly more advanced, remains were later discovered in Java, and an even more highly developed type of man (Sinanthropus or Peking Man) was found in China. Since Java was part of the Asian land mass thousands of years ago, it is generally believed that the early Pitheocanthropoid men of Java spread gradually northwards to China from tropical Southeast Asia, evolving during a journey that must have taken thousands of years.

Outside Influence from the Start

The most striking characteristic of the history of Southeast Asia is the succession of outside influences. From the earliest recorded history, there is evidence that continued contact with other cultures helped shape the cultural development of Southeast Asia.

As early as 300 B.C. the age of bronze and iron (known as the Dong Son culture) had passed from China down into Southeast Asia. Even today, typical Dong Son motifs can be seen in the art of various people in southern China as well as the Bataks of Sumatra and the Borneo Dayaks. Han dynasty pottery found in Indonesia gives additional evidence of Chinese contact as far back as the first century B.C.

References to Southeast Asia appear in the sixth century B.C. Indian epic poem, *Ramayana,* indicating that Indian travelers were already sailing to the "Golden Peninsula" (probably Malaya) and the "Island of Barley" (thought to be Borneo) in search of gold and tin. There are also records of Buddhist missionaries voyaging to the "Land of Gold" (Lower Burma) during the third century B.C. During these early centuries India was trading westwards with Mediterranean countries as well as with those to the east; glass beads of Mediterranean origin found in Malaysia and parts of Indonesia bear beautiful witness to India's Roman contacts.

Indian traders and adventurers were followed by priests and teachers who brought their religion, literature, language and the art of writing. While Chinese influence in the early centuries was largely commercial, the cultural influence of India was far more significant and long lasting. Partly because of the comparative prestige and wealth of Indian traders, their religions and culture took root among the indigenous people of Southeast Asia. Hinduism, a way of life with a clearly defined caste system rather than an organized religion, permeated Southeast Asia. The courts adopted the belief in a god-king and the system of aristocracy, while the traditional animistic beliefs of the common people were gradually overlaid with the cult of the popular Hindu gods, Shiva (symbolizing both destruction and reproduction), and Vishnu (the preserver). Stone carvings of these gods can still be seen enshrined in temples such as the 10th-century Loro Jonggrang in Central Java, and have been unearthed in southern and eastern Thailand.

A new mythology and folk lore slowly developed and have lasted until the present day. Many words of Sanskrit origin are found in the languages of Southeast Asia, while the *Ramayana* forms the background of countless dance dramas. The influence of Indian dance on the court dances of Southeast Asia is strongly evident; the customs and rituals of both palace and village folk reveal their Indian origins.

Buddhism, offering an alternative to the polytheistic Hindu or Brahmanistic caste system, also spread from India. This philosophy of life penetrated deeply in certain areas, particularly Burma and Thailand. For a long time, Hinduism and Buddhism existed side by side in mutual toleration. They were regarded as two different aspects of a single Indian civilization rather than two different incompatible religions. This attitude helps explain why two great monuments, the Buddhist stupa Borobudur and the Hindu temple complex at Prambanan, could be built in Central Java within a century of each other.

The empires of Southeast Asia were influenced to such an extent by India for over a thousand years that these early kingdoms are generally referred to by historians as "Indianized States." In some cases, Indians actually ruled after marriage with local ruling families. The earliest of these states Funan, held power in present-day Cambodia until about A.D. 500. The successor to Funan was a mighty empire that exerted considerable political and commercial influence over Southeast Asia.

This was the Srivijaya, whose sea-port capital in southern Sumatra commanded the sea route between India and China. This sea lane between Sumatra and the Malay Peninsula (later known as the Straits of Malacca) was of strategic importance for centuries, and even today Indonesia and Malaysia acknowledge the importance of controlling sea traffic along this vital waterway. Not only Indian vessels but those of China and the Middle East passed by and constituted the trade on which Srivijaya's commercial power was based. Buddhism was strongly entrenched; a seventh-century Chinese pilgrim noted that over a thousand Buddhist priests were based in Srivijaya.

The increasing influence of Buddhism in neighboring Java coincided with the rise of another powerful dynasty, the Sailendra, which began during the seventh century (the name Sailendra, meaning "King of the Mountain," came from the custom of locating holy places on hills or mountains). Sailendra rule spread from Java up the Malay peninsula into Cambodia, and across into southern Sumatra. By the middle of the ninth century the Sailendras had gained a controlling influence in Sumatra. The union of two powerful dynasties, the Sailendra and the Srivijaya, formed a powerful political and commercial empire that ruled for an amazing 500 years from the middle of the ninth century.

Sailendra influence in Cambodia was eventually replaced by the Khmer kingdom of Angkor, which ruled from the beginning of the 9th to the end of the 12th century. The greatest of the Khmer temples, the early 12th-century Angkor Wat, still bears witness to the powerful Indian cultural and artistic traditions of the period.

With the movement of the Buddhist Sailendras from Java to Sumatra, a new kingdom that reverted to Hinduism and Shiva worship appeared in Java. This new dynasty, the Mataram, moved to East Java in the 10th century and proceeded to build up an empire rivaling that of Srivijaya. The inevitable happened, with a challenge by Mataram (repulsed by Srivijaya) and the destruction of the Mataram capital in the early years of the 11th century. However, the Mataram dynasty recovered under the talented King Airlangga, only to be split less than 50 years later by dynastic squabbles. The new state arising from these, Kediri, soon spread its influence to the eastern parts of island Southeast Asia.

Early Burma, Thailand, and Cambodia

The history of mainland Southeast Asia is characterized by movements of people and shifting borders as successive kingdoms with their expanding and contracting spheres of influence rose and fell. In the same way that the states of Central Europe arose and were later absorbed by more powerful neighbors during the 18th and 19th centuries, so too did the borders of the countries of Indo-China, Burma, and the Malay Peninsula fluctuate.

The area that is modern Burma was inhabited by two major groups of people by the sixth century. The Mons, the original inhabitants of Lower Burma, had been strongly influenced by their contacts with Indian traders as early as the third century B.C., and had accepted Indian literature, art and writing. The Tibeto-Burman people of Upper

Burma moved slowly southwards and founded a capital at Pagan in the ninth century. Their political influence moved farther south, eventually absorbing the Mons and their cities, Pegu and Thaton. For the next 200 years the continued rule of the Pagan kingdom over the entire area of Burma assisted the cultural assimilation between the Mons and Burmans, with Mon religion and culture becoming universally accepted.

Another group of people known as Thai or Shan (the former name being indigenous, the latter a Burmese term) moved southwards into the Indo-Chinese Peninsula from central and southern China. By the ninth century the Thais had an important settlement in north Siam, and 200 years later they were also established in Laos.

The Mongol invasion of China in the 13th century and their overthrow of the Pagan kingdom in Burma further encouraged the south and westward movement of the Thai people; they spread into the north of Burma leaving the Mons in the south to re-establish their own separate kingdom in Pegu. The Thais then overthrew the Khmer regime in what is now northern Thailand and established a kingdom in Chiang Mai around 1275, and by the mid-14th century founded the kingdom of Siam with its capital in Ayutthaya, thus forcing the Khmers to withdraw eastward into Cambodia.

The Traders Come

By the 12th century China, under the Sung dynasty, had become increasingly involved in overseas trade. Delicate Sung porcelain, achieving a quality unmatched elsewhere for centuries, was in demand throughout Southeast Asia and as far away as the east coast of Africa and the Middle East (this "export porcelain" is still being unearthed in parts of Southeast Asia). Siam became an important pottery-producing center in the 14th century as immigrant Chinese began turning out items such as the distinctive greenish glazed ware known as "celadon."

Like their Chinese and Indian counterparts, Arab and Persian merchants were drawn by the rich and often unique produce of Southeast Asia. They came in ships laden with Venetian glassware, wool, gold, and metal items from the Mediterranean. The Chinese carried silver and pearls as well as silk, heavy damask, and rich brocade destined to clothe the elegant and wealthy, while the Indians brought cotton textiles.

To these traders, the old lure of Southeast Asia's gold and tin was reinforced by an abundance of teak, ebony, and camphor, by ivory and the reputedly aphrodisiac rhinoceros horn. But the most important attraction of all that sent the leading merchants of the world to sea in frail boats, risking their lives with piracy, storms and disease, was spices. Although peppercorns also grew in southern India and cinnamon in profusion in Ceylon, nutmeg, its covering mace, and cloves were unique to Southeast Asia. These spices, found far to the east, in the Moluccas group of islands, eventually lured the adventurer-merchants of Europe half way around the world.

The Spice Trade

During the 12th to 14th centuries, major shifts in power took place. The kingdom of Srivijaya still dominated trade passing through the Straits of Malacca, although its strength had diminished sufficiently for the state of Malaya in northwest Sumatra to reassert its independence.

The increasing importance of the spice trade enabled the East Javanese kingdoms to achieve great commercial power. Kediri was, by the 12th century, not only a trading force to be reckoned with but a strong center of Hindu culture and religion. However, a revolution in the early 13th century overthrew the Kediri dynasty and a new kingdom based in Singosari (also East Java) arose.

The Singosari dynasty's brightest star was the great warrior-king Kertonagoro. Toward the end of the 13th century he had gained control of most of Java, large parts of Sumatra, the eastern side of the Malay Peninsula, southwest Borneo and the Moluccas spice islands. But the dynasty was not destined to last for long; a prince of the previous Kediri dynasty killed Kertonagoro and established the last of the great Hindu-Javanese kingdoms, Majapahit.

By the middle of the 14th century the East Javanese Majapahit empire had expanded rapidly under the reign of Hyam Wuruk; this era is regarded by present-day Indonesia as the "Golden Age" of Java. With the 500-year-old empire of Srivijaya finally ended, Majapahit controlled most of Sumatra and the Malay Peninsula, parts of Borneo, the southern Celebes and the Moluccas, and exerted influence over much of the Indo-Chinese Peninsula. But by this time the Thai kingdom of Siam was increasing its domination of Indo-China and began challenging the rule of Majapahit in the states of the Malay Peninsula. Another threat to Majapahit was the increasing independence of the rich coastal ports of Sumatra.

These factors, combined with another important cultural change—the arrival of Islam—meant that the last of the mighty Hindu-Javanese empires was to fade in importance as commercial and cultural power moved back to the Straits of Malacca.

Arrival of Islam

Islam had swept across the Middle East and penetrated as far as the north of India by the beginning of the eighth century. Indian Muslim merchants from the northwestern state of Gujerat became a powerful group in Southeast Asia during the 13th century, bringing Indian goods to the area and acting as middlemen between the spice-producing islands and the Far Eastern and Middle Eastern markets. Centuries of contact with India resulted in its being regarded as the center of power and prestige by the people of Southeast Asia, so although they had learned of the new faith from Arab and Persian merchants, it was not until it was presented by the rich and powerful Indians that Islam became acceptable.

By the late 13th century, these Gujerati merchants had been responsible for the conversion to Islam of a number of important north

Sumatran ports. Not surprisingly, the coastal areas, which had always been in contact with new ideas and peoples from abroad, were more receptive to change than the isolated and more conservative inland districts. However, once Islam became accepted in the commercial ports (often through marriages of Muslim merchants with daughters of leading local families) it slowly spread inland.

The new faith gradually penetrated the northern coastal ports of Java, and spread to the Malay Peninsula where, in the port of Malacca, it received its greatest boost. Perhaps inevitably, Islam was tempered by the old Hindu customs and animistic beliefs that have never been completely erased.

Malacca's Importance

Malacca, founded in 1403, quickly became "the richest seaport with the greatest number of wholesale merchants and abundance of shipping and trade that can be found in the whole world." The beginnings of Malacca are linked by tradition with the island of Temasek (old Singapore). Temasek, part of the weakening Srivijaya empire, was involved in a series of struggles between Siam and the East Javanese Majapahit dynasty, and was eventually destroyed around 1376. According to legend, a prince named Parameswara came from Palembang in Sumatra, killed the ruler of Temasek and set himself up as king. Five years later he was forced to flee by the Siamese, and moving northwards selected a river estuary on the west coast of the Malay Peninsula as the site of a new settlement.

Malacca rapidly achieved a tremendous concentration of commercial power during the first quarter of the 15th century. Parameswara was converted to Islam through marriage, and as later rulers adopted the new religion and hastened its spread throughout the peninsula through judicious marriages, Malacca became the powerful center of Islam in Southeast Asia.

The importance of Malacca as the center of entrepôt trade was largely a result of geography. It was the center of a triangle linking China, Southeast Asia and India. All ships had to pass through the Straits of Malacca, the Chinese sailing junks being borne on the northeast monsoons to Malacca where they traded with the Indians and Arabs who arrived with the southwest monsoons. In return for her recognition of the "Son of Heaven," Malacca was protected against the ever-threatening Siamese by the Ming rulers. During the early 15th century, China sent a number of diplomatic missions throughout Southeast Asia before suddenly reversing her imperialistic policy and withdrawing into seclusion.

Descriptions by Chinese and Portuguese merchants give some idea of the magnificent bazaar that Malacca became, with gold, tin, precious woods, cloth from India and China, and, above all, spices passing through its warehouses. So valuable were these spices that it was possible for a fully laden ship to pay for the cost of the voyage (including the price of the vessel) ten times over!

The Age of Discovery

Malacca was destined to remain independent for only a century before she and the rest of Southeast Asia were affected by the winds of change that were to sweep the world.

News of the fabulous Spice Islands was brought to Europe early in the 14th century by Marco Polo, who had passed through the Straits of Malacca on his return journey from China. Until this time, Europeans knew only that spices came from somewhere to the east, brought to them at exorbitant prices by Arab middlemen. But Marco Polo told of "a very rich island, producing pepper, nutmegs, spikenard, galingale, cubebs and cloves, and all the precious spices that can be found in the world. It is visited by great numbers of ships and merchants who buy a great range of merchandise, reaping handsome profits and rich returns. The quantity of treasure in the island is beyond all computation." This island was Sri Lanka.

This treasure was conveyed from the spice-producing islands via Malaccan, Indian and Arab merchants, making a long and dangerous sea voyage followed by an overland haul through Asia Minor where trading routes were often upset by political turmoil. Eventually the spices reached the European distribution point of Venice, by this time commanding such a price that only the rich could afford them. Indeed, so precious were they that the lady of the household kept them under lock and key. (Before Europeans learned to keep sheep and cattle alive during the bitter winter months, they had to live on salted meat made palatable only through the addition of spices.)

It became imperative that Europe should find a sea route to the riches of the Spice Islands.

Thus began the Age of Discovery. At the end of the 15th and beginning of the 16th centuries, epic voyages took place: Columbus, in his attempts to find the Spice Islands, crossed the Atlantic and found America; a Spanish fleet led by the Portuguese Magellan circumnavigated the globe. Portugal reached the west coast of Africa by 1478 (and access to that country's gold) and rounded the Cape of Good Hope ten years later. The way to the east was open, and in 1505 the Portuguese obtained a concession of a small fort in Sri Lanka, which they gradually expanded until it covered most of the coast regions of the island. By the beginning of the 15th century, Portugal had fought a series of sea battles that enabled her to gain control of the vital sea routes in the Indian Ocean as well as a foothold in India.

The Portuguese acknowledged the necessity of gaining control over Malacca, for as the explorer Pires put it, "whoever is lord of Malacca has his hand on the throat of Venice." In 1511, they attacked Malacca, which eventually fell after great destruction and loss of life. Portuguese economic domination of Southeast Asia was accompanied by appalling brutality and violence, the result of a religious fanaticism that virtually achieved the proportions of a holy war. The detested Muslim traders were treated mercilessly by the crusading Portuguese Catholics.

Unlike later 19th-century European involvement in Southeast Asia, Portugal's interest was not in colonial rule or political conquest but in obtaining control of markets and trade routes. To maintain this control, Portugal constructed coastal fortresses that limited her influence to a very tiny portion of the countries of Southeast Asia. Until the 19th century, the presence of the Portuguese and other Europeans did not affect the structure of the peasant economy in Southeast Asia.

Not content with Malacca, the Portuguese tried to establish control over the Moluccan spice islands. She was not the only nation interested in doing so. In 1521 Magellan headed a fleet of Spanish ships that rounded Cape Horn and eventually landed on the islands later named the Philippines. Magellan was killed not long after, but the Spanish fleet continued south to the Spice Islands where they skirmished with the Portuguese.

The Spanish eventually returned home via the Cape of Good Hope (thus completing the first journey around the world), determined to challenge Portuguese control. The Spaniards and Portuguese backed rival rulers in local feuds in the Moluccas until the Spanish were forced to acknowledge Portuguese control in 1527. However, unwilling to let the treasures of Southeast Asia slip from their hands, they again challenged Portugal's rule. Unsuccessful, they moved north conquering the Philippines island of Cebu in 1565. They advanced on Luzon six years later, overpowering the local Muslim ruler and building their own fortress settlement in Manila.

Portuguese involvement in Southeast Asia increased with the acquisition of the lease of Macau, a peninsula near the estuary of Canton's Pearl River, in 1571. As it grew into the entrepôt center for trade between Southeast Asia, China and Japan, the Portuguese found it prudent to declare total possession of Macau.

Meanwhile, the Spanish were building Manila into the center of the trans-Pacific trade between their silver-rich possession, Mexico, and the Philippines, China and Spain.

The Philippines were to prove an exception to the rule that Europeans had virtually no effect on the customs and culture of Southeast Asia before the 19th century. The Spaniards found in the Philippines a more primitive culture that had been less affected by early Indian influence than any other area of Southeast Asia. The Spaniards were colonizers who had little difficulty in spreading their system of administration, land ownership and religion throughout most of the Philippines. The influence of the Catholic Church was particularly far-reaching, with priests in every village and a system of education established by the church. By the 19th century, the Filipinos had become Westernized and Christianized to such a degree that there was virtually no preservation—let alone development—of indigenous culture although a great deal of native artifacts were sent to Spain to form the basis of such collections as the Museo de los Filipinos in Valladolid. But present-day Filipinos are rediscovering their native heritage through archeological diggings, studies and research.

Portuguese control of Malacca was continually challenged throughout the 16th century, first by the Malays then later by the increasingly powerful Sumatran sultanates. The Achinese of northern Sumatra were particularly troublesome, but as there was no united Muslim front against the Portuguese, they managed to resist.

The Portuguese quickly learned the value of "divide and rule," a policy that was to set the pattern for later European diplomacy in Southeast Asia. They intervened in (or even helped cause) local disputes that enabled them to gain concessions by playing off one side against the other.

Portugal's commercial empire in Southeast Asia was controlled by the State, which did not run it along normal commercial lines. Insufficient money was put back into the countries exploited; administration, manpower, and equipment were neglected; salaries were inadequate, encouraging bribery and corruption.

It was not possible for Portugal to maintain her monopoly indefinitely, and by the end of the 16th century the Dutch had reached the pepper port of Bantam in West Java. A number of Dutch commercial syndicates combined to form the Dutch East India Company in 1602, with the aim of ousting the Portuguese and establishing commercial penetration of Southeast Asia.

The English had been receiving the produce of Southeast Asia via Venetian ships, which in turn carried English wool and cloth to foreign markets. Unlike the Dutch and Portuguese, the English wanted to become Eastern traders not only for spices but to find export markets. A series of English expeditions were made to Southeast Asia (Sir Francis Drake bought spices in the Moluccas in 1579), ending in the formation of the East India Company in 1600.

The Dutch finally forced the Portuguese out of Malacca in 1641, and prevented the English from gaining a firm foothold in Southeast Asia. The English eventually withdrew to concentrate on Indian trade, leaving the Dutch to become the chief European power in Southeast Asia until the 19th century. In the intervening 200 years, the Dutch concentrated on commercial rewards and showed no interest in political responsibilities.

Although the Europeans concentrated on the rich islands in Southeast Asia, Taiwan to the far north was not overlooked. At the end of the 16th century the Portuguese, impressed by the loveliness of the island, named it Ilha Formosa (Beautiful Island). The Dutch and Spanish were not long in following the Portuguese, and by 1624 had established themselves in southern Taiwan. But their stay was shortlived, for in 1661 Koxinga, a loyal supporter of the former Ming Dynasty, took control of the island during his retreat south. In 1683 Taiwan was incorporated into the Manchu empire.

Isolated Burma

During the early years of the 17th century, Burma was regenerated under the Toungu dynasty. She regained much territory that had been lost to the Siamese, including Chiang Mai, which was recaptured in 1615. The capital of the Toungu rulers was moved to Ava, near Mandalay in Upper Burma. Here, far removed from the coastal area and contact with the changing ideas and conditions of the outside world, Burma developed in self-imposed isolation until the middle of the 19th century.

Not that all was tranquil for the next 200 years. Struggles between Upper Burma and the Mons of Lower Burma resulted in the end of the Toungu dynasty and the eventual reunification of the country. And there were continual skirmishes with the Siamese, with possession of Ayutthaya passing back and forth.

Dutch, British, and French Colonies

During the 18th century the Dutch, experiencing diminishing prosperity from their commercial empire in Southeast Asia, moved farther into Java and developed cash crops such as coffee and indigo. The rhythm of rural life and the peasant economy was upset by the enforced deliveries of goods from various districts, some of which were physically unable to meet the imposed quotas.

Holland saw the loss of her position of world leadership in finance and trade during the 18th century and her East India Company, which became more inefficient and corrupt as it got into deeper financial difficulties, did not last into the 19th century.

Meanwhile, England was becoming transformed into an industrialized nation and was looking for a market for her produce as well as supplies of raw materials. Her trade with China increased enormously in the last quarter of the 18th century and she became more deeply involved in India. Once again, Britain began looking towards Southeast Asia. A British colonial official, Francis Light, pressed for the opening of a strategic base that would give naval protection to the China trade and help balance the presence of the Dutch. By 1791, the Sultan of Kedah had granted the British possession of the island of Penang off the northwest coast of the Malay Peninsula. Britain's first territorial possession in Southeast Asia grew rapidly as a commercial center, though it did not prove to be an ideal naval base.

After a five-year period of British occupation in Java, an idealistic colonial officer named Raffles was anxious to put his liberal principles of colonialism to work elsewhere. He negotiated the acquisition of Singapore, the island lying off the southern tip of the Malay Peninsula. Singapore embodied the British concept of a free trading port, where lack of trading restrictions stimulated its growth into a thriving entrepôt center.

By the time the British had exchanged their Sumatran trading base of Bencoolen for the Dutch possession of Malacca in 1824, they were firmly established in the Malay Peninsula, controlling three settlements: Penang, Malacca and Singapore. This British presence helped discourage the southward pressure of the Siamese. As the 19th century wore on, Britain became more deeply involved in the Malay states as a result of the political turmoil and anarchy that were prevalent during the period. In exchange for "protecting" and "advising" the sultans she was granted trading rights.

Britain also became politically and militarily involved in Burma in the 19th century after a series of border attacks on Indian territory resulted in the Burmese Wars. Gradually, parts of Burma were annexed by the British until all of Burma was incorporated into the Indian Empire by 1886.

Siam (which became known as Thailand in 1949) had traded with the Dutch, English and French during the late 17th and 18th centuries. Much of this trade was conducted on an individual basis by adventurers. The most striking of these was a Greek, Constantine Phaulkon, who achieved the post of chief minister to the king of Siam before he was overthrown and killed in 1687.

By skillful diplomacy, by avoiding provocative incidents that might lead to foreign intervention, and by deliberate attempts to modernize, Siam managed to walk the tightrope between the French and British. She avoided letting any European nation become the single dominant power and thus finished up being the only country in Southeast Asia to avoid colonization.

The French built up their interests in Indo-China in the 17th and 18th centuries, gaining eventual control of the kingdoms of Annam and Tongkin (now combined as Vietnam), Cambodia, and Laos. Siam thus became a neutral zone between the French interests to the east and the British areas of Malaya to the south and Burma to the west.

As a result of the first Opium War with China, Britain gained possession in 1842 of a trading post "in the mouth of the dragon"—the island of Hong Kong, which lay off the coast of southern China. Hong Kong quickly developed into a major trading center, which was expanded by the leasing of 370 acres of adjacent mainland territory in 1898.

The Dutch ousted the Portuguese from Ceilao, as they had renamed Lanka, in 1658 (seventeen years after they had taken over from them in Malacca) and corrupted the name into Ceylan. It was over a hundred years later, in 1796, before the British flag was exchanged for the Dutch one, and the British East India Company's expanding fortunes also replaced the then waning Dutch East Indian Company. It was during the juggling of colonies in the period immediately following Napoleon's defeat and the new friendships which were being forged between Dutch and British that Ceylon, as she became, was so firmly entrenched in the growing British Empire.

The rice and coffee crops had suffered disastrous setbacks, and the British introduced tea to the high sweet lands of the mountainous heart of Ceylon. From that time, tea became the mainstay of Sri Lanka's economy and still is, along with rubber and coconuts, although with the bursts of nationalistic feeling immediately following the setting up of the Independent Republic of Sri Lanka there has been much talk of changing this pattern.

Commercialism and Nationalism

A new era in European influence and trade began in the latter half of the 19th century with the introduction of steam-powered vessels and the opening of the Suez Canal. British- and Dutch-built steamships began replacing the old Chinese junks, the sleek tea clippers, and the "East Indiamen" sailing vessels. The much faster sea route to their eastern markets and the opening up of the telegraph speeded up communications and allowed the Europeans a much greater degree of control over colonial governments.

The rise of nationalistic fervor in their homelands was carried by the Europeans (and particularly the British) to their colonies. The expansion of the colonial territories was seen as adding to the glory of the motherland.

During the late 19th and early 20th centuries, peaceful conditions and generally orderly colonial rule resulted in tremendous development and expansion of trade in most Southeast Asian countries. Railways, roads and canals were constructed and harbors improved; irrigation projects opened up millions of acres of *padi* fields. The Dutch developed large-scale sugar, tea and tobacco production in Java; tobacco and hemp were exported from the Philippines; Taiwan's rice, sugar and fruit supplied Japanese demand. Burma's rich mineral resources (oil, tungsten, lead and tin) were developed by the British.

The Chinese-run tin mines in Malaya were more productive than ever now that repeated anarchy had been subdued by the British. The advent of the motor car at the beginning of the 20th century suddenly increased the demand for rubber. Acres and acres of rubber trees replaced virgin jungle, especially in Malaya and Sri Lanka (where the first seedling came from Brazil via London's Kew Gardens).

This rapid economic development was to have a shattering effect on the countries of Southeast Asia. They changed from self-sufficient, subsistence economies producing just enough for their own needs to commercial economies producing goods for export, relying upon Western manufactured goods to replace traditional handcrafted items or to fill new needs.

Western commercialism, with its emphasis on free trade, competition and individualism was in conflict with the traditional Asian communal approach, and the old social order where family and village reigned supreme was undermined. Caught up in an unfamiliar money economy, many peasants became indebted to moneylenders and eventually lost their land. The situation was further exacerbated by the influx of large numbers of industrious Chinese and Indians attracted by the opportunity of making money.

The presence of Chinese settlers was not a new phenomenon; by the early 18th century there were already thousands of Chinese working as merchants, artisans, and tin miners, in parts of Southeast Asia. Their numbers swelled dramatically in the early 1900s as China seethed with political unrest. They were generally industrious and thrifty people who formed a middle class between the Europeans and the indigenous population. Suspicion and jealousy of the Chinese sometimes erupted in bloody pogroms (as early as 1740 over 10,000 were killed in rioting in Java). The presence of large numbers of Chinese and Indians in the countries of Southeast Asia is still a potentially explosive issue today.

The turn of the century saw the gradual development of a nationalistic fervor in Asia. There was increasing discontent with the rule of Westerners and the great economic gulf between the rich and the poor. The spread of education led to higher expectations and bred a sense of frustration among Asians who felt they should control their own destinies.

The Japanese victory over Russia in 1905 was an inspiration to Asians. It was possible, they realized, for Asia to stand up to the West.

Ironically, it was the Japanese who again gave an impetus to the nationalistic movement by their "Asia for the Asians" catchcry during the Second World War.

Under José Rizal, the Philippines demanded release from the crushing feudalism of Spain. This resulted in control of the Philippines being handed over to America (which was at war with Spain) in 1902. America agreed to restore full independence once the Philippines was capable of stable self-government.

Taiwan, which had continually chafed under 50 years of Japanese rule, rebelled frequently until control passed from Japan back to China after the end of the war.

Indonesia also experienced a rising nationalism. Although the Dutch were prepared to grant limited self-government on a village level, this wasn't enough for nationalists such as Hatta and Sukarno, who caused so much trouble that the Dutch imprisoned them in the 1930s.

Nationalism was slower to develop in Malaya and Singapore, since the population of these countries was diverse and times were prosperous. In addition, some of the Malay states had always retained a degree of self-government. In Burma, the British agreed to a gradual handing over of power, but the Burmese itched for full control as quickly as possible, while Ceylon obtained a peaceful independence from the British at the same time as India and became a nation within the Commonwealth in 1948. She was declared a republic and renamed Sri Lanka in 1972. The latest state to achieve full independence is Brunei, the oil rich Sultanate which severed final links with England in January 1984.

The last obstacles to full independence were swept away by the Second World War, 20 years after which all the countries of Southeast Asia except Macau (still a Portuguese province) and Hong Kong (the last major British colony) attained their independence.

Modern events have continued to demonstrate the fluid pattern of Asian history. For centuries the boundaries of Asian countries moved almost constantly, as a result of changing social, political or economic influences. This is still happening, notably in Indo-China, where the eventual pull-out of, first, the French then the Americans in 1975 failed to bring peace to this war-torn area. The power struggle which still engulfs Indo-China has created a major byproduct of misery and disruption, with refugees seeking safety from the strife in all Southeast Asian countries.

One basic change in the region is that, for the first time in centuries, there is no longer any stabilizing Western influence, colonial or military presence in the region. The Portuguese, Dutch, French, British, and Americans imposed imperial conditions and took away basic freedom from the Asian countries, but they did bring relative stability. Now these powers are gone and there is no obvious force for stability to take their place, apart from the constant background struggle between Russia and China, each of which are seeking dominating influence over the region.

In terms of their interrelationship, the countries of Asia are currently very cautious. The early years of independence were traumatic for many of the nations in the region and clearcut new patterns, political and social, have yet to emerge. The region has tended to reject Western political theories, such as democracy, and most Southeast Asian countries presently have some form of autocratic government, which is more in the historical pattern of the region.

Today's Delicate Balance

Commercial and industrial growth within Asia over the past few years has been phenomenal. Such countries as South Korea, Taiwan, Hong Kong, Singapore and, of course, Japan have boomed to a degree no longer seen in the "developed" West and this economic power is gradually encouraging the Asian nations to seek a stronger voice in world politics. Within Southeast Asia the various countries seem cautious indeed in their dealings with each other. Currently almost the only viable international force for regional cooperation is the Association of South East Asian Nations, ASEAN. It has brought Indonesia, Singapore, Malaysia, Thailand, the Philippines, and Brunei into a loose forum which at present involves little more than a getting together regularly to talk, with the only active cooperation being in such uncontroversial matters as postal and communications policies and the promotion of tourism and cultural exchanges. However, the members of ASEAN have recently managed a degree of accord in the creation of a common policy and joint statements over the still-troubled Indo-Chinese countries.

The withdrawal of U.S. military forces from Vietnam in 1975 resulted in the North Vietnamese taking over the South, but this has not been an easy victory with the people of the two halves still following basically different lifestyles. The North Vietnamese still appear prepared to tolerate a low standard of living as part of their continuing "revolution," whereas the Southerners are not, having gotten used to years of growing materialism and profitable free enterprise. With this social conflict of interests still to be resolved and even before the Vietnamese had been able to enjoy a single year of peace, their leaders chose to become involved with the internal civil war taking place in neighboring Kampuchea. This civil war still continues, causing anxiety not only to Thailand, across its western border, but also to the other Southeast Asian nations which greatly fear that the continuing conflict will encourage a greater degree of direct intervention by China and Russia—an involvement that could hardly fail to escalate into a wider military confrontation.

The nations and power forces within Southeast Asia are therefore, in a state of balance—one that sometimes seems delicate, if not precarious. It is, perhaps, the awareness of the delicacy of this situation that causes the local governments to proceed with the greatest care in making too positive statements or forming major new alliances.

The Asians are generally capable of great subtlety in matters of international as well as personal relationships, and it is this natural gift for diplomacy, with its background of centuries of cultural, religious, and social interchange, that is the best hope for long-term security within the region.

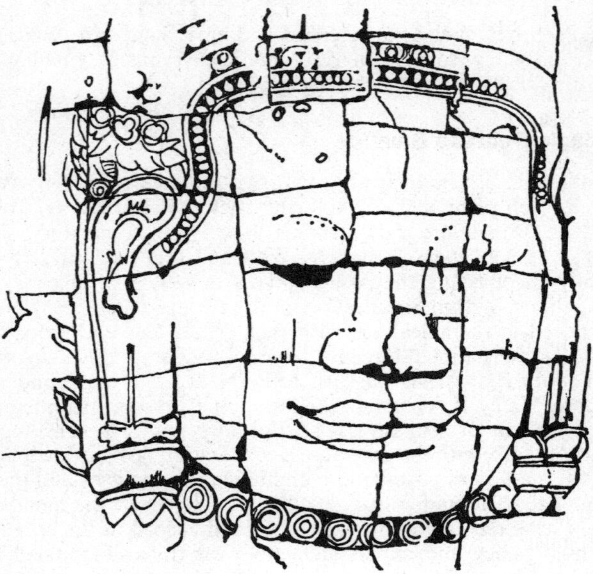

CREATIVE SOUTHEAST ASIA

Inspired Art from Fervent Beliefs

The rich and varied cultures of the countries of Southeast Asia are a source of delight and wonder to travelers, especially those from the West for whom this cultural activity embodies all that is "exotic" in the East.

How could a television show ever compete with the mystery and symbolism of a Javanese shadow puppet play retelling an ancient Indian epic? The excitement of a pop concert could never rival that of a Balinese trance dance where the spirits of good and evil battling for possession of the soul lead to the frenzied stabbing of the body with a steel blade.

Southeast Asian countries are heirs to a cultural tradition that has developed over thousands of years. Nevertheless, the similarity between the temples, sculpture, music, dance and drama of these countries often surprises the visitor. There are a number of reasons for these similarities. Most of the peoples of Southeast Asia are from two ethnic groups, being of either Malay or Chinese/Mongolian origin. They have all been subjected to outside influences, which had a great impact on the development of their cultures. Conquest within Southeast Asia and subsequent borrowing of cultures has further assisted intermixing (some parts of Southeast Asia have changed hands as many as ten times in recorded history!). Two countries covered in this guide fall outside the general pattern of Southeast Asian culture: Taiwan and the Philippines.

Taiwan, far to the north, is not usually regarded as part of geographical Southeast Asia, and has been untouched by most of the influences affecting the development of countries to the south and on the Indo-Chinese mainland. Prior to the influx of large numbers of Chinese migrants in the 17th century and again after the Communist takeover of the mainland in 1949, Taiwan was the home of aboriginal people with a simple culture who devoted their lives to hunting, farming, and fishing. It was thoroughly Sinicized in 300 years. After the Communist revolution it became the repository of some of the most amazing art treasures produced during China's long history. Brief contact with the Dutch in the 17th century and 50 years of Japanese rule at the beginning of this century made no significant impact on the culture of Taiwan.

Indian culture, which had such a profound effect on the rest of Southeast Asia, bypassed the Philippines; only the southernmost islands showed any long-term impression of another great influence, Islam. It was the Spanish, colonizers of the Philippines in the 16th century, who had an enormous effect on its development. Regrettably, the Spanish discouraged as far as possible the animistic and Islamic culture that had existed before their arrival, and superimposed a Europeanized Christian tradition.

Three other countries included in this guide (all of them developed by colonial powers as entrepôt trade centers) cannot lay claim to any indigenous culture. They are Hong Kong, Macau, and Singapore. The Chinese form the majority of the population in each country, thus offering travelers the opportunity of seeing aspects of traditional Chinese culture, despite the absence of any new artistic development.

Spirits, Priests and Traders

Before the arrival of outside influences, the religion of animism or belief in spirits prevailed in Southeast Asia. Early peoples believed that everything had a spirit—a stone, a grain of rice, a river—and dances or ceremonies to placate these were a feature of indigenous cultures.

During the first millennium of our era, Indian traders, adventurers, scholars, and priests became established in the trading ports of Southeast Asia. Their religions (Hinduism and Buddhism), language, philosophy, folklore, literature, dance, and the art of writing were accepted voluntarily by the people of Southeast Asia who respected the more culturally developed and wealthy Indians.

As the great empires of Southeast Asia rose, their influence spread to other areas. Cultural intermixing was especially prevalent on central mainland Southeast Asia between the 14th and 18th centuries when the Burmese, Thais, and Khmers tangled with each other in interminable wars. The entire court of a captured country was regarded as one of the spoils of war: when the Thais sacked the Khmer capital of Angkor in 1431 they carried off the entire court, complete with musicians, dancing girls, poets, and actors; when the Burmese captured the Thai capital some 300 years later, the Burmese adopted Thai arts.

Chinese influence scarcely existed until the Mongol expansion of the 13th century, despite a long history of trade with the countries of Southeast Asia. While China had an effect in the north, it was Islam that added yet another ingredient to the cultural mix of countries like Sumatra, Java, Malaya, and the southern Philippines after it became established in Sumatra in the 13th century. The advent of Islam led to the suppression of Hindu dance, drama and shadow plays, for Muslims believed it to be a sin to make an image of a man, even in plays and dances. Middle Eastern stories were introduced and although they had little effect on the courts, these exciting tales (such as the adventures of the Persian knight, *Amir Hamzah*) formed the basis of much popular theater.

During the 18th and 19th centuries, Western influence increased throughout Southeast Asia. The power, prestige, and financial resources of the courts (always patrons of the arts) declined. They were unable to support the construction of temples and monuments, or to maintain their own artists for performances of dance, drama and music. Many of the Asian élite, as well as the new civil service class, regarded the traditional performing arts as old-fashioned compared with the modern marvels of the West, and, with the exception of Central Java and Bali, there was a great decline everywhere in all forms of art. However, as the art of the courts died away, "popular" theater developed rapidly.

Literature

The earliest literature of Southeast Asia is based on ancient tribal epics that were passed orally from one generation to the next. The Philippines are particularly rich in these epics, many of which were never written down and thus escaped destruction at the hands of the Spanish. These long poems deal with creation, heroic exploits, war, and the supernatural. The most famous of these, the *Darahgan,* comes from Mindanao and takes about 14 days to chant in its entirety.

With the introduction of writing, most tribal epics were recorded as poetic sagas. Many early books were made from long, narrow strips of dried leaf bound together like a venetian blind, a style of book used until recently in areas such as Bali, Lombok (Indonesia), Thailand and Burma. Most of the great literature came from the outside; from India, the Middle East, and, to a lesser extent, from China.

Two famous Indian epics found over most of Southeast Asia are the *Ramayana* and *Mahabharata,* which have inspired countless dances, dramas, puppet shows, and temple carvings; the names of favorite characters from these stories are even used as brand names or adorn buses and pedicabs. Although these Indian epics had the greatest influence on literature and the dramatic arts, later stories such as the Javanese *Panji* cycle, the Islamic tales of *Amir Hamzah,* and the Buddhist *Jataka* legends were important. In some areas Chinese stories such as *The Three Kingdoms* became a popular source of inspiration.

These stories were rarely meant for entertainment alone. Their aim was to educate and spread the philosophy of either Hinduism, Buddhism, or Islam. The *Ramayana,* for example, extolls the virtues of the king and the ruling class, and stresses the duty of the people to serve them. It is the most widespread of all the epics, and is thought to date to the sixth century B.C., although the famous version by Valmiki was probably written around 100 B.C. It was translated from Sanskrit into old Javanese as early as the ninth century; the Thais named their version the *Ramakien,* while the Burmese absorbed the story from the Thais rather than direct from India.

Written in poetic form, the Valmiki version of the *Ramayana* runs to 24,000 verses. The story is of a prince, Rama, who wins the hand of the princess Sita by bending a magic bow. Before he can ascend to the throne of Ayodya, he is forced by a quarrel within his family to go into exile for 14 years. He lives in a forest with Sita and his faithful brother, Laksmana. Rawana, the demon king of Lanka (Sri Lanka or Ceylon), desires Sita and kidnaps her by sending a demon disguised as a golden deer to lure her away from Rama and Laksmana. She is taken to Rawana's palace in Lanka. Rama and Laksmana search for her, aided by an army of monkeys led by the white monkey general, Hanuman. Eventually Rawana is killed and Sita released from captivity. However, her purity is called into question and she begs to be allowed to undergo an ordeal by fire to prove her virtue. She and Rama are finally reunited in Ayodya. This is the barest outline of the story, which includes a thousand and one adventures, great battles and supernatural goings on.

The story of the *Mahabharata* is considerably more complex (and in the original version runs to 100,000 verses). It concerns the struggles between two sets of cousins, the Pandawas and the Korawas, to rule the kingdom of Astina. The best known of the five Pandawa brothers are the refined Arjuna and the impulsive, brave Bima. The *Mahabharata* contains an almost endless succession of conflicts culminating in a great battle that lasts 12 days and 12 nights.

The Buddhist *Jataka,* popular in Thailand and Burma, is a collection of 547 moral tales, some animal stories, some ancient folklore. They are supposed to relate to the earlier lives of Buddha, and provide a source of inspiration for dance, drama, and painting. The most popular tale, known as *Manora,* tells of the romance of a lovely bird-maiden or *kinnara.*

The Javanese *Panji* stories relate the adventures of a Javanese prince who is continually being thwarted from joining his bride, a princess of Kediri. (These stories are known by the name *Inao* in Thailand and Burma.) The adventures of the Persian knight, *Amir Hamzah,* are well known in Muslim areas of Southeast Asia. Tales of romance and adventure taken from Chinese literature are found in Thailand and Taiwan, as well as among the Chinese of major Southeast Asian cities The historical legends of Malaya and its mighty kingdom, Malacca, have been collected in the *Malay Annals* (Hikayat Sedjarah Melayu).

There is also a widespread love for puns, riddles, spoonerisms, and verbal contests; from Burma right through to the Philippines, people delight in quick-witted games, supplying the last line of a verse or poking gentle verbal fun at each other.

Music

Music is an inseparable part of dance and drama in Southeast Asia and is more frequently heard in this connection than on its own.

It is likely that people have sung or chanted songs as part of their religious ceremonies since neolithic times. Tribal singing is still a feature of the more primitive tribes of Southeast Asia, while songs to accompany work such as harvesting can still be heard in the Philippines and parts of Indonesia. Songs are important in Burma, and song festivals are part of the rural tradition in Thailand.

Percussion, wind, and string instruments are known all over Southeast Asia, though the forms they take are often unfamiliar to the traveler. All types of drums (many of ancient origin), cymbals, woodblocks and gongs make up the percussion section. Two-string fiddles (those found on the mainland originating in China, those found in Malaysia and Indonesia of Middle Eastern origin), and zithers are among the stringed instruments. The reed organ of Thailand and Laos, and the Persian *serunai,* a type of oboe found in Muslim areas, give a distinctive sound to the wind section.

Two major types of music are the *pi phat* ensemble of Thailand and Burma, and the *gamelan* of Bali, Java and Malaysia. Both ensembles accompany all types of dance, dance dramas, and puppet shows. There are characteristic melodies for certain situations and characters: a Burmese can identify a tune as being "a woodland melody" or "a royal procession tune," while a Javanese or Balinese audience knows by the sounds of the *gamelan* that a certain character is about to appear on the scene or a battle is to be fought.

The basic *pi phat* ensemble contrasts percussion instruments with one woodwind. An almost hollow sound is produced by the soft sound of wooden xylophones, the pure throaty tones of an oboe and the sharp bell-cymbals. The *gamelan* orchestra consists mainly of bronze percussion instruments with one or two strings and a flute. *Gamelan* has a bright, lingering sound; Bali's *gamelan* is full of vitality and exuberance, like the Balinese themselves, while Java's is more majestic with a slow, hypnotic beauty. The unfamiliar sounds, scales, and rhythms of this music give it an elusive, haunting quality. More familiar to Western travelers are the *kroncong* songs popular in Indonesia and Malaysia. A legacy of Portugal, these romantic ballads are accompanied by 20th-century instruments such as guitars.

In pre-Spanish times Filipino folk songs were sung on every possible occasion. Even then the Filipinos (today regarded as the most skillful musical entertainers in Asia) showed a remarkable musical skill, for, according to an early Spanish Jesuit priest, "they could, without opening their lips but by merely playing their instruments, communicate with one another." Today, the old folk songs are influenced by Spanish music, with Malayan and Chinese touches added for good measure.

Chinese music and singing are heard during Chinese opera, which is performed in the streets of Singapore, Hong Kong, Taiwan, and the major cities of Thailand, Malaysia, and the Philippines where there is a large Chinese population. The high-pitched nasal voices of the singers accompanied by two-string fiddles, zithers, and by much clashing of cymbals give Chinese opera a unique sound that is strikingly different from the rest of Southeast Asian music.

Ingenious instruments abound among some of the tribal people of Southeast Asia. Apart from the reed organ of Thailand and Laos, there are, for example, bamboo *angklungs* (sets of tuned bamboo tubes that are shaken) in West Java, a bamboo "buzzer" dating from megalithic times found in the island of Nias off Sumatra, a bagpipe-like instrument found among the Dayaks of Borneo, a coconut shell resonators in Thailand.

Dance

Since time immemorial, men have believed that through the rhythmic movements of their bodies they could contact magical powers. Ritual dances to ward off illness or misfortunes, to ensure a good harvest, or to assist the soul on its way to another life are still a feature of some of the more primitive peoples of Southeast Asia. Masked dances undoubtedly have magical origins, while trance dances, in which a spirit is believed to enter the body of the dancer, are still performed.

Some of the most striking dances of ancient origin are the masked dance performed by the Bataks of Sumatra when a person dies without a male heir, and the funeral dances of the Torajas of Sulawesi. The trance dances of Bali and Java, which have a religious function, are well-known and frequently performed. Spirit dances are still seen in Burma.

Other simple folk dances less charged with magical or religious meaning are also found throughout Southeast Asia. These include the circle dance (*ramwong*) of Thailand and the gay *malangka* of Jolo in the southern Philippines. Spanish-influenced folk dances are also widely popular in the Philippines, and Chinese dances are a feature in Singapore, Malaysia, Hong Kong, and Taiwan. Every Chinese New Year (and on other auspicious occasions), a number of dancer/acrobats climb into a pile of brightly colored material that is suddenly transformed into a long twisting dragon with snapping jaws or a ferocious lion leaping about, swishing its tail and roaring at unseen demons—all to the accompaniment of clashing cymbals.

The dance and dance dramas of Southeast Asia can be divided into three groups: folk, court, and popular. Folk dance, which is linked with prehistoric beliefs, is connected to village life and is performed by the villagers themselves. Sometimes, folk dance and drama is a simplified version of court art, but there are also instances where the courts have taken a folk style and refined or expanded it. Court dance and drama achieved a very high level of artistry, evolving under the patronage of the ruler. The performers lived at the court, continually practicing and giving performances to mark special occasions. Popular dance and drama belongs to the towns and cities, and is a commercial 20th-century development, absorbing its styles from both folk and court traditions. As it caters to the tastes of the general public and is performed by professional entertainers, the content of popular theater is easily subject to change.

The court dances of Southeast Asia were strongly influenced by the highly stylized dance of India. Every movement of every part of the body is symbolic though the meaning of most of these gestures has been forgotten over the centuries and in many instances the movements have been modified to suit local tastes. Typical of Indian dance are the half-crouch; the balancing on one leg with the other leg raised behind the body; the sideways movements of the head and neck; and the incredibly difficult hand gestures where the fingers seem to have a life of their own, curling and shivering and rotating around the wrist. The main departure from the traditional Indian dance style is with the face, which, in Southeast Asian dance, is kept absolutely immobile and expressionless. Only the Balinese have adopted the striking eye movements of India. In Bali, too, dancing is less slow and sinuous than in other parts of Southeast Asia and, in this, is more similar to the slightly faster pace of Indian dance.

Dancing is taught by imitation and there is no room for individual creativity within a set dance. This is not to say that there is no development, however. In Bali, especially, new dances have been based on old dance styles, particularly since the artistic revival period of the 1930s.

"Pure" dance still exists in Southeast Asia, though many of the folk and court dances have been combined with music, chanting or singing, and dramatic tales to form the dance dramas that are a feature of Burma, Thailand, Java and Bali. In Burma, ancient *nat* dances, developed to pacify the 37 *nats* or spirits known to the Burmese, were incorporated into *nibhatkin,* a type of miracle play. A similar development took place in Thailand where early spirit dances absorbed Indian dance styles and were eventually included in staged dramas.

Thai classical dancing was learned from the Khmers when the Thais captured Angkor in the 15th century; this style was later passed on to the Burmese when they fell to the Thais in the 18th century. The glittering costumes, elaborate head dresses, and stylized movements of Thai and Burmese dance dramas make them one of the most gorgeous spectacles of Southeast Asia.

Java's best known folk dance is a trance dance, the *jaran kepang,* in which riders of plaited bamboo "horses" perform all kinds of acts while under a trance. East Java has a number of colorful folk dances such as *reog.* Animal masks are worn in some of these old dances, which date from the pre-Hindu period, while *topeng* or mask dances telling tales of *Panji* are performed alone or incorporated in dance dramas. Other Javanese court dances that are still performed (like the *topeng,* either on their own or incorporated in *wayang orang*) are the Indian-influenced *serimpi* and *bedoyo.*

Bali absorbed and maintained many of Java's Hindu traditions when courtiers, nobles, and performers fled from the East Javanese kingdoms in the 15th and 16th centuries to escape from Islam. Bali added its own distinctive touches to the art of dance, and Balinese performers are, today, more vigorous and hotblooded than those of Java. Among Bali's religious dances are the *sanghyang* and the *barong,* where the performance itself is a religious act ensuring the proper balance between good and evil. Also performed are numerous less emotionally charged dances such as the *baris* war dance and the *legong,* a dance of the divine nymphs. Many Balinese dances have, like those of other Southeast Asian countries, been incorporated into dance dramas.

Drama

Most of the dramas performed in Southeast Asia have evolved from dances, and are generally termed "dance dramas." Like the dances, they were originally performed "in the round," either in a village or temple square, or in an open court pavilion. The staging of dance drama has always been very informal with only the most basic props, no scenery, curtains or raised stage. Today, however, dance dramas are often performed, Western style, in front of a backdrop. The audiences, too, are very informal. As performances can go on for hours (sometimes from dusk until dawn), it is expected that people should chat, sleep during the dull bits, or wander off to have a snack when they're hungry.

The dance dramas of Burma, Thailand, Java, and Bali are usually based on the Indian epic poems, the *Ramayana* and *Mahabharata,* the Javanese *Panji* stories, or the Buddhist *Jataka* tales.

Universal elements among the dance dramas of Southeast Asia are the much-loved clowns, who assume a similar role to the medieval jester, poking fun at everything and everyone (even the ruler) and dispensing wry wisdom along with humor.

Burmese court drama had degenerated by the time the British annexed Burma in the mid-19th century. Only vestiges of these dramas are now to be seen as the popular *zat pwe* performances, which include singing, dancing, and a lot of clowning. A compact form of the *zat pwe* known as *anyein pwe,* involving musicians, a couple of clowns and two or three dancing girls, is sometimes seen at weddings or similar functions.

In Thailand, the very formal *khon* in which all the actor-dancers wore masks, developed from puppet shows. A later development was the less formal version of the *khon,* known as *khon lakorn,* which dispensed with the masks and enabled actors to speak. The tales inspiring the *khon lakorn* were taken from the *Ramayana* and the *Jatakas.* Historical romances from Sanskrit and Chinese literature form the background of the lively, spontaneous, often bawdy *likay* of Thailand. Related to court drama in terms of music and dance, it is lighter and more popular and is most frequently performed in villages in the open air.

Malaysia, which was often a part of Sumatran or later Javanese empires, was more likely to adopt these styles rather than to create its own. The exception to this was the early 20th-century *bangsawan,* a form of theater with stories taken from Malay history and Islamic literature, which was performed all over the Malay-speaking countries until it faded from popularity about 20 years ago.

The most popular dance drama of Java and Bali is the *wayang orang.* Literally "human puppet," it developed from the extremely popular shadow puppet play or *wayang kulit,* and many of the stances and dance movements imitate the two-dimensional angles of the flat leather puppets. Popular court dances such as the *serimipi* have also been incorporated wholesale into the dance dramas. The stories are taken from the *Ramayana* or the *Mahabharata,* while the masked *topeng* dramas are usually inspired by the *Panji* stories. In Bali, the *wayang orang* is more a simple village production than a refined court drama.

Dramas created in Java during the 20th century, and as popular today as *wayang orang,* are the *ketoprak* (with stories based on Javanese history and legend) and the *ludruk.* The latter, peculiar to East Java, has dispensed entirely with dancing and the theme generally deals with the conflict between traditional and modern life.

Bali's favorite folk opera, the *arja,* is a fast-moving combination of singing, dancing, and lots of clowning, perfectly reflecting the Balinese character.

Some of the earliest known types of pure drama are found in the Philippines, where epics were recited at communal gatherings among many mountain tribes. The Spanish introduced the *moro moro* plays, which dramatized the victory of the Christians over the Muslims. These were folk plays that villagers would rehearse for months to produce scenes of bloodshed and carnage alternating with romantic love. Once very popular, the *moro moro* is now almost extinct. Another legacy of Spain is the *zarzuela,* a type of light opera originally performed for the Spaniards but which attracted the Filipino, too. It was in danger of dying out but is now experiencing a revival. Also a dramatic feature of the Philippines are the Passion plays, which are performed throughout Holy Week.

Chinese opera, with its singing, music, elaborate costumes and make-up, recreates the splendors of Imperial China with its mighty emperors, brave warriors, evil ministers and lovesick heroines. Chinese opera is performed free—usually in the streets—during festivals (especially during the month of the Hungry Ghosts around August) in most Chinese communities of Southeast Asia.

Puppets

The most enduring art form of Southeast Asia is the shadow puppet play, which has been known in Java since pre-Hindu times and was well established there by the 10th century. It has absorbed the relevant and discarded the dross; it has seen (and welcomed, in one way or another) Hinduism, Buddhism, Islam, and the West; and it has survived. It spread to Bali, Malaysia, and Thailand; it influenced dance styles and dance dramas, and it led to the development of their puppet shows.

It is believed that *wayang kulit* performances have always held a religious significance. As one noted historian describes it, "the *wayang* must have satisifed a deep emotional need, providing the Javanese with a stimulus to, and a medium for, mystical meditation . . . the puppets represent an abstract world in which imagination becomes a reality."

The puppets used in *wayang kulit* are cut out of buffalo hide, beautifully etched, painted and gilded. A full set of Javanese puppets includes 300–400 pieces. The shadows of these puppets are cast onto a screen with a light behind. The audience can watch the shadows in front of the screen, or sit on the puppet master's side of the screen and see a puppet performance without shadows. The most important person in the *wayang kulit* is the puppet master or *dalang;* he narrates the story (from memory), sings, adopts the voices of the different characters as they appear, and moves the articulated arms of all the puppets. The *dalang* is accompanied by a *gamelan* orchestra and usually a female singer. As a traditional performance lasts from about 9 P.M. until sunrise, even the most skeptical member of the audience will be convinced that the *dalang* has magical powers.

The Balinese version of Javanese *wayang kulit* is more simple and uses fewer puppets, while the Malays, who eagerly borrowed this drama during the 15th century, put their own stamp on it by telling Islamic tales as well as the *Ramayana* and *Mahabharata* that form the repertoire in Java and Bali. Thailand's shadow puppet drama, *nang,* differs in that each puppet is nonarticulated and is handled by a dancer (clearly visible on the screen) who dances the role of the puppet.

Carved three-dimensional wooden puppets known as *wayang golek* are found in Central and West Java. The faces of these puppets are less stylized than those of the *wayang kulit* figures, and performances are viewed in full light. *Wayang golek* in Central Java draws its repertoire from the Islamic *Amir Hamzah* stories. In West Java, where the *Mahabharata* is usually shown, *wayang golek* has become more popular than the shadow play that inspired it. Other forms of two-dimensional puppets made of wood and leather were once found in Central and East Java, but are now virtually extinct.

Glove puppet shows from China, *pu tai hsi,* tell stories from Chinese folk legends and novels such as *The Three Kingdoms* and *The White Serpent.* These charming and skillfully manipulated hand-puppet shows can be seen in Taiwan, and are occasionally performed during temple celebrations in parts of Java. The Burmese, too, had a puppet theater that originated in marionette shows performed for children. These developed into full-scale puppet plays influenced by court drama in the 19th century, with stories taken from the *Jataka* or based on events in Burmese history.

Painting

Painting has been the least important of the arts in Southeast Asia. Apart from the colorful native paintings of Bali, little is known to travelers of the paintings that have been produced in the area.

There are also the cave and temple murals of Burma and Thailand. The earliest extant paintings dating from the Pagan dynasty of Burma (11th to 13th centuries) depict monks, boddhisatvas, and religious scenes in colors of yellow, black, white, and dark red. They show both Tibetan and Bengali influences, and are akin to the better known cave paintings of Ajanta in India.

Thailand's mural paintings have also suffered from the climate, and have flaked badly. Although many centuries old, the art of murals experienced a revival in the late 18th and 19th centuries. Some of the paintings produced during this period can be seen in such temples as Wat Bang Yi Khan in Thonburi and around the walls of the Compound of the Emerald Buddha Temple (Wat Prakeo) in Bangkok. The purpose of most Thai paintings was not to entertain but to "instruct, guide, and inspire the devout." Drawing on the Buddhist *Jataka* tales, these delicate murals create a fairytale world with mythical creatures, divine beings, and humans as they tell the life of Buddha or his previous incarnations. There are also a few less religiously inspired murals showing scenes from the ever-popular *Ramayana,* which often give delightful insights into contemporary domestic and court life.

The modern paintings of Bali are a product of the artistic innovation of the 1930s, although scroll paintings have adorned temples for many years and painted astrological calendars were also in existence. The most striking example of old Balinese painting is the vivid, horrifying fresco adorning the ceiling the 17th-century Hall of Justice in Klungkung.

In the Philippines, Christianity led to the painting of patron saints and religious scenes, some of which achieved a high level of artistry and originality. However, the modern art now produced in the Philippines is among the most exciting to be found anywhere in Southeast Asia.

Some of the most magnificent paintings ever produced in China are now in the collection of the National Palace Museum in Taipei. The earliest Chinese paintings, like those of Burma and Thailand, served a religious purpose. Later, portraits of generals, emperors and their concubines became the vogue until they were superseded by landscape and "bird and flower" paintings. From about the 10th century, Chinese paintings were executed on hanging scrolls, usually of silk. The landscape paintings have a lovely, haunting quality often enhanced by such poetic titles as "Pure and Remote View of Streams and Hills." The exquisite bird and flower paintings, detailed, yet with a serenity and understatement, provided by judicious use of space, are among the finest of all Chinese paintings.

Architecture

Of three basic groups of architecture—domestic, civic and military, and religious—it is the latter that has produced the superb structures epitomizing the rich culture and creative genius of the peoples of Southeast Asia.

The domestic architecture in rural areas is today basically the same as it has been for centuries. Houses, never intended as permanent structures, are constructed for a generally tropical climate using readily available local materials such as bamboo, wood, and palm thatch. The typical house is a small structure raised above the ground for cleanliness and ventilation; verandahs are a common feature; so too are shutters that can be raised or lowered.

The most interesting traditional domestic architecture is found in parts of Indonesia and Malaysia. The Dayak tribes of Borneo are famous for their longhouses, which may run up to 600 yards long and house 600 people. Beautifully carved and strikingly designed clan houses with curved roofs rising to a point at either end are built by the Menangkabaus of Sumatra, while the homes of the Torajas in Sulawesi are noteworthy for their high-pitched, forward-jutting roofs and dramatic, carved designs.

The civic and military architecture of Southeast Asia, like the 19th-century houses built in many major cities, is basically a product of the West. To maintain a firm grip on their early trading ports, the Dutch, Portuguese, and Spanish were forced to build fortresses. When colonial rule was well established, civic buildings such as town halls, law courts, imposing East India Company warehouses and the like were erected. The remains of these buildings can be seen in many parts of Southeast Asia. Most of those built by the Dutch are in parts of Indonesia (particularly Java), Malacca and in southern Taiwan. The Portuguese left their imprint most strongly on Macau, though remains of fortifications still stand in Malacca and parts of Indonesia. The Philippines hold many memories in stone of the long Spanish period, though the most striking of these, the walled city in Manila (Intramuros), was devastated during the Second World War. However, Vigan in Ilocos Sur, like a mini-Intramuros with its cobbled streets and old houses, still stands to this day.

The juxtaposition of these solid European buildings, especially the forts with their thick stone walls and mighty gates, against a vivid tropical background is startling. The stones have aged through the centuries in the humid climate, and seem to have lost their rigidity and strength.

The creative efforts and finances of the countries of Southeast Asia have, for centuries, been reserved for religious buildings such as temples, *wats,* sepulchral monuments and, later, mosques and churches. All of these have been subjected at some time to outside influences: Indian, Chinese, Dutch, Portuguese, Spanish, or British. The earliest religious structures were megaliths, used in animistic worship all over the ancient world. Huge, flat, tablelike slabs of stone and tall, upright pillars have been found in Sumatra (especially on the island of Nias where a megalithic culture existed until the 19th century), in other parts of Indonesia, and in Malaysia.

Hinduism or Buddhism gradually displaced animism in Burma, Thailand, Cambodia, Malaysia, Sumatra, and Java. Buddhism eventually became the supreme religion in Burma, Cambodia and Thailand and inspired most of their religious monuments. In Java, the two great religions existed side by side or alternated in importance, and a form of syncretism evolved. Magnificent reminders of both Hinduism and Buddhism still stand in Java, although Islam was eventually to become the religion (nominally, at least) of the majority of Javanese. Sumatra, which was the center of the mighty Buddhist Srivijaya kingdom, bears few traces of the monuments that must have been erected.

The eighth-century temples of Burma were, according to a Chinese chronicler, "built of green brick decorated with gold and silver." Among Burma's main attractions are the magnificent temples of the kingdom of Pagan, constructed between the 11th and 13th centuries. Buddhism reached Burma direct from north India, from Ceylon, from the Mons of southern Burma, and from Tibet. The combination of these influences can be seen in the 5,000 temples that dot the plain along the banks of the Irrawaddy River. Solid stupas (bell-shaped structures), sanctuaries, and monasteries were constructed with a central base of brick rather than stone; the base was surrounded by passages with niches holding statues of Buddha and his disciples, and the structure was topped by a tall pinnacle. Stucco friezes were decorated with geometric motifs, flowers, foliage, animals, and mythical beings. Later temples constructed during the 17th to 19th centuries were influenced by Thai architecture and became more decorative; roofs were adorned and the pagodas covered with gold leaf and raw lacquer.

One of Burma's most famous pagodas is the Shwe Dagon in Rangoon which, according to tradition, dates from the time of Buddha. It has been rebuilt and enlarged many times and is now a massive structure towering 344 feet to a pinnacle bearing a solid gold ball studded with diamonds and other precious stones. The whole pagoda is covered with gold leaf.

The Thais modified Indian, Chinese and Khmer styles to create a uniquely Thai style by the time of the kingdom of Chiang Mai (11th to 16th centuries). This style reflected the Thais' feeling for the unity, strength and serenity inherent in Buddhist philosophy. By the late 18th century, however, ornamentation became more important than line and the basic simplicity of Thai architecture was lost. The *wats* of Thailand consist of a number of buildings grouped behind a wall. The most striking of these is usually the *chedi,* a bell-shaped stupa topped by a tall, slender spire. The *prang,* a more solid structure than the *chedi,* is normally built of stone, narrowing slowly to a gently rounded top. The main chapel or *bot* holds the most important Buddha image, while there is a *vihara* for lesser relics. There may also be a *mondop* (library) and *prasad* (throne hall).

The recently restored *chedi* at Phra Pathom, 32 miles outside of Bangkok, is considered to be the oldest Buddhist monument in Thailand. Its solid simplicity is in striking contrast with the most spectacularly baroque work in all Thai architecture, the *prang* of Wat Arun Rajavararam in Thonburi. Begun at the end of the 18th century, this massive *prang* is a riot of ornamentation created with millions of fragments of Chinese porcelain.

One of the best examples of late Thai architecture is the 19th-century Wat Pra Keo (Temple of the Emerald Buddha) in Bangkok. This complex includes buildings with the multi-layered roofs decorated with brilliant glazed tiles, and the tapering ridge poles that are so distinctively Thai.

The greatest glory of Southeast Asian architecture is, of course, Angkor Wat, unfortunately cut off from public view by military activity for the past few years. However, the reconstructed ruins of Pimai, in Thailand, dating from the same period, give a good idea of Angkor Wat's character and quality.

Java is the only part of Southeast Asia where great monuments to both Buddhism and Hinduism still survive. Before the 10th century, the Buddhist Sailendra and Hindu Mataram dynasties ruled large kingdoms from their seats in Central Java until power moved to East Java. Here, the last of the mighty Hindu-Javanese empires held sway until the onslaught of Islam forced the court to flee to Bali, where a form of Hinduism still exists.

The best known of Java's religious monuments is Borobudur, the "cosmic mountain," the largest Buddhist structure in the world. Much has been written about this vast stupa, erected by the Sailendras during the eighth and ninth centuries. It expresses in stone the totality of the universe according to the doctrine of Mahayana Buddhism. The three stages in the attainment of *nirvana* are presented: the material world, the world where man has lost his passions but is still tied to his worldly possessions, and finally the stage where man has lost all cravings and has attained spiritual enlightenment. The rich carving around the lower galleries presents the lives of Gautama Buddha, the *Jataka* tales, and the future Buddhas.

The most striking Hindu monument in Java is the ninth-century *candi* (temple) dedicated to Shiva at Prambanan (near Yogyakarta). Also known as *Loro Jonggrang* ("The Slender Maiden"), this gracefully tapering building achieves a perfect architectural balance that is matched by the delightful carvings surrounding the lower galleries; part of the *Ramayana* is retold, wonderful mythical gargoyles and demonic *kala* heads grimace horribly from above doorways or corners, sinuous *nagas* slither down stairways and *kinnaras* (half-bird, half-maiden) and other charming birds and animals form a recurrent theme.

East Java is also rich in Hindu monuments, the most outstanding being the 14th-century temple complex at Panataran where relief carvings in *wayang* style confirm the early popularity of the shadow play (*wayang kulit*).

Bali's Hindu temples are full of exuberant decoration that begins with the ornately carved split gateways and continues on the buildings and shrines clustered in a series of courtyards. Fantastic demons, flowers and foliage draw one's attention away from the basic shrines or "seats" for the gods. The stone or brick-based temples are topped by a succession of thatched roofs (the maximum number being 11) representing the *meru* or celestial mountain.

Thousands of Chinese temples, some more than 400 years old, are found in Southeast Asia. The Chinese often merge Confucianism, Taoism, and Buddhism, and their temples are an equally fascinating blend. Made from wood or stone, they contain a large worshipping hall, often with small shrines dotted around it. The interior is an exciting combination of carved beams stained with generations of incense smoke, tall altar tables supporting gleaming brass incense holders, jars of divining sticks, cashew-shaped prayer aids, piles of fresh oranges, and carved and painted gods (often with real hair forming their beards or long moustaches). The newer temples seethe with red and gold paint, while the curving roofs of old temples are adorned with delicate colored glass or porcelain figures of dragons, lions, serpents, birds, and flowers. The best places to see old Chinese temples are Macau, Taiwan, Malacca, Penang and Semarang (Java), while Singapore and Hong Kong have a number of lovely 19th- and 20th-century temples.

When Islam came to the southern islands of Southeast Asia, the mosque also arrived to add variety to the architectural scene. Initially, mosques were built in the traditional local style; later, Arabic touches were added. This combination of local and Middle Eastern styles led to some rather bizarre creations, such as a pagoda-topped mosque in the Philippines. At the beginning of the 20th century an intensification of Islam led to widespread copying of Arabic mosques with their round domes (regrettably often executed in tin rather than mosaic tiles). The most striking mosques in Southeast Asia are those recently built in Brunei, Kuala Lumpur, Manila, and Jakarta. There is a particularly interesting old Javanese-style mosque in Kudus (Java), while charming late 19th- early 20th-century buildings that seem to have come straight from the pages of the Arabian Nights exist in places like Kuala Kangsar (Malaysia) and Kuala Lumpur.

The country with the largest number of churches is, of course, the Philippines, where roughly 90 percent of the population are Christians. The Spanish brought the rich baroque styles of Europe with them in the 16th and 17th centuries, styles which the Filipinos happily absorbed and further embellished with their own distinctive touch. The early churches were generally squat rectangular buildings with thick walls built to withstand earthquakes, and a bell tower. The ornamentation of these churches were carried out by Filipino and Chinese craftsmen, the former including traditional motifs like the crocodile and pineapple, the latter adding lions and demons—all these appearing inside a Romanesque Gothic or Baroque exterior!

Sculpture

The sculptural talents of Cambodia, Burma, and Thailand have for centuries been poured into the creation of Buddha figures to assist worshippers in meditation and devotion. Many of the best can still be seen (or rather will be once again in a quieter future) at Angkor Wat, especially in the indoor friezes. There are Buddhas with oval faces and Buddhas with square faces; there are faces with fine regular features and faces with prominent features and bulging eyes; there are completely impassive faces and faces with a gentle, sweet smile. Buddha is shown seated (the most common position), walking, standing or reclining. He is carved out of stone or beautifully cast in bronze. There are so many variations of Buddhist sculpture that all but the expert can become lost trying to distinguish among them. Although styles changed from one period to the next, there is a basic similarity in all Buddhist sculpture, for the appearance of Buddha is prescribed by the scriptures: "his head is the shape of an egg, his eyebrows like drawn bows, his nose as a parrot's beak and chin as a mango stone; his shoulders as massive as an elephant's head, his arms as tubular as an elephant's trunk."

A huge quantity of Buddhist statues are still *in situ* at the ancient cities of Burma, Thailand, and, if you have time, Sri Lanka.

A great many Buddhist statues have also been found in Java, most of them now displayed in museums. The most outstanding Buddhist sculpture still *in situ* is the huge Buddha figure flanked by two companions in the Mendut temple near Borobudur. Java is also a rich source of ancient Hindu sculpture in both stone and bronze. A life-sized stone carving of the bull, Nandi (Shiva's mount), a bronze Shiva with silver-plated lips, a pair of massive stone temple guardians from the East Javanese Singosari dynasty are just three of the many superb legacies of Java's Hindu period.

Unlike the Javanese, the Balinese have never placed images of gods in their temples. Their sculpture, in the form of woodcarving, was reserved for the homes of nobles, for rice barns and communal buildings. Spectacular *girudas,* winged lions, and a host of mythical and real creatures were carved from wood and painted.

The Philippines is another area where sculpture in wood reached a high level of artistry, particularly in the execution of saint figures (*santos*). These lovely sculptures are collectors' items today.

Handicrafts

The handcrafted goods of Southeast Asia are enough to make a traveler long for an unlimited baggage allowance!

Before the arrival of modern methods and materials (in other words, in the pre-plastic era) the majority of the people of Southeast Asia made all their own utensils, furniture, and clothing by hand. In many areas there is still a demand for such items, and even among travelers the most sought-after goods are usually those made for functional rather than purely decorative purposes.

Tempting handmade goods can be found everywhere, from a village market to a large airconditioned emporium. There are hundreds of things woven from dried palm leafs or rattan, all types of bags, boxes, baskets, hats, slippers, fans and so on. There are smooth wooden bowls and carved figures that vie with black and gold lacquer ware; heavy tribal jewelry contrasts with delicate silver filigree; intricate woven cloth from many tribes such as the Dyaks, the Ifugaos (of the Philippines), rivals the beauty of shimmering silks, some of them interwoven with threads of gold or silver. Simple teracotta cooking ware, carved wooden masks, brilliantly colored silk flowers, enameled silver, lengths of pineapple fiber, coconut shell bowls, cast bronzewares, ceramics in countless forms and finishes, carvings in wood and stone, paintings—the list is endless. But among the many handicrafts of Southeast Asia are a couple that deserve special mention because of the high degree of skill involved and their wide appeal.

Batik, the hand-printed fabric of Indonesia, has been produced for several hundred years, reaching a level of superb artistry in the courts of Central Java about 200 years ago. Originally confined to Java, the art of batik spread to Malaysia about 50 years ago. Batik patterns are produced by dipping the fabric a number of times into a dye bath each time covering the portions not to receive the dye with a coating of wax that prevents the dye from seeping through. This brief description gives no hint of the skill and patience required to trace intricate patterns with a small copper *canting* (which holds the melted wax) onto the fabric, or of the knowledge and care necessary for the dyeing process. The finest hand-drawn batik is known as *tulis* ("written"); less intricate patterns are often formed by stamping the fabric with a copper *cap* (stamp), which is first dipped into melted wax. Traditional motifs, either geometric or freer representations of birds, flowers, and butterflies, are produced, usually in dark blue, deep brown, and creamy white. At the other end of the scale are modern batiks in every color of the rainbow with no restrictions on design other than the imagination of their creator.

The art of the armorer reached its peak of achievement with the *kris,* the knife that holds mystical significance for the people of Indonesia (particularly Java and Bali) and Malaysia. The blade of the *kris* is made by combining crude iron with nickel-bearing steel; the metals are folded and beaten, folded and beaten many times; the blade is then dipped into an acid solution that brings out the waving silver patterns of the nickel against the dark background of the iron.

The blade of the *kris,* which has a close affinity with the snake, can be either wavy (with an uneven number of curves) or straight. Although the hilt is often finely carved or decorated, it is the blade itself that shows the skill of the armorer and is believed to hold magical powers. Stories are whispered of curse-bearing *krises* that can bring death to enemies, sometimes flying mysteriously through the air to achieve the purpose. So important is the *kris* even today that no man will ever draw the blade from its scabbard without the appropriate reverential gesture; the *kris* is still an essential part of full dress in Central Java and the sultans of Malaysia always include the *kris* as part of their ceremonial dress.

RELIGION IN SOUTHEAST ASIA

Lotus and Wheel, Crescent and Cross

In the courtyard of the Temple of the Emerald Buddha two monks wrapped in saffron robes walk with graceful, measured tread over the sun-warmed flagstones. The bright Bangkok sunlight shimmers from the mosaic glass and golden tiles that adorn the façade of the temple and also decorate the costume and weapons of two ferocious-looking stone guardians, who protect the sacred grounds with stone muskets—meticulous replicas of 18th-century English weapons. The monks ascend the steps of the verandah leading to the temple and there they remove their sandals. They move past a kneeling woman who is lighting joss sticks to present to the Buddha image. She is dressed in a fine, smartly tailored, blue silk suit; on her fingers glitter diamond and sapphire rings. Inside the temple it is cool; the only sound is the soft whirring of two large oscillating fans. The monks (perhpas they are visitors from a remote village) fold themselves quietly into the lotus position and contemplate the Buddha.

Even though it is midwinter, it is hot in Singapore, for here the thermometer climbs to the low nineties all year long. Inside the Hindu temple the air is heavy with incense and with the crush of people: women draped in their finest embroidered saris; children, their large brown eyes made even wider by the black kohl on their lids and the red slash of their caste mark on their foreheads; the men—less resplendent in white shirts and dark trousers—their dark faces shiny with beads of perspiration. They are friends and relatives who have come to encourage the penitents who at this moment, after days of prayers and fasting, prepare themselves to undergo a day of rigorous self-torment. Some pierce their tongues with sharp silver skewers. Some walk in sandals with nails that pierce the soles of their feet, but they do not bleed. Many make a sacrifice of atonement or of thanks by carrying a *kavadi,* a semicircular steel frame bedecked with flowers, feathers and ribbons, which rests, supported by bars and spikes, on the bearer's shoulders and chest. The air grows murky with the clouds of incense; the thrum of drums grows louder as the crowd prepares for the Thaipusam procession where the penitents, carrying their strange burdens, follow the prescribed route to the Chettiar Temple in Tank Road. In the procession there is dancing and gay music, for this is a joyous occasion. Most penitents are making this journey in praise and thanks to Lord Subramaniam who has fulfilled a request or granted a pardon for some misdeed.

Contrasts in Faith

Sunday morning. It is cool here in the hills of Sumatra. Lingering wisps of morning fog wreathe distant mountains. The path to the church wanders through terraced rice fields where newly planted green shoots stretch toward the sun in muddy rich water, past the fields and through the village where the communal longhouses of the Bataks stand in two rows, facing each other like petrified war ships. Under the houses pigs and piglets snurf and burrow through the garbage. Majestic cocks strut from yard to yard while flocks of chicks scamper after their plump mamas. The people of the village have all gone to church except for a few old folk who doze in the sun. A few rowdy youngsters play a game of ball. Past the village and past the shuttered schoolhouse, the path turns upward toward the sound of a hauntingly familiar melody. The words are strange but the tune has a familiar ring even though the church choir has altered the tempo of the doxology so that it sounds like an operatic overture. Around the last bend of the path is the church itself: a sturdy, whitewashed frame structure with a tall steeple. From the glassless windows pours the sound of Batak voices soaring in their praise of God the Father, Son, and Holy Ghost.

Shafts of light from the setting sun illuminate the towering clouds in the vast arch of the tropical twilight sky in Kuching, Sarawak. In one of the Malay *kampongs* near the river, the early evening is awash with soft lingering light from the sky. At the entrance to the small *kampong* mosque, men and women gather to chat before evening prayer. The men wear sarongs and the women don special white prayer robes before entering the mosque. The light fades down and out. Now, inside the mosque—lit from within like a stage setting, the large open windows forming the proscenium—we see the men assemble in neat rows and bow facing Mecca to the West. An adjacent window frames the women, now completely enveloped in their voluminous white robes, standing behind the men and also facing West. A wall separates the women from the men. The mosque contains no decorations or ornaments; no gilded figures or statues; no multi-limbed goddesses wreathed in flowers; no incense to distract worshippers' thoughts from the words of the daily prayer: *La ilah illa 'llah Muhammad rasul Allah* (There is no god but God, Muhammad is the messenger of God).

It is a sunny bright April day on a hillside near the fishing village of Aberdeen, Hong Kong. In the Chinese cemetery the mood is one of festivity and family joy, for this is the month of Ching Ming when families make their annual outing to clean the ancestral sites, repair any damage done to the stones during the year and to offer paper money to the spirits of the departed. Food is brought for the spirits—some rice and sweets. It is ceremoniously offered to the departed and the leftovers consumed by the family. The dead have been remembered in an honorable way; spirits have been appeased; the family has renewed its bonds with a day of feasting and picnicking.

Like the shifting patterns in a kaleidoscope the rituals, ceremonies, prayers and customs of all of the world's major religions come to the eye of a visitor to Southeast Asia in a series of changing scenes. The intrepid tourist will spend many hours "doing temples" and his weary feet will carry him up hundreds of steps and through miles of courtyards. His camera will click unceasingly, recording images of Buddha, of Jesus, of Rama and the pantheon of Hindu and Chinese gods. He will take pictures of mosques with golden domes and of minarets festooned with loudspeakers. Probably he will view at least one procession, perhaps in Bali, where graceful women bear elaborate towers of bamboo and blossoms, baked rice cakes, and colored sugar to the temple. At night, if he is in Malaysia or Indonesia, he will turn on the TV and listen to the current Koran-reading competition.

Mosque and church; wat and temple; the wheel and the lotus, and the crescent and the cross; Hindu and Buddhist, Muslim and Christian live side by side in Southeast Asia. All are imported faiths and each has undergone some subtle changes in transition.

An interesting example of the anomalous journeyings of a religion can be found in the presence in Penang of a temple of the Pure Land School, a Chinese branch of Mahayana Buddhism. (In order to understand the anomaly, a brief explanation of the main branches of Buddhism is necessary. Therevada Buddhism is based entirely on following the original Pali Canon of the life and teachings of Gautama Buddha. This tradition, which is also known as "The Lesser Vehicle," is followed in Ceylon, Burma, Cambodia, and Thailand. Essentially non-theistic, The Lesser Vehicle (Hinayana) concentrates on following the Way as taught by Buddha and has a monastic tradition that urges every man to spend part of his life as a monk. The second school, which is called Mahayana, or The Greater Vehicle, moved from India up through Tibet to China and Japan. Mahayana Buddhism, in contrast to Hinayana teaching, states that following the Way is not enough. Every person has within him the potential of Buddha: hood, and monasticism is the goal of every right-thinking man. Through prayer, meditation and study a monk may become a boddhisatva whose duty is to teach and help others. (Temples and monasteries spring up around famous boddhisatvas much in the same manner as cathedrals in Europe were dedicated to the glory of certain saints.)

Thus, it is a bit strange that in Southeast Asia, where the majority of Buddhists follow The Lesser Vehicle, one of the largest and most spectacular temples is Penang's Ayer Hitam Temple. Here, in contrast to the begging bowl image of Therevada Buddhism, great emphasis is placed on lavish gifts to the temple in order to obtain the help of Kuan Yin, Goddess of Mercy, for the benefit of the Dead. The temple was founded by a wealthy Chinese immigrant. Thus here, 200 miles from the spot where the first Buddhist missionaries are believed to have arrived, exist the two forms of Buddhism, one brought from Ceylon in the sixth century and the other from China in the nineteenth.

What Year Is It, Please?

A quick glance at the Singapore calendar explains some of the problems faced by a secular state in determining which days should be declared public holidays. The government of multiracial Singapore is basically Chinese. The only holiday when these pragmatic hard-working people close up shop altogether is Chinese New Year. Nevertheless the government recognizes holidays sacred to four religions. Not only the Chinese New Year, but also important Buddhist, Islamic, and Hindu occasions are declared public holidays.

The Muslim holidays give gazetteers the most trouble, because Islamic tradition is that a holiday begins at the first sighting of the new moon. This goes back to the desert region where Islam began and where that first glimpse of the silver crescent was one of the absolute certainties. In the tropics, however, cloudy skies sometimes obscure the moon On those occasions, in the past, the holiday would be postponed until the mullah made an actual observation of the moon. In modern times this has caused some difficulties because purists insist on adhering to the old way, frowning on the heretical proposal that the fact that the moon has indeed risen be accepted on faith. Singapore has firmly set dates for Hari Raya Puasa and Hari Raya Haji, but in neighboring Malaysia some areas still wait for the mullah's official announcement before beginning their festivities.

Even the date of the year is not the same for everyone. After all, the fact that it is 1,981 years after the birth of Christ is not a meaningful date for Muslims, who date the era from the year of Muhammad's hegira in A.D. 622. The Buddhist year goes back to 563 B.C. Christian dating, like the English language, is used for business, banking and all international transactions. Many Asian calendars are bilingual, with arabic numerals and Christian dates on one side and Chinese and Buddhist dates on the other. In Thailand, cornerstones for important buildings usually carry two dates.

The calendar plays an important part in the lives of the people, because elements of astrology (both Hindu and Chinese) are consulted when making important decisions. Statesmen, kings, and peasants refer to astrologers or bomohs or dukuns for help. The Chinese and Thai, for example, attach great importance to the year of a person's birth according to a 12-year cycle. Each year is represented by an animal: tiger, monkey, buffalo, rat, etc., 1982 was the Year of the Dog, 1983 the Year of the Pig, 1984 the Year of the Rat, etc. In considering marriage it is wise to know the birth year of your intended, because certain combinations are said to be fraught with difficulties. A woman born in the Year of the Rat, for example, should never marry a man born in the Year of the Dog and women born in the Year of the Horse are reputed to be terrible nags!

As the Wheel Turns: Buddhist and Hindu

In the Oriental consciousness time moves in circles, whereas for most Occidentals time moves progressively from point to point. For most people in the Judaeo-Christian tradition each individual life is an entity—a unit—created at a specific moment in time. Death is considered the termination of the physical life of that individual, while the soul may continue to exist through eternity. The conditions of the afterlife, according to Christian belief, depend in large part on the behavior of the individual during his earthly sojourn. Christians, according to most dogmas, believe in resurrection, but nowhere do you find any reference to the idea of reincarnation. And here is where the great schism between Eastern and Western thought begins. Hindu and Buddhist beliefs rest on the assumption that life, as well as time, is cyclical. The soul may endure many lives. Often the conditions of the new life depend on the behavior of the soul in its previous body.

A devout Christian seeks Eternal Life through the teaching of Christ. A devout Buddhist seeks *nirvana* or eternal nothingness, and follows the teachings of Buddha as set forth in his sermon "Setting in Motion the Wheel of Righteousness."

The cyclical notion of time and the idea of reincarnation were taken over by Buddhists from older Hindu and Vedic beliefs. Indeed, Buddha was born a Hindu prince and much of his teaching was aimed at a reform of the structure and complexities of Hinduism. For example, Buddha, like another great Indian religious reformer, Gandhi, deplored the Hindu caste system.

The "historic Buddha" (actually the term "buddha" refers to an awakened or enlightened being) was born Gautama Siddartha about 563 B.C. near the borders of Nepal. A wealthy prince, he lived a comfortable, luxurious life, married happily and had a son. Like so many people of his class, he had been protected from viewing the harsher aspects of life. Legend says that one day he went out from the palace and for the first time saw poverty, sickness, and death. Overwhelmed by this sight of reality, he renounced his worldly position and became a wandering mendicant, determined to find a solution to the problems of life. After years of fasting, begging, and traveling, he sat down under a Bodhi tree and sank into a deep meditation lasting 49 days. On the full moon day of the fifth month, Vesak, he achieved enlightenment and Siddartha became a Buddha.

The answer he found after his contemplation was that in order to escape from suffering and misery, human beings must eliminate desire and attachment. In this world, maintains Buddha, evil is caused by desire, which grows from ignorance caused by wrong thought and misdirected action. Buddha, for example, would have considered modern advertising the essence of ignorance, for it promotes desire. Thus, in order to achieve *nirvana,* an individual must extinguish desire from life by renunciation of evil action and also by atonement for wrongs already done, either in this or in a previous life. Each life that an individual goes through is another chance to escape the wheel of life. If the individual ignores opportunities for thinking and right action, in his next incarnation he will have to pay for past mistakes.

The Five Precepts in Buddhist teaching resemble the Ten Commandments and prescribe guidelines for right living. They are: not to kill, or steal, or do sexual wrong, or lie, or to use any intoxicants. Thus, a devout Buddhist should be both a pacifist and vegetarian. How then, one wonders, can there have been so many years of war? I asked a young Thai that question. He answered quite forthrightly: "In my village the church is not so strict. The teacher says that a very good man must follow all five precepts. But, for an ordinary man, he may choose only one and follow not doing that one."

Which precept had he chosen, I wondered? "That is a very difficult decision for me," he admitted. "Because not to kill, well that means no meat and I am a very hungry man. Not to steal? That is a problem because I am in business and sometimes I must cheat and steal a bit. No sex? Very difficult. I am young. I am not married. I like girls very much. That leaves only two. It is my bad luck to like to drink whiskey. So I told my teacher would I tell no lies. I always say the truth." Whether this young man's theology would be acceptable to a learned monk in Bangkok I don't know, but it makes for a lively conversation over a bottle of Mekong.

Burma and Thailand are both Buddhist countries and there religion forms an integral part of the way of life. In Thailand, for example, it is customary for every young man, who is able, to spend at least three months of his youth as a monk, when he will eat only the food he has received as "merit" offerings by the people early in the morning. The remainder of the day is spent in study, prayer, and meditation. Buddhist monks appear at every official function, whether it be the opening of a village school or the inauguration of a gigantic military airfield.

Buddhist Tolerance

Buddhism, being a non-theistic religion, is tolerant of other faiths and beliefs. Thus it is that elements of older religions turn up in the practices and customs of Buddhists in Southeast Asia. For instance, in Sri Lanka where it is believed that the Buddha visited the island three times and where there is evidence of Buddhist beliefs from that early time, the real conversion of the island to Buddhism occurred in 247 B.C., when Mahinda, missionary son of Emperor Asoka of India, converted Devanampiyatissa, King of Anuradhapura, to that faith, but it can be seen that the rudiments of demon and cobra worship still survive, along with the Hindu influences.

In Thailand, pre-Buddhist animistic notions are widely held. The most visible is the spirit house, a tiny replica of a temple perched on a pole, which serves as a dwelling place for the Phra Phum or guardian spirit of the land. Every day this spirit, or *phi* as the Thais say, is presented with an offering of food, incense, and candles. On special occasions, such as New Year or the anniversary of the Phra Phum's installation, grander food offerings are made. As resident *phi,* he gives help to the family in time of trouble or difficulty.

Not all *phi* are friendly. Some are ghosts of people who died suddenly and violently or for whom there were no proper funeral ceremonies. Other *phi* are demons or fairies from other realms who have come to earth to do some mischief. These, too, must be appeased and guarded against. Help often comes from angelic beings who are often visitors from the Hindu pantheon. These beliefs are seen in their most extreme form in the religious practices on Bali.

Hindu Influence

Hindu-Brahmanic influence, which can be seen throughout Southeast Asia from Burma to the island of Java in Indonesia, remains as a relic of historical kingdoms that had come under Indian influence in the sixth to tenth centuries. In Thailand some of these Hindu traditions came from the great Khmer kingdom that flourished in the ninth to twelfth centuries. (The most spectacular example of the Khmer glories, of course, is in Cambodia. The temples of Angkor Wat will hopefully soon again be open to visitors.) Thai royalty retains several court Brahman priests as a holdover from the times when they advised the king on heavenly omens so that he might rule more wisely. In modern times, these priest-astrologers advise only on special matters affecting the royal family and for public ceremonies such as the Annual Opening of the Plowing Season, held in Bangkok on the Pramane Ground.

The Hindu influence in Indonesia stems from the glories of the powerful Srivijaya kingdom, which controlled much of Sumatra and the Malay peninsula in the 10th century. In Java, a succession of empires combined several aspects of Hindu and Buddhist traditions so that in some instances Shiva, the Hindu god of destruction and regeneration, became merged with Buddha—as can be seen in the temple at Prambanam near Yogyakarta.

The grounds of the Prambanam temple provide the setting for the famous *Ramayana* dance performances held during the summer months. One of two great Sanskrit epics (the other being the *Mahabharata*) the *Ramayana* narrates the life and adventures of Rama, an incarnation of Vishnu descended to earth in human form to subdue the demon Ravanna. The *Ramayana* theme is present in dance, painting and sculpture throughout Southeast Asia.

The advent of Islam in the 16th century extinguished Hinduism in Indonesia except on the island of Bali. Balinese religion, which encompasses all aspects of life from work to play, from birth to death, is a rich mixture of Hindu mythology, animist beliefs and an underlying awe of nature and God as manifest in the great volcano Gunung Agung. The Balinese, who accept the Hindu concept of Kali Yug, which is the last of the four great epochs, believe that in such times as these it is imperative to maintain a proper reverence for all the gods and spirits who dwell on the island, for their anger can be very destructive. Many Balinese believe that both the eruption of the volcano in

1963 and the wave of killings during the civil unrest in 1965 occurred because of religious improprieties.

Balinese Hinduism has absorbed so many local island deities as well as mystic practices from Java that it has very little in common with that observed by other Hindu communities in Southeast Asia. During the 19th century many Indians, especially from the southern part of India, emigrated to the Malay peninsula and the Indonesian archipelago. They brought their religion with them, but some of the more rigid rules of Hinduism, such as the caste system, did not survive the journey.

Hindu belief in reincarnation forms the basis of religious practice and faith. Unlike the Buddhist concept of *nirvana,* the Hindu concept is one of attained deliverance. The Hindu dogma teaches that the soul can be released from the wheel of life only by the observance of *dharma,* that is doing one's duty according to one's position in life. The aim of each existence is to perform the *dharma* of that life so correctly that the soul will be rewarded with a higher station in the next life.

The Hindu godhead consists of a holy trinity: Brahma the Creator, Vishnu the Preserver, and Shiva the Destroyer. Each god appears in a number of different forms, or incarnations, and has a consort and many minor deities attached to his worship. Brahma is usually depicted with four heads to indicate his creativity and intellect. Vishnu is usually pictured with four arms stressing his versatility and strength. His consort is the popular goddess of wealth and fortune, Lakshmi. Shiva is probably the most popular of the three, and the most widely worshipped. As he is the god of both destruction and regeneration, he is thought to be sympathetic to the human condition. His consort, who is known by many names, and is worshipped in several forms, is a source of comfort and inspiration. Her more familiar names are Kali, Parvahti, or Dewi. Shiva has two sons: Ganesha the elephant-headed god of knowledge and "the remover of obstacles," and Subramanya, god of war. Worship of the deities takes place daily in the home and in the temple on festival days. Thaipusam, which pays homage to Subramanya, is celebrated widely in Singapore and Kuala Lumpur. The other major Hindu holiday is Deepavali, the autumn festival of lights.

The Movable Feast: Islam

Despite its long cultural and historical role, however, Hinduism is a minority religion in Southeast Asia today. The reason for this was the great Islamic expansion during the 15th and 16th centuries, when part of the Malay Peninsula (including the four southernmost provinces of Thailand), all of the Indonesia archipelago (with the exception of Bali), and the southern islands of what is today the Philippines became Muslim.

Islam, which is monotheistic (believing in one god), exclusive, and highly moralistic, came as quite a contrast to the easygoing pantheism of the Hindu and Buddhist religions it replaced. With the advent of Islam, the way of life in these areas changed. Some of the more obvious changes were in the calendar, the status of women, and the role of the state in regulating the behavior of citizens.

The Islamic calendar is divided into 12 lunar months, as is the Chinese, so that all festivals move forward every year. Unlike other systems of calculation, the Muslim lunar calendar does not attempt to make any accommodation to the solar year by adding 7 months every 19 years, or the Gregorian system of putting an extra day every 4 years into the solar calendar. Muslim holidays, therefore, move forward 11 days each year, which explains why Muslims do not make a fuss over the beginning of a new year. Also, this system ensures that the month of fasting, Ramadan, rotates through the seasons and therefore is never confused with local planting or harvest festivities, which hark back to pagan customs and would be considered taboo for orthodox Muslims.

Islam, with its emphasis on masculine superiority, tended to weaken the position of women in Asian society. In many areas women had held quite a high position. And in a few societies, such as the Minangkabau in Sumatra and Malaysia, property was held by and handed down through the female members of the family.

The Koran has a great deal to say on the position of women in society. The keynote of the Muslim attitude toward women is in the phrase "women are your tillage," indicating that women's primary function is that of producing children and serving as vassals. Partly because of this attitude, and partly for reasons that may be traced to the rigors of nomadic desert life, a Muslim is allowed to have four wives. The husband may divorce his wife for no reason; he has only to say "I divorce thee" three times and the marriage is dissolved. The authority for this attitude is found in the Koran in passages like this: "Men have superiority over women because God has made the one superior to the other . . . so good women are obedient." For a Muslim, the law of Islam is quite clear. In modern times, however, women are given some legal protection by parliamentary action.

In Southeast Asia, Indonesia and Malaysia are avowedly Islamic nations as is the State of Brunei. Government departments include a bureau of religious affairs. Indonesia's constitution has a law that every citizen must profess belief in a single deity. This law is primarily directed against the nontheistic Chinese, and in recent years many Chinese have become Christian to avoid harassment.

Islam, like Christianity, is based on a specific holy scripture: the Koran, or Qur'an, which is a collection of the words of Allah as revealed to his prophet, Muhammad. To a devout Muslim the book is the holy of holies and much time is spent reading and studying it. The book must be treated with reverence, never handled carelessly, and should never be placed beneath any other books. One should never drink or smoke while the Koran is being read aloud, and it should be heard in respectful silence. In many villages children are taught to memorize great numbers of verses and Koran competitions are annual events.

The Koran sets forth the Five Pillars of Islam: the Profession of Faith, the Five Daily Prayers, the obligation to fast, the obligation to make the pilgrimage, and the obligation to give alms. The Profession of Faith is the familiar doctrine of the Unity of God, which is heard in every mosque and from every minaret: There is no God but Allah; Muhammad is the messenger of God.

The Five Daily Prayers are made at specific times of day, beginning at dawn, then at noon, once in the afternoon, once at sunset, and once at night. The Muslim tradition gives specific instructions on how to say prayers: kneeling and bowing in the direction of Mecca (of course, in this part of the world to "face Mecca" means to turn West, not East). Because the Koran demands cleanliness before prayer (preferably a total bath, but if this is not possible then a ritual cleansing of face, hands, and feet) you will see tanks and basins of water outside all mosques.

The third Pillar of Islam is the necessity for fasting. The ninth month of the year, Ramadan, is set aside for ritual fasting. For 30 days all adult Muslims are enjoined against taking any food from dawn to dusk. During this month, as one would expect, work efficiency tends to drop, because in addition to being hungry and thirsty, many Muslims are also sleepy because they have stayed up so much of the night eating. Adherence to the tradition is quite strict, and in some villages special police prowl the streets looking for secret munchers. The Koran does, however, give dispensation to the sick and to those who must take a meal in the course of their work. The end of Ramadan is the great feast, Hari Raya Puasa. After a morning visit to the mosque, the family returns home for a memorable feast that more than makes up for the month of deprivation.

The fourth Pillar is the duty to make a pilgrimage to Mecca. Obviously for Muslims in Southeast Asia this can be difficult, and therefore the pilgrimage is obligatory only for those who can afford it. Nevertheless, because of the honor and prestige accorded to those who have made the journey, every year thousands of men and women, many of them old, swarm aboard pilgrim ships for the long, arduous journey to the West. Those who return are addressed as Haji (or Hijah for women), indicating that they have fulfilled their obligation. The last Pillar is that of almsgiving, similar to the Christian custom of tithing. In Malaysia this money is collected by the Department of Religious Affairs and is used for welfare projects for the poor.

Christianity in Southeast Asia

Because of its universal appeal and the simplicity of its faith, Islam swept through the islands of Southeast Asia up to the Philippines, where it ran head on into the Spanish Catholic Church. With the establishment of Spanish authority in Manila on June 3, 1571, Islam had reached its utmost extent.

The Filipinos often pride themselves on having the only Christian country in Asia, as well as the most westernized. Before the 16th century, the myriad islands that make up the Philippines had never reached the advanced stage of civilization of their western neighbors. The Filipinos accepted the Catholic teaching eagerly for a variety of reasons. In the first place, Catholicism did not have to contend with an organized, established religion because most of the indigenous customs were family-oriented toward household gods and spirits who dwelt in nature. So for the Filipino, acceptance of the new religion did not involve any deep traumatic rejection of old ways. In fact, many of the older customs were absorbed into Catholic ritual. The second factor in the establishment of Catholicism in the Philippines was the language problem. Never having been unified, the islands were a hodgepodge of different languages and dialects. Catholic schools, which taught Spanish as well as the catechism, opened up opportunities for Filipino unification through language. Furthermore, the church offered protection from marauding pirates and outlaw gangs—one of the terms for new Christians was "those who live under the bells."

Needless to say, Catholicism acquired many Filipino characteristics such as the *fiesta.* Just as the pagan religions had been centered in the home, so was the new one. Even today, in some rural areas, the images of saints carried in procession on festival days are kept in the homes of important or well-to-do members of the community, rather than in the church. Indeed, the focus of a fiesta is often on lavish preparations for the family feast rather than on the religious observance in the church. This is not to say that Filipinos take their religion lightly; only that they have added some facets of their own heritage.

As you travel through the Filipino countryside, you will come across some huge, stark, very un-Roman-looking cathedrals. These are the churches of an indigenous new Christian faith, the Iglesia ni Kristo, which incorporates nationalistic feelings into a Protestant liturgy. It is estimated to have almost a million members.

Elsewhere in Southeast Asia, Christian missionaries, both Catholic and Protestant, followed the colonizing European powers. The lovely churches in Macau, Malacca, and parts of Indonesia and along the coastal regions of Sri Lanka, where nearly all the fisherfolk are Catholic, are remnants of the Portuguese presence.

Missionary work in Southeast Asia did not disappear with the departure of the colonial powers. Indeed, in certain areas proselytizing church groups are more active than ever. Much current missionary effort is directed toward the tribal peoples living in remote jungle or swamp, where pagan practices still prevail. Furthermore, the Chinese are able to embrace Christianity without denying their Confucian or Taoist ideals, because neither of them is theistic.

Within the last few years the world has become much smaller and more and more of us travel to areas where once only intrepid explorers or dedicated missionaries ventured. The global village, McLuhan calls it. Spaceship Earth has become a commonplace notion. This global village now includes formerly remote and exotic lands. Anna and her problems with the King of Siam are a quaint subject for a musical, but the portrait of King Mongkut as a barbarian monarch is outdated. If you visit a Buddhist monastery today in Thailand, you may encounter several European faces among the saffron-robed bikkhus—undergoing the same course of study and meditation that King Mongkut did for 27 years. A former prime minister of Malaysia serves as president of an international Muslim organization, and the Pope has visited the Philippines. Yellow-robed Hare Krishna devotees dance and chant on Fifth Avenue in New York, and Oxford Street in London.

Religion in Southeast Asia no longer plays the role it once did, when personal identity was established by an individual's spiritual tenets. Educational, national, and professional ties have superseded the bonds that rituals in the home and ceremonies in the community once forged. Overcrowding in the cities has pushed people closer together, sometimes with unfortunate results, when vastly different customs clash with one another. The Call to Prayer when amplified over a loudspeaker becomes noise pollution to some ears; the clanging cymbals accompanying a Chinese funeral are equally pollutant to the ears of others.

In today's universities boys and girls study together—and sometimes fall in love! Marriages outside the religious community, while still not as numerous as in the West, have become a reluctantly accepted way of life.

In rural areas change comes more slowly. Nevertheless, modern communication techniques have brought once-remote villages into the 20th century almost overnight. An illiterate old farmer may not understand helicopters and moving picture shows or the news that man has landed on the moon, but he is aware that these phenomena exist.

But just as people in the West have become aware of the value of tradition, so in the East old customs and rituals are undergoing a reassessment in terms of cultural identity as well as spiritual sustenance. During these transitional times a visitor to Southeast Asia has a unique opportunity to observe and participate in the customs, rituals, and ceremonies of many different religions. He can visit a mosque or a Hindu temple, and he is equally welcome in a Buddhist wat as in a Christian church. Old taboos about strangers have been relaxed, so that a visitor may find himself overwhelmed by hospitality.

Throughout Southeast Asia, religion has remained a more important feature of day-to-day social activity than it usually has in the West. Although the form and nature of this religious feeling varies widely within the region, a large proportion of the population is actively involved in it. There is still a strong sense of traditional values, reflected in fundamental social attitudes.

THE FACE OF SOUTHEAST ASIA

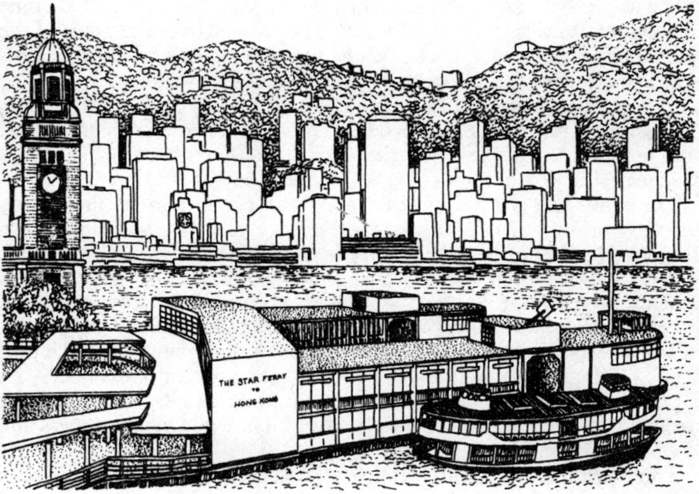

HONG KONG

China Face to Face with the West

Hong Kong is the most interesting and intense package Southeast Asia has to offer. It's the East and West compacted into a tiny space: Western on the outside, Eastern at heart. It's a temple full of money-changers perched on the doorstep of the world's biggest Communist country.

The harbor dominates—in beauty and importance. It brings the many worlds of Hong Kong together. Vessels fat with cargo from all over the world lie at anchor, while junks and sampans nose and cluster around like piglets feeding from mother sows. White cruise ships give birth to blue-haired ladies, who are quickly herded into shops laden with embroidered silk and beaded sweaters. Mighty warships blast forth blond-haired sailors into the arms of bargirls, tailors and electronic-gadget salesmen.

One of the most familiar of Hong Kong residents, perhaps the longest-staying and certainly one of the most awesome, is a scavenger—the Black-Eared Kite, fork-tailed, with a wing span that stretches over two feet. The kites may also be the most envied of Hong Kong residents, envied for the freedom and space they enjoy.

They sail above the pink azalea gardens of Government House where the Governor lives, open to the public one spring Sunday a year, and circle over the concrete slabs of tenement houses, flowered with laundry on bamboo poles. They soar over the packed narrow streets and wheel above the Taoist and Buddhist temples where the devoted come to kowtow to sea gods and goddesses. They sweep over the green of the horse-racing track and cricket club, the grey waters worked by red-sailed junks, and the coves that shelter gleaming white yachts.

The visitor discovers old China as seen in storybooks—rickshaws, rice paddies, narrow and crowded streets festooned with signs in red and gold—side-by-side with the Hong Kong of banking, bikinied beaches, New York-cut steaks, and topless bars.

There are the worlds of the waterfront coolie and of the fishing people, but also of cricket matches, sailing regattas, and diplomatic dinners. He may not find it all in the Yellow Pages, but if he lets his feet do the walking, the traveler will find everything from abacus dealers, acupuncturists, and sellers of aphrodisiacs to snakeshops, street barbers, and dealers in volumes on the *yin* and the *yang*.

The streets throb to the staccato clatter of mah jongg tiles, the beat of rock, pop, and soul, and shrill voices intoning Cantonese opera. As if powered by spring rain, bamboo scaffolding shoots up around the steel and concrete frames of new construction, while jackhammers and piledrivers pound away.

The market stalls of the teeming alleys, selling anything Chinese in flavor from "hundred-year-old" eggs, to paper "ghost" money for burning, are in direct contrast to the boutiques and sophisticated Westernized shops and gleaming department stores with their offerings of the latest in things fashionable from Paris, Rome, London, or New York, or things electronic or photographic from Tokyo.

The people, too, offer great contrasts. The old people still follow the ways and dress of China, but the young are more likely to be dressed in local copies of the latest fashion trend in Paris or Los Angeles. These contrasts can be fascinating and, perhaps, a bit confusing to the new visitor.

Hong Kong is sometimes translated as meaning "fragrant harbor." On hot summer days, the air is heavy with the smells of local markets—not always "fragrant," but always fascinating. At night, Hong Kong becomes a tier of bright jewels—the shimmering reflections in the harbor, the blaze of neon along every street, the shining windows of Mid-Levels, and the orange-yellow necklace of streetlights on The Peak. It's easy then to forget that Hong Kong is a hard-hearted lady, and easy to be seduced by one of her many faces.

History

One writer has asked: "How did this paste jewel come to be hung in the ear of Old China?"

Hong Kong came into British hands in 1841 as something of a war prize. Until then, it was just one of a jumble of hilly and rocky islands at the mouth of the Pearl River, islands which were no more than haunts for fishermen, smugglers, and pirates.

Britain had built up a highly profitable trade with China by bringing opium from India to pay for Chinese goods like tea, silk, and porcelain. That trade was conducted through the south China port of Canton, 144 kms. up the Pearl River from Hong Kong. Britain's merchant adventurers were trying to expand their trade with China at a time when China was trying to stop the import of opium and restrict the activities of the foreign trading community in Canton. London sent a naval expeditionary force to back demands for a commercial treaty or an offshore trading post free of Chinese interference. As a result of the first opium war of 1839–42, Britain ended up with both. Hong Kong Island was ceded "in perpetuity." Ironically, the officer who carried out the occupation was recalled to England in disgrace for accepting what the Foreign Secretary called a "barren island with hardly a house on it."

A second "opium war" (1858–60) resulted in the cession "in perpetuity" of Kowloon Peninsula across the harbor and Stone Cutters Island just offshore from Kowloon. These two acquisitions added 11.75 sq. kms. to the 75.6 sq. kms. of Hong Kong Island. In 1898, Britain negotiated a 99-year lease for mainland north of Kowloon plus 235 islands in the vicinity—an area called the New Territories, comprising 960 sq. kms. As a result of reclamations of land from the sea along the harborfront, the entire colony now measures over 1,066 sq. kms. The New Territories lease runs out in a few years—in 1997—a date that is causing increasing economic unease among the ultra-capitalistic local Chinese, who do not relish the inevitable takeover by China.

The People

There are more than 5.5 million people in Hong Kong. About 98.5 percent are Chinese—mainly immigrants or descendants of immigrants who came to Hong Kong from China in times of war, famine, and political upheavals. Most of the population growth has occurred since the end of the Second World War. It went from around 600,000 in 1945 to 4 million in 1971.

Because the great majority of Chinese in Hong Kong trace their origins to Cantonese-speaking parts of Guangdong Province, the main Chinese dialect in Hong Kong is Cantonese. Other large population groups are the *Hakkas,* who live mostly in the New Territories, the *Chiu Chow,* who migrated mostly from Amoy and Swatow on the South China coast, and the *Tanka* people—primarily fishermen—who have been in the region since time unknown. *Shanghainese,* who came largely after 1949, are among Hong Kong's most prominent manufacturers, businessmen, and financiers.

Many of the immigrants to arrive in Hong Kong came illegally, often fleeing poor harvests or political upheaval in China. The official attitude toward these illegal immigrants has varied over the years from tolerance, to, as at present, a strict policy of returning them across the border. More recently there has been a new influx of refugees, from Indo-China. The so-called boat people have arrived by the thousands, to be held in transit camps until they can be sent to other countries for ultimate resettlement. The unwelcoming attitude of the authorities is, perhaps, understandable in this most overcrowded of environments. The pressure on public housing, education, and social services has been extreme at times of heavy immigration.

China's national language, often called Mandarin and originally spoken mainly in North China, is only occasionally heard in Hong Kong. In recent years, the Government has bent somewhat to popular demands that Cantonese be used more widely or at least concurrently with English in court proceedings, legislative sessions, and Government transactions. English continues to be the idiom of the large business communities involved in international commerce.

The non-Chinese population numbers around 150,000, of whom the majority are British and Australians, followed by Americans, Japanese, Indians, Filipinos, Indonesians, Germans, Koreans, French, and Dutch.

How They Live

Hong Kong residents are mostly city dwellers. More than 95 percent of the population is crowded into urban areas that total only about ten percent of the total land area. In some districts, there are up to 160,000 people per square kilometer living in cramped, high-rise housing—more than ten times the population density of Tokyo. Statistics like these illustrate why housing is considered the number one social problem. Almost half the people live in government or government-aided housing at low rents. As the population grew rapidly, so government efforts to house, educate and provide services for this mass of humanity intensified, but in spite of new housing projects, overcrowding of accommodations and facilities is still widespread. It is, perhaps, this background that has given the people their dominating ambition, to make money to escape to a grander life style—and many do make it in this paradise for capitalism.

The Place

The bustling Central District on Hong Kong Island is the center for commerce and government. Along the waterfront are modern buildings housing hotels, department stores and offices. With the increasing congestion in Central District, business has been pushing to the east of Central into Causeway Bay. The new office buildings have greatly changed the character of Wanchai, which once had a well-justified reputation as a center of sin and sex in the Orient. Hundreds of cargo junks moor along a stretch about a mile to the west of Central. Many of them fly the five-star flag of the People's Republic of China. They bring food from China daily, since the colony produces only a small fraction of what is consumed by residents.

From the edge of Central District, a cable car ascends 400 meters to The Peak where wealthy *taipans* (businessmen) live. Other beautiful residential districts on the Island are Repulse Bay, Shousan Hill, and Shek-O. On the opposite side of the island from Central is the fishing village of Aberdeen where thousands of Chinese live most of their lives aboard junks in its harbor. Here, too, high-rise public housing is replacing the traditional style of living.

Most of the colony's industry is centered in the city of Kowloon, across the harbor from Hong Kong Island on the mainland of China, and in the New Territories, which are behind Kowloon. The colony's agriculture, mostly vegetable farming, is predominantly in the New Territories, although competition with industry for land and the difficulty of competing with food imports from China has meant a steady reduction of acreage under cultivation. The New Territories end at the border of China. Except for travelers going to China, farmers of the area, and those with special permits, no one is allowed close to the politically sensitive border.

The Economy

Hong Kong was born of mercantile interests and remains very much dominated by them. It was declared a duty-free port soon after its cession in 1841 and thrived for about 100 years chiefly as an *entrepôt*—a warehouse for goods being shipped to and from China and other parts of Asia. The Japanese occupation of Hong Kong from 1941 to 1945 made for a big setback in economic growth. And the installation of a Communist government in Peking in 1949 raised doubts about the future of *entrepôt* trade. But the influx around this time of many rich merchants and manufacturers from Shanghai and Canton helped turn Hong Kong in a new direction. In something of an industrial revolution, the emphasis switched to manufacturing—especially textiles and clothing—which are still the dominant money earners. Other important industries include plastic goods, chemicals, leather goods, toys, and electronics. Although Hong Kong has ceased to rely solely on its role as an *entrepôt* port, trade is still the colony's lifeline. Nearly all raw materials come from overseas, so Hong Kong must import to export.

The People's Republic of China is just a coin's toss away. Most people believe that if there is to be any major change in the colony's social and capitalistic style it will come on China's initiative once it regains control. The PRC never officially recognized the British claim to Hong Kong. China could have marched across the border any time and retaken the colony with the simple explanation that the 19th-century treaties were unfair and unequal, imposed on a weak and crumbling Manchu empire by foreign powers, and signed at gunpoint.

China, however, regularly declared that it did not regard Hong Kong as an "immediate problem." The Chinese were content to wait—as a nation with a 5,000 year history can afford to do. The inevitability of the Chinese takeover was obvious, however, also to the British. In recent years they entered into long, drawn-out negotiations to allow for the Chinese takeover by 1997, the end of the 99 year lease period on the New Territories, and to protect the interests of the Hong Kong people, including the basic freedoms not always allowed in China. These negotiations resulted, in 1984, in the signing of a historic agreement under which a gradual changeover will ease the transfer of sovereignty from England to China, through a process of joint consultation.

Although ideological shifts in China can influence Hong Kong in important ways, the economic benefits that China reaps from Hong Kong seem to have more to do with the colony's survival and prosperity than any other factors. China obtains a good part of its foreign earnings through exports sold and shipped through Hong Kong, and through investments in Hong Kong properties like banks, department stores, factories, and restaurants. Hong Kong is also a good customer for commodities from China like oil, water, food, cement, and building materials, plus a whole range of consumer goods.

Hong Kong has developed as the major gateway for both business and tourist visitors to China. It is now easy to take one- to four-day visits by train or air to Guangzhou (Canton) and other cities in China. Visa and other restrictions have been greatly relaxed, but still exist and can take time. Allow at least three working days in advance in Hong Kong to give your agent time to make all arrangements.

Policies and Personalities

Hong Kong has been governed well, but always with an eye to what free enterprise business interests want. To the Hong Kong Chinese, British rule has brought protection of his property and little interference with his local customs. This will inevitably change when China takes over Hong Kong.

At present, the top of the pyramid of this Crown Colony is the governor appointed by London who works closely with a 17-member cabinet-like body called the Executive Council. The 47-member Legislative Council, something like a parliament, is concerned with all matters of legislation, taxation, and expenditure. There is no elected representation to the Executive or Legislative Council. The nearest thing to democracy occurs in the election of 30 members of the Urban Council, which looks after such vital things as sanitation, public health, and cultural and recreational activities. Only about two percent of the population is eligible to vote, and most don't bother, but there is now a growing feeling for more local Chinese participation in government.

Exactly how the form and system of government will change over the coming years is not yet clear, but it appears, from the 1984 agreement between China and England, that China is willing for Hong Kong to retain much of its Western style of commercialism and social freedom, certainly well beyond 1997. Political forces are now developing, but whatever their ultimate form, the balance between free enterprise and communism is likely to remain delicate.

About half the population is under 25 years old. And as in the West, there has been increasing awareness and participation in political affairs by students and young workers, and occasionally some minor clashes with authorities. But most of the people are not politically active; the motivating and binding ethic is "the cult of money."

It's hard to say why people seem to be more money-minded in Hong Kong than in other places of the world. It's not that the desire to get ahead and the willingness to work are qualities exclusive to residents here. But the shortage of everything except people—especially shortages of time and space to live and breathe and play—make the scramble to get a share all the more intense.

The many nationalities and races and cultures make for a fascinating and picturesque place in the eyes of Western travelers. But essentially the worlds of the East and West go their separate ways, and there's less of a blend than might be expected. BBC correspondent Anthony Lawrence, a long-time resident, was asked the question "What brings the two worlds together in Hong Kong, at least to the extent that they do find meeting ground?"

His answer: "All human beings admire the same vital qualities that make life livable—honesty, reliability, respect for family, courage, a sense of humor. There is plenty of common ground at this level between the Chinese and the Westerners, despite the differences. I've noticed the Europeans who get on best with the Chinese are not usually those who spend their time in open-mouthed admiration of Chinese culture, or make great back-slapping efforts to persuade sensitive and suspicious Chinese acquaintances of their love and goodwill; but rather the man who appears relaxed, unimpressed by the more futile conventions of society (his own country's or other peoples')." It may well be that this will be the key to the future development of Hong Kong.

EXPLORING HONG KONG

As we have stated earlier, try an organized tour for your introduction to Hong Kong. One of the most popular water cruises goes by comfortable launch to Yaumatei Typhoon Shelter. This is the anchorage for some 1,000 vessels, most of which are cargo lighters. From there, the boat sails past the western anchorage on the Hong Kong side—the Kennedy Town waterfront. Here Chinese flags fly from many a junk mast and coolies sweat and strain with baskets and boxes being unloaded along a mile of wharves.

The streets of Kennedy Town are noisy, crowded, festooned with bright Chinese signs, and crammed with fish and vegetable shops, ships' chandlers and coolie hotels. The launch proceeds around the island to Aberdeen, port of some 3,000 junks and sampans. Many of the "floating population" here spend most of their lives aboard these boats, which are both their homes and means of livelihood.

At Aberdeen, passengers stop for drinks or a meal aboard a floating restaurant. Dating back to the Mongol dynasty and once famed as a haunt of pirates, Aberdeen is one of the earliest settlements on the Island. Although most of the boat people are fishermen, light, land-based industries are rapidly developing in the area. Not far across the water from Aberdeen is the small island of Ap Lei Chau, which is a junk-building and boat-repair area. From a floating restaurant, you can watch the fishermen repairing nets, setting sail for the day's catch, or buying food from the small sampans that are traveling grocery stores.

The harbor tour takes a look around this fascinating waterway and passes the world inhabited by commercial vessels, the Royal Hong Kong Yacht Club, and Causeway Bay Typhoon Shelter, a water parking lot for the sampans and junks used in unloading cargo from ships moored in the harbor. This is also the home for a number of "kitchen sampans" that will pull up alongside your boat and cook and serve a fresh seafood dinner. The launch returns via the eastern coastline of

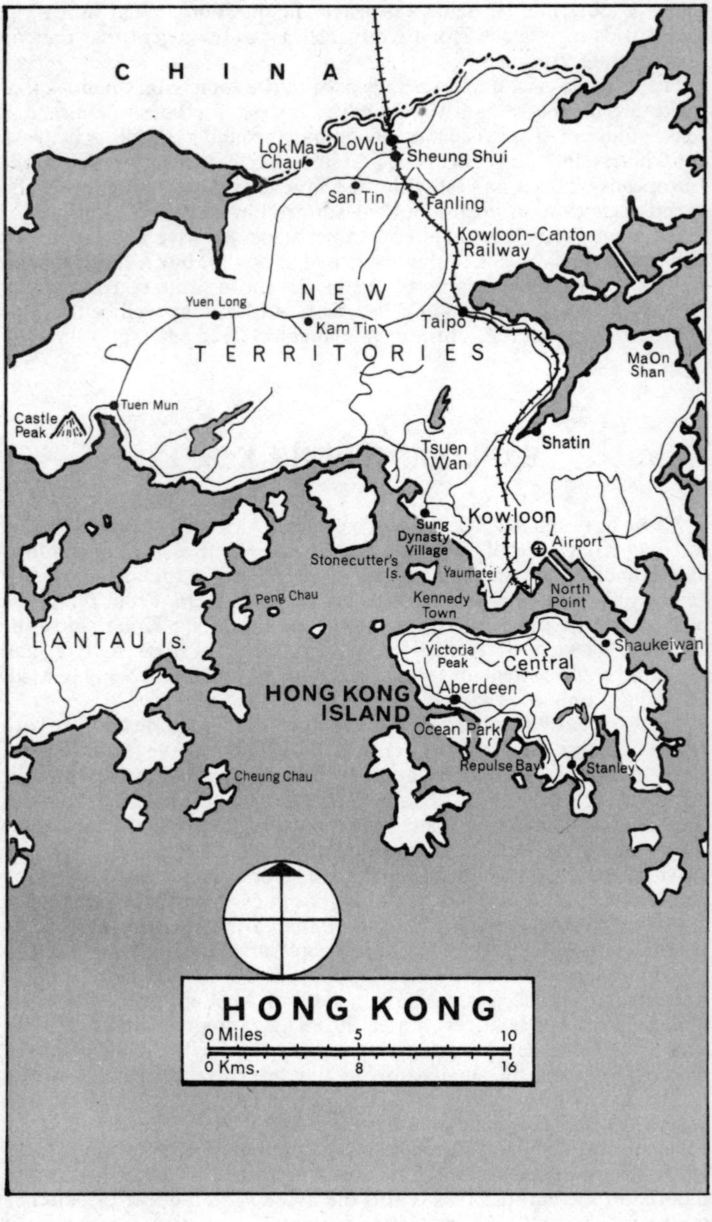
CHINA
Lok Ma Chau
LoWu
Sheung Shui
San Tin
Fanling
Kowloon-Canton Railway
NEW TERRITORIES
Yuen Long
Kam Tin
Taipo
Ma On Shan
Tuen Mun
Castle Peak
Shatin
Tsuen Wan
Kowloon
Sung Dynasty Village
Airport
Stonecutter's Is.
Yaumatei
Peng Chau
Kennedy Town
North Point
LANTAU Is.
Victoria Peak
Central
Shaukeiwan
HONG KONG ISLAND
Aberdeen
Ocean Park
Repulse Bay
Stanley
Cheung Chau
HONG KONG
0 Miles 5 10
0 Kms. 8 16

HONG KONG

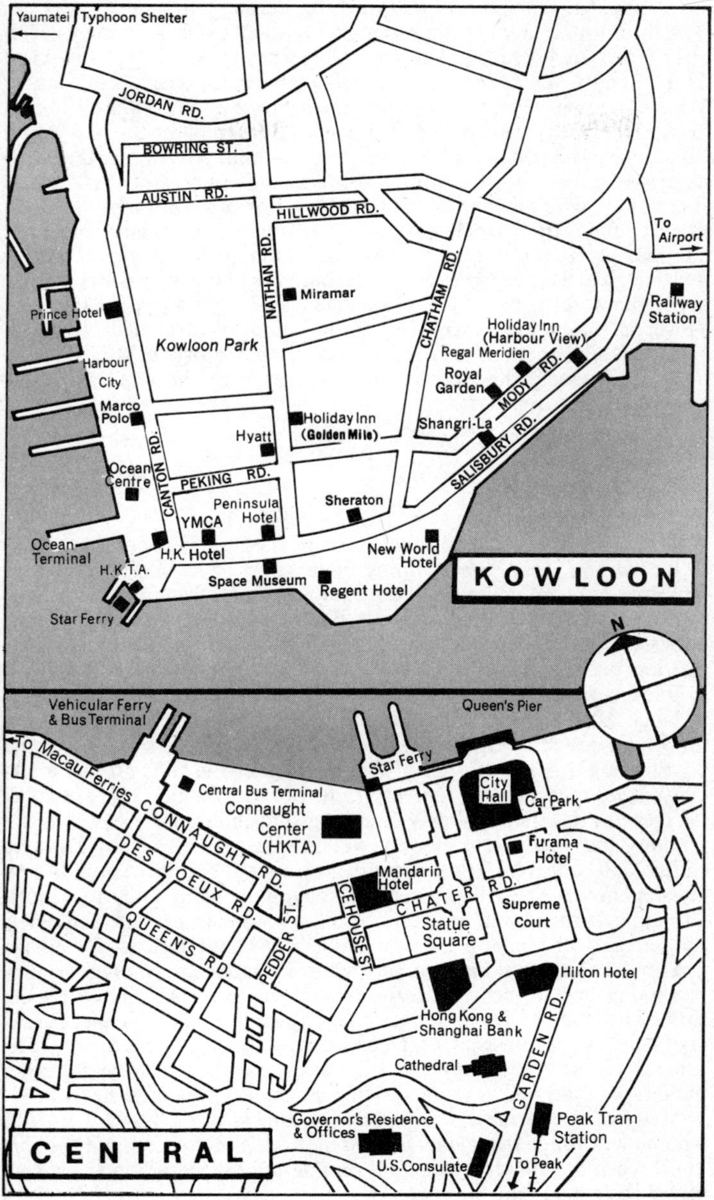

Yaumatei
Typhoon Shelter
JORDAN RD.
BOWRING ST.
AUSTIN RD.
HILLWOOD RD.
NATHAN RD.
CHATHAM RD.
To Airport
Railway Station
Prince Hotel
Miramar
Kowloon Park
Holiday Inn (Harbour View)
Regal Meridien
Royal Garden
MODY RD.
Harbour City
Marco Polo
Holiday Inn (Golden Mile)
Shangri-La
SALISBURY RD.
Hyatt
CANTON RD.
Ocean Centre
PEKING RD.
Peninsula Hotel
Sheraton
YMCA
Ocean Terminal
H.K. Hotel
New World Hotel
H.K.T.A.
Space Museum
Regent Hotel
KOWLOON
Star Ferry
N
Vehicular Ferry & Bus Terminal
Queen's Pier
To Macau Ferries
Star Ferry
City Hall
Car Park
Central Bus Terminal
CONNAUGHT RD.
Connaught Center (HKTA)
DES VOEUX RD.
Mandarin Hotel
Furama Hotel
ICEHOUSE ST.
CHATER RD.
Supreme Court
Statue Square
QUEEN'S RD.
PEDDER ST.
Hilton Hotel
Hong Kong & Shanghai Bank
GARDEN RD.
Cathedral
Governor's Residence & Offices
Peak Tram Station
CENTRAL
U.S.Consulate
To Peak

Kowloon past the runway at Kaitak, a two-mile man-made airstrip for jet planes that reaches out well into the harbor.

A third tour combines the water tour with an overland trip by coach after lunch at Aberdeen. The land trip is past Deep Water Bay Golf Club, Repulse Bay (named after a British man-o'-war), and Stanley Village, a town which has a fishing fleet, some of the loveliest homes on the Island, the main prison, and the headquarters for the Maryknoll Mission Fathers. Many of the land tours take in Aw Boon Haw Gardens where there is a beautiful pagoda near the home of the late Aw Boon Haw, who made millions by selling tins of menthol salve. Open to the public, the garden next to Aw's home is a mass of violently colored, grotesque, sculpted concrete statuary that depicts Chinese mythological figures. From there the tour goes along Stubbs Road, high above the waterfront, to The Peak. The view from the roof of the Peak Tower is the best in town. The entire colony is stretched out in all directions like an enormous living map, with Victoria below, then the harbor, Kowloon, the New Territories, and at the horizon, the misty mountains of China.

New Territories

One of the popular land tours starts at the Star Ferry and proceeds along Nathan Road, the booming main street of Kowloon where old buildings are torn down and new ones go up at a frantic pace. A little over two miles up Nathan Road is Boundary Street, the dividing line between Kowloon (owned outright by the British) and the New Territories (on lease until 1997).

One answer to the problem of squatters can be seen at Shek Kip Mei, in block after block of high-density housing built by the government for former shack dwellers. Nearly every mile there is a sandy cove and beach along Castle Peak Road. Huddled under the cliffs are the weekend houses and clubs of the very rich. Beyond Castle Peak are small villages and farmland, slowly changing into industrial areas.

Many tours stop at a gloomy walled village in the Kam Tin area called Kut Hing Wai. It's surrounded by a moat and has watch towers at each corner. The village was built during the Ming Dynasty (1465–87) and is truly a bit of old rural China with one important difference: the villagers of modern-day Kut Hing Wai hustle tourists for coins.

Yet the farm buildings in the Kam Tin area are among the few remaining ones to be seen in the New Territories. As one writer described it, "the tiled roofs are gone, and there is much tar-paper shackery which is reminiscent of Depression outback America. . . . The cement and textile factories stand up against the green fields rather harshly, and serried skyscrapers of housing estates stand nearby."

Many of the farmers are *Hakkas,* members of a "lost tribe." The women wear huge straw hats fringed in black cloth to keep out the sun. Until recently, they frustrated all photographers by hiding their faces under their hats, but the more enterprising now pose cheerfully for a dollar. In fact, the old girls are now very displeased with the visitor who does not want their services as a model.

Visitors can now also take one-day excursions to China by train. From Kowloon Railway Station one rides through the countryside of the New Territories and crosses the border at Lo Wu, with a visit to the small Chinese city of Shenzhen—not exactly Peking, but very interesting for those who do not have time for a full-scale visit to the People's Republic.

The Kowloon–Canton Railway (British Section) runs frequent trains from the main station in the Hunghom section of Kowloon, north to the border at Lo Wu. Sightseers may ride without formality as far as Sheung Shui, the last station before Lo Wu, where China-bound passengers cross the border bridge and board a train on the other side, bound for Canton. There are eight stations between Kowloon and Sheung Shui—Mongkok, Kowloon Tong, Tai Wai, Shatin, Fo Tan, University, Taipo Market, and Fanling. You may buy a round-trip ticket and ride out and back in around one hour, or buy a ticket for any one of these stations, get off, have a look around, and buy another ticket for the next station an hour later. At the University stop one can alight and visit the campus and see its excellent Art Gallery. Shatin is a popular—and crowded—destination on race days at the big new course there. Visitors with the time and energy can also climb up the hillside and visit the 10,000 Buddhas Monastery.

Much of the New Territories can be explored by means of the Mass Transit Railway, Hong Kong's "metro," which now provides direct links with Central District. A fast, convenient and cheap means of getting around and itself an interesting aspect for "people watchers." But be warned, it does get *very* crowded during rush hours. The Hong Kong Tourist Association has an organized tour of the New Territories.

The Outlying Islands

Lantau Island, twice as big as Hong Kong Island but with a tiny fraction of the population (around 30,000), is a delightful way to get away from it all. It's a place full of fresh air, green hills, and serenity—another world after the noisy, crowded streets of the city. You can go on your own by one of the regular ferries, or have one of several tour agencies plan the trip and provide a guide. The more adventuresome can take an early ferry (weekdays are best) from the Outlying Districts Pier to Lantau's Silvermine Bay. The bus or minibus from Silvermine hugs a steep, winding, and sometimes scary road to *Po Lin Tse* (Golden Lotus) Buddhist monastery—a big, ornate temple fronting a plateau of small pagodas. There is a tea plantation nearby where visitors can sample the tea that is being picked, and buy some to take home. Another excursion goes from Silvermine to the old port and fishing village of Tai O on the west coast.

Most ferries to and from Lantau stop at Peng Chau (an interesting island in its own right with several porcelain painting factories and a woodworking and a metal factory in which to poke around). From Peng Chau it's a short junk or sampan ride and a 15-minute uphill walk to the Trappist Monastery of Our Lady of Joy. This is home for a silent order of monks whose life is a routine of prayer, study, and manual labor, and whose days begin at 3:15 A.M. The Po Lin Monastery can provide a clean, hard bed and a vegetarian meal at nominal prices for the visitor who wants to stay overnight and sample the monastic way of life. The thing at Po Lin is to get up before dawn and go with a guide to Lantau Peak to watch the sunrise.

Cheung Chau ("chau" means island) used to be a pirates' haunt. These days it's the home base for a large boat population, and there's something of a shipbuilding industry along the waterfront. It has a charming, old-style atmosphere and is a nice place to wander through for an hour or two. All these can be reached by regular public ferry from Central.

Rambling Around

Beyond the fancy shops in the hotel arcade and the blue-glazed windows of the air-conditioned tour bus is the other side of Hong Kong. It's just a few steps off the main road, but somehow not many visitors get that far. Tour guides and guidebooks can name names and point the way, but the only way for the traveler to discover it is by himself, unhurried, on foot. It has to be heard, smelled, and felt. So the tourist who really wants to see Hong Kong should put aside some time to just ramble around.

Get up early one morning, say around six-thirty or seven, and go over to the Botanical Gardens or Victoria Park. Watch the early risers doing *Tai Chi Chuan,* literally the "great, ultimate fist." It's a form of exercise also called shadow boxing—a series of slow, graceful, highly controlled body movements developed by Taoist monks 1,000 years ago. Then, if you're at the Botanical Gardens, go take a look at some of the exquisite birds in the aviary. Then go back to your hotel and have breakfast.

Walk around the Peak. Get off the Peak Tram at the top and take Lugard Road, an almost-level, two-mile, circular walk that takes about 45 minutes and gives a bird's-eye view of almost all of Hong Kong. At the upper tram terminus is the Peak Tower Village, an arts and crafts center, with shops and craftsmen at work.

Ride on the old trams. Sit on the top by a window. Take the "Shaukiwan" car and ride to the end and back again. You will see Wanchai, Causeway Bay and North Point. Then take one going the opposite direction from Central District to Western Market. For a good lunch in Causeway Bay, visit the collection of reasonable eating places on Food Street, a parade of restaurants and cafés featuring variations of Chinese and Western food, close to the Excelsior Hotel.

Easily reached from this area, by bus or taxi, is the Aw Boon Haw Garden. Built in 1935 and covering 20,000 square meters of steep hillside, the gardens feature grottos and cement sculptures of beasts, gods, and characters from Chinese mythology. Admission is free, 9–4 daily.

Explore the fascinating area of small streets around Hollywood Road and Queen's Road Central, H.K. side, where old ladies sort bean sprouts in baskets on the sidewalks alongside shops that sell countless exotic wares, traditional foods and crafts. Alongside, others sell reconstituted refrigerators, office files and sewing machines. Stop in at the Man Mo Taoist Temple on Hollywood Road. Breathe in the perfume from the burning spiral incense sticks and look at the curious wooden figures standing on the altars. Have your fortune told here.

There are also shops on Hollywood Road that make carved inlay, Coromandel and other types of furniture, as well as curio shops, porcelain shops, and coffin makers. Take a look at the snake shops on Jervois Street and the egg shops on Wing Sing Street that sell every kind of egg including 100-year-old eggs and salted eggs. Look for the herbalists and umbrella makers on Queen's Road West and take a walk through Cloth Alley (Wing On Street) as you head back to Central along Des Voeux Road.

Plan on spending a day in Aberdeen and visit one of Hong Kong's top touristic attractions, Ocean Park. It's billed as one of the largest marinelands in the world, and features regular performances by dolphins and sea lions in the Ocean Theater. The miniature ocean in the two-million-liter Reef Tank contains around 300 species and offers a view of underwater reef life normally seen only by divers. The 90-meter-long Wave Cove is home for leopard seals, whales, dolphins, penguins, and cormorants. There are two viewing levels to show surface and below surface activity. New attractions are being added all the time, including some thrilling roller coasters.

Shanghai Street, off Jordan Road in Yaumatei District, is a good starting point for a stroll on the Kowloon side. Follow it down to Saigon Street where you will see fortune tellers, street lending libraries, a street barber, and stalls that sell wardrobes for the dead. The stores on Battery Street sell all kinds of paper items including kites and paper houses and luxury items for burning at funerals. Woo Sung Street is full of cooked food, vegetable, and fruit stalls. On the way to Nathan Road you will pass Tin Hau Temple, Yaumatei Typhoon Shelter, more herbalists, wine shops, and medicine shops if you walk up and down Public Square Street, then to Reclamation Street and on to Man Ming Lane. The Hong Kong Tourist Association's various fact sheets offer the best directions to these interesting sights on the Hong Kong and Kowloon side.

Around the junction of Reclamation St. and Kansu St., from 9 to 4 daily is the most fascinating sea of green you will ever see. For about two blocks, the sidewalk and part of the street are literally covered with jade, laid out by hawkers on newspapers and boxes. Rings, bangles, pendants, and beads. Haggle like mad! The HKTA leaflet *Arts and Crafts* also gives a good rundown of places you can visit and watch craftsmen carve ivory, build junks and sampans, carve jade, make carpets, and make rattan furniture. There are also directions if you'd like to visit a brewery, a sandalwood-fan workshop, and a seal-engraving factory.

The "Poor Man's Nightclub" near the Macau Ferry carpark on the Hong Kong side or the Temple Street night market off Jordan Road in Kowloon makes a colorful evening spectacle. They are lantern-lit open-air markets where a variety of food sellers and merchants lay out everything from T-shirts, ties and toothpaste to records, books, and costume jewelry.

Among the newest attractions is the Space Museum and Planetarium opposite the Peninsula Hotel in Kowloon. Admission is free to the main Exhibition Hall and the Hall of Solar Science, HK$15 for the Sky Show. The Planetarium and Space Museum is the first phase of a massive Culture Complex planned on the site of the old Kowloon–Canton Railway Station.

Another attraction is the Sung Dynasty Village at Laichikok, a re-creation of a Chinese community as it may have been a thousand years ago. Not a large-scale construction, but interesting, with cultural and crafts demonstrations against an authentic background of traditional buildings. Best way to see the Village is on a guided half-day tour, which can include lunch, and is arranged by most local tour operators.

There are a number of contrived tourist attractions like those above, but the best sightseeing experiences are the genuine ones, such as a trip on the upper deck of a tram, from Central to Causeway Bay, costing only 60 cents; a ride on the cross-harbor ferry that costs only 70 cents; a half-hour sampan ride around Aberdeen harbor, $40–50 after bargaining; or the free browsing through the old alleys around Hollywood Road and Central. Even better value is the Star Ferry, crossing between Kowloon and Central every few minutes. For only 70 HK cents (First Class!) you can see the harbor and the skyscrapers of the island from a spectacular vantage point. One of the world's greatest, and cheapest, travel experiences.

PRACTICAL INFORMATION

FACTS AND FIGURES. Land area: 1,066 sq. kms. Population: 5.5 million. Birth rate per 1,000: 16. Average per capita income U.S.: $5,300. Life expectancy: 76 years. Number of tourists annually: 3 million.

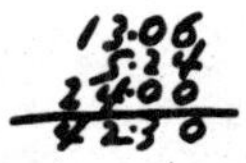

WHAT WILL IT COST? The biggest single expenditure for most Hong Kong residents is rent. It's not unusual for the expatriate businessman to pay HK$15,000 to $25,000 a month for an apartment, most of which is reimbursed by his company. That's about ten times what the average Chinese worker takes home in wages each month. So the term "cost of living" doesn't mean much unless it's clearly defined *whose* cost of living.

The contrast in styles of living in Hong Kong is immense. Expatriate residents generally live in relative luxury; the poorest Chinese exist in poverty, living in crude shanties perched on steep hillsides. But many of the richest millionaires started in those shanties: this is probably the world's greatest place for individual rags-to-riches stories. The tourist who wants to enjoy the very best—luxury hotel, fine food, etc.—can do so, but it is also possible to stay and eat here quite inexpensively.

As Hong Kong imports almost everything it needs—food, raw materials, energy—it is subject to the worst that international inflation can inflict, so prices have tended to rise rapidly over recent years. Local economic problems, however, have lowered the value of the HK$, so this is still a good buy for foreign travelers. (See "Currency," later in this Practical Information.)

A Typical Day's Cost (per person)

Moderate hotel, breakfast and bed (in a double room)	HK$500.00
Lunch (moderately priced restaurant)	50.00
Dinner (moderately priced restaurant)	90.00
Cross Harbour Ferry	1.40
Taxi ride for two kms.	5.00
Coffee	5.00
Beer	6.00
Half-day city or harbor tour	75.00
	HK$732.40

WHEN TO GO? WHAT TO TAKE? The weather is best from October through December. Skies are usually blue and temperatures range from 60° to 80°F. Summer clothing with a lightweight woolen coat or suit, sweaters, and a light woolen dress or two will cover all needs. January and February are generally dank, with temperatures hovering around 60°, but often dipping below 50° and as low as 40°; good topcoat and warm clothing weather. March and April are unpredictable with possibilites of an 80° sunny day followed by a 15-degree drop and a week of rain. The temperature reaches the low 80s by May and stays in the high 80s during June through September afternoons. This is the hot, sticky, rainy season in which humidity averages 83 percent but is often well over 90 percent. Only very lightweight, cool things will do. This is also the typhoon season, which can mean a day or two confined to the hotel. Throughout the year, clothing is mostly informal, although some top nightclubs and hotel restaurants require jacket and tie at night. Air conditioning in Hong Kong hotels and shops tends to be rather frigid. It makes a light sweater indispensable.

ELECTRICITY. 220 volts—50 cycles; shaver adapters are standard equipment in most hotel rooms. American-type electric irons require special adapters. Hair dryers can usually be borrowed from hotels.

LOCAL FESTIVALS. *Note:* Most Hong Kong festivals are based on the lunar calendar; dates therefore vary from year to year. Check with HKTA offices for exact times.

January–February. *The Hong Kong Arts Festival* has become one of the most important cultural events in Asia over recent years. There are visiting drama groups, theater, orchestras, famous soloists and dancers from both East and West. The HKTA can supply a full program, with details of advance booking procedures.

February. *Chinese New Year* is the festival that means the most to the Chinese. It's a family festival, a time for visiting friends and relatives, clearing debts, and buying new clothes. Everyone greets each other with shouts of "Kung Hei Fat Choy," which loosely translated means "Best wishes for a prosperous New Year." Flower markets at Victoria Park in Hong Kong and Choi Hung Chuen in Kowloon burst with peach and plum blossoms, chrysanthemums, and daffodils. The stores are filled with mountains of oranges, apples, and candles. New Year cheer is strung out all over in the form of colorful light displays in Central District and Chinese lanterns in the stores. Just about everything comes to a stop, especially the first day, including stores, restaurants, and nightclubs. *Yuen Siu Festival* marks the end of Chinese New Year. Colorful lanterns deck every home, market and shop.

April. *Ching Ming* is the Chinese Easter when many pilgrimages are made to tombs to honor dead ancestors. Stay out of the New Territories; roads are congested. *International Film Festival,* showing movies from all over the world.

April/May. *Tin Hau Festival* is the birthday of *Tin Hau.* The Heavenly Queen who is Goddess of the Sea and the patron saint of Hong Kong's fishing people. Junks and sampans are gaily decorated with flowers and flags and some with 20-foot-high ceremonial arches. There are big celebrations at Joss House Bay complete with lion dances and traditional rites at the Queen's Temple.

June. *Dragon Boat Festival* heralds the annual boat races, which commemorate an upright statesman of the third century named Ch'u Yuen who drowned himself to shock into reform a ruler who had scorned pleas for better government. International dragon boat races are also held in the harbour. Coxswains pace their crews by beating on huge drums. The races supposedly symbolize attempts to rescue Ch'u Yuen. This is now a big event, attracting international crews.

August. *Yue Lan*—Festival of the Hungry Ghosts. Offering made to spirits of the dead, released from the underworld for just one day.

September. *Mid-Autumn Festival* is also known as the *Lantern Festival, Moon Festival,* and *Moon Cakes Festival.* Bakeries turn out "moon cakes" by the thousands and the thing is to give a box to friends and relatives. The cakes recall a 14th-century uprising against Mongol rulers of China when cakes containing messages calling people to revolt were distributed to compatriots. The parks and hillsides appear to be swarming with fireflies as thousands of children parade around with candles or battery-lit paper lanterns shaped like rabbits, fishes, or airplanes.

October. *Chung Yeung* marks the date that a visionary Chinese and his family escaped death by climbing a high mountain when their village was destroyed. To ward off calamity during the coming year, thousands of Chinese climb to The Peak on this day. The Peak Tram and the roads around The Peak are absolutely jammed from dawn to midnight, so this holiday is not a good one for claustrophobes. *Festival of Asian Arts* attracts participants from all over the region for performances of theater, dance, opera, music, and various visual arts.

SAMPLE ITINERARY. The average stay for most visitors to Hong Kong has been three to four days. That's really too short to enjoy the many sights and things to do. For those who have the time, here is a five-day itinerary that packs in most of the sights.

Day One. Round the harbor boat cruise.

Shopping: Ocean Terminal/Ocean Center/Harbour City in Kowloon, or Causeway Bay area on the island. Dinner: try Cantonese food on your first night in town.

Take tram to The Peak, have a drink at the Peak Café—sit outside to admire the superb view.

Day Two. Take a tram ride to Western District. Stroll through the back streets and lanes including Ladder St. and Hollywood Rd. Visit Cat Street Galleries on Lok Kwu Road.

Lunch at the small restaurant on the end of Blake's Pier. Cheap.

Hong Kong Island coach tour, or a visit to the marineland in Ocean Park, or Aberdeen.

Sunset cruise (HK$230 including dinner).

Day Three. Kowloon and New Territories coach tour.

Rest for a few hours before dinner or buy that watch you like.

Walk down the waterfront to the Macau ferry carpark and stroll through the "Poor Man's Nightclub." Check out the *Wanchai* or *Tsimshatsui* bars—stick to beer.

Day Four. Start out early before it gets too hot and walk around Kowloonside (take the Star Ferry). Visit Yaumatei District or Jade Market, Reclamation St.

More shopping or rest.

Have late afternoon tea in the Peninsula Hotel lobby, then off to a Chinese restaurant for some Peking duck.

If you still have any strength left, stroll through the Temple St. night market before going back to the hotel.

Day Five. Take an early ferry to Lantau Island and visit one of the monasteries. **Or** stay in town and start the day with a visit to the aviary at the Zoological and Botanical Gardens, or Aw Boon Haw Gardens.

Return on the afternoon ferry to Hong Kong, or if you've stayed in town, explore some of the special attractions suggested by the Hong Kong Tourist Association's factsheets.

Dinner and a discothèque (you can rest on the plane tomorrow).

PASSPORTS, VISAS, AND HEALTH DOCUMENTS. Holders of British passports may visit Hong Kong for six months; no visas required. Commonwealth and Irish Republic subjects may come for three months without visas. Americans, West Europeans, and nationals for other non-Communist countries holding valid passports may visit for one month without visas, provided they have onward or return tickets and enough money for their stay.

Visas for longer periods may be obtained from British Consulates or throughout the world or at Immigration Dept. in Hong Kong. Persons who intend to work, study, or live in Hong Kong normally must apply for visas before they arrive and will be subject to income tax regulations before departure. (But it is only 15%!).

Any questions about visas should be directed to the Department of Immigration in the Mirror Tower on Mody Road, Kowloonside.

Certificates of cholera and yellow fever are *not* required unless you are arriving from an infected area.

CUSTOMS. Hong Kong permits the duty-free import of almost everything except liquor, cigarettes, and tobacco. Visitors are allowed to bring in duty-free 200 cigarettes or 50 cigars or 250 grams of tobacco, and one liter of liquor. Don't bring Scotch whisky or brandy from the United States. It's as cheap in Hong Kong, duty included. Imports of arms and ammunition is totally prohibited. Currency and gold may be carried in and out freely. *Note:* Any form of drugs or narcotics are absolutely forbidden. Customs search on arrival can be thorough and penalties for drug offenses are *very* severe.

ARRIVAL IN HONG KONG. The airport. Most visitors arrive by air. Touchdown is at Kai Tak Airport where airplanes of 30 companies land on the runways extending into Kowloon Bay. It's either a white knuckle descent between mountain peaks, then a rooftop skimming pass over Kowloon, or the more relaxed approach over the harbor. Either way, the safety record at Kai Tak is one of the world's best.

The terminal building, nose-in piers, runways, and parking lots seem to be in a constant state of construction, extension, and expansion. Immigration and customs people are perhaps the most efficient in Asia, and except for peak periods, travelers are on the way to their hotels within 30 minutes after touchdown and often much sooner. There are hotel booking, money changing, and tourist information counters beyond the customs area.

There are supermarket-type shopping carts available in the baggage pickup area, which can be used to wheel suitcases and the like up to and through the Customs check aisles, through the lobby, and into the taxi, coach, and hotel car area. There are also airport porters to help with the luggage. They should be given about HK$1 a bag for their services.

Prices in the airport shops for just about everything are the highest in town, except for the duty-free goods (mostly alcohol and tobacco) for sale only to departing passengers. The newcomer should also be on guard against touts and extortion-minded taxi drivers.

The airport coach costs HK$2.50 to Kowloon-side hotels and HK$4 to the Hong Kong side. Taxi fares are fixed to meter charges. Regardless of what type of transportation is used, including regular taxis, the charge should never be more than HK$18 to get to a Kowloon side hotel or HK$45–55 if the hotel is on Hong Kong Island and the driver goes by the cross-harbor tunnel, plus

HK$1 per suitcase. Remember these are Hong Kong dollars, so make sure you and the driver are talking about the same kind of currency. Hong Kong taxi drivers are usually helpful, but often do not speak English well. Airport departure tax is a steep HK$120.

The Piers. Cruise ships dock at the Ocean Terminal, one of the world's best facilities for cruise passengers. This modern complex, together with the adjoining Ocean Center, comprises the biggest shopping center in Hong Kong. In addition to the wide variety of products for sale from Hong Kong and all over the world, there are facilities for cabling or making overseas telephone calls, changing money, or having a meal (Chinese to Hungarian). The traveler arriving by ship can also usually count on being welcomed to Hong Kong by a cluster of pimps and touts. The terminal is in the busy tourist area of Tsimshatsui in Kowloon and minutes away from Hong Kong Island via the nearby Star Ferry.

$P£

CURRENCY. The monetary unit is the Hong Kong dollar, divided, naturally, into 100 cents. Value fluctuates and is reported daily in two English-language newspapers. All major currencies can be exchanged easily into HK dollars, or vice versa. As a rule, moneychangers give the highest rates, banks are next best, and hotels are the worst. Although other currencies will usually be accepted by sellers of goods and services, the buyer is the loser, *so always change your money to Hong Kong currency.* You can get it changed back when you leave. There are no restrictions on the amount of currency that may be brought in or taken out of Hong Kong. Most well-known credit cards are accepted. Personal checks are accepted by many shops if backed up by a passport. Current exchange rates (mid-1985): US$=HK$7.80; UK£=HK$9.20.

TIPPING. Residents tip about ten percent to cabbies, waiters, beauticians, and barbers. Most hotels and restaurants add a ten percent service charge, but waiters expect you to leave some of the change on the tray. Hotel and baggage porters get HK$1 per piece.

ACCOMMODATIONS. With an eye to the fast-growing tourist and convention trade, the colony now offers 19,000 air-conditioned hotel rooms, all with baths and telephones. Hotel representatives will meet expected visitors at the airport and provide transportation to the hotel; they charge more than regular taxis.

Most hotels are running at nearly full occupancy all year round and especially in the peak months of October and November, so reservations are a must. But there's always the chance you can book a room at the hotel reservations center (no charge) at the airport once you clear customs.

For grandeur and elegance, the famous old *Peninsula* remains in a class by itself. The *Mandarin* is most highly regarded by experienced travelers and is rated as one of the ten best hotels in the world. There's a touch less formality and stiffness in hotels like the *Hilton, Excelsior, Hong Kong, Sheraton, Lee Gardens, Plaza, Holiday Inn, Regent,* and *Furama.* This combination of a slightly more swinging atmosphere plus all the comforts of a really first-class hotel goes down well with a lot of people.

Almost all the moderate and inexpensive hotels are air-conditioned and have Chinese and Western restaurants. Most also have television and refrigerators.

Almost all the deluxe and many first-class hotels have doctors on immediate call. Many also offer special services for business travelers, such as secretarial facilities. Few, except the most expensive, newer hotels have swimming pools.

The traveler should also note that a number of leading hotels do not offer single-rate rooms. Many hotels have a wide price range for rooms, standard or deluxe, with or without a harbor view, so specify grade required when booking.

The price ranges listed below are for a double-occupancy room and are in Hong Kong dollars. A 10 percent service charge is added to bills.

KOWLOON

Deluxe—$850–1,500

Peninsula. Salisbury Rd. The "grand old lady" of hotels here, the leading hotel for distinguished guests. The big, high-ceilinged lobby is still a good place to spot Old China hands, film stars and an occasional king or prime minister. *The Pen,* as it's often called, has 210 big and comfortable rooms, and good service. Gourmet French, Swiss and Chinese cuisines, nightclub.

Regal Meridien. 71 Mody Rd., Tsimshatsui East, 600 rooms in magnificent harbor view situation.

First Class—$400-950

Regent. Salisbury Rd. 600 palatial rooms on the waterfront. Luxury class with marble washrooms, huge ballroom, big swimming pool, sauna, health rooms and harborside sundeck. 3 restaurants, conference facilities. Part of the New World Center complex, full of shops.

Shangri-La. 4 Mody Rd. New, luxurious and superb facilities, overlooking harbour. 720 excellent rooms and suites. Pool, sauna, and conference facilities. 4 restaurants. Gemini Lounge offers live music and dancing, and the Tiara Roof Top Lounge superb harbor views.

Sheraton. 20 Nathan Rd., near the harbor. Rich, subdued décor befitting a luxury hotel. A huge ballroom, swimming pool and health club, two landscaped gardens, and two outside glass-enclosed elevators give extra glitter. 5 restaurants and no less than 8 bars. Harbor views from 65 percent of the 905 rooms and suites. The view from the Sky Lounge is worth the trip.

Ambassador. Nathan and Middle Rds., An exceptionally attractive lobby, a nightclub, and a basement bar that attracts like-minded people; 315 rooms.

Holiday Inn Golden Mile. Nathan Rd., has 600 rooms and suites and features a swimming pool, sauna and steambaths, Viennese-style coffee-shop, German/Continental gourmet restaurant, and big shopping arcade. Its sister hotel, the brand-new **Holiday Inn Harbour View,** has 595 luxurious rooms and a good range of restaurants and other facilities including pool and health club. The two hotels are linked by a free shuttle bus service and are popular with business visitors due to their good executive service centers.

Hong Kong. Beside the Ocean Terminal at 3 Canton Rd. A modern spacious first-class hotel. Two excellent restaurants (Taipan Grill and Bauhinia Room), health center, sauna, and swimming pool. Close to Star Ferry, favored by business men, harbor views in around half of the 790 rooms.

Hyatt Regency. Nathan Rd. Right in the center of the action. Lots of facilities, including beverage dispensers in the 774 rooms and discothèques at top and bottom. A good hotel for conventions or big tourist groups.

Marco Polo. 440 comfortable rooms in new Harbour City Complex, Canton Rd., overlooking the harbor. Full range of good facilities.

Meridien Airport. Hong Kong's only airport hotel. 380 rooms and good facilities. Ideal for stopovers, but some distance from business and shopping action.

Miramar. 134 Nathan Rd. One of the first postwar hotels, but newly expanded to 1,200 rooms. In the heart of the shopping district with a spacious arcade of its own. Houses a theater restaurant that offers cultural shows and Chinese opera. Just one of 11 restaurants. Health club and indoor pool.

New World. Smack on the waterfront at 22 Salisbury Rd., and has 735 rather small but comfortable rooms, swimming pool, health club, and one of the biggest shopping malls in Hong Kong. Good value for quality offered.

Park. 61 Chatham Rd. Great harbor views in about one half of the 450 rooms and suites and is close by what's happening.

Prince Hotel. Harbour City. Part of huge new harborside development. 400 rooms. Good restaurants and facilities.

Royal Garden. Tsimshatsui East. 436 luxurious rooms. Spectacular atrium lobby. Range of restaurants, bars, and nightclub. Business and conference facilities.

Moderate—$300–650

Astor. 11 Carnarvon Rd. In the busy downtown district, surrounded by shops. The 148 rooms are smallish, but reasonable.

Carlton. With 60 rooms at Taipo Rd. in North Kowloon. Combines city and country pleasures with an open terrace, swimming pool, bar and nightclub with good dance music, and a beautiful panoramic view of the city and harbor lights. Rooms rather small, about 25 minutes from Star Ferry.

Empress. 17–19 Chatham Rd. Refrigerators in all of its 189 rooms. The Outrigger Bar is just the place to sip long, colorful drinks.

Fortuna. 355 Nathan Rd. has 195 good-sized rooms. A good second-class hotel, near shopping. Rooms are smaller, but also reasonable at the 80-room *Fortuna Court* annex round the corner.

Grand. 14 Carnarvon Rd. 194 rooms, all with refrigerator-bars. Close to shopping.

Imperial. 32–34 Nathan Rd. 220 rooms. Indonesian and Continental food, babysitters, and nightclub. Clean, well-situated, popular with Asian guests.

International. 33 Cameron Rd. A neat little hotel in the heart of Tsimshatsui. The 91 rooms are rather small, but clean. Reasonable value.

Shamrock. 233 Nathan Rd. 150 rooms. Clean, cheap, and near shopping. Geared to visitors from Southeast Asia.

Inexpensive—$150–250

Chungking House. 40 Nathan Rd., and **Washington,** at 15A Austin Ave., are cheap, but scruffy.

Chung Hing and **King's** at 380 and 473 Nathan Rd., are a few minutes' bus ride off the beaten tourist track, but lower prices more than compensate. Adequate rooms, many with TV and refrigerator.

There are four very clean, well-run **YMCA/YWCAs** in the colony, three of which accept male and female guests and families. Not all rooms have private bath and telephone. **Salisbury Rd. YMCA** has a swimming pool and is just a few steps from the Star Ferry. **YMCA International House** on Waterloo Rd. has a steambath, massage room, and gymnasium. Most of the 300 rooms have a private bath. Excellent value.

HONG KONG ISLAND

Deluxe—$1,000–$1,500

Mandarin. 5 Connaught Rd. Central. 540 rooms, and suites, has more than a touch of class. Good harbor view from almost one half of the rooms. Superb French and Chinese restaurants. Indoor swimming pool and separate ladies' and men's health centers. Beautiful green marbled lobby with antique gilded carvings. Excellent service. Current, full-length films shown on room's TV at no extra charge. Expensive, but the top place in town.

First Class—$650–950

The Excelsior. Overlooking the Yacht Club in Causeway Bay. Puts the visitor in touch with the real Hong Kong, yet is less than 10 minutes by taxi from Central. Surrounding area is packed with restaurants, theaters, and stores. The shopping arcade houses Yee Tung village where traditional craftsmen are at work. The adjoining World Trade Center has tennis courts and mini-golf practice area. About half the 952 rooms and suites have full or partial harbor views. 5 restaurants and 3 bars, all good.

Furama Intercontinental. 1 Connaught Rd. Central, has 571 rooms and suites, 4 restaurants, including top-floor revolving restaurant with Continental food and great views. About 40 percent of the rooms have full harbor view—and what a view it is. Buffet dinner in rooftop revolving restaurant is particularly recommended.

Lee Gardens. Hysan Ave. in the lively Causeway Bay district. 820 rooms and suites with most of the usual first-class facilities, including range of good restaurants, Eastern and Western, and lively disco.

Hilton. Queens Rd. Central on the edge of the business and banking district. One of the busiest spots in town. There are six restaurants and six bars. The outdoor swimming pool is surrounded by luxury suites. Two-floor shopping arcade. Chinese-cuisine supperclub, big ballroom, sauna, and good people-watching coffee shop. Full or partial views from most of the 810 rooms and suites, including specially equipped rooms for the handicapped.

Moderate—$350–700

Caravelle. 94 rooms, at 84–86 Morrison Hill Rd. Near the racecourse in Happy Valley. Has seafood restaurant and grill room. The bar is popular with jockeys and soccer players. TV and refrigerators in all rooms.

Harbor. 116–122 Gloucester Rd. 198 rooms, about half have a great view of the harbor. Near Central, also close to the action in Wanchai. Houses a classy Japanese nightclub and sauna. TV and refrigerators in rooms.

Plaza Tower. In Causeway Bay. 850 rooms and suites. Rooftop cocktail lounge, Japanese and Korean restaurants, nice rooms. Japanese-owned and most popular with Japanese visitors. Prices may run slightly higher than this range.

Singapore. 41 Hennessy Rd., in the heart of the Wanchai shopping and bar district. 165 rooms. Modern, clean, reasonable, and stimulating atmosphere.

Inexpensive—$280–350

Luk Kwok. 67 Gloucester Rd., Wanchai. The original Suzie Wong hotel, carries on, but in a more staid tradition. Good Chinese *dim sum,* popular with Asian visitors. 102 rooms, scruffy but reasonable.

TELEPHONES. Direct-dialing. No charge for local calls from most hotels. Public telephones (painted red) cost HK$1. Do not mistake the double ring signal for a busy signal (a single repetitive beep). The prefix "K" or "3" indicates a Kowloon side number and "H" or "5" means it's on the H.K. side. If calling H.K. side from Kowloon, dial 5 first, and if calling Kowloon from H.K. dial 3 first. Dial 108 for information, 109 if you are having any problems.

"NT" or "0" indicates New Territories.

BUSINESS HOURS. *Banks* open 9–4:30 weekdays, 9–12 Saturdays; *offices* 9–5 weekdays, 9–1 Saturdays, lunch usually 1–2; Central District *shops* and *stores* 10–5:30 or 6 Monday through Saturday, closed Sundays; in other tourist areas including Tsimshatsui and Causeway Bay; many shops stay open until 9 or 10 o'clock seven days a week.

HOW TO GET AROUND. Taxis are abundant and cheap. Fares are HK$5.00 for the first 2 kms. and 70 cents for each succeeding quarter km. and all of the taxis are metered. Drivers know their territory and speak some English, but if the address is not well known, ask someone to write it in Chinese, or ask the hotel doorman to tell the driver. Do not rely on a taxi for a tour. The legal fare to cross the harbor via the tunnel is HK$20 plus what it shows on the meter. If possible use the Star Ferry to cross the harbor.

There are regular bus services on both sides of the harbor, and trams on Hong Kong side only. The top deck of trams and buses offers a treat to photographers and people-watchers for only 60 cents to $2.50.

Two ferry companies offer regular cross-harbor service on comfortable boats. Fares are from 50 cents upwards on "Star" and Yaumati ferries. The Star Ferry takes around seven minutes and leaves every three to five minutes until 8 P.M., and every eight to ten minutes from 8 P.M. to 11:30 P.M. except on a few holidays when the ferries run later. If you miss the last Star Ferry crossing, you can cross by taxi via the road tunnel, or by the MTR underground railway. Ferries going to islands like Lantau, Cheung Chau, and Peng Chau leave from the Outlying Island Services Pier on Connaught Rd. in Hong Kong.

Rickshaws can be a bad scene and the Tourist Association stops just short of advising against them. Bargain like mad and make sure the fare is settled beforehand with the understanding that it is Hong Kong, not U.S. dollars. Theoretically it should be around HK$20 for each five minutes, but consider yourself lucky if you can get it for this.

A cablecar service called the Peak Tram runs from Garden Rd. (opposite the American Consulate) to Victoria Peak from 7 A.M. to midnight. Splendid view at the top. Avoid busy Sundays and holidays. Fare is HK$4.00.

Tickets for the Kowloon-Canton Railways can be purchased at the Hunghom Railway Station. First-class fare to Sheung Shui costs HK$10.

Unless you have a special reason for renting a car, you can save yourself a lot of expense and bother by simply joining a tour. Traffic can be maddening and parking is almost impossible. There are several car-rental agencies here, but the emphasis is on chauffeur-driven cars. For chauffeur-driven tours, rates are around HK$85 per hour, usually 3-hour minimum.

The MTR (subway or underground) is the fastest way to get around. Fares are HK$2.00 to $4.50. The MTR is worth getting to know, as it is by far the cheapest way to get around, but avoid the rush hours—8 to 10 A.M. and 5 to 7:30 P.M.

TOURS. An organized tour, or a trip by car with an experienced chauffeur-guide, is the best way to get an introductory, comprehensive view of Hong Kong.

Tours around Hong Kong and Kowloon and the New Territories take 3–5 hours and cost HK$70–$275 depending on itinerary and whether you travel by coach, limousine, or private car. Most tour vehicles are air-conditioned. Night tours include dinner and a visit to a nightclub plus a drive to The Peak or a vantage point in Kowloon and a visit to a night market or typhoon shelter. Figure 4–6 hours in the HK$175–350 range.

The easiest way to see the New Territories is to take "The Land Between" tour, operated by the Hong Kong Tourist Association, with Mon.–Fri. departures at 8:30 A.M. from Queens Pier Central. Price, including lunch, is HK$180.

BOAT TOURS Are the coolest and easiest way to see Hong Kong, especially in the hot summer months. Here are some of the more popular cruises from *Watertours of Hong Kong,* the biggest operator.

Harbor Tour. 9 A.M. or 3 P.M. HK$85. Here's a two-hour trip through the heart of Hong Kong that will show you what makes it tick—the harbor. Boats of every kind: junks, sampans, ferries, tugs, freighters, liners, and warships.

Sunset Cruise. 5 P.M. HK$165. Free drinks as you cruise through the harbor and out to Aberdeen. Includes an hour aboard a floating restaurant for dinner (at your expense). Back by 9 P.M.

Dinner Cruise. 8:15 P.M. HK$230. Follows the same route to Aberdeen, skips the drinks, but includes the dinner. Takes three hours. A variation of this includes a tram ride, with drinks provided.

China Sea Happy Hour Cruise. 5:30 P.M. HK$135. Music and unlimited drinks for a two-hour cruise.

Watertours also offer combined junk and coach tours. Daytime tour from HK$200, evening tours from HK$290; and include drinks, dinner, and a show.

The *Wan Fu,* a 110-foot brigantine owned by the Hong Kong Hilton Hotel, goes out for HK$140, two-hour harbor cruise every day at noon (includes lunch) and again at 5:00 P.M. for $165, 2½-hour cocktail cruise to Aberdeen (unlimited drinks and snacks). It also goes out every Tuesday and Saturday at 5 P.M. for a dinner and drinks cruise (HK$240). The *Wan Fu* is a beautiful reproduction of British Navy ships used in the 19th century to protect merchantmen in these waters from pirates.

Sea View Harbour Tour Co. runs a 211-foot, three-deck floating restaurant and nightclub around the harbor every night for only HK$60, including Chinese dinner. It's called the *Man Kin* (great value for money).

Day trips to two areas in China—Shenzhen or Zhongshan–can be arranged through *China Travel Service* for HK$280–390. Present passport to C.T.S. at least two days before departure.

The cross-harbor ferries aren't tours but are good vantage points for views of the city. See "How to Get Around," above.

WHAT TO SEE? The Peak (go up on the Peak tram), a night view from Stubbs Rd. or a sunset view from the top floor of one of the hotels facing the harbor, take tea in the Peninsula lobby and, for contrast, sample an excerpt from a Chinese opera. Visit Ocean Park (a must), Aberdeen at sunset from a floating restaurant. Take Chinese *dim sum* lunch, visit a Wanchai or Tsimshatsui bar, the discothèques in the big hotels at full swing. See the Connaught Rd. West wharves, Shanghai St.

The "Poor Man's Nightclub," the Temple St. night market, Aw Boon Haw Gardens, the Botanical Gardens, or Victoria Park early in the morning when the local residents do Chinese shadow boxing. Ladder St., Cloth Lane, the Man Mo Temple on Hollywood Rd., a typhoon shelter from a sampan, Hong Kong from the upper deck of a tram, the Ocean Terminal and Harbour City, the harbor from aboard a sunset cruise boat, the Hong Kong Museum of History.

Peak Tower Village, City Hall and Art Museum, Lantau Island's Buddhist and Trappist monasteries, Lei Cheng Uk tomb, the replica Sung Dynasty village at Lai Chi Kok, a shipbuilding yard (Aplichau for Chinese junks), one of the housing estates, an ancient walled village, the fishing village of Lau Fau Shan, a lion dance, the ladder streets off Queen's Rd. Central, the Space Museum and Planetarium. HKTA's *Places of Interest by Public Transport* and other excellent leaflets list all possible sights and experiences whether costly or free. One should not miss the chance to take a ferry to one or more of the outer islands, such as Cheung Chau, Peng Chau, or Lantau.

PARTICIPANT SPORTS. Swimming is the most popular sport in the colony. The government has developed and maintains 40 of the beaches along the coastline, most of which are in sheltered bays of the South China Sea. The biggest and most accessible beaches—Repulse Bay, Deep Water Bay, and Shek-O on the Hong Kong side, and Castle Peak beaches and Silverstrand at Clearwater Bay on the Kowloon side—are fair to good, but unfortunately very crowded and often dirty on hot Sundays from mid-March to mid-December. Big Wave Bay has the only real surf to speak of, suitable at least for some body surfing, and is one of the nicest beaches with a beautiful stretch of sand. There's an excellent long stretch of clean white sand along the south coast of Lantau Island (Cheung Sha Beach), but it's 70 minutes away by ferry and another 15 minutes by minibus. One of the best sports complexes is in Clearwater Bay, where the Golf and Country Club makes its facilities available to visitors. Enquire through the HKTA for tour arrangements here covering swimming, golf, tennis, squash, etc.

Water Skiers can rent skis and a speedboat with operator for around HK$180 an hour at Deep Water Bay. Call 5–920391 for reservations.

Skin Diving is best from April to October with best visibility in May (25–50 feet and occasionally up to 90 feet). Visiting divers can rent equipment and join launch outings organized by the Sea Dragons Diving Club, call 5–721629 for details. The best diving area is in the northeastern part of the colony (Clearwater Bay, Mirs Bay) where the waters are suitable for spearfishing, underwater photography, and specimen collecting.

Rowboats can be hired at Silvermine Beach. There are sailing dinghies for rent at the Hong Kong Yacht Club (across from the Excelsior Hotel) but only to visitors who are granted reciprocal privileges by virtue of membership in a yacht club back home. Call 5–7902817. *Sampans* are available at the nearby Causeway Bay typhoon shelter for around $80–100 per hour, after negotiating. Check with the Hong Kong Water Tours for details on how you can hire a Chinese junk with crew.

A motorized junk can be hired for a *deep-sea fishing* trip in Clearwater Bay for upwards of $400 a day. Other fishing areas include Tsing Lung Tau and Tai Po Kau and sampan fishing in Tolo Harbor. Contact HKTA.

Hiking. There are some excellent, scenic hiking routes in the New Territories, Lantau and Cheung Chau islands, and on Hong Kong Island. The best map guides for hiking trails are the *Hong Kong Countryside Series* and *New Territories West,* which are sold for HK$10 each at the Government Publications Center,

Star Ferry Concourse, H.K. side. The various free "facts sheets" issued by the Hong Kong Tourist Association give full details on interesting rural and urban excursions. For **joggers,** several top hotels offer routes and transport. One of the most popular areas is around Bowen Rd., in Mid-Levels.

Tennis. There are public courts at Victoria Park in Causeway Bay, in Wong Nei Chong Gap Rd, and on Bowen Rd. in Mid-Levels. Both are on a first-come, first-served basis. Easiest times to get a court are mid-mornings and mid-afternoons. Fees are HK$15–30 per hour, depending on the time and day. Victoria Park has the only public **squash** courts in town.

Golf. The Royal H.K. Golf Club welcomes visitors weekdays only to play its 9-hole course at Deep Water Bay on H.K. side for HK$100, or one of the three 18-hole courses at Fanling in the New Territories for $400. You can apply to play at the Royal Hong Kong Golf Club, Fanling (0–901211). Take the train to Fanling, and the Golf Club minibus from the train to the Club. Fine fairways and greens, very heavy rough at Fanling. Also a driving range and small 9-hole course. Caddies are available from $40, and clubs from $20. The Hong Kong Open Golf Championship at Fanling in February attracts professionals from all over the Asia-Pacific region.

Horseback Riding. The Shatin Riding School hires out horses and offers tuition for $200 per hour, Tuesdays to Sundays. There are paths for a steady trek round the valley, or more exciting rides on hillsides for more experienced riders. Call H.K.T.A. for more details on this activity also.

SPECTATOR SPORTS. Horse Racing. There are race meets most Saturday afternoons and some Wednesday nights from October to May at either the racecourse in Happy Valley or the beautiful new track at Shatin. The fans are as interesting to watch as the races. Tickets for *bona fide* tourists are available for HK$50 at the RHKJC office at Sports Road. The HKTA also operates a special tour, for $200, inclusive of bus transfers and lunch or dinner. or dinner.

On winter and spring weekends, Commonwealth expatriates gather for **cricket** matches at the Hong Kong and Kowloon Cricket Clubs. There are **football** (soccer) matches from September to May. Sports car buffs are off to Macau for the annual **Grand Prix** in November, a 60-lap, 228-mile event. Macau also has year-round **greyhound racing** at the Macau Canidrome on Saturdays, Sundays, and public holidays, plus a very big and plush **jai-alai** stadium.

POLLUTION REPORT. Air pollution is not as serious in Hong Kong as in most other big Asian cities. This is partly because of the fresh air currents that sweep through here, cleaning the atmosphere and blowing the smoke out to sea.

Water pollution has already closed down some beaches nearer to population centers, and other popular swimming beaches are under the constant threat of oil slicks and debris. Untreated sewage and factory waste discharged into the sea and rivers is another problem. A recent survey showed that over half of the streams in Hong Kong are polluted, and according to a Water Works spokesman, some of the streams in the northwest part of the New Territories are "grossly polluted."

The government has moved in the area of noise pollution to control the use of air compressors, pneumatic drills, and concrete vibrators from 8 P.M. to 6 A.M. Nevertheless, several areas in Hong Kong register over the 80-decibel level. Among the biggest offenders are the side street record and cassette stalls.

An intensive "Clean Hong Kong" campaign that started several years ago has had noticeable effects, but there is still a lot to be done. One of the most resistant areas is the very crowded district of Mongkok.

WATER. Absolutely safe according to the government, but old ideas die slowly and most residents prefer commercially bottled water or water that has been treated first.

CULTURE AND ENTERTAINMENT. *The Museum of History,* Kowloon Park, off Nathan Rd., has old photos, prints and maps, an archeology display and display of model junks and sampans, authentic in every detail. The *Museum of Art* in City Hall features monthly exhibitions plus a permanent display of Chinese ceramics and paintings, Old Hong Kong prints and Museum publications are on sale at both museums. The *Fung Ping Shan Museum* at Hong Kong University houses a good collection of Chinese ceramics and bronze, plus a number of Ming and Ching dynasty paintings. Daily 9:30–6:00, closed Sunday. The art gallery at *Chinese University* has an outstanding collection of paintings and calligraphy by Kwangtung artists dating back to the 16th century. Daily 9:30 to 4:30, Sunday 12:30 to 4:30.

Of archeological interest is the ancient Chinese tomb, *Lei Cheng Uk,* Tonkin St., 20 minutes by taxi or bus from downtown Kowloon. Excavated in 1955, the tomb is adjacent to a small building in which *Han Dynasty* objects found in the tomb are displayed. Closed Thursdays.

City Hall has a large auditorium for concerts, a theater, rooms for art exhibits, a dining room, ballroom and cocktail lounge. Concerts, plays and exhibits are well advertised in Hong Kong newspapers, and a list of the day's events is posted in the main lobby. The *Hong Kong Arts Center* in Wanchai, supplements the City Hall offerings with culture in depth—everything from Chinese opera and puppet shows to art exhibitions, lunch-time recitals and evening concerts. Open every day.

The *Hong Kong Arts Festival* in January–February (see preceding section *Local Festivals*) attracts internationally famous orchestras, dance troupes, rock stars, chamber music ensembles, folksingers, opera companies (Chinese and Western), and other performers and groups—something or someone to suit just about everyone. Every October another festival, dedicated to Asian arts, attracts superb presentations from around the region, including theater, dance, music, art, and a varied selection of cultural exhibitions and lectures. Participants from up to 20 countries usually take part, coming from places as far apart as India, Australia, and Japan.

To many Western eyes and ears, a little *Chinese opera* goes a long way. Occasionally there's a performance at City Hall or the Lee Theater. For the real thing, culture freaks and anthropology majors should follow their ears to the clashes, bangs, and shrieks coming from one of the improvised, outsized, tin and bamboo "theaters" of the neighborhood variety. Perhaps a Chinese friend can point the way, or the Hong Kong Tourist Association can give directions. Costumes are ornate to the point of gaudiness; the plot contains one or two main story lines with a half dozen subplots. Members of the Chinese audience watch intently during the portion that interests them, then sit back and chat with friends, drinking tea and eating water-melon seeds, whenever their interest wanes. If no operas are playing local theaters, you can always try the *Lai Chi Kok* amusement park next to the Sung Village tourist attraction where a general admission ticket entitles you to watch the open-air opera.

American, European, Chinese, and Japanese films with subtitles are shown at a number of good, air-conditioned theaters around town, all listed in the daily newspapers. Seats are all reserved and it is sometimes necessary to phone in advance to make reservations, in which case tickets must be picked up at least 15 minutes before the show. The best seats cost HK$25. Cultural shows of many kinds—music, art, and dancing—are held in the central lobby area of the new Landmark Shopping Center on Des Voeux Rd., Central, including lunchtime performances for city office workers. On Sundays, at 2:30 P.M. there is a free cultural show sponsored by the HKTA here. On Saturdays another show is presented, at 2:30 P.M. at the New World Centre. On Wednesdays, at 6:30 P.M., free cultural shows are also presented in the lobby of the Ocean Terminal. In April, films from all over the world are shown in Hong Kong during the annual International Film Festival.

LIBRARIES. The biggest public library occupies four floors in the City Hall High Block near the Star Ferry, H.K. side. Closed Thursdays, half-day on Sunday. Also in Central District; the U.S.I.S. library in Pacific House and the British Council library, 255 Hennessy Rd., Wanchai, are closed Saturday afternoons and Sunday.

SHOPPING, BARGAINING, KICKBACKS, AND COMPLAINTS. Hong Kong is still one of the world's great shopping places; careful buyers can find some good bargains and shopping continues to be the biggest drawing card in this duty-free port. Jewelry, watches, perfumes, cameras, optical goods, rosewood furniture, and Asian curios are among the best buys. The name of the game is comparison shopping and, in smaller stores without price tags on their goods—bargaining.

The Official Guide to Shopping, Eating Out, and Services in Hong Kong, available free at the H.K. Tourist Association information centers, is a useful guideline. Bargaining is an essential part of shopping in Hong Kong.

In small shops and stalls where goods are not tagged, offering prices should be around one-half the asking price. The Cantonese love a joke, and buyers with a sense of humor will find bargaining is not difficult. Gentle manners in every good shop will be returned. If salesmen are rude, it means the place is seeking a fast sale of inferior goods to tourists who have no knowledge of what they are buying.

Avoid touts and remember that tour operators are also often getting a kickback from the stores to which they bring groups. The best thing is to keep recommendations in mind but go shopping on your own. Take the time to check around before you buy. Buy only brands that can be serviced back home, get a manufacturer's guarantee, check that electrical equipment is compatible with voltages and cycles at home, and get insurance coverage on breakable items to be mailed or shipped.

The H.K. Tourist Association has a shopping enquiry service and although it has no legal power to resolve disputes, most shops cooperate, particularly HKTA member shops.

Antiques, Gifts, and Curios

There's an abundance of antique shops and some very nice pieces in Hong Kong. There are also a lot of fakes. Stay out of this game unless you know what you're doing. Prices for the real thing are often cheaper in London or New York.

If you want to minimize the risk, check out the offerings in the mainland Chinese outlets. You can be certain that you are getting just what the store says it is. Other reliable stores:

Charlotte Horstmann, Ocean Terminal and Mandarin Hotel, and *Ian McLean Antiques,* 73 Wyndham St., are among the best in their lines, but costly.

Amazing Grace, 242 Ocean Terminal; Excelsior Hotel lobby and arcade; and Landmark, Central, is a rare find. A tasteful choice of Asian crafts and clothing —everything from Chinese junk compasses and ceramic elephants to antique chests and buddhas—at reasonable, fixed prices. A favorite with residents.

Welfare Handicrafts has small, inexpensive gifts at its shops in Ocean Terminal, and in the Connaught Center.

Cameras

Hong Kong offers a wide range of cameras for sale including almost all famous brands. In most cases, prices are as cheap as, and in some cases cheaper, than in the country of origin. A good approach is to check prices of models you are interested in back home before you come to Hong Kong. A favorite sales strategy is the "loss leader" concept of selling the basic item at a low price, in this case the camera, and overcharging on accessories. So do a thorough job of price comparison. Most camera shops also sell binoculars. Don't depend on a binocular test inside the store. Go outside and try focusing at various distances.

Hong Kong is chock full of good reliable camera shops in or near every hotel, but as with every type of shopping here, it pays to buy at those places endorsed by the HKTA. Insist on a full guarantee.

Carpets

The best carpet buys are the thick luxurious, all-wool Tientsin rugs from China, although a few local manufacturers do a very good job of producing Chinese-style carpets comparable in quality and price. Prices have shot up in the last few years, but are still cheaper than in Europe, the U.S., or Japan. The best-quality carpets are treated with chemicals that make them resistant to dirt and liquid and give them a shimmering gloss.

Among the best places to buy made-in-China carpets are the various mainland stores, e.g., *Chinese Arts & Crafts* in Kowloon and Hong Kong. There are also a wide range of oriental rugs available in Hong Kong imported from Afghanistan, Pakistan, and Iran, as well as those made locally.

Department Stores

There are several chains that sell products exclusively from mainland China. Prices are fixed and fair.

Most convenient from the tourist standpoint and abundant in the best of Chinese jewelry, antiques, and artifacts are: *Chinese Arts and Crafts* in Star House on Salisbury Rd. and 233 Nathan Rd., Kowloon, and Shell House on Hong Kong side. *Chinese Merchandise Emporium* at 92–104 Queen's Rd., H.K.; *Yue Hwa Chinese Products Emporium Ltd.* at 300 Nathan Rd. in Kowloon. A little farther out are *Chung Kiu Chinese Arts and Crafts Center,* 528–532 Nathan Rd., Kowloon, and *China Products* at 488 Hennessy Rd., H.K.

The *Ocean Terminal, Ocean Centre* and *Harbor City* shopping centers are joined to form one terrific complex of stores on the waterfront near the Star Ferry, Kowloon side.

The Landmark, Gloucester Tower, Central District is the most prestigious shopping center in town with stores like *Gucci* and *Hermes.*

Daimaru & Matsusakaya are Japanese-owned department stores diagonally opposite each other on Paterson St. in Causeway Bay. *Mitsukoshi,* Hennessy Rd., also Japanese-owned. Prices are fixed and for the most part fair.

Other good department stores are *Lane, Crawford Ltd., Wing On, Isetan, Shui Hing, Sincere,* and *Yashan.*

Furniture

Woods like rosewood, teak, and blackwood must be properly dried, seasoned, and aged to prevent future cracking in less humid climates than that of Hong Kong. Rosewood should have floating panels to allow for natural shrinking and expansion; with large teak surfaces, it is advisable to use ply. Solid teak is otherwide preferable. Look carefully at the workmanship and the small details of the finished piece. Brass fittings, for example, should always be inserted and never tacked on. Tables and chairs must be perfectly stable and drawers should slide in and out easily and smoothly.

There are a number of rosewood furniture dealers in the Ocean Terminal/ Ocean Center complex and in hotel shopping arcades.

Also *Chinese Arts and Crafts* in Star House, 3 Salisbury Rd., Kowloon, sells a wide variety of attractive, made-in-China chests, cabinets, screens, and tables.

For carved camphorwood chests, try Canton Rd. behind the Ocean Terminal or Hennessy Rd. and Wanchai Rd. in Wanchai, H.K.

For Chinese blackwood and inlaid furniture, try the shops along Hollywood Rd.

Rattan furniture can also be a good buy, but beware of the high cost of shipping large or heavy items home.

Ivory

Hong Kong antique dealers still have many old and expensive pieces of ivory, but unless the buyer is a good judge of them, he had better find a friend who is, before buying. Most of the ivory on sale is new, but has been dyed to appear aged. To distinguish the real thing from plastic or bone, look for a crosshatch pattern on a flat, unpolished portion of the piece, usually underneath. It should resemble a magnified square of linen. New ivory is available in a wide price range. Controls are tight in many countries, including the U.S. and U.K., on people returning with ivory. This rule also affects imports of snakeskin and most wild animal skins. Many countries now have bans on the importation of ivory and other materials that come from endangered species, so check before you buy.

Jewelry and Watches

Hong Kong is a major jewelry center of the world and is said to be the third biggest retailer of diamonds after the U.S. and Japan. The uninitiated should, however, be extremely cautious when buying. With no import duty or sales tax on precious and semi-precious stones and many shops to choose from, it does seem there are some bargains to be found in stones by the careful and knowledgeable shopper.

Another advantage in buying jewelry in Hong Kong is that settings, custom-made by expert craftsmen, will cost far less than in most Western capitals.

The Hong Kong Tourist Association advises shoppers always to get a receipt noting the gold or silver content, the names of the stones with approximate weights, and some recognizable feature of the design. Check the setting and stones carefully, preferably with a magnifying glass.

Although there is a field of selection in Hong Kong unmatched elsewhere, good jade is still very expensive. Size, shade, evenness of color, and absence of flaws determine the price. Hard jade (called jadeite) is for jewelry, as opposed to soft jade, used for art objects. A third kind, Jasper jade, is actually an opaque variety of quartz, also used for art objects.

The price of pearls has also shot up in recent years, but they are still cheaper than in the U.S. and, in many cases, even Japan. What counts is color, shape, luster, and size. According to experts, the order of color quality is: silvery white, light pink, darker pink, yellow, and plain white. The perfect shape is round, free of imperfections and tiny bubbles. And this shape is more likely to be found in a cultured than in a natural pearl. Luster can be found only in older pearls and never in synthetics. The final criterion of worth is size. Cultured pearls from the South Seas—including the Philippines, Borneo, Indonesia, Australia, and Burma—are relatively large, ranging from 10 to 15 millimeters in diameter. Japanese cultured pearls are smaller, ranging from 3 to 10 millimeters. Price is proportionate to the various criteria of quality.

There is a wide variety of semiprecious stones and costume jewelry available at fair prices in the Chinese department stores (see section on *Department Stores*).

By taking pearls back unstrung through U.S. Customs, the returning traveler can save the difference between 3 and 33 percent in duty charges. Unset and unmounted jewelry enters at ½ to 4 percent while set jewelry costs 14 percent duty. One way to avoid questions at customs is to carry the stone and airmail the setting.

Buying a watch in Hong Kong is difficult, only because there are so many styles, prices, and famous brands from which to choose. Imported duty-free, they are often cheaper than in the country of origin, where a local sales tax increases the price. Beware of the small shop which may use the famous brand's casing but put local mechanisms inside. The business of faking well-known names is rife, so buy from an official agency and insist on a full guarantee.

Linens

Most of the finest hand-embroidered and appliquéd linens and cottons sold here come from China; local manufacturers produce only machine-made embroideries. Pay attention to the cloth used. China imports some Irish linens and Swiss cottons. Of their own materials, the best quality fabrics are Chinese linen followed by linen-cotton and Chinese cotton. The best of the handwork is done in Swatow and is known as Swatow drawn work. A favorite with American visitors is the "Army and Navy" pattern. Examine workmanship with a magnifying glass which the dealer will provide. Make sure the edges are properly overcast on hand-embroidered items. With machine-made goods, the fabric may unravel unless the edges have been carefully trimmed. The best places to shop for linens are the *Chinese Arts and Crafts* stores on both sides of the harbor (no bargaining), and on "linen row" (Wyndham St. and On Lan St., in Central), where you can compare the wares of a dozen shops and bargaining is very much in order.

Men's Clothing (Tailor-made)

Be prepared to pay at least HK$1,500 for a suit (less if it is light tropical weight). Don't rush the tailor and get at least two or three fittings. Don't be afraid to be fussy and insist that everything is to your satisfaction before accepting the suit. Allow at least three days. It helps to have a clear idea of the style you want, perhaps aided by a picture clipped from a magazine. Don't pay more than 25 percent in advance.

Optical Goods

Eyeglasses and contact lenses are among the lesser publicized bargains in Hong Kong. But prices are generally much cheaper than in the U.S. or Europe for the latest style and best quality frames and lenses imported from Germany, France, and the U.S. Opticians are not always as well trained as in the U.S. and Europe, so it is better to have a written prescription or let the optician take a reading from the lenses you are using, rather than having the store test your eyesight.

Radios, Hi-Fi Sets, Tape Recorders

Hundreds of shops carry Japanese, German, English, Swiss, and American radios, stereos, and tape recorders, all well known brands at low prices. Competition is fierce, and asking in three or four stores before buying will assure a purchase at lowest possible cost. Manufacturers in this field often come out with "new" models which may have a few changes or minor improvements. But it's really nothing more than an excuse to charge higher prices. Last year's model may be essentially the same thing and a much better bargain.

Shoppers who take the trouble to read up a little on the kind of thing they want will come off best. The price of a magazine may save you a lot.

If you are looking for a particular brand, call Community Advice Bureau (H-245444) and ask for the agent's name. The H.K. Tourist Association's booklet *Official Guide to Shopping, Eating Out and Services in Hong Kong* lists the names of many reliable dealers as well as the names and addresses of agents.

Shoes

Women and men who wear a standard size shoe at home have no difficulty in getting a good fit from custom shoemakers here, but those with unusual foot measurements are taking a chance. Shoes can be made to measure very quickly in Hong Kong or one can buy top name Italian or other European names in many shops.

Women's Clothing

A woman simply cannot walk into any tailoring establishment in Hong Kong and be sure of getting a dress that fits properly. However, a woman with irregular measurements may be far happier with clothes made here than with things off a rack at home. A woman who knows the mysteries of draping and insets can assist the tailor by pointing out any errors, and together, they can produce something perfect.

One fashion expert has concluded that there's more of a saving in silk than cotton garments since the silk is woven here and the best cotton fabrics are imported. Wool garments are good buys, too, since they are easier to cut and thus involve less risk of a poor fit. Another good buy: Hong Kong-made brocades.

Fine dress lengths, locally made or imported from Thailand, China, or India, are good buys for women adept at making clothes. A good place to browse for dress lengths is Wing On Lane and Cloth Alley in Central, Lee Yuen St., East and West. Here you can also find imitations of top boutique names in leather goods, at rock-bottom prices.

One of Hong Kong's greatest exports is fashions, and in the Colony's factories are made many of the top-branded names for the fancy shops of New York and London. If you hunt around some of the street markets you can often find these named-fashions, still with the labels on, at really low prices. These are often end-of-range items or seconds, but are truly bargain buys. If you are looking for good things in silk, try the silk factory area around Man Yue St., Hunghom, Kowloon, near the airport. Take a taxi to Kaiser Estate, Phase 1 and 2, and seek out such factories as *Camberley, Four Seasons, Genti Donna, Bonaventure,* and *Wintex.* These places produce for the top fashion houses in Europe and the U.S. and you can buy at a fraction of the price you will have to pay at home.

Open-Air Markets and Bazaars

It is a fact of life that Hong Kong's shops have become much more expensive in recent years, due mainly to higher rents and staff costs, but one area in which Hong Kong is still tops is in the bargains to be found in the open-air markets. These provide not only really cheap shopping opportunities, but also the chance to people watch, so one can both buy souvenirs and sightsee at the same time. Among the best are:

Jade Market, Reclamation St., Kowloon. Every morning from about 9 A.M. till 4 P.M., with a huge array of jades set out on the pavements.

Temple Street, in Kowloon, is best seen at night, for all sorts of household items, clothes, handbags, and electrical goods. Granville Road, Kowloon, is a daytime market full of bustle and action.

On Hong Kong side, the area around the Central Market, Lee Yuen Lanes and Cloth Alley, off Wing On Lane, is fascinating for strolling and browsing.

Stanley Market (bus 6 or 260 from outside Connaught Center) is in what was once a picturesque fishing village. It offers wonderful bargains in designer jeans and sportswear, mostly end-of-range and seconds, but with some top international brands to be found. Here you can also find rattan and household goods.

In Causeway Bay, *Jardines Bazaar,* off Hennessy Rd., behind the Lee Gardens Hotel, also offers wonderful buys in clothes and sportswear, often with top names, either genuine or imitation.

RESTAURANTS. Outside of China and Taiwan, gourmets and gluttons will find some of the best Chinese food in the world in Hong Kong at generally reasonable prices. The secret is in knowing what to order and where. Don't be fooled by gold braid on the waiter's jacket or big, fancy menus; the advice of a friend is far more valuable, and few people are more expert on eating than the Hong Kong Chinese.

There are also some excellent restaurants serving Western, Japanese, Korean, Indonesian-Malaysian, and Indian food. The choices for a traveler to Hong Kong range from a T-bone steak and *escargot Bordelaise* to *teppanyaki, pulgogi, satés* and curries, from Hankow beggar's chicken to Peking duck.

The décor in Chinese restaurants is usually pretty rough. And don't expect a nice, quiet romantic dinner. Going out to eat for Hong Kong Chinese is often a family affair, which comes off as a vigorous and joyful but noisy occasion. By almost unanimous opinion, Cantonese is not the most beautiful-sounding language in the world, and even less so at high volume. The effort to make yourself heard across the table may make dinner sound more like a shouting match.

There's a wide variety of Chinese food available, but the most popular and common kinds are Cantonese, Northern (Peking), Chiu Chow (Swatow), Shanghai, Szechuan, and Hakka. Cantonese is big on parboiling, steaming, and quick frying to retain natural juices and flavors. The food is not salty or greasy and seafoods are prepared especially well. Served usually with steamed rice. The emphasis in Northern food is on bread and noodles, deep-frying and spicy sauces. Peking duck and hotpot dishes are the most famous. Shanghainese like their food diced or shredded, stewed in soya sauce or fried in sesame oil with lots of peppers and garlic. Chiu Chow food is flavorful with lots of rich sauces, and Hakka food is generally earthy, simple and peasant-like with baked chicken in salt among the very best of dishes. Szechuan food is hot and spicy, with plenty of chilis. Barbequed meats are a specialty.

It's best to have at least four people for a Chinese meal since there will be a greater variety of dishes.

The Tourist Association publishes an excellent booklet called *The Official Guide to Shopping and Eating Out.*

The most popular lunchtime fare for Cantonese is *dim sum* (snacks), which is served by young girls circulating among the tables with big trays. Try spring rolls *(chun guen),* pork dumplings *(cha siu bao),* dumplings of shrimp *(ha gau)* and pork *(siu mai)* with a dish of soup noodles or crab and vegetables. The bill is computed by the number and design of plates on the table at the end of the meal. Cheap and good.

Chinese do not usually order a drink before dinner, but often have beer or brandy with the meal. Among the popular Chinese wines and liquors are *hsiao hsing,* a rice wine served hot like *sake; liang hoa pei,* a potent plum brandy; and the even more potent *kaolian* whisky (similar to American White Lightenin'), and *mao tai.* The most popular beers are the locally brewed *San Miguel* and *Tsingdao* beer from China.

In a top hotel grill room one could easily pay over HK$500 a head for food alone, excluding drinks, while four could eat in a small "peoples" restaurant for under HK$250, including beer.

Briefly, the fancier the atmosphere and the more elaborate the décor and food, the more expensive the bill, as in any country. But as a rough guide, you can expect to pay between $300 and $450 per head, excluding drinks, in the most expensive Western or Japanese restaurants, and perhaps $100 less per head than this in a good, lavish, Chinese or other Oriental-style restaurant.

A simple meal for two in a leading hotel coffee shop will cost around $150 while a more lavish dinner in the same place could run up to $500 for two. A room service Continental breakfast in such a hotel would cost $30 upwards, including service charge, a full breakfast $15–25 more. Hotel restaurants are generally much more expensive for all forms of eating and drinking than those found outside.

Dinner in a family-style restaurant, not fancy, would cost from $60 to $120 per head for a reasonable selection of dishes. For the really economy-minded traveler there are the various branches of McDonald's and other hamburger or spaghetti-house chains of quick-service restaurants or, in street markets, open-air stalls or cheap cafés where one can have a bowl of noodle soup or a plate of fried rice for around $10–15.

The selection and the cost will depend very much on the taste and budget of the individual. Until one gets the hang of the place, it pays to study and compare menus carefully in various places in advance—although this can be difficult in many Chinese restaurants where menus are sometimes only printed in Chinese and prices not quoted at all! To cut eating costs, which have tended to escalate rapidly in recent years and which can now make up a substantial part of your budget, you should take a good breakfast, perhaps a buffet in the hotel, have just a snack lunch, and then make up with a good dinner.

Because it is nearly impossible to give price ranges accurately in dollars, we have simply broken down the restaurants according to *Deluxe, First Class, Moderate,* and *Inexpensive* to serve as a general guide.

KOWLOON

Chinese

Deluxe: **Fook Lam Moon.** 31 Mody Rd. Shark's fin, plus other delicacies such as bird's nest, abalone game stews and seafood.

Lai Ching Heen. Regent Hotel Arcade. Exquisite Cantonese food in an elegant re-creation of Imperial surroundings.

First Class: **Peking Garden.** Star House. Good for Peking Duck, beggar's chicken and other northern specialties.

Siu Lam Kung. 22 Hanoi Rd. Superb shrimp baked in salt, lobster in black bean sauce, *dofu* (bean curd) with shrimp's egg sauce, oysters with shrimp sauce, steamed garoupa, minced beef with egg soup. Book early.

Moderate: **Spring Deer.** 42 Mody Rd. Fine Peking dishes. Try the barbecued fish, onion cakes, crunchy jellyfish with chicken, dumplings, and fried shredded beef.

Tien Hong Lau. 18 E. Austin Ave. Praised for its beggar's chicken.

Tsui Hang Village. Miramar Hotel and Holiday Inn Harbour View. Serves up shredded beef in taro nest, sautéed mixed vegetables, grilled chicken with honey and ginger, and some wonderful fish dishes.

Inexpensive: **Great Shanghai.** 36 Prat Ave. Best for its "drunken chicken" in wine sauce, braised duck with green onion, noodles with eels, and crab.

Home. 19 Hanoi Rd. Serves the simple and good peasant food of the Hakka people. Best dishes are baked chicken in salt, stuffed bean curd, and preserved vegetables. No frills, clean.

Western

Deluxe: **Gaddi's.** In the Peninsula Hotel. Among the best restaurants in town serving Western food and despite the expense, worth the price. Favorites are *terrine du chef,* prawns with sherry, oyster soup, stuffed quail, Irish coffee.

Plume. Regent Hotel. Excellent *nouvelle cuisine,* stunning setting, superb wine cellar, but dinner only.

First Class: **Hugo's.** In the Hyatt Regency Hotel. Best bets are champagne pea soup, rabbit stew, roast prime rib eye, Cornish game hen, venison, roast pigeon, roast lamb, and cold avocado soup. Elegant, opulent, amusing, overpriced.

Baron's Table. In the Holiday Inn. Specializes in German provincial cuisine. Hotel's own smokehouse provides smoked eel, trout, and sausages. *Eisbein* (braised pig's knuckle) and the venison are super. Rustic atmosphere.

Chesa. Also in the Peninsula Hotel. A lovely Swiss restaurant with understated décor and friendly service. Serves good schnitzel, sausages, and best fondues in town.

Grandstand Grill. In the Sheraton Hotel. Eager to please and well on its way to proving it's worth its salt. Beautiful beef and a house-specialty ham.

Lalique. In the Royal Garden Hotel. Beautiful art deco setting, fine continental cuisine and wines.

Margaux. Shangri-La Hotel. For Continental food of fine quality in a luxurious atmosphere.

Moderate: **Au Trou Normand.** 6 Carnarvon Rd. Serves French food of varying quality. Friday is *bouillabaisse* day. For dessert, the apple tart for two.

Beverly Hills Deli. New World Center. Overstuffed sandwiches and prices to match. Best choice of Kosher-style dishes in the tropics.

Le Mistral. In the Harbour View Holiday Inn. Mediterranean food and atmosphere, with music.

The Sheikh. 89 Kimberly Rd., Kowloon. The only Middle Eastern restaurant in town and well thought of by lovers of stuffed vine leaves and *hummus.*

Stoned Crow. 12 Minden Ave. The colony's only Australian food and wine cellar, specializing in steaks and seafood.

Verandah. Peninsula Hotel. Has perhaps the best lunch buffet in town, with lots of smoked salmon.

Inexpensive: **Marseille.** 5–5A Hart Ave. Serves generous portions at good prices. Big choices but emphasis is on French cuisine. Best bets are black pepper steak, stewed duck, *bouillabaisse.*

Rick's Café, Hart Ave. Small pub-café with good atmosphere, music, and snacks like tacos to build a thirst.

HONG KONG

Chinese

Deluxe: **Fook Lam Moon.** Lockhat Rd. Causeway Bay, same high standards as other branches in Kowloon, offers a wide range of popular favorites.

Sun Tung Lock. Wongheichong Rd., is famous for its shark's fin and bird's nest soups, fish and game dishes.

Sunning Unicorn. Sunning Rd., Causeway Bay. Elegant setting for exceptional Cantonese and Szechuan cuisine. Famous for drunken prawns.

First Class: **Island Room.** In the Furama Hotel. Basically good Cantonese, but with some Peking specialties. Set courses, good wine list.

Jade Garden Restaurants are scattered around town at different locations, and combine good Cantonese food with nice décor. Specialties are shark's fin soup with chicken, crab meat au gratin Toi Shan style, deep-fried shrimp roll, fried vegetable puff, shrimp sauté, and double-boiled fresh sweet milk for dessert.

Moderate: **Orchid Garden.** 481 Lockhart Rd., Hong Kong and 37 Hankow Rd., Kowloon. Great lemon chicken, roast duck stuffed with minced taro, and stuffed crab claws. Reservations essential.

Pep 'n Chili. Blue Pool Rd., Happy Valley. Newer trendier Szechuan restaurant. Try smoked duck or aubergine braised in garlic and chili.

Red Pepper. 7 Lan Fong Rd. Specializes in fiery hot Szechuan food. Try minced beef with vermicelli, shrimps in hot garlic sauce, braised beef tendon, and sour pepper soup.

Riverside. Food St., Causeway Bay. Offers suckling pig, roast goose, braised brisket of beef in a clay casserole pot. Very good.

Sze Chuan Lau. 466 Lockhart Rd., Causeway Bay. Specializing in the deliciously spicy Szechuan cuisine. Extensive menu and waiters who speak English make ordering easier than usual.

369. 32 Wellington St. in Central District. Some excellent Shanghai food plus some Szechuan and Peking dishes. Try the fried or braised eels, if you go that route.

Tung Hing Lau. At the corner of Gloucester and Percival Sts. in Causeway Bay. The best Peking duck in town. Also well known for its hotpot, a winter favorite with residents, beggar's chicken, and roast fish in soybean sauce served on a sizzling platter.

Vegi Food Kitchen. 8 Cleveland St., Causeway Bay. Vegetarian food. Try stuffed eggplant, bitter cucumber, and green chili in bean sauce, deep-fried taro rolls, and nest of gems—a deep-fried potato basket of crunchy vegetables.

Yung Kee. 36 Wellington St. in Central. Famous for its roast goose. Try also their chicken with black beans, fillet steak Chinese-style, fried frog legs, or steamed garoupa.

Inexpensive: **American Restaurant.** 20 and 23 Lockhart Rd. Actually two restaurants famous for their roast spring chicken, onion pancakes and dumplings.

Chiu Chow Restaurant. 485 Lockhart Rd. Serves food special to an area in Kwangtung Province. The steamed crab is superb, the lemon duck a specialty of the house. The food is as perfect as the décor is undistinguished.

Muikiang. 483 Jaffe Rd. in Causeway Bay. A Hakka restaurant with delicious salted chicken, beef balls with vegetables, and roast duck with chop suey.

Nanking Beef Noodles. Food St., Causeway Bay. Basic noodle dishes from northern China.

Pak Lok Chiu Chow Restaurant. 23–25 Hysan Ave., in Causeway Bay. A few steps from the Lee Gardens Hotel. Specialties are minced pigeon, steamed crabmeat balls, and fried *e fu* noodles.

Western

Deluxe:

Pierrot. In Mandarin Hotel. Plush decor, unmistakably French—and expensive.

The Rotisserie. Furama Hotel. Deserves a place among the very best restaurants in town. Quiet, comfortable, classy.

First Class: **Grill Room.** In the Hong Kong Hilton. Some very fine charcoal-grilled steaks, lobsters, prawns, and crabs and excellent roast beef and salads.

Mandarin Grill. In the Mandarin Hotel. Good at charcoal-broiled steaks, Swiss fondues, apple strudel and flambé dishes. Quiet and almost comfortable. Reserve your table.

Moderate: **California.** 30 Aguilar St. Hamburgers and juke box favorites, great for people watching.

Galley. Connaught Centre, Central. Seafood specialty restaurant, best fish 'n' chips in town. Music nightly.

Jimmy's Kitchen. 1 Wyndham St., H.K., and Hotung House, Kowloon. One of the oldest and best restaurants in town.

1997. 9 Lan Kwai Fong, off D'Aguilar St., Central. One of the newer, trendier eateries, friendly atmosphere makes up for average food.

The Pavilion at Lee Gardens Hotel, **Golden Lotus** at the Hilton, and **La Ronda** at the Furama all serve acceptably good buffet lunches, but best to arrive early.

La Taverna. On Hing Terrace off Wyndham St. **La Futura** in D'Aguilar St., both in Central, another branch of **La Taverna** at 24 Percival St.,Causeway Bay, **La Bella Donna,** 51 Gloucester Rd., and **Rigoletto,** 16 Fenwick St., both in Wanchai, are among the best that Hong Kong has to offer in the way of Italian restaurants.

Inexpensive: **Blake Pier.** On the tip of the pier next to the Star Ferry. Another great find. It's open air so choose a nice sunny day if possible.

Peak Tower Restaurant. Above the Peak Tram. Offers fairly good but overpriced food. Certainly the best view in town.

Poor Man's Nightclub. From around 7 P.M. the Macau Ferry car park converts into an open-air eating place. Try the fresh seafoods and noodle dishes. Characterful.

Peak Café. Sit out on the terrace and enjoy a beer and sandwich or a more substantial meal while taking in the magnificent view.

Other Asian Food

Among the best Japanese restaurants in town are: **Okahan,** Lee Garden Hotel and Plaza Hotel; **Kanetanaka,** 21 Kimberley Rd., in Kowloon; and in Plaza Hotel, Causeway Bay; **Benkay,** in the Landmark complex in Central, **Nandaman** in the Shangri-La Hotel; **Sui Sha Ya,** Chatham Rd., Kowloon and Leighton Rd., Causeway Bay. First class to deluxe. In the moderate range: **Yamato,** 74 Queen's Rd., **Saito,** 50 Queen's Rd., and **Nagoya,** Hyatt Regency Hotel. Most feature *sushi* (raw fish) bars and *teppanyaki* (beef, salmon, or prawn grilled at your table).

Cristal Palais and **Arc En Ciel,** at 57 and 57B Paterson St., and **Viet Hoa,** 1 Canon St., all clustered in Causeway Bay, are among a number of Vietnamese restaurants.

Ginseng Garden, 32 Cannon St., Causeway Bay, is our choice for *pulgogi* and stewed beef spareribs. Others worth a mention are **Koreana** on nearby Paterson St. (moderate) and **Mynna** at 32B Mody Rd., 83B Nathan Rd., and 6 Humphreys Ave. in Kowloon (inexpensive). **Korea Garden,** 119 Connaught Rd., H.K., has passable food, good view, band, and sexy but expensive Korean hostesses for unattached men (moderate).

Gaylord, 43 Chatham Rd., Kowloon, and the **Ashoka,** 57 Wyndham St., Central, are among best Indian restaurants in town. The *tandoori* specialties are rated highly (moderate).

Indonesian Restaurant, at 28 Yun Ping Rd. near the Lee Gardens Hotel in Causeway Bay and at 10 Prat Av. in Kowloon, has good *saté* (skewered, barbecued meat), hot curries, fried noodles, and *gado gado* (mixed vegetable salad) (inexpensive). **Java Rijstaffel 1974** at 38 Hankow Rd. is said by some connoisseurs to have the best Indonesian food in town. The buffet is popular and inexpensive.

NIGHT LIFE. Most of the "respectable" entertainment for an evening is centered around the hotels. The other kind has more to do with the exotic and erotic and mysterious Orient and is found in the bars and clubs and dancehalls scattered around Wanchai, Tsimshatsui, and Causeway Bay. It's possible (just barely) to enjoy both kinds without spending too much money or getting into too much trouble.

Supper clubs and dinner dancing: Occasionally a name performer plays a top hotel restaurant, although this type of entertainment has become rather rare in Hong Kong. On an irregular basis, several hotels offer live stage plays with dinner.

Several places offer music with dinner but no floor show. There are strolling musicians and a dance area at the *Peak Tower Restaurant.* In Kowloon, *Gaddi's* in the Peninsula and *Pink Giraffe* at the Sheraton Hotel offer dinner-dancing music, *Hugo's* in the Hyatt Regency Hotel has the music but no dancing.

Lovers of kitsch and camp, perhaps masochists as well, will enjoy a visit to a Chinese-style supper club. Bejeweled mistresses, the Big Band sound, or Chinese opera excerpts can benumb the mind.

The biggest and the best of the "so bad they're good" places in Kowloon are: *Highball,* 74 Nathan Rd.; *Golden Crown,* 66 Nathan Rd.; *Oceania,* Ocean Terminal; and *Kingsland,* 134 Nathan Rd. Most serve very good *dim sum* at lunchtime. Prices can be steep at night. The most recently opened supper club is *Ocean City* in the New World Center, Kowloon, while if one is staying in a Causeway Bay hotel, *Pearl City* is worth a look-see.

Hotel bars with music: On the Hong Kong side, *Captain's Bar* in the Mandarin has some of the smoothest music in town by excellent Filipino and Chinese musicians. Small, jam-packed dance floor, older but still swinging clientele. *Yum Sing Bar* at the Lee Gardens has a long "happy hour," pretty waitresses, intimate atmosphere, and usually a singer. *Dragon Boat Bar* in the Hilton is great for people watching, flirting, and drinking weirdo drinks like the "Big Bamboo." The Hilton Hotel's *Eagle's Nest* is an exciting rendezvous with music and Chinese food.

In Kowloon, *L'Aperitif* piano-bar at the Peninsula is chic and intimate. Also recommended for some quiet music (often a singer or small group but no dancing) and good drinks are the *Chin Chin Bar* in the Hyatt Regency, the *Gun Bar* in the Hong Kong Hotel, the Ambassador's *Cellar Bar* (some strange and interesting people). There are also atmospheric bars in the newer hotels such as Regent, Shangri-La, Royal Garden, and Holiday Inn Harbour View (all on Kowloon side).

Discos and pubs: *Underground,* D'Aguilar St., attracts straights and gays and has proven to be the most popular. Two of the most popular discos in the Tsimshatsui area are *Hollywood East* in the Regal Meridien and *Faces* in the New World Hotel. Among others of note are *Another World* (Holiday Inn); *The Manhatten,* Gloucester Rd., Causeway Bay; *Canton,* and *Hot Gossip,* both on Canton Rd., Kowloon; and *Polaris* (Hyatt). Best of the English-style pubs are *Bull and Bear* (Hutchison House), *Dickens Bar* (Excelsior Hotel), and *The Jockey Pub* (Swire House). The *Go Down* around the corner from the Furama has English lasses serving good draft beer and reasonably priced food. *Bar City* in the New World Center offers half a dozen different styles of theme bar. The Furama's *Lau Ling Bar,* with a good trio, is popular with the young, "in" Chinese crowd.

Hostess Clubs, Escort Services, Ballrooms: For bachelors (in fact or spirit), Wanchai is the center of the girlie area on the Hong Kong side, Tsimshatsui in Kowloon. There are dozens of girlie bars in these areas that cater to foreigners, priced about the same, except for topless bars, which are more expensive. Some have a juke box, some live bands, and dancing. Companionship is pushed at HK$40 to $50 per thimble of Coke or 7-Up by delectable but thirsty lasses. Caution is advised; otherwise the bill mounts rapidly. Girl willing, you can take her out by paying the bar. Compared to Bangkok and Manila, the bar scene in Hong Kong is a big disappointment. One important piece of advice—pay each round as you go.

Some of the places have upgraded and geared themselves to the growing number of Japanese businessmen and tourists. The classy ones with "international" hostesses are *Kokusai and Gekkesai* in Tsimshatsui, and *Club Dai-Ichi* and *Aoishiro* on Gloucester Rd., in Wanchai. Low lights, good bands, well-dressed and undressed girls, and expensive. Girls can be hired out as "escorts" at some places, but for more than it would cost in an ordinary bar.

There are several escort services that "provide attractive companions for all occasions." Such services are much less expensive in Bangkok or Manila.

Ballrooms are patronized mostly by Chinese, although many big ones like *Tonnochy* in Wanchai and *Oriental* on Jordan Rd. in Kowloon have a fair number of English-speaking hostesses.

HAIRDRESSERS. Most of the hotels have good hair stylists and offer the quickest and most convenient solution, although not the cheapest.

LAUNDRY. Available seven days a week in all hotels, but some charge extra for same-day service. For those on a budget, there are coin-operated machines listed under "Launderers—Self Service" in the Yellow Pages.

LETTERS, CABLES, AND PACKAGES. Postal service is very reliable. Main branch hours are 8–6, subbranches 9–5. Main branches are beside the Star Ferry Terminal, Central District, and Hermes House, Middle Rd., in Kowloon. Air mail letters are $1.30 per 10 grms. to Europe, America, and Australia. Almost all hotels have wrapping and mailing services for those purchases you don't wish to take with you.

For overseas cables and phone calls, check with your hotel. Most add a service charge, so it may be cheaper to go over to one of the Cable and Wireless offices in the Ocean Terminal, New Mercury House in Wanchai, or Mercury House in Central, and Lee Gardens in Causeway Bay, and place the call or send the cable yourself.

CHURCHES. There are many English-speaking churches of every denomination in Hong Kong; a few of the more conveniently located churches and a synagogue are listed here.
St. John's Cathedral, Anglican, Garden Rd., Hong Kong; *St. Andrew's Church,* Anglican, 133 Nathan Rd., Kowloon; *English Methodist Church,* 271 Queen's Rd. East, Hong Kong; *Kowloon English Baptist Church,* 300 Junction Rd.; *Union Church* (Interdenominational), Kennedy Rd., Hong Kong; also at 4 Jordan Rd., Kowloon; *St. Joseph's Church* (Roman Catholic), 7 Garden Rd., Hong Kong; *St. Theresa's Church,* Roman Catholic, 258 Prince Edward Rd., Kowloon; *Ohel Leah Synagogue,* 70 Robinson Rd., Hong Kong. The Yellow Pages list many more.

MEDICAL SERVICES. Western medicine as practiced here is up to the best standards. Travelers suffering illness or accidental injury receive first-class care. Hotels have a list of government-accredited doctors to call, including British and Chinese physicians, the latter trained in the United States or England.

QUESTIONS AND COMPLAINTS. Services offered by the *Hong Kong Tourist Association* (HKTA) represent the best deal in town. All reasonable questions answered by their charming young ladies at information centers or desks at the airport just outside the customs area, and the Star Ferry Concourse on the Kowloon side. There's also an abundance of free materials available including a shopping guide plus information leaflets on hotels, festivals, sightseeing (tours, or on your own with public transport), things to do, beaches, and arts and crafts. Information and a wide range of leaflets are also available at the HKTA head office on the 35th floor of Connaught Center, H.K. side.

Visitors may report any complaints about shops, restaurants, hotels, taxis, etc., to the HKTA at the head office or through the information centers. There's no promise they can solve the problem, but they do say they "will be pleased to mediate on behalf of visitors."

FOR THE BUSINESS TRAVELER. Although Hong Kong is an expensive place for foreign businessmen to work and live, it does offer the advantages of excellent communications, a skillful and versatile labor force, a good harbor and strategic location in the Far East, good supporting facilities, a free trade climate and low tax structure. Permission to take up residency and work beyond the time allowed by an ordinary tourist visa must be obtained beforehand from the nearest British Embassy, High Commission, or representative of the Crown. Holders of British passports issued in the United Kingdom enjoy a six months' exemption.

The industrial work force is large and flexible and there are no minimum wage laws. Trade unions are not very strong and big strikes are rare.

The Trade Section of the Department of Commerce and Industry, Ocean Center, is geared to assist in matters related to trade and industry. The Trade Development Council (Connaught Center) offers a wide range of services and is especially helpful to businessmen interested in buying Hong Kong products. T.D.C. officers will quickly arrange meetings with factory or export agents. Other useful contacts are the Hong Kong General Chamber of Commerce at 9th floor, Swire House, Chater Rd., and the Chinese General Chamber of Commerce at 24–25, Connaught Rd., both in Central District.

Useful publications aimed at the overseas businessman include *Hong Kong Trader,* a newspaper published quarterly, and *Hong Kong Enterprise,* a monthly periodical put out by T.D.C.

The Miramar Hotel has a 23,000-square-foot convention center with six languages simultaneous translation equipment, seating for 2,000 persons, and cocktail or banqueting facilities for up to 2,500. The World Trade Center Club in The Excelsior has a business library equipped with telex, private board meeting room, health club and restaurant—for use by visiting members. The HKTA publishes a range of useful literature for convention and conference planners.

The *American Chamber of Commerce* (Amcham) has office space in the heart of town which can be rented on a temporary basis by executives in town for a short period of time. Facilities include bilingual secretarial assistance, receptionist and telephonist, telex, duplicating and mailing, printing, a reference library and advice on how to do business in Hong Kong. Amcham also publishes a number of books and pamphlets including *Living in Hong Kong.*

Most top hotels provide Business Centers for visiting businesspeople, providing typing, duplication, translation, and other services.

EMERGENCIES. For real trouble, dial "999" and say police, fire, or ambulance as applicable. English-speaking policemen wear a red shoulder tab.

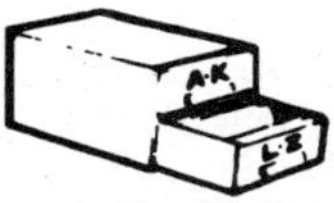

USEFUL ADDRESSES. Consulates. The *American Consulate* is at 26 Garden Road. *British* subjects needing assistance should call the Inquiries Section of the Government Information Office. They will be directed to the correct office for their particular problem. *Japanese Consulate:* Bank of America Tower, Harcourt Rd., 24th floor, H.K.; *Portuguese Consulate,* 14th floor, Central Bldg., Pedder St.; *Thailand,* Hyde Center, Gloucester Rd., Causeway Bay; *Australia,* 11th floor, Connaught Center.

Others (All addresses in Yellow Pages). American Chamber of Commerce. British Council. Foreign Correspondents Club. H.K. Export Center.

There are regular meetings of the following clubs: Jaycees, Kiwanis, Lions, Round Table, Rotary, Shrine, and Toastmasters.

FIVE-MINUTE CANTONESE

Most of the Chinese with whom the visitor comes in contact will be able to speak good English. But there may be times when a few words of Cantonese will be useful. If nothing else, the five-minute investment will pay off in goodwill and a few laughs. In the following vocabulary list, the accented words are capitalized:

English	*Cantonese*
Please	Cheng n*a*y (*a* as in *a*pe)
Thank you (for service)	mmM'GOY (*mmM* as in "mmM, that's good" but said much quicker; *goy* rhymes with boy)
Thank you (for a gift, e.g.)	D*o*ugh-jeh (*Dough* rhymes with mow, *jeh* as in *Jeh*ovah)
One	Yaht (rhymes with tiny *tot*)
Two	Eee (as in *e*ven)
Three	Som (as in *som*bre)
Four	S*ay* (*a* as in *a*pe)
Five	Ng (try just saying the last two letters in si*ng*)
Six	Look
Seven	Chut (as in *chut*ney)
Eight	Baht (as in *bot*tom)
Nine	Gau (as in *gou*ge or *gau*cho)
Ten	Sup (as in *sup*per)
Sunday	Lye bye YAHT (*yaht* is low tone)
Monday	Lye bye YAHT (*yaht* is high tone)
Tuesday	Lye bye EEE
Wednesday	Lye bye SOM
Thursday	Lye bye SAY
Friday	Lye bye NG
Saturday	Lye bye LOOK
Yes	High
No	mM'HIGH
Good	Hoe (Very good—Hoe Hoe)
Bad	mM'HOE
Good morning	JOE sun
Goodbye	Joy G*ee*n (*ee* as in *E*ven)
I love you	Ngo jung-ee n*a*y (*a* as in *a*pe)
How much money?	G*a*y dough ch*ee*n? (*a* as in *a*pe, *ee* as in *e*ven)
Too expensive	Tie gway (tie rhymes with my, gway is like saying *goo* and *why* together but fast)
Hurry	F*ie* dee (f*ie* as in b*i*te, d*ee* as in *e*ven)
Never mind, it doesn't matter	mM gan yow (*gan* rhymes with *bon*fire, *yow* with *no*)

MACAU

Six Square Miles of History

Just 21 years after Columbus discovered his New World, a Portuguese merchant and mariner, Jorge Alvares, was establishing a European foothold in South China. Alvares sailed in a Chinese junk from Malacca to the Pearl River, where he opened trade negotiations with the Guangzhou (Canton) authorities. By 1555 the trade had grown so valuable that it was consolidated on a small peninsula on the west coast of the Pearl estuary, with good protected anchorages.

The site was called A-Ma Gau (the Bay of A-Ma) from the small temple to A-Ma that was found amid a tumble of boulders and trees in a sheltered cove near the harbor entrance. Over the years, the name changed and was shortened until it became known as Macau (although the city's official name is much longer and more striking: "City of the Name of God in China, Macau, There is None More Loyal").

Seizing a monopoly of trade between China and Japan—and improving relations with the Canton authorities by curbing piratical attacks on shipping and coastal villages—the Portuguese in Macau prospered and the city quickly grew in size, stature, and commercial importance. In the century from its official founding in 1557 it became one of the most important trading cities of the world, with links from China and Japan, back to Malacca and Goa and thence to Portugal, across the

Pacific through Manila to Acapulco and thence to Europe, and through the Spice Islands of what is now Indonesia.

The city that grew up became renowned for its magnificence. Antonio Bocarro, writing in Goa about 1635, said: "It is one of the noblest cities in the East, on account of its rich and noble traffic in all kinds of wealth to all parts; it has all kinds of precious things in great abundance, and more and wealthier citizens than any other in this State." Peter Mundy, the first English visitor to Macau, wrote in 1637 of a banquet served in "a very faire house retchely furnished"; his description indicates the sumptuous lifestyle of the merchant princes. "Our dinner was served in plate, very good and savoury to my Mynde, only the Manner much different From ours, For every Man had a like portion of each sort of Meat broughtt betweene 2 sillver plates, and this often Chaunged, For before a man had don with one, there was another service stood ready For him; Allmost the same Decorum in our Drincke, every Man his silver Goblett by his trencher, which were no sooner empty butt there stood those ready thatt Filld them againe with excellent good Purtugall wyne. There was alsoe indifferent good Musick of the voice, harpe and guitterne."

Macau has been Portuguese for over 400 years, although the Dutch, British and Chinese have at various times fought for its possession. As the political winds have changed, Macau has gone from being a Portuguese colony to an overseas province of Portugal to its present status as simply "a territory" under Portuguese administration.

Relations with China have become warmer in recent years, following re-establishment of diplomatic relations between Lisbon and Beijing. In 1979, the Border Gate was opened to local and foreign visitors, and daily tours now operate into the "special zone" of China that adjoins Macau. In this "special zone" a number of tourism developments have been completed, including small resort-type hotels, a safari park and shooting range. China Travel Service (Macau) operates tours in conjunction with a number of Macau travel agencies. The business climate has thrived on the new feeling of confidence, and a great deal of property redevelopment is under way. Some 10 new hotel projects were among the numerous building schemes undertaken, while the influx of visitors has passed the four-million-a-year mark.

Macau comprises a peninsula, on an island in the Canton delta, and two small islands, Taipa and Coloane, with a total area of 6½ square miles. On the isthmus which links it to mainland China stands the century-old barrier, Portas do Cerco. On the other side, beyond a short no man's land, is the five-starred red flag of the People's Republic of China. One of the most densely populated areas in the world, Macau now accommodates about 420,000 people. Fewer than 7,500 are classified as Portuguese, and of those less than 1,000 are actually Portuguese from Europe. The rest are *Macaenese*—Portuguese-speaking Eurasians with a distinctive but disappearing *patois.* There are probably more churches, Catholic and Protestant, per square mile than in any other city in the world, plus Chinese temples and a mosque.

Officially founded in 1557, Macau is said to have been given to Portugal as a reward for destroying the rule of pirates over the South China Seas. In the following centuries Macau grew in wealth and importance as the controller of all trade between China and Japan and between both nations and Europe. In later centuries, when China trade opened to other nations, Macau prospered as the summer residence of the great *tai-pans* or trader barons of the old China Coast days.

Macau was also a port of refuge for the persecuted. Sun Yat Sen, founder of the Chinese Republic, lived here while he planned the overthrow of the Manchu Dynasty. From 1937 until 1945, thousands of refugees flooded into Macau, to escape the invading Japanese.

A visitor to Macau today sees a delightful old Portuguese seaside town with broad tree-lined waterfront avenues and cream, red and ochre villas on which the paint may be peeling a bit. Pedicabs cycle slowly along quiet streets. Although, as one writer put it, "the place is enjoying an economic boom for the first time since 1685 when the Portuguese lost their monopoly on trade with Canton," it is still possible to enjoy a stroll down the cobbled side streets, have a cup of tea in one of the sidewalk cafés, and relax under the shade of centuries-old banyan trees along the *Praia Grande,* the city's promenade. But the serenity and charm are fast disappearing, victims of the motor car and pile driver, while the delightful and handsome stucco colonial buildings, Mediterranean in style, are giving way to 15- and 20-story apartment blocks garnished with plastic marble and stick-on mosaic tiles. Go before it's too late.

EXPLORING MACAU

If you take a jetfoil, hydrofoil, or a daytime ferry, the boat journey affords marvelous views of the Pearl River estuary, of fishing junks and of the coast of mainland China. Once there, the visitor to this small part of Portugal can see almost everything of note in two days, and this by leisurely walking, with perhaps a few rides over long stretches between spots of interest. Maps dispersed at hotels and the tourist bureau indicate what to see, and one can choose any route desired. Principal spots of interest are:

The Leal Senado (literally "Loyal Senate," its functions are that of a town hall and houses municipal offices), built in 1876, contains the oldest European public library in the Far East with over 40,000 volumes. One writer described it thus: "The two main galleries are splendid examples of decorative wood carving and the two antique crystal chandeliers are magnificent reminders of a lost age of elegance. But for the scholar, the great attraction of the library is its books, some of which date back to the 16th and 17th centuries."

Nearby is Santa Casa de Misericordia, a charitable institution established by the first bishop of Macau in 1569. Farther along this way are S. Domingos Church, built by Spanish Dominicans, and the Convent of Sta. Clara, founded by Franciscan Sisters of St. Mary, both 300 years ago.

A road around Guia Hill has a fine bird's-eye view of all of Macau. The lighthouse in the old Fort of Guia is now open to the public. The

Fort and Chapel of Our Lady of Guia within its grounds date back to 1626, the lighthouse to 1865 (the oldest on the China coast).

Camoens Gardens, a park named for Portugal's great poet, who was said to have come to Macau in 1557, has a grotto where he may have written part of his epic poem *Os Lusiadas.* Nearby is the Luis de Camoens Museum. The building itself is of interest for it once served as headquarters for the Select Committee of the powerful British East India Company. Exhibits inside are well displayed and include old paintings of early Macau, early colonial and Chinese furniture, and some very nice examples of Chinese pottery and bronzeware. Adjacent is the Old Protestant Cemetery, a quiet retreat shaded by frangipani trees where many early residents and visitors were reinterred after the Protestants were given permission to establish their own burial ground. Included are Chinnery, the painter; a forebear of Winston Churchill who died on his ship in Macau Roads; and Morrison, translator of the Bible into Chinese. Many other English, American, and Scandinavian pioneers of Macau's trading heyday are buried here.

The ruins of the ancient Church of St. Paul, Macau's most famous landmark, are quite impressive. Only the face is left, the rest having been destroyed by fire in 1835. It is considered a masterpiece of interpretation of Christian thought with an Oriental background, done by Japanese Christian artisans. The façade is covered with *bas relief* in three tiers. There are magnificent steps leading to the Baroque-style ruins.

The fort of Sao Paulo do Monte in the middle of the peninsula was built by Jesuit fathers in the 16th century. Its culverins and old bronze cannons are preserved in the embrasures of the fort. Another fort, the Barra, or Sao Tiago Fort, guards the Inner Harbor. Near this is the Ma Kok Temple, built before the Portuguese came to Macau. Still another temple antedating the Portuguese is that of Kun Iam Tong, the Goddess of Mercy. In its garden is a stone table erected for the signing of the first treaty between the U.S.A. and China, signed by Mr. Caleb Cushing and Viceroy Yi, in 1844. The treaty declared a "perfect, permanent and universal peace" between the two countries.

The Portas do Cerco is the entry point on the border between China and Macau. Built in 1849, it replaced a crumbling wall which the Chinese had erected in 1573. The opening of the border to tourism traffic in 1979 enables visitors to Macau to take a daytrip into China. This can be arranged after your arrival.

A 4,000-seat sports complex in front of the ferry terminal has given the Macanese and many visitors their first look at the fast and furious game of jai alai.

The mile-long bridge provides the fastest and most convenient way to get to Taipa, the nearby but tranquil and secluded island. Taipa was best known for its firecracker factory and its quaint Portuguese-style village. But this is changing, with three major developments there: a massive trotting track opened in 1980, the University of East Asia occupied its new campus in 1981, and two big hotel projects. As well, a satellite town for 15,000 people is being built on the island.

MACAU

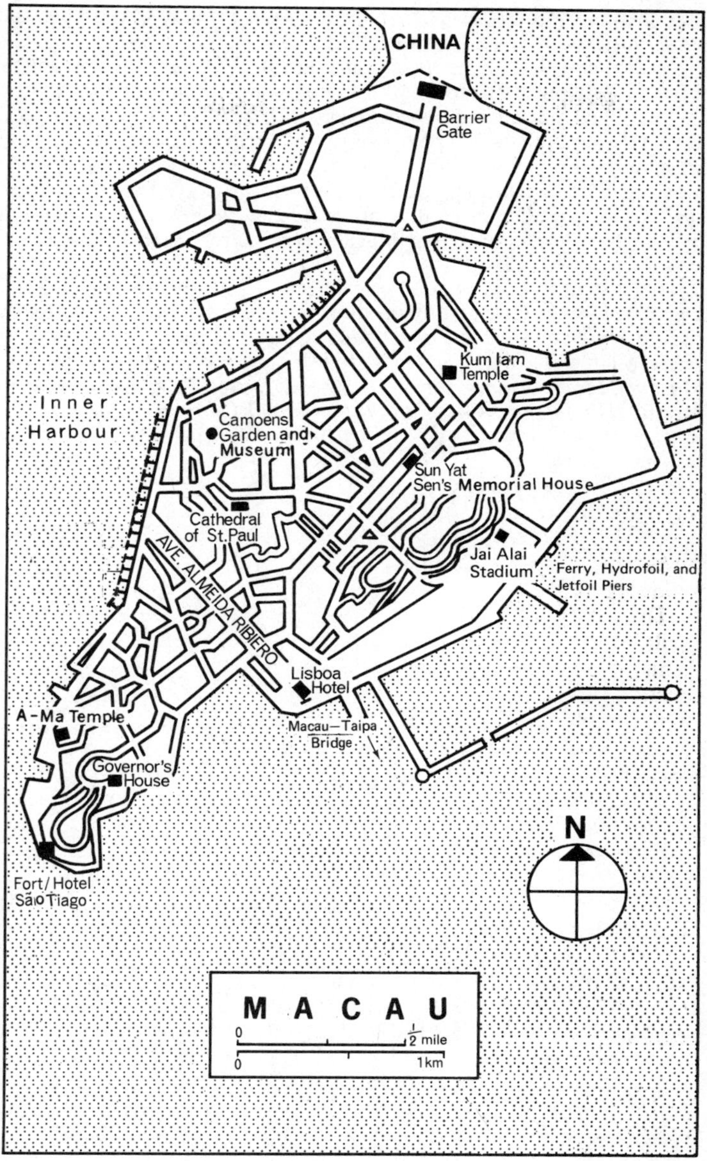

CHINA
Barrier Gate
Kum Iam Temple
Inner Harbour
Camoens Garden and Museum
Sun Yat Sen's Memorial House
Cathedral of St. Paul
AVE. ALMEIDA RIBIERO
Jai Alai Stadium
Ferry, Hydrofoil, and Jetfoil Piers
Lisboa Hotel
Macau—Taipa Bridge
A-Ma Temple
Governor's House
Fort/Hotel São Tiago
N
MACAU
0
1/2 mile
0
1km

Across a causeway from Taipa is Coloane Island, with its beautiful pine groves and beaches. It's worth an overnight stay if you have the time, but even a day trip is of interest.

Among new developments expected around 1986 are the opening of a $1,500 million ferry terminal in Hong Kong, designed to handle up to 15 million passengers a year. There will also be a new high-speed ferry service carrying 700 passengers on the trip to Macau, taking only 90 minutes. For sightseeing, there are plans to open a folk museum in a converted colonial home on the Taipa village praya (waterfront), as the first of five units in a cultural center that will eventually house a gallery, handicrafts museum, Macanese restaurant, and heritage museum.

To get the most out of your stay, check in with the Macau Tourism Department and pick up any or all of the following brochures, free of charge: *Guide to Macau; Tourist Map; Unique Macau; Hotels; Restaurants; Shopping Guide for Gold and Jewelry; Your Trip to Macau; Macau; Macau Casinos; Jai Alai; Macau Travel Talk; Eating Out in Macau; The Islands; Churches, Temples and Gardens of Macau.*

PRACTICAL INFORMATION

FACTS AND FIGURES. Population: 420,000. Land area: 15.5 sq kms. Birth rate, per 1,000: 26. Number of tourists annually: 4 million.

WHEN TO GO? Temperatures are similar to Hong Kong's, but a few degrees cooler. The rainy season is from June through September, summer heat continuing through October. November and December are perfect months for sightseeing. In January and February the thermometer drops to 50 degrees or below and March can be cold and wet.

WHAT TO TAKE? Since the weather is almost the same as in Hong Kong, whatever is comfortable there will do in Macau. Summer months require the lightest of clothing and an umbrella. Informality is the rule, even for evening wear.

ELECTRICITY. Electricity in the "old" section of Macau is 110v 50c, and in the "new" section, 220v 50c. Power supplied to the hotels is normally 220v 50c, but it's a good idea to check before plugging in.

LOCAL FESTIVALS. January–February. *Chinese New Year* is welcomed here with a salvo of firecrackers, colorful confusion around cascading flower stalls and dragon dances. Good opportunities for filming Oriental color, but always very crowded.

February–March. *Feast of Our Lord of Passos,* featuring an impressive procession of religious images winding through the streets from the cathedral to St. Augustine's Church. Many of Macau's Chinese populace are Roman Catholics.

May 7. *Feast of A-Ma.* The exact date is fixed by the Lunar Calendar. A-Ma is the patroness of fishermen and seamen and it was after this Chinese goddess that the Portuguese named Macau. The entire fishing fleet comes to port to honor the goddess in her 600-year-old temple at the entrance of the Inner Harbor.

May 13. *Our Lady of Fatima Procession* winds its way through the narrow streets from Sao Domingos Church to the Penha chapel in this commemoration of the vision of the Portuguese children 50 years ago.

June 10. *Portuguese Communities Day* is celebrated in conjunction with *Camoens Day,* with high pomp at the Camoens Grotto.

October 1. China's *National Day* is not an official holiday in Macau but is widely celebrated. Since 97 percent of the population is Chinese, a large number of people join in the celebrations, which include the colorful decoration of buildings, theatrical performances, cocktail parties, and many, many firecrackers.

November. *Macau Grand Prix,* held on the third weekend of the month, is one of the world's most exciting sports car races, run on the winding Guia circuit. The main event is backed up with numbers of other motor car and cycle events over the weekend. Booking is required long in advance.

HOW TO GET THERE. A fleet of 12 jetfoils, each seating 260 passengers, makes the 40-mile run from Hong Kong to Macau in just under an hour. There are more than 40 round-trips daily, starting about 7:00 A.M. and ending about 5:15 P.M. in winter and 6:30 P.M. in summer; there are round-trips on a special night service between sunset and 1:30 A.M. A variety of other vessels serve the same route, and all leave from the same departure points in Hong Kong and Macau. Hydrofoils, seating 115 or 160 passengers, make about 30 round-trips a day (only in daylight hours), three jetcats (a jet-engined catamaran seating 215) make 10 round-trips daily. In 1983 a new company started hover-ferry service from Shamshuipo Pier in Kowloon, making 11 daily round-trips in the 200-passenger craft. A limited jetfoil service also operates from Kowloon to Macau.

All these vessels take about 70–80 minutes for the crossing. Three conventional ferries operate six round-trips daily, including night trips, with extra weekend and holiday services; they take about three hours. There are luggage limits on jetfoils and hydrofoils.

One-way fares (in HK$) are: *Jetfoils*—upper deck: weekday daytime, $66; weekend and holiday daytime, $72; night services, $88; lower deck: weekday daytime, $57; weekend and holiday daytime, $63; night services, $77. *Jetcats*—weekday, $46; weekends and holidays, $58. *Hydrofoils*—weekday, $46; weekends and holidays, $58. Hover-ferries—weekday, $45; weekends and holidays, $56. Ferries—ranging from $30 (for aircraft seats) to $150 (for VIP cabin for two). Jetfoil bookings can be made up to 28 days in advance through the computerized Ticketmate service. Information and bookings can be obtained from Far East Hydrofoil Co. Ltd. (H–457021) or Hong Kong Macau Hydrofoil Co. Ltd. (H–438648). The Hong Kong government imposes an HK$15 departure tax on all passengers.

All services leave from the Macau Ferry Terminal, Connaught Rd., Hong Kong Island.

PASSPORTS AND VISAS. Anyone who may enter Hong Kong can go to Macau. Visas are not necessary for Hong Kong residents and nationals of the U.S., Canada, Australia, New Zealand, Japan, Malaysia, Philippines, Thailand, Brazil, Austria, Belgium, Denmark, Spain, France, Greece, Italy, Norway, Netherlands, United Kingdom, West Germany and Sweden. For those who need them, visas can be obtained on arrival in Macau for HK$50 (individual), $75 (family) or $25 (per person in a bona fide group of 10 or more). In Hong Kong, a visa may be obtained from the Portuguese Consulate-General, Room 1407, Central Building, 3 Pedder Street. International inoculation certificates are not normally required unless either cholera or smallpox has been detected in Hong Kong or Macau. No Customs, but you are allowed to bring only one quart bottle of wine or spirits and 100 cigarettes back into Hong Kong duty-free.

CURRENCY. The Macau pataca, like the Hong Kong dollar, may be bought at any licensed money-changer or bank. There is no black market and the rate, which fluctuates slightly, is published daily. The Macau pataca is now officially tied to the Hong Kong dollar at the rate of 103 patacas=HK$100, with a permissible fluctuation of 5 percent above or below this rate. The pataca is divided into 100 *avos,* but the dollar sign ($) is commonly used to refer to patacas and the *avos* are often called cents as is the practice in this text. Do not bring patacas back into Hong Kong as it is difficult to change them into HK$.

TIPPING. Ten percent is average but waiters are disappointed if they don't get a little extra.

HOW TO GET AROUND. Taxis are plentiful and all of them are metered. The flagfall cost is $4, which is about what it should cost to get from the ferry pier to the Lisboa Hotel, for example. There is a $5 surcharge for trips to Taipa and a $10 surcharge for trips to Coloane. Pedicabs (rickshaw-bicycle combination for two) are about the same price as taxis, but bargain for a price in advance.

Bus services are quick and cheap at 50 cents per journey on routes in Macau proper. The ride to Taipa costs $1 and $2 to Coloane.

Bicycles can be rented from the Excelsior or Hyatt hotels, or from roadside shops. Hotels charge $18 for the first hour and then a lower rate.

Drivers with an international license can hire a moke (a small jeep-like vehicle) for self-drive. Details from *Macau Mokes,* phone H-434190, or Macau 78851. Weekend rate is $270 a day, but it is cheaper mid-week or for longer periods.

ACCOMMODATIONS. Macau's accommodations range from luxury suites at the *Hyatt* to delightfully quiet and reasonable rooms in tiny Portuguese inns. Hotels are less expensive than in Hong Kong, but some increase rates on weekends, holidays, and special occasions like the *Grand Prix.*

You can make reservations in Hong Kong for the *Lisboa* and *Sintra:* 5-807193, *Hyatt:* 5-661311, *Excelsior:* 3-268888, *Royal:* 3-422033, *Presidente:* 3-41056, *Pousada de Sao Tiago:* 3-8910366, *Matsuya:* 5-686181, *Metropole:* 3-444441, *Mondial:* 3-449283, and *Pousada de Coloane:* 5-696922.

The price ranges quoted below are for double-occupancy rooms. These prices include a 10 percent service charge and a 5 percent government "tourism" tax.

Deluxe—500–1,000 patacas

Excelsior. 438 rooms, some with sea views; decor in public rooms has strong Portuguese flavor. Bars, with restaurants featuring European, and Chinese cuisine; banquet and meeting facilities, health club with sauna; swimming pool, tennis and squash courts. Convenient location near ferry wharf.

Hyatt Regency Macau. Situated on Taipa Island. 335 rooms, many with views across the harbor to the city. Warm Mediterranean décor with lots of greenery; good seafood and Japanese restaurants, coffee shop and disco; pool and fitness center.

Pousada de Sao Tiago. Converted from the Barra Fortress (Fort Sao Tiago.) to a tiny hotel. It has 24 rooms, each with individual décor. The tiny chapel has been restored and the barracks has become a wine cellar. The site is steep, commands views of both the Inner and Outer Harbors and has two good restaurants. Full of history.

First Class—300–600 patacas

Lisboa. A huge, hotel-casino complex with ten restaurants, three nightclubs, shops, bowling alleys, swimming pool, and sauna. One of Macau's best hotels, and despite its garish appearance ("a giant ornate marmalade jar" according to one writer, "like a helicopter landing on a giant artichoke" to another), its 1,000 rooms and suites are tasteful and comfortable.

Royal. Businessman's hotel in quiet garden setting; 380 rooms; European, Chinese and Japanese restaurants; lobby lounge and coffee shop; indoor pool, fitness center, squash court.

Presidente. A 340-room first-class property on Avenida da Amizade with rooms facing the harbor or Guia Hill. It has a lobby lounge bar and coffee shop, specialty restaurants and disco/nightclub. Just a few minutes from the ferry wharf and the main casinos; close to the city's commercial and shopping areas.

Moderate—200–350 patacas

Matsuya. 40 pleasant rooms overlooking the Outer Harbor from Guia Hill and a terrace bar.

Metropole. A high-rise with 109 rooms, including several duplex suites on the top floor. Plain modern décor, good location on Rua da Praia Grande, and value for money.

Pousada de Coloane. 22-room resort set in a pine forest overlooking Cheoc Van Beach on Coloane Island. A great place to get away from it all.

Sintra. Ave. da Amizade. 260 rooms, pleasant and moderately priced. Good harbor view and 24-hour coffee shop, nightclub, sauna, and health club.

Inexpensive—100–200 patacas

Bela Vista. An old, charming, hotel overlooking the bay. A local favorite but not well maintained and downright cold from around January to March. 26 rooms. First floor front suites best. Have a drink or breakfast on the verandah.

Central. In the business district. 149 rooms, some with no windows, at very reasonable rates. Clean and comfortable rooms, a few of which are usually available when all other hotels are booked solid.

Estoril. 89 rooms. Still a favorite with those who prefer its more quiet and leisurely pace and air of shabby gentility. Swimming pool, a dining room with good food and dancing, and a popular bar. Rooms in the "New Wing" best.

Grand Hotel. A stone's throw away from the Floating Casino and popular with gamblers from Hong Kong. Big, rambling hotel, which is also suitable for those on a budget and travelers who do not demand every comfort.

London. Praca Ponte e Horta. 43 clean and comfortable rooms at moderate prices.

Man Va. Upgraded from villa to hotel; it has 27 rooms and a Chinese restaurant. Economical.

INFORMATION. For maps, guidebooks, and information, there are Information Centers in Travessa do Paiva, next to Government House, and at the ferry pier.

TOURS. Macau has a number of Government approved and licensed tour companies with guides who speak several languages. They can custom a tour to fit your interests, pocketbook, and time. Among the better known are *Asia Tours,* telephone 82687 in Macau and K–693847 in Hong Kong, *Estoril Tours,* 73614 and H–445161, *Hi-No-De Caravela Tours,* 77272 and H–236683, *International Tourism,* 86522 and H–412011, *Sintra Tours,* 86394 and H–444451, *Macau-Zhuhai,* 87278, *Macau Tours,* 85555 and K–661158. If you book from Hong Kong, these agencies can take care of your ferry tickets, visas, transportation from hotel, and will meet you upon your arrival in Macau. A four-hour bus tour of the city, including lunch, costs $62–67; by private car, it's $100–150.

If you prefer to go a more independent route, you can hire a taxi or go by bus and walking. The *Guide to Macau* distributed free by the Macau Tourist Information Bureau (see under *Casinos*) contains some useful advice for the budget traveler on how to see Macau by city bus.

WHAT TO SEE. The primary object of a visit to Macau is to view the ruins, churches, forts, cemetery and other evidences of Western man's first attempts to penetrate the mysterious Orient.

Macau information can be secured in Hong Kong from the Macau Tourist Information Bureau by calling K-677747 or visiting their office in Star House, Kowloonside, close to Star Ferry Terminal.

Note that day tours across the Macau border into China are now available through local travel agents.

SHOPPING. The antique and souvenir hunter may luck upon a nice piece of Chinese porcelain or a temple carving in the junk market located in the maze of streets below the Sao Paulo façade. Good stores are scattered round the city, but be prepared to get dirty hands if you are going to investigate them thoroughly. It can be a lot of fun, and rewarding. One of the most interesting areas is the "flea market" in Rua de Tercena, best approached from behind S. Domingos Church. Good buys in Macau are Portuguese wines (but watch the Hong Kong Customs restrictions) and local Chinese-style cookies. Chinese goods are readily available in stores. Portuguese wares can be bought at a shop on the ground floor of Hotel Lisboa. Locally made clothing can be good value, especially if you can locate export overruns.

Shoppers should exercise great care when buying goods at street stalls near the Border Gate, St Paul's, or on Penha Hill; they are not likely to be much of a bargain. Those interested in buying gold or jewelry should first obtain the Department of Tourism's guide on this subject, which lists approved shops.

RESTAURANTS. An interesting development in Macau has been the opening of a number of small restaurants serving Portuguese-style food. These can be found in the city and also in Taipa and Coloane villages. With the demise of the *Pousada de Macau,* one of the most popular city restaurants is *Henri's Galley,* on Avenida da Republica. Excellent spicy prawns, African chicken, and a unique fried rice.

Extra guidance can be obtained from the tourism department's brochure on *Eating Out in Macau;* restaurant names are listed in Chinese. The major new hotels all feature good restaurants, but these tend to be expensive.

A Galera, Caesar's Palace, and **Portas Do Sol** are worthy restaurants serving international cuisine in the Lisboa Hotel.

Fat Siu Lau on Rua de Felicidade is the oldest restaurant in town and specializes in roast pigeon. Reasonable.

Pinnochio, in Taipa village, is not easy to find, but well worth the effort. Excellent food, ranging from curried crab and roast quail to leg of lamb and whole roast pigs (if ordered in advance).

Solmar, a popular meeting place for Portuguese residents. Try the chicken à la Portuguaise or the fish soufflé.

Among the good **Chinese restaurants** are *Chiu Chau Restaurant, Golden Crown, Lee Hong Kee,* Lisboa Hotel's *Lisboa Restaurant, Long Kei, New Macau Palace, Palace, Jade, Jade Garden, Fu Wah,* and *Estoril* at the Hotel Estoril.

NIGHT LIFE. Most of the night life is centered around the hotels, particularly the Lisboa. *Portas Do Sol Supper Club* at the Lisboa is Macau's most popular nightclub with the best band in town and Portuguese folk dancing to boot. At the Estoril Hotel, the main attractions in the *Sun Fa Un Cabaret* are the Mandarin singers, and hostesses, Cantonese cuisine and good dance music. One of Macau's popular attractions (day or night) is the sauna at the Estoril, complete with Thai girls famous for the kinds of massage they give. If you're looking for girls and don't mind paying for their company, try the *Mermaid Night Club* in the Lisboa. The Hyatt has an excellent disco, *The Green Parrot;* there are other discos at the Royal and Presidente hotels.

A sophisticated strip show is offered at the charming and historic Dom Pedro V Theatre. Produced in the style of the Crazy Horse show in Paris, it uses a changing cast of European artists. Crazy Paris shows twice daily (three times on Saturday).

CASINOS. Gambling is the big attraction for most visitors to Macau. There's not as much glitter or big-name entertainment as in other gambling centers of the world, but the gambling is just as serious and the stakes are just as big or bigger. There are five casinos. The one at the Excelsior Hotel is the most lavish, while that at the Lisboa is the biggest. The *Macau Palace* Floating Casino moored in the Inner Harbor is a three-deck Oriental fantasy with a Chinese restaurant on the top deck and casinos on the lower decks. The casino at the *Jai Alai Palace* is just a few bounces away from the jai alai courts. Hours are 6 P.M. to 1 A.M. on weekdays, 1 P.M. to 7 P.M. weekends. There's a small casino just off Avenida Almeida Ribeiro, downtown, that offers only Chinese casino games.

Even if you don't gamble, it's interesting to go and take a look. Admission is free. Dress is informal and jackets and ties are very much the exception. The Lisboa casino is open round the clock every day of the year; all are usually jammed on weekends.

All the casinos are run by an aggressive, multimillion-dollar gambling and tourism syndicate called the *Sociedade de Turismo e Diversoes de Macau* (STDM). The rules are the same from casino to casino but vary slightly from those at Las Vegas and Monte Carlo. It's a good idea to get hold of the official *Guide to Macau* which is distributed free at the Macau Tourist Information Bureau in Star House (Kowloon), Hong Kong. This booklet outlines the house rules for the various casino games.

The games offered are baccarat *(chemin de fer),* craps, blackjack, roulette, *fantan,* and *dai-siu* (big and small). There is also keno and one-armed bandits (called "hungry tigers" in Macau).

The Chinese games *fantan* and *dai-siu* are fun to watch. In *fantan,* the house man shovels a pile of white buttons on to the table and with a baton removes four at a time until the pile is reduced to none, one, two, or three. Bettors have to guess at how many will be left after the last withdrawal of four. Conversation is unnecessary, and it is an easy game to play.

Dai-siu is played with three dice. Bets are made on any number from 4 to 17, three of a kind, combined value of the dice, or whether the combined value is big or small.

Minimum bets are 10 patacas for most games. machines start at 1 pataca.

The players are as fascinating as the games, ranging from tourists who have played at Las Vegas and Monte Carlo, to working people of Macau gambling an entire month's wages. It is not unusual to see a wealthy Chinese businessman playing $15,000 on a single turn of the wheel. Don't bring your camera as it is strictly forbidden to take pictures of the patrons. There are many guards watching for cameras, concealed or otherwise.

Jai Alai. This spectacular and entertaining sport was imported, along with the players, from Spain, where it originated among the Basques. It is played in the huge "Palacio de Pelota Basca," opposite the ferry piers. Singles and doubles are played nightly, with professional teams from Spain. Much betting, by totalizator. Restaurants and bars are also found in the stadium.

Lottery. A new lottery has been established, with profits going to the government-sponsored Macau Foundation. "Instant" prizes up to 100,000 patacas. Tickets are $5 each.

RACING. There is greyhound racing at the Macau *(Yat Yuen)* Canidrome on Avenida General Castelo Branco in the evenings on weekends and Hong Kong public holidays. Races begin at 8 P.M. Admission fees are $1 and up. Betting is by totalizator. A spectacular harness racing track is in operation on Taipa island, with year-round meetings, up to three times a week. Air-conditioned grandstands and splendid views of the sea and adjacent islands.

CHURCHES. St. Agostinho is one of several Catholic churches where Mass may be celebrated and which hear confession in English. There are Protestant services in English on Sundays at 9 A.M. at the East India Company Chapel, Praca Luis de Camoes. There are a number of other Protestant churches, but services are mostly in Cantonese.

TAIWAN

The Island Republic of China

Taiwan, more commonly known as Formosa or Nationalist China, has within the last few years established herself as a major stop for tourists on their swing through Southeast Asia. Visitors numbered less than 15,000 in 1956 but jumped to more than 1,516,138 by the end of 1984 (last figures available). It is easy to visit Taiwan. The island lies midway between Japan and Hong Kong, the Orient's two major tourist attractions, and a stopover costs no extra airfare, although visas or letters of recommendation by approved agencies are required for all visits. The way of life is authentically Chinese although cities are rapidly industrializing.

Early Portuguese mariners exploring the trade routes to the Far East in the late 1500s came upon this lush, leaf-shaped island, 100 miles off the southeastern coast of the Chinese Mainland. Sailing down the length of its some 325 miles, these venturesome lads were so impressed by the majestic mountain ranges and magnificent shores, that they set it down on their chart as *Ilha Formosa,* "Beautiful Isle," the name by which it has been most popularly known ever since. It was this discovery that started the historical chessgame.

Connected by land to the China Mainland during the Ice Age, the island was named Taiwan, which means "Terraced Bay" in Chinese, during the 13th century. The Portuguese charts soon claimed the attention of the Spanish and Dutch who were tiring of earlier conquests in Luzon and Java and eager to seek new and more lively outlets for their energies. By 1624 the Dutch were occupying the south, and two years later Spaniards were busily building the cities of Keelung and Santa Domingo at Tamsui in the north. The Dutch finally drove the Spaniards out, securing virtual control of the island, and erecting dozens of forts, the remains of which can still be seen.

In 1661 a colorful Chinese patriot, Cheng Cheng-kung (called Koxinga), driven south by the invading Manchus, overcame the tiny Dutch garrison and claimed Taiwan for the former Ming Dynasty. Two decades later, his grandson surrendered the throne when the Ch'ing Dynasty attacked Taiwan and occupied Penghu Island, finally forcing an unconditional surrender. The island eventually became a province, and the Chinese retained control for 212 years, in spite of separate abortive attempts by the Japanese and the French to invade. At the end of the first Sino-Japanese war in 1895, the Taiwanese attempted to establish their own republic rather than be governed by the Japanese, but Tokyo had its way, and Formosa became a part of the Japanese Empire. Under Japanese occupation, good roads and a rail system were established, and the economic strength of the island was enhanced. Education for the Taiwanese beyond middle school was nearly impossible, and during the 50 years Japan ruled the island active armed resistance led by the Taiwanese never completely ceased.

Japan's possession of Taiwan was the realization of a long cherished ambition and the island was looked upon as a prospective base for expansion into the South Seas, and future granary for the Japanese people. A central link in the chain of islands bordering the east coast of Asia, it commands the sea lanes between Japan and the ports of Southeast Asia, and was used by the Japanese as a major military outpost and springboard for attacks on South China, the Philippines, and Malaya during the Second World War. The Japanese surrender in 1945 found Taiwan restored as a part of the Republic of China.

After Self-Defense Comes Development

In 1949 when the mainland fell, and China's government-in-exile was set up in Taiwan with Generalissimo Chiang Kai-shek as president, the primary concern was self-preservation and preparation for the eventual return. After the Formosa Straits Crisis of 1958 and the establishment of the present status quo, the Chinese government, weighted down by the high cost of maintaining its large army and by long term U.S. aid obligations, became conscious of the economic rewards to be had from tourism and foreign investments. They therefore embarked on a campaign to promote Taiwan. The results have been phenomenal.

This backwater beauty of the China Sea has bloomed, and readied itself for a place among its older, more sophisticated, tourist-wise counterparts. After the sparkling Crown Colony of Hong Kong with its array of tax-free treasures, sparkling nightlife, and skyreaching structures, or Japan with its dazzling Ginza, geisha girls, and barterable baubles, bangles, and cultured beads, you may arrive in Taiwan still aglow with memories of what you have left behind. If you have dreams of finding even greater variety of gaiety and glamour awaiting you here, you will be in for a disappointment.

But if you're looking for something uniquely Chinese, as well as up-to-date, then you will be amply rewarded. The island has made economic strides in recent years, and the progress has changed the face of Taiwan. Bustling Taipei houses Hsimenting, a nighttime carnival of neon, movies, and entertainment that rivals Ginza. Live Western music in many Taipei restaurants and flashy discos in many hotels rock with action every night. At the same time, the island's people have not succumbed to crass commercialism. They retain much of their heritage, living with beliefs and customs whose roots reach back thousands of years. A delightful blending of ancient and modern Chinese culture, fast-disappearing traces of a half-century of Japanese influence, decaying evidence of Dutch and Spanish visits, and the glow of healthy economic progress are some of the themes of today's Taiwan.

The past years have seen an unprecedented boom in industrial growth, including both foreign companies and local industries, which has caused a movement of population from the countryside to such urban centers as Taipei, Kaohsiung and the new industrial area around Taichung. Because of this economic expansion, Taiwan is becoming a nation unto itself; a unique blend of Chinese and Taiwanese culture combined with Western technology. But once out of these rapidly developing urban areas, visitors still wander through tranquil villages, miles of seemingly uninhabited paddy lands terracing up from the floor of valleys to mountain tops—and wonder where the population of over 18 million has gone. Of the total population all but approximately a quarter million are Chinese, descendants of early migrants from the coastal southern provinces of China, or refugees who came after the fall of the mainland. The nine aboriginal tribes account for the best part of the other quarter million, and are believed to be of Polynesian and Malayan origin.

Many in Taiwan insist on a clear distinction between the early Chinese immigrants and those who came during the fall of the mainland, pointing to the fact that the islanders speak several southern Chinese dialects, notably Amoy and Hakka versions, while the later arrivals mainly speak Mandarin. Until 1949, very few Taiwanese knew the official Chinese language, having used their own dialects at home and the Japanese language imposed between 1895 and 1945 for business purposes. Since then, however, there has been a campaign to encourage everyone to learn Mandarin. The culture remains basically Chinese, with the family, not the individual, the unit of society. Elders have obligations to provide for both descendants and younger siblings; in return, they still receive respect and support in their old age. One of a person's responsibilities is to give his children as much education as possible. The major goal is a graduate degree on the "new mainland," the U.S. Most middle-class families thus have at least one member studying or working in the States, and many upper-class families have packed off all but one child, who either returns or remains here running the family business and taking care of Mother and Father.

"Reconstruction," rather than recovery of the mainland, has become the dominant theme in recent years, so government investment and building have accelerated the island's economic progress. Land-reform laws, in addition, have broken the landlords' and moneylenders' (China's traditional vultures) backs. The "crown" has passed to Chiang Ching-kuo, President Chiang's first son. A much greater number of native Taiwanese have also been absorbed into the government. Indeed, many international economic experts consider the island one of the greatest success stories of U.S. and U.N. aid.

A Storehouse of Chinese Culture

Buddhist, Taoist, Muslim, and Christian centers of worship fill the need for spiritual refreshment in the people's daily lives, religious tolerance being one of the better aspects of Chinese society on Taiwan. Festivals of ancient origin are celebrated enthusiastically and holiday programs are important to the Taiwanese. Dragon and lion dances, local pai-pai's, lantern festivals, and a variety of parades often enlivened by the popping of firecrackers lend an air of wholesome exuberance found in too few countries today. Many of this year's exotic lanterns, handmade for the colorful lantern festival, were lighted by electricity and mechanized. A custom originating long ago to guide the spirits of departed ancestors through the dark, this observance illustrates the grand mixture of ancient customs with a modern touch.

Colorful wedding processions are fading from the scene and future tourists will have to seek assiduously to find a glimpse of gifts as they are drawn on carts from the bride's old home to her new residence. Carefully arranged on red paper for all to see, these presents indicate the station in life of the bride, who is enjoying the privacy of her childhood home for the last time. Today's wedding parties are characterized by speeding taxis decorated with red bunting streamers. In many parts of Taiwan, the funeral procession of bier and pallbearers, accompanied by long lines of mourners and bands dressed in mourning clothes, has been replaced by columns of motorized vehicles decorated with floral pieces.

By far the most popular entertainment in the countryside is Taiwanese opera, the provincial version of classical Peking opera. Traveling troupes go from village to village during festivals and attract large crowds at each performance. Almost equally popular are the hand puppet shows called "Pu Tai Hsi." Both the Pu Tai Hsi and the Taiwanese opera have been televised, and boast the largest audiences of any entertainment shows.

As the repository of Chinese culture, Taiwan is in a unique position. With the Peking Communist regime destroying many classical books as inconsistent with Marxism, forbidding the practices of certain of the arts, and simplifying the Chinese traditional characters, the ideographs, beyond recognition, the importance of classical and artistic endeavors on Taiwan becomes increasingly apparent. Meanwhile, enjoy while you can a relatively peaceful culture.

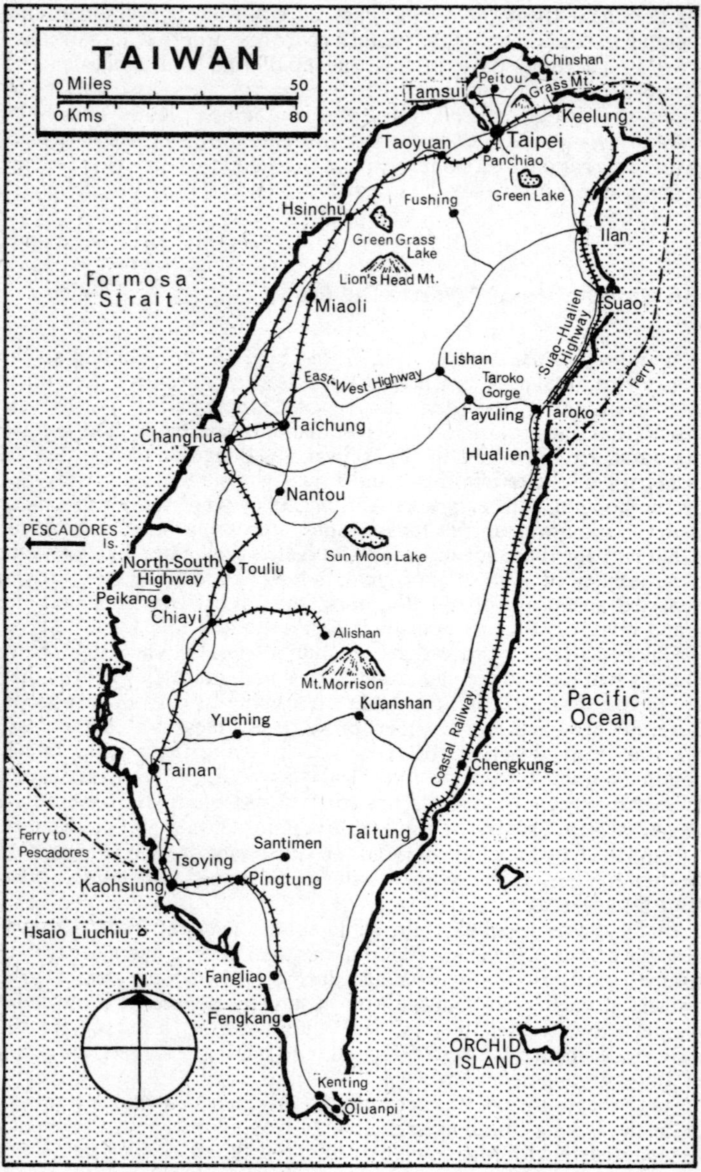
TAIWAN
0 Miles 50
0 Kms 80
Chinshan
Peitou
Grass Mt.
Tamsui
Keelung
Taipei
Taoyuan
Panchiao
Green Lake
Fushing
Hsinchu
Ilan
Green Grass Lake
Lion's Head Mt.
Formosa Strait
Miaoli
Suao
Suao-Hualien Highway
Lishan
East-West Highway
Taroko Gorge
Ferry
Tayuling
Taroko
Taichung
Changhua
Hualien
Nantou
PESCADORES Is.
Sun Moon Lake
North-South Highway
Touliu
Peikang
Chiayi
Alishan
Mt. Morrison
Pacific Ocean
Kuanshan
Yuching
Coastal Railway
Tainan
Chengkung
Taitung
Ferry to Pescadores
Santimen
Tsoying
Kaohsiung
Pingtung
Hsaio Liuchiu
N
Fangliao
Fengkang
ORCHID ISLAND
Kenting
Oluanpi

TAIPEI
N
to Museum
Grand Hotel
KEELUNG R.
To Airport
FREEWAY
ZOO
TAMSUI R.
SUNGSHAN AIRPORT
Minchuan W
Minchuan E
CHUNGSHAN N. RD.
HSINSHENG N.
SUNGCHIANG RD
TUNHUA RD.
NANKING W. RD.
NANKING E. RD.
Chang an
Stadium
Station
Chang an
PATEH RD.
Post Office
Executive Yuan
CHUNGSHAN S. RD
New Park
Presidential Building
Jenai Rd
Hsinyi Rd.
Botanical Gardens
Chiang Kai-shek Memorial
American Institute
Taipei Mosque
Roosevelt Rd.
Taiwan University

EXPLORING TAIWAN

When you fly into Taiwan, you will land at either the southern seaport of Kaohsiung or at Taoyuan's new Chiang Kai-shek (CKS) Airport, which opened in February 1979. The Taiwan Auto-Transport Co. runs two routes into Taipei. One bus makes nine stops, including the Ambassador Hotel, the Taipei Hilton Hotel, Taipei train station, and the Lai Lai Sheraton Hotel, en route to the Chunglun Bus Station. The other goes directly to Taiwan's domestic airport (Sungshan Airport) in northeastern Taipei. Buses run every fifteen minutes to and from the airport. The buses are comfortable, air-conditioned, and cost about $1.80 one way. Tickets are available in the airport's arrival lobby to come into Taipei. The bus service is an economical alternative to a cab which could cost you up to $25. Because airport cabs are specially licensed, expect your fare to be calculated at one and a half times the meter price. So you won't miss your departing flight, allow plenty of time to get to the airport. If you're traveling by sea, the chances are your first port of call will be Keelung, the northern port near the capital.

With a history of little more than a century, and a population of more than 2.4 million inhabitants, Taipei is the largest and most modern city in the country. The name "Taipei" was first given the city in 1879 by the Ching Dynasty and an 18-foot wall was erected around the settlement with huge gates strategically located at the points of the compass. Removal of the lacquer from the North Gate was completed in 1979, returning this historic edifice to its original appearance of dark red brick and yellow-gray stone. The other gates have been reconstructed in the Chinese Palace style, so only North Gate shows the actual style of the original gates.

With a city map, the adventurous tourist can explore on foot some of the historic sections of Taipei, like Wanhua, famous for its snake stalls and outdoor food stands.

Directly in front of the East Gate is the Presidential Building, which is the chief executive's office, rather than residence, and hub of the city. Nearby New Park covers a block or two and contains the Provincial Museum where you will find interesting exhibits of Taiwan's history. With its classical pagodas and gardens, the park is a favorite rest spot.

To the east is the towering Chiang Kai-shek Memorial Hall, a striking example of classical Chinese architecture, set within pleasant gardens. A concert hall and Chinese opera house are now also being constructed on the 62-acre plot.

The Botanical Garden, just south of the Presidential Building on Nanhai Road, provides a comfortable and attractive place to walk leisurely through tall palm trees and gaze at thousands of different tropical plants. Also within its confines are the National Historical Museum, the National Taiwan Arts Hall, the Central Library, and the National Taiwan Science Hall, whose towering dome resembles that of the Temple of Heaven in Peking.

One of the largest and most colorful Buddhist temples in Taiwan is the Lungshan Temple in the Wanhua district in the southwest section of Taipei. Wanhua is the oldest district in the city, and Lungshan was the first temple to be built there. The magnificent stone sculpture, intricate woodcarving, gold-leafed idols, and ornate roof decorations of this 200-year-old edifice fascinate many visitors. It was built by settlers coming from three districts in Fukien province who wished to continue their worship of Kuan Yin, the Goddess of Mercy, and Ma Tsu, the Goddess of the Sea, as they had done in their home province. Although first constructed in 1738, it has been rebuilt twice, once after a severe earthquake in 1816, and again after bomb damage during the Second World War.

Temple touring is a major attraction in the city, and there are several of interest within this area. The Confucian Shrine, located in the North Taipei District of Tatung, west of the Taipei City Zoo and the Chungshan Amusement Park, is dedicated to the great Chinese philosopher and is similar in architectural design to a Buddhist temple. The interior, however, is quite different. Unlike a temple, where images and icons are displayed, the shrine has only a wooden plaque carved with the Chinese ideographs "The most sacred, respected Master Confucius" on the altar. This, if nothing else, should remind any visitor that Confucianism is a philosophy, not a religion.

Nestled against a hillside near the Grand Hotel is the Martyr's Shrine modeled after the Hall of Supreme Harmony in Beijing's Forbidden City. It is one of two shrines honoring the nation's war dead.

Yangmingshan (Grass Mountain) and the Suburbs

Shihlin Institute of Horticulture is only a five-minute drive from the Grand Hotel, and next door to the late President Chiang's winter residence. The butterfly orchid and the Mei Ling variety named for Madame Chiang Kai-shek were first cultivated in this experimental station where innumerable varieties of chrysanthemums are also exhibited in season. From this point you can drive to the National Palace Museum in Waishuanghsi, to Yangming Park on Grass Mountain, or to the famous Peitou hot springs resort.

If Taipei had nothing else to offer, the National Palace Museum, north of Taipei, would make the trip worthwhile. Housing over a quarter of a million objects of Chinese art, it is undoubtedly the world's best collection of works of beauty from this gifted people. The exhibits change quarterly (6,000 to 8,000 items each time) and can be best seen on weekdays, as the weekends find the beautiful museum thronged with school children. Daily English-language tours start in the main lobby at 10 A.M. and 3 P.M., lasting for one hour. Most items are labeled in both Chinese and English.

Yangmingshan (Grass Mountain) is probably the best place near Taipei to sample the near virginal beauty of Taiwan. Cool, quiet, with a rich variety of scenery, it has a swimming pool and an excellent park. The China Hotel, very modern, complete with sulfur baths, is just a short ride from the park. The late President's summer residence and those of many wealthy Taipei citizens are also located here.

Only seven miles south of Taipei is Pitan, or Green Lake. This tranquil waterway tempts visitors to try the ancient royal sport of leisurely spending a day afloat, far removed from worldly cares. Besides rowing, Pitan offers a nice setting for a picnic.

Another picturesque spot north of Taipei is Tamsui, a town which was once the main northern port of Taiwan. Today the town resembles a sleepy Spanish fishing village. Fort San Domingo, known as "the old Dutch fort," towers above the town, its salmon-colored walls glowing in the afternoon sun. The British formerly used it as their consulate.

Farther up in the mountains south of Pitan is Wulai, about an hour's drive, a mountain reserve inhabited by very commercialized aborigines who pose for pictures and perform old tribal dances (for a price) beneath a huge waterfall that cascades down a towering cliff. There is a side attraction, tiny hand-pushed railcarts to carry you up the rather long trail to the waterfall.

The stout-hearted and long-winded may wish to visit Chihnan Temple, a Taoist temple standing near Mucha, accessible by car or bus in about 45 minutes. The temple, perched halfway up the slope of Monkey Hill, can be reached by climbing a thousand steps.

Yehliu Park to Keelung

Along the north coast lies the beautiful Yehliu Park, famed for its rock formations that have been sculptured through the ages by nature.

For the adventurer who has time to continue on to Keelung, the North–South Freeway carries you there quickly, or the slower, old Taipei–Keelung road takes you on a ride through a region of old, worn-out gold mines. The highway tunnels through several steep mountains to reach Keelung, one of the largest, oldest, drabbest, rainiest, and busiest cities on Taiwan. More than 300 years ago, Spanish forces built Fort San Salvador overlooking the harbor. Although little remains of the old Spanish fort, the rain remains, and Keelung is known as the world's rainiest seaport, just as Formosa sometimes claims itself to be the country with the highest annual rainfall. Shopping is somewhat cheaper than in Taipei. Keelung isn't a pretty city, but it is full of history, as your shoes will be full of water.

The Long Road South

Taoyuan, site of Taiwan's newest international airport, is approximately 25 miles southwest of Taipei and easily accessible by car. About 8 miles farther south, Shihmen Dam, a huge hydroelectric and irrigation project, attracts tourists with its manmade as well as natural beauty. Tahsi Park is partially enclosed within wall-like cliffs where the reverberations of the sound of running streams and driving rain give the visitor a strange thrill. The suspension bridge and distant view of the white sails on the Takokan River are memorable scenes. Deeper in the mountains is the Northern Cross Country Highway which stretches on to Ilan. Tzuhu, the temporary resting place of the late President Chiang Kai-shek, is located about 4 miles down this road. Another spot in this area is Chiaopan Shan, or Fushing village, with an elevation of around 2,000 feet making for wonderful scenery and cool air. This village is located at the headwaters of the Shihmen reservoir and motorboats are available for a trip along the reservoir to Shihmen. A number of Ataya aboriginal settlements exist in the more deeply wooded areas. Aboriginal villages still not up to the commercial approach welcome visitors.

Hsinchu is on the route south. Green Grass Lake is a short two miles from the city, and is a manmade reservoir in the mountains. By the lake stand three temples, with Lingyin Temple the best for a good view. Boating and fishing are the usual forms of relaxation here. A short distance south of Hsinchu is Lion's Head Mountain, or Shih Tou Shan, the major center of Buddhist worship on the island. It can be reached either by car; going through the small town of Toufen, by bus, taking a bus to Hsinchu then transferring to one headed for Nanchuang, or by train, getting off at Chunan and then taking the same Nanchuang bus, which drops you at the foot of the mountain.

Over 10 Buddhist temples are located on the 1,500-foot-high peak. Many of the temples are built so that the interior is actually part of a natural cave. The nuns and monks living on the mountain grow tea and vegetables to trade for rice.

This is a great trip—either by day or overnight. But be sure to wear comfortable shoes. Buses and cars must stop at the foot of the mountain and the rest is on foot. Several of the temples—notably Chuan Hua T'ang, Kaishan and Haihui—welcome guests. There are no hotels in the area, but staying in the dormitories adjacent to the temples is an unforgettable experience. Chuan Hua T'ang has evening services at 8:30 P.M. which are very colorful, and all the temples welcome the dawn with drums and gongs.

The dormitories are fitted out with straw mats, or *tatami,* for sleeping, and bedding and mosquito nets are available. Food and water are also provided. The visitor should be warned, however, that the monks are vegetarians, so the food is strictly meatless. There is no charge for a meal or staying overnight, but a donation for incense-oil money is welcome.

Sun Moon Lake

Continuing along the southern route you'll find Taichung, a two-hour ride from Taipei on the North–South Freeway and two and a half by fast express train. Here is the jumping-off spot for Sun Moon Lake or the East–West Cross Island Highway. However, the town itself is interesting.

An attraction in Taichung is I. M. Pei's magnificent modern chapel, located at Tunghai University, about fifteen minutes outside the city. Set on a grassy field, the triangular chapel soars proudly up against the blue sky, its yellow glazed tiles glittering in the sun. It blends in well with the rest of the bucolic campus, which is modeled on the architectural style of the T'ang Dynasty, about 8th century A.D.

Kukuan Hot Springs, about two hours' drive from Taichung, is where the East–West Cross Island Highway begins winding its way, over the Central Mountain range, through the middle of the island. A great part of the 115 miles of the highway was hand-chiseled from sheer rock by thousands of retired Chinese servicemen over a three-year period. If you like mountain scenery, this trip is for you. However, the winding highway makes the ride tiring. One way to get around this is to stop overnight at the Lishan House, about a four-hour drive from Taichung. This breaks up the eight-hour trip to the east coast and Hualien, and also enables you to taste some very good Chinese food.

Backtracking a bit we find Sun Moon Lake. Of all the scenic spots in Taiwan, this is perhaps best known, and also the most overrated. Although the lake itself is attractive, its beauty has been marred by commercialization. Still, Sun Moon Lake is a good place for relaxation and rest any season of the year. A small islet emerges in the center of the lake, and is used as a gauge to measure rainfall as it changes in size. As the lake is a natural reservoir of water, its power is utilized by two hydroelectric plants. Rowboats and motor-launches take the visitor on a cruise of the lake, to several renowned Buddhist temples and an aboriginal village. Along the lake shore are several hostels and modern hotels.

Within half an hour's drive from Taichung, in the suburbs of Changhua, stands Pakua Shan, a small hill with spas and a good view of the city of Changhua, the surrounding plain, and to the west, the sea. In 1895, when the Japanese took over Taiwan, this was the scene of a fierce battle that went on for days until all the defenders were killed, and four old cannon remain as a testament to this battle. There is also a large concrete Buddha which stands 72 feet high.

From here it is a quick trip south to Peikang, famous for its Ma Tsu temple, and Chiayi, surrounded by some of Taiwan's most beautiful farm country. The route from Changhua takes you across the Hsilo Bridge, which spans the Choshui River, 6,232 feet wide. It is the longest bridge of its type in Southeast Asia and handles not only motor traffic and pedestrians, but a narrow-gauge train.

Next along the line south is Chiayi. From here, a 30-minute drive will bring you to Wu Feng temple, honoring a 17th-century Chinese official and interpreter of aboriginal affairs. Wu reformed these primitive people and was respected and loved by them. He is now regarded by the aborigines as a saint.

Then uphill trains take you on a seven-hour ride from Chiayi through 50 tunnels to Alishan. The four-hour journey on the old narrow-gauge railway built by the Japanese is thrilling and costs about $4.50. A reserved seat on the quicker Chung Hsing Express is about $9.00, and on the first class, air-conditioned Alishan Express train about $10.50. A highway has recently been opened between Chiayi and Alishan, making it possible to travel by bus between these two points. The Taiwan Bus Company runs buses between Taipei and Alsihan that leave Taipei at 8:30 and 9:30 A.M. The $9.50 ticket price includes the Alishan entrance fee. Buses run from Chiayi to Alishan once an hour. Tickets cost about $2, excluding an entrance fee of $.75 each. At the top, about 9,184 feet, the Alishan guest house offers a good place to stay overnight. A steep climb from Alishan village takes you to Sisters Pond which, in addition to its romantic setting, has a small museum of local wildlife, artifacts, and logging exhibits. There are plenty of mountain paths for hiking, which are particularly colorful in March and April when the wild orchids and cherry trees bloom.

Historic Tainan

Way down south now, we reach Tainan which some people consider the most charming of Taiwan's cities. Without a doubt it is the most interesting, historically. Here you can see the temple dedicated to Koxinga, the patriot who threw the Dutch out. A hall to the rear of the temple honors Koxinga's mother. Then there is Fort Zeelandia, that took the Dutch six years to complete. The foundations still stand, with a newly erected lighthouse surrounded by the ancient cannons of the fort. Another Dutch bastion was their headquarters, Fort Providentia, renamed Chihkan Tower 300 years later. Two buildings, all that is left of a large complex, house some documents and relics of historical interest. The whole city of Tainan can be viewed from the tops of these buildings.

On now to the next and southernmost port city of Kaohsiung. The Love River cuts the city in two. Both banks have been made into public parks. Hsi-tzu Wan nearby has the best beach in southern Taiwan. Cheng Ching Lake, five miles northeast of Kaohsiung, is a pleasant retreat for picnics, or visiting the gardens and aquarium. The lake boasts the famous Bridge of Nine Bends, dragon- and ghost-proof.

Kaohsiung's shipbreaking wharves are one of its major attractions. They are the largest in the world, and a tourist can not only watch the fascinating dismantling process, but also pick up such items as ships' lanterns, wheels and clocks which are for sale.

Off the southern tip of the island is a small isle called Lanyu, or Orchid Island, still relatively unexplored by tourists. It is best known for its orchids and Yami aborigines. The Taiwan Airlines Company flies to Orchid Island from Kaohsiung and Taitung and also has daily flights from Taitung to the extinct volcano Lutao (Green Island) just east of Taitung. TAC will arrange charter flights all around Taiwan, but there must be a minimum of eight people and the flights can be expensive. A relatively inexpensive charter flight flies even farther off the beaten path, to and from the seven-square-kilometer island of Little Ryukyu (Hsiao Liuchiu) which is home to many Buddhists, fishermen, and over thirty temples. Contact TAC (591–4156) for detailed information.

A two-hour drive south of Kaohsiung is Kenting Park, located on the windswept Hengchun Peninsula. The park abounds in rare butterflies and exotic flora and fauna. Nearby are beautiful beaches for swimming and skindiving. Two government guest houses and numerous small hotels operate there, and a luxury hotel will open in early 1986 as part of a project to develop the area into a major resort.

Hualien, a city about halfway down the east coast, has several tourist attractions. It is from here that the excursion through scenic Taroko Gorge (the easternmost segment of the East–West Highway) starts.

Taroko Gorge

The Gorge is one of the great natural wonders of the world. A round-trip from Taipei to the 12-mile-long Taroko Gorge can be made between morning and evening for about $68. The cost of the tour, which is offered daily, includes a round trip by air to Hualien, as well as lunch and attendance at a lively song-and-dance performance by aborigines of the Ami tribe. If visitors wish to make the round-trip to the gorge from Hualien by taxi, the cost is about $30. For those who have time, Tien Hsiang Lodge at the far end of the gorge offers good overnight accommodations and food.

The Pescadores

The Pescadores (Penghu Islands), composed of 64 islands midway off the west coast of Taiwan, are one of Taiwan's few tourist attractions which are not included in any package tour. Situated right on the Tropic of Cancer, the islands are flat, and windswept from October to March. During the summer, however, there is only a mild southwesterly breeze, except for occasional typhoons. Rainfall is light, and because of the wind, any vegetation must be protected by stone walls. Most of the 120,000 inhabitants earn their living from the sea.

Penghu, the largest island of the group, composes about half of the total area, and is connected to Paisha, the third largest, by causeway, which is in turn linked to the second largest, Hsiyu, by a 5½-mile-long bridge, the longest across open seas in the Far East. Beautiful beaches are everywhere.

In addition, this windy archipelago is one of the two places in the world that produce the famous veinstone used in jewelry. If you like coral, moreover, this is the place to find it at bargain rates.

The largest town on the islands, Makung, is connected to Taipei, Taichung, Chiayi, Tainan, and Kaohsiung by air. If your plans include a visit to the south, it would be cheaper to fly from Kaohsiung (one way about $15) than from Taipei (one way about $25). Even more inexpensive (about $5–$11 one way, depending on the type of passage booked) is the ferry between Makung and Kaohsiung, but it takes 4½ hours travel time one way.

Once in Makung, the *Shen Kuo* and the *Pao Hwa* offer overnight accommodations. A double room (with bath) costs $25 or so. Western food on the islands is poor, but, predictably, the seafood is excellent.

PRACTICAL INFORMATION

FACTS AND FIGURES. Population: 19 million. Birth rate per 1,000: 19.51. Life expectancy: 72 years. Average per capita income: US$2,755. Land area: 36,000 sq. kms. Percentage cultivated: 32 percent. Number of tourists (1984): 1,516,138 of whom 180,616 were American.

HOW MUCH WILL IT COST? Taiwan has not been untouched by inflation over the past year, but is still considerably cheaper than her neighbors Japan and Hong Kong, and the traveler from Japan, especially, may be delighted with the comparatively inexpensive accommodations and food. Even lacking the duty-free climate of Hong Kong, local products such as coral and jade jewelry are inexpensive.

Outside of Taipei prices go down even more. Naturally, other major cities such as Taichung, Tainan, Keelung, and Kaohsiung are more expensive than the countryside and smaller towns, although still cheaper than Taipei. It is therefore worth your while not to limit yourself to the Taipei area.

Other than the standard package tours, which are available at all large travel services with little price variation, an inexpensive way to spend a week is hiking in Taiwan's beautiful mountains. One path through the mountains follows the same route as the East–West Cross Island Highway, and takes about 5–7 days. There are youth hostels along the way for cheap bed and board, administered by the China Youth Corps, which is headquartered at 219 Sungchiang Rd., Taipei (tel. 543–5858). There is also a 6-day trip starting in Chiayi. Take the train from Chiayi to Alishan, then to Tungpu, and from there hike to Mount Morrison and back. For other treks, try the areas around hot spring resorts on the east coast.

A Typical Day's Cost

Moderate hotel (per person in a double room. *Not* including breakfast)	NT $1500
Breakfast at moderately priced restaurant	160
Lunch at moderately priced restaurant	300
Dinner at moderately priced restaurant	400
Taxi for 3 kilometers	48
City bus (per district)*	6
Movie or Chinese opera ticket	120
Most popular local brand of cigarettes	22
Taiwan beer in an expensive restaurant	110
Miscellaneous (10% of above sum)	260
	NT$2926

* Air-conditioned city bus cost NT$8 per district.

Other items: one bottle of Shao Hsing wine, the best local rice wine, costs NT$200; an American-style cocktail NT$150; a 295 ml. bottle of Pepsi NT$20; man's haircut NT$200; woman's shampoo NT$300; movie or Chinese opera NT$90; film (Kodak color slides, 36 exp.) NT$220; cup of coffee NT$80; package of American cigarettes from NT$75; and English-language newspaper from NT$25.

Salaries in Taipei are not high. The per capita income for 1984 was around US$3,000. For those not working in a government organization, or in a large company with similar arrangements, the salaries are a little higher.

Food is quite cheap in Taiwan. The exception is beef, most of which is imported, and therefore more expensive. Pork, which is excellent and trichinosis-free, is the most common meat. There are also countless varieties of fish, which are generally cheaper than pork. A large variety of tropical fruit and interesting vegetables are readily available according to the season.

Housing varies in cost as in any other large city. Outside Taipei the housing is much cheaper.

WHEN TO GO? This subtropical island enjoys moderate temperatures in the north, where there is a distinct winter season, and a topcoat is necessary (mid-December to mid-March). If you plan to go on the Cross-Island Highway, or up some of the higher mountains in the central part of the island during these months, a heavier coat is advisable. The south enjoys sunshine nearly every day, and it is a trifle warmer, with no winter. Light summer clothes and autumn suits are comfortable throughout the island. It rains a lot around Keelung and Taipei, so bring an umbrella. Typhoon season is June to October. But fair days alternate with foul in the north; the south is always pleasant.

WHERE TO GO? Taipei is a gray but modernizing city with opportunities to view many aspects of Chinese life and culture. The northern section and suburbs include a zoo, National Palace Museum, the Fine Arts Museum, Shihlin Institute of Horticulture, Peitou Hot Springs, and Yangming Park. South of the Taipei bus–train station and north of Hoping West Rd. are government buildings, the Provincial Museum, the National Museum of History, several parks, the National Science Hall, as well as many shopping areas. Throughout the city are fascinating night markets including the Food Circle (Yuanhuan), Shihlin Market, and Snake Alley. And all over Taipei are Buddhist, Taoist and other temples. The Taipei area offers many day tours: Tamsui, a picturesque fishing village, is the site of a Dutch fort and the earliest British missions; Yangmingshan (Grass Mt.) Park, Peitou; The Lin Family Garden in Panchiao and the National Palace Museum with its world-renowned collection of Chinese art.

About an hour's ride south, near Hsinchu, is Lion's Head Mountain with numerous Buddhist monasteries which accept overnight guests but no cars or other transportation.

The Central Mountain Range and East Coast offer rugged scenery. Sun Moon Lake, Taroko Gorge with its solid marble cliffs, the Chitou Forest Recreation Area and mountain resorts at Lishan and Alishan, in the Alishan Forest Recreation area, are all pleasant refuges. Near Alishan is Mt. Chu; from the observation deck here one can see one of the most spellbinding sights in Taiwan: the Sea of Clouds that rings Yushan, loftiest peak in Northeast Asia.

Also of interest are the islands off the coast of Taiwan, which may be reached by air or water. Off the eastern shore are the Yami aborigines and the orchids of Lanyu (Orchid Island), as well as the extinct volcano of Green Island. To the west, the Pescadores offer warm water for snorkeling and skindiving.

WHAT TO TAKE? Taiwan's climate is subtropical with an average annual temperature of 71.2F (21.7C) in the north and 75.5F (24.1C) in the south. Summer weight clothing is best from April through November. Sweaters and light top-coats are advised from December through March. Sports clothes are acceptable during the day, and informal dress is acceptable after 6 P.M., except in a few Western and more expensive Chinese restaurants, and nightclubs. Raincoat and walking shoes are a must.

ELECTRIC CURRENT. In Taiwan the current is 110 volts, 60 cycles, A.C.

LOCAL FESTIVALS. February 9 on the Western calendar in 1986. *Chinese New Year.* This is the time when work stops, families are reunited, and everyone spends from four days to two weeks enjoying large dinners and visiting friends. The holiday starts the first day of the lunar New Year and ends the 15th.

February 23. *Lantern Festival.* The Lantern Festival on the 15th of the first lunar month ends New Year. To celebrate the winter moon, lanterns of many shapes are made. Lantern festivals abound, and are best seen at the Lungshan Temple.

March 28. *Kuan Yin's Birthday.* Elaborate celebration for the Goddess of Mercy in Taipei's Lungshan Temple.

March 29. *Youth Day.* Parades and ceremonies commemorate the 72 young martyrs who died in the 1911 overthrow of the Manchus.

April 5. *Tomb-sweeping festival and anniversary of death of President Chiang Kai-shek in 1975.* A national holiday.

May 1. *Ma Tsu's birthday.* Since the sea goddess Ma Tsu is the patron saint of Taiwan, her birthday is a great occasion for celebration. Starting one or two weeks before her birthday, people flock to the mid-island towns of Peikang and Lukang which have the oldest Ma Tsu temples on the island. Celebration includes stilt dancers, floats, and dragon dances.

June 11 *Dragon Boat Festival* commemorates the futile attempt of boatmen centuries ago who tried to rescue China's greatest poet, Chu Yuan, from drowning. Legend says that each year since their futile attempt in 221 B.C., the races have been held, gradually becoming more and more elaborate. Despite the growing expense, dragonboat races are still held in Taipei, Kaohsiung, Tainan, Keelung and Chinshan bays.

August 6. *Ghost Festival,* or Feast of the Dead. The seventh full moon each year is the Ghost Festival. Everyone burns paper money in the evening to keep their forefathers financially solvent in the other world.

September 18. *Mid-Autumn Festival* is held one month after the Feast of the Dead. Falling on the eighth full moon, it is also called the Moon Festival. It is a time for family reunions, lavish dinners, seasonal offerings, and above all, the baking and eating of the famous moon cakes.

September 28. *Confucius' Birthday,* or Teachers' Day. All-day ceremonies are held at Confucian Shrines in Taipei and Tainan.

October 10. *Double Ten Day,* the anniversary of the founding of the Republic of China in 1911. Big military reviews, speeches, and athletic meets in Taipei.

October 25. *Taiwan Restoration Day,* commemorating the return of Taiwan to China in 1945 after 50 years of Japanese occupation. More parades in Taipei.

October 31. *Birthday of Chiang Kai-shek (1887).* A national holiday.

November 12. *Birthday of Dr. Sun Yat-sen* (1866), founder of the Republic of China. A national holiday.

HOW TO GET THERE. By Air: *Cathay Pacific, Thai International, Korean,* and *Malaysian Airlines* all have flights from Hong Kong and Japan, with free stopovers in Taipei. Also serving Taipei are *Northwest Orient, Philippine Airlines, Singapore Airlines, Japan Asia Airways, Air Nauru, KLM Royal Dutch Airlines, Pan American, Aloha Airlines,* and *South Africa Airways. China Airlines,* the Republic of China's designated flag carrier, has three trans-Pacific routes, one to San Francisco, one to Los Angeles, and one to New York. They also run several flights a week between Kaohsiung and Hong Kong, besides the regular Taipei route.

The new Taipei international airport at Taoyuan has opened. Located 25 miles south of Taipei, the airport is connected to the city by the new North–South Freeway—a drive of about 40 minutes. A bus into the city costs NT$73; a taxi about NT$1000; hotel limousine NT$100.

By Sea. *Norway American, Costa Cruises,* and *Cunard* have cruises that stop at Taiwan. *American President Lines,* which has container ships with limited cabin space, has services from Taiwan to the West Coast.

PASSPORTS AND VISAS. Persons entering the island must be in possession of a valid passport. Visas are required for any overnight stay. Visas can be obtained easily by nationals of a country recognizing Nationalist China for two weeks (transit visa), or one month, with an option of a one-month extension. Citizens of countries which do not recognize Nationalist China, such as the U.S., Great Britain and Canada, can obtain a visa by either writing or visiting any of Nationalist China's consular offices or nongovernmental organizations around the world. A visa can be obtained on arrival in Taipei if a letter of recommendation from an accredited representative abroad is provided. British citizens, for example, should get such letters from the *Free Chinese Centre,* Dorland House, 14–16 Regent Street, 4th floor, London SWIY, 4PH. Other representatives: *Far East Trading Co.,* 71 Queens Road, 7th floor, Melbourne, Vic., 3004, Australia; *East Asia Trade Center,* 155–161 The Terrace Alley, IBM House, 7th floor, Wellington, New Zealand; *Chung Hwa Travel Service,* 20 Des Voeux Road, Hong Kong; *Association of East Asian Relations,* 3F., 39th Mori Bldg., 4–5, Azabudai 1-Chome, Minato-ku, Tokyo; *Coordination Council for North American Affairs,* 801 Second Ave., New York, New York 10017; *CCNAA,* 300 Montgomery, Suite 535, San Francisco, California 94104. Group tourist permits (minimum of 15 people) are valid for a single visit of up to 2 weeks within 3 months of issue date. Each group must arrive and depart as a whole by the same conveyance. An International Health Card is no longer required upon entry except when the traveler has passed through a cholera-infested area. If traveling with children note that Taiwan has experienced an outbreak of polio, so children should have completed their vaccines.

CUSTOMS regulations are no longer as rigid as they once were, and the visitor may bring in nearly everything he needs for his personal use, such as clothing, toilet articles, etc. One bottle of liquor, 200 cigarettes, or 25 cigars, or 1 pound of tobacco are examples of limits for these personal effects. It is *extremely important* that you declare movie cameras, radios, etc.

CURRENCY. The New Taiwan Dollar is legal tender here. NT$40 equals US$1 (at press time). A foreign currency can be conveniently changed at the CKS Airport, any appointed agency, or branches of the Bank of Taiwan. You may bring in as much foreign currency as you wish, but you must declare all kinds and amounts in order to be able to take it back out. Otherwise, only US$1,000 cash or its equivalent in other foreign currencies can be taken out of the country. A maximum of NT$8,000 is all you can bring *in* or *out* of the country in Chinese currency. Keep all your exchange receipts for departure.

Foreign banks in Taipei include *American Express, Bank of America, Bankers Trust Company, Chase Manhattan, Chemical Bank, Citibank, Continental Bank, Irving Trust Company, Seattle First National Bank, Société General of France, Morgan Guaranty Trust, Manufacturers Hanover Trust, Banque Paribas, Toronto Dominion Bank,* and the *Royal Bank of Canada.*

WATER. Drinking water provided at hotels and restaurants is distilled or boiled.

HOW TO GET AROUND. Trains, buses, and planes are punctual and well run, but there are not enough of them. Buy bus and train tickets one day before departure, preferably through a travel agent or your hotel. Although a little more expensive, this will save you frustration and valuable time. Meter-taxis are available in every major city and are still relatively inexpensive: the first kilometer costs NT$24, and every half-kilometer thereafter, NT$6. Few taxi drivers speak English, so have your destination written down in Chinese.

Most travel agencies offer a selection of special tours to various parts of the island. The prices are about the same. Among these are a 2-day trip to Sun Moon Lake for NT$3,200 per person (assuming you share a double room, a single is more expensive; not including meals), and a 4-day round-island excursion for NT$8600 (same arrangement).

Both *China Airlines (CAL)* and the domestic carrier, *Far Eastern Transport Corporation,* have numerous daily flights from Taipei to both Kaohsiung (one way NT$1,090) and Hualien (one way NT$737). There are also daily flights to Tainan, Taichung, and the Pescadores.

There are a number of trains and buses daily to and from Taipei. The ride to Taichung on the Tzuchiang train (NT$259) takes about 2 hours—to Kaohsiung on the Chu Kuang train (NT$497) is about 5 hours. You can pick up a *Travel Gazette* with train, plane and bus schedules at the Taiwan Tourism Bureau on the 9th floor of 280 Chunghsiao E. Rd., Sec. 4 in Taipei. Remember you can't buy roundtrip tickets! Your return ticket must be purchased either by you or your hotel the day before you intend to leave. Railway stations in Taipei, Taichung and Kaohsiung take phone reservations for the Tzuchiang Express and Chu Kuang Express. The Taipei telephone number is 371–5558.

Kuo Kuang (National Glory) Greyhound buses traverse the North-South Highway from Taipei to Kaohsiung on the southwest coast in 4½ hours for NT$424. Taiwan Highway buses carry passengers over roads all around Taiwan, even in the most remote mountain areas.

Buses operated by the *Taiwan Auto-Transport Company* ply all roads in Taiwan, even those in remote mountain areas. The most spectacular area is the East-West Cross Island Highway which links east and west Taiwan through the great north-south Central Mountain Range.

TIPPING is rare in Taiwan. About the only persons the tourist authorities recommend tipping are those who wait on you directly, such as waiters, room maids, bar boys, barbers, and beauty parlor operators. Ten percent. Porters: NT$20–30 for 1 or 2 bags. Taipei hotels and restaurants add 10 percent service charge. It is not customary to tip taxi drivers.

ACCOMMODATIONS. Taipei has many new hotels. They are listed according to district—starting with the *Grand* in the north and working south through the uptown, *Chungshan,* district. All have an English-speaking staff and Western and/or Chinese dining room. Unless specially noted, hotel restaurants offer nothing special. The large, expensive hotels have standard facilities such as air conditioning, giftshops, tour reservation service and barber and beauty shops. Virtually all hotels have Western coffee shops and most of the larger ones a nightclub as well, usually with live entertainment. Buffets are also fairly standard during the day. Price ranges quoted are for double rooms, singles average about NT$100 less. All rates are on a daily basis; they do not include a 10 percent service charge that will be added to your bill. *Inexpensive:* NT$800–1500; *Moderate: NT$1500–3000. First Class:* NT$3000–4000. *Deluxe:* over NT$4000.

TAIPEI

Chungshan North Road

First Class

Ambassador. 500 rooms. The Szechuan restaurant on the 12th floor is one of the best in Taipei, and offers a good view of the city, as does the cocktail lounge on the same floor. The International Room on the second floor is a good place for Cantonese snacks from 8 A.M. to 2 P.M., and doubles as a nightclub from 8 P.M. to 12 midnight, with floorshows and dancing. Largely Japanese guests. Pool.

Grand. 576 rooms. On a hill at the north end of Chungshan N. Rd., it is the choice of the government for their VIP guests. The three old wings, a replica of the Imperial Palace in Beijing, have now been over-shadowed by a new addition of rooms in the "pregnant pagoda" combination of Western structure and Chinese decoration. Much of the charm has gone. It has one of the best Western dining rooms, another one serving good Cantonese snacks, and a tea room serving northern snacks. The recreation club offers a swimming pool, bowling alley, and tennis courts.

Imperial. 600 Linshen N. Rd. 392 rooms. Accommodations in old or newer wing. Good Cantonese and Japanese food.

President. 423 rooms. 9 Teh Hwei St. Popular with Western businessmen. Its nightclub, the *Champagne Room,* is also a great favorite of visitors to the city.

Royal Taipei. 201 rooms. Smaller, elegant hotel opened in 1984 under Japanese management.

Taipei Fortuna. 304 rooms. Older hotel, recently renovated and brought under attentive new management.

Moderate

Empress. 68 rooms. Near the President and Imperial. Modern and well managed.

Olympic. 200 rooms. Right next to the Majestic.

Inexpensive.

Majestic. 421 rooms. At the corner of Chungshan N. and Minchuan E. Rds., one of the main intersections of uptown. The Elite coffee shop is a convenient meeting place. Mostly Japanese clientele. Good breakfast buffet with a fine view.

Uptown, Chungshan District

Deluxe

Asiaworld. Nanking E. and Tun Hwa N. Rds. New, large hotel with restaurants and bars, atrium lobby, shopping arcade and health club.

First Class

Taipei Ritz. 218 rooms. On Minchuan E. Rd. Boasts an excellent French restaurant, Paris 1930. Decorated in French art deco throughout; English movies; health club.

Brother. 292 rooms. Located on Nanking East Rd. The Western food is standard but good. Very pleasant coffee shop which has a sidewalk-café atmosphere. Excellent Taiwanese restaurant.

Moderate

Gloria. 250 rooms. On Linshung N. Rd., which runs parallel to Chungshan N. Rd. one block east of it. Caters mainly to Japanese tour groups. Recently underwent expansion and renovation.

Leofoo. 168 Chang Chun Rd. 237 rooms. "The Inn of the Sixth Happiness," like the Grand's new addition, it has Chinese "icing" but modern interior.

Mandarin. 350 rooms. Near the domestic airport in new business district. Thai facade and public rooms with a flavor akin to Singapore's Tiger Balm Gardens and Hong Kong's Aw Boom Haw Gardens. Tennis courts and indoor swimming pool. Restaurants include a Mongolian barbecue.

Inexpensive

Taipei Miramar. Minchuan E. Rd. Large hotel with Chinese, Japanese, Western restaurants. Swimming pool, sauna.

First. 202 rooms. Modernized and well managed. On Nanking East Rd. in a lively commercial district. The Hillman Discotheque has guest performers and is popular with the younger set.

Downtown (South of Taipei Station)

Deluxe

Lai Lai Sheraton. 687 rooms. On Chunghsiao E. Rd., near the city's government and financial centers. Ten gourmet restaurants featuring various cuisines. Super-modern convention facilities, pool, disco, and health club.

Taipei Hilton. 527 rooms. Across the street from the Taipei train station. A central meeting place for foreign residents of Taipei. Trader's Grill serves standard Hilton U.S. beef. La Pizzeria offers complete Italian cuisine. Tiffany's provides Cantonese *dim sum* at lunch and a disco every night from 9 to 12. Sauna. Good Sunday brunch.

Inexpensive

China. 153 rooms. Directly across from the station. Mostly Japanese and overseas Chinese visitors. Superb Hunan restaurant.

Flowers. 280 rooms. The basement restaurant and bar has an electric organ at night, and is popular with Taipei's young office workers.

Hsimenting (West Gate)

Moderate

Century Plaza. 250 rooms. One block from the Western edge of Hsimenting. Roof garden.

Southeast

First Class

Beverly Plaza. 118 units, all suites. Friendly atmosphere. Three restaurants, including good Italian cuisine at Fellini's.

Howard Plaza. 606 rooms. Located on Jen Ai Rd. in pleasant residential-commercial neighborhood. Six restaurants, swimming pool, health center, conference hall, 4-story shopping arcade, and large parking lot. One of Taipei's newest hotels.

San Polo. 407 rooms. Restaurants, coffee shop, bar. Near the Sun Yat-sen Memorial Hall.

United. 250 rooms. Located near the Sun Yat-sen Memorial Hall. Three restaurants; convention and banquet facilities.

Inexpensive

International House. On Hsinyi Rd., at the intersection of Hsinsheng S. Rd. Mostly a men's dorm, but it has a few rooms open to women and married couples also. It is usually full of students, so reserve.

Taipei International Youth Activity Center (TIYAC). A large dormitory for Chinese and international students. Has cheap rooms for transients. Dining facilities.

Yangmingshan (Grass Mountain)

Inexpensive

China Yangmingshan. 50 rooms. Out of the hustle and bustle of the city. Hunan restaurant. Hot sulfur baths, and a good outdoor swimming pool.

Taoyuan

Moderate–Expensive

Holiday Hotel. 269 Dashing Rd. Near airport outside Taipei. Restaurants, conference rooms, swimming pool, fish pond, shopping arcades.

Moderate

CKS Airport Hotel. 526 rooms. At the airport, run by Civil Aeronautics Administration. Tennis courts and practice golf range.

CENTRAL TAIWAN

Alishan

Inexpensive: **Alishan House.** 54 rooms. Inexpensive but comfortable. To reach this mountain retreat requires a 4-hour train ride on single-gauge tracks through spectacular scenery or a shorter bus ride. Japanese-style rooms and group chambers available.

Hualien

First Class: **Marshall Hotel.** 346 rooms. Meeting and banquet rooms. Pool, sauna, golf.

Moderate: **Astar.** 170 rooms. Faces the ocean on one side and the mountains on the other. A very convenient stopover if you're going on to the Taroko Gorge and Tien Hsiang. Pool, garden, and bowling alley.

Li Shan

Moderate: **Li Shan Guest House.** 60 rooms. The halfway point on the East–West Highway. Palace-style architecture. Set against a mountainside that is the apple and pear raising center in Taiwan. Excellent dining room. Pool and bowling.

Sun Moon Lake

Moderate: **Evergreen.** 120 rooms. Cocktail lounge with a beautiful view on the top floor. Located on a hill high above a village overlooking the lake. Quiet surroundings. An oldtime favorite among Taiwan's resort hotels.

Sun Moon Lake. 116 rooms overlooking the water. Restaurant, bar, and coffee shop. 9-hole golf course and pool.

Teachers' Hostel. Near the Evergreen. Distinguished by exclusive use of local building materials and products. Has a swimming pool (indifferent maintenance) and tennis court. Bath and room partitions often open at the top but noise is controlled by a 10 P.M. curfew.

Taichung

First Class. **National.** 320 rooms. 5 minutes from the freeway.

Moderate. **Taichung.** 124 rooms. Western and Chinese food.

Inexpensive. **Apollo.** 127 rooms. Very popular. Right in the center of town.

Taroko Gorge

Inexpensive. **Tien Hsiang Lodge.** 40 rooms. A peaceful mountain refuge at the western end of the gorge. Your travel agent can arrange transportation to and from Hualien.

SOUTHERN TAIWAN

Kaohsiung

First Class. **Ambassador.** 457 rooms. On Min Sheng 2nd Rd. New deluxe hotel with convention and banquet halls, a night club, shopping arcade, pool, sauna, garden.

Kingdom. 302 rooms. Harbor view, attentive management, convenient for shopping. Good restaurants.

Moderate. **Holiday Garden.** 313 rooms. Free transportation to and from the airport. Shanghainese and Western dining rooms. Chinese decor. Pool, bar, and nightclub.

Kaohsiung Grand. 108 rooms. Out of the way and deserted. Same management, elegance, comfort, and service as Taipei's *Grand.* Overlooking Cheng Ching Lake, 6 miles from the city.

Oluanpi

Inexpenive. **Kenting Guest House.** 71 rooms. Near Kenting Park (see *Exploring Taiwan*). Eight motel rooms are right on a magnificent isolated beach. An extension of the Guest House perches on the hill behind, luxurious with spectacular view. Western and Chinese food.

Tainan

Inexpensive. **Tainan.** 151 rooms. Across from the railroad station. Pool, nightclub, and restaurant.

TOURS. The travel agents most frequently used by English-speaking tourists to make hotel reservations, buy tickets and arrange tours are the *China Travel Service* (551–5933) at 56 Linsen N. Rd. (affiliated with *Tai Travel* in L.A., 800–421–8908) and the *Shangri-La Tour and Travel Service* (591–1111) at 626 Linsen N. Rd., President Building, 4th floor. Both of these companies, as well as hotels, can arrange tours of Taipei. The most popular is the city tour, which includes temples and the National Palace Museum. It costs about NT$450 and lasts 3½ hours or more. Tours of industry or farms are available upon request. There is a 4-hour trip to the aborigine village of Wulai near Taipei, but many tourists find it commercialized. Another way to visit aborigines is to take the day trip to Taroko Gorge. This includes a stop to see aborigine dancing. Travel agents can also arrange reservations at Taiwan's mountain and seaside lodges.

SPORTS. The sports-minded tourist in Taiwan can **bowl,** play **golf, tennis,** or **ping-pong, swim, rollerskate** or **ice skate, fish,** or enjoy the best mountain climbing in Southeast Asia. Bowling is the most popular indoor sport in Taipei. Among the many alleys with modern facilities are the *Yuan Shan Bowling Center* at 6 Chungshan N. Rd., Sec. 5 and the *Jen Ai Bowling Center* at 466 Tunhua S. Rd. For golfers, the *Taiwan Golf and Country Club* reputedly has the finest course in Southeast Asia. Located in Tamsui, about 30 minutes from Taipei by taxi, the club is open to non-members, providing they limit their play to before 10 A.M. Green fees are NT$1300. You must be accompanied by a member on Sundays. Other golf courses include the *Peituo Kuo Hua Golf and Country Club* and the *Kaohsiung Country Club.* There are 17 public golf courses in Taiwan. For swimming enthusiasts, beaches on the north are open between May and September. *Chin Shan* is the most popular public beach, but is usually packed. *Fulung Beach,* 2 hours from Taipei on the Suao railroad line, is much nicer. Beaches in the south are more beautiful, cleaner, and less crowded than in the north. *Oluanpi* is particularly outstanding. Public pools within Taipei, though multiplying rapidly, are usually crowded. The best bet is a hotel pool. The Yangming Park pool is quite nice. For tennis, courts can be found at most universities and colleges, some hotels, and at the *International House,* 18 Hsinyi Rd., Sec. 3. Badminton can be played at 10 Nanking East Rd., Sec. 4.

POLLUTION REPORT. For years the prevailing attitude was that pollution control was less urgent than industrial development. But with the rise in living standards in recent years, both the government and public have gradually become more concerned with environmental problems. A government agency, the Bureau of Environmental Protection, is tightening up on enforcement of existing regulations and proposing new ones.

Despite the improvements, one can still come across factory smokestacks belching black fumes into the air, and the rivers that flow through highly populated areas are badly polluted with sewage and industrial waste. In some areas, private individuals add to the problem by burning garbage or dumping it haphazardly.

In the absence of strict vehicular emission controls, the main problem in the cities is the large number of buses, cars and motorcycles. Only after a rain or steady wind does the smog lift and blue skies appear.

Noise pollution in the cities, from car horns and construction, is also severe.

MUSEUMS. The new *Fine Arts Museum,* the largest of its kind in Southeast Asia, should not be missed. It is located at 181 Chung Shan N. Rd., Sec. 3, and is open daily except Mondays. Admission is NT$10. In the suburbs is the *National Palace Museum,* which has one of the best collections of Chinese scrolls, porcelain, jade and bronze in the world. Open from 9 A.M. to 5 P.M. daily, the museum offers English-language tours at 10 A.M. and 3 P.M. Admission is NT$20. *The National Museum of History,* 49 Nan Hai Rd., also has a good collection; and the *Taiwan Provincial Museum,* 2 Hsiang Yang Rd., houses an interesting selection of Taiwan aboriginal artifacts.

SHOPPING. Taiwan is coming into its own, shopping-wise, although it can't compare with Tokyo or Hong Kong. The major problem is getting where you want to go, since it is important to include the section number in the address. Since the numbering starts from the beginning in each section, it is possible to arrive at the correct street number but wrong place if your taxi goes to Section 1 rather than Section 3, and most taxi drivers don't speak English. The easiest way to get around is to make a list of where you want to go and then show that to your hotel clerk. He will be happy to write down the names and addresses in Chinese, and you can give these directions to your taxi driver.

The range of ceramics, handicrafts and curios for sale in Taipei is vast. Many things are moderately priced, but bargaining is expected except in the larger department stores. Shop-owners can be expected to take off at least a third or half if the tourist is not afraid to bargain. A timesaver is a trip to the *Taiwan Handicraft Mart,* 1 Hsuchow Rd., although if you buy the same item in the Chunghua arcade you can generally bargain the price down further. Even nicer is the *Taiwan Crafts Center,* 7th floor, 110 Yenping South Rd. in downtown Taipei. A larger variety of quality jewelry, furniture, metalware, among other goods are nicely displayed there.

Bamboo is abundant in Taiwan and you will find items range from toothpicks to rattan furniture. Go to Shihlin, a suburb of Taipei, for marvelous rattan items.

Sea Grass, found growing in the coastal area, is plaited and made into the same Formosan Sea Grass mats many a visitor has on his floor back home. This material is also used for many styles of hats, handbags, and slippers.

Coral, Veinstone, and **Taiwan Jade.** The sea girding Taiwan abounds in coral, which is of excellent grade and expensive. There is everything from tiny buttons to large Chinese figures, all beautifully handcarved. Veinstones from the outlying Pescadores Islands, reputed to be one of the two places in the world where these stones are commercialized, make unusual and lovely gifts. Inexpensive, but elegant looking, the stones are fashioned into bracelets, rings and necklaces. Taiwan jade and marble products are also earning worldwide recognition for their beauty. While coral and jade jewelry stores are well scattered all over the city, many are concentrated along Hengyang Rd., Chungshan N. Rd., and Nanking E. Rd., Sec. 3 (especially Lane 89, Alley 3).

Dolls. Enchanting figures out of the past and present are ideal for a little girl's collection or display. Dressed in every fashion from palace to farm, they come in all sizes, shapes, and forms.

Palace Lanterns are a reminder of the days when China was an empire. The first palace lanterns appeared during the Han Dynasty (206 B.C. to A.D. 200) and these sold on Taiwan today are almost identical. Usually made of wooden or horn frames covered with silk, they are hand-painted with scenes symbolic of the grandeur of old Cathay.

The above-mentioned handicrafts can be found at handicraft stores all along Chungshan N. Rd. Try *Haggler's Alley* on Chunghua Rd. near North Gate for wonderful Taiwanese puppets and colorful remnants from Buddhist temples.

Furniture. Teak abounds in Taiwan but be sure to check whether furniture has been kiln-dried to prevent splitting, if you want to ship it to a less humid climate. Best bets: *Unicorn Artwares Ltd.,* 65 Lane 65, Da-yeh Rd., for unique furniture designed around old temple carvings; or try *Ricardo Lynn & Co.,* 1–9 Chungshan N. Rd., Sec. 6, Shihlin.

Ceramics. One of China's oldest arts was recently revived by a group of young artists who blend modern techniques with the ancient. The stoneware that resulted can now be found in the ceramic shops slong Chungshan N. Road. Sec. 2 and 3. Another place selling more conventional lines of pottery is *China Pottery and Porcelain Arts Co.,* 69 Nanking East Rd., Sec. 2. If you would like to see these articles made, visit their factory at 14 Central S. Rd., Sec. 2, Peitou, and enjoy their adjoining museum.

Brass, like silver, is something not to be overlooked. Ashtrays, dinner bells, wall planters, huge copies of ancient Chinese coins, to name but a few of the items, are found in many of the souvenir shops. Also available are lanterns and other fixtures from dismantled ships.

Rugs. Taiwan is the only place in the world where ramie fibers are woven into rugs, handbags, placemats, etc., and the result is lovely. Traditional Chinese wool carpets following the old Tientsin patterns can also be bought in Taipei. They can also be made from your own design, if you want. *Veteran Rug & Blanket Manufactory, VACRS,* 31 Chungshan N. Rd., Sec. 2, *Lioho Rug Corp.,* 105 Peihsin Rd., Sec. 2, Hsintien, and *Lovely Rug Mfg. Co.,* 147 Sungchiang Rd., are recommended. Many other rug stores are located along Chungshan N. Rd.

Shoes, handmade of snakeskin, are great buys. Taiwan has a large variety of reptiles, and puts them to good use. You may also have matching purse and belts made at the same time. Good shops can be found along Chungshan N. Rd., Sec. 1, and many other sections of the city.

Fabric. The silks and damasks traditionally used for Chinese chipaos can be found at *Hung Hsiang Department Store,* 122 Po Ai Rd., and *Hsiang Tai Silk and Cotton Piece Goods Store,* 63–65 Hengyang Rd. These two streets are the center of yard goods sales, so you will find many other good shops there besides the ones recommended. If you are interested in brocades two manufacturers, *Dah Tong* and *Siang Tai,* have sales outlets in the outlying town of Taishan.

Chops. These decorative little sticks of ivory, wood or marble are used by Chinese to affix the characters of their names, much the way Westerners once used signet rings. You can either have your Western name carved on a chop, or ask for a Chinese equivalent. The stores along Chungshan North Rd. have a large variety, but the place where the Chinese themselves go is Hengyang Rd.

Antiques. Watch out! But if you insist, try the antique stores on Chungshan N. Rd., Sec. 2, right around the Ambassador Hotel. If you are really adventurous poke around in *Haggler's Alley,* a row of antique and junk shops located all along Chunghua Rd., but especially on the third floor of building one. Custom regulations do not allow valuable antiques to leave the country. A wiser alternative is to purchase reproductions.

Packing and Shipping. The Central Post Office has a wrapping service that is convenient and fairly inexpensive. Take whatever you want sent, any extra cushioning material, and a magic marker, go in the large side door on Po Ai Rd., and there will be signs directing you. They have a range of different-sized boxes there and will bind the package with light metal stripping. You can thus pack everything and have it checked by Customs all at once.

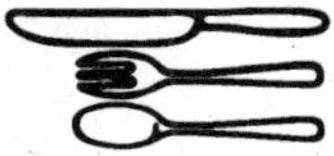

TAIPEI RESTAURANTS. If anything equals the scenic beauty in Taiwan, it is the island's Chinese food. Taipei is an ideal spot to experience a gourmet's voyage of discovery. Because of the influx of mainland Chinese after the Second World War, the island has every kind of Chinese food imaginable. Expect a 10 percent service charge to be added to most bills. *Deluxe,* NT$600 on up; *First Class,* NT$300–600; *Moderate,* NT$150–400; *Inexpensive,* under NT$150. The usual custom is to order at least as many dishes as the number of persons served. It is advisable, whenever possible, for visitors unfamiliar with Chinese food to be accompanied to non-hotel restaurants by a Chinese friend or tourist guide. Tipping is optional. Only some of the bigger non-hotel Chinese restaurants accept credit cards. Restaurants close early and most diners arrive before 6:30 P.M.

SZECHUAN

Hot spicy dishes based on red chili pepper and garlic. They often make Mexican food seem bland, so the phrases *bu la* and *ching hung,* both meaning not so hot, are useful. Hot foods: Mother Ma's bean curd, eggplant with garlic sauce, palace-style *gung bao* chicken, twice-cooked pork. Not-so-hot: *bon bon* chicken, camphor tea-smoked duck, dry-cooked string beans. A pleasant change from rice are the steamed and fried breads and pancakes.

First Class

Lien An Restaurant. 425 Tunhwa S. Rd. Has a good reputation and quick service.

Rong Shing. 45 Chilin Rd. The biggest and the best. Even though it is large, service and food excellent.

Moderate

Fortune Restaurant. 160 Chunghsiao E. Rd., Sec. 4. Recommended.

Kuo Ting. 25 Nanking E. Rd., Sec. 3. Very popular at lunchtime. Their special dishes are liberally spiced. Try fish in red sauce.

PEIPING

Mild dishes combining roast meat, vegetables, and flat pancake wrappers. Most famous is Peking Duck (remember that one is more than enough for 4 people), also live carp cooked three ways, and eel in pepper sauce.

First Class

Tao Jan Ting. 16 Chunghsiao E. Rd., Sec. 4, Lane 49, Alley 4. Excellent atmosphere and meticulously prepared food.

Moderate

Celestial. 1 Nanking W. Rd., 3rd floor. Avoid the standard Peiping fare and try some of the special dishes, which are seldom found elsewhere in town.

Real Peiping. 37 Chunghua Rd., Bldg. 6, 2nd floor. (Just south of the circle.) Plain décor, but excellent duck, and smiling service. Inquire about prices though; they are not always marked on the menu.

HUNAN

Hunan has both spicy foods and steamed dishes. Steamed ham with honey sauce, chicken "à la viceroy" (Duke Tso chicken), mushrooms and bamboo shoots, minced pigeon in bamboo cups, and steamed silver thread rolls are all fantastic delights.

First Class

Les Copains de Chine. In the Taipei Ritz Hotel. Excellent cuisine in the true spirit of Hunan.

Moderate

Treasure House. 152 Sungchiang Rd., 3rd floor. Recommended.

SHANGHAI

Mostly seafood dishes with rich, somewhat salty sauces. "Drunken" chicken, bean curd pork, Ningpo-style fried eel, West Lake fish, green cabbage hearts with dried mushrooms, and shark's fin soup.

Deluxe

Asiaworld Shanghai Castle. Luxurious restaurant in new luxury hotel. Asiaworld, 337 Nanking E. Rd., Sec. 3.

Shangri-La Garden. Located at the Lai Lai Sheraton Hotel on Chunghsiao E. Rd. First-class elegant dining.

First Class

Chu Feng Yuan. 46 Kuanchien Rd. Luxurious and has excellent service.

Sunny Garden. 92 Nanking E. Rd., Sec. 1. Good service and excellent seafood dishes.

CANTONESE

More colorful and sweeter than the other schools of cooking. Its more mundane forms are what passes for Chinese food in the U.S. Fried shrimp with cashews (often listed on menus as "walnuts"), onion-marinated chicken, beef with oyster sauce, and sweet-and-sour pork are the best dishes.

Expensive

Fung Lum. 72 Linsen N. Rd. Topnotch restaurant. Tasteful décor, and a friendly atmosphere.

Moderate

An Lok Yuan. 232 Tunhua N. Rd. One of the best. Food and service are both always dependable.

Mei Hwa. Second floor of the *Brother Hotel,* 255 Nanking E. Rd., Sec. 3. Reputed for its *dim sum,* served from 8 A.M. to 9 P.M.

TAIWANESE

The native food here. Mostly seafood with thick sauces. It relies on garlic in the north; in the south, on soy sauce. Seafood is superb. Spring rolls (with crushed peanuts), sweet-and-sour spareribs, bean curd in red sauce, oyster omelette.

Moderate

Flour Meal of Tainan. 31 Hwa Hsi St. Seafood is the freshest, kept alive in tanks and on ice-blocks.

Hong Lin. 36 Poai Rd., 2nd floor. If you are interested in getting a good vegetarian meal cooked Taiwanese style, Hong Lin offers more variety and creativity than most vegetarian restaurants in Taipei.

Mei Tzu. 5 Linsen N. Rd., Lane 107. Good food in a casual atmosphere. Popular with the younger set because it is frequented by movie stars.

Taiwan Shiao Diao. 71 Chungshan N. Rd., Sec. 2, 9th fl. Famous for food and old-style Taiwanese decor. Live Chinese folk music at mealtimes. Honeyed chicken with black dates is especially good.

Inexpensive

Wan Hua (Lung Shan Arcade). Across from the Lung Shan Temple, this, plus Huahsi St., sells about every type of food imaginable—and then some! Popular for firepot in the winter; draft beer in the summer. Although the cleanliness leaves something to be desired and virtually no English is spoken, the adventurous can avoid the "Taipei trots" if they stick to sign language, the cleaner stands, and just-cooked food.

MONGOLIAN

Popular with the "do-it-yourselfers" and those who feel they can beat the "all you can eat for NT$220" crowd. Only 2 basic dishes exist: firepot, which is similar to Japanese *sukiyaki,* but is not sweet and is dipped in a sauce based on sesame paste, shrimp oil, ginger juice and bean paste; and barbecue. The second one starts with various thinly sliced meats and vegetables on which you put condiments and give to a chef to cook on a big iron grill. Then you stuff the mix in a sesame bun.

Moderate

Genghis Khan. 176 Nanking East Road, Sec. 3. The most famous and the biggest. Popular with Westerners and tours. There are three big grills outside.

Great Wall. 1 Linsen S. Rd. Less well known to foreigners, but the choice of many Chinese. Cheaper than the Genghis Khan.

SNACKS

A wide variety. The places mentioned are clean, but since they are so popular, they don't offer a very relaxed setting. Neither are they fancy. Expect "erratic English." Basic dishes are *gwo-tieh,* a fried meat and vegetable roll, *jyaudz,* a meat dumpling, and beef or pork-chop noodles. All snack places are inexpensive.

Acme Co. Ltd. 71 Chunghsiao E. Rd., Sec. 4. French bread, curry turnovers, and baked goods.

Du Yi Chu. 53 Wuchang St., Sec. 2. Delicious *syan bing,* or *shao bing,* two northern snacks.

Evergreen (Hojo's). Behind the Oasis Hotel. *Jyaudz* and green peppers with beef.

Old Fatty Chou's. 53 Hanchung St. The best *gwotieh* in town.

Ruby. 135 Chungshan N. Rd., Sec. 2. The best place for Cantonese *dim sum,* or snacks, from 8 A.M. to 5 P.M.

WESTERN

Taipei has a number of Western restaurants, mainly steak houses, and all expensive. A *Kobe* steak may cost up to NT$850, but most are around NT$350. Don't expect steaks served in the typical U.S. steakhouse manner, however. The cooking methods and the spices are different, and the result is an appetizing variation. Most steak houses include an appetizer soup, salad, a few vegetables, and coffee in the price of the steak. Western restaurants tend to be dressier than Chinese restaurants on the whole.

Deluxe

Europa Haus. 21 Changan E. Rd., Sec. 1. Offering a wide selection of otherwise "rare foods" in Taipei. Excellent buffet.

Mediterranean. Nanking E. Rd., Sec. 1, Lane 13, Alley 7, No. 1–1. Features Portuguese cooking but also offers dishes from Spain, Greece and Yugoslavia.

Paris 1930. Ritz Hotel, 2nd fl. French food in plush surroundings; attentive service.

First Class

Fellini's. In the Beverly Plaza Hotel, 576 Tunhwa S. Rd. An Italian restaurant that even the Italians in Taipei recommend.

Ploughman's Pub. 9 Shuangcheng St., Lane 25. It's like stepping straight into England. Great place for meeting and making friends. Good food. Excellent steak and kidney pie. Draught beer and darts. Its sister restaurant, Ploughman's Cottage, located at 305 Nanking E. Rd., Sec. 3, offers the same quality food.

JAPANESE

Japanese food is less expensive in Taipei than in Japan. The preparation is authentic, due to Taiwan's historical contact with Japan and the large number of Japanese tourists.

The best Japanese restaurants are the *New Hama* at 10 Nungan St., and the *Tsu-ten Kaku* at 8 Chungshan N. Rd., Sec. 1, Lane 53, which is a little less expensive.

OTHER CUISINES

First Class

Gaylord's. 328 Sungchiang Rd., Taipei's first authentic Indian restaurant. Luxurious decor and excellent service.

Moderate

Bali. Upstairs above Taipei Theater at 118–17 Wuchang St., Sec. 2. Delicious Indonesian cuisine in tasty sauces, for an interesting change from Chinese food.

Seoul Korean Barbeque. 4 Chungshan N. Rd. Sec. 1, Lane 33. Korean barbecue, which is different from the Mongolian variety. The sauce is spicier, and the meat is cooked right at your table.

Jen Ho Yuan. 16 Nanking E. Rd., Sec. 4, 2nd Fl. Yunnan food which is in a category by itself when it comes to Chinese cuisine.

NIGHT LIFE. Authorities claim that no one need fear being out at any time. Taipei isn't known for its lively nights except for single men. The major "girlie" area is in the back alleys off Chungshan between Minchuan Rd. and Mintsu Rd. "Bar" girls are for sale, and, unless you are in the market, you aren't welcome. "Clubs" vary from undercover "bars" to cocktail lounges where the hostesses are nice college girls. Nothing to recommend any of them, but the best kept-up ones are around the President Hotel. Taxi dance halls: the *MGM, Singapore,* and *International;* and wine houses: the *Queen, Pai Yu Lou, Tung Yun Ko,* and *Mayflower* all have some girls who speak erratic English.

If you already have a partner, much less selection exists. The *Champagne Room* in the President, the *Dynasty* in the Hilton, the *Mahbuhay* in the Imperial, and the *Discothèque* in the First all have dancing and dining. The Mahbuhay and the Disco alternate rock and slow bands.

Theater restaurants such as the *Hoover* and *First* offer variety shows featuring Chinese singers and acrobats. All have a cover or minimum ranging from NT$160 to NT$400, not including 30 percent tax and service charge.

For off-beat entertainment, try a sword movie, or visit the night market near Lungshan Temple in Taipei S.W.

Another idea is to go see Peking opera *ching hsi.* There is a show daily at 7:30 P.M. at the *Armed Forces Cultural Activities Center,* 69 Chunghua Rd., southeast of the circle. Tickets are US$4–10 apiece. Saturday *ching hsi* matinees are staged at 2 P.M. in the Sun Yat-sen Memorial Hall at the corner of Jenai and Kuangfu S. Rd. This hall also presents exhibits and a wide variety of other performances such as theater, music and dance. *The New Aspect International Arts Festival* is held from February to April.

MAIL. Post offices are usually open from 8 A.M. to 6 P.M. except Sundays, when they close at noon. The *Taipei General Post Office* remains open until 10 P.M. daily. Airmail letters to any country outside Asia cost NT$18 for 10 grams and NT$7 for each additional 10 grams thereafter. Postcards are NT$9 and aerograms NT$12.

TEA. The traditional tea ceremony can be sampled at the *Lu Yu Tea Center* at 64 Heng-Yang Rd., 2nd fl., at the *Cha Tao Tea Shop* at 229 Min-Chuan East Rd., and at the *Wisteria Tea House* at 1 Hsin-Shen S. Rd., Lane 16, Sec. 3.

TELEPHONE AND TELEGRAPH. Overseas phone calls or telexes can be placed through your hotel, of course, or through the *Chinese Government Radio Administration Office* at 118 Chunghsiao W. Rd., Sec. 1 (tel. 344–3779 or 344–3781), or any of its branches. The Overseas Operator may be reached on a private phone by dialing "100." One NT dollar coin will give you 3 minutes. The English-language information operator is at 311–6796.

MEDICAL SERVICES. *Central Clinic,* 77 Chunghsiao E. Rd., Sec. 4, Taipei (tel. 751–0221); *Country Hospital,* 61 Jen Ai Rd., Sec. 4, Taipei (tel. 771–3161); *MacKay Memorial Hospital,* 92 Chungshan N. Rd., Sec. 2, Taipei (tel. 543–3535); *Veterans General Hospital,* 201 Shihpai Rd., Sec. 2, Tienmu (English information 871–2121, ext. 3530).

USEFUL ADDRESSES. Embassies and Consulates. United States American Institute in Taiwan at 7 Hsinyi Rd., Sec. 3, Lane 134 (tel. 709–2000); South Africa, 205 Tunhua Rd., 13th floor (tel. 715-3251). There is no U.K. consulate in Taiwan. If you have problems check with your airline or the police.

General Information. *Taiwan Visitors Association,* 111 Minchuan East Rd., 5th floor (tel. 594–3261); *Taiwan Tourism Bureau,* 280 Chunghsiao E. Rd., Sec. 4, 9th floor (tel. 721–8541).

Emergencies. For police, call 110; fire, 119.

FIVE-MINUTE MANDARIN

Unlike the Chinese populace of Hong Kong, who are for the most part natives of the bordering province of Kwantung and therefore speak the Cantonese dialect, the officials of the Nationalist Government of China on Taiwan are encouraging the use of Mandarin. Originally the language for officials (hence its name), Mandarin is now known as National Speech, or Ordinary Speech.

Mandarin is based on the dialect spoken in Beijing, but without that city's regionalisms. With slight modifications, it is spoken by the vast majority of Chinese from Manchuria to Szechuan. Coastal dialects such as Taiwanese (a slightly modified form of a dialect used in Fukien) and Cantonese, however, are related to Mandarin, roughly the way German is to English or French to Italian.

The government of the Republic of China on Taiwan has encouraged the teaching of Mandarin in the schools, and therefore, in addition to the Chinese who moved to Taiwan from the mainland in 1949, most Taiwanese under the age of 50 now speak Mandarin. Older Taiwanese will usually be more fluent in Japanese than in Mandarin, however.

Although all Chinese dialects are tonal (some having up to 11 tones), the spellings below do not take the tones into consideration. The context of your conversation will usually make your meaning clear. In difficult conversations, the tones become more and more important, and in expressing complicated thoughts, even the tones will not always serve the purpose, and resort to the written ideograph is frequently necessary. Writing out the word is often done between natives of different regions in China who pronounce one written word in two completely separate ways; if the two know English, as is frequently the case in such places as Hong Kong and Singapore, they may resolve their difficulty by using that language. Do not be surprised, therefore, if words which sound the same have different meanings; some sounds have several meanings. The word for *money* in Mandarin, for example, differs from *thousand* only in tone, the pitch used in pronouncing the words.

English	*Mandarin*
	Pronunciation Guide
Airport	fay gee gee (soft g) chahng
Railroad station	hwaw (as in l*aw*) chuh (as in *chu*rl) jan (as in *John*)
Hotel	fahn dyen
Where?	nah lee
Which way?	dzemmah dzou (ou as in *toe*)
Where is?	dzai (*xy*lophone, with an initial *dz*) nah lee
Right	yo (as in *yo*ke)

Left	dzaw (as in l*aw*)
Straight	ee jih (as in *Ji*m) dzou
Stop	ting
Restaurant	tsahn ting
Where is the toilet?	shee shou (as in *show*) jyen dzai nah lee
Thank you	syeh syeh ni (as in *knee*)
You're welcome	boo syeh
Good morning	dzau (as in *ou*ch with an initial *dz*)
How are you?	ni *how* mah
Goodbye	dzai jyen
How much? (money)	daw (as in l*aw*) show (as in *shower*) chyen
I	waw (as in l*aw*)
You	ni
To buy	mai (as in *my*)
To drink	hu (as in *hu*rt)
To eat	chr (as in *chir*p)
Water	shwei (*shoe-ei*ght)
Tea	cha (as in *cha*-cha)
One	ee
Two	*are*
Three	san (an as in *on*)
Four	sz (as in *cer*tainly)
Five	*woo*
Six	lee-o (as in *row*)
Seven	chee (as in *cheat*)
Eight	bah
Nine	jyo (as in go)
Ten	shr (as in *shir*t)
Eleven	shr-ee (ten plus one)
Twenty	*are* shr (two tens)
One hundred	ee *buy*
One thousand	ee chyen
Ten thousand	ee wan (as in *on)*

THAILAND

Contrast in Old Values and New Temptations

The tourist visitor to Bangkok will find a bustling modern society, frantic and noisy, overlying the stylized and devout culture of an easygoing and happy people. If this sounds a paradoxical statement, it is, because Thailand *is* a paradox, a visible contrast in values that can be both enchanting and confusing for the visitor.

A brief and casual visit to Thailand, involving a quick dash round the most obvious attractions, is unlikely to be very satisfying for the sensitive traveler, but time spent in going a little deeper, searching out the original and genuine behind the slick façade of the country, can lead to richly rewarding experiences. It is worth the effort.

Throughout Asia traditional values and cultural patterns are being eroded under the impact of Western styles of materialism and political change. In no country is this conflict between old and new ideals more pronounced than in modern Thailand. The Thai people are probably the most physically attractive race in Asia and are endowed with the most delightful traditions and culture, but the old concepts are being challenged by new temptations. The Thais are adopting foreign social and material attitudes at an amazing pace—television, for example, with foreign films and productions, has taken over from the temple fair as the major source of entertainment and the Thais' easygoing approach to life is being forced into the background.

Thailand as It Used to Be

Perhaps it is easier to describe Thailand as it used to be, rather than as it is now. By understanding the original, one is more likely to be able to keep the later changes in perspective.

Life in Thailand used to be easy—the climate is hot, the land fecund and there are no natural disasters such as earthquakes or typhoons to disturb the easy rhythm of life. Apart from the fierce wars that swept the country and neighboring lands every few centuries, the people could concentrate on cultivating the art of "sanuk," the all-pervasive sense of fun that runs through so much of their social exchange.

One of the wisest of the old kings of Thailand had a stone tablet engraved in the 13th century: "During the reign of King Ram Kamhaeng the city of Sukhothai is great. In the water there is fish, in the field there is rice. The King does not levy tax on his people. They are free to travel, leading on their way to trade. A happy citizen. . . . " The tablet can still be seen in the National Museum with its convincing description of a peaceful and rich nation in its first glorious flowering of creative and social achievement. Although there have been great changes down the centuries, that phrase about there being fish in the stream and rice in the field has been a keystone to the basic philosophy of the Thai people. It is an attitude that led them to develop one of the gentlest versions of Buddhism and to accept gracefully a very rigid class system in which people acknowledged easily their own position relative to others.

The Thai attitude to their religion is interesting. Over 90 percent of the population are Hinayana (Theravada) Buddhist. Most Thais could be considered devout, but they usually have only a minor theoretical knowledge of their faith and the priestly chanting is done in a language that few can understand. There are also elements of Hinduism, animism and even epic fairytales that have crept into the religion. A figure in a shrine to which, or through which, an honestly devout Thai Buddhist might pray could be a former king, a famous but nonecclesiastical person of long ago, or even an animal associated with Rama, the mythical god king and hero of the epic story of the *Ramayana.* It can be confusing to an ecclesiastical scholar from abroad to study the day-to-day practice of Thai Buddhism. But although the connections with "pure" Buddhist doctrine may apparently be rather loose in the ordinary Thai's appreciation of his religion, he is nevertheless entirely and deeply sincere in his devotion. Perhaps this is a question of application to a basic principle rather than to specific dogma.

There are trees in Thailand that have been made into venerated shrines, and no Thai home is considered secure or safe from harm without the presence of a "spirit house" on the grounds. These small, templelike models, set on posts, can be seen everywhere. Looking like an elaborate cross between a doll's house and a bird house, the houses are set up to accommodate the spirits of the land on which the humans have erected their house, shop or office. The spirit houses are usually elaborately decorated (to prevent the land spirits from becoming jealous), and are kept well supplied with offerings of fresh flower garlands, food and fragrant incense.

Because they are tolerant toward the manifestations of their own religion, so the Thais are equally tolerant toward other faiths, allowing by long-established practice the freedom of worship for anyone. It is noteworthy, however, that very few converts have been made to the Western religions.

There are many practical problems facing Thailand. The economic gaps between rich and poor, the urban and rural populations, are too great for security or comfort. The political problems of neighboring Laos, Cambodia, and Burma are widely known abroad and these problems may well involve Thailand more actively in the future. A *laissez-faire* attitude and a natural gift for the more devious forms of diplomatic handling in the balance of power may not, in future, be enough to save the independence of Thailand, as it has been in the past. The changeover from absolute monarchy to the awareness of the theoretical value of democracy has taken place over barely 50 years and this developing involvement of the people in the running of their country has happened against an almost continuous backdrop of conflict, war, revolution, and civil war within the Southeast Asian region. In spite of this, or perhaps because of it, the Thai people remain basically apolitical.

With the growth of foreign trade, alien military presence and tourism into the region, the influence of Western material and cultural patterns has been enormous. The Thai people are giving up their traditional styles of dress, colorful and practical, for Western clothes. The fact that they wear these with a delightful sense of style and elegance does not counter the fact that they are abandoning a form of costume that could turn a festival or public holiday gathering into a "painter's shimmering palette of vividly colored sarongs and silk trousers."

Thai girls look exquisite in any kind of clothes, but one can be forgiven for yearning for the old demure simplicity of the Thai silk or cotton "panung," a garment wrapped tightly round the hips and falling in a soft drape to the feet. Worn with their waist-long gleaming black hair, and bare feet, this dress is surely the epitome of femininity.

Most urban-dwelling Thais now aspire to live in a modern-style concrete house, which needs air conditioning, in preference to a traditional wooden building, which is naturally cool and airy. There are many examples of the clash between tradition and modernity, but the majority of Thais take it all as it comes, with the same carefree sense of self-indulgence that has marked their attitude to all their social evolution.

Thai Culture

Thai culture originated from a mixture of Chinese and Indian influences, although it would be difficult to say exactly where one begins and the other leaves off—the two have become so intertwined into a single entity that is distinctly Thai. One aspect of Thai culture clearly reflecting a strong religious background is the classical drama, including dancing. Perhaps the country's most conspicuous forms of art, classical drama and dancing are ancient forms of entertainment said to go back as far as the sixth century, when they were first performed in India. The impact of radio, television, and Western music has cut deeply into traditional dancing. Performances are given less frequently and the dancers are less skillful than their predecessors. In Bangkok the waning of classical dance has been accompanied by a waxing of nightclub culture. Despite official attempts aimed at controlling its excesses, Bangkok remains a swinging city. The new type of entertainment has developed along with traffic jams, pickpockets and armed robbers. However, violence is still alien to most Thais, and Bangkok is not a dangerous city for any tourist with a modicum of discretion.

Classical drama is divided into two categories, the Khon, or the masked play, and the Lakhon. In the Khon, all male characters wear masks as they perform plays taken from parts of the famed Hindu epic, the *Ramayana* (the Thais call it the *Ramakien*). Communication is through gesturing, with occasional dialogue orated by someone else. Khon dances, postures, and gyrations are strenuous, and an actor needs years of training before he is ready for the stage. It is presented by an all-male cast.

Lakhon, generally performed by an all-female company, is more graceful. The dialogue is nearly always sung by a chorus, but at times players do speak. Again, communication of emotion is portrayed through the dance, the gesture, and the posture, but movements in the Lakhon are more graceful than in the Khon and flow in a way reminiscent of Western ballet. Here, too, the *Ramayana* is the source for most of the plays, although the Lakhon does not confine itself to the religious epic.

The literary heritage is not particularly rich, if for no other reason than that an immense number of manuscripts and writings were lost when the former capital city of Ayutthaya was sacked in 1767. Against an ancient background of folk tales, Thai romantic verse of the 17th and 18th centuries is most strongly represented. Prose came into use in the 18th century. Some historical works and several renditions of the *Ramayana* are best known here, but very little has been translated into Western languages.

Best seen in most of Thailand's temples, Thai painting is essentially mural painting in the linear tradition. The murals are done in natural colors, depicting both secular and religious themes, but almost always inspired by the *Ramayana.* The country's architecture is a mixture of Chinese, Burmese, Indian and Khmer influences, but has evolved into a distinctive Thai style best expressed in the temples. Thai music uses the diatonic scale, and thus has neither major nor minor keys in the Western sense (which simply means it will all sound off-key to you). Music accompanying the classical drama is similar to the drama's gesture language in that the same tune is always used to accompany a particular action—for example, a weeping tune, walking tune, etc. Thai popular music is greatly influenced by Western music but the result of East and West meeting on musical grounds is a rather weird sensation.

All of this may serve to illustrate the contention that, above all, Thailand is a tolerant country. Through hundreds of years rich with history, Thais have examined, at length, the cultural traits and achievements of others, have absorbed into their own what was acceptable and have either reshaped it to their liking or wholly rejected what was not. In part, at least, this grows out of the theory that people are not meant to fight one another, that problems should be avoided, if at all possible, rather than worried to death.

Throughout, Thailand has managed to preserve its independence and its own way of life. It has succeeded in achieving this because of the political shrewdness and sophistication of Thai kings and ministers who employed the art of gentle diplomatic compromise and the renunciation of absolutes to gain their ends. In the long run, these were the traits that saved the Thais from falling under Western colonial rule. By inference, these traits, which kept them on good terms with foreigners, maintained Thai interest in seeing outside ways and tolerating foreign ideas—if only with a smile that seemed to say that Thailand, after all, knew better. Whether such ideas would be accepted in their entirety, was quite another matter.

Thai History—Melting Pot of Conquest

Some 50 million people live in Thailand. Their ethnic and cultural background is mixed, the result of a thousand years of influence, by peace and war, from many surrounding countries. The country is rich in beauty and natural resources and has tempted many jealous neighbors, keen for plunder and power. But the Thais, too, have engaged in imperial conquest, and the tides of war and fortune have swept back and forth across the whole of Southeast Asia, bringing the growth and decline of many great empires—Funan, Champa, Angkor, Annam. The names and very few archeological sites are all that remain of some of these powerful states, which, in their day, were known and respected throughout the Eastern civilized world, from Peking to Persia.

Nothing is known for sure about the earliest history of Thailand, although recent discoveries in one small village, Ban Chiang, indicate that a sophisticated Bronze Age culture existed there as long as 5,000 years ago. It is assumed that the original Thais gradually migrated southward from the Yunnan Valley province of South Central China around the fifth to seventh centuries, as a result of pressure from warlike northern neighbors. Most of what is now Thailand would have then been under the control of the Khmer empire, with its capital in Angkor.

Chinese pressure continued to force them south, and so they trickled into the plain, slowly at first, but with greater impetus during the centuries that followed. The great push of the Thais finally came in the 13th century when Kublai Khan's hordes forced them out of China. At first they were divided into principalities, all of them vassals to the kings of the Khmer and small pawns in the powerful empire that the Khmer had built throughout most of Southeast Asia. In 1238, however, they founded the kingdom of Sukothai, the "Dawn of Happiness." The period's most important ruler was King Ramkamhaeng, a man of wisdom and foresight and a man who took over the Khmer alphabet, thus giving the Thais, already united in the spoken word and in cus-

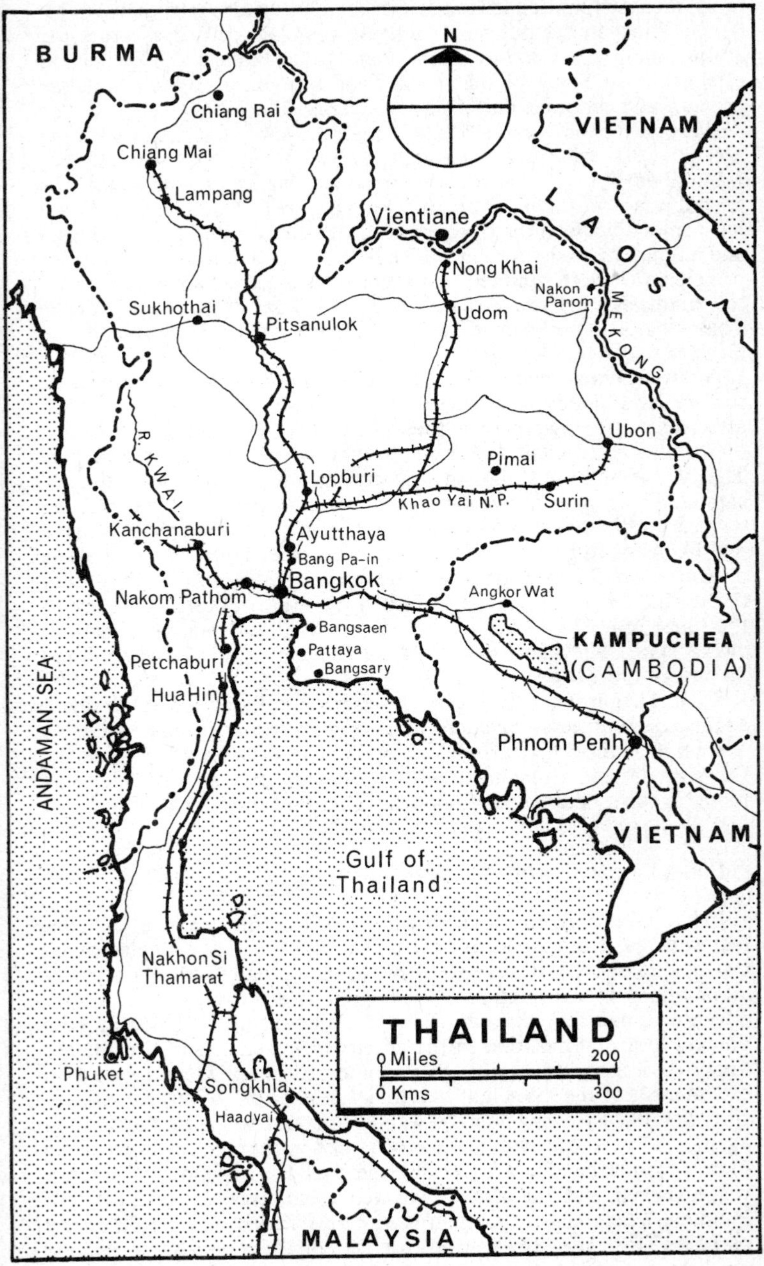
BURMA
Chiang Rai
Chiang Mai
Lampang
VIETNAM
Vientiane
LAOS
Nong Khai
Nakon
Panom
MEKONG
Sukhothai
Pitsanulok
Udom
R. KWAI
Ubon
Pimai
Lopburi
Khao Yai N.P.
Surin
Kanchanaburi
Ayutthaya
Bang Pa-in
Bangkok
Nakom Pathom
Angkor Wat
Bangsaen
Pattaya
Bangsary
KAMPUCHEA
(CAMBODIA)
Petchaburi
Hua Hin
ANDAMAN SEA
Phnom Penh
VIETNAM
Gulf of
Thailand
Nakhon Si
Thamarat
THAILAND
0 Miles 200
0 Kms 300
Phuket
Songkhla
Haadyai
MALAYSIA

toms, their first written language. Ramkamhaeng also introduced to his people Hinayana Buddhism, a religion that had drifted up from the South where missionaries and traders from India and Ceylon had established it. Some of the finest Thai antiquities, Buddha images, bronzes and ceramics date from this period.

But however happy the "Dawn" might have been, it didn't last long and Sukothai was in for a rough awakening in 1350 when Prince Ramatibodi split off and founded his own kingdom to the south. His capital was Ayutthaya, in the midst of the Chao Phya plain, and soon his armies advanced the frontiers of the realm into the Kra Peninsula and all the way to the Andaman Sea in the west. Sukhothai fell, smaller principalities were subdued. And while Ayutthaya's soldiers took on the mighty Khmer to the east, Ramatibodi, considered the first of the Thai kings, showed himself an enlightened ruler who presented an original set of codified laws.

Ayutthaya was to last 417 years, over 300 of which were years of struggle and bloody wars—with the Khmer in the east and the Burmese, a newly rising power, in the west. In 1431, the Khmer abandoned their magnificent capital of Angkor Wat, which was within reach of Thai war expeditions, and moved into an area southeast of the old capital. The Thais did not subdue the Khmer; the struggle continued for years, although attacks became less frequent as long as Ayutthaya had its hands full with the aggressive and expansionist Burmese. The pressure from the west mounted, and in the middle of the 18th century the Burmese invaders took and sacked Ayutthaya (at that time one of the finest cities in Asia), carried away slaves and made Thailand a vassal state. They also destroyed all the city's official records and histories—a great loss.

Soon Thai prince Naresuan became the rallying point of revolt against the Burmese yoke, and in a series of successful campaigns he overran first the newly-arisen Cambodians in the east, then killed the Burmese pretender in combat with a force of war elephants. The Burmese, in turn, became vassals of the Thai, but only for a while.

Initial Contact with the West

In the meantime, the beginning of the 17th century saw initial contact with the Europeans, first with the Dutch and the English, who established trade relations with Ayutthaya, and later with the French, all of whom were then empire building in Asia. At this point, a Greek adventurer named Constantin Paulkone showed up at the court, rose quickly to a high position in the country's treasury, and became the king's adviser and first minister. Paulkone, a Catholic and a man with the interests of the French at heart, had designs to convert the king to Christianity. The king merely wanted an alliance with the French against the powerful Dutch who controlled important positions at the mouth of the Chao Phya River into the Gulf of Thailand. The alliance was achieved, but the French showed themselves greedy and with Paulkone's help insisted on getting more privileges than the Thais had bargained for. The Greek adventurer attempted a conspiracy against the king in 1688, causing the court nobles to band together in self-defense, deposing the king and assassinating Paulkone. For 150 years thereafter, the Thais, wary of foreign interference, tried to keep out Western influence, but with much less success than their counterparts had achieved in Tokugawa Japan.

The squabbling with the Burmese and the Khmer had not, of course, stopped and a slowly declining Ayutthaya finally fell to a massive assault by the Burmese in 1767, in an attack that ruined the once mighty capital and killed most of its inhabitants. Only a young general managed to escape with a few men. Under him the Thais rallied and drove out the invaders, with the general, Taksin, becoming king. When he went insane, another army man, General Chakri, became King Rama I and founded the present dynasty, of which King Bhumibol Adulyadej is the ninth ruler.

Modern Development and Political Problems

Thailand's modern phase begins with Rama IV, also known as King Mongkut, of *The King and I* (from a Thai point of view a most offensive portrayal of a revered ruler). A wise and farsighted man who studied Western ways extensively, Mongkut opened Thailand to the West, becoming the father of modern Siam. He was a man of many interests (they included astronomy); he encouraged foreign (Christian) missionaries to bring his predominantly Buddhist people the advantages of Western medicine and education; he put an end to cumbersome court traditions and taboos; he liberalized trade. At the same time he managed to keep at bay Western nations intent on colonizing in Southeast Asia. His successors, King Chulalongkorn and King Vajiravudh, carried on the work of modernization in government, administration, education, communications, and social reform. Chulalongkorn became the first Thai king to travel abroad, signed decrees outlawing slavery, and, most important, maintained Thailand's precarious buffer position between the British (India, Burma, Malaya) and French (Indo-China) colonial spheres.

With the steady influx of Western ideas, the absolute monarchy, despite its reforms, was doomed to end. In 1932, a junta of army officers took over, giving Thailand a constitutional monarchy, and introducing a limited measure of democracy. The story after 1932 is one of succeeding coups d'état, but an underlying stability. The most publicized feature of Thai politics, the coups and attempted coups, affected relatively few people, and were rarely accompanied by violence. Before and during the Second World War, the Thais formed an alliance with Japan. Although the Thais declared war on the Western allies, it was made clear that the alliance with Japan was one of necessity and that Thailand's real sympathies lay with the West. In certain ways this attitude was shown when Allied soldiers were repeatedly given refuge and aided in Thailand during the Japanese occupation of the country. One aspect of this unique period was the refusal of the United States to accept the Thai declaration of war, the State Department saying that America never considered her an enemy, but as an area under Axis domination waiting to be liberated. Others of the Allies were not so willing to treat the matter lightly, however, once hostilities ended in 1945.

After the war, except for short intermittent periods, power belonged again to Field Marshal Pibul Songgram, one of the so-called promoters of the revolution of 1932 and prime minister of Thailand for much of the prewar and war years. Several attempts to overthrow him failed until 1957 and 1958 when two successive coups d'état (the latest in a series of 28 coups or power plays since 1932) brought to power the late Field Marshal Sarit Thanarat, who headed the government until his death in 1963.

Again, the Sarit years marked the beginning of a new era for Thailand. The country was under a benevolent, rarely enforced version of martial law throughout the years of his rule. But if Sarit was tough, he was also a man of vision, a trait that gained him grudging respect from the people. The Sarit period, particularly the early sixties, brought a time of building and development, of healthy economic gains, and, for the first time in Thailand's history, of a searching look by the Bangkok government at the problems of the people in the countryside. The emphasis was on the Northeast and, to a more limited degree, on the deep South—two areas threatened by Communist subversion. Backed in his resolve by U.S. aid, Sarit's government hammered out a wide-ranging development program worth millions of dollars. It concentrated on the country's backward areas, utilizing so-called Mobile Development Teams as well as Mobile Information Teams to carry Bangkok's message to the countryside.

The Northeast was the prime target. There, more than eight million Thais, in language and custom more oriented toward Laos than the central Thai plains, were scratching subsistence living out of the dry soil. For centuries, they had been ignored by Bangkok. Now, from across the Mekong River, Laos' pro-Communist Pathet Lao—and, indirectly, from a greater distance, Hanoi and Peking—began to spread the propaganda gospel of a new order.

Did Sarit's development push come too late? When he died in late 1963, the government of his successor, quiet, soft-spoken Field Marshal Thanom Kittikachorn, continued it with the same sense of urgency, but discovered that the Communists had already made headway. As a result of this, and other factors, the promised democratic constitution and the holding of free elections were delayed until 1969.

Constitutional democracy with such inconveniences as elections, critical opposition, and unfettered press did not appeal to Thai leaders. In late 1971 Marshal Thanom and his military cohorts consolidated their power through a bloodless coup which abolished all those hampering nuisances of democracy. The NEC, as the new group of old leaders called itself, cracked down on minor corruption and made gestures aimed at convincing the population that they were the best possible form of administration for the country.

The people of Thailand, however, especially the students, were *not* convinced and pressure mounted against the military régime, climaxing in a series of student demonstrations that grew in intensity through the summer of 1973. In October 1973 a series of circumstances, mostly unplanned, turned a mass student demonstration into a bloody revolution in which public buildings were burned down and some 90 students were killed by soldiers' gunfire.

A civilian government was called, under strong influence from the king, with university rector Dr. Sanya Dharmasakdi as Prime Minister heading a provisional government.

Free democratic elections were held early in 1975, and out of the 40 political parties competing a rather shaky coalition was formed, making some socialist noises, but rather solidly right wing, under the prime ministership of M. R. Kukrit Pramoj. The government seemed to gather strength during 1975, but was shaken by the collapse of Vietnam and Cambodia. This, together with the political developments in Laos, led the Thais to launch a policy of rapprochement with the Communist rulers of the region and to turn against America. The Kukrit government was forced into general elections in 1976 and Kukrit himself was ousted. A rather stronger coalition, somewhat more to the right in political views, was elected with Kukrit Pramoj's elder brother, Seni Pramoj, becoming Prime Minister, with a rather more solid base. But this government also failed to achieve political stability and once again, in October 1976, civil disorder erupted among students in Bangkok and a strong military régime took over running the country. The new military leaders appointed a civilian government and took a hard line in dealing with such problems as Communism in border areas and economic imbalance between the urban and rural areas. The final political position of Thailand has yet to be established, with the, mainly, military influence still in control, but influences towards a wider form of democracy are still growing.

The country is, after all, an integral part of Southeast Asia. Phnom Penh, the capital of Cambodia, is a little over 200 miles from the Thai border. Only the Mekong River separates Vientiane, the capital of Laos, from Thailand. The Thais have in the past, however, demonstrated a considerable skill in balancing external forces to their own advantage in achieving internal sovereignty.

If, despite its problems, Thailand is relatively stable—and, by comparison with some of its neighbors, it certainly is—that circumstance is in no small measure the merit of the progressive King Bhumibol Adulyadej (or, officially, King Rama IX). For, as all Thais will acknowledge, the throne is the symbol of the unity of their country.

Bhumibol is a modern king, the ninth in a dynasty that dates back to the years immediately following the fall of Ayutthaya. He was born in the U.S. (at Cambridge, Mass., where his father studied public health) and educated in Europe. He is as thoughtful as he is studious. His interests range widely: he is a good jazz saxophonist, he composes, he paints, he experiments in rice culture.

More important than all that, however, he takes a deep interest in his people, for whom he is the most deeply revered and respected man in the country. Bhumibol has traveled to all sections of Thailand, and has made it part of his job to hike to remote hamlets in the northern hill country where government and royal family are often but vague entities. On trips inside Thailand, as well as on state visits abroad, the king is usually accompanied by radiant Queen Sirikit, whom the king is once said to have called "my smile."

The royal couple live in the middle of Bangkok, at Chitrlada Palace, inside a sprawling green compound surrounded by a moat, with the two younger princesses. The Crown Prince of Thailand, having completed his studies in a military college in Australia, is now assuming wide official duties to aid his father.

EXPLORING THAILAND

The capital of the country and its heart is Bangkok, a sprawling city hugging the banks of the Menam Chao Phya River and less than 30 miles from the Gulf of Thailand. Thais call their capital of five million people Krung Thep, the "City of Angels," to whom the glittering rooftops of the Grand Palace, and countless beautiful *wat,* seem to reach.

Below are hundreds of hotels, bars, massage parlors, shops, and modern business buildings. There are also bowling alleys, movie theaters and horrendous traffic jams. But from the numerous slum areas it is never more than a few blocks to a flowering bush or graceful palm tree.

Bangkok is a young city. Barely 200 years ago, it was the site of a little fishing village and of a Chinese trading post on the swampy and jungled shore of the wide brown river. Sailing ships and barges glided by on their way to and from the splendid capital of Ayutthaya, some 40 miles up river, and to the upcountry provinces of the kingdom. But when Ayutthaya fell under a Burmese onslaught in 1767, General Taksin, one of the survivors of the bloodbath and the man who routed the Burmese after their initial victory, made himself king and established his court across the river from Bangkok in Dhonburi. Only 13 years later, another general, Chakri, became king and moved the capital to the opposite shore. That's how Bangkok was founded. It became the capital, the seat of the court, and the hub of the country in 1782; and celebrated its bicentennial, with considerable pageantry, in 1982.

In the beginning, it was a city whose lifelines were water. Canals, or *klongs* as the Thais call them, crisscrossed Bangkok. Canals were the city's first line of defense, canals were its mainstreets along which people lived a water-oriented life and on which flat barges brought food and resources from the country. Trade boomed as ships from foreign countries moved slowly up the river from the gulf laden with cargoes and the influence of the West. The city did not build its first road till the 1860's. Running parallel to the river this first street followed the Chao Phya's winding course, never more than three or four blocks away from it—and soon "New Road," as it was called, became the center of the business communities.

Today, "New Road" is still one of the city's main arteries and one of the major business sections. But now the narrow thoroughfare is choked with traffic and people. In the early sixties, caught in the automobile revolution, Bangkok built miles and miles of four- and six-lane avenues, sacrificing in the process long stretches of klong that paralleled the old roads. The "Venice of the East" has almost aban-

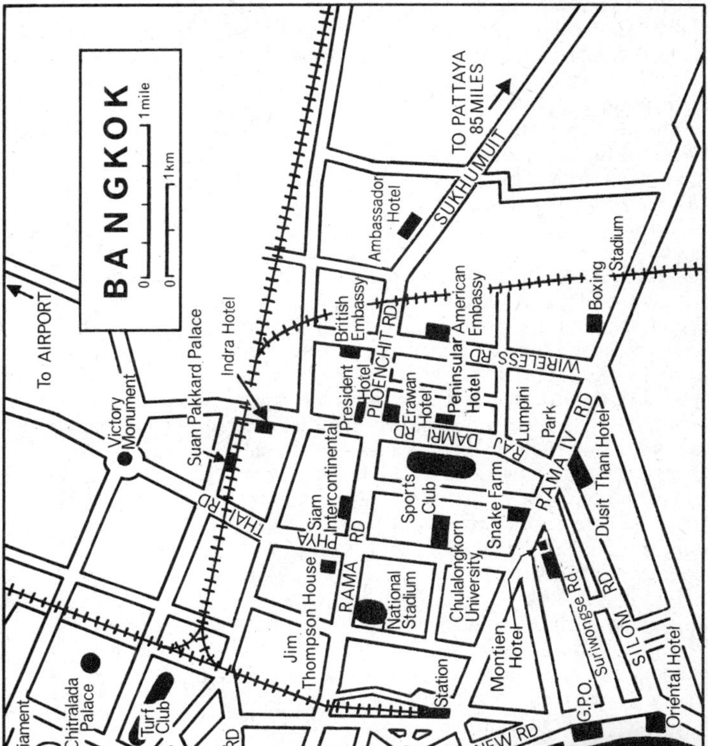
BANGKOK
0 1 km
0 1 mile
To AIRPORT
Victory Monument
Suan Pakkard Palace
Indra Hotel
British Embassy
Ambassador Hotel
TO PATTAYA 85 MILES
SUKHUMUIT
PLOENCHIT RD
American Embassy
Boxing Stadium
President Hotel
Erawan Hotel
Peninsular Hotel
WIRELESS RD
Lumpini Park
RAJ DAMRI RD
RAMA IV RD
Dusit Thani Hotel
Siam Intercontinental
PHYA THAI RD
Sports Club
Snake Farm
RAMA RD
Jim Thompson House
National Stadium
Chulalongkorn University
Montien Hotel
Suriwongse Rd.
SILOM RD
Station
G.P.O.
Oriental Hotel
NEW RD
Royal Orchid Sheraton
CHAO PHYA RIVER
Parliament
Chitralada Palace
Turf Club
Boxing Ring
LANLUANG RD
RAJADAMNERN AVE
MAHACHAI RD
TAT Office
TRI PETCH RD
Thieves Market
Pramane Ground
National Museum
Emerald Buddha and Palace
Wat Arun
N

doned its watery heritage. Yet the problem of "the inner city" does not plague Bangkok, because there is none. A noodle-seller parks his cart outside the iron gates of a mansion. Across the *soi* (lane) from a modern California-style home is a two-story frame house of unstained teak. The ground floor front is open in the daytime. At night, before the wall is closed, the family car is parked in the living room. Rich are not isolated from poor.

The new constantly and steadily replaces the old in Bangkok today. Modernistic structures mark the site where rice fields and swamps were seen just a decade or so ago. Slum districts are razed and give way to cleaner residential quarters and tall office buildings.

Yet despite the unhalting influx of the modern, the city has maintained its particular character in a way that seems possible only in Bangkok. Beside the multicolored façade of the modern building shine the glazed tiles of an ancient temple or *wat,* and while ferocious traffic thunders by on the street, saffron-robed monks sit calmly in the shade of a tree in the temple courtyard, protected from the outside and the noise by the high walls. On the river high-powered water taxis with special outboard motors throw up white spray while a boat-woman, chanting rhythmically and slowly handling her single oar, moves her sampan along the side of the canal—in the same fashion in which her ancestors would have done it a hundred or more years ago. When night falls, the metropolis glitters, its neon signs advertising the good life. Until the late hours, streams of buses, cars, taxis, little three-wheeled samlor taxis glide along the avenues, and restaurants, night clubs and cinemas do booming business, day-in, day-out.

This is Bangkok—a city of color and contrast, in its buildings which range from strictly Thai to strictly Victorian to a mixture of Thai and Western modern, in its people, and in its daily life. But beneath the tropical sun, the colors, the smells, the contrasts are never obnoxious. Instead, they seem to merge into an amalgam that is often confusing, but never without charm.

All about Bangkok

More than 300 *wat,* some of which are chapels, others monasteries, etc., but none of which are really "temples," adorn the city, and on your tour you should take in some of these fine examples of Thai religious architecture. Thailand's *wat* have a style all of their own. Believed to have sprung from a mixture of Indian, Khmer, and Chinese influence, the style developed over the years into something uniquely Thai, and the colorful temples with their glittering and multi-tiered roofs, their curved gables, are as joyous an expression of religious feeling as one can find anywhere.

Most *wat* hide their main chapel, or *bot,* behind a high wall that shuts out the stares of the curious and the noise of the street. The *bot* houses the figure or figures of the Buddha and is the main shrine. Sometimes there is a smaller chapel, the *viharn.* Almost always there is a *cheddi,* an ornamental, sharply pointed spire rising on top of a bell-shaped base, or a *prang,* a more thickset stone column tapering slowly to an almost rounded top, its sculpted sides lavishly ornamented.

The Chapel of the Emerald Buddha and Royal Palace

One of the most beautiful and most famous *wat* in Thailand, Wat Phra Kaeo, sits in the compound of the Grand Palace, formerly the seat of the court of old Siam. It was built by the founder of the *Chakri* dynasty, King Rama I, and houses one of the world's most venerated Buddha images, the Emerald Buddha, a 31-inch-high figure carved out of translucent emerald-colored jasper, and seated on a very high altar. The image is supposed to have originated in Ceylon, but no one knows when it was made nor when the Buddha was originally brought to Thailand. The Chapel itself is a tall structure with a golden, three-tiered roof. Murals inside depict the earthly life of the Lord Buddha. Another item of interest is the inside of the wall that rings the temple. On it murals depict the great Hindu epic, the *Ramayana* (or *Ramakien* as the Thais call it). Wat Phra Kaeo is open daily, 60 baht. Next to the Chapel of the Emerald Buddha is the Grand Palace (closed Saturday/ Sunday), that huge, formerly forbidden city where the kings of Siam once held court. Main attractions in the compound are the Amarindra Vinichai Hall, Dusit Palace (a fine example of Thai architecture), and Chakri Hall, most lavish with a strange mixture of European and Thai architectural styles. For the tour of the Royal Palace grounds ladies are asked not to wear shorts. Another thing: no pictures may be taken inside the Chapel of the Emerald Buddha. You may click your shutter as much as you like in the compound of the Royal Palace, but only 8 mm. movie cameras allowed. Shoes must be removed before entering this, or any, temple in Thailand.

The Reclining Buddha and Giant Swing

Wat Po, also called Wat Jetubon, is close to the Royal Palace. Its main attraction is the 160-foot statue of the Reclining Buddha, symbolizing the passing of the Lord Buddha from this life into *Nirvana.* Other items of interest are the Chinese and Thai figures in its courtyard, its famed *bhodi* tree, said to have sprung from a branch of the tree under which Buddha once sat, the *Ramayana* epic in bas-reliefs along the walls, and the four tall *cheddi* said to represent the first four kings of the present dynasty. Entrance fee, 10 baht. Open daily 8:00–5:00.

Again close to the Grand Palace stands the Giant Swing in a square in front of Wat Suthat. In ancient days it was used for a ceremony of Brahmanic origin, long since forgotten. The tall, red-colored, teak frame still stands, but there is now no "swing." Wat Suthat has two massive main halls, elaborate multitiered roofs, murals inside the chapel, and superb door panels carved in the time of King Rama II.

The Temple of the Dawn

One of the city's most striking landmarks, Wat Arun, sits on the banks of the Chao Phya River, conspicuous with its five tall *prang* or spires. The Khmer-style pagodas which stand on a raised platform a bit away from the actual chapel (which once held the Emerald Buddha before it was taken to the Grand Palace) are decorated with colorful broken pieces of pottery and porcelain. Wat Arun, its tallest central spire, more than 260 feet high, was completed in the last century when King Rama III built it up to its present height. An extensive renovation project of the main spire was recently completed, but the mass of cheap souvenir stalls in front of the temple is an eyesore. Near Wat Arun is the collection of the King's Barges—ornate gilded and carved craft that were the original form of royal water transportation. There are over 30 barges in all; the largest is the graceful "Suvannahong," manned by 60 oarsmen on ceremonial occasions. Both the temple and the barges can be seen on organized tours or individually. Entrance fee, 5 baht.

The Marble Temple and Golden Mount

Built at the turn of this century out of white Carrara marble, this monastery, called Wat Beujamabhopit, is considered the most beautiful expression of Thai religious architecture. Its symmetry is pure and uncluttered and its brilliantly colored roof tiles set off the blazing marble of the main structure. King Chulalongkorn, who built the monastery, filled it with Buddha images from many countries to give the Thai people an idea of Buddhist iconography in other countries.

Elevated on a huge brick mound just outside the old city wall, at one end of Rajadamnoen Avenue, Wat Saket is one of the high points in the city. It has a brilliant golden spire. In its shrine it also shelters one of the largest bronze Buddha images in Thailand. It is best known for its one-week fair toward the end of October or the beginning of November, when thousands flock to worship in front of the Buddha and then enjoy themselves at the hundreds of fair attractions that ring the base of the "Golden Mount" which gives the monastery its name.

Temple of the Golden Buddha

In the rather uninspiring surroundings of Wat Trimitr, you suddenly enter an open-fronted pavilion in which sits a huge solid gold Buddha image, reputedly made of some 5.5 tons of the precious metal. The image was originally encased in plaster and housed in a semi-ruined temple by the docks. Its true nature was discovered only when it was being moved by a crane and was dropped—a piece of plaster fell off and showed the gold beneath. The origin of the statue is not known, but it is believed to have come from the 13th-century former capital of Sukhothai.

After Wat, What?

If you have any energy left after a tour of Bangkok's *wat* you should take a look at the National Museum where archeological finds from the pre-Christian era and ancient art work bring back the time when Southeast Asian cultures were at their peak. Other displays include royal vehicles and barges from Thailand's past; weapons, coins, traditional garments, and dancers' garments. There are regular guided tours in English (closed Monday). Admission 10 baht. The National Library contains a large collection of books and ancient Thai and Pali manuscripts.

Another spot of interest is the Snake Farm. The compound of Chulalongkorn University houses Thailand's Pasteur Institute. The snakes, including cobras and *kraits,* are fed and venom for serum is extracted every day at 11 A.M. Admission 10 baht. (Closed Saturday, Sunday, and public holidays.)

There is a fine zoo in Bangkok, set in a large and beautifully landscaped park. The main entrance to Dusit Zoo is on Rajavithi Rd.; admission is 6 baht. The park is open from 7:30 A.M. to 6 P.M. Among the many interesting animals to be seen here are the royal white elephants (actually they are pinky-gray—and that only around the edges!). These traditionally belong to the king and are regarded as sacred by the Thais.

Among the best of the public parks in the city is Lumpini Park, overlooked by the Dusit Thani Hotel, and a popular place with Thais on weekends. There are ornamental lakes, a children's playground, and numerous food and fruit stalls offering refreshment for the stroller.

The many monuments and statues in the city are dedicated mainly to past kings or former glories. The Democracy Monument, in Rajadamnoen Avenue, was a rallying point for the students in the October 1973 revolution and has therefore assumed a special place in the hearts of the Thais. On Phaholyothin Road, one of the main roads to the airport, is the Victory Monument, a swordlike memorial to a campaign fought with Cambodia during the early years of World War II.

The Markets

Perhaps one of the most typical sights to be seen in Bangkok are the many markets—most fascinating places to wander around, although often rather too pungent in smell and startling in experience for the unaccustomed foreign visitor. The most famous is the floating market, no longer the fascinating experience it used to be, due to touristic overexposure and to the fact that the area formerly served only by canal for communications now has new roads. Today shoppers tend to travel by minibus rather than miniboat to collect their shopping. There are, however, so-called rural floating markets, further away from the capital, which still present authentic atmosphere. The best is at Damnoen Saduak, a half-day's excursion out of the city. Still a fascinating experience is the "weekend" market, held Saturdays and Sundays on the outskirts of the city near the main airport road, opposite the North Bangkok Bus Terminus. Here, hundreds of stalls sell all the necessities of life and some luxuries—such as orchid plants, myna birds, puppies, antiques, and gems. And, as anywhere in Bangkok where something is sold, you will be struck by the bargaining and the haggling about prices. This is only one of the interesting markets in Bangkok. Among the most colorful are Bangrak, off New Road at the end of Sathorn Road. This becomes an open-air restaurant at night with dozens of small stalls, tables and chairs set out in the open. The food is good, if spicy, but may be a bit too much for the foreign visitor used to different standards of hygiene. Pratunam Market, by the overpass on Rajdamri

Road, is also well worth visiting for its masses of closely packed stalls offering merchandise from food to fabrics.

From beside the Pinklao Bridge, by the National Museum, you can take a small outboard motor-propelled boat along the river and into one of the many klongs. For about 300 baht an hour the boatman will race along the main canals that still exist in the suburbs, with their shops, houses and restaurants set facing the water, as if they were ordinary streets and will divert into the narrow backwaters where farmhouses and rural family life can be seen. Late afternoon is a good time to take this trip. This is also the subject of a tour—look for the "Rice Barge" tour, which operates with bus pick-up service from hotels.

For a look at a traditional Thai house you might go to Jim Thompson's Thai House in Soi Kasemsan 2 (opposite the National Stadium) which is open to the public weekdays 9 A.M. to 4 P.M. The Thompson House is actually a composite of five houses. Its teak woodwork and collection of Oriental antiques are admirable. Admission 50 baht. Another beautiful teak house is on Sri Ayutthaya Road and is called the Suan Pakkard Palace. It once belonged to one of the ministers of King Mongkut, and has a small lacquer pavilion in the garden, and is packed with antiques. Open every day except Sundays, 9 A.M. to 4 P.M. Admission 50 baht.

Next, go to Chinatown. Although Chinese businessmen are to be found throughout the city, the large concerns and many smaller ones are still concentrated in Bangkok's teeming Chinatown, around Yawarad Road. Walking or riding along the wide street with its hundreds of shops is an exexperience, especially in the early hours of the evening when the street is ablaze with lights and neon signs. While you're in the area walk over to Sampeng Lane, not far from Yawarad, where all sorts of inexpensive goods are for sale. Also, look for the traditional gold shops, their brilliant lights reflecting off chains, necklaces, bracelets, rings and belts of the rich, and expensive, metal.

Day Tours

Apart from the wide variety of attractions within the city itself there are a large number of worthwhile excursions you can take into the nearby countryside. Set down below are the main places you can reach within a day's itinerary. Subsequent sections deal with beach resorts and major upcountry destinations.

To the south of the Rose Garden is the city of Nakhom Pathom, conspicuous from miles away with its huge Golden Cheddi. The famous shrine, in the form of a large bell surmounted by a sharp spire, and completely covered with shiny, golden glazed tiles, rises 380 feet into the air to dominate the skyline of a whole region. Largest pagoda in Southeast Asia, it was built in the middle 19th century by King Mongkut over the ruins of an ancient sanctuary. Nakhom Pathom is 30 miles from Bangkok by car or train.

About 80 miles from Bangkok by road or railway and the last good-sized outpost of the central plain before the mountains in the west, Kanchanaburi is best known for its role in the Second World War when it marked the starting point of the Japanese "Death Railway" built by Allied prisoners of war to connect Thailand with Burma over the mountains. A large cemetery where 5,000 Allied prisoners lie buried is situated on the outskirts of the town and is beautifully maintained by the Thai government. Another attraction is the bridge over the River Kwai, although it's not the one shown in the movie. This one is made of steel, not of wood. It was built by prisoners, bombed by the Allies, and repaired after the war by the Japanese. One can now go over the bridge by train or take a newly completed road, for some 40 miles to a jungle-set hotel named the River Kwai Village. From here one can explore the lovely scenery, river life, caves, waterfalls, and remains of the old wartime railway. Here one can also stay in a charming Raft Hotel, with simple accommodation built on bamboo rafts floating in the exquisitely scenic river.

Ratchaburi, about 90 miles from Bangkok, is noted for its caves which have become Buddhist sanctuaries.

Often included with coach excursions to the Rose Garden and Nakhom Pathom is the rural floating market at Damneon Saduak, a less commercialized version of the more famous Bangkok attraction.

Most travel agents offer tour packages to include all or several of the above-mentioned attractions, with bus pick-up from main hotels.

Nineteen miles to the southwest of Bangkok is the small riverside town of Paknam (also known as Samut Prakan) where you can see a bustling market and busy fishing boat quay. The town is also renowned for its small seafood restaurants and the simple temple, Cheddi Klang Nam, on the other side of the Chao Phya River, a brief trip by ferryboat.

Close to Paknam are two unusual attractions, a crocodile farm and the Ancient City. Entrance fee for the crocodile farm is 100 baht, and you can see thousands of the animals being cultivated for their hides. They range in size from newly hatched babies to full-grown giants. You can watch them being fed daily at 3 P.M. Possibly the world's largest outdoor museum, the Ancient City consists of a 200-acre piece of ground some miles from Bangkok. The site has the rough shape of a map of Thailand and laid at appropriate spots in this area are reproductions, many of them in full scale, of all the major architectural styles of the various periods of Thai history. You would not have the time to travel the length and breadth of Thailand to see every ancient city site and ruin, but here, in one place you can study some 65 monuments, reconstructed, and see typical rural villages, waterways, hundreds of statues and montages of epic sagas from Thai history. The project, a life's work for a very rich industrialist, represents the investment of some US$25 million. The project is incredible in scale—5,000,000 tons of earth were moved, 200,000 trees planted and 30,000 tons of rock together with 120,000 tons of concrete were used in the construction. There is even a 150-foot-high miniature mountain with a cascading waterfall. This is probably the largest development of its kind in the world and is very uncommercialized in comparison with, say, Disneyland. The best way to see it is with an organized tour out of Bangkok. Admission 50 baht or 250 baht, including transportation from any city hotel. Opening times 8:30 A.M.–6 P.M.

Out to the north of Bangkok lies the ancient city of Ayutthaya. A day's trip to the old ruined capital can be combined with a river excursion and a visit to the former Royal Summer Palace at Bang Pa-In. Pleasantest of all the tours offered is on the *Oriental Queen,* a luxury, air-conditioned river cruiser that leaves the Oriental Hotel each morning, except Monday and Friday, at 8 A.M. and takes visitors up river, past all the fascinating river traffic, and serves lunch on board before transferring passengers into buses for the summer palace and Ayutthaya visit. For bookings contact the Oriental Hotel or any travel agent. Cost 750 baht, including lunch.

Also out to the north lies the game reserve of Khao Yai. It is covered fully later in this chapter.

One place you must not miss, especially if you have no time to go upcountry, is the Rose Garden Country Resort, where you can see a "Thai Village Show," featuring a wedding ceremony, Thai boxing, swordfighting, classical and folk dances (you'll be dragged into it if you sit in front), a hill tribe dance, Bamboo Dance (similar to that of the Philippines), and watch umbrellas being made. There is also a display of elephants at work. Every afternoon 3–5 P.M.; bookings through your hotel or travel agent. It is just 90 minutes from the city. Cost, with transportation from Bangkok, 250–300 baht. There is a good 18-hole golf course and a small comfortable hotel in the Rose Garden, or traditional-style antique wooden Thai houses which one can rent—a delightful and relaxing escape from a busy touring schedule.

Upcountry Destinations

Most tourists who come to Thailand do not leave time to see much of the country beyond Bangkok and, perhaps, Pattaya. This is a pity because there is much to see and do outside the capital. There are ruined cities, some of which can rival Angkor Wat in importance, and superb beaches, only a few of which have been developed. To the north is Chiang Mai, so different in culture from Bangkok, and to the south lies the long road to the Malaysian border and picturesque towns, fine beaches and fishing villages.

Many worthwhile places and experiences can be reached in just a day spent away from Bangkok—these have been covered above. For those of you who have the time, however, we include brief descriptions of some of the more important upcountry destinations. Travel within Thailand is easy—as air, road and rail systems are well developed. In some of the smaller towns, you will have to sacrifice standards of comfort by comparison to Bangkok, but modern hotels and facilities are increasingly found throughout the country.

Perhaps the easiest way for travelers to see upcountry Thailand is to take advantage of the increasingly diverse range of tours offered by the imaginative Bangkok travel agents. No major attraction in Thailand is more than two hours away from the capital by air, so you can see more of this varied country than just Bangkok.

One excellent upcountry tour, by Diethelms, offers a 7-day around-Thailand itinerary, departing every Wednesday, for 11,000 baht.

The upcountry destinations below are divided into two sections to cater to culture-vultures as well as to would-be beachcombers.

Ayutthaya

Barely 50 miles from Bangkok, in the wide fertile plain that is Thailand's rice bowl, lies Ayutthaya, the old capital of the Kingdom of Siam. Easily reached by train, bus, or boat (on the Chao Phya River), Ayutthaya is today little more than a sleepy provincial town. But on its outskirts lie the remains of ancient grandeur. The old city was founded in 1350 by a prince U Thong, who subsequently became king with the name of Ramatibodi. It remained the capital until it was captured and destroyed by the Burmese in 1767. During that time the city prospered until its center alone covered an area of 5 square miles. The French and Dutch traders who saw it in the 17th century left vivid descriptions of its size, culture and richness.

The city lies in a large loop in the river. The fourth side was guarded by a wide moat and canals interlaced the whole area, amid palaces, temples, magnificent public buildings and houses. At the height of its power the Kingdom centered on Ayutthaya covered much of what is now Burma, Laos, Cambodia, and Malaysia as well as Thailand.

Ayutthaya was sacked by the Burmese in 1767 in a bloody drama that ended with the "canals of the city running red with the blood of the killed" and with its splendid buildings no more than smoke-blackened ruins. Today, the crumbling reddish walls of the royal palace, of old government buildings and temples fight for survival and light with the lush tropical vegetation that is trying to hide them. Special items of interest are the Buddha Mongkol, a huge image of the Lord Buddha, now housed in a modern temple, the Chao Sam Phraya Museum, the elephant kraal and a number of key ruins.

The Phra Sri Sanpet Monastery was once the Royal chapel. In 1500, a standing Buddha figure, 42 feet high, was erected and covered with 580 pounds of pure gold. The Burmese set fire to the chapel to release the gold covering and caused the total collapse of the building.

The former Royal Palace consisted of five "main buildings." The remaining pillars, walls, porticoes and brick foundations give a good idea of how vast the original must have been.

The Pagoda of Sri Suriyothi is the famous memorial to the brave queen who risked her life to save her husband during combat on elephant-back during a great battle in 1563.

The *cheddi* (pagoda) of the Poo Khao Thong Monastery is 260 feet high. It was built in 1569 and remodeled in 1745.

Bang Pa-In

A tour to Ayutthaya usually incudes a visit to the Royal Palace of Bang Pa-In on the banks of the Chao Phya river. The palace dates mostly from the turn of the century when King Chulalongkorn was happy to show his taste for European architecture. Amid handsome gardens you can therefore find two Greek-style buildings, a replica of the Peking Palace, a Renaissance hall and a small Gothic church (which actually contains a Buddhist *wat*!). In the middle of a lake is the exquisite orange, green, and gold pavilion that is seen in so many guidebooks and posters of Thailand. Watch particularly in one corner of the palace park for a monument that King Chulalongkorn built for his Queen who was accidentally drowned. In the King's own moving English the inscription on the small stone monument reads: "To the Beloved Memory of Her Late and Lamented Majesty Sunandakumaviratn, Queen Consort, who wont to spend her most pleasant, and happiest hours in this garden amidst those loving ones and dearest to her. This Memorial is Erected by Chulalongkorn Rex Her Bereaved Husband whose suffering from so cruel an endurance through those trying hours made death seem so Near and Yet Preverable [*sic*] 1881." A small museum (closed Mondays) has displays of ceramics and antiques.

Chiang Mai

Chiang Mai, Thailand's second largest city, lies in a wide valley sprawled at the foot of Doi Sutep, one of the high mountains that surround it. As the altitude is about 1,000 feet, it is less humid and considerably cooler during the winter months than Bangkok. It is a hill station people in Bangkok dream about—evenings beautifully fresh, cool enough to stroll around without becoming a wet rag.

The rectangle wall, with its fine gates running along the moat, is not very old and not the original city walls that many people think them to be. The originals, built sometime in the 13th century, lie further away by the Menam Ping—where only a little trace of them remains. Legend has it that King Mengrai, the founder of Chiang Mai, had 90,000 men working day and night to complete the city walls in four months.

The impact of modernization is being felt in this northern city, and already it has had to spread its business and commercial activities outside its ancient walls. Most of the new commercial area is to be found between the east gate and the banks of the river, while the residential area has spread to the very foot of Doi Sutep. The modern campus of the Chiang Mai University is situated there. Chiang Mai still seems to have retained its old charm, however, and preserved comparative quiet from the horrors of traffic noise. The people speak the northern Thai dialect still and have maintained their traditional cultural forms of music and song, customs and art.

Places to visit and see in the city are the very stylized temples and the villages of various handicrafts, such as weaving, umbrella-making, silverware and woodcarving. Tours can be easily organized by your hotel if you do not feel brave enough to venture out by yourself. Chiang Mai certainly is the place to buy your teakware, silverware and Thai celadon. Most of the shops selling these goods are to be found grouped together. Ladda Land features cultural shows, craft displays and Thai-style buildings. Rather more interesting is the "Old Chiang Mai" cultural center, a gathering of hill-tribe people in reconstructed village settings. One can also take the typical Chiang Mai-style "Kantok" dinner here and watch the elaborate cultural show.

The temples to see are Wat Phra Tat Doi Sutep, which is built on a hill some 3,500 feet high; Wat Suan Dork, which has one of the largest bronze Buddha images in the country, and Wat Phra Sing, where there are fine historical murals of northern traditional art. For half-day trips, go to the caves at Chiangdao, or the waterfalls of Mae Klang. The zoo and the Botanical Gardens too are worth a visit.

To the south of Chiang Mai lie the smaller towns of Lampoon, famous for its orchids, hand-loomed silk and cotton and also for its pretty girls, and Lampang, where you can see the sights from a horse-drawn carriage. These include the Burmese-style temple of Wat Phasang, the ancient Wat Phra Keo Don Tan and Wat Lampang Luang, one of the finest temples in the whole area.

On a day excursion out of Chiang Mai you can also visit several hill tribe villages—Meo, Yao and Ekaw. There are approximately 20 distinct tribes living in the green mountains around Chiang Mai who have, for the most part, steadfastly retained their own cultures and traditions. The origins of these peoples are somewhat mysterious, but most of them are believed to have come from the southern provinces of China, some as recently as a few hundred years ago. The majority are nomadic, living for a spell in one place and then moving on to another. Their costumes and ancient crafts are distinctly beautiful and unusual but their villages are rather dirty and depressing. You can reach Chiang Mai by air, in an hour from Bangkok, by overnight sleeper train, or by road. There are several luxury bus services with day or night time travel to Chiang Mai, the return fare being from 500 baht; return airfare is 2,200 baht; first-class train return 1,500 baht; second class is only 750 baht.

Haadyai

Haadyai, in the deep south of Thailand, is one of the country's richest commercial and trading cities, bustling with activity. It is made up of shops—up and down the streets and all the way to the outskirts of town—offering anything from great varieties of local fruit and fish to imported items. One specialty is cloth, Thai silks and cottons and especially batik, that exotically patterned cloth.

The town itself is modern and not very attractive from the historical or esthetic point of view. It is, however, a convenient center for touring the southern attractions such as Songkhla or Phuket and has reasonable hotels and a busy nightlife. It can be reached by train, bus or domestic flight. Airfare is 3,060 baht, return train, first class, is 1,750 baht, second class 1,020 baht. The bus is a very long and tiring non-stop journey, but costs half the rail fares.

Kanchanaburi

Lying 75 miles northwest of Bangkok, Kanchanaburi is one of the most picturesque provinces in the country, with great forests, wild jungles and rugged hills. It has achieved a great archeological importance since the discovery of Neolithic burial sites. The town of Kanchanaburi is a departure point for many interesting trips to some of Thailand's most notable scenic and historical attractions.

The bridge on the River Kwai was made internationally famous by the book and subsequent film, but it does have an actual place in history and to many is worth a visit. The famous bridge was built to link the valley of the River Kwai Yai to the valley of the River Kwai Noi. At Kanchanaburi lie the British, Dutch, Indian, and Anzac prisoners of war who died in the building of the notorious "Death Railway" during the Second World War. There is a poor, but interesting museum here, devoted to the railway and the prisoners who built it. The Erawan Falls, a restful boat cruise from Kanchanaburi are named after Erawan, the three-headed elephant steed of the mythical God Indra, because of their shape. Discovered as recently as 1957, they are made up of 15 large falls and numerous smaller ones, in a peaceful setting of forest scenery. Stay at the new 60-room hotel or on delightful raft houses. A three-day, two-night tour from Bangkok, inclusive of travel, meals, and the hotel, costs 3,000 baht. Booking through Diethelm or other Bangkok agents.

Khao Yai National Park

In the early sixties, at the persistent urging of Thai naturalists, the Government set aside a wildly beautiful chunk of central Thailand as a national park. The decision has paid off handsomely: today the park is one of the favorite weekend excursion targets of Bangkokians who want to get back to nature.

There is plenty to get back to. Khao Yai covers more than half a million acres, spills out into four provinces. Its green hills, covered by evergreen and deciduous forest, rise to 4,000 feet. It is the home of the wild elephant, of bear, deer, boar, tiger, monkey, of tropical birds, of wild orchids, but few tourists currently report seeing game.

Khao Yai is northeast of Bangkok, about 125 miles from the capital by a new road. Most picturesque are the last ten miles in which the road winds along the flanks of the hills, climbing higher and higher above the green valleys below. Khao Yai's main attractions are the jungle paths which finger out from Non Khing village, the center of the park. Three miles from the village, along one of these paths, is Pha Klaoy (Orchid Cliff) waterfall, so named because of the wild orchids which grow near it in profusion. Somewhat farther is another, equally picturesque, fall, Hew Suwat.

Khao Yai is also excellent for golf, climbing, picnics and camping out. One suggestion: avoid making the trip on the weekend when the park is crowded with Saturday–Sunday overnighters. (Bungalows are available for rent through the TAT should you decide to spend a few days here, but they are not very luxurious and services are poor.) TAT also arranges transportation from Bangkok.

Lopburi

On the rail and highway route to the north, almost 100 miles from Bangkok, lies Lopburi, another of Thailand's ancient cities dating from the 6 to 11th centuries.

Once a Khmer outpost in a Siam that paid tribute to the kings of Angkor, Lopburi's main attraction is the Triple Prang, a temple consisting of three huge Khmer-style pagodas. The city is also well known for the old summer palace of 17th-century King Narai who employed French engineers in the construction of the residence, now mostly in ruins. There is also the Renaissance-style house of Greek adventurer Constantin Paulkone. To the Thais, Lopburi is known for the Kala Shrine (Monkey Shrine). In the compound a large tree serves as home for hundreds of monkeys, regarded as descendants of the warrior monkeys who aided Rama in his fight against Ravana.

Nakorn Nayok, about 100 miles by road from Bangkok, is famed for its impressive Salika and Nang Rong waterfalls. Pitsanulok, about 200 miles by train from Bangkok, is close to Thailand's first capital of Sukhothai whose ruins can still be seen. Pitsanulok is famous for its 600-year-old Buddha, the Phra Buddha Jinaraj and a number of 15th-century ruins.

Nakhon Sri Thammarat

Some 750 miles south of Bangkok, this is one of the oldest of Thailand's cities. Since its foundation 1,400 years ago Nakhon Si Thammarat has been a religious center and it still contains very many temples. Wat Mahathat, one of the oldest monasteries in Thailand, is said to contain relics of the Lord Buddha. Today the city has a population of some 40,000, but it still has a peaceful and sleepy atmosphere. One of the local sports is bullfighting, setting one animal against another. This takes place on weekends. The city can be reached by rail or by the domestic airline TAC.

The Northeast: Pimai and Surin

The ancient remains to be found around Korat (Nakhon Ratchasima) date mainly from the Angkor period when this region was controlled by the Khmers.

Korat is an important—and rather ugly—modern city with a population of 80,000. It has a few remains of a 17th-century fort and city and is a convenient center to explore the ruins of the area.

Pimai is built on a very ancient site. In the Khmer period in about the 11th century it was an important town linked by a fine road with Angkor, 150 miles away. Now that Angkor cannot be visited, Pimai offers one of the best opportunities to study the exquisite architecture and sculpture of the period. The main temple at Pimai has been extensively renovated.

Surin is best known abroad for its annual elephant roundup in November, which features hundreds of the beasts put through their paces for an audience from all over the world. The TAT and travel agents arrange inclusive two-day tours to cover the roundup.

Sukhothai and Around

Some 375 miles north of Bangkok is the first capital city of the Thai nation which grew to great power and influence during the period 1257–1389. Here the Siamese culture flourished under a series of wise kings who encouraged the adoption of the Ceylonese forms of Theravada Buddhism. This religious inspiration produced a highly developed style of art and architecture, examples of which can be seen in ruins or as artifacts in the Ram Kamhaeng Museum at Sukhothai. Some of the ruins are under renovation in this huge old walled city; combined with the many crumbling palaces and temples they give a good idea of the power that must have existed in the Kingdom that first released an independent Thai nation from the control of the Khmer empire to the east.

In the same district are Pitsanulok and Sri Satchanalai, two other cities of this period of former greatness. Sri Satchanalai, particularly, offers the historian or amateur archeologist a fascinating glimpse of the beauty and grandeur achieved by the ancient builders who chose this lovely setting between high hills and the river. The ruins are unrestored and very peaceful. It was in this area that much of the early Thai celadon and Sawankalok ceramics were produced and bargains can still be obtained here, if you really know what to look for.

Other attractions in the area include the Wang Nang Am Waterfalls and Toong Slang Luang National Park with its mountainous terrain and rushing streams. The most convenient way to reach these sites is by taking an inclusive tour from Bangkok.

Pattaya

In a sandy bay, some 85 miles southeast of Bangkok, has developed the largest beach resort in the Asian tropics. Only 20 years ago this bay was almost completely deserted, with land costing only a few dollars an acre. Now it is one of the hottest pieces of real estate development in the region, with hotels, nightclubs, shops and restaurants fighting for shorespace. Pattaya is not yet Acapulco or Cannes—it still has an air of informality and it is not yet as well organized or as efficient as it should be, but things are changing, fast. Along with the growth of hotels and other tourist facilities have come problems such as lack of municipal planning and pollution, but compared with, say, the Mediterranean, the level of pollution is low indeed. Touting and overpricing are present as well, but again these are much less serious in Pattaya than elsewhere. Reports of security problems, especially bag snatching, have been received, so visitors should observe basic, common-sense precautions.

Tourist bus services from any Bangkok hotel cost 120 baht one way, 220 baht return, and the journey takes about 2½ hours. In the resort there are plenty of accommodations, except at the very high season of Christmas and the New Year when visiting Thais swell the numbers of foreign tourists. Hotels are excellent, from the large and expensive to the smaller, less formal, establishments; most have swimming pools, restaurants, bars, nightclubs, shops, tennis, and access to a very full range of watersports. There are also bungalow complexes, very suitable for families with children.

You can take a fishing boat out to the offshore islands, sail, waterski or parasail. Pattaya is one of the few resorts in Southeast Asia where you can hire a full range of good quality scuba gear, and take scuba lessons from qualified instructors. Underwater swimming is excellent. There are no sharks, although jellyfish are occasionally a problem. Large fish have been hunted out of the near-shore areas, but there are plenty of excellent opportunities for boat fishing in deeper waters. On land you can hire a motorcycle (but check insurance coverage carefully) and explore the many solitary bays or go inland to explore hills and forests. There are three good golf courses, tennis or squash at the hotels and horseback riding.

There is plenty of nightlife and the quality of both Asian and Western food in the many restaurants is good. There are lively nightclubs ranging in style from respectable to frankly seedy. The vice squad is not too active in Pattaya, but this problem is not unpleasant enough for a family group with children to have to avoid the place. The late night parade of "characters" in the village is extraordinary.

Bangsaen and Bang Saray

To the north and south of Pattaya are two other beach resorts, both different in character. Bangsaen is one of the beaches most popular with daily bus-trippers from Bangkok. The resort is packed on weekends and almost deserted during the week. On holidays the beach is crowded with vendors of straw hats, soft drinks, rubbishy souvenirs of sea shells or carved coconuts, kites and an endless array of snacks and eats. You can hire a deck chair, sailing boat or tire inner tube to float in the sea amid the thousands of paddling city folk. As a foreign visitor you are likely to be stared at and have your peace constantly disturbed by curious Thais. If you want the feel of an authentic beach resort, local style, this is it. Other non-beach-oriented attractions in the area include a nearby monkey hill, fishing villages, oyster farms and the shrine of Chao Mae Khao Sammuk, the sacred protectress of the local fishermen.

Bang Saray is different again. More of a holiday resort development, it offers privacy, a good beach and facilities and the chance to explore an adjacent fishing village which is small, but which has great character. Here are bungalows for rent and a reasonable restaurant. It is also the best place for hiring game-fishing equipment and boats.

Both resorts can be reached by bus or hire-car from Bangkok.

The Deep South

On the other side of the Gulf, 140 miles southwest of Bangkok, is the small town of Hua Hin. It became Thailand's first beach resort in 1920 when King Rama VII built a summer palace there. It offers good beaches, an excellent 18-hole golf course and relaxation. The local nightlife and shopping are not very exciting, but small restaurants in the town serve good Thai- and Chinese-style seafood. Hua Hin is reachable by train, car, or bus from Bangkok and the journey takes about 2½ hours, passing such places as the Rose Garden and Nakhon Pathom en route.

Koh (meaning island) Samui is an exquisitely beautiful, relatively undeveloped island in the Gulf of Thailand halfway between Bangkok and the Malaysian border. It can be reached by air or overnight train to the small port of Surat Thani from which a daily ferry takes approximately five hours over usually calm seas to reach the island. Perhaps the easiest way to reach it is to take one of the organized tours arranged by agents in the capital, but these tend to be short and you are likely to want to stay longer. Accommodations are limited and restaurants modest, serving only Thai and Chinese food.

Phuket is Thailand's only island province, located over 550 miles south of Bangkok on the west coast, in the Andaman Sea. It has a population of 150,000, a lush green pastoral landscape and good beaches. Its economy is based on fishing, copra, rubber, tin dredging—and, increasingly, tourism. Best way to reach Phuket is by air, via daily TAC flights from Bangkok, or by luxury bus services. Accommodations are reasonable, both in quality and price, and European food is available. Local dishes of lobster, shrimp, crayfish, and crab are superb, but nightlife and shopping opportunities are limited. This is essentially a retreat rather than a resort, but if you need mental stimulation just watching the local community and its activities will keep you busy. There are a number of excellent beaches around the island and underwater swimming is good. Equipment, including scuba, is available. Good fishing is available, but no good game-fishing gear is to be hired locally. There are a number of boat excursions available, including those to the spectacularly beautiful islands in Phang Nga Bay. The bay is scattered with huge limestone outcrops, pillars rising as high as 900 feet, between which the green water is calm and clear.

Songkhla is the most southerly large town on the east coast of Thailand. It is reached by a two-hour flight from Bangkok, or 21 hours by train and bus through Haadyai, a bustling, modern and unattractive town. Songkhla is set between the sea and a huge lagoon, both of which offer good, if unorganized, excursion opportunities. The area has long stretches of white sandy beaches, lush vegetation and is famous for its great variety of native fruits and seafood. The buildings in this rather relaxed small city show the influence of Chinese and early Portuguese settlers for whom this was an important trading center. Accommodations are good and standards of Western-style tourist services are improving since it was designated by the TAT as a major area for development. It is not likely to grow too fast, however, due to the general air of relaxation among the community—one of the best reasons why you should visit the place. You can now take a seven-day luxury tour from Bangkok to Singapore, some 850 miles, a comfortable and interesting way to see a great deal of southern Thailand, Malaysia and its key cities. Accommodations are good all the way.

PRACTICAL INFORMATION

FACTS AND FIGURES. Population: 51.5 million. Land area: 513,000 sq. kms. Population percentage engaged in agriculture and fishing: 66%. Birth rate per 1,000: 26. Life expectancy: 61 years. Average per capita income: US$800 p.a. Number of tourists annually (1984): 2.4 million.

WHAT WILL IT COST? If you stay at one of the best hotels, your daily accommodation will cost between US$100 and $160, including service and tax for a double. Food should be less expensive and you should be able to eat for around US$25–35 per day per person. For a typical day then, including transportation, sightseeing, you should count on something like US$90–150 or more per person. Staying at one of the smaller and cheaper hotels will drop the accommodations cost to something like US$40–70 for a double. Your food bill, however, will run about the same—unless you eat in the simpler Thai or Chinese restaurants that do not cater to tourists. In that case, your food bill per day should be no more than US$12–20 each.

Inflation in Thailand has remained relatively steady over the past few years, at around 10–12 percent annually, and the recent strength of the US dollar has lowered the value of the local currency, the baht. Although no longer a bargain destination, Thailand does represent a good tourist buy in terms of the diversity of its offerings.

Bangkok, the capital, is naturally the most expensive city in Thailand, but the main beach resort, Pattaya, comes close to the big city's prices, especially in the quality hotels and plush restaurants. Once you get into the smaller towns (as one should try to do), the prices come down noticeably, but Western styles of comfort and cuisine are less available. As you get away from Western standards of sophistication, prices descend rapidly and life becomes simpler and, usually, less hectic.

Of the upcountry cities, Chiang Mai is the next most expensive after Bangkok. After that there is a big gap in both size and cost before you reach other provincial cities such as Lampang, Khon Kaen, or Nakhon Si Thammarat.

Of the beach resorts, Pattaya is certainly the most expensive, as already mentioned. After this come Hua Hin and Bangsaen, both quite a lot less expensive. Such resorts as Songkhla or Phuket are fishing or trading towns, but are beginning to attract international tourists, so prices have risen over recent years. Once you reach a retreat such as the island of Koh Samui, the prices are probably some 60% of those in Pattaya—but the facilities are, naturally, rather basic. Forget about filet steak or coq au vin and, instead, explore the delights of local Thai seafood—it is truly delicious.

The actual costs for, say, one- and two-week periods are difficult to give, as the difference in price ranges is wide between living Western-style in Thailand and seeking to live the local way. As a very general rule of thumb, your basic hotel cost might represent about half a day's expenditure.

There are a number of opportunities for bargain seekers in the off-season which is, roughly, May till September. A tough bargaining attitude toward hotels, jewelry and souvenir shops at that time, when business is relatively poor, can produce worthwhile discounts, although meal prices are not usually the subject for bargaining!

The cost of drinking in hotels or bars is quite high, but can be reduced substantially by buying hard liquor outside and taking it into the hotel with mixers. Buy in a supermarket.

The cheapest way to see upcountry destinations if you are short of time is to take the tours organized by local travel agents. Overnight sleeper train services are good (recommended are second-class couchettes on expresses).

A Typical Day's Cost (per person, at Approx. 27 Baht to US$1)

	Baht
Tourist class hotel—bed and Continental breakfast, including tax and service charge, double room, per person	1,100
Lunch at moderately priced restaurant	300
Dinner at moderately priced restaurant	500
Taxis for 2 miles (two journeys)	80
Cinema—good seat	40
Pack of cigarettes—best local brand	12
Coffee in popular café	15
Small beer in medium-quality bar	35
Half-day sightseeing tour	250
Total	2,332

One word of warning on drinking: do avoid drinking wine in Thailand. A bottle of very indifferent French red wine can cost 400 baht and a good vintage 1,200 baht, so it's best to forget wine till you reach a country where import duties are lower.

Note that everything costs considerably more in hotels and hotel shops, than it does outside—this includes jewelry, antiques and souvenirs, too.

If wine is prohibitive in cost, spirits are reasonable (imported Scoth 190–300 baht, depending on the place purchased outside hotel—local gin, 150 baht a bottle).

Anything imported is expensive, as heavy duty applies. If you are coming into Thailand via Hong Kong or Singapore, buy all cosmetics, cigarettes, liquor, etc., in advance.

Cost of Living. For local residents, Thailand is still relatively much less expensive than other Southeast Asian cities, although prices for expatriate residents have tended to increase over recent years—especially rents.

A typical two-bedroom apartment in a reasonably good area of Bangkok would cost, barely furnished, 9,000–20,000 baht per month, which would be considerably less than in Hong Kong or Singapore. A good housemaid would be paid 1,900 baht per month. Local residents often comment that schools are expensive, and medical costs very reasonable. (There is no national health scheme in Thailand.)

Local foodstuffs, including meat, are rather cheap by international standards. Excellent pork costs 40 baht a pound and chicken about 35 baht a pound. Any imported supermarket items, including canned or packaged food, is high in cost. A tin of ordinary baked beans, for example, can cost up to 80 baht.

Cars are expensive to buy, as are washing machines, but taxis are relatively cheap, if rattling.

This is a country where the minimum industrial wage is still only US$5 per day, so personal services are cheap, while manufactured products, especially imported ones, are expensive.

WHEN TO GO. It is generally quite hot. The heat reaches a peak of 94–96°F during the hot season which falls between the middle of February and the middle of June. From June to November it's monsoon time in Thailand. It's still hot but monsoon-laden clouds bring torrential rains, sometimes several times a day. It cools down then, but as soon as the rain is over, it's muggy and hot again. Thailand's most pleasant period is between November and February, the cool season or winter, as the Thais say. But it never gets really cold and the most you'll ever need is a sweater in the early morning or late at night. This is the best time of year for visitors.

WHERE TO GO. Most important, of course, is Bangkok (called Krungthep, or *City of the Angels,* by the Thai people). There you should visit the most important temples, take a boat ride along the canals, watch Thai-style boxing, see the classical dances, visit a Thai home, and look in on Chinatown. Also go to the Weekend Market (Saturday and Sunday), opposite the North Bangkok Bus Terminus. Outside the capital, you may have time to visit Chiang Mai, the ruins of Ayutthaya, or rest on the white-sand beaches to the south if you really want to take it easy. We can recommend a trip to Kanchanaburi, where you can see a bridge over the River Kwai, although it's not the one on which the picture by the same name centered. Beyond the bridge is a small jungle resort for an adventure holiday in relative comfort.

WHAT TO TAKE. Don't bring anything heavier than a sweater or a stole—that is if you arrive during the cool season. Otherwise, lightweight suits and dresses, preferably washable, are just the thing to bring. It's hot most of the time and you will go through plenty of clean clothes in one day. There are good same-day laundry services in most hotels. British and American tobaccos and cigarettes, a wide range of cosmetics and toiletries, and imported luxury goods from the United States and Europe are available in Bangkok shops.

ELECTRIC CURRENT. Mostly 220 volts, but check. Adaptors available for appliances in any good hotel.

LOCAL FESTIVALS. The festivals listed below are all in Bangkok, unless otherwise noted. In case of inclement weather or some other unforeseen happening, some of the festivities are occasionally postponed a day or two, so it is always wise to check with your travel agent before setting out to see one of these events.

December 31–January 2. *New Year* celebrations, especially colorful at the temples. Ceremonies and games at Pramane Ground, special Thai dances performed.

February. *Magha Puja* commemorates a gathering of 1,250 disciples who heard Lord Buddha deliver his sermon summarizing his cardinal doctrines. Buddhists recite prayers, after which they make a clockwise candle procession round the temple.

February–April. *Kite Flying Contests* at Pramane Ground (in front of Royal Palace). Barbs attached to the kite strings are used to destroy the other contestants' kites. So-called male (chula) kites battle female (pakpao) kites during the contests.

April 6. *Chakri Day* commemorates the enthronement of King Rama I, founder of the present dynasty, in 1782. It is now observed as the Dynastic Day of the Kings of Thailand.

Mid-April. *Songkran Festival,* a folk festival of throwing water as well as the setting free of fish and birds. Water is sprinkled on Buddha images, on the monks, parents and elders, as a gesture of veneration. Everyone joins in the fun and there is much splashing of water on passers-by. Especially worthwhile in Chiang Mai, where processions, dancing in the street, fairs and beauty contests are added to the general festivities and waterthrowing. A boisterous and fun-filled occasion.

May. *Ploughing Ceremony,* a traditional ritual performed before the King and Queen at Pramane Ground to open the rice-planting season.

May 5. *Coronation Day Anniversary,* when the King and Queen proceed to the Royal Chapel to preside over ceremonies commemorating the anniversary.

May. *Visakha Puja* commemorates the Buddha's birth, enlightenment and passing into Nirvana. Illumination of the many temples with thousands of paper lanterns and torchlight processions.

July. *Khao Parnsa* (Buddhist Lent), when the Buddhist monks return to their monasteries for study and meditation. Many young men join the monkhood for the period of Lent. The ceremony of accepting a novice into the priesthood is interesting and very photogenic.

August 12. *Queen's Birthday,* a celebration of Queen Sirikit's birthday, when she attends religious ceremonies at Chitralda Palace. A public holiday.

October–November. *Tod Kathin* and, during some years, the *Procession of Royal Barges* on the river, marking the official end of the rainy season, when the annual offering of new yellow robes is made to the monks. The King goes to the Monastery of the Dawn, on a specially chosen day, to present robes to the monks there. The Royal Barge procession has been revived in recent years with the boats having been extensively restored. It is a uniqùe and spectacular sight.

October. *Phra Cheddi Klang Nam Festival,* at the pagoda in Paknam, south of Bangkok. The festival is celebrated with colorful processions, games, and boat races.

October 23. *Chulalongkorn Day* commemorates the date of the death of the fifth king of the Chakri Dynasty, who died in 1910. Thousands of people place floral tributes and incense at the foot of his statue in front of the National Assembly Hall.

November. *Loi Krathong Festival,* when thousands of banana-leaf boats, each carrying lighted candles, are launched into the rivers and canals. Some of the best-loved folk songs are sung at this time. A truly delightful festival at the time of the 12th lunar month at full moon. The natural charm and gaiety of the Thai people seen at its best.

Golden Mount Festival. One of the most spectacular temple fairs to be seen in Bangkok. Sideshows, foodstalls, all the fun—and noise—of the fair set around the base of Bangkok's largest "hill"—a man-made mountain on the top of which is a golden temple.

Elephant Round-up at Surin. (Day trip possible.) 200 elephants in action, with demonstration of agility in a race; how wild elephants are caught and trained; and tug-of-war between 100 men and one elephant (the men usually lose).

December 5. *The King's Birthday.* National holiday. Illuminations of buildings and a parade of the royal household troops. Boat races on river.

December. *Fairs* are held all over Thailand, climaxing the year for the villagers.

HOW TO GET THERE. By air: Planes of more than 35 airlines touch down at Bangkok's Don Muang airport every week. Occasionally, cruise liners make Pattaya beach resort a port of call. The majority of tourists reach Thailand by air. The Thai government has spent much time and money renovating the airport and now it is one of the most pleasant in Asia.

Once in the airport, officials are generally pleasant and efficient, and baggage collection relatively quick, except at peak traffic times. Transportation into the city can be arranged at the special desk immediately after customs. To any downtown hotel: air conditioned limousine, 300 baht; seat in a minibus, 100 baht. On the main road outside the airport one can get an ordinary cab to city center hotels for 150–200 baht. Airport departure tax is 120 baht. **By train:** There's also an approach to the city by rail—and an exciting and picturesque one at that. You get on a train in Singapore, then travel the length of the Malayan or Kra Peninsula through Malaysia and southern Thailand to Bangkok. Air conditioning, sleeping car, lounge car, and a just passable dining car highlight its service. There are three "express" trains each week. They leave Singapore at 9 A.M., taking 52 hours, via Kuala Lumpur, Ipoh, and Butterworth, to Bangkok. Crossing the border of Malaysia and traveling up the long, narrow peninsular strip on the west side of the Gulf of Thailand affords some fascinating jungle scenery and lovely landscapes. The cost, first class, is about 2,200 baht, excluding food and drink. Since the dining car leaves much to be desired, many passengers bring biscuits and buy fresh fruit and soft drinks from vendors along the way. Second class (no air conditioning, a short pullman berth) is 1,050 baht. There are also inclusive overland luxury tours from Bangkok to Singapore.

PASSPORTS AND VISAS. All foreign nationals arriving in Thailand must have valid passports. A 15-day "transit" visa is granted to most nationalities on arrival, provided they can show confirmed onward travel arrangements (i.e., confirmed air ticket), to leave within 15 days. No extensions are usually granted for this type of visa. "Tourist" visas are valid for 90 days from date of issue and are good for a stay of up to 60 days in Thailand. They can be extended if a cash deposit or bank guarantee is lodged with the Immigration Department. Tourist visas are issued by overseas Thai embassies and consulates, free to some nationalities, $5 to others. Note that a "multi-entry" endorsement is needed if one is touring out from Thailand and returning later. No exit visas required. For a longer stay, or for the business traveler, a "non-immigrant" visa is preferable, valid for 90 days, but for this type of visa one may be required to present a tax clearance certificate on departure if one has been earning while in the country.

HEALTH CERTIFICATES. An international certificate of vaccination for cholera and yellow fever is only required if coming from contaminated areas. Health certificates are not, now, usually checked at Bangkok Airport on arrival.

CUSTOMS. Immigration and customs clearance forms should be issued to you for completion on your flight, before arrival in Bangkok. 200 cigarettes or 250 grams of smoking tobacco are allowed. One quart of wine or liquor is allowed and all personal effects for your trip may be brought into Thailand duty-free. Prohibited are all kinds of narcotics, obscene photos or literature, firearms and ammunition, certain species of fruits, vegetables, and plants. Currency of more than US$2,000 per person must be declared on arrival.

TRAVELING IN THAILAND. Air, rail, and road communications networks within Thailand are all efficient and modern, thanks to massive expenditure of aid and international loan money over the last two decades. The visitor can combine the various means of travel to see a lot in a reasonably short upcountry schedule. Some would claim that Bangkok and upcountry Thailand are as different as two separate countries; try to visit both.

By air: The *Thai Airways Company,* 161 Larn Luang Rd., is the goverment-owned domestic airline and operates services to all major towns and cities in Thailand, using Avro 748 and Boeing 737 equipment. The airline that transports you to Thailand can arrange domestic flights in advance, or it is easily done on arrival in Bangkok. Thailand is a large country, the road distance from north to south being over 1,430 miles. If time is limited, air travel is the most practical and convenient way to reach such cities as Chiang Mai in the north (1½ hour's flight) or Phuket in the south (over 1 hour's flight). Airfare from Bangkok to Chiang Mai is 2,200 baht, return; to Phuket is 2,680 baht, round trip. Domestic services operate from Don Muang, the same airport as for international flights. Domestic flight departure tax is 20 baht.

By Train: The *State Railway of Thailand* operates a modern system over 2,480 miles of track. There are four main trunk lines, to the north, northeast, east, and south. Sleeping cars and/or air-conditioned carriages are available on all long-distance trains; dining cars offer adequate, but not very interesting, food. Trains are clean and comfortable and timetables reasonably punctual. Recommended.

Daily services cover all main destinations within the country from Bangkok. There are two main stations in Bangkok, Hualampong, and Bangkok Noi, which is in Thonburi, on the farther side of the river from the main city. Be sure to check which one your train leaves from.

Fares are reasonable and tickets can be efficiently reserved in advance. Second-class couchette sleeper berth to Chiang Mai, is under 1,000 baht round trip, 1st class only 1,500 baht and the overnight sleeper express leaves Bangkok at 5:00 P.M. daily for the 14-hour journey, which is very pleasant and relaxing. To Haad Yai, first-class round-trip rail fare is 1,750 baht, including sleeper charge.

The greatest travel opportunity offered by the railroad system out of Bangkok is a direct link to Singapore at the southern end of the Malay Peninsula. The journey takes 52 hours, but is a fascinating experience and traveling conditions are comfortable in first class, the fare for which, with sleeping car supplement, is 2,200 baht. Travel by rail is a good way to see something of rural Thailand and, in combination with air transport, need not take up too much of a busy itinerary. The hustle and bustle of Asian railroad stations, with food vendors and extensive loadings and unloadings of goods and passengers, can give wonderful opportunities for photography. Tickets and reservations at Hualampong Station or through certain travel agents, who may charge a small service fee.

By bus: Long-distance buses reach into every corner of the country. They are extremely cheap and extremely uncomfortable. Increasingly, however, there are major trunk routes where air-conditioned luxury, scheduled tour buses are offered. There are several major terminals from which buses leave Bangkok, but the communications problem and lack of spoken English in these hectic stations make bus travel for the inexperienced foreign visitor a rather unnerving and harrowing experience. Any travel agent will direct visitors to reliable and comfortable private luxury bus services upcountry.

If you enjoy bus travel then the best way to take advantage of the excellent Thai road system is to use the very good services operated by some of the Bangkok travel agents. There are regular bus tours to most major tourist attractions in the provinces and a direct daily express service to Chiang Mai and Phuket by air-conditioned bus. Recommended is the Diethelm 7-day "around Thailand" bus tour and their 8-day overland trip from Bangkok to Singapore, using train, boat, and plane, as well as bus.

By boat. Within the country there is an extensive network of rivers and canals that carries much trade and passenger traffic. The lack of fixed schedules, large-scale operators, or facilities suitable for visitors from abroad, however, make this means of transportation rather impractical for the tourist. Within Bangkok there are several excursions offering travel on the river or canals, and leading travel agents offer luxury launch services upriver to Bang-Pa-In and Ayutthaya.

There is no longer a regular shipping service from Bangkok down the western coast of the Gulf of Thailand, but plans are being made for a hydrofoil service from Bangkok down the coast to Songkhla and to Pattaya, the main beach resort. For availability, check with local travel services.

By car: Self-drive motoring cannot be recommended to the tourist visitor to Thailand; indeed, it cannot be recommended to anyone except a dedicated Kamikaze pilot. There are a number of contenders for the title of "city most likely to cause the driver to have a heart attack," but Bangkok must certainly be close to the top of the list. Insurance coverage is not compulsory in Thailand, but it is strongly recommended for any foreign driver—the financial consequences of an accident can be very serious. Once in the country, roads are good and gasoline (petrol) readily available. Most city street names are in Thai, which makes navigation rather difficult, especially as English is not spoken widely outside the capital. Traffic flows on the left (most of the time!) and speed limits are technically 60 kmph in Bangkok and 90 kmph outside. Few Thai drivers would even know what the limits are, let alone observe them. International driver's license required.

Car hire: If you're not daunted by the preceding "motoring" section, you can find a number of self-drive hire companies in Bangkok. If you go to the expense of hiring a car, which is higher than in the U.S. or other developed self-drive countries, you might as well go for the small extra cost (not more than $15 a day total) of engaging a chauffeur as well. On upcountry trips, however, you are usually expected to provide in addition an allowance for the driver's food and lodging.

Avis offers the best service in Thailand and operates from the Rama Tower Hotel; other leading hire organizations include *Hertz,* on Ploenchitr Rd., or *Asoke Car Rent,* 79 Sukhumvit 21. If using one of the smaller local car or motor-cycle hire companies you are advised to check most carefully on the insurance coverage provided.

MONEY. The basic unit of currency is the *baht.* There are 100 *satang* in one baht. Easy to distinguish by color, bills are marked with Thai and Arabic numerals. Four different bills are in use: ten baht—brown, twenty baht—green, one hundred baht—red, five hundred baht—purple. Coins in use are twenty-five satang, fifty satang, one baht and five baht. The baht is considered one of Asia's most stable currencies. But nowadays even the most stable currencies can fluctuate widely in relation to others, so check the $ and £ rates of exchange before—and during your trip. At presstime for this edition (mid 1985) US$1.00=27.50 baht, UK£1=33 baht.

There is no limit on the amount of foreign currency visitors may bring into the country provided that they declare the amount on entry and that the amount brought out does not exceed that brought in. No traveler may bring into the country or take out local currency in excess of 1000 baht. There is no import limit on travelers' checks and drafts. Foreign currencies (cash) in excess of US$2,000 should be declared to the Customs on arrival. Money can be changed at any bank, moneychangers, in hotels, and in most downtown shops that cater to tourists. Hotels usually offer very poor rates of exchange.

Banking hours are from 8:30 A.M. to 3:30 P.M. Banks are closed on Saturdays.

HOW TO GET AROUND BANGKOK. Within the capital you have the choice of bus, taxi, *samlor* (a small and risky three-wheeler, two-seat vehicle propelled by a motor scooter engine), and water buses.

By bus: Buses are crowded, especially in rush hours, when crowds of extra passengers hang on to the outside like bunches of human grapes. The city bus network is efficient and comprehensive, with fares from 2 baht. However, all buses are identified only by color and numbers. Bus route maps can be obtained from book stalls or, sometimes, from the Tourist Authority of Thailand offices. There is also a system of air-conditioned buses operating on long-distance routes within the city. Fares vary according to distance, ranging from 5 to 15 baht.

By taxi: Best bet for the new visitor are taxis. Cabs have meters but no drivers will use them, so you must bargain for each journey in advance, which makes a little preliminary research with a map desirable. Hotel doormen will assist with this bargaining, but visitors usually soon get to enjoy the process, counting it a great triumph if they can win a big reduction. Generally, you should reckon on not paying more than 25 baht for a short journey and not more than 100 baht for any trip within the city. This rough rule will prevent at least the worst level of exploitation. Most taxi drivers speak some English, but general comprehension of directions and destinations is poor, so be sure of your destination and be able to describe it in simple words, or have it written in Thai by a hotel or shop employee. Prices tend to be higher during the morning and evening rush hours, which are dreadful and should be avoided if possible. An increasing number of taxis are air-conditioned. Those seeking the most reliable and comfortable taxis can use hotel taxi services, more expensive than ordinary cabs.

By samlor: *Samlor* (meaning "three wheels") travel can be fun if you are young or have nerves of steel. If you have neither, they are best left alone. Samlors are cheaper than taxis, but generally the drivers do not speak English and have a poorer knowledge of the touristic aspects of their city.

By water: On the Chao Phya River and major canals there are waterbus services. The sleek white motor launches on the river provide a wonderful excursion. You pay 5–15 baht for the trip and can go up or downstream for several fascinating miles from the centrally placed landings next to the Oriental or Royal Orchid hotels. You simply climb on to one of these craft and go off anywhere to explore the riverside streets for a while before getting back aboard the next one going back the other way to your starting point. All the waterbuses stop at all the same landing stages, so it is difficult to get lost.

TIPPING. Most of the hotels will attach a 10 percent service charge and an 11 percent government tax to your bill. Tipping then is not necessary, but if the service has been good, a small tip is in order. When no service charge is mentioned, tip between 10 and 15 percent of the cost. Cab drivers are *not* tipped. Hotel porters, 5 baht per piece, or 10 baht minimum. Airport porters, fixed fee of 5 baht per bag, no extra tip.

ACCOMMODATIONS. A tremendous boom in hotel construction over the past few years has eased what used to be a chronic room shortage in Bangkok. The city has more than 19,000 hotel rooms, offering something for just about everybody's pocketbook—from luxurious hostelries to economy-class accommodations. All hotels are air conditioned. All first-class and most moderately priced ones have swimming pools, coffee shops, restaurants, shops, bars, and nightclubs. The service will be courteous and the staff exceptionally friendly by world-wide hotel standards. English may not always be easily understood, so speak slowly and clearly.

All hotels listed below operate on the European Plan, which means you are paying only for your room. Meals are not included. A 10 percent service charge and 11 percent government tax will be added to room charges.

The hotels listed are classified as *Deluxe, First Class, Moderate,* and *Inexpensive.* Prices quoted are for double-occupancy rooms in Thai baht. Where prices are *not* shown, grades of hotels do not exist in that locality. Also, as no accurate grading system exists in Thailand, the rates must be considered approximate.

BANGKOK

Deluxe—2,200–4,000 baht

Dusit Thani. Saladaeng Circle, Rama IV Rd. Topped by a golden spire, its triangular shape affords a view from all 580 rooms. There is a rooftop nightclub with a magnificent view, plus restaurants, bars, shops, and a disco.

Hilton. Delightful new luxury hotel with 400 rooms in a charming tropical garden setting off Wireless Rd., near to U.S. and British embassies. Good restaurants and facilities; it is proving popular with business travellers.

Oriental. 48 Oriental Lane. The best! This oldest of Bangkok's large hotels is loaded with charm. On the banks of the Chao Phya River, the Oriental offers outstanding service, 420 luxurious rooms, and every facility. Popular barbecue dinners on riverside terrace. The superb Normandie Grill, swimming pool. Delightful gardens and riverside terrace.

Regent. Rajdamiri Rd. Superb new hotel with 420 rooms built around 2 open air atriums and overlooking grounds of Royal Bangkok Sports Club. Excellent restaurants, Asian and Western, plus tea served elegantly in the huge lobby.

First Class—1,700–2,400 baht

Airport Hotel. Next to the International Airport. New and comfortable. 300 rooms. Convenient for overnight transits, but 17 kms out of city. Comprehensive range of facilities and services.

Ambassador. Soi 11–13 Sukhumvit Rd. 1,050 rooms. Pool, shopping, plus range of excellent bars, restaurants, nightclub, etc. Out of city center.

Asia. 296 Phyathai Rd. Comfortable, 360 rooms, with reasonable facilities.

Hyatt Central Plaza Bangkok. 1601 Phaholyothin, Central Plaza Complex. Out of the city center, but new and with full range of facilities.

Indra Regent. Rajparop Rd. Has 440 rooms, shops, restaurants, bars, and a theater-restaurant in 18th-century Thai style. Conventioneers' and shoppers' paradise near a busy Thai market area.

Montien. 54 Suriwong Rd. In the center of the business district, the Montien has good restaurants, swinging night club, pleasant pool, and shopping inside and outside. 580 rooms. Close to Patpong nightlife.

President. 135/26 Gaysorn Rd. In shopping center, convenience is the key word, with shopping inside and outside. The Fireplace Grill is first rate and so is the coffee shop. 400 rooms.

Royal Orchid Sheraton. Capt. Bush Lane, off New Rd. Sparkling, new, quality hotel impressively located on the river. 780 big rooms, plus good range of restaurants and all amenities; excellent service.

Siam Intercontinental. 195 Rama I Rd. Built in an attractive mixture of traditional Thai and modern architecture, the Siam sprawls over a huge landscaped site. Shops, postal and travel agency offices, plus 414 rooms and a reasonable choice of restaurants. The gardens and swimming pool are particularly beautiful.

Sheraton Tawana. 80 Suriwongse Rd. Rooms are slightly small for an otherwise luxury hotel, but good service and facilities. Convenient location. 265 rooms.

Moderate—900–1,800 baht.

Erawan. 494 Rajdamri Rd. Among Bangkok's older hotels, the Erawan is still a favorite for many returnees to Bangkok. The tables around the swimming pool are comfortable for morning coffee and afternoon tea, and Le Cave serves delicious seafood. Le Chalet, good Swiss food. 245 rooms.

First. 2 Petchburi Rd. Rather noisy 222-room tourist-class hotel.

Mandarin. 622 Rama IV Rd. 419 rooms, nightclubs, shops and other facilities, reasonable.

Manhattan. 12 Soi 15, Sukhumvit Rd. 200 rooms, adequate facilities but well away from city center.

Manohra. 412 Suriwong Rd. 216 rooms. It is across the street from the Bank of America in a good shopping district.

Narai. 222 Silom Rd. 500 rooms, a revolving rooftop restaurant and a German beer cellar make this a convenient tourist hotel with full range of facilities.

Rajah. 18 Soi Nana North. 450 rooms in the main residential area for foreigners, 30 minutes from downtown. Lively after hours coffee shop, unusual clientele. *Not* a family hotel.

Inexpensive—500–900 bahr

Park. 6 Soi 7, Sukhumvit Rd. 129 air-conditioned rooms, swimming pool and restaurant.

Royal. 2 Rajdamnoen Rd. Close to government buildings, Grand Palace and National Museum. 140 rooms. Frequented by tour groups, especially German.

Rose. Just off Suriwongse Rd., close to Patpong. Modest, but inexpensive and convenient rooms. Small coffee shop. Popular with bachelor visitors.

Trocadero. 343 Surawongse Rd. Older style, with 212 rooms and limited facilities. Full of character, in convenient location. Restaurant is poor, but good ones are close by.

Viengtai. 42 Tanee Rd., Bang Lam-Poo. Good reputation among low-priced hotels. 130 air-conditioned rooms and swimming pool, restaurant, and bar.

Others, even cheaper, are *Federal, Malaysia* and *Swan.* Rates around 300 baht.

A few older-style guest houses, such as the centrally located *Swiss Guest House* on Convent Road, off Silom, still exist and provide good, inexpensive accommodations. Both YMCA and YWCA are located on Sathorn Rd.

BANGSAEN

(65 miles southeast of Bangkok, on Pattaya Road)

Bangsaen Beach. Covering 190 acres by the beach in the favorite seaside resort for Thai people from Bangkok. 150 bungalows and hotel block of 30 air-conditioned rooms with bar and restaurant serving Thai, Chinese, and not very good European food. Inexpensive compared to Pattaya.

HUA HIN

(144 miles southwest of Bangkok)

Railway Hotel. In Thailand's oldest seaside resort, on the west coast of the Gulf and close to a good course, the Old Railway Hotel is a delightful return to the days of Somerset Maugham. The food is poor, but the atmosphere more than makes up for it. There is a new wing of air-conditioned rooms, but those in search of character should try the un-air-conditioned rooms in the old wing, with high ceilings, fans, and mosquito-netted beds.

Royal Garden. New and delightful beachside resort hotel on the Gulf of Siam near Hua Hin. Limited, but good facilities. 171 rooms. Tennis, pool, disco, and nearby 18 hole golf course.

CHIANG MAI

Chiang Inn. Probably most luxurious in Chiang Mai. 175 good rooms and facilities. 100 Changklan Rd.

Chiang Mai Orchid Lodge. 267 comfortable rooms in this modern hotel. Good facilities. 100 Huay Kaew Rd.

Poy Luang. 227 rooms, good facilities and service. Out of town center, rather "plastic." 146 Super Highway.

Prince. 121 rooms, plain but comfortable.

Railway. Near the station, and a long way to the town center. Well-kept gardens, and 77 old-style air-conditioned rooms.

Rincome. Popular first-class hotel with 150 air-conditioned rooms, a nice pool and lobby, and good service. Huay Kaew Rd.

Suriwongse. Good location with 200 rooms. Cheerful service and inexpensive meals. 110 Changklan Rd

KORAT

Chomsurang. A good base for seeing the Khmer monuments of northeastern Thailand. Air-conditioned rooms, pool, coffee shop.

PATTAYA

(85 miles southeast of Bangkok)

Asia Pattaya. 320 rooms, superb pool and private beach, good nightclub and charming modern atmosphere. "Over the hill," away from the main bay.

Grand Palace. Newest hotel in bay, with its own beach. 460 rooms and full facilities.

Merlin Pattaya. 400 rooms, modern and luxurious with good convention and other facilities. In central position on main beach. Good restaurants and lovely pool, garden area.

Montien Pattaya. Under same management as Montien Bangkok, 320 delightful rooms, all with sea view. Lovely pool and tropical gardens, good restaurants and facilities. Among the best.

Nipa Lodge. 145 rooms. Pattaya's original beachside quality hotel. Now a little worn around the carpets, but with a delightful atmosphere. Offering good restaurants and service. It also offers a large freshwater pool, tennis, watersports facilities, deep-sea fishing, and skindiving. Good swinging disco. The excellent open-air *Buccaneer* is one of several good restaurants.

Orchid Lodge. With 243 rooms and loggias set in lovely tropical gardens on slight hill overlooking the sea and sunset. Under the same management as the Nipa Lodge and with the same informal atmosphere. Lively discothèque, tennis, and watersports facilities.

Royal Cliff Beach. The largest hotel in the resort, with 750 rooms, convention facilities, nightclub, shops, and restaurants, full sporting and recreational facilities. The Royal Cliff has its own beach and bay, overlooking the sea and offshore islands. It is about a 15-minute drive from the main bay of Pattaya and away from the village. Good range of restaurants, but the food is indifferent.

Siam Bayshore. Closest to the characterful village, where most of the resort's nightclubs, eating places and shops are; offers delightful facilities and 270 rooms, many set in smaller blocks overlooking exquisite gardens. Good tennis facilities.

Tropicana. Pleasant low-rise hotel in landscaped setting; the main building is a mass of flowers and trailing plants. All rooms have balcony and refrigerator. 200 rooms.

There are many smaller, less expensive hotels in Pattaya, but their facilities and services are nowhere near the quality of those listed above. In the village and along the beaches of adjacent bays there are a number of cottages that can be rented by the day or week and that offer better value for a family on a longer stay. Many of the cottages along the shore have Bangkok contact addresses, obtainable from the TAT or Bangkok agents. Cottages are furnished and most have limited cooking facilities. Among the best are *Moonlight on Sea, Golden Sands. Wongse Amataya* is most recommended, with good restaurants and facilities. Many small, inexpensive hotels in and near the village cater to the budget traveler; advance booking is usually not necessary.

PHUKET

(572 miles south of Bangkok)

Coral Beach Hotel. Superb beachside location for this pleasant new resort hotel. 124 rooms on Patong Beach. Good restaurants and facilities. Run by Siam Lodges. Tennis, big pool, water sports, etc.

Pan Sea. 40 rustic-style, informally grouped bungalows and cabanas set on stilts among the palm trees. Simple but delightful facilities and good beach location.

Patong Beach. Pleasant beachside location and good facilities. 104 rooms.

Pearl Hotel. 250 rooms of modest facilities but better than older accommodations. Not on the beach.

Phuket Island Resort. 100 rooms and 50 bungalows in this delightful beachside development, ideal for peace and rest, or watersports, including excellent skindiving. Good seafood restaurant, but not a sophisticated resort.

Phuket Merlin. Not on beach, but 210 comfortable rooms and reasonable facilities make this a convenient base for exploring.

Thavorn Hotel. A total of 90 rooms and limited facilities, including dining room and pool. Air-conditioned singles.

PHANG NGA BAY

(Spectacular scenic bay 3 hours drive from Phuket)

Phang Nga Bay Resort. 100 reasonable rooms in this new hotel in spectacular setting.

SURAT THANI

(Southern fishing town and port, reached by air or train from Bangkok, jumping off point for Koh Samui)

Wang Tai Hotel. 238 new comfortable rooms. Chinese and seafood restaurants, night club and other good facilities.

SONGKHLA

(826 miles from Bangkok, close to Malaysian border)

Samila Hotel. A modern and comfortable hotel with 100 rooms, set on fine beach. The town is some 20 miles from the nearest airport, at Haadyai, and is a rapidly developing resort. Service and food are not the best, but local open-air seafood restaurants offer excellent meals. Golf, sea, and land excursions.

CLOSING HOURS. Most tourist shops are open from 9–10 A.M. till around 7 in the evening. Smaller shops and local markets stay open even longer.

TOURS. There are numerous tour operators in Thailand who are both efficient and competitive. The problems of the language barrier, particularaly upcountry, and the difficulties in using the local means of transportation make the organization of one's own individual upcountry tour program rather hard work. Bangkok is a big and confusing city. It is difficult to communicate with taxi drivers, impossible with bus conductors, and it is easy to get lost. Better by far to let someone else have all the practical problems and just get on with enjoying the sights. Once you have seen the major attractions you can relax and "people watch"—a fascinating pastime that can be done anywhere and needs no organizing.

Most of the attractions listed earlier in this chapter under *All about Bangkok, After Wat, What?* and *Upcountry Destinations* (including the sites of Pimai, Nakhom Pathom, and Kanchanaburi) can be seen through organized tours, but to see them all would take weeks, so get a detailed schedule of tours from any operator and plan your itinerary in conjunction with that, after arrival.

The standards of knowledge among tour guides are not usually very high in Thailand so if you have specific interests on which you need detailed information it is better to undertake research from books.

Among the most reliable agencies offering tours in Bangkok and upcountry are *World Travel Service,* office at 1053 New Rd., and in a number of leading hotels; *Boon Vanit,* 420/9 Soi 1 Siam Square; *Diethelm Travel,* 544 Ploenchit Rd.; *East West Tours,* Soi 3, Sukhumvit; *Arlymear Travel,* 109 Surawong Road.

Costs range from 300 baht for the morning floating market tour that includes the Temple of the Dawn or a three-hour city and temples tour, to upwards of 11,000 baht for a seven-day trip upcountry. For example, a full-day tour of Nakhom Pathom will cost about 600 baht, including a rural floating market and the afternoon Rose Garden Village Show. A full-day boat tour to Pattaya and the off-shore coral islands, including a seafood lunch, costs around 650 baht. There are frequent inclusive tours by road, rail or air to most major attractions, but it is worthwhile to compare prices, if you have time, as they do vary quite widely among operators. Generally you can expect to save money by taking a tour, relative to the amount you can see in any given time.

The *Tourist Authority of Thailand* (TAT), Rajdamnoen Ave. (next to Boxing Stadium) tel. 282–1143/9, does not arrange tours, but can assist with leaflets and information.

All Bangkok hotels operate efficient tour desks.

SPORTS. Spectator: Thailand's most popular spectator sport is *football* (soccer). There are no professional teams in the country but some of Bangkok's elevens stack up well among the elite of Asia. Big games are played at Bangkok's spacious National Stadium.

A real sport is *kite-fighting.* This is performed in the windy season during the early months of the year, when "male" kites fight "female" kites in the air, steered by expert handlers on the ground. This should not be confused with the simple kite flying of Western children. Kite-fighting in Thailand is an elaborate, complicated, and skilled procedure seen during March-April.

Then, of course, there is *Thai boxing* performed regularly during the week at Bangkok's *Lumpini* and *Rajadamnern* boxing stadia. Thai boxing is far from Marquis of Queensberry rules (he would probably pale if he could see it) because it allows elbowing and kicking besides the use of the hands. Because of this ability to use extremities with equal facility, the Thais have been called "the race of eight arms." Bouts are fought over five rounds and begin with a prayer and ceremonial solo dance in which one fighter tries to impress his prowess on the other. As a rule, however, the other boxer is too busy going through a performance of his own to pay much attention to his opponent. If you go to see "the ferocious Somsook, the Tiger of Raiburi," battle "hard-smashing, lion-killing Deang of Bangkok," don't forget to take a look at the huddled groups of betters in the corners of the stadium. Thais love to bet on anything and they're at their best at the fights, which can be seen at *Rajadamnern Stadium* on Mondays, Wednesdays, Thursdays, and Sundays, and at *Lumpini* on Tuesdays, Fridays, and Saturdays.

Something you might like to take in is *fishfighting* and *cockfighting.* They even have *cricket fighting* in some areas outside Bangkok.

For *horseracing* fans there are regular meetings at the *Royal Bangkok Sports Club* or the *Turf Club.* There are a number of bowling lanes in Bangkok, and all good hotels have swimming pools. Some also have tennis facilities. Joggers usually work out in Lumpini Park, as street running is out of the question.

Participant: For *swimming* you'll have to go anywhere between 45 to 150 miles from Bangkok (unless you like the pool at the hotel) to the beach resorts of *Pattaya* and *Hua Hin.*

Pattaya offers good opportunities to learn and participate in *scuba diving.* A day's excursion costs around 800 baht, including rentals. Also good for *sailing, parasailing,* and *water skiing.* Motor fishing boats for a day at the off-shore coral islands can be rented for 400–600 baht.

Bang Saray is the best place to hire *game-fishing* equipment and boats. Such a trip costs around 1,500 baht a day.

Golf is a growing game in Thailand. Bangkok, has ten 18-hole courses and the beach resorts of *Hua Hin* and *Pattaya* possess several good courses. *Tennis* is available in several Pattaya hotels.

MUSEUMS. *The National Museum,* on the far side of the Pramane Ground from the Royal Hotel, is open daily 9–4, except Mondays. Admission free on Sundays, otherwise 10 baht. Housed in a former Royal Palace, built in 1782, with later exhibition halls, the museum contains a fine collection of prehistoric items as well as a representative selection of all major art forms and styles from the different periods of Thai history. The museum is strongly oriented toward religious exhibits with comparative material from other countries and cultures in Asia. There are regular guided tours in English.

Jim Thompson's House, Soi Kasemsan 2, Rama I Rd. (near the National Stadium). American Jim Thompson came to Thailand with the American forces at the end of World War II and stayed to develop the Thai silk industry, in which he saw great business potential. His love of Asian art led him to assemble a huge and very fine collection, which he housed in a series of antique buildings that were moved from various parts of Thailand and reassembled on the present site. Thompson disappeared mysteriously while on holiday in Malaysia in 1967. His house is now a museum and gives a wonderful chance to see a typical rich Thai house of traditional design. Open 9 A.M.–4 P.M. on weekdays; admission of 50 baht goes to charity. Guided tours.

Suan Pakkard Palace, Sri Ayudhaya Rd., A delightful traditional palace complex, housing the art collection of a leading aristocratic family. Fine examples of Thai antiquities, bronze, stone carving, furniture, and ceramics. A fine lacquer pavilion is probably the best of its type still to be seen in Thailand. Beautiful gardens in formal Thai style. Open daily except Sundays, 9–4; admission 50 baht.

Small museums are sometimes found at major archaeological sites. (See sections covering upcountry destinations.)

READING MATTER. English and American publications are available at good bookshops found in all main shopping centers and hotels. Bangkok has two English-language morning newspapers, the *Bangkok Post* and *The Nation,* and one afternoon paper, the *Bangkok World.*

SHOPPING. There are lots of beautiful things to buy in Bangkok. The secret of success is to shop in the vicinity of your hotel, rather than to sit in a taxi for hours in traffic-jammed streets attempting to reach a specific store. Each hotel is surrounded by shops carrying the same goods as those located at the other end of the city. The great local markets where Bangkok residents buy their food, clothing, and household items are also scattered throughout the city. One will be a walk or short ride from your hotel. After mastering the logistics, the second "must" is to bargain. All but the most elegant stores expect you to do so. The price tag is a hint as to what they hope to get, but they often settle for less.

Thai Bronzeware

Uniquely handicrafted bronzeware can be bought in complete table services, in coffee and creamer and bar sets, letter openers, bowls, tankards, trays, and candlesticks. Designs vary but the older horn-handle and dancing-angel motif is being replaced by smarter, simpler lines. Solid bronze handles go into very hot water, or the dishwasher, the horn do not.

Nielloware

Thailand is famous for this special kind of silver with its inlaid designs that look black when held against the light at an angle, and white when looked at straight. Nielloware is now also available with colored inlays, green, red, and blue being the preferred colors. Neilloware articles cover a wide range—from cufflinks to lighters, jewelry, ashtrays, tie clasps, and cigarette boxes to coffee and creamer sets. The variety of articles is almost endless and you're sure to wind up with at least one piece of Thai neilloware.

Tailoring

Bangkok is now probably cheaper than Hong Kong for tailoring and dress making, though not perhaps as stylish. Tropical weight suits, safari outfits, and light dresses are the best buys. Good bargains are the local versions of top-name sports shirts, sold along with cheap leather goods from street stalls.

Thai Silk

Probably the best-known of all local products, Thai silk is luxurious, but the price in Bangkok is conservative compared to what you would have to pay at home. Thai silk is available in some of the brightest and happiest colors and patterns you have laid eyes on. Weights differ—thus you will find material for a man's suit just as easily as for a cocktail dress or a stole. Yardage runs about 40 inches wide. Available also are ready-made articles.

Widely known throughout the Orient is the *Thai Silk Company,* owned by the late Jim Thompson, at 9 Suriwong Rd. His selection, one of the best in town, includes plain silks as well as the relatively recently perfected, colorfast, washable prints.

Thai cotton, with its vivid colors and striking designs, has achieved almost as much popularity as the more expensive silk. Today it can be had in drip-dry and "wrinkle-free" fabric. Less prevalent than formerly is the handsome hand-woven cotton from the Chiang Mai area. A number of boutiques around town offer smart ready-to-wear clothes in Thai cotton.

Precious and Semi-Precious Stones

Lovely zircons, garnets, turquoise, sapphires, and rubies are the best buys, plus, of course, good Thai gold and silverwork in old and modern designs. One of the finest examples of Thai jewelry is the so-called Princess Ring, cone-shaped and resembling the tall, ornate crown which Thai dancers wear. Princess Rings, also called Nine-Gem Rings, are made of gold and carry nine stones in circular form—diamond (in cheaper rings a zircon), cat's eye, ruby, emerald, sapphire, topaz, moonstone, garnet, and zircon. The same design is also available for earrings and bracelets. Designs on other rings and bracelets vary, but if you have found the right stone and have the time, any Bangkok jeweler will be only too glad to make you anything according to your own design or wish.

The more reliable jewelry stores are now registered by the Tourist Authority of Thailand and carry a special sign. Always insist on a guarantee and full receipt, written in English, when buying in the smaller shops. If doubtful about choosing stones buy in better hotel shops but still bargain fiercely.

Mention should also be made of the very inexpensive watches sold in Bangkok, carrying famous names, but priced at a small fraction of the originals.

Dolls

Best examples are Thai classical dancers or mythological characters, dressed in brocade costumes and adorned with shimmering rhinestones. More expensive dolls dressed in Thai silk.

Lacquerware

Lightweight, comes generally in a gold and black color scheme. Small tables, vases, trays, cigarette boxes.

Carved Wood

Teakwood carvings, figurines, trays, boxes, bowls, bookends—and elephants in all sizes. Carved wood, dolls, and lacquerware are carried by most stores.

What look like antique carvings are often new, but made of old wood. Often in groups of figures, these are a very good buy.

Thai Celadon

The ancient art of celadon pottery which died out in China and Thailand many hundreds of years ago has been revived and craftsmen today use the same methods and designs that once produced sleek green pottery. The best bet is *Celadon House,* Silom Rd. Somewhat expensive, but good.

Sukhotai Stoneware

This name is used to distinguish the blue and blue-green pottery recently developed in another kiln in Chiang Mai. Handsome modern pieces with an Oriental flavor, mostly inexpensive.

Temple Bells

Made of brass and graduated in size, they are small replicas of the kind of bells that tinkle in the compounds of Thailand's wat. Available anywhere and everywhere. Prices don't differ much. Neither does selection or quality, but bargain in all but major department stores.

Festival Barges

Delicately carved and ornamented replicas of the royal barges that once plied the Chao Phya River carrying the king and the royal family, with tiny oarsmen made of lead, body of ship carved from teak, then lacquered in red and gilt. Also made in glass and buffalo horn.

Antiques

Of particular interest are stone and bronze statues and figures, woodcarvings, Burmese carvings, embroideries, laquerware, and ancient Thai (and Chinese) pottery, and paintings. The Thai government has become extremely strict about the export of Thai antiques and religious art. By law no antique may leave the country, and even reproduction items not sold as antiques may need an export permit issued by the Fine Arts Department. Better antique shops can arrange permits in about a week.

A good place for just browsing around for antiques is the *Thieves Market,* just off the upper end of New Road in Chinatown. Several fascinating shops, with Chinese as well as Thai pieces. This used to be a great place for bargains, but no more. Many good shops also in Siam Sq. and New Rd., Suriwong and Silom Rds.

Note: The Thai government has, technically, banned the export of all religious art, whether antique or modern. In practice visitors are still buying carvings, paintings, and other Thai art, most of which has a religious theme. There is no indication as to whether commercial desire will continue to overcome stated ethics: Buddha images, however, may be a problem to try to take out of Thailand and this includes those made in Burma and even those obviously brand-new.

RESTAURANTS: Bangkok has more restaurants than New York has bars. Occidental food is easily found, but not always first rate. What is good is fairly expensive. Dinner without drinks will be from 200 to 800 baht per person. Chinese food in the better restaurants is around 150 to 450 baht per person, and is excellent. Almost every national style of European and Asian food is available.

Trying to establish eating costs in Thailand is like asking "how long is a piece of string?" It depends entirely on what your tastes are.

An à la carte dinner in a top Bangkok hotel restaurant, without drinks, would cost around 500 baht—a bowl of noodle soup on a corner stall will cost 20 baht. The happy medium lies somewhere between the two, exactly where depending on whether you prefer Chateaubriand or Tom Yam Gung.

The à la carte menus of top restaurants can be very expensive indeed, with a meal for two costing up to 2,000 baht, without drinks, but you have to be a real gourmet to hit those heights.

It is best to try Thai food in one of the restaurants catering to tourists. The Thais are well known for their addiction to hot (spicy) food. Although most tourist-oriented restaurants tone down Thai food, watch for the *pri-kee-noo,* a tiny red or green pepper. It is safest to eat around these. If one slips down, cram down rice as quickly as possible. It removes the worst of the heat.

Here are a few Thai dishes (plus ingredients) that really shouldn't be missed:

Tom Yam Gung—A soup to end all soups and probably quite unlike anything you've ever eaten anywhere else. The broth is prepared with some special leaves called *makroot,* an herb known as lemon grass, and water. Prawns are generally placed into the broth, but chicken, fish, or pork may be used instead. Once the meat is tender a bit of lemon juice is added along with a kind of fish-flavored soy sauce and *pri-kee-noo.* The whole concoction—and it's a good one—is served piping hot in a charcoal brazier.

Gang Pet—Literally means "hot curry" and can be made with pork, chicken, beef, fish, or prawn. Despite the fact that it's a common dish the preparation is somewhat elaborate and the ingredients are almost innumerable. *Gang pet* has a very faint sweetish taste which comes from using coconut milk (more accurately water squeezed from grated coconut) for the liquid base. To this is added a paste consisting of lemon grass, garlic, chilies, shrimp paste, caraway seeds, coriander, and of course, pepper. All of this is mixed well and brought to boil. Before serving, more spices, the inevitable chilies, and a bit of soy sauce are added. Eaten with rice.

Gai Yang—Might be called barbecued chicken and is really quite similar to that Western dish. A whole fresh chicken is rubbed inside and out with salt, pepper, butter, and sometimes bacon. Inside is stuffed with grated coconut and the prepared bird is rotated on a spit over glowing charcoals till it's golden brown. The coconut stuffing is removed before serving.

Haw Mok—Following ingredients are pounded into a paste: dry chilies, shrimp paste, lemon grass, onions, garlic, and salt. Then the paste is carefully blended with coconut milk, soy sauce, an egg, and sliced raw fish. Mixture is placed over variety of local greens in a banana leaf and topped off with coconut milk before being steamed and served in the leaf.

Kao Pat—Thailand's version of fried rice, it contains bits of crab meat, chicken, pork, onion, egg, and saffron—and plenty of rice. Usually served with side dish of green onions, sliced cucumbers, and soy sauce along with chopped chilies.

Among favorite desserts you can choose from the following:

Salim—Thin strings of sweet noodles floating in coconut milk and small chips of ice.

Songkaya—A kind of pudding made from coconut milk, eggs, and palm sugar. Can be eaten both hot and cold and is often served in empty coconut shell after having been chilled.

Sticky rice and mangoes—One of the favorite sweet dishes during the mango season (from March till May). Glutinous rice is cooked in coconut milk and served with juicy slices of delicious mango.

These are but a few of the delicacies which Thai cuisine can produce and which you should taste—even in their toned-down tourist forms. One more word—about fruit: If you're on a fruit diet, Thailand is the place to be. Depending on the season, there are mangoes (perhaps the East's most delicious fruit), mangosteens, durian, oranges, melons, a whole slate of different kinds of bananas, rambutans, papayas, pineapples and grapes.

Also, don't be surprised if in a Thai restaurant the waiter does not bring you a knife. Thais use only spoon and fork for their meal since food is cooked in bite-size morsels.

Chopsticks, of course, are the order for Chinese food, which is excellent in Bangkok and readily available just about anywhere in the kingdom. Most small restaurants in the cities and the small towns are owned by Chinese. The Southern Chinese food which most serve is popular with Thais, if for no other reason than that it is fairly well spiced. Tai Chew (Southern)-style Chinese cooking is prevalent in Bangkok, but the city also offers Canton, Shanghai, Hunan, and Hakka food. If you get a chance, try shark's fin soup, or roast duck (Kwa Lo Da-ark), or fried crab claws.

Another word of advice: Try to go in a group if you're out to taste Thai or Chinese food. That way, with everyone at the table ordering a different dish, you'll be able to sample more of the range of delicacies which Bangkok cooks can concoct. In a Chinese restaurant, you will be handed hot (or sometimes chilled) towels before and after the meal. Use them to wipe your face, neck, and hands. At the end of the meal they take the place of finger bowls.

BANGKOK

Authentic Thai

The following places present the authentic product, with no concessions made to foreign palates. Here you can try Thai food at its best.

Bankeo Ruenkwan, 212 Sukhumvit Rd. (opposite Chavalit Hotel). An old house, modernized and partly air-conditioned, that offers reasonably priced meals, full of flavor. Specializes in seafood, which is among the best in Bangkok.

Chitr Pochana, 62 Soi 20, Sukhumvit Rd. Open-air gardens complete with fountains or air-conditioned rooms are the settings for the serving of some of the finest Thai food available. Good service, but now more for tourists than for locals. One of the few Thai restaurants where some of the waiters speak English. Highly recommended is the *Chitr Pochana* branch operated in conjunction with the Oriental Hotel. On riverside terrace with free ferry from hotel's own landing. Delightful atmosphere and excellent food.

Silom Village. Silom Road, a block from the Central Department Store. Atmospheric compound of several restaurants, open air food stalls and a cultural theater restaurant, serving really good genuine Thai food. The complex also has some good antique and souvenir shops, nightly Thai music and shows.

Sorn Daeng. Rajadamnoen Ave. A pavement-side café overlooking the Democracy Monument. Delightful for people watching and good, inexpensive Thai-Chinese food.

Thai Room. Patpong 2. Serves good Thai dishes (also Mexican and Italian!), though decor is not the finest. Waiters speak English. Convenient location.

Toll Gate. 245, Soi 31 Sukhumvit. Moderate prices and good traditional Thai food. The set six-course table d'hôte menu is excellent and saves having to choose dishes from a strange menu. Closed Sundays.

Touristic Thai

The restaurants listed cater to a mainly tourist audience, offering rather subdued versions of Thai food and traditional dancing or other entertainment. All these will arrange pick-up from any Bangkok hotel.

Baan Thai. 7 Soi 32, Sukhumvit Rd. An old Thai house with tropical gardens, good food, and Thai dancing. Show at 9–10 P.M.

Maneeya Lotus Room. 518/4 Ploenchit Rd. The décor of ancient Siam, with classical dancing and good food.

Piman. 46 Soi 49 Sukhumvit Rd. This beautiful theater-restaurant is a replica of a Sukothai-era house (14th century). For 400 baht, you are served reasonable Thai food while watching Thai dancing.

Sala Thai. Indra Regent Hotel. Replica of a 13th-century Thai house on a rooftop of the hotel provides a delightful setting for relatively unspicy set menus. Good classical dance and music show. Showtime 8:30 P.M.

Sukothai. Dusit Thani Hotel makes it easy for guests to see Thai folk and classical dancing while they eat Thai food. Elaborate traditional setting.

Chinese

Chai Talay. Opposite Lumpini Boxing Stadium, Rama IV Rd. Famous for many years for its barbecued chicken, the original small restaurant expanded and is now in a big modern office building. In addition to the chicken specialty, a good range of Cantonese dishes.

Golden Dragon. 108–114, Sukhumvit Rd. Clean, comfortable, and serves a variety of authentic Cantonese dishes. Recommended for large parties.

Happy Restaurant. Siam Square. Offers genuine Hunan food of Central China. The dishes are spicy. Two of the best are chicken with wine sauce and Empress Fish.

Hong Teh. Ambassador Hotel, Soi II, Sukhumvit. Splendid surroundings and excellent, if rather expensive, menu.

Jade Garden. Montien Hotel, 54 Suriwongse Road. Good Cantonese menu. The buffet luncheon is among the best in town.

Maple Leaf. 602 Petchburi Rd., opposite Paramount Cinema. Szechuanese food at its spicy best. Vinegar pepper soup, fried duck. Rather expensive, but unusual food.

Shangari-La. Two branches, both on Silom Rd. Specializes in Shanghai dishes, although others are available, and good. Try the Peking duck here.

European

Beefeater Steak House. 9/4, Thaniya Rd. (off Suriwongse). Fine beef, good value. Popular business lunch place.

Charly's. Sathorn Rd. Northside. Swiss décor and cuisine in delightful house-setting.

Fireplace Grill. In the President Hotel. Offers French and Swiss food. Try the roast lamb loin Provençal, or pepper steak from New Zealand prime beef.

Italian Pavilion. 19 Soi 4 Sukhumvit Rd. Good Italian food for those wanting a change from more exotic fare. Homemade pasta a specialty in pleasant garden.

Captain Bush Grill. In Royal Orchid Hotel. Good continental grillroom menu and pleasant deluxe atmosphere.

La Cave. In the Erawan. Serves excellent seafoods and has a good wine list.

Le Châlet. In the Erawan Hotel continues to be a favorite with locals as well as visitors. The dishes are French and Swiss.

Le Gourmet Grill. In the Montien Hotel. Good service in a luxurious setting. Steaks, fish, and game are all specialties.

Ma Maison. In Hilton Hotel. Superb, if expensive gourmet menu in elegant surroundings.

Le Metropolitan. Reasonable French restaurant on Gaysorn Rd. Excellent food, intimate atmosphere.

Nick's No. 1. South Sathorn Rd. Features Hungarian dishes, Kobe steak, and Viennese chocolate cake, as well as other European cuisine. Characterful, in extraordinary old house.

Normandie Grill. The Oriental Hotel's rooftop restaurant. French cooking and a view of the river. At ground level, beside the Chao Prya River, the Oriental's Terrace Barbeque is also recommended.

Paesano. 34/1 Soi Lang Suan, off Ploenchitr Rd. A modest place, specializing in good, inexpensive Italian, French, and Thai food.

The Two Vikings. 2 Soi 35, Sukhumvit Rd. Regarded by many as Bangkok's best. A Scandinavian place, with six different rooms, in an old house, it is relatively expensive.

Indian

Cafe India. Suriwongse Rd. (opp. Trocadero Hotel). Some of the best Indian food in S.E. Asia. *Tandoori* chicken and North India curry specialties.

Himali Cha Cha. 1229/11 New Rd. Behind Trocadero Hotel, off main street. Superb North Indian food in this highly recommended small restaurant.

Japanese

Aoyama. 960/1 Rama IV Rd. Expensive, but one may have a Japanese bath before dinner and a walk in the garden after. Geishas in attendance.

Benkay. Royal Orchid. Wide menu of specialities in peaceful surroundings, overlooking the river.

Hanaya. 683 Siphya Rd. Serves traditional dishes in traditional style. Set menus are more reasonable than the 150-item à la carte list.

Tokugawa. In the Ambassador Hotel. Excellent, with some good, reasonably priced, set menus.

Korean

Arirang House. 106 Silom Rd. Good set menus or à la carte. Barbecued meats a speciality.

Korea House. 510 Ploenchit Rd. Has "stamina barbecue" and "hormone barbecue," which are enticing names for standard Korean barbecued dishes.

OUTSIDE BANGKOK

For the most part, restaurants outside Bangkok are not very good, with the exception of a few places in Chiang Mai and in Pattaya.

Chiang Mai: *Chiang Inn, Orchid, Rincome,* and *Poy Luang* hotels are best. Chinese food is good at *Wagon Wheel;* pleasant outdoor terrace is preferable to noisy pop music indoors. Homely, friendly atmosphere can be found at *The Pub,* where fish and chips are the specialty. Thai food with a Burmese influence available at a restaurant with *no discernible name* in Fa Hram Rd. At *Pat's Tavern* you will find snacks, light meals and efficient service.

Pattaya: *Dolf Riks* is tops for European food. Try also *The Coral Reef, La Gritta,* or *Buccaneer* in Nipa Lodge Hotel. The *Mai Kai* offers Polynesian and European food with seafood, naturally, the specialty. Good evening barbecue buffets served in *Montien* and *Merlin* Hotels. *Nang Nual,* overlooking the sea in the village, also serves fine Oriental seafood.

NIGHT LIFE. Bangkok has the reputation for being one of the most wide-open cities in Southeast Asia, an image that is entirely justified.

Entertainment, mostly Grade B, Las Vegas-type floorshows, make Bangkok a stop on their Asian tour. Some of the nightclubs and most of the bars have B-girls, or hostesses, as they are called here. There are also "Go-Go" dancers, scantily clad and extremely vigorous. In night clubs, hostesses are usually available at an hourly fee, and arrangements for after-working-hour get-togethers can generally be made quite easily, although most good hotels do not allow extra "guests."

Among the better known of the city's night spots (without hostesses) are the Erawan Hotel's dignified *Ambassador,* the Royal Orchid Hotel's *Silks,* the Montien's lively *Casablanca,* the Oriental Hotel's atmospheric *Bamboo Bar, Diana's Disco,* and the *Tiara,* Dusit Thani Hotel. With hostesses are the *Café de Paris,* on Suriwongse; and *Honey,* Suriwongse Rd.

Discothèques and cocktail lounges with music of all sorts, from soul to baroque jazz, are numerous. Popularity varies with the quality of the music and this week's "in" spot may be tomorrow's damp dishrag. Currently among the best discos are the Oriental's *Diana's* and Dusit Thani's *Bubbles.* "After hours" places are secret but available. Ask a friend or at the hotel desk. The lights are usually low and the noise level high in these places and female companionship is invariably available. The 99 on Silom Rd. has a good atmosphere; popular with residents. Clubs are supposed to close at midnight on weekdays, 1:00 A.M. on Saturdays.

In addition to the nightclubs there are a mass of bars and go-go establishments that do not pretend to be subtle, but which offer most of the things a bachelor visitor might be seeking in Bangkok. Main center for this type of activity is Patpong Rd., in front of the Montien Hotel, between Suriwongse Rd. and Silom Rd. Foreign female visitors are liable to be scathing about the quality of the bars and entertainments available in these places, but some knowledgeable bachelors claim that the girls are less materialistic and more feminine in Bangkok than in Hong Kong or Manila. Nightspots in Thailand are generally more lively than anywhere else in Southeast Asia, though they are no longer cheap. Bangkok also has a lively "gay" night life.

One form of "entertainment" that cannot be ignored in Bangkok is the massage parlors, of which there are hundreds. These range in style from the opulent to the degenerate. Better-quality establishments provide pretty masseuses and clean and pleasant surroundings and are entirely suitable for a respectable visitor. Unfortunately they cater mainly to men, though brave foreign female visitors have also been known to try, and few have complained afterwards.

RADIO, TV, AND MOVIES. Thailand has 4 television channels as well as a bewildering number of radio stations, all of which are in Thai. Of Bangkok's 60 major movie houses, a few screen English-language films. For programs and times see local English-language newspapers.

DRINKING WATER. Insist on boiled water or commercially bottled water. Bangkok authorities say that water from the tap is fine—perhaps it is—but it's better to be on the safe side. Some water served you in Bangkok or the upcountry will be slightly yellow. That's your best indication that it has been boiled with a tea leaf or two thrown in and that it is safe.

MAIL AND TELECOMMUNICATIONS. Minimum letter airmail rates to the United States are 9.50 baht; 8.50 baht to the United Kingdom. Airmail postcards will cost you 7.50 baht to the U.S. and 6.50 baht to the U.K. Aerogram letter forms cost 6.50 baht to any destination. Cable, telex and telephone facilities are available, 24 hours a day and 7 days a week, from the General Post Office on New Rd. Telegrams can be sent from any post office. Most of the better hotels have telex, but may add a substantial service charge to overseas telephone charges. Upcountry telephone services are not good, but overseas calls can be arranged from Bangkok. You may have to pay cash for these telecommunications because international credit cards, although technically acceptable, are usually not accepted in practice. Best bet is to go to the main G.P.O. on New Rd., where an international telephone office is open 24 hours a day. Most post offices open 8:30 A.M.–5 P.M. weekdays, till noon on Saturdays.

CHURCHES. *Roman Catholic:* Assumption Cathedral, Oriental Ave.; Holy Redeemer Church, Ruam Rudi Rd.; *Protestant;* Christ Church (Episcopalian), Convent Rd. Calvary (Baptist), 88 Soi 2 (Sukhumvit Rd.). International Church (Presbyterian), 67 Soi 19, Sukhumvit, and Seventh-Day Adventist Church, 57, Soi Charoenchai, Ekamai Rd., Sukhumvit.

MEDICAL SERVICES. Hospitals: *Bangkok Sanitarium and Hospital* (Seventh Day Adventists), 430 Pitsanuloke Rd.; *Bangkok Nursing Home,* Convent Rd. All major hotels have doctors on immediate call.

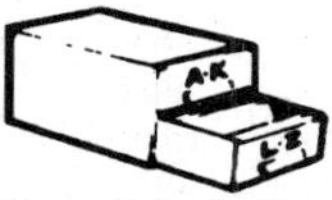

USEFUL ADDRESSES. Immigration Department. Soi Suanplu, Sathorn Tai Road.

Embassies. *American Embassy,* Wireless Rd.; *British Embassy,* Ploenchit Rd.; *Australian Embassy,* 37 South Sathorn Rd.; *Indian Embassy,* 46, Soi Prasarnmit, Sukhumvit 23; *Indonesian Embassy,* 602 Petchburi Rd.; *Japanese Embassy,* 1674, New Petchburi Rd.; *Philippine Embassy,* 760 Sukhumvit Rd.; *Burmese Embassy,* 132 Sathorn Rd. N.

General Information. Contact the *Tourist Authority of Thailand* for information. Their central office is at Rajadamnern Nok Avenue. Tel. 282–1143/7. Next to Rajdamnern Boxing Stadium. There are also TAT information offices at Don Muang Airport and at major upcountry tourist destinations.

Emergencies. In any emergency dial "191" and say, in simple words, whether you want police or fire services and the exact location. The only ambulance services in Bangkok are attached to individual hospitals or clinics.

Police numbers are 579–1370/9.

Note that most accident cases are taken to the Police Hospital, opposite the Erawan Hotel.

FIVE-MINUTE THAI

The Thai national language is written in a script derived from Sanskrit and Pali, and looks quite different from Western alphabets or Chinese and Japanese. The spoken language has five different tones, so transcription from Thai into romanized alphabets is, at best, only approximate. Most persons in hotels, restaurants, and shops understand some English. Just in case you get lost, or if you want to try out your linguistic ability, we have listed a few important words.

(The words *khrap* and *kha* are polite expressions for "Sir" and "Madam" and are added at the end of many Thai phrases. Their use depends on the sex of the *speaker,* not the addressee.)

English	*Thai*
Good morning, hello, goodbye (i.e., all greetings)	Sawat dee khrap (if spoken by a man) Sawat dee kha (if spoken by a woman)
Please	Dai prod
Thank you	Khob khun krap (or kha)
Never mind, or, it doesn't matter	Mai pen rye
How much?	Tao rye?
I don't understand	Chun mai kao chai
Too expensive!	Paeng mark
I don't want it	My ow
Very good, delicious	Dee mark, aroy
Water	Nam
Stop, go	Yoot, pai
Here, there	Teenee, teenun
Go left, go right	Lee-o sai, lee-o kwah
Wait here	Koi tee nee
Today, tomorrow	Wun Nee, proong nee
Hotel	Rong Ram
W.C.	Horng Nam
Red	See daeng
Blue	See nam ngun
Black	See dum
White	See kao
Green	See kee-o
Yellow	See Luang
Telephone	Torasap
Zero	Soon
One	Nung

English	*Thai*
Two	Song
Three	Sam
Four	See
Five	Hah
Six	Hok
Seven	Jet
Eight	Paat
Nine	Khow
Ten	Sip
Twenty	Yee sip
Thirty	Sam sip
Forty	See sip
One hundred	Nung roi
One thousand	Nung pan

BURMA

Another Place, Another Time

The Government of Burma does not at present encourage tourism. Limited to one-week-only visas, few travelers are now visiting Burma, a truly "adventure" destination. The government places increasingly severe restrictions on the areas which may be visited, due to dangerfrom one or another of the country's many insurgent groups. Most overseas operators have canceled their regular tours owing to the unreliability of upcountry air transport, but access is still easy from Bangkok, where several reputable agents offer package tours of 4 to 7 days. Travelers should check on the current security situation with leading Bangkok tour agencies and can depend on their advice.

While off the beaten track, Burma offers much that the tourist will want to sample. Although accommodations are not luxurious, they are relatively comfortable. First, there are the people—polite, kind, fun-loving, happy to see you and willing to show you parts of an attraction, and answer your questions, generally without expecting payment, although Rangoon has now become rather more commercial.

Next, the pagodas. Burma is known as the Land of the Golden Pagodas. They are everywhere. These places of worship with monasteries attached are the religious and, frequently, the commercial and social centers of daily life. It is a rare Burmese who does not visit one several times a week.

Third, Pagan may be the major archeological attraction in Southeast Asia now that Angkor Wat is off limits. For more on this unique ancient capital, see *Exploring Upcountry* below.

Burma is reasonably untouched by Western life and here lies another of its charms. You will not be engulfed by hordes of tourists taking photographs and monopolizing the time of your guides. No Burmese custodian will seem to exact a toll to open a religious area for your inspection. You will feel privy to a unique culture where you can spend your moments relatively undisturbed.

One problem visitors face is that local people who are not government officials or directly connected with tourists are, by law, not supposed to be in contact with foreigners, but the natural friendliness of the Burmese often overcomes this rule.

Sarongs for Everyone

One of the things you will notice immediately on arrival is that both Burmese men and women have retained their traditional dress. The men wear a cotton or silk *Xongyi* (sarong-type dress) and, over a collarless shirt, a very smart short-length jacket known as the *ingyi.* As in the West, few men wear hats, except on formal occasions. The Burmese type of hat, a *gaung baung,* is made of pastel-colored silk, wrapped around a wicker framework.

Women wear a similar style of *longyi* (sarong) of all patterns and colors, whereas men are restricted by custom to either plain colors or checked type of patterns in more somber tones. As much controversy has arisen over the types of blouses (*ingyi*) that women wear these days as ever sprung up over skirt lengths and waistlines in Europe. The *ingyi* is carefully shaped and is with or without sleeves and is often made of silk and nylon. It is this latter that has, by being transparent, caused so much discussion. Note the very decorative buttons of gold, silver, and jewels worn on the *ingyi.*

Many women still keep their hair long, binding it high up above the nape of the neck. On ceremonial occasions, as when they get married, they often go back to the court dress of the past. It is then that the hair is worn high on top of the head with a switch of hair flowing over the shoulders. Great pride is taken in decorating the top knot, with bejeweled combs and delicate sprays of artificial flowers. All women love wearing flowers in their hair, and a red rose worn in jet black hair catches any man's eye.

Many women and some young children wear Burmese make-up, *tanaka,* on their faces and arms. The make-up is made by grinding a special plant into a powder. While at first it may appear odd to a visitor, its continued use is one indication of a desire by the Burmese to retain their customs and not succumb to Westernization.

Arts, Umbrellas, Htis, and Zat

Unfortunately much of Burma's craftsmanship and artistry began to die once the patronage of a king was removed. One of the artistic achievements had been the ornate and complex woodcarvings that used

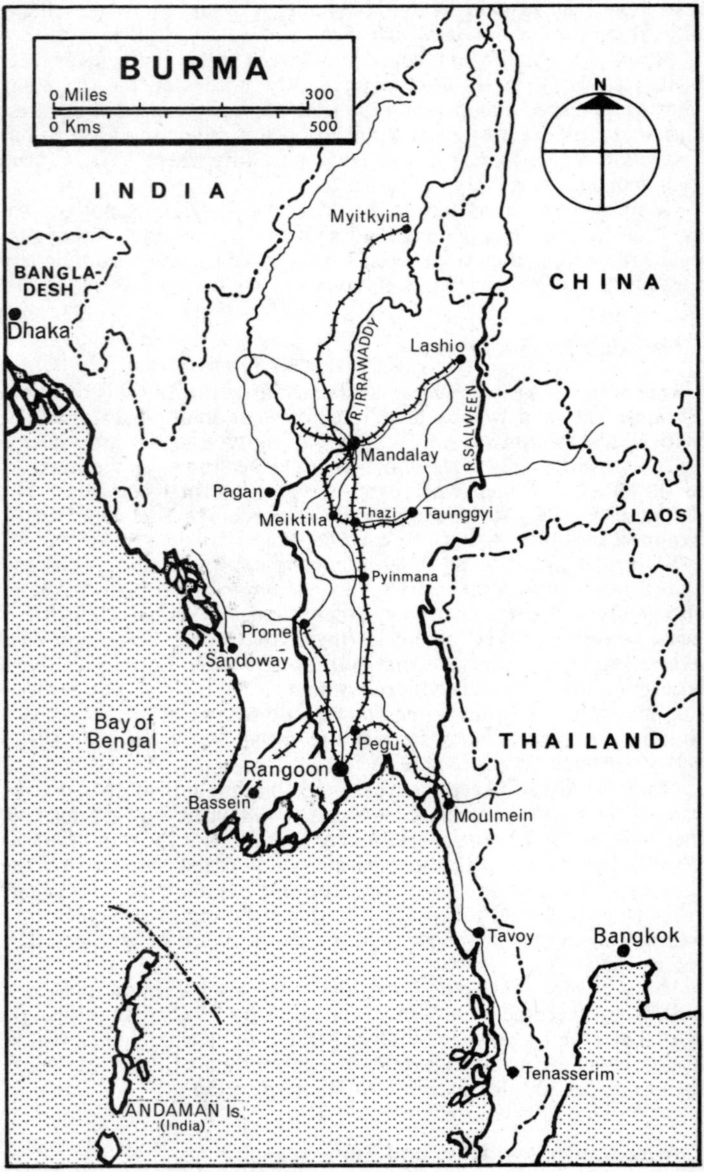
BURMA
0 Miles 300
0 Kms 500
N
INDIA
BANGLA-DESH
Dhaka
CHINA
LAOS
THAILAND
Myitkyina
R. IRRAWADDY
Lashio
R. SALWEEN
Mandalay
Pagan
Meiktila
Thazi
Taunggyi
Pyinmana
Prome
Sandoway
Bay of Bengal
Pegu
Rangoon
Bassein
Moulmein
Tavoy
Bangkok
Tenasserim
ANDAMAN Is.
(India)

to adorn pagodas and palaces. (One impressive example is the Shwe Nandaw Monastery in Mandalay, a "must-see.") In the hot, sometimes intensely dry, sometimes intensely wet, climate, woodwork has a life of about only a hundred years. For what the weather does not destroy, white ants and other insects quietly attack, burrowing deep into the timber and leaving only a shell that an idle touch or a gust of wind will send toppling down.

But in some pagodas, one can still find some exceptionally fine work, with lacquered Buddha figures made from a form of papier-mâché applied to a wooden framework. Metal and stone Buddhas are also found, but less work has been done on dating them than in Thailand and other Buddhist countries, and it is difficult for the amateur to find reference books that will help him to date what he sees. However, the art of building pagodas, surrounded by a great cone of bamboo scaffolding, still lives in every village and town. And the most exciting moment comes on the day when a new pagoda is consecrated. Then the *hti* (umbrella), a fine piece of metal work encrusted with jewels and gold in the richer pagodas, is swung aloft by a carriageway strung from cane ropes.

If you stay on after the ceremony, you will be able to witness the greatest expression of Burmese art, the *zat,* or dance drama, that starting in the evening will last all through the night. There are two words you will hear frequently when you reach Burma. One is *pwe* which means a fête or celebration, and the other is *zat.*

The zats are based on the Indian stories of the *Ramayana* and on Jataka tales, the stories of the Buddha's many reincarnations before his last life as Gautama Buddha, when he attained Nirvana. The whole performance is extempore, although the general outline of the story and musical themes have, of course, been decided on long before both by tradition and the troupe's earlier performances.

Nobody would expect you, if you do not understand Burmese, to spend a whole night at the zat. But an hour or two, seated on the floor eating pickled tea leaves and asking questions, will show you the kings and queens, the gods and devils, the dancing girls, the clowns and buffoons who by their pageantry touch the Burmese imagination. The performances combine the troubles, problems and humor of the present with stories of the magical past when men were, after all, not so very different from what they are today.

These and other pleasures of Burmese life in towns and villages are yours to see and enjoy if you visit the country. If you do not visit Burma, your picture of Asia will be incomplete, and you will have lost an opportunity to discover the different and unique experiences it has to offer.

The Original Pagan Kingdom

The Burmese began to enter the country, from the direction of Tibet, in the early centuries of the Christian Era. But it was not until 1044 when King Anawratha seized power in Pagan (pronounce *pah-GUN* with the stress on the second syllable) that the numerous little Burmese kingdoms were welded into one nation. The great kingdom of Pagan was to be destroyed later, but it created a national identity among the Burmese that has never been completely forgotten, although two contending Burmese characteristics have ever since bedeviled Burmese politics: the tendency to join into groups, to be followed immediately by a tendency to split apart!

Anawratha was one of the greatest of Burma's kings. He gave the Burmese not only political strength but also brought them into contact with the accumulated knowledge of South Asia. From the Mon capital, Thaton, which he captured, he brought back Buddhist Theravada monks and their scriptures. To the Burmese language he gave a recognized script. Out of the wealth and skills he gave Pagan, it became one of the greatest cities of the world. In magnificence and splendor it remains today the most notable of Burma's historical monuments. But Pagan was doomed. Its greatness, its beauty, its wealth produced an overwhelming self-confidence in which there was little room for diplomacy, or understanding of the power of other nations. In 1287 after unsuccessful engagements against the forces of Kublai Khan, the King fled and the power of Pagan was destroyed by the Mongol invaders.

The Mongols influenced Burma in another way. In 1252–53 Kublai Khan's brother crushed Nan Chao, the capital of the Tai (or Thai) race in Yunnan. Driven from their homes the Tais began a second wave of immigration into Laos, Siam, and Burma. Soon they took over the power that Pagan had held and extended it even further, setting up new kingdoms throughout the center and north of the country.

In 1519 the Portuguese were granted trading privileges at the seaport of Martaban to the south. This was the beginning of European influence that culminated in 1885 in the Third Burmese-British war, a war that ended by King Thibaw handing over his Mandalay capital to the British. Thibaw and his queen were sent into exile on the west coast of India. But in the few years of their reign, they had tried to ensure their power by terrible palace massacres. Weakened first by these, then by the assumption of power by the British, the Burmese aristocracy (such as it was) ceased to play an important role in Burmese affairs.

Independence and Civil War

After many years of resistance against the role of the British, producing many notable freedom fighters, Burma was granted her independence in 1948. The years that have followed have been marked by almost constant civil war and rebellion. Very soon after the Japanese had surrendered, an extremist group of the Communist Party went underground, to be followed soon after by other Communists and extreme leftists. Unfortunately, however, the various insurrections have not been only political, since both stern police action and political compromise could then have brought about a solution. Racial and intertribal problems have complicated the matter.

The Union of Burma, to give the country its full name, is composed of many different racial groups. Members of these groups have also taken up arms so that in 1948 Rangoon itself was besieged and the government was in control of little more than the capital and a number of airfields and towns upcountry. The first and largest rebellion was by the Karens, who have always had a reputation for being exceptionally fine soldiers. The Karens live largely in the Irrawaddy delta and to the northeast and south of Rangoon. Some are Christian, but the insurrection was based not on religious cause, but political. They wanted a separate state of their own within the Union. Since then, members of other ethnic groups, such as the Kachins, Chins, and Shans, have also gone underground.

In March 1962 General Ne Win decided that U Nu, then premier, was too ineffectual in containing minority separatist desires (especially those of the Shans), had caused the economy to deteriorate, had created religious frictions by establishing Buddhism as a state religion, and had failed in his renewed attempt at effective Parliamentary democracy. He staged a *coup d'état,* imprisoned the President, the entire government and all the important Shan princes and members of Parliament. The Constitution was declared void and the country was then ruled by the revolutionary committee headed by Ne Win. By 1968, Ne Win had released nearly all prominent leaders and hundreds of other detainees. U Nu, one of those released, was permitted to leave Burma in 1969. From exile in Thailand he organized a coalition of several ethnic groups then in rebellion. The coalition was known as the United National Liberation Front. Additional groups still in rebellion included the Kachins and the Shans. The Burmese government has, however, been able to contain these various rebellions so that at the present time, the country's major tourist areas are secure. These secure areas include upcountry destinations such as Pagan, Mandalay, Tounggyi, Sandoway, and Moulmein.

Ne Win attempted to establish state socialism in Burma. As part of this policy, all large and moderate size industries and the agricultural marketing system have been nationalized. This has caused many foreigners, including hundreds of thousands of Indians who lived in Burma for several generations, to leave the country. The system has encouraged the growth of smuggling, which now exists on a large scale for many commodities. Unfortunately, this economic policy had disastrous consequences and was subsequently replaced, in part, by a system of cooperatives. This is why Burma will not look like a prosperous and bustling country to the tourist, although, as will be readily apparent, there is enough food for everyone.

EXPLORING BURMA

Burma has hardly begun to organize itself to meet the modern requirements of tourists and visitors. "Exploring" is therefore a more accurate description of what your visit will be like than for some other Asian countries. If you really wish to enjoy your stay, it is very important to make up your mind well in advance how much time you will have. If it is to be only a few days then it is best to reconcile yourself to seeing only Rangoon, a city you will never regret visiting, but one that is only a shadow of the country as a whole. If you have slightly longer, then you must plan your arrival so that you can fly to Pagan

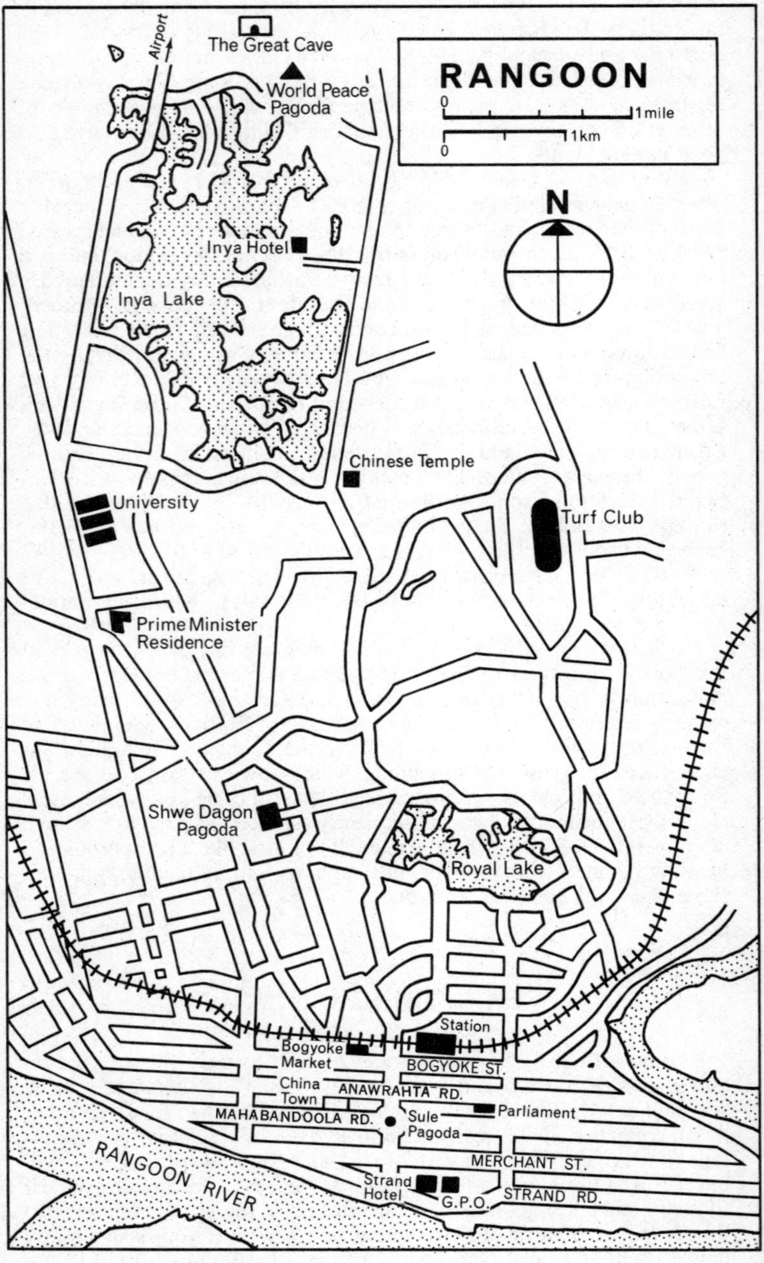
RANGOON
0
1 mile
1 km
0
N
The Great Cave
Airport
World Peace Pagoda
Inya Hotel
Inya Lake
Chinese Temple
University
Turf Club
Prime Minister Residence
Shwe Dagon Pagoda
Royal Lake
Station
Bogyoke Market
BOGYOKE ST.
China Town
ANAWRAHTA RD.
Parliament
MAHABANDOOLA RD.
Sule Pagoda
MERCHANT ST.
Strand Hotel
G.P.O.
STRAND RD.
RANGOON RIVER

for one day at least and see this magnificent capital city of more than 2,200 pagodas, all that remains after the destruction of the city by the Mongols in the 13th century and subsequent earthquakes.

The way to enjoy Burma, then, is to plan ahead (or have your travel agent do it for you). Otherwise your time will be wasted as you try to find connections that do not exist or make trips that would have fitted perfectly if you had only started, for example, yesterday.

Due to the limitations of time and difficulties in organizing your own tours and transportation, it is recommended that you take a "package" tour arranged by a travel agent outside the country. By doing this, you will see the most in the short time available.

There is not a great deal to be seen in Rangoon. Two full days are sufficient for most visitors and it is therefore important to make the most of the very real pleasure that is to be found there. Rangoon (pop. 800,000) is a new capital (1875) though it has a long history going back to earliest times when it was a small fishing village. Most of the building took place at the end of the 19th century. During the Second World War it suffered a large amount of damage.

After other Asian capitals you will find Rangoon rather quiet and staid with an atmosphere reminiscent of prewar more than postwar years. The large office buildings, the modern cinemas, flourishing businesses, hosts of taxis and diesel buses, all these have hardly made their mark. But against this you will find beautiful tree-lined streets once you leave the center of the town and residential areas that are scattered among the lakes and half-hidden valleys. Embassy Row on University Avenue is a good example of this.

The Shwe Dagon Pagoda

The Shwe Dagon is one of the greatest Buddhist shrines in the whole of Asia. This great golden spire stands dominating the whole city from the last of the hills of the Pegu Yoma as they reach down from the north to the delta plains and the sea. Nobody knows exactly when the first pagoda was built on that site but guides will tell you it is well over two thousand years old. This is a subject that has for long been in dispute among Burmese historians and it is perhaps better to remain on the safe ground of legend rather than to search for historical fact.

By tradition the Shwe Dagon contains relics (four hairs) of the Gautama Buddha and of three Buddhas who were born in ages before him. For this reason it is visited by Buddhist pilgrims from all over the world who come to pay homage and respect to the great teaching the Buddha gave to the world.

The pagoda spire rises 326 feet above its platform. From its base which is 1,420 feet in circumference, it first curves upward like an inverted bowl, then soars nearly to a point before blossoming into a bud, on top of which stand the tiered umbrellas representing royalty and greatness. The whole of the Shwe Dagon is covered in gold. The Plaintain Bud itself has been covered since the beginning of the century in foot-square sheets of gold. There are 8,688, each worth over $10,000 in today's money. As well as this there are many thousands of diamonds and semiprecious stones which encrust the umbrellas and the vane.

The Shwe Dagon is the real heart of Rangoon and in many ways the real heart of modern Burma. It is therefore worth every moment that you spend on looking at it, not in a wide-sweeping casual glance but in detailed and careful study. To do this you must plan your day so that you are there either before the heat of the morning, say between 7 and 10 or late in the afternoon after 4 o'clock. In the cool of the evening the pagoda, usually floodlit, is particularly impressive. Official closing time is 10 P.M. Even if you have already made a daytime study of the pavilions encircling the central dome and the fascinating shops on the approach stairways, an evening visit is unforgettable for the aura of tranquility that the shrine inspires. A lift has been built by the south gate for those who do not wish to climb the stairs. Try to obtain a printed guide to the pagoda from the government tourist office. (None available at pagoda.)

Other Points in Rangoon

The Sule Pagoda in the center of the city holds a representation of the Sule Nat (or god) who is the legendary guardian spirit of the Shwe Dagon hill. Another place of interest is the Kaba Aye (The World Peace Pagoda) built by U Nu as the meeting place for the sixth Buddhist synod in 1953–54. The first object you will see on entering the Kaba Aye will be a great mass of boulders. This represents the great cave in which the first Buddhist synod was held. The cave is open from 8:00 A.M. to 5:00 P.M. Unfortunately the two nearby pagodas show few signs of original Burmese craftsmanship and are not of great historic interest. To the north of the compound can be seen a building designed in a mixture of Western and Burmese styles. This is the Buddhist Library which is intended to be of international importance.

A visit to the Rangoon River is well worthwhile. There you will feel the pulse of the city. You can observe the storage and loading of rice and teak, Burma's leading exports. There are frequent ferries down and across the river to Syriam, taking 45 minutes each way. In Syriam one can take a short bus trip to visit a small pagoda.

The Kodagi Pagoda contains a huge Buddha, approximately 65 feet high, built in 1905 by a wealthy Burmese. On the walls of the metal enclosure are scenes of the events in the Buddha's life.

The Botataung Pagoda has been rebuilt after being bombed in World War II. It is one of the few pagodas where you can walk into the interior, which contains a series of rooms covered with semiprecious stones. A hair reputedly belonging to the Buddha is in one of these rooms. The treasure house across the street contains a Buddha taken to the British Museum in 1824 and returned to Burma in 1954.

The University and Rangoon Institute of Technology are also worth a trip especially if school is in session. The university consists of old and new buildings on a tree-shaded campus. Perhaps your guide will point out the site of the old student union, destroyed by Ne Win's government at the time of the student riots in 1968. The Institute is an example of an aid project built by the Soviet Union.

The Martyr's Mausoleum contains the tombs of General Aung San, the revolutionary leader who led the country toward independence before his untimely assassination in 1947, and his advisers.

Finally, a visit to Rangoon is not complete without a stroll through the Chinese and Indian sections, which provide a distinct contrast, and a boat trip on the river from opposite the Strand Hotel. This should cost about 10 to 15 kyat per hour.

Exploring Upcountry

Pegu

Pegu, which is 50 miles from Rangoon, can be visited by road or rail, each route taking about two hours. If you are driving it is best to leave as early as possible and return to Rangoon by about 5 o'clock in the cool of the afternoon. You will find a picnic basket and bottles of beer most welcome after a hard morning's sightseeing although you can enjoy a good Burmese meal at a local restaurant such as the one at the Myazuke Hotel, or the government rest house.

Pegu was once a great city and a capital of the lower part of Burma in the days when the Mon dynasty stretched across Siam and Cambodia. The city was founded in 573 A.D. In the 16th and 17th centuries it was visited by a number of European travelers who remarked on its importance as a seaport and the magnificence of the reception they were given. But King Alaungpaya, who forged the modern kingdom of Burma, destroyed the town utterly in 1757. It was rebuilt by King Bodawpaya (1782–1819) but its days of greatness were past and the changing of the river course finally deprived it of its sea trade.

The greatest of the pagodas is the Shwemawdaw (means: "On the tip of the land") which is said to contain two of the Buddha's hairs. As you enter the main entrance and climb up the steps to the platform you will see murals that show how the pagoda was almost completely destroyed by an earthquake in 1930 and how after the war it was rebuilt. Across the town lies the Shwethalyaung, the Reclining Buddha. It is over 200 feet long and 46 feet high at the shoulder. King Alaungpaya's destruction of Pegu was so thorough that for many years the Reclining Buddha was lost in the jungles; it has since been extensively renovated.

The Kalyanisima (Hall of Ordination), built in 1476 by a Mon king, stands nearby. Pali and Mon inscriptions can be found on ten large tablets within the pagoda. Kyaikpun, two miles down the Rangoon road, contains four 90-foot-high Buddha figures seated back to back. This is an ideal spot for your picnic, as is Shwehinthagone, the remains of an old pagoda on a hill behind the Shwemawdaw pagoda, which is on the way from Rangoon to Pegu.

The 2,000 Pagodas of Pagan

Pagan, 350 miles north of Rangoon, is the greatest of all Burma's historical monuments and you should do everything you can to include it on your itinerary. If possible do not fail to see it at sunrise and sunset.

It was the first capital of a united Burma and was founded in the 10th century. Pagan reached its zenith in the times of King Anawratha (1044–77) who built, or added to, so many of the pagodas that still stand today. The former capital lies on a bend of the Irrawaddy in the desolate dry zone that stretches across the center of Burma.

Of the estimated 50,000 pagodas that existed in Pagan before time, natural catastrophy and neglect caused their destruction, only a little more than 2,200 stand today. Some of these are actually temples built in a square design with projecting porches or vestibules, an image of the Buddha usually inside. Ananda temple is one of the best examples of this type—it should be seen at length as it is of great architectural significance. But spread across the many square miles of sandy desert-like soil, they create an impression of majesty and haunting beauty that makes Pagan one of mankind's great achievements. It was a tradition in Burmese architecture that stone was reserved for pagodas and occasionally for the monasteries or parts of the royal palaces. But, generally, palaces, houses, and shops were built of wood and the poorer people, as today, used woven bamboo and thatch. Only the pagodas and a part of the massive city walls now stand. These walls were constructed mainly of bricks, taken from the older pagodas by Mongol invaders.

The first thing that will strike you is the utter calm. As the breeze blows gently, you can hear the bells in the *htis* (the umbrella-shaped objects at the top). Even the searing sun will not dissuade you from visiting as many temples and pagodas as time permits. You may also want to linger at the excellent archeological museum. Try to buy the *Pictorial Guide to Pagan.*

In July 1975 a massive earthquake occurred in the Pagan area. At the time there was worldwide alarm that as many as 80 percent of the famous temples, including the superb Shwezigon Pagoda, had been destroyed and a major international project of restoration was launched. After the initial sensational reports had been more fully assessed, it appeared that the damage was not so bad. Restoration of the most important monuments was started at once and it is estimated that most of the more urgent work will be completed within 15 years.

Pagan has basically been a city of ruins since it was "visited" by a few thousand Tartar horsemen in 1287.

Among Pagan's many temples are:

Ananada. Built in 1091 in style of Indian cave-temple. Four standing Buddhas inside; terra cotta glazed tiles on walls illustrate the *Jakata Tales.* Its top was broken off in the 1975 earthquake but scholars claim that this portion was only an 18th-century addition.

Bupaya Pagoda. Right by the bank of the Irrawaddy, an unforgettable sight, especially at sunset. It has a bell-shaped dome resting on a series of receding terraces.

Htilominlo Temple. Built in 1211, it is 150 feet high and 140 feet on each side at the base.

Manuha Temple. In Minkaba, a few miles away, it contains huge images of Buddha standing and reclining; built by a king long held captive.

Nanpaya Temple. Manuha's residence during his captivity; intricate carvings of Brahma along frieze.

Sulamani Temple. Built in 1183 by King Narapatisithu; excellent frescoes in the arches.

Shwezigon Pagoda (at Nyaung-U). A "must see," started by Anawartha and finished by Kyanzittha; a difficult approach on foot but once near the huge terraced strip (reputedly containing the frontal bone and tooth of the Buddha), well worth the effort.

Notice the pilaster crowned with a Hintha, the statues of the 37 royal *nats* and the four small temples, each with a 13-foot Buddha.

Thatbyinnyu Temple. 201 feet high, shaped in a nonsymmetrical cross; the temple symbolizes the omniscience of Buddha. One of the more seriously damaged temples in the 1975 earthquake.

Upali Thein. Ordination hall: marvelous frescoes.

After your tour, enjoy a boat trip on the Irrawaddy River and then see the lacquerware village at which skilled cottage artisans take up to 18 months to fashion bowls, dishes, and trays. Products bought here are alone worth the trip to Burma.

. . . Where the Flying Fishes Play

Mandalay, a hundred years old, was founded by King Mindon in 1857. It remained capital of Burma only until 1885, when the British annexed the country. Only 248 feet above sea level, Mandalay is exceptionally hot, dry, and dusty, especially in the summer months. It has very little rainfall. In many ways, Mandalay is far more a Burmese city than Rangoon. It was not constructed by the English and, therefore, its buildings are not in the colonial style. It is the seat of Burmese arts and Buddhism. The national school of dance and music is there, and you should not miss it if you are in the city between July and March. Be sure to watch the stonecutters, leather craftsmen, and the makers of gold leaf, which the Burmese buy to gild images of the Buddha at their favorite pagoda. The Zegyo Bazaar and night market must also be seen, although it suffers from the austerity imposed by the current economic crisis.

After you have sampled the handicrafts and arts, you can begin your tour of the pagodas and the Royal Palace.

For many hundred years before Mandalay became the capital there was a large village on the site. The Shwekyimyint dates back to 1167 and is the oldest pagoda in the town. It contains early Buddha figures and other valuable historical objects that were dedicated to the pagoda by King Minshinsaw, the founder.

Near Mandalay Hill (934 ft.) is the Kyauk Tawgyi pagoda, built by King Mindon. The Buddha figure is carved from a single block of Saggaing marble and is of immense size. Also worthy of notice are the 80 figures around the pagoda, representing the disciples of the Buddha.

Another famous pagoda built by King Mindon is the Kuthodaw (Royal Bounty) which was started in 1857. It is on the grounds of this pagoda that 729 white marble tablets, each covered by a small temple, were set up to preserve the definitive text of the entire Buddhist scriptures decided upon by the fifth Buddhist Synod. The pagoda is modeled on the famous Shwezigon at Nyaung-U.

The Shwe Nadaw Monastery contains a royal couch and a copy of the royal throne because it was the place where Thabaw, one of the last Burmese Kings, lived. Now a Buddha image sits on the throne. The most remarkable aspect of the monastery is the elaborate wood carving on its exterior and its brilliant mosaic glass interior. The carving is similar to what was on the walls of the buildings which constituted the Royal Palace before it was destroyed.

The Maha Muni to the south of the city is also called the Arakan Pagoda because the ancient, heavily-gilded image inside was brought to Mandalay from that part of southern Burma. Also inside are two bronze warrior figures which people believe have the power to cure any disease if the patient touches the appropriate place on the warriors. Remains of a road built by King Bodawpaya from his then capital at Amarapura to the pagoda can still be seen.

During the Second World War the wooden pavilions and houses of the Royal Palace caught fire and were burnt to the ground, but the great walls with their very fine watchtowers and gates still surround the square mile which was once the royal city. These walls are over 20 feet high and 10 feet thick. They are surrounded by a moat 225 feet wide and 11 feet deep. There are also some old cannons. But in all, the palace is a great disappointment and your visit to it can be short so that you can spend time in the museum if possible. Special permission is unfortunately required to visit the museum, which contains fine examples of royal household furniture.

All around Mandalay lie deserted capitals, some of them quite easily reached, others inaccessible to the average tourist because one has to reach them by boat. Amarapura (City of the Immortals) was founded by King Bodawpaya in 1781 as capital of his kingdom. When you buy "Mandalay" silk or cotton, you will find that most of the weaving is done in Amarapura. Sagaing, another former capital, lies on the opposite bank of the Irrawaddy, which can be crossed by the magnificent mile-long road and railway bridge, the only bridge across this river. It is on a hill and has many old pagodas. You should also see the Kaumudaw, one of the most unusual pagodas in Burma. Fronted by two stone lions, the solid stone hemisphere (circumference 400 feet) is modeled on the Mahaccti of Ceylon. Legend has it that its builder was inspired by his view of a young lady as her blouse dropped while he was passing the site. There are 160 images of *nats* or *devas* around the base and 812 stone posts with places for oil lamps which can floodlight the pagoda at night. You can buy some exquisite hand-crafted brassware at a workshop on the road between Mandalay and Saggaing. Mingun can only be reached by river and lies seven miles north of Mandalay. It is famous for its bell, the largest uncracked bell in the world. (There is a slightly larger bell in Moscow, but it is imperfect.)

Hill Stations

The Shan State is a must for tourists with a few days to spare. On arrival at Heho, you have the choice of making Kalaw your base, or Taunggyi, the seat of the Shan State government. From either of these two places you will be able to do a leisurely tour of the surrounding areas in two days. Kalaw (alt. 4,340 ft.) stands among pine-covered hills. It used to be one of the favorite hill stations where tired and worn officials and families went to escape from the heat and humidity of Rangoon. There are many lovely walks around Kalaw among the sweet-smelling pines, though one is limited to an area of one kilometer outside the towns. The air is fresh and clear and it is pleasantly cool any time of year. Your hotel will organize excursions by road to Taunggyi, Yawngshwe and Inle Lake.

In Taunggyi (4,675 ft.), as in Kalaw, there are many walks and good climbing. At the daily market you will see a number of hill people all in their unusual costumes. There will be the Pa-o, Taung-yo, Ung-sa, and Danu peoples. Yawngshwe lies in a valley, and it is where you will find a boat for your trip on the Inle Lake. A request to visit the Yawngshwe Haw (residence of the Yawngshwe Saopha, or local ruler) can be made on arrival. There is usually someone at the Haw to show you around.

The Inle Lake is famous for its leg-rowers and floating island gardens. The lake dwellers are known as the Danu. The "Bangkok" and "Zimme" silks are products of Inle, and you can be taken to see the weaving villages. The Paung-Daw-U Pagoda at Nam-Hu contains the five Buddha figures which over the centuries have been so frequently gilded that they have almost become balls of gold. The Buddha figures are very sacred, and people from all over the country come to worship. There is a special festival every year.

Maymyo, 50 miles southeast of Mandalay and 3,000 ft. above the hot plains, is worth a visit for its botanical gardens, bird life, and the old houses dating from the British reign.

Note on Remote Burma

The more remote parts of Burma may usually not be visited due to security problems. When in doubt, check with travel agents in neighboring countries or the authorities in Rangoon, who are very cautious regarding the safety of visitors and will recommend accordingly.

PRACTICAL INFORMATION

FACTS AND FIGURES. Land area: 676,000 sq. kms. Cultivated area: 12%. Population: 39 million. Population engaged in agriculture and fishing: 66%. Birth rate, per 1,000: 39. Average life expectancy: 54 years. Average per capita income: US$180. Number of tourists annually (1984 est.): 40,000.

WHAT WILL IT COST? If you stay in an air-conditioned room you must expect your hotel to run to US$20 for singles, US$25 more for doubles. Set meals at the main hotels are around US$3 for breakfast and US$10 for lunch or dinner. A taxi if hired all day costs US$25. Official taxis are now almost unobtainable; private taxis charge US$5 per hour, by negotiation. A safe top estimate for hotel, food, and sightseeing would be US$50. By staying at a smaller hotel you could bring this down to US$40. It is almost impossible for a Westerner to eat satisfactorily outside hotels and a very few restaurants. Do not risk changing foreign currency on the black market.

WHEN TO GO. The best time to visit Burma is during its so-called winter, which runs from October to March. The mornings and evenings are cool and fresh—in some years for ten days around Christmas you are glad to wear something heavier than tropical suiting—but the days are warm and sunny. In the hills, the days are crisp and sunny but at night the temperature may fall below freezing.

February to May is the hottest season. In Rangoon temperatures in the daytime are between 90 and 100 degrees Fahrenheit and the traveler is well advised to do his sightseeing in the early morning or late afternoon.

Toward the end of May the rains come and the monsoon lasts until about the end of October (Rangoon has about 100 inches of rain). The heavy clouds cut out some of the heat but the humidity is high.

WHERE TO GO. Because of the seven-day visa limitation and the overwhelming problems in arranging one's own travel and accommodation needs within the country, a "package" tour is the only practical way to see Burma. The easiest jumping-off point is Thailand. One Bangkok-based travel agent, *Diethelm* (544 Ploenchit Rd.) handles about 30 percent of all tourists visiting Burma and they offer five-, six-, and eight-day tours.

The places you can visit within Burma are limited. Rangoon, the capital, is relatively easy to tour and you can make several day excursions from there. Pagan and Mandalay, reached by air and having reasonable accommodations, are also practical, but smaller upcountry destinations, including hill stations and seaside beaches, may be restricted due to security problems, or poorly provided with facilities if you can get there.

The Hotel & Tourist Corp. of the Burmese government (77–91, Sule Pagoda Rd., P.O. Box 559, Rangoon) can provide information and arrange tours and accommodations upcountry, but, as with all aspects of the tourism industry in Burma, letters from abroad are answered slowly, if at all.

WHAT TO TAKE. Bring the lightest suits and clothes and, especially in the monsoon season (May to October), remember that you have to change at least twice a day and the laundry can take a long time to come back. If you are going up into the hills between November and February, also bring light sweaters. American and British drinks are either impossibly expensive or unobtainable, as are tobacco and cigarettes (local English-type brands available). Cosmetics are expensive and only a limited selection is to be found.

Very limited duty-free facilities at Rangoon airport are available to *departing* passengers. Take also all personal needs for such things as razor blades, camera film, and toiletries. Pharmaceutical needs should also be purchased before your visit. Many visitors take advantage of local shortages by carrying in foreign cigarettes, liquor, and cosmetics for use in bartering, at greatly inflated value, for souvenirs. Best bartering items are English cigarettes and Scotch. Do not have film developed locally.

ELECTRIC CURRENT. 220 volts, 50 cycles—voltage fluctuations are often serious, especially in the evening. Better bring your own adapter.

LOCAL FESTIVALS. Most of the festivals are of a religious nature and are held simultaneously throughout the country. Nearly all festivals take place on a Full Moon day and are based on the lunar calendar. The days therefore differ from year to year. For secular holidays the dates remain the same every year and are shown below.

January 4. *Independence Day,* parades, sports events, folk dancing and carnivals throughout the country.

February 12. *Union Day* is celebrated in much the same manner as January 4, with the addition of boat races.

Early March. *Full Moon of Tabong.* Alms offerings to monks at various pagodas and monasteries.

Mid-April. *Maha Thingyan or Water Festival.* The Burmese New Year celebrations. It is a time when everyone goes on holiday for at least three days. For the older people it is a period of prayer and fasting, but for the younger people everything is sacrificed to fun and amusement. From the ancient ceremony of sprinkling scented water over one's elders as a token of respect, has developed a free-for-all water fight in the streets—even fire hoses are often used. Also competitions in singing, dancing and comedy skits. It is a festival in which tempers must be kept down, and one must accept getting wet gracefully. After all, the water is supposed to wash away all your sins of the past year.

May. *Full Moon of Kason.* Celebrations in most temples to mark the birth, enlightenment and death of the Lord Buddha.

July. *Full Moon of Waso.* Another widely observed religious festival commemorating the Lord Buddha's first sermon and marking the beginning of Buddhist Lent. Among the ceremonies carried out are the distribution of alms and special prayers at major temples, especially at the Shwe Dagon in Rangoon.

Late August. *Taungbyon Festival* held at Taungbyon, 20 miles north of Mandalay, is a seven-day raucous affair of propitiation of the *nats,* spirits whose worship is a secular counterpart of Buddhism, and dancing by those possessed of nats, who are known as *nat kadaw.*

Early October. *Paung-daw-U Festival of Yawnqshwe,* which is in the Shan States. Five Buddha images tour the entire Inle Lake district in a specially constructed state barge. A colorful occasion, with leg-rowers of the Inle towing the enormous gilded barge over the limpid waters of the lake.

October–November. *Full Moon of Thadingyut.* The end of Buddhist Lent, and the first day of gaiety and light-heartedness after three months of fasting and strict observance of the precepts. For some weeks starting from this day, there is always a great rush of engagements and weddings.

November. *Tazaungdaing Festival,* Tazaungdaing and the previous festival, Thadingyut, are both celebrated with lights. All pagodas, monasteries, and houses are beautifully illuminated. Streets are lit with colored lights. In Rangoon, Lanmadaw, and Kennedy Point, you can usually see the most brilliant illuminations. There are foodstalls, zats (Burmese dancing and drama), Chinese and Indian conjurers and other numerous side shows. There is a special weaving competition of robes for Buddhist monks at the Shwe Dagon Pagoda the night before the full moon.

HOW TO REACH BURMA. You can *only* enter Burma at Rangoon. The easiest way is by air from Bangkok.

The following airlines call regularly at Rangoon: *Thai International, Bangladesh Biman,* and the national airline, *Burmese Airways Corporation,* which flies to Calcutta, Bangkok, Singapore, Kathmandu, and Dacca. Of these airlines, only Thai can be recommended.

VISAS. If you are going to Burma as a tourist, it is essential to see that the Burmese Embassy or Consulate (or British Mission where Burma is unrepresented) gives you an entry visa. Visas cost $10, and you'll need three photos with your application. A minimum of six weeks may be required for getting a visa, in a Western country, although most tourists now report getting one in a much shorter time. Visas are usually issued within two working days at the Burmese Embassy in Bangkok. This can be handled by travel agencies there. International health regulations must be met for cholera.

CUSTOMS. Duty-free allowances include 200 cigarettes, 8 oz. tobacco, one bottle of alcohol, one bottle of perfume, one still camera and reasonable quantity of film, one movie camera and limited film, as well as your personal effects. Foreign-made clothes are an excellent form of barter for local handicrafts, so take some spare ones as there are no customs restrictions. You will be required to declare such equipment as cameras on arrival, for rechecking before you leave. Customs formalities are very strict, both on arrival and departure, but visitors arriving with a tour group are usually less hassled.

AT THE AIRPORT. Visitors will find formalities slow and frustrating at Rangoon Airport, and officials generally unhelpful. Be careful to declare all currency (including credit cards if you intend to use them), cameras, jewelry, and other salable effects to Customs on arrival; they will probably be checked in detail on departure.

Proof of immunization against cholera is required; also for yellow fever if arriving from an infected area.

Transportation from the airport into the city (19 kms.) is usually by taxi, fare around 30 kyats, or less if you are a good bargainer. Airport Departure Tax Ks. 15.

TRAVELING IN BURMA. At the time of writing, internal security continues to be a problem and one cannot advise either road or rail travel without first asking the advice of your travel agent.

By air: Air travel is regular, but flights to some parts may be only on a once or twice weekly basis, so make certain you have a return reservation. Before now, tourists on a tight schedule have visited the beautiful sands at Ngapali for a two-day rest only to find that they could not get back to Rangoon and had to spend four or five days of rather primitive lotus-eating waiting for a plane. Flight delays, sometimes long ones, are usual, and priority in seating is always given to groups, so individual travelers, even with firm bookings, get "bumped."

By surface transport: There are no long-distance buses; only 3-ton trucks that have been converted to carrying passengers—and the conversion, to say the least, has been extremely unimaginative. Cheap, but you had better be young and possessed with infinite patience. One of the most leisurely and thorough ways of seeing Burma is by river boat. The finest trip is undoubtedly from Bhamo to Mandalay through the river gorges. But both Mandalay to Pagan, and Mandalay to Rangoon, are excellent routes from which to see river life and enjoy the landscape. Pagan is accessible either by air from Rangoon (one-day trip) or by jeep, taxi, or boat from Mandalay (three to five days, allowing two nights at Pagan). There are also daily flights up to Heho. Advance booking is essential. Pegu, 50 miles from Rangoon, is accessible by road or rail. Taxi fare, for up to five people, will cost about 300 kyat.

Travel by boat or train in Burma can be quite difficult and time-consuming. Engines tend to break down and day-long delays can occur for many reasons, which makes the foreign tourist nervous about overstaying his visa, which is a serious offence. If you do attempt a boat or train trip, take your own food. Advance arrangements cannot be made through travel agents.

MONEY. The basic unit of the Burmese currency is the *kyat* (pron. *jut* as in *shut*) which is divided into 100 *pyas.* At presstime the official rate is Ks. 8.35 = US$1. On the open market people are willing to give Ks. 15 to 18 for a dollar. Currency restrictions therefore are very strictly enforced and the traveler is warned absolutely not to risk breaking them. Under current regulations, travelers are not allowed to bring *any* Burmese currency into the country.

On entry you will be given a currency form. All foreign exchange transactions must be entered on the form by an authorized foreign-exchange agent. This form must be presented on departure and will probably be checked.

Travelers' checks, drafts, and foreign currency are unlimited, but must be declared on entry. On departure, your currency transactions and remaining balances may be rigidly checked, so do declare everything on arrival; you may change back up to 25 percent of what you have cashed into kyats in Burma. Banking hours: 10 A.M.–3 P.M. weekdays.

Note. The only credit card that can be used in Burma is American Express and this card must be declared to Customs officials on arrival, as if it were currency.

GETTING AROUND RANGOON. By bus: Japanese buses are to be found on some routes, but the vintage of Rangoon's buses varies greatly, and the ride will be cheap, but usually uncomfortable. Recently imported foreign buses are often inoperative due to lack of spares, so the standard bus service is often a converted truck of Second World War vintage.

By taxi: There are numerous kinds of taxis, from the large and antiquated that hover around hotels hoping to catch the unwary visitor (expensive) to the little three-wheeler which, if its meter is working, is very cheap. But if you wish to drive firmly on four wheels, ask for a Jeep taxi. Always try to arrive at a price before making the journey as they are meterless. Approximate charge is Ks. 35 for the first hour, Ks. 20 for each additional hour. With the smaller taxis and three-wheelers, allow Ks. 8 for every ten to fifteen minutes of driving.

TIPPING. This is expected. Most of the hotels add a service charge of up to 10 percent to your bill. It is then only necessary to give Ks.2 or 3 to your room boy if he has looked after you well and Ks. 1 to anyone else who has been particularly helpful to you. It is unusual to tip taxi drivers and you can take it as a rule that any price arrived at by bargaining *includes* the tip . . . plus, most probably, quite a lot more, unless you know the East well.

ACCOMMODATIONS. Rangoon's few hotels range from the expensive *Inya Lake* to very modest inns. It will doubtless be many years before Rangoon can offer the accommodation found in other great cities in the world, although plans have been announced to build new hotels in all major tourist centers.

RANGOON

Inya Lake. Built with Russian aid and first run by an Israeli firm. It is now operated by the Burmese government hotel corporation. The hotel has a magnificent site overlooking Inya Lake and lies off the road from the airport to town. There are six VIP suites, six two-room suites, 125 double and 75 single rooms, restaurant serving European, Chinese, and Burmese food, coffee shop, etc. As well, it has the modern pleasures of swimming pools and putting green. It is by far the best hotel in Burma. Prices subject to 10 percent service charges, from US$20, single; US$27 double.

The Royal Lake Hotel, also called **Kandawkyi Hotel.** A former British Raj club, has reasonable facilities and 19 air-conditioned rooms. Reasonable prices.

Strand. One of two first-class establishments, is government run, has 100 rooms and three suites at prices ranging from US$17 (nonair-conditioned single) to US$28–35 (air-conditioned double). Older than Inya Lake but situated downtown and recent attempts have been made to renovate the hotel and all facilities. The restaurant serves European, Chinese, Burmese, and Indian food. The hotel also has a tourist shop and is an authorized moneychanger.

Thamada. Newer than the Strand, has 57 rooms, air-conditioned, with showers. Located downtown, near the Shwe Dagon pagoda, the food is quite good. US$17 for a single, or US$25 for a double.

There is also a **YMCA** in Rangoon which offers poor quality, but cheap accommodations. Also for budget travelers, the **Garden Guest House** is possible.

OUTSIDE RANGOON

Pagan: The *Thiripyitsaya Hotel,* by the Irrawaddy, has 48 rooms, all air-conditioned. Prices are expensive, the same as the Inya Lake. Also in Pagan, the *Irra Inn* has 30 rooms, all doubles, with primitive facilities, but a renovation program in hand promises better things. Singles are priced from US$6 and doubles from US$10. Reasonable European-style food is available.

Mandalay: The *Mandalay* is government-operated, same as the Strand in Rangoon. It has 50 rooms, all air-conditioned and with showers. There is a dining room and bar. Single $15; double $18. *The Htun Hla Hotel* is also just possible; small, and old, but cheap.

Taunggyi: *Taunggyi* has 60 double rooms, with showers but no air conditioners. At the beach town of Sandoway, the *Sandoway* hotel on the beach is of quite reasonable standard. Both are inexpensive, with double rooms from $15.

CLOSING HOURS. The larger shops are open from 10 A.M. to 5 P.M. or 5:30. The smaller shops are usually open from about 9 in the morning until 7 or 8 in the evening.

SPORTS. Every Saturday afternoon, except in the hottest weather, you will see crowds pushing their way across the railway bridge into the Aung San Stadium. They are going to watch a *football match* (soccer), Burma's most popular sport. Cricket and hockey are also played, but they do not have the same immensely large following. The most popular Burmese sport, after football, is *boxing.* It is very similar to Siamese boxing and has nothing to do with the Queensberry rules. Kicks, jabs with the knee, as well as good hard punching, are all a part of the fight.

All these are spectator sports, but the one game played by everyone from the rapidly advancing young civil servant to the ordinary villager is *chinglone.* It has all the appearance of simplicity and ease that only years of skilled practice can bring about. It is played with a ball of woven cane and the object of the game is to prevent the ball hitting the ground. The players stand round in a circle, kicking the ball into the air with their insteps, knees, elbows, shoulders and even, when it falls behind their backs, with their heels. If it all looks too easy, ask if you can join in. Rangoon has two *golf* clubs, the *Rangoon Golf Club* and the *Burma Golf Club,* and a *swimming* club (for members and guests only).

For a day by the sea, *Tourist (Burma) Corp.* arranges trips to *Sandoway* or *Ngapali Beach,* and the *Union of Burma Airways* has a Sunday (day return) excursion flight during the dry season. Although there are other small beaches in the south along the Tenasserem Coast, Ngapali has been the only seaside resort opened up for tourists.

MUSEUMS. *The National Museum,* Phayre St, houses archeological and art treasures. Of special interest is the display of Mandalay court regalia, including the famous Lion Throne, returned to Burma by the British in 1948. Note two separate entrances, one marked Ministry of Union Culture—then up three flights. English signs on exhibits, but ask for guide book as well. Open daily, except Sunday, 10 A.M. to 3 P.M. The *Museum of Natural History,* on Royal Lake, has a collection of Burmese flora, fauna, and minerals. For a fascinating look at live Burmese flora and fauna, take a trip to the Rangoon zoo and gardens, on King Edward Ave. Two white rhinoceroses are on view. If you are lucky you may even catch a snake-charming show on Sundays—Burmese snake charmers specialize in kissing cobras!

SHOPPING. Rangoon's day as one of the great shopping centers of Southeast Asia is long since gone, as are many of its shops and all of its department stores (vanished with nationalization). But there are still finds for the eager shopper. The Strand and Inya Lake hotels both house government-run (foreign exchange only) shops with very limited goods, and the government also operates the large *Diplomatic Shop* (for diplomats and tourists only—that is, foreign exchange) on Sule Pagoda Road, where you can get an overall glimpse of fine Burmese craftsmanship: handmade silver and lacquerware, mother-of-pearl, ivory and teak carving, handwoven silk and cotton, Burma's famed cheroots, cigars and fancy pipes, and an exciting, but very limited, selection of Burma's even more famous gems—rubies, sapphires, jade, pearls, and a variety of semiprecious stones—only available here. Prices here are rather high. The main shopping center for Burmese is the *Bogyoke Market* on Bogyoke St., with many stalls selling traditional local products. You can buy material there for a *pasoe* or *longyi,* and have a Chinese tailor make one for you in three days. Also have a look at the *Pagan Shop Moonlite,* and *Burma Craft,* all on Sule Pagoda, and the row of shops on Edward St., (between Merchant and Mahabandoola Sts.) specializing in fascinating lacquerwork designed chiefly for use at Buddhist ceremonies. *Gallery Orient,* 555 Merchant, has interesting collection of contemporary Burmese artists.

One of the best areas to search for antiques, bric-à-brac, silver and bronze, or just good old junk is in the stairways leading to the Shwe Dagon pagoda, while Bogyoke (Scott) Market, close to the Railway Station on Aung San St., offers a mass of covered shops selling all kinds of local products, including silver and jewelry. It is important to note that the exportation of all antiques and religious articles is forbidden. Customs authorities can be very unhelpful and difficult.

Best shopping in Mandalay is around Mahamuni Pagoda.

In Pagan the best buy is local laquerware.

There is a small tax-free shop at Rangoon airport carrying a limited range of liquors and cigarettes, available only to departing passengers.

DINING OUT. Good-quality restaurants serving Burmese food are very limited. One, the *Burma Kitchen* on West Shwe Dagon Road, is popular with expatriates and serves a reasonable selection of both Burmese and Chinese food. Some Burmese food is offered at hotels or one can buy *Khao-swe* or *Mohingna* at a wayside stall. This is an idea that does not strike the average traveler as particularly attractive, since however good the food may look and taste, it is only too obvious while much thought has been given to its cooking, virtually none has been accorded to the simpler problem of washing-up. *Myakanda* restaurant offers inexpensive seafood.

Although a number of hotels offer Burmese cuisine, this is seldom a very satisfactory way to try it out for the first time. Burmese cooking has much in common with English cooking . . . . it can be extraordinarily dreary and rather strong to the uncultivated taste, unless it is prepared with considerable attention. A real Burmese meal is a mixture of contrasting and, to the Westerner, delightfully novel tastes. The table is covered with a large number of small dishes in which will be found many different sauces, most of them based on differing varieties of dried and fermented fish or shrimp, known as *nga-pi.* A little *nga-pi* will go a long way for the beginner and like gorgonzola cheese is a taste one likes immediately or only acquires after an arduous apprenticeship.

The main foundation of the meal is rice. On this you put two or three of the curries that are to be found surrounded by the sauces. One curry will certainly be fish, another possibly chicken, and another prawn, shrimps, or some other type of fish curry may also be present. There will be some green salad, also some uncooked vegetables such as cucumbers and green mango, when it is in season, served to be eaten with a particularly strong, sharp sauce. The great art is to take a very little of each dish until you know what its flavor is and then to concentrate on those you like, blending and adding them to suit your own taste. Some Burmese hostesses are very fond of pressing you to take piles of food from every dish for fear you might be too shy and go away hungry. But a gentle refusal of anything you do not like very much, and judicious praise for what you want to have, will ensure that both you and the hostess will be happy.

Remember that all bars and restaurants in Burma close early, usually by 9:30 P.M.

RANGOON

Chinese

Most Chinese restaurants prefer their clients to arrive by 7:30 P.M.; they usually close by 9:30. For a late snack (Chinese fried noodles and pancake rolls or Indian *chapati* and chicken curry), try the open-air night bazaars.

Hai Yuan. On University Ave. Serves good casual meals of mostly Cantonese cooking.

Hwan Chyu. 98 Kaba Aye Pagoda Rd. Cantonese-style. Specialty: sticky rice-stuffed chicken.

Kwan Lock. 67 22nd St. Specializes in elaborate meals to 24-hour order (suckling pig, bird's nest soup, etc.).

Nam Sin. At 8th mile, Prome Rd., 20 minutes from city center. Peking or Shanghai specialties.

New Oi Hkun. 75 Latha St. Another place which would like advance notice for elaborate meals.

Palace. 84 37th St. Specializes in Shanghai and Szechuan cooking. Many residents consider it the best.

Western

Inya Lake Hotel. Dining rooms are also open to nonresidents, European, Burmese, and Chinese. Serves a passable buffet lunch.

Karaweik. Floating restaurant, intended for tourists. It is built like a boat and offers quite good Burmese cuisine and cultural shows on several days a week. Beautiful location and unusual architecture—worth a visit.

Mya Nanda. Open-air snack bar in park opposite Strand Hotel. Good chicken kebab and Indian dishes. Open evenings only, until 9:00 P.M.

Nanthida. Opposite the Strand Hotel (and managed by them). Serves snacks and Mandalay beer. Moderate prices. Overlooking Rangoon River.

People's Patisserie. Sule Pagoda Rd. Snacks only.

Strand Hotel. Dining room is open to nonresidents, but like all restaurants, bars and clubs in Burma, closes very early by Western standards.

Yatha. On Merchant St. Offers coffees, teas, and ice creams.

NIGHT LIFE. Sophisticated night life is not to be found in Rangoon. Soft lights, danceable music, and romantic settings are completely out.

If you like spending an evening at the cinema better, you will find *The Thamada* a comfortable theater. There is also a bar attached. There are other cinemas, but the local movies are an acquired taste and the few Western ones, like every other imported item in Burma, are of extreme vintage.

MAIL AND TELEGRAMS. A letter to the United States costs between Ks2.85–3.15 cents, to Great Britain about Ks2.50. The postal system is not reliable, and outgoing mail is often censored. Better to mail material from your next destination. Cable and international telephone facilities are available, but unreliable.

DRINKING WATER. Do not use the water from the taps. Insist that all water you drink has been boiled (tea is usually safe) or use bottled drinks. In most places the tap water is so bad that visitors are even advised to brush their teeth in soda water.

MEDICAL. Upcountry Burma is malarial, so take appropriate precautions, especially if visiting higher altitudes between May and December. Stomach disorders are also common, so carry along an anti-diarrhea remedy as recommended by your doctor at home. Be sure that all water has been boiled, or drink hot tea. On no account drink tap water, or eat fruit that has already been peeled. Also be cautious about salads and any food from street stalls.

PHOTOGRAPHY. Film rarely available in government's hotel and diplomatic shops. Have any developing you may need done at home or in your next port of call.

FIVE-MINUTE BURMESE

Although English is used officially in Burma, and all educated persons speak it fluently, you may find yourself off the beaten path and in need of a few words of Burmese. In addition to this, the people you deal with will always be happy to hear you say something nice, especially "thank you."

English	*Burmese (phonetic)*
Hello	hey
Thank you	chay-zoo tin pah-day
Please	chay-zoo pyu-pah
How do you do	nay kah-oong thah lah (accent on kah-oong)
Goodbye	thwah pah taw may ("t" is very close to "d")
Airport	lay yin p'yan kwin (kwin is like Quinn)
Hotel	hoh tay
Toilet	eing thah
Water	yea
Please may I have the check?	chay-zoo pyu-pah sayin logindey
Tea	le phet yee

English	*Burmese (phonetic)*
How much does this cost?	bear loud kyat the le
Expensive	shah day
Where can I eat?	bear mhar sar ya mhar le
Excuse me	won ne par de
Very good	ah lung kaung pa da
Good	kah-oong day
Not good	mah kah-oong boo (accent on boo)
Come	lah pah
Go	thwah pah
Hot	pu de
Twenty-five pyas	nhe se ngar peya (the "n" sound is like French un)
Fifty pyas	peya ngar se
Yes	hoke ket
No	ma hoke boo
One	h'tit (h like huh, but very short)
Two	h'nit (h like huh, but very short)
Three	thone (like an Alabaman saying "thorn")
Four	lay
Five	nga
Six	chauk (chalk without the "l")
Seven	cone h'nit
Eight	she-it
Nine	koh
Ten	h'tit say
Eleven	say h'tit
Twelve	say h'nit

MALAYSIA

Minaret and Skyscraper; Jungle and Kampong

Malaysia is a place that does not immediately create strong visual impressions as does Thailand, where saffron-clad monks stroll serenely among the impassive gilded Buddhas, or Bali, where exquisite dancers perform under the stars in a velvet magic night. On the map Malaysia is just sort of there: hanging down below Thailand, snuggling up to the huge Indonesian island of Sumatra to the west. And then to the east, way over on another island on the north of that other island, are another two states of Malaysia: Sabah, just a hop and skip from the southern islands of the Philippines, and Sarawak, a blanket of jungle and rivers covering the top half of Borneo.

Malaysia conjures up several outdated images: beefy British plantation managers sipping stenghas and playing bridge with Somerset Maugham; jungles where pirates and smugglers make secret rendezvous on hidden airstrips that exist more in the novels of Eric Ambler or Gavin Black than in real life; or the trails of the Emergency as depicted in the film *The Virgin Soldiers.* East Malaysia is even less well known, except among anthropologists who arrive regularly to study remote tribal peoples such as the peaceful, nonheadhunters, Punan, who live in the backwaters of Sarawak.

Nevertheless, Malaysia has become a real attraction in Southeast Asia for visitors who want to relax in a strange land without worrying about exorbitant prices, crowded sightseeing attractions, or impassable language barriers. Malaysia admittedly doesn't offer much for the culture vulture. The country does, however, contain some of the loveliest beaches in the world, unusual social situations with opportunities for a visitor to explore various cultures, and last but not least, adequate facilities for the tourist: good hotels in every price range, moderately priced transport, and friendly, helpful people. It is also the only Southeast Asian country in which the visitor can safely enjoy the delights of self-drive car touring.

Through the ages the Malayan Peninsula remained relatively unexplored and underdeveloped, except along the coasts where river harbors offered anchorage. The reason for the sparse settlement of the interior lies in one of the many paradoxes in Southeast Asia: despite the lavish jungle growth that appears so lush and rich, the red laterite soil is not very fertile. Jungle growth results from a delicate balance of abundant rain, hot humid air and rapid decay, so that in effect the jungle feeds on itself. Until rubber, which grows well in this climate, became a worldwide commodity, the interior of the Malayan peninsula enticed only a few settlers and some nomadic hunting tribes.

A Short Trip through History

In prehistoric times the general movement of migration was from north, around China-Burma, to the south, all the way to New Guinea. The earliest inhabitants of the Malayan Peninsula were Negrito neolithic peoples whose descendants can still be found in jungle uplands. Several waves of "progressively more Mongoloid peoples" brought Iron and Bronze cultures to the peninsula and spread out over the entire island archipelago. Thus, many of the people throughout Southeast Asia share certain characteristics, and there are similarities in the life style among such widely scattered peoples as the Jakuns of Malaya, the Batak of Sumatra, and the Iban in Borneo.

During the early years of the Christian Era in the West, several kingdoms rose and fell in this area, some on the islands of Java and Sumatra, as well as in the lands below China. The Chinese established a center called the "kingdom" of Funan at the mouth of the Mekong River and trade flourished and expanded. Several river valley kingdoms appeared in Malaya, the best known being that of Lankasuka, centered in the north, near Kedah.

In the eighth century, the rise of Sri Vijaya, a kingdom centered near the present-day city of Palembang in Sumatra, focused attention on the Straits of Malacca. Later, with the emergence of the Majapahit (about which there is considerable controversy among historians) with its base in Java, the Malay Peninsula came under the influence of a Hindu-Javanese empire that exerted little political control. Culturally, however,the Hindu influence was strong and can be seen in the *wayang kulit,* plays still performed in villages, and also in the forms of many ceremonies and customs.

Thus, until the arrival of Islam and the rise of Malacca, the predominant influences on Malaya were migrations of animistic, simple, village-oriented peoples who settled in small groups in river valleys.

Then came sailors, traders, and merchants who set up organized towns structured around a central leader and his entourage. The basic schism between agriculture and trade societies was never quite bridged in the centuries following.

In the 15th century, Islam came to Malaya from northern Sumatra and became the state religion of the powerful state of Malacca during the reign of Sultan Iscandar Shah/Parameswara. Islam brought not only a new religion, but it also solidified the political system of the sultanates in which one person (and his family) provided both political and religious leadership.

For the next 200 years the entire area from Kedah to Johore at the tip of the peninsula was a hornets' nest of warring sultanates, marauding pirate bands and European adventurers, who, searching for spice and gold, introduced guns and cannons. The Portuguese conquered Malacca and evidences of their stay remain to this day. Following them came the Dutch, who established a stronghold in Java and outposts in Sumatra and Malacca. In Malaya, intrigue and minor wars kept the sultans occupied as power flowed across the Straits to Aceh in North Sumatra and then down to the kingdom of Johore. Meanwhile, Islam became established as the majority religion and gradually the notions of modern Malay culture and law began to evolve.

Peace and Prosperity: 1824–1942

British settlements in the Straits of Malacca, Singapore, and Penang flourished. The treaty of 1824 separated the Malayan Peninsula from Dutch-held Sumatra, and the two regions, so similar in historical development, cultural traditions, and religious customs began to split and follow the lead of the new colonialists from Europe.

The political influence of the British on the sultans consisted mostly of advice on economic matters and intervention in interstate squabbles. Moreover, the British presence kept the Dutch away and also settled the disputes with the Siamese over the northern border.

The European Industrial Revolution created a demand for tin and the closing decades of the 19th century saw the rapid enrichment of the tin-mining states of Perak, Selangor, and the area around the present national capital—Kuala Lumpur. Railways followed tin production and thus pinpointed those areas which were then cleared to make way for rubber plantations. A glance at today's map of Malaysia shows that the west coast, first because of the strategic position of control of the Straits and later because of rail links with the ports of Singapore and Penang, developed much more than the states on the east coast. These remained economically, politically and culturally isolated until the late 1960s. It was not until 1983 that an east–west road link was finally completed across the mountainous north of the country, from Penang to Kota Bharu.

British influence on life in Malaysia remains indelibly stamped on the national educational and political systems. Despite the fact that Bahasa Malaysia is the teaching language in schools, English remains the language that is mandatory for anyone wishing to enter the fields of commerce, industry, or civil service.

With the increase in Malay nationalistic feeling, the remnants of the British presence are slowly vanishing. British governors were immortalized (or so they thought) in the names of towns such as Port Swettenham or streets such as Jalan Weld. They established clubs such as the old Tudor-style Selangor Club in Kuala Lumpur. That somnambulist sport—cricket—became popular and nearly every town has a central *padang* where even today Sunday cricketers dressed in starchy whites wield their bats. Cricket and the club remain, but the imperial names, reminders to the Malaysians of a colonial past, have already all been changed.

The British imported organized horseracing, which attracted the gambling fervor of the Chinese and the sporting instincts of the Malays. The racetracks, themselves a tribute to the British talent for gardening, support several thousand workers who care for and train the horses and lovingly tend the shrubs, trees, and grass surrounding the track.

More important than the importation of sports was the introduction by the British of national legal, communications, and transportations systems, which gave the country, actually a group of rather loosely knit independent sultanates, its basic social infrastructure.

Tongs and Towkays: The Chinese

Rapid expansion in the tin-mining industry resulted in large-scale Chinese immigration in the middle of the 19th century. China itself, where the Manchu dynasty could no longer enforce emigration restrictions on its subjects in the southern states of Kwangtung and Fukien, was beginning to disintegrate and millions fled the twin scourges of war and famine. Malaya was sparsely populated; more to the point, the heavy work demanded by the new industry did not particularly attract the easygoing Malays. Another deterrent to the Malays was the hazard of malaria and other mosquito-borne fevers that were endemic in the jungle areas where the tin mines were. The Chinese, fleeing terrible conditions in their homelands, provided a steady source of expendable labor. They were usually brought by the shipload, single men without families, hoping to earn enough to return to China and buy some land. Employers met the ships and paid the shipowners for passage in return for the services of their human cargo. Terms were usually fair for those times and after the contract period was up the laborers were free to seek employment on their own or to set up a small business.

The Chinese are a hardy, frugal, and thrifty people and soon their numbers swelled. By 1870, for example, the district of Larut had a larger population of Chinese than Malays. The Chinese brought some problems with them. One, which caused trouble in Hong Kong and Singapore as well as Malaya, were the secret societies or *tongs* and the bitter fighting that arose between rival groups. The secret societies were similar to early Mafia organizations in that they were essentially mutual protection agencies that looked out for the illiterate, naive and homesick immigrant. The societies had their origins in China and were militant groups dedicated to the overthrow of the Manchu dynasty. They had a strong militaristic bent, and sometimes aggressive internal conflicts erupted and spread throughout the entire community. When these disturbances became severe the British police and military were forced to step in—as in the Penang riots of 1867.

Chinese immigrants, most of whom were poor, illiterate and unskilled farmers from the southern provinces, encountered a small but well established Chinese community in the Straits settlements. These were the descendants of early Chinese traders and adventurers. Often, because the Manchu dynasty actively discouraged emigration, they had fled for political or criminal reasons. Therefore, they had come to Malaya to settle permanently with no plans to return to the homeland as did the later immigrants. These families, known as *babas* or Straits Chinese, adopted many Malay customs and styles of dress. Their food, called *nonya* cooking, is a delicious blend of Malay and Chinese cuisine, which can still be found.

After the Chinese arrived to work the tin, another new commercial enterprise developed: rubber. The strange elastic substance, first found in Brazil, seemed a ridiculous commercial venture until the bicycle and automobile industries created a huge demand for tires. Coffee planters, discouraged by market uncertainties, eagerly experimented with seedlings introduced by Henry Ridley, the Director of Gardens for the Straits Settlements. Soon stately rows of rubber trees covered the hills.

Rubber requires intensive labor and again workers were brought in from outside. This time the Indian subcontinent supplied workers. Willing to accept low wages, the Indians, mostly from the south and from Ceylon, were brought in under an indenture system. Most arrived with the idea of returning to their homeland. Many, however, remained and even today the majority of workers on rubber plantations are Indian. In addition to the workers for the rubber plantations, other groups arrived from India following traditional occupations of trade, shopkeeping and money-lending. The British in India had trained many civil servants and professionals and these also came to Malaya to practice.

Because of India's proximity, ties with home remain strong in the Indian community. It is not unusual to send a request to the ancestral village for a bride or groom (many marriages are still arranged). Many Indians still return to their native land after retirement, something that the Chinese are no longer able to do.

Thus the patterns of life in Malaya were well established until the disruptions of the Second World War. Malay communities continued their traditional life in kampongs where time flowed slowly. The sultans prospered under the British protection and lived quite expansively, combining pleasures of East and West. The Chinese, growing ever more numerous and powerful, became the economic backbone of the peninsula, with the Indians performing various middlemen roles. The British continued their easy benevolent rule as they sat contentedly on the wide verandahs of their clubs, sipping stengahs and watching glorious tropical sunsets. Each community continued to exist separately, each independent of the other with little cultural interchange.

Upheaval and War

The early years of the Second World War in Europe had little effect on life in Malaya and life proceeded much as it had in the preceding decades.

The Japanese attack on Pearl Harbor and their subsequent invasion of Malaya jerked the complacent population into the worldwide turmoil. Japanese forces landed in the northern state of Trengganu and marched, or rather cycled, rapidly down through the jungle, taking Singapore in March 1942. Overnight, life for the inhabitants of the Malayan peninsula changed under the new administration.

Japanese ideals of a "Greater Co-Prosperity Sphere" attracted many at first, particularly in the Indian community. Many joined an abortive Indian Liberation Army that was to have been led by a noted Indian Independence leader, Chandra Bose, who died mysteriously on his way to Malaya.

The British, of course, underwent the most dramatic change in life style. Although most wives and children were evacuated to Australia, the men remained. Former planters, bankers, executives as well as soldiers were suddenly jolted from a life of ease and thrust into the rigors of prison life. Many of the prisoners perished working on railway construction in Siam. Loss of life was horrendous enough, but almost as excruciating for those surviving was the loss of face as the indignities of life in captivity undermined traditional self-images of white superiority.

The Malays, by and large, did not suffer greatly from Japanese rule and kampong life continued as it had for centuries. Shortages of food, clothing, and commodities, however, created difficulties and hardship for everyone.

The Chinese, particularly, received harsh treatment from their Japanese conquerors, bitter and suspicious after their experiences in China. In addition to economic hardships resulting from the disruption of world trade markets, the Chinese faced constant harassment from Japanese forces who arrested, jailed, and executed thousands. Many fled to the jungle, where, aided by remnants of the British Army, they formed guerrilla bands. Just as happened in Europe, those most adept at underground organization were Communist-trained. By the end of the war, Communist influence among the Chinese was much enhanced by the years spent in the jungle fighting the Japanese.

The Indian community, after the brief euphoria of alliance with the Co-Prosperity Sphere had evaporated, also suffered during the occupation. The Japanese conscripted 60,000 rubber estate workers as laborers for the Siam-Burma railway. Less than 20,000 survived.

Although Malaya escaped large-scale destruction from bombings and marauding armies, the war's end found the people floundering in economic uncertainties. Added to this difficulty was the obvious defanging of the British Lion when the native population saw their former masters stripped of power and prestige after their years in the prison camps.

Until independence under a federation of Malayan states, which was declared in 1957, politics was mostly concerned with jockeying and maneuvering for power between the two major racial groups. The Malays, realizing that independence would remove British protection and leave the Chinese in control, became politically active. Meanwhile the Chinese, their ranks decimated and demoralized by the rigors of the occupation, were not able to organize effective political power, despite their control of the economy. Thus the years of communal separatism began to take their toll in terms of national unification and development.

The developing communal divisions, exacerbated by economic hardships, led to bitter disputes among the leadership. Added to this tension came a full-scale rebellion led by Chinese who had been training for the struggle as guerrilla fighters during the Second World War. Inaugurating a campaign of terrorism in 1948 the rebels, many of whom had fought with the British, harassed plantation workers as well as owners and managers. Travel along the lonely jungle roads was hazardous, and many, including a British High Commissioner, were killed in ambush. The insurgents were pushed back into the jungle and by the time of independence they were under control. In 1960 the Emergency was lifted.

Political factionalism based on communal loyalties plagued the Federation. Finally in 1963 the nation of Malaysia was created and included the two British protectorates in northern Borneo. In the new nation the Borneo states were to serve as an ethnic balance against the power of the Chinese in Singapore. Indonesia, however, viewed the creation of Malaysia as a threat and Sukarno declared Confrontation, a sort of mini-war that finally fizzled out in 1967.

Today the racial and political power balance is still delicate. In terms of population 54 percent are Malay, 35 percent are Chinese, and 10 percent Indian, with other nationalities making up less than one percent. In terms of social influence, however, the Chinese are still relatively strong, and in spite of legislation to promote the "Bumiputra," or ethnic Malay interests, they still control much of the commercial and industrial sector. Much has been done to diffuse tensions between the ethnic groups, but pressures do still exist.

Sarawak and Sabah

These two states added 1.2 million people to the Federation and more than doubled the area of the new nation. Most of the new territory, however, was dense jungle and remote mountain ranges, accessible only by arduous travel up dangerous rivers. Except for coastal towns, much of the land was sparsely inhabited and unexplored. Moreover, the peoples in the two states had closer ties with Borneo and neighboring islands than with the Malayan Peninsula. The boundaries, established by European colonialists, followed river watersheds and took little notice of tribal territorial traditions. Because the mountain ranges run every which way, unlike the hills of northern Thailand and Burma, the terrain is so complicated that even an experienced explorer can get disoriented and lost.

THAILAND
N
Langkawi Island
PERLIS
Kangar
Alor Star
KEDAH
Khota Bharu
Beach of Passionate Love
South China Sea
Keroh
Georgetown
Butterworth
PENANG
East-West H'way
Gerik
Jeli
PERAK
KELANTAN
Taiping
Kuala Kangsar
Kuala Trengganu
TRENGGANU
Ipoh
Lumut
Cameron Highlands
Pangkor Island
National Park
Talok Anson
Kuala Lipis
Fraser's Hill
Kuantan
SELANGOR
Genting Highlands
PAHANG
Kuala Lumpur
Klang
NEGRI SEMBILAN
Seremban
Port Dickson
Strait of Malacca
Tioman Island
Malacca
MALACCA
Mersing
Keluang
JOHORE
SUMATRA
Johor Bahru
Singapore
INDONESIA
PENINSULAR MALAYSIA
0 Miles 100
0 Kms 150

In 1846, after Sir James Brooke settled a dispute between the local rajah and the Sultan of Brunei, the history of Sarawak began. Establishing peace and bringing relief from constant harassment by marauding pirate bands, Rajah Brooke instituted a benevolent family regency that lasted more than a century until the arrival of the Japanese. Their intrusion was deeply resented by the tribal people who eagerly resumed their practice of headhunting, which had been banned by the Brooke Rajahs.

But except for the interruption of the war years, and to a lesser extent the fighting during the Confrontation, Sarawak has remained peaceful, unspoiled and serene. The town of Kuching, capital of Sarawak, is charming and has one of the finest museums in the entire region.

The dense jungle forest, which broodingly dominates the atmosphere of Sarawak, has changed little since explorer Odoardo Beccari wrote in 1904: "the Bornean forest is so varied and so different at different hours and seasons . . . infinite and ever changing are its aspects as are the treasures it hides. In the forest man feels singularly free."

A visitor fortunate enough to take a trip up one of the rivers and spend a night or two in a longhouse will encounter a strange and wide spectrum of noise: insects hum and whine and buzz, invisible creatures bark and grunt, water slips gurgling and sighing steadily throughout the night. Even more mysterious are the ominous groaning and screeching noises of a tree that, burdened by age and accumulated debris, breaks and finally crashes thunderously and slowly through the dense jungle growth. Even more unnerving are those noises one does *not* hear: the tiny noiseless tread of hundreds of centipede feet marching across the foot of the bed or the padded pawsteps of a silently approaching hungry civet cat.

A newcomer to the jungle is often surprised by the absence of any readily visible wildlife. Except for varied and rather pesky insects, most jungle wildlife is shy, eager to avoid contact with man. Moreover, many jungle animals are nocturnal. Extended travel might, however, enable an exploring and enterprising visitor to encounter the shy mouse deer, the lovely clouded leopard and certainly several chattering gibbons.

Also, lurking in the undergrowth, there are snakes! The most dreaded are pythons, which sometimes reach 20 feet in length. Many horrendous python stories (and you will hear some dillies) should be greeted with skepticism—until you tell one of your own. The Dayaks have a superstition that if you plant the last bone of a python's spinal cord, you will soon have produced another entire snake.

More dangerous than pythons, who tend to be reticent and retiring unless extremely hungry, are the aggressive king cobras which have been known to pursue their prey for miles. One 1930s account of jungle lore prescribes the following sure-fire method for escaping: "throw off one garment after another at fixed intervals . . . when the cobra stops he attacks them furiously, thus giving his victim a certain start." Today's visitor, however, is unlikely to see even one snake.

The other Borneo state, Sabah, covers the northern tip of the island. Much smaller but wealthier than Sarawak, this state was also once part of the loosely held Brunei Sultanate. Dispute with that monarch, as well as trouble with the neighboring Sultan of Sulu (now part of the

Philippines), led to a confusing sale of concessions and territory to wandering European and American adventurers. Sabah's primary resource through the years has been the vast timber operations on which fortunes have been made.

Politically, the state is part of Malaysia but it is ruled by its chief minister with a fairly free hand. Internal politics are complicated but this political bickering should have little effect on the casual tourist.

The Sabah government is spending a great deal of money on tourist promotion and the people themselves are friendly and delighted to meet foreigners, and the standards of tourist facilities are improving every year.

Malaysia Today

Since 1963 Malaysia has prospered and flourished, although occasional setbacks have plagued the nation; most notably the interracial riots of May 13, 1969. Communal division between Malay and Chinese ethnic groups remains a problem, but much has been done to reduce the causes and the community is enjoying a rapidly improving standard of living.

Continued economic growth makes Malaysia one of the most interesting and pleasant countries in this region. Expanding tourist facilities draw an increasing number of foreign visitors who are delighted by the natural beauty and hospitality they discover. Because Malaysia survived the turbulent years of the late sixties intact and without the wrenching internal upheavals that plagued its neighbors, it has retained its national flavor. Thus despite increasing foreign investment, Malaysians do not feel they are being exploited. The foreign visitor will feel little of the anti-foreign attitudes that lie smoldering under the surface in other parts of the world.

EXPLORING MALAYSIA

When you set out to travel the length and breadth of Malaysia, you will find a most beautiful and changing landscape that moves from the tropical lowlands to the hilly temperate regions, the latter ideal for walking and golf. You will also find well-appointed hotels and resthouses. Malaysia has one of the highest standards of living in Asia, so that one need not travel first-class in order to be certain of good accommodation and food. The health record of the country is excellent, and hospitals and medical services are of a high standard. When they withdrew, the British left the finest highway system in Southeast Asia, and on the mainland the Malaysian government has added to this legacy, building new paved roads into many remote *kampongs* (Malay villages). The Communist terrorists have been defeated, and while minor elements of the "C.T.'s" are still hiding in the hills along the Thai border, they pose no danger to the tourist who restricts himself to even moderately traveled places. Water can be taken directly from the tap anywhere in mainland Malaysia without worry.

Any tour of Malaysia begins with odors: the smells of frangipani, of Malay *satay* and Indian curries, of steamy rubber plantations, dense jungle, and Chinese food stalls. While there are many specific things to see and do in Malaysia, the major attraction, as anywhere, lies in the people themselves, and the Malaysian people are particularly fascinating, for several cultures exist side by side; the Malay, Chinese, Singhalese, Punjabi, Sikh, Pakistani, Dusun, Dayak, Murut, and aborigine, as well as the Dutch, Portuguese, British (and now, increasingly, Australian) cultures, mingling into one of the region's most cosmopolitan societies. The sights and sounds, the odors and tastes of Malaysia are unique and, mostly, delightful.

You will be struck by the various forms of dress. Male attire may be Western, shirtsleeves and trousers with coat and tie added for the evening, but female dress generally is distinctive. The Malay women in their graceful *sarong* and transparent *kebaya:* the Indian women, in shimmering, flowing *sari,* with red caste marks on their foreheads; the Chinese woman can still be seen in the loose *samfoo,* a pajama-like uniform common to *amahs* (household servants and nursemaids). The men, too, have their distinctive dress, from the stately Malay national costume (or the simple *baju,* or Malay shirt) to the white Indian *dhoti,* from the briefest of shorts and undershirts, worn publicly, to the turban and beard of the Sikh.

Religion in Malaysia is as varied as food and dress, and visits to the many Chinese temples, Muslim mosques (the faith of Mohammed is the national religion of Malaysia, and the Sultans of each state are the heads of the faith within their areas, this being their primary modern function), Hindu temples, and Catholic and Protestant churches should be high on any visitor's list. Chinese temples are usually the most interesting, being highly decorated with many chambers, and there are several dozen worth visiting in Kuala Lumpur, Ipoh, Malacca, and Penang.

Kuala Lumpur and Central Malaysia

Kuala Lumpur, the administrative capital of Malaysia, is a rapidly growing educational, governmental, and industrial center. Cooler than many parts of the peninsula, and with all modern facilities available, "K.L."—as it is always called—is an ideal staging point for making forays into the rest of Malaysia.

The city itself was founded on the juncture of the Klang and Gombak rivers as a tin-mining center, and it has retained its commercial flavor. Architecturally it is a mixture at once weird and attractive, ranging from the delightful arabesque flavor of its public buildings, post office, town hall, and railway station, to the sweeping, functional lines of its new high-rise buildings. In distinct contrast to the new buildings is the lovely old Masjid Jame mosque, located by the river in the commercial heart of the city, dating from the time of its foundation.

Exploring Kuala Lumpur can be fun for the intrepid shopper, for the city is not yet totally overwhelmed by modernization. To be sure, shopping centers and hotel arcades offer good buys and convenient shopping. But if you have time, it is more interesting to wander around

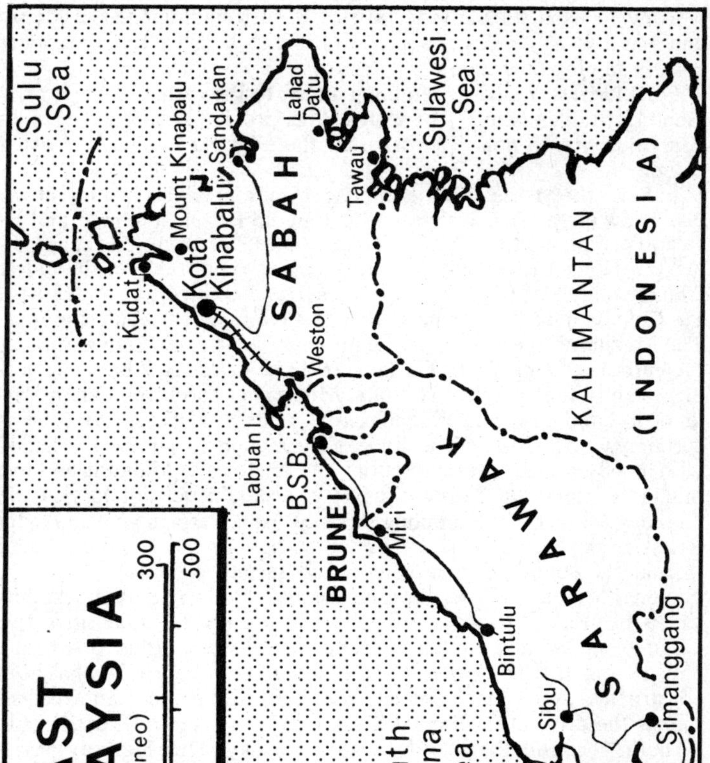
EAST MALAYSIA
(Borneo)
0 Miles 300
0 Kms 500
N
South China Sea
Sulu Sea
Sulawesi Sea
Kudat
Kota Kinabalu
Mount Kinabalu
Sandakan
Lahad Datu
Tawau
Weston
Labuan I.
B.S.B.
BRUNEI
Miri
Bintulu
Sibu
Simanggang
Kuching
SABAH
SARAWAK
KALIMANTAN
(INDONESIA)

the older sections of the city where a purchase may take more time, but the transaction itself becomes part of the bargain.

From one's base in Kuala Lumpur it is easy to make a number of worthwhile excursions into the attractive surrounding areas of forests and plantations. Among the interesting sights here are rubber tapping and tin mining operations.

For those interested in gambling a visit to the casino in the nearby Genting Highlands might be worthwhile, provided you don't take all your money with you. The drive up there by car or bus is a visual delight.

In K.L., the Merdeka (Independence) Stadium is well worth visiting; just below it, on Jalan Maharajalela, is an old Buddhist temple, and on Jalan Petaling are two Chinese temples. On Jalan Cheng Lock, adjoining the Hong Leong Building, lies the See-Yeoh Temple, the oldest Chinese temple of Kuala Lumpur, which is dedicated to Yap Ah Loy, the Chinese adventurer who is said to have founded Kuala Lumpur. The Muzium Negara, or national museum, is on Jalan Damansara, at the entrance to the Tasek Perdana, or Lake Gardens. Above the gardens stand the impressive National Monument and ultramodern Parliament buildings. The magnificently modern National Mosque is certainly worth visiting. The dome of the main hall is umbrella-shaped with an 18-pointed star representing the 13 states of Malaysia and five pillars of Islam. On Saturday night you should not fail to visit the "Sunday Market," in Kampong Bahru. Wisma Peringatan Tun Abdul Razak is the memorial and museum to honour the late Tun Abdul Razak, the country's greatly respected second prime minister. The National Museum of Art, opposite the main Railway Station, exhibits works by leading regional artists. There are several quite attractive Chinese temples along Jalan Ampang, a road which leads to Ampang Village, and at Klang Gates, a break in the hills where a dam has been constructed. A National Zoo has been built in this area. An excellent tour is the drive over Gombak Pass, or via the Gap to Fraser's Hill, or both, a circuit that can be made in a day. This highway passes through magnificent jungle.

Seven miles north of Kuala Lumpur are the Batu Caves, which until modern times remained unexplored. The caves are approached by a flight of 272 steps, but the steep climb is worthwhile. A wide path with an iron railing leads through the recesses of the cavern. Colored lights provide illumination for the unique features and formations of this limestone cave. Stalagmites, such as the fancifully named "Onyx Rock," have been tinted over the years by internal chemical processes and now can be viewed in all their glory. It is here, during January or February, that the spectacular, but gory, "Thaipusam" festival takes place in its most elaborate form. In the main cave is a Hindu Temple dedicated to Lord Subramaniam. Behind the Dark Cave lies a third cave called Art Gallery, displaying colorful and elaborate sculptures of Hindu mythology. Around Kuala Lumpur one can also visit a rubber plantation or tin mine.

Eleven miles outside Kuala Lumpur is the 300-acre Mimaland recreational resort, featuring boating and swimming, mini golf and restaurants.

The Peninsula: The Southern Half of West Malaysia

If you are starting from Singapore, one of the best ways to see Malaysia is to drive the 250 miles up to Kuala Lumpur. One can in this way see Malacca en route, and, after K.L., a visit can be made to the tin-mining center, Ipoh, and Penang farther to the north. All these cities are linked by air, but a journey by train, taxi, or car (easily arranged through your hotel) gives you a real picture of Malaysian life and culture.

As you drive across the causeway from Singapore on to the mainland of Asia, you enter the southernmost point of the continent. Johor Bahru, the capital of Johor, has little of interest itself, although the grounds of the Secretariat building provide excellent views across the strait to Singapore island. The ruins of the ancient capital of Johor Lama, downriver from Kota Tinggi, is only a half-day excursion from Johor Bahru. There is a particularly attractive waterfall near Kota Tinggi, with a pool, which is an excellent goal for a day's picnic outing from Singapore. Some 20 miles to the south, a beach resort destination, Desaru, has been developed, offering first-class accommodation and watersports facilities. Recently, the Johor state government has opened a Safari Park to show wild animals in their natural habitat. Visitors to the park, for their own safety, should not leave their cars.

To the north of Johor is Negri Sembilan, literally meaning "Nine States." Negri Sembilan is unique in Malaya, for it's an internal union of ancient states, and it is a matriarchy—tribal lines descend from women rather than from men. Seremban, its capital, is a pleasant city with attractive botanical gardens. An old Malay palace has been moved to the gardens and serves as a museum; there also is a reconstructed Malay house, so that you may study the early Minangkabau (or Sumatran) architecture. At Sri Menanti, near Kuala Pelah, is the Sultan's headquarters, where both a new and an old *Istana,* the latter in Sumatran style, as well as an ancient royal burial ground, may be visited. The drive to Sri Menanti takes you through some of the hill country where, during the Emergency, battles were most intense. Bougainvillaea and hibiscus are everywhere. Port Dickson, on the coast, is a seaside resort area, where Casuarina trees line the shore. Near the Malacca border, south of Port Dickson, is Pengkalan Kempas. Here are three famous stones, inscribed in cuneiform, that remain an archeological mystery, and the tomb of Sheik Ahmad, dated 1467.

Intriguing Malacca

One of the most exciting cities in Malaysia is the ancient port and capital of Malacca. Once the center of Malay civilization, then dominated by the Portuguese, Dutch, and finally the British, Malacca is rich in Western as well as Eastern history. The visitor will probably find more to see in Malacca than anywhere else on the peninsula.

The city is built in a series of twisting, turning alleys along a river. It was founded in 1403. The Chinese sent envoys beginning in 1409, and Malacca, despite the many other influences so obviously present, remains predominantly a Chinese community. Bukit China, set onto a hill, is the largest and oldest Chinese graveyard outside mainland China itself. At the foot of the hill is a fountain which according to Malacca belief, will guarantee return to the city for those who visit it. The oldest Chinese temple in Malaysia, the Cheng Hoon Teng, is in the very center of town. Here you can walk from shop to shop to search for antiques. Just on the edge of town, along the coast road to the North is Tranquerah Mosque, one of Malaysia's oldest. The carved doors to the old merchant's houses and the Chinese clan associations are particularly noteworthy.

The Portuguese arrived in 1511 and occupied Malacca until 1641. They built a fortress, *A Famosa,* and the gateway still remains. In front of *A Famosa* is reclaimed land, the site of the original harbor. A block away is the Malacca museum, in one of the city's oldest buildings. Just under a mile to the southeast, along the coast road, are the ruins of St. John's fort (reached by climbing from the back, or landward, side of the escarpment), and slightly beyond, the "Portuguese Village," where descendants of the original Portuguese settlers still live.

The most famous sights of Malacca center around the old Dutch *Stadthuys.* Built in the 17th century, and until recently used for the chief government offices, this series of connecting buildings is the oldest Dutch remnant in Asia. It has now been converted into a museum. The history of Malacca can be traced through its exhibits. On the wall to the grounds of the *Stadthuys* is the symbol of Malacca, the Makara stone, a Hindu relic. Directly across the road is a red clock tower and Christ Church, built in 1753 by the Dutch. High on the hill above, reached by steps 100 yards from the clock tower, is the ruin of St. Paul's Church. Built by the Portuguese in 1521 (but renamed by the Dutch in the 17th century), this church was once the burial place of St. Francis Xavier. His statue crowns the summit of the hill.

The journey south along the coast to Muar and Batu Pahat is particularly attractive. It passes through several *kampongs* and past an unusual variety of Malay houses. Inland can be seen Mount Ophir, or Gunong Ledang, "Shimmering Mountain," the Olympus of Malay legend.

Perak State

Perak is one of the richest states in Malaysia. Tin seems present everywhere, providing a substantial base to the economy. Some of the wildest country in Malaysia lies within its borders, and it was not very long ago that elephants were used to maintain communications in the Gerik area. Statutes to these elephants stand in both Gerik and Keroh. A new highway runs close to the Thai border, through spectacular mountain scenery, from Gerik to Jeli and on to Kota Bharu, on the East Coast.

Three sights stand out in Perak. Ipoh, one of Malaysia's major cities, is a thriving, modern, predominately Chinese commercial center. Just south of town, on the K.L.–Penang highway, are a series of exceptionally fine Chinese rock temples, literally cut into limestone cliffs. Visit the Sam Po Temple in particular, and be certain to climb through the many chambers of the first temple until you reach the uppermost room, where a magnificent view of the surrounding countryside will reward you. Then move another hundred yards down the road to the second temple where, by a narrow opening behind the central "altar," you will be able to enter a huge and almost hidden valley, surrounded on all sides by sheer limestone cliffs, but open to the sky with only a tunnel from the temple giving access.

An hour's drive north of Ipoh brings you to Kuala Kangsar, a fairytale royal capital. Here, in a single riverside area two miles south of the city, is the royal compound, with an "Arabian Nights" *istana,* a royal burial ground, mosque, and *balai besar* (or coronation hall), all open to visitors. Twenty-two miles farther north on the road to Penang is Taiping, famed for its lovely Lake Gardens, an excellent museum, and one of the three hill stations in mainland Malaysia—Bukit Larut (formerly Maxwell Hill). The road to the summit is so narrow, private cars are not permitted on it, but regular landrover service operates daily from the Rest House, beginning at 8 A.M. The elevation is 4,700 feet and the journey takes 40 minutes.

Easily accessible from both Ipoh and Kuala Lumpur is the premier hill station of Malaysia, Cameron Highlands. The road branches at Tapah from the main north-south highway (designated Route 1) and for 35 miles you will climb by winding, paved road to 3,000 feet above sea level. Good hotels and bungalows are to be found here, from which one can explore the mountain trails and aboriginal huts (and probably aborigines walking along the roadside) which are features of the lovely highland landscape. A narrow but good road leads to the summit of Mount Brinchang, the highest peak in the area. Another drive carries you to the Boh Tea Plantations, where regular tours through the tea processing plant are a feature of any visit. Aboriginal carvings may be purchased, and an interesting exhibit building explains the importance of the hydroelectric project. Accommodations are excellent, if simple.

For those seeking a lovely beach holiday Pangkor Island is ideal. Reached by road and ferry from Ipoh, via Lumut, there is a government rest house and several hotels with chalet accommodation. Main beaches are Pasir Bogak and Telok Belanga. Superb beaches, swimming, and coral beds.

Penang

Penang is at that delicious state where the knowledgeable visitor can take advantage of a beautiful, exotic resort which is now easily reachable and comfortable yet remains uncrowded. For many years, people who know Asia have cherished Penang for its serene beaches, unspoiled scenery, and colorful blend of Malay, Chinese, Thai, and Indian cultures. Now, overlaying the charms of Penang is a network of expanded tourist facilities: new luxury hotels, increased shopping and excursion opportunities, and a variety of transportation.

Here in Penang you will find the Oriental charm and exotica which has been overwhelmed, if not entirely obliterated, in other Asian cities and towns. So far, suffocating concrete jungles, automobile-choked streets, and polluted water have not yet arrived.

The most convenient and comfortable way to get around the island's capital, George Town, is the trishaw, a marvelous combination of the rickshaw and the bicycle. The drivers, who pride themselves on their English, are eager to serve the visitor—for a modest price.

George Town is a jumble of Malay, Thai, Indian, and Chinese cultures. The busy shops and elaborate temples reflect the multiplicity of Penang. A walk down Campbell Street takes you past shops selling perfumes from Paris, electronics from Japan, nylon shirts from Hong Kong, and music from everywhere. Record shops advertise their products using loudspeakers turned to ear-splitting volume.

Canarvon Street is full of Chinese shops, with several antique stores worth poking around. Here also are shops which create rattan and paper goods to be burnt as offerings for the Hungry Ghosts. Effigies of paper TV sets, automobiles, houses, and wads of paper money are purchased by Chinese families for offerings at the graves of the recently departed relatives.

One of Penang's most elaborate temples is actually not a religious shrine, but a clan house: Khoo Kongsi. Located at the dead end of a small alley off Cannon Square, Khoo Kongsi reflects the prosperity and devotion of the Khoo Clan, whose ancestors migrated from Fukien Province in China. Ceramic tiles and glittering stone mosaics decorate the roof and eaves. The outer walls depict legendary stories from Chinese history. Huge carved stone guardians ensure the wealth, longevity, and happiness of all who come under the protection of the *kongsi*—or Benevolent Protection Society.

Fort Cornwallis dates from the time of Captain Francis Light who, in 1786, first claimed the island for the British. Also in the town are temples, both Hindu and Buddhist, Christian churches, mosques and shrines of many faiths. By the road to the airport lies the famous Snake Temple, built in 1873 and occupied by dozens of deadly pit-vipers, rendered drowsy and safe by the heady fumes of incense.

On the outskirts of George Town is Penang's most spectacular temple, the Kek Lok Si Temple, or as it is sometimes called, Million Buddhas Precious Pagoda. An incredibly complex series of structures, the temple consists of three main levels: one that honors the Goddess of Mercy, Kuan Yin; one that praises the familiar "Laughing Buddha"; and one that commemorates the Gautama Buddha with thousands of gilded statues. The temple complex has a vacation air about it. The long walk up the hill is lined with shops selling souvenirs, as well as joss sticks, flowers and gold leaf to be used by worshippers at the shrine. As always with the Chinese, many food shops line the way selling snacks.

A complete change of pace awaits the visitor to the Buddhist Temple in Burma Lane, where an 108-foot Reclining Buddha smiles enigmatically down at the well-dressed worshippers who kneel at his side. The temple building is elaborately decorated with crystal chandeliers from Czechoslovakia and fine paintings depicting the many stages of Buddha's Path to Enlightenment.

A unique experience is a ride on the Penang Hill funicular railway. Ascending the steep slope of the hill in cable cars, the visitor passes through several layers of jungle vegetation until, at the top, he finds himself in a cool, semitropical atmosphere, where the gardens are full of roses and gardenias.

Much of a visitor's interest centers on Penang's lovely beaches. The most popular is Batu Ferringhi where many hotels provide comfort and luxury. Other remote beaches await the explorer—the north end of the island abounds in secluded coves with white sand.

The best way to explore the island is by self-drive car, obtainable in George Town, or by organized sightseeing tours.

The Northern Part of West Malaysia

Kedah is, together with Johor, the richest in pre-European history of the Malay states. Archeological sites abound; most of them hold little interest for the average visitor, but one, Bukit Chandit Batu Pahat, or the Temple of Cut Stone, is well worth the effort to visit. Quite small, the base of the temple has been reconstructed. It shows both Javanese and Indian influence. The ruin is reached by a short, rough, but motorable road from Merbok, itself on a paved highway.

At Alor Star, the capital of Kedah, there is an outstanding group of royal buildings, matched only by those in Kuala Kangsar. The *balai besar,* showing Siamese influence, is the finest in Malaysia; in front of it stands the *balai nobat,* or the tower for the nine musicians of the *nobat* group, the only one in Malaysia. Across the road is the mosque. The road to Alor Star from Prai, opposite Penang Island, is unique in Malaysia, in that from Gurun, it follows a Thai-style klong, or canal, along which a great variety of village activity may be observed.

The East Coast

Readily available rental cars, both from well-known international firms and cheaper but less reliable local outfits, have opened up the East Coast of Malaysia. These isolated states abound with empty white sand beaches, coral-ringed islands (which during the dry season rival the Caribbean) and mysterious first-growth jungle inhabited by crocodiles and the elusive aboriginal Orang Asli people.

The East Coast is about five hours' drive from Kuala Lumpur. The beaches from Kuantan up through Trengganu are famous as the homing ground for giant leatherback turtles. From late May to September these huge beasts which roam the seven seas come home to Malaysia to lay their eggs. The older turtles weigh up to a thousand pounds and may measure as much as six feet in diameter. Rantau Abang is the best among the many beaches which have been set aside for turtle-watching. But you will be sharing your beach with local egg gatherers. Conservation authorities have imposed controls on wholesale looting of turtle nests, but they have not yet been able to eliminate it entirely. Accommodation is now available at Rantau Abang itself in the Rantau Abang Village Motel, which offers chalets in typical Malay design. Also close to Kuala Trengganu, the Tourist Development Corporation of Malaysia opened the Tanjung Jara Beach Resort with first-class accommodations.

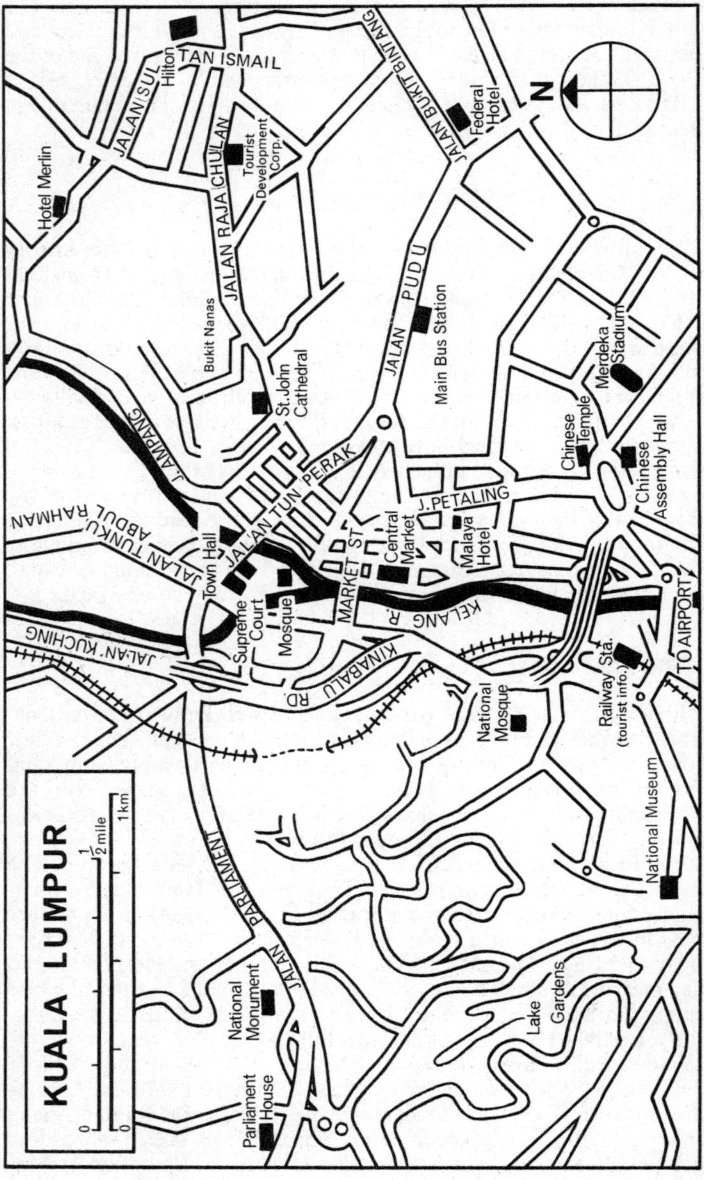
KUALA LUMPUR
0
½ mile
1 km
N
Hilton
JALAN SUL TAN ISMAIL
Hotel Merlin
JALAN RAJA CHULAN
Tourist Development Corp.
Federal Hotel
JALAN BUKIT BINTANG
Bukit Nanas
JALAN PUDU
Main Bus Station
Merdeka Stadium
St. John Cathedral
J. AMPANG
JALAN TUN PERAK
JALAN TUNKU ABDUL RAHMAN
Town Hall
Supreme Court
Mosque
MARKET ST
Central Market
J. PETALING
Malaya Hotel
Chinese Temple
Chinese Assembly Hall
KELANG R.
JALAN KUCHING
KINABALU RD.
National Mosque
Railway Sta. (tourist info.)
TO AIRPORT
National Museum
JALAN PARLIAMENT
National Monument
Parliament House
Lake Gardens

The drive from K.L. to Kota Bharu can be made nicely in two days, breaking the journey conveniently in Kuantan where there are now excellent resort hotels. Along the East Coast road the last rivers have been bridged, making it no longer necessary to schedule your trip to coincide with the ferry service. From Kota Bharu one can continue the circle tour, vià the new east–west highway, over superb mountain scenery to the West Coast and Penang.

East Coast States retain a more distinct Malay flavor than the rest of the country. Poor soil supports few plantations, and tin deposits are less accessible than those on the West Coast. Thus the Malays, unhindered by outside elements, developed their cultures, and the old way of life still flourishes in the agricultural and fishing communities. The MARA shop in Trengganu and the Tourist Information Center in Kuantan will direct you to the sites of cottage industries which produce hand-printed batik, silverwork, shellcraft and brocade weaving.

Driving up from Singapore the closest beach resorts are Desaru or Mersing. In Mersing you can stay at the new hotel and hire a fishing boat to take you on a day excursion for snorkeling, swimming, and sunning on the nearby islands. Better yet, you can stay in a small bungalow on Rawa Island, or in the resort hotel on Pulau Tioman, leaving your car at the pier at Mersing.

East Malaysia (Borneo)

Borneo is one of the world's remaining undeveloped spots, from the tourist's viewpoint. The very name, "Borneo," remains one of the most romantic in the traveler's vocabulary. The island of Borneo, one of the largest in the world, is divided into four areas; the largest portion, Kalimantan, is a province of Indonesia. The smallest, Brunei, is an independent sultanate, oil-rich and isolated. Sarawak and Sabah, or the former British North Borneo, together about the size of Kentucky, were crown colonies which have merged with the mainland Federation of Malaya, to form the new nation of Malaysia. The three non-Indonesian areas can be visited fairly easily by the tourist, with convenient travel from Singapore or Hong Kong.

Your first stop if traveling from Singapore or Peninsular Malaysia will probably be Kuching, and as the plane begins its descent you will see an incredible, strange landscape. Down below, wide brown rivers snake through impenetrable green jungle and mangrove swamp. Limestone hills and outcroppings dot the landscape. You will see signs of human habitation—cleared land, palm-thatch huts—but few roads except around the town of Kuching itself.

Kuching is a pleasant town, easy to get around by foot or car. The town center is a busy market area where traders come by river to sell fish, fruits, vegetables and of course rice, in order to buy shoes, plastic wares, clothes. Around the *padang* (village green) are handsome modern structures housing government offices. Off in the distance gleams the gold dome of Kuching's principal mosque. In the evening you can take a hand-poled sampan across the river and stroll along the serene streets of the prosperous Malay kampong. As the sun sets, you will hear the call to prayer, as men in sarongs and women in white prayer robes gather at small neighborhood mosques.

A visit to the Sarawak Museum is a prerequisite to any upcountry traveling you might want to do. The founder, Tom Harrison, traveled all over Sarawak collecting nature specimens as well as anthropological lore. In the museum are exhibits of artifacts and customs of the varied tribal peoples of Sarawak. Several grave sites have been reconstructed, such as the Melanu burial where ceramic dishes were placed beneath the hands and feet of the deceased. Some exquisite Chinese porcelain has been discovered in those sites and the museum has an excellent collection of Ming blue and white.

After a visit to the museum you will want to go to a longhouse yourself. This can be arranged through one of the tour agencies or an introduction through a friend. One frequently visited longhouse is a Bedayuh (Land Dyak) community which is a 1½-hour drive from Kuching. The headman and villagers are delighted to receive visitors; the people are friendly and do not mind being photographed. A great deal of the daily activity in a longhouse concerns the preparation of rice for the evening meal. Dry *padi,* or unhusked rice, keeps for months, but once it has been polished it must be eaten quickly. The rice is polished by women who stand and use long poles to pound away at the padi in a stone urn. The husk is gradually shaken off and spills out over the lip of the urn. This looks fairly easy until you try it, as you may be asked to do. You will find that pounding the rice without spraying precious grains out all over the floor requires great skill. The pigs and chickens who live under the wooden floor of the longhouse are delighted, however, by the unexpected rice-fall.

For those with more time, an overnight trip up to the Skrang River is an unforgettable experience. Unfortunately, the first part of the trip is a long, hot, dusty car or bus ride, interrupted only by a quick stop for a drink in the uninspiring town of Serian. You may want to stop and visit one of the many pepper plantations along the road. Mostly cultivated and produced by Chinese families, pepper is one of Sarawak's most lucrative exports. The vine (yes, pepper is a vine although it looks more like a tree) is trained to grow around a cone-shaped trestle to a height of 10–12 feet. The plant requires careful cultivation and it takes from two to five years before the plant becomes fully productive. Surprisingly, both white and black pepper come from the same vine. White pepper results from a special treatment after picking, whereas black pepper is merely the sun-dried kernel. Pepper picking is a great family occasion when relatives, including children, gather to help in the harvest.

After the long road journey you will get into a canoe and travel up the Skrang River. The trip is beautiful; the river runs clear and green through towering jungle. The ride feels like an experience in Disneyland and a Westerner finds it difficult to overcome a strange sense of familiar unreality about the jungle atmosphere.

At the longhouse you will be greeted with great warmth and polite indifference, which is not quite the paradox it seems. Longhouse living is communal and has a tradition of "you do your thing and I'll do mine," which gives visitors both freedom and hospitality. Iban dances are colorful and rather informal. The dance is for the delight of the performer rather than a show for an audience and often ends abruptly in what seems like the middle of a sequence. It almost seems as if the dancer had decided it was enough. He then goes and shakes the hands of the foreign visitors as another dancer takes the center and begins.

From Kuching you can also make a trip downriver by boat to Santubong, about 18 miles away on the coast. A Government Rest House affords rudimentary accommodations. Here, in addition to swimming on the beach, you can visit some archeological sites. This area was an ancient trading center more than 1,000 years ago.

Those eager to explore further archeological sites should travel over to Miri and up to the Niah Caves. Miri is about 40 minutes by air from Kuching (there is as yet no proper road) and is the site of formerly productive oilfields. Otherwise Miri is a sleepy little port town with two adequate hotels and a lively fish market.

From Miri you can hire a taxi or land rover to take you to Batu Niah about 2½ hours away. You pass through rather uninspiring scrub country and vast acres of oil palm plantations until you see the limestone escarpments rising in the distance. There, at Batu Niah, a tiny town of no distinction, you will get into a long boat and travel down the river for about 15 minutes until you reach the settlement from where Tom Harrison directed the exploration and excavation of the caves. If you have made arrangements in Kuching you may stay overnight at the bungalows or at the nearby longhouse. There is a Chinese trading post right out of Somerset Maugham. The proprietor will provide you with an excellent birds' nest soup if you give him advance notice and are willing to pay his price, which compared to San Francisco or Hong Kong is cheap.

The caves are an hour's walk from the river landing. Most of the path up through the jungle is a long plank walk consisting of 12-foot-long boards, each one inch thick and ten inches across. There is no handrail. Traversing the plank walk, however, becomes easier after the first 100 yards as you become more sure-footed and a trifle ashamed as you see the guano pickers lope across the planks carrying 100-pound sacks down to the river.

In addition to their archeological value, Niah Caves provide an economic resource for the people of the area. They collect guano, sold as fertilizer, from the floor of the caves, and birds' nests for soup from the ceilings. Collecting the nests, which are considered a great delicacy by the Chinese all over the world, is a difficult and dangerous task. Thousands of tiny swiftlets make their homes on the roofs of the caves. In order to reach them pickers must clamber up bamboo poles, some of them 100 feet from the ground. Some nests are even higher and they are reached by rope ladders from holes in the roof of the cave. There, perched precariously in the darkness, illuminated by a single flickering candle, the picker spends up to eight hours plucking off the tiny nests. If the candle should go out, the picker must find his way out by touch aided by the dim filtered light coming from the cave entrance. Little wonder that the profession is dying out! Nowadays all the pickers are old men; the younger men prefer the less dangerous labor of digging out guano.

Extremely adventurous travelers might want to go through the caves and out another entrance, track through a treacherous swamp up to another cave where some old Punan grave boats have been discovered. The Painted Cave, as it is known, contains some primitive drawings of mysterious age and origin. The trip is really worth it, but you must have a guide who can find his way through the darkness of the caves and also through the labyrinth of jungle foliage. If you want to make this trek, ask for directions and permission at the main office of the Sarawak Museum in Kuching.

After Miri and Niah, if you are touring North Borneo, you will want to spend a few days in Brunei (see separate chapter).

From Brunei you will fly to Sabah, sometimes called "The Land Below the Wind," because it is below the typhoon belt. It is also possible to fly from here to Hong Kong, Singapore, or the Philippines to continue one's tour.

The capital of Sabah is Kota Kinabalu, formerly known as Jesselton. It is a relatively new town, built and expanded after the devastation of the Second World War. The town contains little of interest.

The main attraction for the tourist in Sabah is of course the National Park where you can see rare flowers, trees and climb Mount Kinabalu. Those with extra time will find several interesting side excursions. The little town of Kota Belud has an excellent *tamu* (open-air market) where Bajau tribesmen, noted for their superb horsemanship, come to sell and trade every Sunday. To visit a different tribe, go to Papar and see the Kadazan whose women wear elaborate chain belts and caftans decorated with silver coins. Only a few minutes from Kota Kinabalu is the delightfully relaxing Tanjong Aru Beach Resort, with good accommodations.

Also in Sabah is the small coastal trading town of Sandakan, which can be reached by a bad road, sea or air. It is famous as a loading port for the rich tropical hardwoods felled in the interior. About 15 miles out of Sandakan, at Sepilok, is the Orang Utang Sanctuary. Set on the edge of the jungle it is one of the only places in the world where one sees these rare apes in their natural surroundings.

PRACTICAL INFORMATION

FACTS AND FIGURES. Population: 15.3 million. Birth rate per 1,000 population: 31. Life expectancy: 64 years. Percentage of population in agriculture and fishing: 38%. Land area: 330,000 sq. kms. Proportion of land area cultivated: 13% (80% forest). Average per capita income: US$1,950 p.a. Number of tourists annually: 2.6 million.

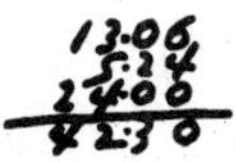

WHAT WILL IT COST? With the rapid escalation of prices in neighboring Singapore and Thailand and the continued competitive situation in Malaysia, the country has become one of the better travel bargains in the region. Hotels, particularly, are now noticeably cheaper in Peninsular Malaysia than in other major tourist destinations and the inexpensive convenience of various forms of domestic travel enable the visitor to see the country at a relatively low cost. Meal prices have tended to increase in hotels, but are still very good value in outside restaurants.

Unlike most ports of Southeast Asia, inexpensive accommodation is still available, although the luxury, international "group" hotels have pushed their prices up rapidly in recent years.

Taxis in Malaysia should charge 70 cents (M) for the first 1.6 km. and 30 cents for each .8km. thereafter, but over recent years the practice of bargaining a fare before the ride has grown. Taxi charges are 20% higher if the vehicle is air-conditioned.

A Typical Day's Cost (In KL) US$ = $M2.30

Hotel, per person, including service and tax	$M95
Continental breakfast (coffee, fruit juice, toast, butter)	12
Tour, a morning's sightseeing	22
Lunch at a local café (fried Chinese noodles, tea and fruit)	6
Trishaw or taxi for shopping	5
Dinner at a moderate hotel, no drinks	45
Nightcap (whisky and soda) at your hotel bar	15
	$M200

Outside KL the prices are 10–15% cheaper.

Cinema $3, or cultural evening show $20.

WHEN TO GO. Malaysia is a tropical country, but is blessed by a moderate climate with a lack of extremely high temperatures. The days are sunny but often humid, while the nights are fairly cool. The western half of West Malaysia enjoys excellent weather the year-round, while the eastern part is best visited between March and October. From November to February, the east coast is drenched in rain, while December is the wettest on the west coast. In East Malaysia, Sabah has heavy rains from October through April and Sarawak, from October through February.

WHERE TO GO. Most visitors will probably enter Malaysia from Singapore. Improved transportation has increased the flow of tourists from Bangkok and Hong Kong direct to Kuala Lumpur, Malaysia's capital, which will probably be your base of operations. Highlights in this city are the Sunday Market (on Saturday night), the Moorish railway station, the National Mosque, Mimaland, the Selangor Pewterware showroom, Parliament House, the National Museum and National Monument. Nearby are the famed Batu Caves, Templer Park, and several open-cast tin mines, all of which are worth visiting. To the north is the island and resort of Penang, with many tourist facilities, including the Snake Temple and 99 others, a funicular railway, and good roads for motoring to the more secluded beaches on the island. The hill station resorts, for which Malaysia is famous, are good places to rest if you feel the need during your Southeast Asian journey. Cameron Highlands is set in a natural forest at 5,200 feet above sea level. It is 40 miles northwest of Tapah on the Perak-Pahang border. Fraser's Hill, about 5,000 feet above sea level, is 64 miles north of Kuala Lumpur. Another resort is at Bukit Larut (Maxwell Hill), above Taiping in the state of Perak. The newest hill resort to be developed is the gambling casino and hotel/recreational area in the Genting Highlands, 32 miles north of Kuala Lumpur.

To the south, also on the west coast, lie the fabled city of Malacca, the Sultan's former capital at Johor, and the lure of neighboring Singapore. For those who do not have time to travel very far from Singapore, a visit to Johor will give some idea of the complete Malayan character, which the visitor will quickly discern is something quite different from the Chinese. To the north of Johor is Negri Sembilan, famous for its typical Malay architecture, and the new SafariWorld with many game animals to be viewed as one drives through. On the east coast, there is Malaysia National Park, in the state of Pahang. A game reserve, it is ideal for camping and fishing, boating through rapids, stalking big game with camera, jungle walks, and mountain climbing. Rest House and bungalow accommodations and camping facilities are available in the park. This is not a luxury tour. There are fishing lodges and observation hides for game watching and photography. For a successful visit, you should write well before your arrival date, giving as much information as possible on your special interests, to the Chief Game Warden, Wildlife Department, Kuala Lumpur, Malaysia. The department will help plan your itinerary. Asia Overland Services, Kuala Lumpur, Hotel Malaya, Jalan Hang Lekir, specialize in inexpensive adventure tours throughout Southeast Asia.

In Borneo, the longhouses, aboriginal life, and one of Southeast Asia's best and most famous museums are some of the many highlights to be visited.

In the northwestern tip of Borneo is the state of Sabah, called by the Sulu pirates of old, "The Land Below the Wind." Its capital, Kota Kinabalu, is the eastern gateway to Malaysia. Kota Kinabalu is near the highest mountain in Southeast Asia, Mount Kinabalu. This 13,455-foot peak is a goal for mountaineers. Kinabalu has a national park through which you can travel by landrover.

In Kuching, the capital of Sarawak, Borneo, are the superb Masjid Besar mosque with gilt domes, several old Chinese temples, Fort Margherita, and the former palace of the White Rajahs.

WHAT TO TAKE. Dress in Malaysia is informal, and you would be wise to confine your wardrobe here to lightweight clothing. The ladies will not need formal attire, although some European women do dress in garden-party style for early evening. Most first-class restaurants and the better hotel dining rooms expect gentlemen to wear a jacket and necktie in the evening, but most of these places are air-conditioned so you should not be uncomfortable.

ELECTRICITY. Malaysian current is 220 volts, AC, 3 phase, and 50 cycles. Many of the hotels will supply an adaptor for your razor or hairdryer.

LOCAL FESTIVALS. January–February. *Chinese New Year,* with everyone dressed in his colorful best, visiting friends and relatives and the Buddhist temples.

January–March (luna). *Thaipusan.* Hindu festival devoted to God Subramaniain, when devotees pierce cheeks, tongues and bodies with steel hooks and spikes. Gory but fantastic spectacle. Best seen at Batu Caves, near Kuala Lumpur.

February. *Thaipusam,* annual Hindu religious festival. It is the birthday of Lord Subramaniam, and rites of penitence are performed on this day. Huge crowds of Hindus go to the Waterfall Temple in Penang, many with large needles driven into their bodies. Procession at nights through the streets. In Kuala Lumpur the celebrations take place at Batu Caves, 8 miles from the capital. On the eve of the festival, the image of the Lord Subramaniam is taken out in procession to the caves. The next day, crowds of Hindus and devotees with long, steel rods skewered through their tongues, backs and chests make the long climb up 272 steps to the limestone cave-temple. *Snake Temple Rites,* Penang. Chinese pray and then go to the compound facing the temple where a theatrical performance is staged.

Early March. *Chingay,* featuring colorful parades in Penang and Johor Bahru by the Malayan Chinese. Clan flags and temple idols are carried in the parades, accompanied by plenty of noisy music.

March–April. *Birthday of the Goddess of Mercy.* Malayan Chinese visit temples dedicated to her, the largest number of the faithful going to the temples in Malacca, Penang, and Kuala Lumpur.

May, June or July. *Birthday of the Prophet Mohammed.* A procession through the city is the main feature of the day. A Koran reading competition for Muslim youth is an interesting event of the day. At night, shops and houses are gaily illuminated. *Mandi Safar,* usually about the middle of April, is the day when Malaysians go down to the river and proceed to wash themselves in ceremonies to avoid dangers and sin. This is supposed to be the most unlucky day of the year.

May–June. *Vesak Day,* celebration of the Buddha's birthday. Buddhist religious rites at temples throughout the day, followed by lantern processions in Kuala Lumpur, and in Penang, where an image of the Buddha is carried.

Mid-May. *Kadazan Harvest Festival,* a public holiday in Sabah. A traditional ceremony celebrating a successful harvest, with colorful Kadazan dances.

June. *Dragon Boat Festival,* celebrated to mark the anniversary of the death of ancient China's leading poet, is celebrated in various villages, but is most spectacular in Penang city.

June 3. *Birthday of H.M. the Yang Di-Pertuan Agong,* Malaysia's Supreme Head of State. Parades in every state. Best is in Kuala Lumpur, where the trooping of the colors takes place in Merdeka Stadium.

August–September. *All Souls' Day, Feast of the Hungry Ghosts,* is celebrated toward the end of the month. Ancestors traditionally return at this time to visit their descendants on earth. Shops display colorful paper religious objects. Large tables covered with food are offered to spirits of departed Chinese ancestors. Artificial money, houses, and paper clothing are burned as offerings.

August 31. *Merdeka Day,* Malaysia's independence day. Illumination of buildings and parades. In Kuala Lumpur, a variety show of Indian, Malay, and Chinese classical songs and dances is held outdoors in the Lake Gardens.

Early September. *Market Festival,* celebrated by the Chinese community in a splendid outburst at the Market Place in Johor Bahru. Classic Chinese drama is performed every night just outside the market.

October. *Hari Raya Haji.* This holiday marks the tenth day of the twelfth month in the Moslem calendar. Pilgrims who have gone to Mecca visit the Baitullah and this completes their pilgrimage. All male Moslems who've made the pilgrimage to Mecca are called *Haji* and on this day families fête and honor those privileged to have made the journey.

October. *Festival of the Emperor Gods.* Kew Ong Yeah Temple, on Pava Terubong Hill in Penang. A procession winds up the 1,200 steps to celebrate the return of the nine celestial kings to heaven. Some of the images are masterpieces of sadistic vulgarity. The K.L. festival features a fire-walking ceremony. Kew Ong Yeah Temple, at Ampang Village.

October. *Birthday of the Sultan of Johor.* Johor city. Boat races, Chinese opera troupes and other entertainment.

October-November. *Deepavali* or the Festival of Lights, commemorating the slaying of a mythological king by Lord Krishna, an annual celebration in which houses and business premises are decorated with thousands of lights.

October-November. *Hari Raya Puasa.* The Mohammedan calendar is lunar and Moslem holidays tend to wander through the year. This day is the first day of the tenth month and marks the end of a month of fasting. During this time all Moslems have gone from dawn to dusk without any food or water passing their lips. As you can imagine, the end of this time of self-denial is a day for feasting and rejoicing. The day begins with Thanksgiving prayers in all the mosques. Then families put on new clothes and go visiting; each matron tries to outdo the other in offering sumptuous cakes and sweets. The day ends with a large, elaborate feast.

HOW TO REACH MALAYSIA. By air: Kuala Lumpur and Penang modern jet airports are served by many lines coming in from Europe, Australia and all key Asian cities. *Malaysian Airline System* (MAS) operates many direct flights, and provides good domestic services throughout East and West Malaysia.

One can also fly to Penang from Phuket or Had Yaai in South Thailand, or from Medan in Sumatra.

By car: If you wish to drive into Malaysia by car from Singapore, make sure that your rented car has a valid entry permit.

By boat: *Blue Funnel* and other regional cruise lines operate limited services from Australia, the Indonesian islands and Hong Kong, via Singapore. The *Shipping Corp. of India* operates a twice-monthly link between Penang and Madras in South India. There is also a ferry link from Malacca to Dumai, on Indonesian Sumatra.

By train: You can reach Malaysia by train from Bangkok or Singapore. There are express rail services between Bangkok and Penang, departing Bangkok at 4:10 P.M. on Saturdays, Mondays, and Wednesdays, and arriving at Butterworth, on the mainland, opposite Penang, at 6:45 P.M. on Sundays, Tuesdays, and Thursdays and continuing direct to Kuala Lumpur and Singapore. The six-hour train journey from Singapore to Kuala Lumpur is interesting and convenient, with departures in the afternoon or evening.

PASSPORTS AND VISAS. Tourist visitors from Britain, Commonwealth countries, America and most non-Communist European countries must have valid passports, but do not require visas for a stay of up to three months. Anyone looking remotely like a "hippie" (an ill-defined term throughout the region to cover undesirable, non-rich travelers), may be required to show an onward air ticket, a visa for the proposed next destination, and adequate funds before being allowed in. Otherwise, restrictions are minimal in Malaysia. Smallpox, cholera and yellow fever vaccinations are only necessary if arriving from infected areas.

CUSTOMS. The usual international rules apply here, 200 cigarettes and one liter of liquor being permitted duty-free. Firearms and other weapons forbidden. Any drugs or form of marijuana will get you in trouble. Restrictions exist on the export of antiquities, so, if in doubt about purchases, check with the Director of the Museum Negara in Kuala Lumpur.

AT THE AIRPORT. Formalities at airports are usually courteous and straightforward. One usually taxis from the airport into town. At Kuala Lumpur special taxi vouchers cost between $M14 and $M20, depending on destination. There is also a public bus service, number 47, between the airport and central bus station in the city. Penang Airport to city $M8, to beach $M15. Airport departure tax is $M15 for international flights, $M7 to Singapore and $M4 for domestic flights, including East Malaysia.

LANGUAGE. Bahasa Malaysia is the official language of East and West Malaysia. English is spoken and understood widely. Though the majority of the people are learning Malay, a significant percentage still use mainly their ethnic tongue, often dialects of Chinese. Various Indian languages are also found among minority groups. Road signs are now mostly only in Bahasa, so care is needed with map reading.

TRAVELING IN MALAYSIA. By train: The *Malayan Railways* operate comfortable trains throughout the country, (except Borneo), many with air-conditioning, sleeping compartments, and dining cars.

A "travel anywhere" Rail Pass is available: M$150 for 14 days, $75 for 10 days. Fares are reasonable, the rate between Singapore and Kuala Lumpur, for example, being only M$28 by air-conditioned express. Sleeping accommodations are also reasonable, a single-bed cabin in an air-conditioned first-class coach costing only $15, in addition to the M$55 fare. The main line runs from Singapore through Kuala Lumpur to Ipoh and Butterworth, where a branch line goes to the Thailand frontier and thence on to Bangkok via the Thai railway system. Branch lines connect Kota Bharu on the east coast with Kuala Lipis.

By air: *Malaysian Airline System.* Provides international and domestic transport and it operates a full schedule of flights with 747s, DC-10s, Airbus, Fokker Friendships and 737s. Service is delightful and plentiful. Some of the domestic stops are so close the staff barely has time to serve snacks, but they manage cheerfully. MAS has international services from Penang as well as Kuala Lumpur with flights to a wide range of regional and intercontinental destinations.

By bus: Malaysia's roads being among the best in Southeast Asia, you can take long distance express buses throughout the country. All seats are reserved. Kuala Lumpur-Malacca express buses leave those cities simultaneously at 8 and 10 A.M., and 1 and 3 P.M. daily. Fare: $M7. Kuala Lumpur-Butterworth (where you catch the ferry to Penang Island) services leave Kuala Lumpur at 8:30 A.M. and Butterworth at 9 A.M. Fare $M18. Kuala Lumpur-Kuantan express buses leave both terminals simultaneously at 8 and 10:30 A.M. and 1 P.M. The journey takes six hours, approximately. Fare $M12. Butterworth to Kota Bharu buses take six hours and cost $M18. The express bus service from K.L. to Singapore costs $M17.

Luxury tour bus service between Kuala Lumpur, Singapore, and Penang is available by *Masmara Tours.* Included are air-conditioning, English-speaking guides, accommodations at first-class hotels.

By taxi. In Malaysian cities, one of your best means of transportation will be inexpensive taxi. Charges are 70 cents (Malaysian) for the first 1.6 km, 30 cents for each additional .8 km. but bargaining might be necessary, especially in rush hours. Prices are 20% higher for air-conditioned vehicles. Between major cities an extensive system of shared taxis operates. A seat in a full cab costs only $M25 (approx.) from K.L. to Johore Bahru, across from Singapore. The price from Butterworth to Kuala Lumpur is about $M25.

In Penang and East Coast towns you can still find the inexpensive *trishaw* (bicycle rickshaw). Bargain in advance.

By car: Malaysia is an excellent place in which to use a self-drive car. *Avis,* and *Hertz, Mayflower, Sintat,* have a wide range of cars for hire and operate offices in several key cities, so cars can be collected in one place and left in another. Avis is reckoned to be tops in service and number of local offices, and will help with hotel bookings. Daily rate from $M100 per day plus from 40 cents per km. Weekly "explorer" rates from $M650, with unlimited mileage. Gasoline is not included in the price and costs $M1.10 per liter.

By boat: Ferry services, every 20 minutes, connect Butterworth and Penang. All resort islands can also be easily reached by ferry services from nearest mainland towns.

CURRENCY. The Malaysian dollar is referred to as the *ringgit.* At press time, M$2.50=US$1; M$3.10=£1. There is no limit to the amount of money you may bring into the country with you. Credit cards are widely accepted in tourist centers.

TIPPING. Tipping is now officially discouraged. In the capital and other large cities, 10 percent is added in hotels. Give porters 50 cents (Malaysian) per bag. In restaurants or other places where a service charge is not already added to the bill 10 percent is usual. No tips to taxis.

ACCOMMODATIONS. The advent of a fully developed tourist industry in Malaysia has altered the hotel scene considerably. The new hotels are large and offer a variety of facilities: several restaurants, swimming pool, trained and responsive front-desk personnel, and efficient service. The hotels provide a resort atmosphere and are popular with tourists and businessmen who desire familiar comforts.

Package deals in conjunction with airlines or tour operators will get you the best deal in accommodations. For those on a tight budget Chinese hotels and Government Rest Houses are still the best bet. For information concerning Rest Houses contact Tourist Development Corporation, P.O. Box 10328, Kuala Lumpur; or overseas T.D.C. offices in San Francisco, London, Frankfurt, Tokyo, Sydney, Hong Kong, Bangkok or Singapore.

Accommodations in Malaysia vary greatly in price and quality. Prices generally are highest in Kuala Lampur, up to 25 percent less in smaller towns. Malaysia is one country where the budget traveler will find a good range of accommodations.

Prices are for double-occupancy rooms and in Malaysian dollars. To all prices must be added 10% service charge and 10% government tax.

KUALA LUMPUR

Deluxe—$200–$320

Holiday Inn. Jalan Pinang. 200 rooms offering convenience and comfort. Swimming pool and shopping arcade. Taverna Restaurant, K.L.'s only Greek restaurant, is small and cozy. Especially recommended is the Malay buffet. (A second Holiday Inn, with 280 deluxe rooms, is due to open by 1986.)

Kuala Lumpur Hilton. Jalan Sultan Ismail. 600 luxurious rooms and a wide range of excellent facilities. A good swimming pool with bar service and a view of the K.L. skyline and the hills beyond. *Melaka Grill* for gourmet dining.

Ming Court. Jalan Ampang. New and luxurious, 450 rooms. Five good restaurants, all facilities.

Petaling Jaya Hilton. Jalan Barat, P.J. 400-room deluxe hotel in satellite town between K.L. and airport. Facilities include pool, health club, three restaurants, and disco.

The Regent. Jalan Sultan Ismail. 400 rooms up to the best international standards. Located near the center of town. Prides itself on true Malaysian character and service, while providing the latest in modern luxury.

First Class—$160–$220

Federal Hotel. Jalan Bukit Bintang. 450 reasonable rooms in the older style. Revolving restaurant at top provides spectacular view of the city and surrounding mountains. Central location. Bowling alley as well as swimming pool.

Hotel Equatorial. Jalan Sultan Ismail. 300 rooms, 16 stories high right next to the Hilton. Large shopping arcade, swimming pool, and several restaurants.

Hotel Merlin. Jalan Sultan Ismail. 700 rooms. Provides a full range of facilities and friendly efficient service. Not as "swinging" as the newer luxury hotels, but still a favorite with experienced travelers.

Moderate—$85–$140

Malaysia Hotel. Jalan Bukit Bintang. 50 rooms, all air-conditioned. A favorite with local travelers.

Shah's Village Motel. Lorong Sultan. Located in suburban area, this hotel offers a Malay resort atmosphere. Malay cultural dances at the *Hut.* Swimming pool and bowling alley.

Malaya Hotel. Jalan Hang Lekir. 250 rooms, convenient location.

Inexpensive—$40–100 and up

KL Station Hotel. Shades of the British Raj can be experienced in this renovated, though somewhat faded old hotel of 20 rooms, above the main railway station. 20-ft. high ceilings and, unfortunately, the original plumbing, but a great travel experience.

Among other inexpensive hotels are the 150-room **Grand Central,** Jalan Chow Kit, and the **Grand Pacific,** Jalan Ipoh, 110 rooms, offering restaurants and simple, clean rooms.

PENANG

In Penang you must choose either an in-town hotel 30 minutes away from the beach, or a beach hotel 30 minutes from town. Transport, both public buses and hotel cars, is readily available. The beach hotels are all located at *Batu Ferringhi,* which means "foreigners' mile." *B* indicates beachside location, *C* means city.

First Class—$150–200

Casuarina Beach Hotel. B. 175 rooms. A popular beach hotel especially for families. Nursery center and indoor games for rainy days. Swimming pool, tennis courts.

Eastern and Oriental Hotel. C. The E & O is one of the remaining colonial hotels. Located in town, its rooms are comfortable and the bathrooms huge. Small, but lovely, swimming pool by the sea, where waiters bring gin and tonic to you as you sun by the palms. 100 rooms.

Golden Sand. B. New luxury resort hotel. 310 rooms, full facilities.

Holiday Inn. B. 160 good rooms with modern amenities, including TV. Two restaurants. Excellent facilities.

Hotel Merlin. C. 144 rooms. Right across from the E & O. Swimming pool. Edinburgh Restaurant serves good chops and steaks. Disco with live band.

Rasa Sayang Hotel. B. 320 rooms centrally air-conditioned. Exceptional recreational facilities; freshwater pool, boating, waterskiing, golf, tennis. Disco with live band. A busy resort hotel.

Moderate—$90–$150

Hotel Ambassador. C. 78 rooms, all air-conditioned. Central town location. Not much atmosphere, but has a good steak restaurant.

Hotel Ming Court. C. 100 rooms. Swimming pool. Excellent Chinese restaurant. Friendly bar and two cocktail lounges.

Palm Beach. B. 147 modern rooms with reasonable facilities. Poor restaurant, but good beach-side service.

Inexpensive—$50–$90

Bellevue Hotel. Located on Penang Hill overlooking the island, this small hotel is more of a hill station resort. Cool nights and warm days. A great place to get away from it all.

Lone Pine Hotel. B. On the beach. An old-fashioned family resort hotel with a British flavor. Rates include breakfast and morning tea. Dining room serves good fish and chips. Centrally located so you can mosey up to one of the fancier hotels for elegance.

Paramount Hotel. C. Old-fashioned hotel in residential area between beach and town. 24 rooms, all air-conditioned. Cheap.

Peking Hotel. C. Central location. Very cheap but also noisy.

There is also a small YMCA and a YWCA, very cheap.

EAST COAST MALAYSIA

The lovely beaches of the entire east coast have attracted a number of new hotels as well as encouraging modernization of more established resorts. Bookings are heavy during local holiday seasons, as the east coast is popular with Singaporean residents who want to get away from the city.

Kemaman

Inexpensive: **New Motel Kemaman.** Air-conditioned rooms and chalets. Ideal for families. Dining room with superb Chinese cook. Ask for "chicken in the basket" for a gourmet surprise. Marvelous beach, ideal for long, solitary walks and shell collecting.

Kota Bharu

First Class: **Hotel Perdana.** 136 rooms, international standard, swimming pool.

Moderate: **Temengong Hotel.** 36 rooms. Among the best of poor selection. Coffee shop.

Kuala Trengganu

First Class: **Pantai Primula Hotel.** Good beach resort with full facilities, 264 rooms.

Tanjong Jara. Good, modern 100-room resort-style hotel with reasonable facilities.

Moderate: **Motel Desa.** 20 rooms, air-conditioned. Standard dining room. Pleasant facilities. Close to beach.

Rantau Abang. 40 rooms and chalets. Moderate facilities.

Kuantan

First Class: **Hyatt.** Superb resort hotel with 185 rooms and suites and all facilities, 6 bars and restaurants, disco, tennis and squash courts, health club, pool and lovely beach.

Club Meditérranée. First of the Club Med-style resorts in Asia, this lavishly equipped beachside hotel offers excellent facilities—for an escapist holiday with all the comforts. 47 kms. north of Kuantan.

Moderate: **Hotel Merlin.** 105 rooms. 50 yards from the beach. Attractive swimming pool and terraces for lazy breakfasts.

Samudra Hotel. New. 75 rooms. In town. Coffeehouse and disco.

Inexpensive: **Chendor Motel.** Right on the beach. 21 rooms and 31 chalets. Dining room serves undistinguished Western and Chinese food.

Mersing

First Class to Moderate: **Merlin Samudra** on Tioman Island (boat ride from Mersing). Comfortable hotel with good facilities at a superb location.

Moderate: **Rawa Island.** A very special island. Accommodations are sparse but adequate. Cozy atmosphere. Diving, fishing, and snorkeling equipment available.

Sri Mersing. Small, modern hotel. Convenient stopover en route to Tioman. 34 rooms.

HILL RESORTS

Offering a variety of sports and recreations, as well as lovely walks in the jungle, a good escape from the tropical lowland heat.

Cameron Highlands

First Class: **Ye Olde Smoke House.** Only 20 rooms in this re-creation of English pub atmosphere in Cameron Highlands. Close to golf course.

First Class to Moderate: **Merlin Cameron Highlands.** 65 rooms. Close to the golf course, restaurant, bar, and disco.

Fraser's Hill

First Class to Moderate: **Merlin Fraser's Hill.** 109 rooms, modern; restaurant and limited facilities.

Inexpensive: **Fraser's Hill Hotel.** Two hours from K.L. Popular family-style hotel. Intimate dining room and bar where you get to know everyone quickly.

Genting Highlands

First Class to Moderate: **Genting Highlands.** Only 32 miles from K.L., this resort hotel is most famous for its casino. Tourist and sports facilities are being added, including golf and tennis. Several bars, indifferent restaurants and coffee houses. 1,000 rooms in various hotels, at differing price levels. Access by bus or car.

WESTERN MALAYSIA

Alor Star

Moderate: **Kedah Merlin Inn.** 130 pleasant rooms, reasonable facilities.

Samila Hotel. Most popular; 52 comfortable rooms.

Inexpensive: **Federal Hotel.** Older, originally the only place in town, except for the Government Rest House.

Ipoh

Moderate: **Hotel Eastern.** 30 rooms. Central air-conditioning. Restaurants serve Western food of sorts. Chinese restaurant is good, but noisy.

Inexpensive: **Tambun Inn.** 100 rooms, 10 minutes from airport in residential area.

Kowloon Hotel. Downtown hotel. Favorite with exotic dancers and students.

Johor Bharu

Moderate. **Bali Hai Hotel.** 100 yards from the beach. Nightclub.

Holiday Inn. New hotel with full facilities. 200 rooms.

Merlin Tower. 104 new rooms; good service and facilities.

Inexpensive: **Regent Elite.** New, rather spartan, with limited facilities. 70 rooms.

Straits View. 30 old-style rooms, overlooking straits and Singapore. Good atmosphere, lively in evening.

Langkawi Island

Moderate: **Langkawai Island Country Club.** Isolated beach resort. 100 rooms. A place to get away from the mobs. It offers a variety of activities such as sailing, riding, waterskiing. Access by air charter from Penang, or boat from Kuala Perlis.

Mutiara Beach Hotel. 20 delightful rooms on excellent beach.

Malacca

First Class: **Malacca Straits Inn.** 45 modern rooms with TV, restaurant, discothèque.

Malacca Village Resort. 150 chalets, swimming pool, golf course, tennis, and squash. Out of town, 7 miles inland.

Moderate: **Shah's Beach Motel.** 50 chalets. Close to poor beach, but the motel swimming pool offers cool refreshment after a day of tropical sightseeing. Chalets around the pool. Outdoor dining room with good food and atmosphere.

Inexpensive: **Palace Hotel.** Downtown, air-conditioned. Restaurant and bar. Not much atmosphere, but comfortable enough. Friendly. 48 rooms.

Other inexpensive hotels of passable quality include the **Wisma, Regal, Sentosa** and **Lotus Inn.**

Pangkor Island

Moderate: **Hotel Pantai Puteri Dewi** (Princess Hotel). Resort hotel on island. Catch the ferry from Lumut. 55 rooms and chalets, some Malay-style. Good beach. Some sailing and waterskiing available. Also day excursions.

Pangkor Bay Village. 67 rooms; simple but pleasant.

Port Dickson

First Class: **Ming Court Beach Hotel.** New, 154 rooms. Charming beachside setting plus full resort facilities.

Moderate: **Si-Rusa Inn.** Resort hotel with full range of beach facilities. Boating, sailing, waterskiing. Some air-conditioned rooms and chalets. Very much a family place.

Small and *inexpensive* are the **Lido Hotel** and **Sea View.**

EAST MALAYSIA

Sarawak and Sabah

Kota Kinabalu

First Class: **Hyatt International.** 345 luxury rooms, on waterfront. Good facilities, swimming pool, several restaurants.

Capital. 102 rooms. Located in residential area near center of town. Not too far to walk in the cool of the evening. Air-conditioned and eager to please.

Tanjong Aru Beach. 300-room resort hotel; superb beach and excellent facilities.

Moderate to Inexpensive: **Ang's Hotel.** 35 rooms, air-conditioned, located in center of town.

Jesselton. Close to the seafront in town center. Good Western cuisine. 49 old-style rooms.

Kuching

First Class: **Holiday Inn.** 165 rooms. Kuching's most modern and luxurious hotel. Pool and full facilities.

Moderate: **Aurora.** In city center. Pleasant lounge, where you can sit, sip beer and watch the people. Air-conditioned. Friendly service, cozy rooms. 85 rooms.

Miri

The *Fatimah* or *Park* hotels offer moderately clean accommodations and poor facilities at moderate prices.

Sibu

Moderate: **Premier Hotel.** 120 modern rooms, good facilities.

Inexpensive: Just passable are the **Li Hua** (70 rooms) and **Sarawak** (24 rooms) hotels.

Sandakan

Moderate: **Nak Hotel.** 60 functional, modern rooms. Chinese restaurant and coffee shop.

TOURS. A number of regional airlines, including *MAS, S.I.A.,* and *Thai International* offer inexpensive inclusive tours as a way of promoting their ticket sales. Leading agents in the U.S. and Europe also arrange short or long inclusive package tours covering the whole country. A trip through Malaysia can be included on an overland tour between Bangkok and Singapore, usually taking from 7 to 10 days. In Kuala Lumpur, *Masmara* and *Mayflower Acme* offer coach tours around Kuala Lumpur and the surrounding countryside. If your have 2 days, hire a car and make the roundtrip to Malacca through some beautiful unspoilt country. A complete circle tour of Malaysia by self-drive car should take a minimum of 5 days. In Penang, *Star of Penang Island Tour* takes you on a 2-hour cruise and can be arranged through *Ensign Travel.* For safaris into Malaysia National Park, contact *Malaysian Holiday* in Kuala Lumpur or *Asia Overland Services,* c/o Hotel Malaya, Kuala Lumpur. *Sarawak Travel Agencies* and *Harpers Tours* (M) sdn. bhd., both in Kuching, can arrange visits, including overnight stay, at longhouses. *Dakco Tours,* also in Kuching, offer Dyak longhouse visits and 3- to 12-day river and jungle safaris.

NATIONAL PARK. Malaysia's National Park, one of the largest national parks in the world, is a highlight of any visit to the peninsula. A minimum of three days is necessary, four is better, and five would be comfortable. You can drive to Kuala Lipis or Jerantut from K.L. and store your car; from Kuala Lipis you take the train to Tembeling Halt, where a river boat will meet you. The trip up the Sungei Tembeling to Kuala Tahan, where bungalow accommodations are readily available, takes from 2½ to 4 hours, depending on the water level. You may see wild seladang, otter, and possibly python or crocodile from the boat, and you will ship a bit of water on the rapids, so dress for a wet ride. Salt licks have been located throughout the park to attract animals, and if you are lucky you may see elephant, tiger, tapir, black panther, deer, and wild pigs. Shelters have been provided for photography. Ideally, you should spend the first night at Kuala Tahan and then proceed by boat and track to Jenut Kumbang, the "high hide," built well up into the trees, where 6–7 adults can spend the night. Fishing in the area is excellent, and the entire park provides the visitor with an opportunity to experience real jungle (and probably to encounter an aborigine with a blowpipe) without great inconvenience. You must apply in advance for accommodations, guides, boatmen, and to be met at Tembeling, by writing to the Chief Game Warden of Malaysia, Kuala Lumpur, and sending a deposit of $M100 per party and $1 per person for entry permits. The total cost of a four-day trip from K.L. and return would be about M$700 per person, if you need to hire a car or take a taxi to the rail junctions, or there are organized group tours from around M$500 for 4 days. The park poses no danger for the sensible visitor.

Nature lovers—especially botany buffs—will find Kinabalu National Park in Sabah a rewarding experience. Covering an area of 265 square miles, it contains Southeast Asia's highest mountain: Mount Kinabalu, 13,455 feet. The climb requires no special skills but takes a minimum of two days. The park provides overnight accommodations at various stages. Facilities include a new hostel, visitor cabins, and luxury chalets. *Poring Hot Springs* has campground facilities. During local school and public holidays—April and July–August—the park is heavily booked. Reservations, including a M$10 booking fee, should be made through the Park Warden, P.O. Box 626, Kota Kinabalu, Sabah, Malaysia. The park also provides charter landrovers.

SPORTS. The British influence can be seen in the polo grounds, excellent golf courses and horseracing courses dotted about the country, but Malaysia's favorite sports are *soccer* and *badminton.*

Participant Sports: Among the well-to-do, *golf* has taken over. *Watersports* are delightful on the many white sand beaches on both coasts. Most beach hotels have pools, and all the new hotels in larger cities have one. Golf is best in hill stations, such as Cameron Highlands, and near Kuala Lumpur, Malacca and Penang. Tennis facilities are also available, especially in resort areas.

Some *hunting* opportunities are available throughout the year in most Malaysian states. Licenses may be obtained from state game wardens through your hotel or travel agent. For further information on game hunting contact the Department of Wildlife and National Parks, Government Offices Complex, Jalan Duta, Kuala Lumpur. River and sea *fishing* is excellent, but good equipment is not easily available for hire. Fishing excursions during the period March-October. Limited game fishing opportunities can be found on the East Coast of Peninsular Malaysia.

Spectator Sports: The native sport, *bersilat,* is the stylized Malay art of self-defense handed down from father to son over the ages. It is more a dance form today than an effective exercise in personal combat. It is performed on ceremonial occasions, especially in the presence of Malay royalty. The combatants, dressed for the occasion in colorful costumes, go through the motions of combat with the Malayan *kris* (a dagger with a wavy blade). It is a combination of fencing, all-in wrestling and even boxing, in which agility of step, engagement, and quick disengagement, thrust, counter-thrust, and climax are all stylized into movements of grace with a touch of the deadly and the sinister.

MUSEUMS. *The National Museum,* **Kuala Lumpur**, has a rare collection of gold- and silver-mounted Malay kris and historical Malay weapons, silver and brassware, extensive examples of aboriginal life and customs and a river estuary diorama where reptiles, birds and insects are shown in their natural habitat. Entrance free. Open 9–6 every day. The *National Museum of Art,* opposite the main railway station, in Kuala Lumpur has works by important regional Asian artists. Open 10–6 daily. Admission free.

The Perak Museum, **Taiping**, is Malaysia's first museum and has a wide variety of exhibits. One of its most important exhibits is the black table upon which the Treaty of Pangkor was signed in 1874 between the Sultan of Perak and Britain.

Both **Penang** and **Malacca** have small, but interesting, museums. Old maps, photos, documents, and other colonial mementoes convey a sense of the towns' historical development. Both are open 9–6 daily. Admission free.

The *Sarawak Museum* in **Kuching** is well known throughout Southeast Asia for its excellent anthropological exhibits. The collection includes rare examples of tribal art—weaving, carving, basketry—which are surprisingly sophisticated in design and concept. The museum also has an exhibit of neolithic remains excavated at Niah Caves. The museum shop has a fine selection of artistic native crafts.

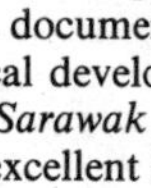

SHOPPING. Malaysian handicrafts are simple and attractive. Batiks are colorful and washable. *MARA* (the Malaysian Government board) turns out handsome tablecloths and bedsheets as well as fashion items for men and women. *Selangor Pewter* produces reasonably priced vases, bowls, ashtrays, and goblets in traditional and modern designs. Antique furniture (Chinese, Dutch, Portuguese) is becoming scarcer, but there are still some good buys around. Shopping opportunities in East Malaysia, Sabah, and Sarawak, include woven hats, baskets and mats, folk weaving and pottery, silver jewelry (often featuring old coins) and wood carving.

Kuala Lumpur. For a peek at Malaysian art, old and new, drop in at *Wisma Loke,* off Jalan Tunku Abdul Rahman, an old Chinese mansion converted to an art gallery and an antique shop. For the best batik, Kelantan silver, straw baskets, mats and purses, go to *Puspamara,* MARA building, or the *Karyarneka Handicraft Centre,* Jalan Raja Chulan, with 14 different buildings, featuring crafts of the various states.

Malacca. One can comb old junk stores for Chinese porcelain and Malacca furniture. Try shops along Jalan Hang Jebat.

Penang. Browse through shops on Campbell St., Bishop St., and Penang Rd., or visit the big new shopping complex called *Komtar.*

DINING OUT. Eating is a tourist's delight anywhere, and especially so in Malaysia. The variety of foods produced by this "plural society" is as great as the national traditions of the groups themselves. One of the pleasures of visiting Malaysia is the opportunity to sample the many different types of Chinese cuisine. Restaurants are classified by the type of food they serve—Cantonese, Peking, Hakka, Szechuan, etc.—and the visitor can sample a different type each night beginning with the elaborate Peking menu, to the hot and spicy Szechuan. Malay food, especially *satay* (beef or chicken on bamboo skewers, with a hot sauce based on peppers and peanuts), is excellent, and differs from Indonesian, even though the words for dishes frequently do not. A Madras or Bombay curry, or roasted crabs (served up whole in little cafés in Port Klang), are delicious and not unduly challenging. You can move on to snake meat and other dishes later, if more adventuresome. And if you object to local foods, European cooking can be found everywhere—although it generally is not so tasty as the national dishes and, in particular, the Chinese ones. For those who do prefer Western food, the best bet is to stay in the major hotels, which offer an excellent choice of restaurants from those specializing in fancy Continental cuisine to the ubiquitous international-style coffee shop.

Among the most popular drinks to be recommended in Malaysia are the local beers, *Tiger* and *Anchor.* The famous Singapore Gin Sling will never fail to cool you. It is a mixture of gin, cherry brandy, and a little Cointreau, red wine, and lemon juice.

SABAH AND SARAWAK

Outside the hotels only the following can be recommended: Western food: *Gardenia,* in **Kota Kinabalu.** In **Kuching,** Chinese food at *Rock Café* and the *Coq d'Or.* Also "the Chinese restaurant in the cinema building" for good food and live music. *Upcountry:* Not to be missed: birds' nest soup at *Mr. Sim's* shop in **Batu Niah.** Food in the good hotels in East Malaysia is surprisingly expensive, although only reasonable in quality.

KUALA LUMPUR

For Chinese food, the *Inn of Happiness* (Hilton Hotel); *Golden Phoenix* (Equatorial Hotel), Tai Thong, off Jalan Barat. *Imperial Room* (Hotel Malaysia), *Mandarin Palace* (Hotel Federal) are good. Also good food, but with no décor, can be had at *Kum Leng* (Jalan Pudu), and, for Malay food, *Bintang* (Jalan Ismail). First-rate European cuisine in an elegant setting can be found at *Le Coq d'Or,* 123 Jalan Ampang. Best seafood on Old Klang Rd. in a number of excellent open-air restaurants. To see a bit of the life of a rubber plantation manager's day in town, try a steak and beer at the *Coliseum.* Good pub atmosphere and excellent steaks in *The Ship,* Jalan Sultan Ismail. *Yazmin,* Ampang Shopping Complex, and *Indah Ku* on Jalan Raja Lau, opposite the new City Hall, offer Malay-style food and cultural shows. Kaula Lumpur offers an opportunity to sample various types of Indian cuisine. *Bilal* serves Indian Muslim dishes such as *murtaba; Shiraz* and *Akbar* are noted for North Indian dishes such as chicken *tikka, tandoori* chicken, *paratha. Satay,* Malay-style barbecue served with a spicy peanut sauce, can be found in Jalan Bunnus.

PENANG

Chinese food is recommended at the *Ming Palace,* in the *Ming Court Hotel* Cantonese style. If you want other kinds of Chinese food, you can get Teochew cuisine at the *Tai Tung Restaurant,* 51 Cintra St. Hokkien-style Chinese food is served at the *Ocean Inn,* **Batu Maung,** and at the *Towne House Hotel.* At the latter hotel you can also get Hylam food. Malaysian food is good at the *E & O Hotel,* the *Ocean Inn, Meera,* 166 Campbell St., and the Dawood Restaurant, 61 Queen St. Western cuisine is best at the *Ming Court* and *E & O* Hotels, or at the new luxury hotels along the beach at **Batu Ferringhi,** several of which offer delightful al fresco barbecue dinners under the palm trees of their beachside gardens.

IPOH

There are many little stalls along Cowan, Clarke, and around the market area, which sell the type of egg noodle famous to Ipoh. If the sanitary conditions of these little shacks do not please you, you may prefer the Chinese food at the *Winner* or *Hollywood* hotels, or *Kun Loong Net,* 6 Anderson Rd. Muslim food is supposed to be best at the *Federal Moslem Restaurant.*

MALACCA

Good all-round food at the *Malacca Straits Inn,* or in various national styles at several new and good restaurants in nearby harbor reclamation area. *Kacil Restaurant,* below the tourist information office opposite the Malacca Museum, is worth a try. Charming are the many small open-air cafes along the sea wall, by the padang. Portuguese food is found at the *Portuguese Settlement* in the Jalan D'Albuquerque.

DRINKING WATER. Water from taps in every city of the Federation is safe.

MAIL, TELEPHONE, AND TELEGRAPH. Airmail letters to Britain will cost you 80 cents Malaysian for each 10 grams; 60 cents to Australia, and $1.10 to the United States. Airmail postcards to the same places are 40 cents, 30 cents, and 55 cents, respectively. Local telephone calls cost 10 cents; international calls may be made through major hotels and main post offices.

USEFUL ADDRESSES. Embassies. All in KL: *Australia High Commission,* 6, Jalan Yap Kwan Seng. *British High Commission,* Wisma Damansara, 5 Jalan Semantan. *Burma,* 7 Jalan Taman U. Thant. *Canada High Commission,* 5th floor, A.I.A. Building, Jalan Ampang. *India High Commission,* Oriental Building, 32 Jalan Tun Perak. *Indonesia,* 233 Jalan Tun Razak. *New Zealand High Commission,* 193 Jalan Tun Razak. *Philippines,* 1 Changkat Kia Peng. *Singapore High Commission,* 209 Jalan Tun Razak. *United States,* 376 Jalan Pekeliling. *Thailand,* 206 Jalan Ampang.

Tourism information offices are located in K.L. opposite the railway station and airport, or the MTDC head office at Wisma MPI, Jalan Raja Chulan; in Penang at the airport and at 10 Jalan Tun Syed Sheikh Barakbah.

Emergencies. For police, fire, or ambulances, dial 999 anywhere in Malaysia or ask the operator. English is spoken by all operators.

FIVE-MINUTE BAHASA (MALAY)

The same words and phrases can be used in both Malaysia and Indonesia.

English	*Bahasa*
Good morning, afternoon, evening	Selamat pagi, tengah hari, petang
Goodbye	Selamat tinggal
Thank you	Terimakasih
Excuse me	Maafkan saya
I understand	Saya faham
I do not understand	Saya tidak faham
I want a taxi	Saya hendak teksi
How much?	Berapa
Expensive	Mahal sangat
Yes, no	Ya, tidak
This, that	Ini, itu
I want this	Saya mahu ini
Stop here	Berhenti di sini
Left, right	Kiri, kanan
Turn left	Pusing kiri
Road, building, office	Jalan, bangunan, pejabat
Post office	Pejabat pos
Hotel, restaurant	Hotel, Kedai makan or restoran
Food, drink	Makan, minum
Island, beach	Pulau, pantai
River, sea	Sungai, laut
Coconut	Kelapa
Tea, coffee	Teh, kopi
Milk, sugar	Susu, gula
Water, ice	Ayer, ayer batu
Good, bad	Baik, tidak baik

English	*Bahasa*
Today, tomorrow	Hari ini, esok
Week, month	Minggu, bulan
Dollar	Ringgit
One	Satu
Two	Dua
Three	Tiga
Four	Empat
Five	Lima
Six	Enam
Seven	Tujuh
Eight	Lapan
Nine	Sembilan
Ten	Sepuluh

BRUNEI

The Oil-Rich Islamic Sultanate

The tiny sultanate of Brunei occupies a sparsely populated area between the two East Malaysian states in Borneo, Sabah and Sarawak. Having once held suzerainty over most of North Borneo, this small state, financially secure because of rich oil and natural gas, had no desire to join the Malaysian Federation in 1963 and opted for independence under the protection of Great Britain until it achieved full independence in January 1984. The kingdom is under the benevolent, autocratic rule of His Highness Sir Muda Hassanal Bolkiah, who organizes his court and government on traditional Islamic patterns.

Brunei resembles no other country in Southeast Asia. Although 65 percent of the 220,000 population is Malay, the weather is hot and steamy, and the terrain jungle and river, Brunei does not share the poverty or internal political strife of its neighbors. The reason is oil. Thus, despite its location, Brunei has much in common with the oil sheikdoms of the Middle East. The oil revenues are spent, subject to the Sultan's approval, on the welfare needs of the people—from medical aid to cultural enrichment and educational programs.

A visitor to Brunei can sample the hospitality and warmth of the Malay life style, view unspoiled tropical river and jungle, and learn the culture of a relatively unexplored region. Because Brunei has not yet developed tourism as an industry, an individual or a small group will not be overwhelmed and crowded by busloads of tourists. Nevertheless, Brunei is modern enough to provide comfortable facilities for the enterprising traveler who will find a relaxed traditional society no longer common in Asia.

Rajah Brooke and the Sultan of Brunei

The history of Brunei State is actually the history of North Borneo. In fact, the very name is a British misdesignation of the entire island. Modern history of the area begins with the advent of Islam during the great conversion era of the 15th and 16th centuries.

Brunei did not at first attract the interest of the colonizing European powers because it possessed no great agricultural resources or any important discovered minerals. When rubber came to Southeast Asia, the previously colonized areas of Indonesia and Malaya were already more fully explored and settled; thus Borneo remained an unexplored, unsettled backwater wilderness. Nevertheless, the British, in the person of James Brooke, the first of the White Rajahs, became involved in the politics and wars of North Borneo. In 1839 he set sail from Singapore into a whirlpool of palace politics, endemic piracy and internal revolts. The throne of Brunei was weak and, after centuries of exploitation of the inland tribes, unpopular.

Brooke settled his administration in Sarawak by invitation of the local ruler and then proceeded to nibble away, river by river, the territory of the Brunei Sultans. As you fly over the North Borneo area the problems of warfare among petty rulers and pirates become clear. Each river mouth afforded a superb location for settlement and subsequent control over the interior, for the jungle was so thick that overland travel was difficult and dangerous. The Brunei nobility were Malay, Islamic and skilled warriors. They often harassed and even enslaved the tribal peoples up the rivers. It was for the protection of these primitive peoples that the Brookes established their suzerainty over much of the area.

Brunei was thus isolated and developed more slowly than its neighbors until the discovery of vast oilfields in 1929. It did not receive a British Resident until 1905 and unlike Sarawak and Malaya did not attract any great numbers of Chinese.

Because of its geographic position Borneo suffered during the Japanese occupation. After the war, the Brookes ceded Sarawak to Great Britain while Brunei remained a British Protectorate. Oil revenues flowed in and the state prospered.

In 1962 A. M. Azahari led a revolt against the Sultanate in the hope of establishing closer ties with the rest of Borneo. The Sultan, aided by British regiments, quelled the rebellion and secured the political stability of the small kingdom. Today the country is ruled by a Legislative Council largely appointed by the Sultan. The present Sultan acceded to the throne in 1967 when his father abdicated in favor of the eldest son. He is the 29th Sultan of Brunei.

A new era in the history of Brunei began in 1984 when the sultanate gained full independence, yet this has not made any difference in the basic form of government or the social patterns of the country.

EXPLORING BRUNEI

A visit of 2 to 3 days is recommended for Brunei, either as a side trip from Singapore or Hong Kong, or as a stop en route between them.

From the moment you land at the new, modern air terminal at Bandar Seri Begawan, Brunei's capital—usually referred to as "Bee Ess Bee" or just "Bandar"—you will be impressed by the cleanliness of the country. The people are courteous and friendly; arrival formalities, which in this region can often be time-consuming and irritatingly complicated, proceed smoothly and swiftly.

Your first sight of BSB will be the huge golden dome of the Sultan Omar Ali Saifuddin mosque, which dominates the town's low skyline. As you drive into town you will notice many attractive well-landscaped buildings: the Language and Literature Bureau Office with a mosaic mural, the Youth Center, the Parliament House, the Churchill Museum (one of the only memorabilia museums in Asia) and, off in the distance, the parapets of the Sultan's Palace. In fact, unlike most Asian cities where imposing modern structures, offices, and hotels dominate the skyline, BSB still presents a traditional appearance with few buildings over three stories, although this will no doubt change in the future as the growing impact of prosperity from the country's rich oil and gas fields is felt.

Bandar Seri Begawan is situated on a wide, lovely river, the port being at Muara 17 miles away. Many of the people live in the water village across from the main part of town. Kampong Ayer (which translates as water village) is an entire town of houses built on stilts. BSB is a clean and quiet town—traffic jams, air pollution and litter have not yet encroached seriously on this lovely place. The pace of life is accordingly slow; after nine o'clock the streets are deserted. Population of the town is just over 60,000.

Upriver is the jungle. Here tribal peoples as well as Malays and Chinese have settled to farm, fish, hunt, and trade. Ibans (Sea Dyaks), many of whom have drifted over the border from Sarawak, live in longhouses (to which visits can be arranged) that reflect an increased standard of living. But even though many of the families are able to afford cars, smart clothes, watches and transistor radios, the Iban still maintain many of their traditional habits and cultural values. Other tribes inhabiting the interior are the Dusun, Muruts, and some Settled-Punan, who have abandoned the uncertainties of nomadic life for the security of the village which offers medical services, employment, and above all, education.

Downriver from BSB and all along the coast are beautiful unspoilt beaches of white sand. The warm South China Sea provides pollution-free swimming, although the slope of the shore is too gentle to create much surf. A few islands lie offshore, and there you will find marvelous fishing and coral. On the horizon you will see some oil and gas rigs.

Kampong Ayer

You will certainly not want to miss a visit to Kampong Ayer, where an entire community dwells on the river. The houses are astonishingly modern and most sprout tall TV antennae. Prahus and small motor launches ply the watery streets, ferrying children to school, housewives to market, and men to their jobs in town, providing interesting sights for visitors.

Kampong Ayer is actually a series of villages, each centered around a traditional occupation: weaving, fishing, metal-working, carpentry. Today, however, most men traverse the water to shore and then drive their cars to work, while the women maintain the house, watch over the children and visit their immediate neighbors.

Life in the water village is paradise for small children who invent an amazing variety of games to play in their confined space. A major in the Brunei Army fondly recalled his childhood days when he and his friends flew kites, made boats, and held swimming competitions. His favorite recollection is waiting for low tide, when he and his friends would jump down into the mud, rolling and wallowing in the ooze until they slathered in mud from head to toe.

Two interesting places to stop in Kampong Ayer are Haji Sulaiman's shop for antiques, and the home-workshop foundry of Brunei's last brass-smith. Brunei was famous throughout the region for the quality of its decorative brass, particularly cannons which were used as gifts and dowry items. In modern times the art has died away, except for Ibrahim who still produces small brass cannons for souvenirs, as well as teapots, handles and tools. At the foundry several men, clad in sarongs and undershirts, sit on the dirt floor preparing scrap metal for melting and shaping clay molds for the molten brass. The smith uses a version of the lost-wax method, but is reluctant to share his formula with anyone.

The best examples of antique Brunei brass can be seen at the Brunei Museum about four miles from BSB. Opened with great ceremony by the Sultan and Queen Elizabeth in 1972, the museum is a handsome building with excellent displays. Of particular interest are exhibits concerning the life of the people. An astonishing variety of fishing methods, some of them no longer used, is on display as well as exhibits on oil production, rice culture, and life in a longhouse. The museum has a small, but good, collection of Chinese ceramics as well as a full collection of Malay *kris* (elaborate inlaid swords).

PRACTICAL INFORMATION

FACTS AND FIGURES. Population: 220,000. Birth rate per 1,000: 28. Life expectancy: 66 years. Land area: 5,800 sq. kms. Percentage cultivated: 2% (85% forest). Number of tourists (1984 est.): 375,000. Per capita income: US $21,000 p.a.

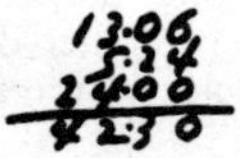

WHAT WILL IT COST? First-class air-conditioned rooms start at B$200 for a double room, per day. More modest accommodations, which are hard to find, range from B$100–B$150. Taxis are reasonable: B$18 to the airport, B$6 to the museum, B$50 to Maura, the nearest beach. Buses are cheap and go to Muara, Seria (oil town) and Kuala Belait, the second largest town. Restaurant food is expensive considering this is a non-tourist town. Breakfast (eggs, toast, coffee) costs about B$10, up to B$16 in the top hotel. A Chinese dinner at leading restaurants is also not cheap, but you can visit a cafe for a plate of fried rice or noodles and spend only a few dollars.

WHEN TO GO, WHAT TO TAKE. Brunei lies between 4° and 6° north of the Equator and it is hot. Very hot. Bring light, loose clothing and a floppy hat for protection from the sun when you go sightseeing. Sandals or any comfortable, airy shoes will do. Many people invest in one of the colorful Asian paper umbrellas (available throughout the region) as a shield against both sun and sudden downpours. The major monsoon season lasts from December-January, but even during the rainy season the sun shines fiercely. Hotels and better restaurants are air-conditioned to an alarmingly arctic degree and a light sweater is necessary. Brunei is not a formal town unless you are going to be involved with royalty on official occasions, at which time you will need proper formal national dress and all your medals. Local shops carry most necessities such as toothpaste, film, etc.

GETTING THERE. *Royal Brunei Airlines, MAS,* and *Singapore Airlines* run direct Singapore-Brunei and Kuala Lumpur-Brunei flights. *Cathay Pacific* operates from Hong Kong. *British Airways* flies direct London-Brunei. *MAS* also connects Brunei to neighboring Borneo states. *Thai International* serves BSB from Bangkok. *Royal Brunei Airlines* has flights from Singapore, Kuching (Sarawak), Hong Kong, Kota Kinabalu (Sabah), Bangkok, Kuala Lumpur, Darwin, Jakarta, and Manila, using Boeing 737s. Be sure to reconfirm onward flights as services tend to be full at certain times.

PASSPORTS AND VISAS. At the time of writing (mid-1985) visas are a problem for all nationalities except neighboring Asian countries. Brunei has just introduced new visa laws which are still not settled in full. American, British and Commonwealth visitors must now obtain visas from overseas Brunei embassies, found in London, Washington, D.C., and leading Asian capitals. For details, check with the airline from which you buy your ticket or your travel agent.

CUSTOMS. Personal effects, 200 cigarettes, and one quart of alcohol are permitted duty free for the tourist. Customs are strict about imported electrical goods, so if you have been buying such items in Singapore, or Hong Kong, declare them on arrival. Officials may also be fussy about imported cameras, so proof of purchase may be useful.

AT THE AIRPORT. Formalities are minimal and officials friendly at the small, ultramodern and greatly under-utilized international airport at BSB. The only congestion occurs during the annual Hajj, the Islamic pilgrimage to Mecca. Inoculation certificates are not required for cholera, smallpox, and yellow fever unless coming from an infected area. Taxi to downtown hotels costs around B$18. There is a duty-free shop in the departure hall of the airport, but this being a strict Muslim country, it does not sell alcohol. There is no airport departure tax.

LANGUAGE AND RELIGION. The official language is Bahasa Melayu, almost the same as in Malaysia and Indonesia, but English is widely understood. Religion is overwhelmingly Muslim though the country is multiracial and Chinese, Hindu, and Christian holidays are also observed.

MONEY. Until 1973 Brunei, Singapore, and Malaysia shared a common currency. At the changeover, Brunei (with one of the region's largest foreign reserves) did not suffer. You may use any of the currencies in Brunei and use your Brunei dollars on par with Singapore money but must go to a bank or moneychanger for Malaysian *ringgit.* At press time (mid-1985) exchange rates were US$1 = B$2.15, UK£1 = B$3.40. Major credit cards accepted in leading hotels only.

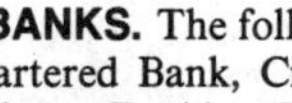

CAR HIRE. Self-drive is practical, but only necessary if one plans to explore outside BSB as the town itself is small enough for seeing by foot. *Avis* rates start at B$90 per day, unlimited mileage. International driving license required, minimum age 23. Traffic drives on the left, with road signs following the British style. Chauffeur rates from B$40 per hour, $250 per day. Hotel pickup can be arranged, in advance, for your arrival at the airport.

BANKS. The following banks have branch offices in BSB: Bank of America, Chartered Bank, Citibank, Hong Kong and Shanghai Banking Corporation, Malayan Banking Bhd., National Bank of Brunei. Banks close for lunch from 12 to 2. Daily hours are 9–3:15. On Saturday they are open from 9–11 A.M.

BUSINESS HOURS. Generally 8:00 A.M. to 4:00 P.M., Monday to Saturday, closed Friday and Sunday. Most local markets open soon after dawn, however, and many shops stay open until late evening.

ACCOMMODATIONS. The State of Brunei is as yet undecided about its commitment to tourist development. Plans have been drawn up for a resort hotel at Jerudong 10 miles from BSB, and it was only recently that a really good hotel became available for the first time in BSB, but the government makes no effort to actively promote tourism, perhaps due to their being so much revenue from offshore oil and gas to fill their coffer. Confirmed advance bookings are advisable. Apart from the Sheraton the other hotels are clean and comfortable, but undistinguished. They have a 10 percent service charge.

First Class—B$230–260

Sheraton-Utama. 170 rooms. The opening of this modern luxury hotel gave Brunei its first good hotel. It has excellent facilities, including The Heritage restaurant and a good coffee shop.

Moderate—B$100–175

Ang's. 86 air-conditioned old rooms. Poor restaurant and bar but a renovation scheme currently in hand promises to improve matters all round.

Brunei. 59 rooms. Renovation has upgraded this centrally located hotel closer to first class, but it still lacks decent facilities.

National Inn. 118 rooms. Modern and air-conditioned, utility rather than luxurious, with reasonable facilities including an adequate restaurant and bar.

Inexpensive—B$80

Capital Hostel, near Civic Centre, is favored by economy travelers. 36 rooms, mostly air-conditioned, some with private bath. Coffee shop.

TOURS. Borneo Discovery Tours offers several trips upcountry and can arrange for overnight visits to a longhouse. *Borneo Discovery Tours,* P.O. Box 234, BSB, Brunei. The other leading tour agency is *Travel Centre Borneo,* P.O. Box 1829, BSB. A half-day tour of city highlights would cost from about B$70 per person, for two, by car. A full-day excursion to a longhouse, from about B$190 per person for a couple, or much less if joining a group. Longer jungle safaris, of a week or more, can be arranged through above agents.

WHAT TO SEE. The *Brunei Museum* should be one of your first stops (closes Monday). A boat ride over to the water village—catch a boat for B$2 or so right by the Brunei Hotel—is a pleasant trip and especially beautiful for photographing the famed *Sultan Ali Saifuddin Mosque* at sunset when the golden dome glows in the evening light. Hiring a boat for a look around the Kampong area will cost between B$20 and B$30 per hour depending on number of persons and on your ability to bargain.

The mosque itself, a superb example of modern Islamic architecture in white marble with gold mosaic and stained glass, is worth a visit. The mosque is closed to oudsiders (non-Muslims) on Thursday afternoon and all day Friday. Near the mosque is the *Churchill Museum,* which contains not only Churchill memorabilia but an exhibition explaining Brunei court customs. (Closed Tuesday). Near the Brunei Museum is the *tomb of Bolkiah,* the fifth Sultan of Brunei, who ruled during the height of the Brunei Sultanate in the 15th century. Set in a contemporary mausoleum the ancient tomb, recently restored, has a mixture of Chinese, Javanese, and Islamic carving. *The Ceremonial Hall and Parliament* is a lavish modern complex with lots of gilding. Outside Bandar Seri Begawan you can arrange to travel up the river to visit an Iban longhouse. The most interesting of these is at Limbang, half an hour away by boat and bad road, actually in Sarawak, so one needs to take a passport.

Other side trips are the short, 20-minute flight from BSB, by Royal Brunei Airlines, or MAS, to Kota Kinabalu, in Sabah, from where one can visit the National Park, or the one-hour flight to Kuching, in neighboring Sarawak.

One interesting river trip from BSB is by the regular ferry to Temburong and Banya, taking 45 minutes, fare B$10 each way. On the journey one gets a good sight of riverside life and scenery, including, perhaps, crocodile and the large monitor lizards.

A worthwhile drive is 1½ hours to the south, past Tutong with its silica sands to Seria, where one can see signs of the oilfields that give the country its wealth. The coast road continues to the most southerly town, Kuala Belait, which is uninspiring as a tourist destination, but an enjoyable day's excursion to see the coast and countryside. From Kuala Belait it is possible, via a ferry and sand road, to cross the Sarawak border and reach the town of Miri.

SHOPPING. Brunei is an excellent place to buy gold jewelry. Residents insist on 24-carat gold for most items; 22-carat is not uncommon, but 18-carat and less are not readily available. Gold traders have their reputations to maintain among the local clientele, so they tend to deal honestly.

BEACHES. Brunei's most popular beach is at Muara, 17 miles from BSB. Here, on weekends, families go for picnics, boating, and swimming. A river beach, only lovely at high tide, is within 10 miles of BSB; ask to be taken to *Pang-Kalan Si Babau.* Six miles from BSB is *Tunku Beach, Gadong,* at the end of a bumpy road. The drive is lovely, however, passing by Kedayan farms where ingenious scarecrows dangle in the rice fields. This beach is a favorite with foreign residents in Brunei. There are shade trees, but you must bring your own food and drink. Also bring insect repellant to discourage the sand flies which can be a serious problem on some beaches. At *Tutong,* 29 miles from BSB is *Pananjong Beach,* where one finds a playground and shade trees; good beach for picnics and swimming. Although in certain seasons stinging jellyfish are found close to shore and it's wise to be careful.

WATER. Do not drink tap water. Hotels provide purified water in flasks in room; otherwise drink tea or bottled soft drinks.

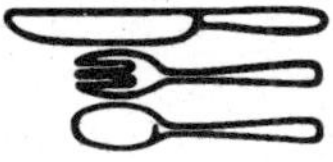

RESTAURANTS. Hotel coffee shops, or try the Rasa Sayang restaurant. Local food shops offer standard Chinese noodle and fried rice dishes or *nasi padang*—Indonesian/Malay rice and curry dishes. Brunei is a strict Muslim state, so your beer may be served in teacups, even though alcohol is freely available to non-Muslims. There is an open-air area of excellent, cheap food stalls, rather like Singapore's "Satay Club," by the Brunei River on the edge of BSB, opposite Kampong Ayer but standards of hygiene might upset the fastidious. There are more reasonable restaurants in the Gadong area close to the center of town. At Muara, about 16 miles from BSB, there are two good restaurants.

Chao Phaya, in Klasse Department Store, Jalan Tutong, offers delicious Thai Muslim food.

The Grill Room. Above Dairy Farm Ice Cream Parlour, Jalan Sultan, for the best Western food. Excellent steaks and seafood, not expensive for quality offered.

The Heritage. Top place for good Continental cuisine is now the Sheraton's signature restaurant. It is also the town's "in" place for local society.

The Lucky and Shiang, both in Jalan Tutong. Excellent Chinese food. A favorite lunch place.

Rasa Sayang, beside the Chinese temple, is also reasonable.

Regents Raug Mahel, 1st Mile, Jalan Tutong, is good for northern Indian cuisine, including Tandoori specialities.

Re's, in Gadong, offers good Indian and Malay curries.

POST AND TELEGRAPH. The General Post Office is open Monday to Thursday and Saturday from 7:15 to 4. Remember that Brunei is a strong Muslim nation and that the Post Office is open on Friday for only one hour: 8:30 to 9:30. Your hotel will supply stamps. Minimum airmail letter rate to USA is $1.20(B), to UK $1. Postcards 75 cents.

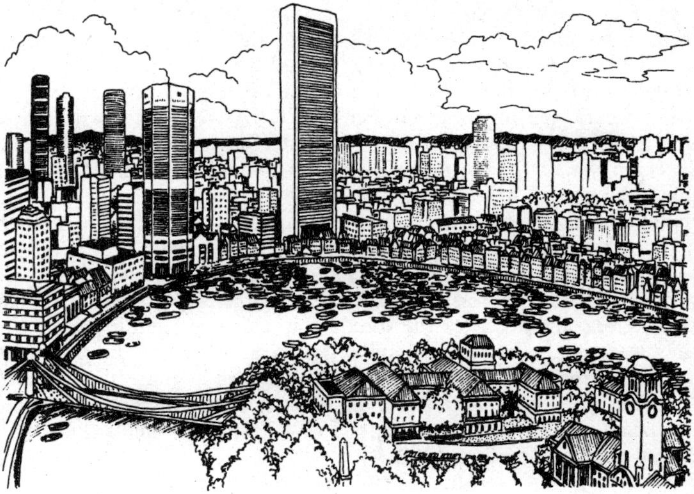

SINGAPORE

Instant Asia

Visiting Singapore is rather like visiting an open-air schoolroom on a summer's day, for the people of this speck on a map live under the Calvinistic, schoolmasterly rule of Prime Minister Lee Kuan Yew. Mr. Lee's idiosyncrasies needn't bother the tourist—unless your hair falls below collar length: the "pupils" are the people who'll interest you.

They offer a remarkable opportunity to see racial harmony at work —because here, just a couple of degrees north of the equator, you'll find a unique mixture of people and religions performing something of a human miracle: living together in peace. They've been working on it since 1819, when a rangy young merchant named Stamford Raffles founded a Trading Post of the East India Company. He then proceeded to develop Singapore into what Joseph Conrad was to call "the thoroughfare to the East." The British knighted Raffles for his trouble. As Raffles turned the tiny island into a staging point for the world's ships, news of its newfound prosperity began to attract immigrants from India and China and to this day it is they, together with the indigenous Malays, who form the basis of Singapore's multiracial society.

They were joined by Indonesian laborers from nearby Java, and within a decade of Raffles planting the British flag in Singapura—Lion City as the Malays called it—handsome, square-rigged merchant ships were calling there, more than one a day. Today, you can see at least

300 great ships there at any one time, for Singapore is now the world's second busiest port. For the next century, Singapore and its British masters prospered from entrepôt trading, and especially from the tin and rubber that were won from the jungles of Malaya, then shipped out to the world's markets from Singapore's bustling harbor.

Then came the Japanese. On February 14, 1942, just ten weeks after Pearl Harbor, a Japanese Army rode into Singapore on bicycles and accepted the surrender of the British garrison. The ceremony was to mark the end of white supremacy in Southeast Asia. Singapore was renamed Shonan by the conquering Japanese, and for the island's people there began three and a half years of horror. The Chinese, especially, suffered cruelly at the hands of the new colonialists.

But eventually it was the turn of the Japanese to surrender. The British formally accepted the standard of the rising sun in 1944—but they were not to be imperial rulers for long. It was a young Chinese with a degree from Cambridge who made sure of that. "We decided that from then on, our lives should be ours to decide, that we should not be the pawn and plaything of foreign powers," he said after his return from England in 1950.

His name was Lee Kuan Yew. And today he is Prime Minister of Singapore and strongman of the People's Action Party (PAP), which rules the island almost without opposition. It is his strength that has brought Singapore economic wealth despite being ejected from the Federation of Malaysia and despite the withdrawal of the once-mighty British garrison. It is he who has turned Singapore into the cleanest, most efficient and most corruption-free country in Southeast Asia.

He is a man who has a knack of making dreams come true. When Lee's PAP came to power in 1959, Singapore's Kandang Kerbau Hospital had the unenviable record of turning out more babies than any other maternity hospital in the world. This staggering birthrate had in turn led to massive overcrowding and slum dwelling.

Lee set about changing that: today, KK Hospital still turns out children, but in greatly reduced numbers. Family planning is subsidized or free and government houses and flats are being erected at the rate of one every half hour. Despite 2.5 million people being crowded into a few square miles, Singapore now has the highest average living standard on the mainland of Asia, and its economic growth rate is second only to Japan's. For a country with no natural resources except its geographical position, this is a truly remarkable achievement and a success story certainly worth studying at first hand.

But Lee and the band of intellectuals who have helped him perform this feat have not just had to fight economic adversity. They have also faced the complicated problems that a polyglot society can throw up. The Chinese, for example, have, by tradition, nurtured secret societies to push opium and prostitutes . . . and kill. Lee has managed to stamp them out almost completely by training an incorruptible force of police. Don't hand a Singapore traffic cop a five-dollar bill concealed in your license if he stops you for speeding. It won't pay.

One Million Teenagers

Despite tussles with the British over the years, the Prime Minister of Singapore has retained a special place in his heart for the English—and he has recognized that if Singapore is to continue as a successful international center for trade and finance, English, the international language, should be learned. So, now, all children have the opportunity to learn English, as well as their mother tongue, Mandarin, Malay, or Tamil, at school. Trilingual cabbies are common in this global city. Schools play an essential part in Lee's plan for the island's future and one of the most refreshing sights for the visitor will be the hundreds of children of many races walking to and from school each day in their immaculate uniforms. The young hold the key to Singapore's continuing prosperity and so Lee is licking his island's million teenagers (the boys at least) into shape by drafting them into the armed forces for a two-year stint.

But this pocket republic isn't all rules and regimentation. Its people's wealth of cultural heritage is reflected in a host of colorful festivals.

But if traditions remain, most traditional buildings don't. Singapore will give you an opportunity to see a state in transformation. For while in many tropical countries you can almost watch the grass grow, here you can watch the buildings grow. Hotels, apartments, offices, and shopping blocks spring up at an incredible rate. Even the island itself is growing—outwards—as land is reclaimed from the sea on which to build multi-lane highways, parks, and new building developments.

Lee, who finds it advantageous to communicate with his people through slogans, might well have this one writ above his desk: "The impossible we have done. The miracles are taking just a little longer."

EXPLORING SINGAPORE

One problem you won't have is seeing all of Singapore: with the same amount of land as the Isle of Man and not even as many people as Philadelphia, its size is no problem to the tourist. But, frankly, it's not a place to be seen from the window of an air-conditioned bus. You'll miss too much that way.

Of course, your guide will take you to the fabled Tiger Balm Gardens, where obese gods of Chinese mythology guffaw silently on a hill. And you'll see the world-famous Botanic Gardens, rich with all that nature can grow in the tropics. Naturally you'll see the garish Hindu temple of Sri Mariamman, where descendants of those first Indian settlers thank their Lord for being delivered into a land of plenty.

The downtown business districts, complete with skyscraper office blocks, are now purely Western, but some areas still retain some of their own unique character, and if one gets away from the newer parts of the city, one can still discover remnants of the old charm.

But only on foot will you be able to turn off the main streets into the alleys where live the amazing cross section of Oriental types which has

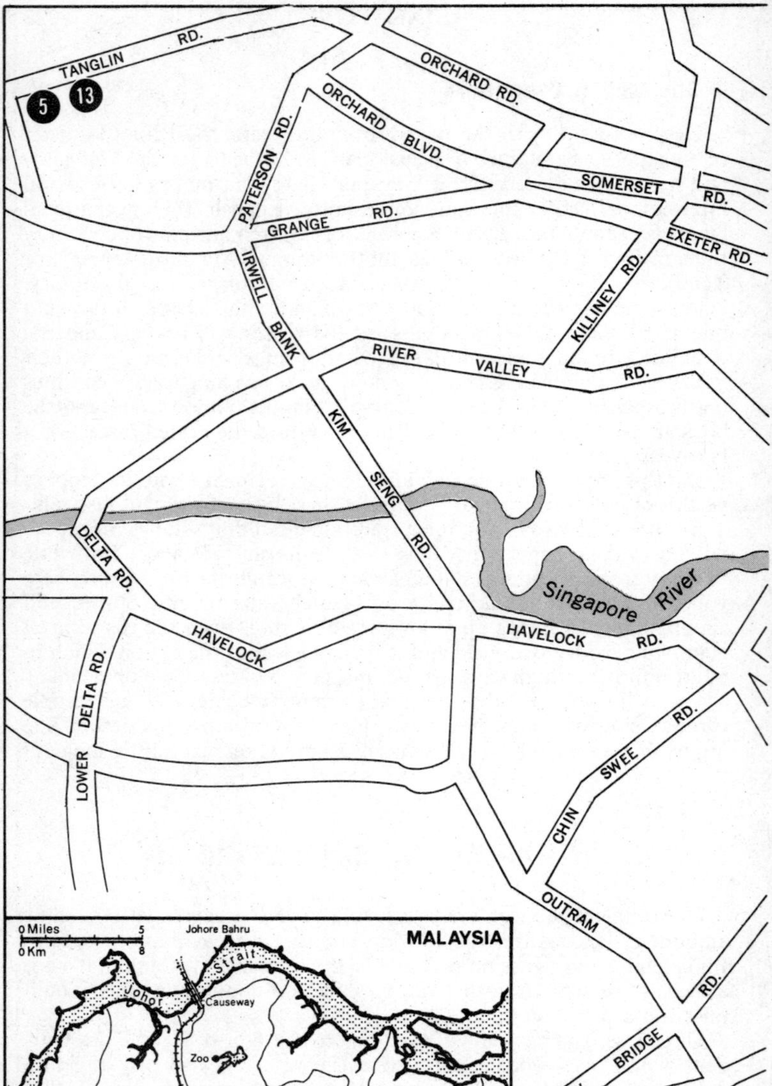
TANGLIN RD.
5
13
ORCHARD RD.
ORCHARD BLVD.
PATERSON RD.
SOMERSET RD.
GRANGE RD.
EXETER RD.
IRWELL BANK
KILLINEY RD.
RIVER VALLEY RD.
KIM SENG RD.
DELTA RD.
Singapore River
HAVELOCK
HAVELOCK RD.
LOWER DELTA RD.
CHIN SWEE RD.
OUTRAM RD.
NEW BRIDGE RD.
NEIL
CANTONMENT RD.
0 Miles 5
0 Km 8
Johore Bahru
MALAYSIA
Johor Strait
Causeway
Zoo
Changi Airport
Race Course
Jurong
Singapore
Clifford Pier
Singapore Strait
SENTOSA

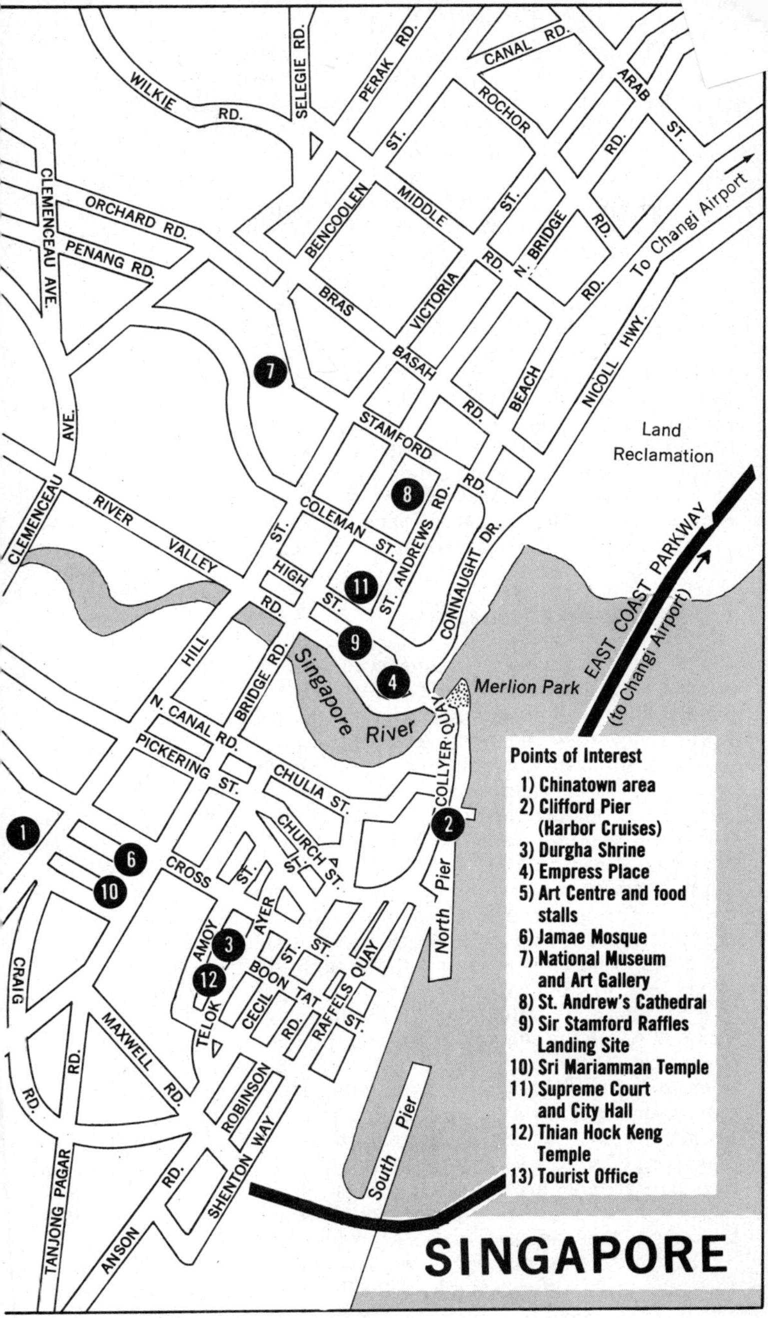
SINGAPORE
Points of Interest
1) Chinatown area
2) Clifford Pier (Harbor Cruises)
3) Durgha Shrine
4) Empress Place
5) Art Centre and food stalls
6) Jamae Mosque
7) National Museum and Art Gallery
8) St. Andrew's Cathedral
9) Sir Stamford Raffles Landing Site
10) Sri Mariamman Temple
11) Supreme Court and City Hall
12) Thian Hock Keng Temple
13) Tourist Office
Land Reclamation
Merlion Park
Singapore River
To Changi Airport
EAST COAST PARKWAY
(to Changi Airport)
North Pier
South Pier
WILKIE RD.
SELEGIE RD.
PERAK RD.
CANAL RD.
ROCHOR RD.
ARAB ST.
CLEMENCEAU AVE.
ORCHARD RD.
PENANG RD.
BENCOOLEN ST.
MIDDLE RD.
N. BRIDGE RD.
BRAS BASAH RD.
VICTORIA ST.
BEACH RD.
NICOLL HWY.
STAMFORD RD.
COLEMAN ST.
ST. ANDREWS RD.
CONNAUGHT DR.
RIVER VALLEY RD.
HIGH ST.
HILL ST.
BRIDGE RD.
N. CANAL RD.
COLLYER QUAY
PICKERING ST.
CHULIA ST.
CHURCH ST.
CROSS ST.
AMOY ST.
AYER ST.
BOON TAT ST.
CECIL ST.
RAFFLES QUAY
TELOK
CRAIG RD.
MAXWELL RD.
ROBINSON RD.
SHENTON WAY
ANSON RD.
TANJONG PAGAR RD.

caused Singapore to be called "Instant Asia." Only on foot are you likely to stumble across the Chinese medicine men who claim to cure everything with frightening concoctions of animal bones, snake soup, and lizard skins. Only on foot are you likely to stop in an open-fronted café where a grand-bellied Indian will serve you spiced meat doused with curry sauce, which you'll eat with your fingers from a banana leaf.

What remains of the old Chinatown area lies between New Bridge Road, through South Bridge Road, to Robinson Road. "Little India" is around Serangoon Road.

On foot you can also explore the many shops along Beach Road, behind the Raffles Hotel, to Arab Street, one of the few "old" areas where you can buy anything in brass from small cannons to cameras.

It has become much more difficult to find these "traditional" areas of the city over recent years. Lee Kuan Yew's dream of making Singapore into a major international financial and commercial center has come closer to reality. Perhaps too late the Singaporeans are coming to realize that something of the past must be preserved. Apart from the major public buildings, the bulldozer has claimed all but a few fragments of the old city. This is certainly the cleanest, most gardenlike city environment in Asia, a most regulated and organized society, but it has lost much of its former charm and character in the process.

Contrasts and Scenes

You will still discover that Singapore is a land of contrasts. You can, for instance, sun yourself on one of the islands to the south of the mainland, yet still be within sight of the sci-fi silhouette of one of the world's biggest oil refineries, which is on another of the offshore islands.

If you're hunting bargains, then you can find some here. Change Alley, just off the waterfront, is known to every sailor in the world for its bargains. But haggle or you'll be taken! Cameras, watches, and audio equipment are duty-free. The bright shopping complexes are exciting places to shop as well, but you may do a better deal in the tiny "shophouses," where two or three different merchants may share the same counter. The open markets, too, are fascinating. Nighttime shopping is a fine feature of Singapore. Shops rarely close before 8 and you'll find some still in business at midnight although the major shopping complexes tend to close by about 9 P.M.

If the shops are selling food . . . well, you can sip *Tiger* or *Anchor* beer and watch the sun go down at many a corner café. Even the most sophisticated of local people enjoy the inexpensive and varied gastronomic delights of the open-air food stalls, such as the area near Newton Circus, or the stalls close to the Singapore River in Empress Place. From early morning to past midnight there are food markets all over Singapore offering a wide range of many styles of Asian cuisine, and hygiene standards are surprisingly high.

For those who prefer less exotic fare, there are European restaurants, bars, nightclubs, and discos to suit every taste.

There are also a number of worthwhile sightseeing opportunities. Jurong Bird Park, for example, is the finest of its kind in Asia, with a vast acreage roofed with nets to allow the birds as natural an environment as possible. The park also contains a huge manmade waterfall. Also in Jurong are splendidly laid out formal gardens in traditional Chinese and Japanese styles. Singapore's Zoo, showing many animals in their natural surroundings, in the "open concept" style rather than in bare cages, is very fine.

To the south of the main harbor, where once giant British guns sat, pointing impotently out to sea while Japanese invaders crept up from behind, the government is turning the island of Sentosa into a tourist resort. The island was once a dumping ground for the bodies of pirate victims. Now it has a fine lagoon protected by an underwater boom. It is also linked with Mount Faber, on Singapore Island, by a cable car; but try to use the car midweek—Singaporeans queue to use it at weekends. On Sentosa one can stroll, or take a bus or monorail car to drive amid lovely scenery to the Maritime Museum, Surrender Chambers, golf course, swimming lagoon and art gallery. The latest attraction is a musical fountain—colorful jets of water dance to music ranging from the classical to pop each evening.

From Mount Faber and nearby Kent Ridge, now a university campus, you get a similar view to one enjoyed by pukka British officers who once messed there, watching the sun set over the Indonesian islands.

PRACTICAL INFORMATION

FACTS AND FIGURES. Land area: 619 sq. kms. Population: 2.5 million. Ethnic breakdown: 77% Chinese; 15% Malay; 6% Indian & Pakistani. Birth rate, per 1,000 population: 17. Average life expectancy: 71 years. Average per capita income: US $5,300 p.a. Percentage of population engaged in manufacturing and commerce: 78%. Number of tourists annually: 2.9 million.

WHEN TO GO. Singapore is a tropical country, with no distinct wet or dry season. December/January the wettest months; July, the driest. Temperatures range from 87°F. to 92°F. daytimes to 75°F. at night. Humidity is usually high.

WHERE TO GO. Take a harbor cruise from Clifford Pier or go out to Kusu Island by ferry from the World Trade Centre Ferry Terminal and visit the Tua Peh Kong temple. Drop in at Tiger Balm Garden—a sort of Charles Addams Disneyland East. Ride out to Jurong to see the Bird Park. Drive through Toa Payoh or Queenstown low-cost public housing and then to the Botanic Gardens to get away from the urban bustle. War buffs might like the Surrender Chamber (recalling the Allied and Japanese surrenders of WW II) on Sentosa, where there is also a maritime museum, golf course, swimming lagoon, and other attractions. Sentosa is reached by ferry from the World Trade Centre Ferry Terminal or cable car from Mount Faber. Peace and beautiful surroundings are found also in the Japanese and Chinese gardens, in Jurong. The vast grounds have been landscaped and include pavilions in two styles, that of the Sung dynasty and of the Summer Palaces in Peking. If you are interested in Asian arts and crafts visit the Handicraft Center in Tanglin Rd., where you will find not only shops, but also craftsmen at work. Next to the Handicraft Center is the Rasa Singapura food center, containing stalls of many types. Temples to be seen include the Hindu Sri Mariamman, South Bridge Rd.; Chinese Buddhist Siong Lim on Jalan Toa Payoh, and Muslim Hajjah Fatimah Mosque on Java Rd. The National Museum is also interesting.

WHAT TO TAKE. Dress in Singapore is informal, and you would be wise to confine your wardrobe here to lightweight clothing. Most first-class restaurants and the better hotel dining rooms expect the gentleman to wear a jacket and necktie in the evening, but most of these places are air-conditioned so you should not be uncomfortable. Many women wear long skirts or dress pants for evenings out. Singapore is one of the world's great shopping centers, a good place to stock up on cosmetics, film, etc. during an Asian tour as these are often expensive or unobtainable in nearby countries. Every possible need can be covered from Singapore's fabulous shops.

ELECTRICITY. Common voltage is 220–240 volts, 50 cycles, but most hotels can supply transformers for 110–120-volt appliances.

LOCAL FESTIVALS. Most local festivals are based on the lunar calendar, dates varying from year to year. To discover what celebrations occur during your stay, call the *Singapore Tourist Promotion Board,* tel. 235–6611 or study local "what's on" publications.

January-February. *Thaipusam,* annual Hindu religious festival. In Singapore, devotees dance through the streets in a trance carrying decorated arcs on spikes. Steel rods are skewered through their flesh. At night the Lord Subramaniam made all of gold, bejeweled and resplendent in his chariot, is taken round town, watched by thousands of people of all races.

January–February. *Chinese New Year,* with everyone dressed in his colorful best, visiting friends and relatives and the Buddhist temples. During Chinese New Year are held the Chingay processions, colorful and noisy, with the theme of the Chinese animal zodiac for the new year.

February and September–October. Twice annual *Birthday of the Monkey God, T'se Tien Tai Seng Yeh.* Penitants pierce themselves with skewers. Street operas and processions.

February–March. *Birthday of the Jade Emperor.* Whole roast pig, piles of decorated sweets, oranges and other lucky fruits are offered on homemade altars in front of the Chinese home. Drive at night through Chinatown.

March–April. *Birthday of the Goddess of Mercy.* Chinese visit temples dedicated to her.

May–June. *Vesak Day,* celebration of the Buddha's birthday. The center of celebrations in Singapore is the Buddha Gaya Temple in Race Course Road. Mass rally in the heart of the city, followed by a grand procession.

June. *Dragon Boat Festival* and races.

July–August. *Hari Raya Puasa.* This most important holiday for Muslims signals the end of the fasting month of Ramadan. New clothes and elaborate food spreads highlight this day.

August 9. *National Day of Singapore.* The one holiday which everyone from sweeper to President celebrates. National Day usually opens with a grand parade at the "Padang." The President of Singapore takes the salute from the steps of the gaily decorated City Hall. On the same day are held many other local and community celebrations throughout the island.

August–September. *All Souls' Day, Feast of the Hungry Ghosts,* is celebrated toward the end of the month. Ancestors traditionally return at this time to visit their descendants on earth. Shops display colorful paper religious objects. An excellent day for picture taking. In market places throughout the country, large tables covered with food are offered to spirits of departed Chinese ancestors. Artificial money, houses, and paper clothing are burned as offerings. Performances of Chinese opera and puppet shows.

August–September. *Market Festival,* celebrated by the Chinese community in a splendid outburst at the Market Place in Johore Bahru and in Singapore. Classic Chinese drama is performed every night just outside the market.

September. *Hari Raya Haji,* a Malay festival in honor of the pilgrims who return from Mecca. The faithful gather in the morning in great numbers at the Sultan Mosque in North Bridge Road, Singapore, for a picturesque ceremony of prayer. A day of festivities follows.

September–October. *Mooncake Festival.* Commemorates the overthrow of the Mongol overlords in ancient China. Elaborate cakes and fruits are exchanged and children are given brightly colored cellophane lanterns. Competition for the best lanterns is also held in several locations.

October. *Festival of Nine Emperor Gods.* Processions and celebrations at main temples, on Upper Serangoon Rd. and at Lorong Tai Seng.

October-November. *Deepavali* or the Festival of Lights, commemorating the slaying of a mythological king by Lord Krishna, an annual celebration in which houses and business premises are decorated with thousands of lights. It is Open House at Hindu business establishments with refreshments.

October-November. *Thimithi.* Hindu festival in honor of goddess Droba-Devi. Firewalking and procession starting at Perumal Temple, to Sri Mariamman Temple.

December. *Birthday of the Prophet Mohammed.* A Koran reading competition for Muslim youth is an interesting event of the day.

HOW TO REACH SINGAPORE. By air: Singapore has become a crossroads of Asia, with over 30 airlines providing service, with direct links from all key points in Europe, North America, Australia and Asia.

By boat: There are a number of cruise and shipping routes from and to Singapore. *Blue Funnel Cruises* operate the *Princess Mahsuri* with links from Sydney, the Indonesian islands, Hong Kong, Manila and Japan. Another regular caller is the *Royal Viking Line's Pearl of Scandinavia.* There is also a twice-monthly service to Madras, India, via Penang on the *S.C.I.* ship *Chidamboram.* Several other major cruise lines include Singapore more infrequently.

By train: You can reach Singapore by train via Malaysia either from Bangkok, which is a two-and-a-half-day journey, or by six-hour train ride from Kuala Lumpur. First-class, reserved, air-conditioned compartments are comfortable and inexpensive. Second-class sleepers are also good—and *cheap.*

PASSPORTS, VISAS, AND HEALTH DOCUMENTS. Everyone must be in possession of a valid passport. Visa regulations are relaxed. Most nationalities are visa free for stays of up to 14 days without prior formalities. Travelers arriving from yellow fever infected areas are required to have valid international certificate of vaccination.

CUSTOMS. The usual international rules apply here, 200 cigarettes and one liter of spirits being permitted duty free. Puritanical customs officers may confiscate "lewd magazines" such as *Playboy, Penthouse,* etc. Rules against drugs are *very* strict.

AT THE AIRPORT. Formalities on arrival at Singapore's superb new Changi airport are smooth and efficient. Taxis cost about S$12–18 to downtown hotels. A surcharge of S$3 is added on the airport taxi fare. Departure tax is S$12 for international flights, $5 for journeys to Malaysia. Duty-free shops are available. A public bus service operates from the lower level of the airport, costing only S80 cents to Orchard Road. There is no transfer bus service to hotels.

CURRENCY. The currencies of Singapore and Brunei are almost interchangeable, with the Malaysian Ringgit worth a little less. It is legal to change money in the street, and often a better rate can be found than in hotels. Check the bank rate and then go to Change Alley or money-changing kiosks in major shopping centers, and bargain. There is no limit to the amount of money you may bring in. Banks are open 10–3 weekdays, 9:30–11:30 A.M. Saturdays. Credit cards are widely accepted. Current (mid-1985) exchange rates: S$2.15 = U.S.$1; S$2.60 = £1.

HOW TO GET AROUND. In Singapore, your best means of transportation will be by taxi, no longer cheap, but still the most convenient. Air-conditioned taxi charges are S$2 for the first 2 kilometers, plus about 10 cents for each additional 275 meters. Rates are for two, with each additional passenger or suitcase 10¢ more, and between midnight and 6 A.M., an additional 50 percent on metered fare. There are also surcharges for entering the restricted central zone of the city at certain times, and $3 for the journey from the airport. Before you start make sure your driver understands where you are going and the meter has been reset. For 24-hour radio-cab service, phone 452–5555.

MOTORING. To hire a self-drive car in Singapore one needs only an international license. Traffic is well disciplined and drives on the left.

Hire cars, some air-conditioned, or self-drive cars can be obtained from your hotel or a car agency. Street signs in English, a complete and comprehensive street guide, and a good map will keep the visiting driver from becoming hopelessly lost. Car rental costs start at S$60, which doesn't include gas. International firms—*Avis, Hertz,* etc.—offer the most reliable service, but if you're on a budget, investigate local car rental outfits, such as *Sintat.* A car with a driver in Singapore will cost from S$200 per day, but using taxis for individual journeys is just as easy, and cheaper.

Singapore is a compact island, and there are restrictions on cars entering the downtown area during rush hours, so self-drive car hire is really more trouble than it is worth. If one is proceeding to Malaysia, however, then driving oneself is a good way to go.

A Typical Day's Cost

Hotel, half double in moderate tourist hotel, including Continental breakfast, service charge, and tax:	S$150.00
Snack lunch in small outside coffee shop	12.00
Dinner in reasonable restaurant, table d'hôte (range S$25–50)	35.00
Taxis, two 2-mile journeys	8.00
Coffee in small café	1.50
Small beer in outside bar	4.00
Three-hour sightseeing tour by coach	22.00
Total	S$232.50

TIPPING. Tipping is now discouraged in Singapore as there is a 10 percent service charge and a 3 percent government tax added onto hotel and restaurant bills. Do not tip taxis. For baggage and small errands: S$1.

TIME. Singapore is 16 hours behind San Francisco, 13 hours behind New York and 8 hours ahead of London.

ACCOMMODATIONS. Singapore hotels offer more in terms of spacious and varied facilities, attractive décor, and friendly service than most European and American hotels in the same price range, but the strength of the S$ against other currencies has now made this a relatively expensive destination. A hotel reservations desk at Changi Airport can assist with bookings on arrival.

All the large, new hotels provide a full range of services. Most have a range of room styles and rates, usually designated as standard, superior, or deluxe. It is necessary to specify which grade you want or you will automatically be given the most expensive. The price ranges given are for standard double rooms and are in Singapore dollars, excluding 10% service and 3% tax.

Deluxe—$220–320

Century Park Sheraton. Superb luxury 464-room hotel in delightful setting, full range of facilities.

Dynasty. 400 superb new rooms, with full facilities in excellent Orchard Road location.

Goodwood Park. 300 rooms. Spacious grounds cover 15 acres and include three swimming pools and playground. Split-level suites, good restaurants. Prices deluxe, though facilities are first class. 22 Scotts Rd.

Hilton. 410 rooms. One of Singapore's busiest and best. *Rooftop Inn of Happiness* features Chinese food and cultural show. 581 Orchard Rd.

Hyatt. 824 rooms. Big and very busy; something's always going on. Good location and facilities. 10 Scotts Rd.

Mandarin Singapore. Towering 40 stories above Orchard Rd., this hotel has some of the most modern décor in Asia. 1,070 rooms.

Marco Polo. 600 rooms. Located near Cultural and Handicraft Center, Tanglin Rd.

Meridien. On Orchard Road. A sparklingly new 420 room hotel, with French flavor. Good restaurants, delightful rooms.

Ming Court. 1 Tanglin Rd., next to Tanglin Shopping Center. 300 rooms.

Pavilion Inter-continental. Magnificent, new, 440 rooms. Spectacular lobby, top-name shops, range of fine restaurants, and full facilities. 1 Cuscaden Rd.

Royal Holiday Inn. Good location across from Hyatt and next to Shaw Center. 600 rooms. Good coffee shop and full facilities.

Shangri-La. 700 rooms, all with a view of Singapore below. Just off Orchard Rd. Lovely swimming pool plus a small golf course. Nightclub and superb facilities.

Off Tanglin Rd.

First Class—$160–230

Cockpit. New wing with 15 stories dwarfs charming original Colonial-style building. 182 rooms. 6 Oxley Rise.

Equatorial. 225 rooms. Located in suburbs, about 10 minutes from Orchard Rd. 429 Bukit Timah Rd.

Ladyhill. Located in a cul-de-sac near the Shangri-La. Suites open onto the pool. Good for families. 180 rooms.

Oberoli Imperial. Location is a bit out of the way, but ambience and service are good. 550 rooms. 1 Jalan Rumbia.

Plaza. Located in an expanding commercial district near the new stadium. Good swimming pool. 260 rooms. 7500 Beach Rd.

Raffles. The grand old lady of Singapore. Style and old-fashioned service, but rooms and facilities somewhat run-down. 127 rooms.

Moderate—$85–170

Apollo. On Havelock Rd. near port area. 332 rooms.

Duke. Located near the new stadium. Ten minutes to town. 170 rooms.

Miramar. Next to Apollo. Clean, comfortable, unpretentious. 350 rooms.

Negara and **Cairnhill** are both good value, with limited facilities, but convenient locations at top end of Orchard Rd.

Novotel Orchid Inn. 320 rooms. Patterned after American motel. In residential area; offers family-style accommodations. 215 Dunearn Rd.

Peninsula. Located right in center of town. 315 rooms. Restaurants. Pool. 3 Coleman St.

Phoenix. Occupies part of a shopping and medical complex. 300 rooms. Somerset Rd.

Sea View. 435 rooms. 20 minutes from town, but provides transport for its guests. Pleasant restaurants. Amber Close.

Tai Pan. Ramada property located near town center. Rather spartan and plastic. 269 rooms. 101 Victoria St.

Inexpensive—$40–90

Several Chinese-style hotels have double rooms for about this price. Not all are air-conditioned. Among the best: *Station, New Mayfair,* Armenian St., *Hotel Ben,* Bencoolen St., *East Coast,* Upper East Coast Rd. There are also several YMCAs for around $50.

TOURIST INFORMATION. For further information and assistance, travelers will find the Singapore Tourist Promotion Board particularly helpful. Their head office is located at 131 Tudor Court, Tanglin Rd., Singapore 1024. Telephone 235–6611. Overseas offices can also be found in New York, San Francisco, London, Frankfurt, Sydney, Paris, Tokyo, Taipei, and Hong Kong, and representatives in Perth, Auckland, Seoul, and Zurich.

TOURS. The visitor with enough time can easily get to know the city on his own. City tours, which will give a hurried traveler a glimpse of the standard sights, are available. These may be booked through your hotel or by calling any tour agencies.

The best way to get an idea of what Singapore is really all about is to take a harbor tour. A range of harbor tours start from Clifford Pier or World Trade Centre pier. Morning or afternoon harbor cruises cost S$5–20, or one can visit Kusu or Sentosa Island by regular ferry. A harbor tour with a difference is provided by *Eastwind Tours* aboard their remodeled Chinese junk *Fairwind.* Drinks and buffet dinner make their Starlight Cruise a pleasant experience, S$36. A cultural show plus dinner at the old Raffles Hotel is a tourist "regular." The 45-minute "Instant Asia" show, held at Pasir Panjang every morning at 11:30, is included on most morning tours. Worth a visit is the Handicraft Center, also near the S.T.P.B. offices on Tanglin Rd. The Tiger Balm Gardens, Pasir Panjang Rd., is not always included on tours, but is well worth visiting.

GUIDES. The Singapore Tourist Promotion Board licenses guides, and one should always use these trained and official guides rather than amateur assistance. Beware of "touts" offering shopping or other services.

WARNING. The government of Singapore has strong rules on such "antisocial" matters as litter and jay-walking. Fines of up to S$500 can be, and are, imposed, even on visitors, so use litter bins and pedestrian crossings in "double yellow line" areas. Smoking is also discouraged in many public places and fines can be imposed, so check before lighting up. Some consider these rules a major source of irritation in Singapore, but it is part of having this as the most organized and disciplined tourist destination in the region. Most serious offenses of all are connected with drugs and narcotics; penalties are *very* high.

SPORTS. No city in Southeast Asia has as many golf courses as Singapore. With nine in all, six are available for play throughout the year. The best known is the Singapore Island Country Club at Upper Thompson Road. The newest course has been laid out at Sentosa. **Waterskiing** has become an increasingly popular sport. *Ponggol Boatel* will arrange to pick you up at your hotel and will provide boat, driver, and equipment. The charge is S$55 per hour for a boat which can hold up to five persons. There is **roller skating** on Sentosa. **Windsurfing** and **swimming** available in new East Coast Park Lagoon, and on Sentosa. Most hotels have good pools and a number of the newer ones offer health centers. **Sailing** can usually be arranged through the Changi yacht club.

Singapore has one of the most beautiful **race courses** in the world, and betting on the races is a favorite pastime with the gambling Chinese. Check the local paper to see if the races are being held in Singapore on the weekend. Ask the taxi to take you to the *Turf Club,* where you may get an entrance ticket for S$5. **Tennis** is popular, with courts available in sports complexes, clubs and at a few hotels. **Jogging** in the Botanical Gardens is delightful; some hotels issue jogging maps.

POLLUTION REPORT. Singapore has succeeded in creating a justified image as being the garden city of Asia. Its roadside gardens and parks are exquisitely maintained. But Singapore has also major industrial centers, such as at Jurong where one meets some air pollution. The offshore islands, with oil refineries and the many ships in the harbor also provide water pollution which spoils the island as a place for swimming, although the new artificially created lagoons have helped to ease this problem.

WATER. Tap water is safe everywhere.

MUSEUMS. *The National Museum* is open every day from 9 A.M. to 5:30 P.M. The Museum is a hodgepodge of history, art, and anthropology and contains the National Art Gallery and the superb Haw Par Jade Collection. *Coral* and *Maritime Museums,* on Sentosa, house a superb display of shells and sea life. Also on Sentosa is the Waxworks "Surrender Chambers."

SHOPPING. Singapore is a free port, there being neither purchase tax nor luxury tax (though there are protective duties to foster local industry).

Singapore wages a constant struggle with Hong Kong for the title "best shopping center in Asia." Prices are probably higher here now due to the S$ exchange rates. Hong Kong may claim a wider selection of electronic and photographic gear and watches, but Singapore is probably a better place for antiques, handicrafts and international boutique items.

In Singapore the range of imported manufactured items available at substantially lower prices than in America or Europe covers not only the obvious consumer items like calculators, movie and still cameras, watches, hi-fi equipment, radios, television sets, luggage, and household appliances, but also sporting goods such as golf clubs and scuba gear, technical and scientific instruments, cosmetics, perfumes, carpets, and leather goods. Singapore also offers an increasingly wide range of top-name boutique items from famous French, British, and Italian producers. Fashions, footwear, jewelry, pens, cigarette lighters and all the other items which are produced under the names of top-name houses are now available in Singapore, which has become much more fashion-conscious.

It is impossible to list here all the types of available merchandise, let alone to recommend specific shops to visitors. Instead we have set down below some of the major shopping areas and types of store through which one can browse. The longer that one can spend on comparative shopping in Singapore the better. Prices do vary considerably, even on "fixed-price" items, such as major makes of cameras and watches. Be very wary of any apparently large saving on a famous-name item: there are many imitations. Insist on a guarantee and receipt showing the name of the seller. The Singapore Tourist Promotion Board, will help if one has a genuine grievance over goods purchased from one of their member shops.

Department stores and the higher-class shops have fixed prices, and bargaining is out of order, but when you get down to the moderate and inexpensive price levels, haggling is expected. Avoid "shopping guides," touts who approach you in the streets and hotels and offer to take you to a particular shop.

Chinese Emporiums

Even if you don't get to Peking this time, you can bring back a bit of the new China from one of Singapore's well-stocked Chinese Emporiums. The People's Republic of China sends attractive, well-made, inexpensive products to the Singapore market. It is fascinating just to browse through the foods section and to look over the hardware, sewing machines, and household goods. Most visitors cannot resist some of the attractive brocades, or the embroidered tablecloths. Despite Singapore's tropical climate, the Emporiums carry limited stocks of heavy clothing which are a real bargain, although not always very stylish.

The *Chinese Emporium* in the International Building caters to the Singapore middle class and to tourists and carries the best assortment of clothing, laces, accessories, stamps, and knickknacks.

Chinese Emporium in *People's Park* is large and carries a wide range of goods. Here one can also find good restaurant and entertainment facilities.

Other Chinese emporiums are *Yuyi* on Orchard Rd., the *Oriental* in Raffles Place, *Klasse* in Lucky Plaza, Orchard Rd., and on High St.

Department Stores and Shopping Complexes

Perhaps one of the most amazing developments in Singapore over the past few years has been the incredible boom in the development of new shopping facilities. Time was when the major shopping areas were confined to Change Alley, Raffles Place, and the small shops along North Bridge Rd. Change Alley is still a fascinating experience and a "must" on any tour itinerary, although one really has to bargain hard, now, to get a good price, and the range of goods is not so wide. The economic "miracle" of booming Singapore has, however, produced half a hundred alternatives to the old stores.

Every hotel now has its own shopping arcade, and some of these are very extensive, although prices tend to be somewhat higher than can be found outside for the same items.

Among the most famous department stores are *Tang's* in Orchard Rd., now in a big new building, the Japanese *Isetan* on Havelock and Orchard Rds., the various branches of *Metro,* the *Specialist Center,* in Orchard Rd., and *Galleries Lafayette* in Goldhill Plaza, Thomson Rd. But even the largest department stores seem small beside the huge new shopping complexes, which seem to expand in number every month. There are now over a dozen large shopping centers along Orchard Rd. alone, and more are being opened in every part of Singapore. In these complexes one tends to find the exclusive boutiques for local and imported items as well as the main showrooms for big-name consumer products and jewelry. One of the best value complexes is People's Park. Many will accept credit cards and they tend to be more reliable over matters of guarantee, etc.

Antiques

Singapore has one big advantage over all Southeast Asian countries (except Hong Kong) in that it has few restrictions on the exportation of art and antiques. This makes it a better place to buy than, say, Indonesia or Thailand, whence old things may not be exported, legally, without a special permit. Opinions differ as to whether one can buy antiques more cheaply in Singapore than in other countries in the area. Generally one probably does pay more for *good* items, but one has less problems over export limitations and may have a better guarantee of authenticity. In this field, particularly, one really needs to know what one is buying, for investments can be considerable and the difference in value between the genuine and the fake can be very great.

Only a few years ago antique and curio shopping in Singapore was a matter of exploring back alleys and discovering wonderful little shops that nobody had ever heard of. Prosperity and the tourist invasion have exploded the myth of the ignorant trader in his torn shirt who reluctantly allows you to purchase a "bargain." He's revealed himself as the successful entrepreneur he always was, and is now usually to be found in an elegant shop on Orchard Rd. or in one of the new shopping complexes. Right now the Chinese, Thai, and Burmese antique market is booming. Prices are high and are rising. Most shopkeepers, however, are quite friendly to the browser and sympathetic to the tourist with a keen interest and a lean purse. Shops here tend to be more reliable about shipping purchases home than those in other Asian cities.

Handicrafts and Asian Art

Singapore is a vast storehouse for the arts and crafts of Asia. Here one can find, in department stores, shops, and market stalls the craftsmanship, best and worst, from every part of the region. Japan, Korea, China, Taiwan, Thailand, Malaysia, Indonesia, India—all are represented here with every type of creative work in any imaginable medium.

It is impossible to advise the visitor on where to find the best bargains. One could start, perhaps, in the hotel or big shopping complexes, then work down through the shops of North Bridge Rd., High St., Arab St., and Serangoon Rd. and the stalls of Change Alley, Chinatown, and Club Street. A good idea of the full range available can also be had in the Singapore Handicraft Center on Tanglin Rd.

Asian fabrics, such as batik, cotton or silk, are typical good-value buys, but there is also woven work in rattan or cane; metals, both precious and base; ceramics; wood; leather; ivory and gems. Stone, whether jade or soapstone, is unlimited in its carved variety as are glass, carpets and painting and prints on fabrics, paper or wood. The range and selections are unlimited; one needs only time and, of course, money!

DINING OUT. Food, glorious food! In Singapore you will eat yourself silly if you are not careful, because the city teems with superb restaurants in every price range. The variety is not limited to Oriental cuisine, either. Here you will find some of the best French and German cooking outside Europe. All schools of Chinese cooking are well represented from spicy Szechuanese to familiar Cantonese. Hotel coffee shops and cafés in shopping centers provide tasty quick lunches at reasonable prices. Because Singapore is a hotel-oriented town most gourmet dining, both Eastern and Western, is to be found in the larger hotels.

Food prices vary considerably in Singapore. In a top quality Western style restaurant, a table d'hote lunch can be S$60–80 per person, dinner S$70–100, excluding drinks. In a first class hotel coffee shop a set lunch would be around S$25 and dinner S$35. In an open air food stall one can have a filling meal for under S$10, including beer. All restaurants, but not all food stalls, charge 10% service charge and 3% government charge.

WESTERN CUISINE

Beefeater. River Valley Rd. Offers authentic British pub atmosphere, draft beer and good lunches.

1819. Tuan Sing Towers, 30 Robinson Rd. Currently perhaps the best eating place in Singapore. Traditional atmosphere, excellent menu, and calm, good service.

Elizabethan Grill. At the Raffles Hotel. Also The Palm Court for elegant dining under the stars. A favorite with foreign residents, the service retains its colonial flavor amid opulent décor. Food is excellent and not oversauced as in many European-style restaurants. Moderately expensive.

Maxim's de Paris. Pavilion Inter-continental hotel. Superb French food, but expensive.

Frisco Grill. Orchard Towers, opposite the Hilton. All imported U.S. beef, pricey but excellent.

Gordon Grill. At the Goodwood Hotel. Another local favorite for steak and convivial atmosphere. Fresh oysters here are really fresh or else they do not offer them. Moderately expensive.

Harbour Grill. Hilton Hotel. Good French cuisine in plush surroundings.

Hugo's. At the Hyatt. Elaborate French menu and wine list. Food lives up to elegant surroundings.

La Rotonde. Marco Polo Hotel. Patterned after famous Gaddi's in Hong Kong. Food is French cooking at its best. Expensive.

La Taverna. Emerald Hill Rd., off Orchard Rd. near Cold Storage, also DBS Building, Shenton Way. Everything Italian from its décor to its anchovies.

Mövenpick. Scott's Building, 6 Scotts Rd. In heart of shopping-complex land, the Swiss chain has opened a delightful restaurant offering excellent, reasonably priced food. Daily set menus recommended.

Pete's Place. In the Hyatt Hotel. Good for Italian food.

The Stables. Mandarin Hotel. Quiet, masculine atmosphere. Usually has excellent food. Expensive.

Troika. In DBS Building, Shenton Way. With harbor view. Russian food; *borscht* and *shashlik* served in quiet surroundings. Moderately expensive.

Nutmegs. Hyatt Hotel. Art deco surroundings, American menu, live jazz on Sundays.

CHINESE CUISINE

The term "Chinese food" covers a wide range indeed. A visitor to Singapore can sample varied schools of cooking at different restaurants. He should also try some of the food at the stalls in the night markets. At lunchtime he might want to pop into one of the many restaurants featuring *dim sum:* tasty steamed and fried tidbits prepared by Cantonese cooks.

Ordering food in a Chinese restaurant can be a frustrating and bewildering experience. Before you settle for just sweet and sour pork and fried rice look over the whole menu. You will see that the restaurant is geared to serving groups, rather than individuals. Dishes are listed according to size. In most places a small order serves four to six; medium is enough for six to eight; large feeds eight to twelve people. (It is linguistically impossible to order "sweet and sour for two" . . . you will be served a "small.") Look at the menu and decide how many dishes you want. It is customary to order according to the meat. Thus, if you have sweet and sour pork, you will want a bland chicken dish and a beef dish with vegetables. Sweet soups (such as sharks' fin) are served as a first or second course. Clear or "sour" soups are served toward the end of the meal. Some restaurants also offer set menus, supplying a range of dishes suitable for two or more.

Cantonese

Ming Palace. Ming Court Hotel. Lunchtime *dim sum* for shoppers who are weary after a morning along Orchard Rd.

Neptune Theater Restaurant. Essentially a supper club catering to wealthy Chinese. The food is good and the entertainment an interesting introduction to Chinese pop entertainers.

New Hong Kong. Taipan Hotel. Good view of Singapore harbor and speedy service. Noisy, but the food is good.

Paradise. By the sea at Pasir Panjang. Specialty is chili crab—delicious, but messy!

Shang Palace. Shangri-La Hotel. Serves a wide variety of subtly spiced dishes. Crowded at lunch for their fabulous *dim sum.*

Peking/Shanghai

Mayflower. In the International Building on Orchard Rd. Long established as a Singapore favorite for *dim sum,* it is also recognized as one of the best Cantonese restaurants in town with a few Peking specialties.

Pine Court. Mandarin Hotel. Superb, but expensive. Specialties Peking duck and baked tench.

Peking

Prima Tower. Revolving restaurant, in Keppel Rd., has good Pekingese food plus fine, changing views of city and harbor.

Szechuan

Golden Phoenix. Equatorial Hotel. Spicy dishes made with red chili peppers. Also sour cabbage soup. In the evening a Chinese classical orchestra plays light selections.

Great Shanghai. Armenian St., sparse décor but very popular with local people, for excellent Szechuan and Cantonese cuisine. Try drunken chicken, roast Szechuan duck, sliced beef with chili.

Hua Palace. Specialists' Center, Orchard Rd. Try the fish stew or smoked duck.

Inn of Happiness. Top floor of Hilton Hotel. Expensive but excellent range of Szechuanese specialties.

Omei. At Hotel Grand Central between Orchard Rd. and Clemenceau Ave. Hard to find but worth it once you're there! Genuine Szechuan food with no concessions made to tender Western palates. Watch those red chilis.

INDIAN CUISINE

Singapore has several first-rate Indian restaurants, both Northern and Southern. In addition to air-conditioned, classy restaurants with tablecloths and bar service in well-decorated Oriental atmosphere, there are several foodshops where the waiters wear dirty shirts, there is one lazy fan and the food is marvelous and cheap. In the vegetarian restaurants, where your food will be served on a banana leaf, you will eat to your heart's content for S$5. The best known are: **Komala Vilas** on Serangoon Rd., **Sri Krishna Vilas** on Selegie Rd., and **India Coffee House,** Market St. For tasty *murtaba* and curry try the **Victory** and **Islamic** on North Bridge Rd., **Motimahal** on Murray St.

Banana Leaf Apollo. At Race Course Road. To eat with one's fingers, off a banana leaf plate, superb meat, fish or vegetarian curries is a gastronomic delight.

Omar Khayam. Hill St. Superb North Indian specialties. Tandoor chicken, mutton curries, and *nan* (a special baked bread).

Rang Mahal. Oberoi Hotel. Chefs from Delhi prepare tandoor dishes, including fish, in a special oven visible to diners. Pleasant décor, friendly service, with regular classical Indian musical performances.

OTHER CUISINES

Indonesian

Borobudur, Goldhill Square, 101 Thomson Rd; **Elizabethan Grill,** Raffles Hotel; **Cempaka,** International Plaza, Anson Rd.; **Indonesian Restaurant,** Apollo Hotel, Anson Rd.; **Ramayana,** Plaza Singapura, Orchard Rd., all serve Indonesian specialties such as chicken and beef curries, *udang sambal* (prawns), *gado gado* salad.

Rendezvous, Bras Bason Rd., is cheap, but good.

Japanese

Kampachi. Hotel Equatorial. Very Japanese. Sit on the floor. Exquisite service and food presented in Japanese manner.

Okoh. Supreme House. In addition to *sashimi* and *tempura,* this restaurant serves Korean-style barbecue.

Unkai. In the Century Park Sheraton hotel. Expensive, but very popular with visiting Japanese, who know what is good.

Also: **Tsuru-no-ya,** Mandarin Hotel, a favorite with visiting Japanese; **Shima Japanese Restaurant** in the Goodwood Park Hotel, and **Atami** in Yaohan supermarket, Plaza Singapura, Orchard Rd. **Yamagen,** Yen San Building, Orchard Rd. **Hoshigaoka-Saryo,** Apollo Hotel, Havelock Rd. Cheap set menus, especially popular for lunch.

Korean

Han Do. In the Orchard Shopping Center, Orchard Rd. Popular Korean restaurant.

Korean. Specialists Center, Orchard Rd. Serves a spicy *kim chee* and beef barbecue.

Korean Barbeque. In the People's Park, Eu Tong Sen St.

Malay

For good Malay food, try the open-fronted coffee shops on Tanglin Road, or the food stalls at Empress Place. **Azizah's Restaurant,** or **Longtong House,** both in Emerald Hill Rd., offer rather classier surroundings. **Rumah Melaka.** Far East Shopping Centre, Scotts Rd., offers good value Chinese Malay food. In all of them, the basic rice is eaten with side dishes of fish, beef, prawns, and vegetables, rich curries or spiced with chilis, onions, and tamarind. The tiny deep-fried dried fish, *ikan bilis,* are wonderful as an appetizer with beer.

Thai

Thai Restaurant, Bencoolen St., **Siamese Seafood Restaurant,** in the Cockpit Hotel and **D'Jitpochana** in Hotel Taipan serve this spicy style of food.

Seafood

Kheng Luck Seafood. Upper East Coast Rd. An old bungalow converted and serving fresh seafood in local styles. Chili crab a specialty.

Singha Inn. East Coast Pkwy. Dining is under thatched roofs in this simple environment, serving good Siamese and Cantonese dishes.

Seafood International. In the Big Splash recreation park on East Coast Rd.

Vegetarian

Kwan Inn. 190, Waterloo St. Range of Eastern and Western vegetarian specialties.

FOOD STALLS AND STREET MARKETS

Singapore's most famous food experiences are the various food markets. Each hawker cooks one or two special dishes and you can choose from Malaysian *satay,* spicy barbecued meat on a skewer; Hokkien *mee,* fried noodles with prawns, pork, and vegetables; *pao,* steamed doughy white buns filled either with grilled pork bits or a sweetened bean paste; *muhrtaba,* Indian egg and flour pancake with a chopped meat stuffing served with a curry sauce; *Hainanese chicken and rice,* steamed chicken and broth with a delicate ginger flavor; *kway teow,* white or yellow noodles, either fried or as a soup, with fish balls, or shreds of meat, and bean sprouts.

Each hawker has a "territory," so first pick out one dish you want. Sit down and the proprietor or one of his small helpers will come and take your order. Then, one person in your party should go to the other stalls and ask for whatever appeals (pointing is perfectly permissible), making sure the cook knows where the diners are seated. The food will be brought to you. Most stalls display their prices and in most cases you will now be asked to pay when you are served. Dishes range from a dollar or so per plate, up to twenty or more for the most expensive, such as large prawns in chili sauce.

There are several market stall "eateries" around town frequented by foreigners. One of the best is **Newton Circus** where you can get every type of Asian food from over a hundred stalls. Another is at the **Rasa Singapura,** behind the Handicraft Center in Tanglin Rd.; a wide variety of Asian foods offered. Try also **Satay Club,** by the harbor on Elizabeth Walk, and the **Telok Ayer Market,** a converted Victorian-period vegetable market on Shenton Way—Chinese or Indian dishes from individual stalls. A superb, cheap lunch.

NIGHT LIFE. There are lively but expensive nightclubs or discothèques in most top hotels. Those in the Hyatt, Mandarin, Shangri-La, Hilton, Marco Polo, and Sheraton hotels are among the best. Supper clubs, such as the *Belvedere* in the Mandarin Hotel, feature pop singers and comedians. Popular with tourists is the *Neptune Theater Restaurant* and the *Tropicana,* which offers food and spectacular shows. One can have a variety of Asian cultural shows with appropriate dinner at places like the Hyatt, Mandarin, and Raffles hotels. Prices range from S$30 for show only and $50 upwards, to include buffet dinner.

New features of the entertainment scene are the theater restaurants, showing good plays, usually comedies from London, in hotels such as the Hilton and Shangri-La.

MAIL, TELEPHONE AND TELEGRAPH. Hotel mail service is always reliable. Airmail letter to Europe is 75 cents Singapore; to Australia and Japan 50 cents, and to the United States S$1.00. Airmail cards to U.S. are 55 cents, to Europe 40 cents, Australia 25 cents. Aerograms to anywhere, 35 cents.

Overseas phone calls may be booked through your hotel but most charge a handling fee, sometimes unreasonably high. Telegrams and telex may be sent at the Post Offices or from major hotels (24-hour service).

MEDICAL SERVICE. Health care is exceptionally good. *Singapore General Hospital* receives emergency cases, tel. 222–3322. All hotels have doctors on 24 hour call.

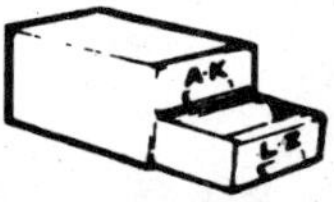

USEFUL ADDRESSES. Singapore Tourist Promotion Board. Tudor Court, Tanglin Rd. (tel. 235–6611). Tourism has become a major industry in Singapore and the government works hard to keep the customers satisfied. The Tourist Promotion Board maintains an information desk where attractive receptionists dole out attractive brochures and useful information. The Center is open daily from 8 to 5 weekdays, Saturdays 8 to 1, closed Sunday and public holidays.

Embassies and High Commissions. *Australia,* 25 Napier Road; *Canada,* 8th floor, Faber House, Orchard Rd.; *Great Britain,* Tanglin Rd.; *U.S.,* 30 Hill St; *Thailand,* 370 Orchard Rd.; and *Malaysia,* 301 Jervois Rd.

Emergency Phone. Police, fire, ambulance, dial 999.

INDONESIA

Tourist Paradise and Traveler's Despair

The modern traveler gets an impression of Indonesia's riches as he approaches the capital of Jakarta, on the northwest coast of Java, by plane. First he glimpses some offshore islands, rich green against the sea, and then he sees the orange tile rooftops of Jakarta, surrounded by verdant woods, fields and glistening rice paddies. Java is the richest, most heavily populated of Indonesia's 13,677 islands, stretching some 3,000 miles from Sumatra to Irian Jaya, uniting the Indian and the Pacific oceans and Australia with Southeast Asia. Once the source of exotic spices for European nobility, Indonesia in modern times supplies the world with oil, tea, rubber, spices, tin, and a host of other products. The home of over 360 tribal and ethnic groups, Indonesia today is governed largely by proud and cultivated Javanese, who comprise about 60 percent of the population, plus a smattering of powerful leaders from the outer islands.

Indonesia, throughout its recorded history, has been involved with maritime trade and the import of external religious, cultural, and ethnic influences.

Hindu and Buddhist elements, introduced from India, built great empires based in South Sumatra and Java, which spread their maritime power far abroad, even to Thailand and Indo-China. The riches of these empires led to enormous creative and artistic energies and centuries of relative peace. The introduction of the Islamic faith by Arab and Malay seafarers in the 9th century gradually changed social control from the Indo-originating faiths and the Hindu communities gradually retreated to the East up to the 15th century when Majapahit, the last and greatest of the Hindu-Javanese empires, succumbed to rising Muslim kingdoms. Only in Bali were they finally allowed to stay, and where the remains of the Hindu faith in Indonesia is still found today. Elements of all the varied cultural stages of history still remain, however, in the hearts and minds of most Indonesians. They have absorbed many outside forces and molded them into their local characters.

Other important influences were the Chinese, who have traded into Indonesia from as early as the 2nd century B.C. and the later, if more imperially minded Europeans—Portuguese, Spanish, Dutch, and British. The Dutch exploited the riches of Indonesia for over 300 years, after the formation of their East India Company, almost monopolizing the rich spice trade which was the archipelago's major attraction for all foreign traders.

After the Japanese occupation independence brought Indonesia the chance to develop its resources for its own benefit, but many growing pains have beset the community and, in spite of its huge potential wealth, it still has problems to sort out. With economic expansion, however, have come better facilities for the foreign visitor in terms of first-class hotel accommodations, transportation, shopping and restaurants. Since late 1984, tourism has been given top priority, in an effort to move it behind oil as the number 2 foreign exchange earner. Steps are being taken to open Bali to more foreign airlines, and new areas are being developed as tourist destinations.

Jakarta's new airport at Cengkareng opened in 1985 and caters to international and domestic flights. Located 20 kms west of the city, it is linked by new highways which have been built to bypass more congested areas.

The Years of Independence

Understanding the string of changes which this country has gone through since it proclaimed its national independence on August 17, 1945, is imperative to fathom modern Indonesia. Although the national constitution provides for a strong executive somewhat in the style of that of the United States of America, the young nation began its history, under internal political pressures, as a parliamentary democracy. The president was a mere figurehead, while the real executive power rested in the hands of a prime minister accountable to parliament. Squabbles and bickerings soon arose among the proliferating political parties, still unaccustomed to the responsibilities of democracy.

The fifties were known as a period of political instability. Cabinets fell and were replaced in rapid succession and the republic was torn by secessionist rebellions. The national economy deteriorated rapidly.

In 1955, the first general elections held in Indonesia failed to bring the much hoped for stability and the next year President Sukarno declared a policy of Guided Democracy. Reinstating the 1945 Constitution, which was amended and replaced during the years of liberal

KAMPUCHEA
(Cambodia)
VIETNAM
Ho Chi Minh City
THAILAND
South China Sea
PENANG
WEST MALAYSIA
Kuala Lumpur
EAST MALAYSIA
Medan
Lake Toba
Singapore
SAR
Nias
Padang
KALIM
SUMATRA
Palembang
Teluk Betung
Java Sea
Jakarta
MADURA
Surabaya
JAVA
Yogyakarta

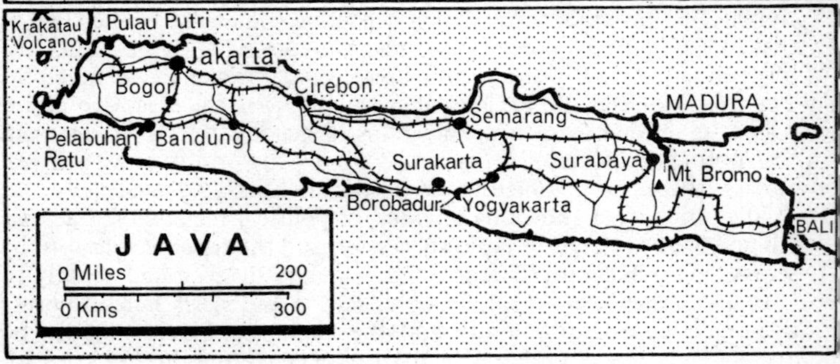
Krakatau Volcano
Pulau Putri
Jakarta
Bogor
Cirebon
Semarang
MADURA
Pelabuhan Ratu
Bandung
Surakarta
Surabaya
Mt. Bromo
Borobadur
Yogyakarta
BALI
JAVA
0 Miles 200
0 Kms 300

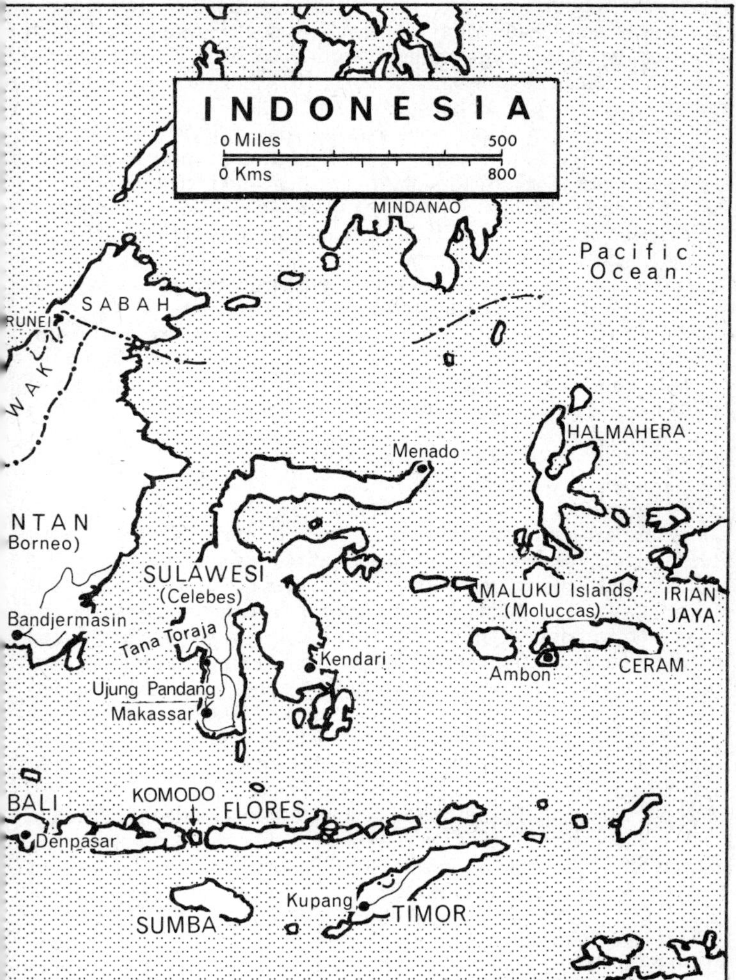
INDONESIA
0 Miles 500
0 Kms 800
MINDANAO
Pacific Ocean
SABAH
RUNEI
WAK
HALMAHERA
Menado
NTAN
Borneo)
SULAWESI
(Celebes)
MALUKU Islands
(Moluccas)
IRIAN JAYA
Bandjermasin
Tana Toraja
Kendari
Ambon
CERAM
Ujung Pandang
Makassar
BALI
KOMODO
FLORES
Denpasar
Kupang
TIMOR
SUMBA
Darwin
Indian Ocean
AUSTRALIA

democracy, Sukarno made himself the effective Head of Government as well as Head of State. Many political parties which opposed the new policy of the Sukarno government were disbanded. The legislatures were "streamlined" by the hand-picking of their members by President Sukarno and voting was abolished.

As Sukarno's power increased, however, his policies began to veer more and more toward the left. The late fifties and early sixties were known as a period of leftist revolutionary élan which proved fertile for the spectacular growth of the Indonesian Communist Party, the PKI. By the middle of the 1960s, the Communist Party had well over 3,000,000 card-holding members. The PKI could also claim some 20,000,000 followers in scores of Communist-front organizations, from student groups to artists and writers.

In the early hours of October 1, 1965, the Communist Party supposedly saw itself compelled to launch a pre-emptive coup d'état in the midst of rumors of President Sukarno's illness. Communist-trained agents kidnapped six army generals and one officer from their Jakarta homes and took them to a wooded spot at Crocodile Hole near Halim airbase, where mobs of Communist cadre executed them and threw their mutilated bodies into a well.

The assassinations were meant to precede a coup d'état in which the Communists began by setting up a "Revolutionary Council," with Sukarno still president, and take over control of the entire country. In fact, General Suharto, now the country's president and then a major general, swiftly rounded up support against the Communist troops and drove them out of the capital. Then the Indonesian army, spearheaded by red-bereted paracommandoes, decimated Communist forces in Central and Eastern Java, two areas where they were said to have considerable strength. The armed forces soon had the backing of the overwhelming majority of Indonesia's Muslims, who turned against the Communists in virtually every part of the country and slaughtered them by the thousands. The number of persons killed from October, 1965, to February, 1966, has never been determined with any certainty, but estimates have ranged from 100,000 to one million. Most journalists and diplomats have settled on 300,000 as the best guess. No matter how you figure it, the purge was the bloodiest single defeat for Communism in the history of the Communist movement.

President Sukarno, lost in the dream of the "Great Revolution" which he so often had propounded, refused to abandon his policies. In speech after speech he proclaimed his faith in socialism and refused to act against Communists in key positions in his cabinet. Gradually, however, General Suharto and his allies rounded up enough political power to strip Sukarno first of his authority and then of his titles. Sukarno's most faithful political allies, notably Dr. Subandrio, the foreign minister who had forged the alliance with China, were jailed and later tried and sentenced to death for their alleged roles in the coup. Sukarno, in March, 1966, was forced to sign a decree transferring his power to General Suharto and outlawing the Communist Party. The People's Consultative Congress, Indonesia's highest policy-making body, removed Sukarno's title of "President for life" and finally, in early 1967, voted him entirely out of office, and he remained out of the public eye until his death in 1970. The Congress the same year named Suharto as acting president and, a year later (March, 1968), elected him as president.

The fall of Bung—for "brother"—Karno brought about vast changes in Indonesia's policies. First, the country in the spring of 1966 began to make overtures for private foreign investment, an element of capitalism that Sukarno had officially abhorred and discouraged. Next, after a bitter struggle, Suharto and Indonesia's new foreign minister, Adam Malik, forced Sukarno to abandon his costly policy of diplomatic and military confrontation against Malaysia. After a series of secret diplomatic missions, Indonesia resumed trade relations with Singapore, also cut off by "confrontation," and then, in late 1966, joined in an agreement to "normalize" relations with Malaysia. At almost the same time, Indonesia also rejoined the United Nations, from which Sukarno had withdrawn his country in early 1965.

Indonesia's post-Sukarno generation of leaders has now been in control long enough so that its achievements can be analyzed. General Suharto and his colleagues have succeeded in bringing the economy back from the brink of bankruptcy and have attracted a phalanx of foreign investors. The runaway inflation of the Sukarno years has been checked and the rupiah is a stable currency.

Despite Indonesia's economic success, life for the ordinary citizen still needs to be improved. The average per capita income is around US $600 a year. As in many countries, Indonesia faces a widening gap between rich and poor with the country's oil wealth and new industrial development tending to benefit the wealthiest classes.

Indonesia's economy has recently been affected by the declining price of oil and other export commodities, and other sources of revenue are being sought to cover costs of ongoing national development projects. Consequently, Indonesia, with Suharto as president, is paying serious attention to tourism and formulating new policies. For the first time, tourism affairs have been elevated to the ministerial level, incorporated into the Department of Tourism, Post, and Telecommunications.

Indonesian people are friendly toward foreigners, and except perhaps in a few obvious "tough" areas, the foreigner is probably safer walking around than he is in his home town. Even if violence against foreigners is rare, they are not altogether free from occasional pickpockets. So the visitor should be careful, both in Jakarta and provincial towns.

Indonesia's most consistent problem since independence has still been that of intramural squabbling—Sumatrans against Javanese, modern against traditional Muslims, Muslims against Communists. And yet the Indonesians, despite the quarrels that always threaten to shatter their nation, have traits in common. Most of them are basically Malay in ethnic background, with brown complexions, wide open faces, flat noses, round, dark eyes and wavy hair. Most of them are polite and will extend endless courtesies to foreigners whom they trust and like. Most of them, in the years since independence, have developed a sense of national pride and deep sensitivity, capable of inspiring the most profound national hatred or the warmest devotion. On the other side,

Indonesians also have the reputation for a frustrating combination of inefficiency and inertia. All too often the tourist will find that service is poor and dining inadequate except at luxury hotels.

And still Indonesia remains a source of wonder and awe. Since the country reopened to Western tourists and journalists, they have arrived in increasing numbers despite all the inconveniences of travel and service, year-round heat and seasonal monsoons. In their stubborn desire to savor Indonesia's beauties and riches, the controversial Westerners are following a trail blazed by Marco Polo, who arrived nearly seven centuries ago in search of Oriental spices and other wonders of the East. And Marco Polo himself followed visitors from all the important Asian countries, to which Indonesia owes its basic racial, religious and cultural heritage. It would be quite in keeping with the mercurial Indonesian character, once humiliated by three centuries of Dutch colonialism, to turn against the new wave of foreign influence. It is not at all unlikely that a fresh generation of Indonesian nationalists will eventually rise up to oppose the renascent influence of American, Japanese, and other foreign investment. In the meanwhile, the doors to Indonesia are open, tourist and Customs officials are smiling again, and the country's wonders are yours for the asking.

EXPLORING INDONESIA

Today, Indonesia has put aside her preoccupation with politics and is busy getting on with the business of development, including the expansion of tourism. Improved communications and new tourist facilities make both inter- and intra-island travel easier; however, you should be prepared to encounter some delays and inconveniences, particularly if you are interested in visiting the less tourist-frequented areas. Nonetheless, if you have time and some flexibility, you will be rewarded by your contacts with the lush tropical landscape, rich and ancient cultures, and a warm and friendly people. Perhaps the most pleasant way to begin after your arrival in Jakarta, where most visitors enter Indonesia, is by a drive across the western end of Java to Pelabuhan Ratu on the southern coast. The city of Jakarta has vastly improved in appearance during the past few years. It does contain, however, plenty of sightseeing to occupy a 2- to 3-day itinerary, with several worthwhile side trips. On the way to Pelabuhan Ratu (a three-hour trip if you go nonstop) one can see Bogor, a little city nestled in the foothills of the extinct volcano Salak and the active but dormant Pangrango and Gedeh, visible on a clear day from Jakarta. The ride to Bogor over the new toll road takes about half an hour. In these highlands you will see farmers tending their vegetable plots and rice paddies and workers on farms and plantations—or else dense green forests occasionally broken by thatched-roof or simple brick homes.

As you reach Bogor, make a sharp right turn to come out on the main road leading to the famed Bogor Botanic Gardens. Following the road which circles these gardens you will eventually confront the enormous, white-painted porticoed mansion set several hundred yards back from the road, behind a front lawn crowded with grazing deer and tall oak trees. You are looking at the palace once occupied by Indonesia's Dutch governors general, now a retreat for the country's presidents. It is here in Bogor that Sukarno gave his most lavish parties and often presided over cabinet meetings. Sukarno took special pains to ensure that the grounds were as neatly manicured under his rule as they were during the era of Dutch colonialism. He kept statues put up by the Dutch and added some of his own, with an emphasis on the female figure. Although Sukarno inherited deer from the Dutch who nurtured them for venison banquets, he banned the killing of deer on the palace grounds and let the flock multiply to almost a hundred head.

The palace may now be visited by arrangement, which is easiest done through a good travel agent. If you cannot get the opportunity to view the inside of the palace and its immediate grounds, it is easy to gain access to the Botanic Gardens, which occupy some 217.5 acres and back up to the palace. The gardens, famous throughout the world, were first inaugurated in 1817 and now include some 15,000 species of plants. Attached to them is a zoological museum and a library containing some 60,000 volumes. It also has an orchid house with 3,000 registered hybrids. The gardens were originally laid out at the orders of Sir Thomas Stamford Raffles, who was lieutenant governor of Java and its Dependencies during the short British colonial period, prior to his establishing Singapore.

Across the Puncak

After Bogor, the road starts twisting through hills and then through deep mountain passes and terraced rice paddies. Here in the Puncak Hill Resort well-to-do Indonesians and foreigners spend their weekends in hundreds of well-kept cottages and estates. You see swimming pools and tourist lodges, often almost completely empty during weekdays, but full on weekends. From here, the mountain range rises to heights of around 10,000 feet, dominated by Mount Pangrango and Mount Gedeh, both active, but dormant volcanoes, and Mount Salak. Flower- and plant-lovers may wish to stop at Cibodas, on the shoulders of Mt. Gedeh, where the Botanical Gardens has a separate branch for species that cannot stand the warm temperatures of Bogor. Small signs on the road southeast of Bogor point the traveler either toward Bandung, the capital of West Java, or to Pelabuhan Ratu. Turning right toward Pelabuhan Ratu, you drive through more mountains, sometimes along a road that is spectacular but pocketed with potholes. Two or three hours later, you cross a final crest of hills and before you, like a mirage in the distance, stretches the turquoise blue of the Indian Ocean, its waves forming a narrow band of white on the sandy yellow beaches.

The drive to Pelabuhan Ratu takes about 3 hours and can be done by taxi or rented car. In Pelabuhan Ratu you can stay in the Samudra Beach Hotel, swim in its pool and soak up sun and atmosphere to your heart's content, but never, *never* go more than chest-deep in the ocean. The reason is that the beach suddenly drops off, and a sharp undertow can then carry even the strongest swimmer to his death. The waters, what's more, are infested with sharks, which more than once have darted in to attack a tempting human target. Signs warn swimmers away and tourist officials have considered remodeling part of the beach to protect against both sharks and drop-off. But it's not likely that Indonesia will soon invest in such a scheme, especially since the excellent Samudra Beach Hotel is nearly empty (except on weekends) and is losing money. For variety, you can drive along the rough, unpaved roads near the beach or hike to Cisolok hot springs. There is also a small fishing village with a flourishing fishermen's market, seen at its best early in the morning.

Bandung and Yogyakarta

Without returning to Jakarta, you can reach Bandung from Pelabuhan Ratu in three to four hours by car. The seat of the Afro-Asian Conference in 1955, Bandung is a famous educational and cultural center and also the home of Indonesia's quinine industry, which depends on the bark of cinchona grown on nearby plantations. Bandung, in sharp contrast to Jakarta, exudes a distinct charm. Its streets are wide and lined with trees and its downtown shopping area neat and efficient. Bandung's citizens, totaling one and a half million, often take a patronizing attitude toward their countrymen in other large cities. Reflections of their high-spirited outlook are their dress, which runs to flowery shirts and batiks, and their choice of food, which includes carp caught in nearby ponds and *tape,* or fermented rice, or cassava roots. At 2,000 feet above sea level Bandung is relatively cool and pleasant. Be sure to drive to the *Tangkuban Perahu* (Upside Down Boat) crater 12 miles north of Bandung, where you can see steam escaping from the volcano or view the panoramic Sundanese countryside. Bandung is also the home of one of the most famous forms of Javanese puppet play, the *Wayang Golek.* The elaborately carved and painted figures make wonderful souvenirs.

After Bandung, you have a choice. Should you go to Central Java by the northern, coastal route or drive through the mountains, across the center of the island? Most chauffeurs would by far prefer the former. The road, while potholed in parts, is generally better kept and certainly flatter. The difficulty, however, is that the scenery assumes a dull sameness after you leave the mountains, while the latter route offers the variety of sweeping views, rich landscape and thickly populated villages. One can take a ten-hour train journey to get the same superb views, but the trains have no first-class seats and the trip can seem long and hot in the sometimes crowded carriages. Either way, your goal at the end of a hard day's journey is Yogyakarta, the home of Sultan Hamengku Buwono. If you decide to take the coastal road, the *kratons* (palaces) in Cirebon are of interest. The Kesepuhan *kraton* of the Sultan of Cirebon has a museum of ancient arms and Islamic carvings. In the carriage house see the rather strange carriages, one of which is in the shape of an elephant head with wings. The custodian will open the museum for visitors and a small donation is expected. Note the Chinese porcelain inset in the walls and Dutch Delft tiles portraying biblical stories in this former stronghold of Islam. Opposite the *kraton* is the Grand Mosque with the Javanese "meru" roof architecture.

The royal graves at Astana Gunung Jati, five miles out of town, tell the story of Sultan Gunung Jati and his Chinese wife. Chinese porcelain vases and plates which were brought by the Chinese princess in the 15th century are kept in the museum and some are placed among graves and on the walls.

Also see the port area with its brightly colored fishing boats, old East India Co. warehouses and those of the tobacco companies. Known for its seafood, particularly shrimp, try the local food at Lembur Kuring or seafood at Chinese restaurants.

Yogyakarta, a focal point of Javanese culture, is a city of about 300,000 people, whose residents take a deep pride in its heroic past. The sultanate of Yogyakarta was born in 1756 after a rebellion against the increasing Dutch encroachment on the integrity of the once-mighty kingdom of Mataram. Then, from 1824 to 1830, Prince Diponegoro led a bitter war against the Dutch which ended only when the prince was tricked into surrender. During the 1940s, the city was the heart of Indonesia's war for independence. Indeed, "Yogya" became the capital of the newborn republic when returning Dutch troops occupied Jakarta after the Japanese surrender at the end of World War II.

Yogya is at present a separate administrative region—an enclave in the province of Central Java but not legally part of it. The sultanate's special status reflects in part the prestige of Sultan Hamengku Buwono, whose staunch support for the republic during the war of independence is legendary. The sultan allowed the Indonesian republican guerillas, including General Suharto, now the nation's president and at that time a lieutenant colonel, use his vast palace or *kraton* as a base. The Dutch, although they occupied the city for less than a year, dared not move against the sultan for fear of arousing the anger of millions of Javanese, to whom he was a heroic, almost godlike figure.

The sultan's palace contains a vast number of elegant pavilions with ornate gilded pillars and beams, carved in delicate designs. Here, the sacred royal heirlooms are kept. During certain Muslim holidays, the sultan's palace becomes the focal point of elaborate traditional ceremonies known as "Sekaten." The *kraton* is open to the public every morning except on Muslim holidays. Across the palace square or *alun-alun* there is a good museum (closed on Mondays).

Yogyakarta is perhaps best known among foreign visitors for the beautiful ancient Hindu and Buddhist temple sites which surround it, for its *wayang kulit* shadow plays and dance dramas, as well as for its silver and leather work and batik cloth. Shops along the main street, Malioboro, sell all these products at lower prices than those found in Jakarta and other large cities. Silver craftsmen in nearby Kota Gedeh execute intricate designs, reflections of Java's ancient past by punching patterns on the metal supported by wax. Another favorite product is the kris, a wavy-bladed dagger used in traditional ceremonies. Yogyakarta has a number of factories where batik is made by etching colors into cloth. The traditional form and most valued batik is drawn by hand by women. The newer technique of block printing was introduced in the twenties. Yogya leather, made from dried and smoked buffalo hide, also comes in intricate patterns and is used for a variety of purposes ranging from simple decorations to fans, luggage, purses, shoes and *wayang kulit* puppets.

It happens that Central Java was the center of some of the most violent conflicts between Communists and Muslims after the Communist coup in 1965 and was a hotbed of Communist activity. But you won't see a trace of violence or sense any danger at all as you tour the region in search of ancient attractions, the cultural survivors of centuries of wars and upheavals. The most impressive of all the local sights is Borobudur, a mass of carved stone and rock rising in nine terraces atop a hill 30 miles northwest of Yogya. Built by Central Java's rulers in the ninth century, Borobudur was abandoned soon after completion and started to crumble and was covered with centuries of volcanic ash and overgrowth when discovered in 1814. It was later reconstructed by Dutch archeologists. Borobudur, the largest Buddhist temple in the world, includes delicate stonecarving depicting Buddhist scenes as well as massive images of Buddha. The temple, after massive restoration which took more than ten years, was partly destroyed by terrorist bombing in December 1984. Nine of the latticed Buddhas were bombed and the main stupa was struck by lightning two weeks later. Repairs are expected to be completed by 1986.

Other architectural wonders near Yogya include the Mendut Temple, only two miles away from Borobudur, with a statue of a seated Buddha between two Bodhisatvas, and eight small temples northwest of Borobudur. Then ten miles northeast of Yogyakarta on the road to Surakarta is the Prambanan Temple complex, a series of temples built slightly later than Borobudur. The Prambanan, with separate temples for each of the important Hindu gods, Shiva, Brahma, and Vishnu, forms the background for the Ramayana Ballet performances over each full-moon period during the dry season from May to October. Like Borobudur, Prambanan is to be the center of an extensive park which will also include other temple ruins in the vicinity. The next stop after the temples is Surakarta, 27 miles away. Like Yogya, Solo, as it is commonly known, has two *kratons* or palaces. The older, belonging to the *sunan* or prince of Solo, was partly burned in a fire in January 1985. The main pavilions were gutted, but plans are already underway for reconstruction, with donations initiated by President Suharto, pouring in from the public. For the time being the kraton will remain closed to the public. Solo, with broad, tree-shaded streets seems better kept, less dirty than Yogya, with which it competes for cultural prestige. Solo also produces batik and is famed for its gamelan music and *wayang wong* dance dramas, held most evenings in the Sriwidari Recreation Grounds from 8:00 P.M. to midnight. There is a fascinating shopping area for colonial relics in the Pasar Trewindu antique market. Pasar Klewer is good for batik. Candi Sukuh is 23 miles from Solo, very difficult to find, but rewarding to those intrigued by erotic religious cults.

Surabaya and Mt. Bromo

From Solo, you can take several routes into East Java; however, the most spectacular if not harrowing is the road crossing Mount Lawu. The drive is best accomplished during daylight hours so that you can arrive in the mountain town of Sarangan before sunset. The cool weather, picturesque walks and lovely lake will probably convince you to spend at least one day here before descending into inviting and unexplored East Java. As the center of the Majapahit Kingdom in the 14th century, the area is rich in cultural antiquities in addition to having its fair share of lovely scenery.

Surabaya, the capital of this eastern province and the second largest city in Indonesia is hot, dusty and has relatively little of interest from the tourist's point of view. Its distinction is that it is the main base for Indonesia's navy and for centuries has been one of Indonesia's most important ports. Nonetheless, using it as a starting point, drive south to Mojokerto where there is a small but quite excellent museum next to the regional *(kabupaten)* office. Official hours are from 8 A.M. to 2 P.M. weekdays (until 11:00 A.M. on Friday, 1:00 P.M. on Saturdays; closed Sundays), but in a pinch you can always ask for the guard to open the gate. Inside are some fairly well preserved and variously dated stone carvings including Airlangga's posthumous image as Vishnu being carried by the mythical garuda; the statue dates from a kingdom of unknown name, finally consolidated by the famous half-Balinese prince, Airlangga, between 929 and 1047. The nearby village of Trowulan is believed to be the approximate site of the old Majapahit capital.

Traveling by road through East Java is an exhausting but interesting adventure. The road, usually no more than a one and a half lane thoroughfare, handles an amazing variety of traffic: cars and trucks, ox-drawn wooden carts, pony traps, motorcycles, bicycles and pedestrians. Doubtless you will want to hire a car *with* driver.

The old Dutch hill stations provide an exhilarating change of climate from the steaming plains of East Java. One of the best is Tretes (pronounced tray-tess), about an hour's drive from Surabaya. Situated about 2,800 feet above sea level, it nestles in a high green valley. From Tretes you have spectacular views of the surrounding mountains: Welirang and Penanggunan.

The road to Tretes is rather ordinary at first, passing through numerous villages with teeming markets selling papayas and rambutans in season. Past the town of Gombal it begins to climb and twist like a demented corkscrew. As you near Tretes you will see lovely villas with carefully tended gardens; these are weekend retreats for wealthy Indonesians. The several small hotels on the wooded slopes of Mount Welirang are comfortable and arranged like motels with separate entrances and balconies or terraces where you can sit and drink in the view.

Aside from taking walks in the crisp, cool air, you can hire ponies and make a day trek over to a resort at Prigen. Or you can take a half-day trip by car to Singosari and its famous Hindu temple. But mostly Tretes is a place in which to relax, walk and explore—and escape from the crowded noisy cities.

Undoubtedly, one highlight of an East Java trip would be a visit to Mount Bromo whose vast crater and smoking cone in the center provide an unforgettable sight in the misty dawn. However, you should be prepared to rough it and pack accordingly, including a heavy sweater, jacket, and warm slacks. While Bromo's 7,000-foot altitude is not particularly high when compared with its lofty neighbor Mount Semeru, seasonal fluctuations can cause night temperatures to drop below freezing thereby reducing the pleasure of the trip for the unprepared. To reach Bromo, take the main road toward the town of Probolinggo. At the village of Tongas, follow the sign which indicates a right-hand turn to Sukapura. You should reach Sukapura within 45 minutes but continue your journey on to Ngadisari which is the end of the line. To enjoy this beautiful ride and catch the spectacular sunrise, try to time your arrival so as to reach Ngadisari no later than 4 A.M. Apart from one small hotel, there is really no suitable accommodation close by, but one can arrange a tour or taxi from hotels in Malang or Surabaya. The distance between Ngadisari and the Bromo crater is about two miles. Taking a horse will not save you any time but it may make the journey more comfortable. On a moonlight night, the sight of falling stars and towering peaks along the route to the crater can be almost as memorable as a glimpse at dawn of the crater floor with its smoking cone veiled by the morning mist. In 1948, the volcano erupted burying the Dutch-built iron staircase which led to the top of the cone; however, it has recently been excavated and is a tremendous improvement over the treacherous final climb which tourists had to make as recently as eight years ago. If you reach the top while it is still dark, you will have the awesome experience of looking down at the glowing lava bed as it churns and smokes. Equally impressive is the sunrise which reveals the vastness of the crater as well as the weird lava formations at the foot of the cone. The Tenggerese villagers who live in this area visit the crater annually to make offerings ranging from live animals to rice and nuts for the god of fire.

Returning to Surabaya, you may wish to visit the island of Madura, a thirty-minute ferry ride away. Madura's claim to international fame is the bull races, held in local communities and ending in October with a Great Karapan in the stadium in Pamekasan, the capital, some 60 miles from Surabaya. The hill towns of Tretes, 30 miles south of Surabaya and Selecta, near Malang, have several swimming pools and inns, perhaps the best in the area.

Bali, Morning of the World

For most tourists, Mount Bromo, even Central Java or the Puncak, are secondary to the fabled island of Bali, off the eastern tip of Java. Bali can be reached directly from Singapore, Tokyo, and Hong Kong by Garuda, and from Melbourne, Sydney, Perth, and Darwin by both Garuda and Qantas. In addition Garuda's network connects Bali with Jakarta, Yogya, Surabaya, Ujung Pandang, and other cities in eastern Indonesia. Despite the dramatic influx of tourism, Bali has, fortunately, remained largely unchanged. However, to find the "real" Bali, you must venture away from the Sanur beach area, where the major hotels are located, explore the back roads by car or motorcycle, stopping in villages and, with luck, chancing on some religious ceremony or spontaneous dance.

"The morning of the world" was how India's late prime minister, Jawaharlal Nehru, described Bali during a visit to the island in 1954. The tinkling notes of the gamelan drift gently on the afternoon breezes, farmers and housewives walk lazily down the streets and roads, dogs and pigs lounge in the sun while little children play hide-and-seek in the rich green woods beside the road. The idyllic picture of rural life on Bali, a land of forests and rice paddies, soaring volcanic peaks and alternately roughhewn or sandy seacoasts, remains almost unchanged after generations of Dutch colonial rule, Japanese occupation and Indonesian independence. The beauties of modern Bali have survived, what's more, despite the ravages of a volcanic eruption in 1963 and a bloody purge in late 1965 and early 1966 in which some 50,000 Communists and Communist sympathizers were believed killed and whole villages burned to the ground. You begin to understand Bali's attractions as soon as you leave the airport. Alongside every road are small brick villages and Hindu temples, often decorated with ornate carving and sometimes piled high with offerings wrapped in leaves or gaily colored cloth.

Bali, in fact, is known as "the island of a thousand temples," and some officials think 10,000 would be a more realistic figure. The special artistic and cultural life of its 3,000,000 residents revolves almost entirely around the Hindu religion, which arrived on the island about 2,000 years ago and survived the Muslim onslaught that all but destroyed Hinduism on Java. The devotion with which Balinese Hindus revere their gods is readily apparent from the stream of religious holidays, which they celebrate at the temples with enormous feasts, dance performances and prayer sessions. The Balinese year has 210 days and temple festivals occur almost daily. The most important holiday is Galungan, celebrating the creation of the world and lasting for ten days. The Balinese New Year, Nyepi, is a day of silence and no activity is allowed anywhere on the island, in a ruse to drive out evil spirits. There are temple anniversary celebrations and days commemorating important dieties.The most sacred and festive of Balinese religious observances is the cremation of the dead. Bodies are carried to cremation grounds in tall carved towers, covered with decorations and weavings, and there placed in carved coffins, again covered with expensive material. The cremation is a ceremony in which the entire village participates. The procession, with a high priest ensconced in a sedan chair, begins at the village and ultimately ends at the seaside, where the last ashes are thrown in the water.

Town, Beach, or Ubud

The tourist, if at all possible, should spend at least four days in Bali, and preferably a week. The leading tourist center on the south side of the island, Denpasar, the small capital, has become hectic and commercial with frantic traffic and contains little of the "real" Bali one has come to see. The Balinese people are famous for their artistic abilities which are expressed in wood, stone, horn, bone, ivory, and painting. They also create delicate ornaments of gold, silver, and copper, all of which are available in varying quality in the island's shops. The city markets, where mainly the women sell goods, are colorful with tropical fruit, vegetables, and other exotic produce. The women sitting in the markets plait coconut and *lontar* palm leaves into lovely decorations used in Bali's numerous festivals. The Bali museum in Denpasar is adorned with many beautiful art treasures. Just outside Denpasar is the new Bali Cultural Center with an art gallery and large open-air theater in delightful garden setting. Entrance Rp 200.

Major hotels are mostly close to Denpasar, on Sanur and Kuta beaches. Hotels and tour operators arrange island tours or one can bargain for one's own car with driver (US$50 upwards for full day), which gives one freedom to explore out beyond the reach of the tourist buses. Big hotels are expensive but the many charming seaside bungalows are cheaper. Still cheaper hotels are located in Denpasar itself, or at Kuta beach, which has become a major center for "hippie"-style travelers. One can also stay inexpensively at one of the small guesthouses in Ubud, a delightful little artists' colony some 15 miles north of Denpasar. A trip to Ubud, in fact, would be an excellent way to begin your Balinese vacation. There you will find the studios and galleries of several prominent European artists who have devoted most of their lives to depicting Balinese life on canvas. And you will find the equally enchanting studios of Balinese painters, some of whom have staged a renaissance in Balinese art by combining the traditional Balinese approach with European techniques.

Ubud is the home of Puri Lukisan Palace of Paintings, which contains a magnificent collection of modern Balinese paintings and sculptures from 1930 to the present day. Also here is a school for music and dancing unparalleled on the island. In spite of the arrival of television in the village community centers, one can still sometimes find a spontaneous dance being put on by the village girls. From an early age they begin to develop the qualities of beauty, line and grace required for the *legong,* the most popular of Balinese dances. A legong performance, featuring three girls in bright, bejewelled costumes and characterized by quick body and eye movements, often tells the story of a cruel king who tries to woo an unwilling princess.

Another delightful dance sometimes encountered is the *Joged Bumbung,* the only dance in Bali where an exuberant male onlooker can join the girls. The dance begins when a flirtatious girl solos across the dance floor, and with her fan taps the shoulder of the male of her choice. Then begins a love game of enticement, but traditional Balinese restraint always wins in the end because the male is not permitted to hold his partner. The music for the dance is provided by an orchestra comprised only of bamboo instruments, called the *Bumbung.*

Mount Agung

The oldest, most sacred temple on Bali is Pura Besakih, on the slopes of volcanic Mount Agung. Much of Besakih was destroyed or damaged when Mount Agung erupted on March 17, 1963, but the temple has since been restored. Many of Agung's 2,000 victims were devout Hindus praying at the temple. (Balinese guides say their priest told the worshippers not to fear the onrushing lava since the gods would protect them.) In order to reach Besakih, you have to drive to the east of the island, into the area of black volcanic sand beaches, the drier, less fertile part of Bali, and to walk the last mile as cars are no longer allowed to come close to the temple. You should start early in the day and plan to leave the temple by the middle of the afternoon, when rain often falls. Besakih is actually a complex of temples dominated by Pura Panataran Besakih, at the height of a slope of terraces. Anthropologists believe that Besakih was first built before Hinduism arrived on Bali and then turned into the seat of Hinduism on the island. The old temple was the sanctuary where the spirit of the great mountain received prayers and offerings. Today it is the place where the Balinese practice ancestral worship.

The structure consists of three main parts, each connected with the Hinduistic trinity: the north in black for Vishnu, the center in white for Shiva, and the south in red for Brahma. The large central temple is built on a slope of terraces. Entrance is made through a split doorway, and a broad terrace leads to the Gapura Gateway which opens onto the pagoda-like *merus.* The *merus* are dedicated to the spirits of the deceased rulers of the Samprangan dynasty, who are the ancestors of the present princes of Klungkung.

Other important temples include Pura Goa Lawah (Bat Cave); Pura Ulu Watu, perched on the cliffs in southern Bali; Pura Batur, which is believed to be linked with Pura Besakih; Pura Pusering Jagat ("Navel of the World"); and Pura Batukaru, in the forest of Batukarau mountain. Another small temple by the sea, Tanah Lot, provides spectacular scenery at sundown.

One of the earliest centers of Hinduism on Bali is the Tampaksiring sanctuary which includes the holy spring, the source of the Pekerisan river, with its ritual bathing place, plus temples, large and small. Nearby are 11th-century royal tombs and the hermitage of Gunung Kawi. Of equal interest is the Elephant Cave, once a monastery for both monks and hermits. The T-shaped cave outside the village of Bedhulu includes niches in which the monks are said to have slept. Outside it is a medium-sized bathing pool with water-spouting statues, all cut out of stone and only recently unearthed by excavation. Another indication of the fascination of pools on ancient Bali is the water palace, once the home of the richest raja on the island, is a complex of lakes, statues, gardens, and a pavilion with stone animals overlooking the Indian Ocean. The palace was seriously damaged during an earthquake, but efforts are being made to restore it.

Villages of the Dance

Another attraction is Gianyar, 30 km from Denpasar. It is a weaving center and across the town square is one of the few traditional Balinese palaces still in existence. Its courtyards are decorated with beautiful stonework and carved pillars. Near Gianyar is the delightful town of Bona, the center of the plaiting industry. Nearly all of Bona's inhabitants plait baskets, hats, sandals, bags, fans, and build bamboo chairs and tables. They also plait bamboo birds and flowers. The tingling *kecak* (monkey) dance is performed in several villages by groups of nearly 200 men sitting in concentric circles. In the center stands a large, branched torch which is ablaze. The *kecak* dance depicts fragments of the Ramayana story when Sita, the wife of King Rama, is captured by the demon King Rahwana. The dance shows the battle to get Sita back, when Rama kills Rahwana. Hanuman, the leader of the apes, and his hordes of monkey-soldiers help to carry Sita back home. The dancers, at a signal, sway together, circling and bending, stretching out their arms and waving them, all the time issuing hisses, chattering and other inarticulate monkey-like sounds.

In Trunyan is the largest statue in Bali, that of Natu Gede Pancering Jagat, powerful guardian of the village. Also in the town is a dancing school putting on daily shows, and the longest council house in the whole island, built to provide a residence for Kbowa, a fearful giant of pre-Hindu days whose appetite was so great that there was never enough food for him. He ate people to keep satisfied. Near Trunyan lies the frightening "dead rock" where the dead are laid and the corpses picked by birds. Elsewhere in Bali, burial is by cremation. If you hear of a cremation taking place, do make a special point of attending. These are among the most spectacular and important social and religious events on the island.

Another dance performed often in Bali is the *janger,* in which ten men face a female partner across a square in the center of which is the dance leader, the *dag.* This modern Balinese dance begins with the group dancing and singing toward the *dag,* who in the second part of the dance relates a legend which the dancers enact. A rather weird dance is the *jalon arang,* depicting a combat between an evil witch who is feared for her great magical power, and a famous priest, who finally wins the battle and restores peace and prosperity to the country. The witch, Rangda, wears a frightening mask, plus a costume which is set off with long sharp nails. The facial mask has an out-thrust tongue and flowing hair. Also in the dance is the *barong,* a legendary animal with attendant soldiers. The most frightening part of the dance is the battle between Rangda and the *barong,* whose followers become entranced and who, in order to display their invulnerability, stab themselves repeatedly with their sharp, wavy *kris* knives, yet remain unscathed by the realistic stabbings.

As a contrast to the richness of the Bali hinterland, you might visit Uluwatu, the site of the area's holiest temple, situated on a limestone peninsula at the southern tip of the island. The curious limestone plateau gives the impression of having been at one time the bottom of the ocean. It is joined to the mainland by a low, narrow, isthmus, but its sides rise almost vertically from the sea. At the end of a rock, over a drop of 250 feet straight down, is the Uluwatu temple. The projecting rock is believed to be the ship, turned to stone, of Dewi Danu, the goddess of waters. Religious rites involving the sea are frequent on Bali, reflecting the islanders' fear of the fierce demons which inhabit the ocean.

Mas

The village of Mas, 20 kilometers from Denpasar, is famous for its wood carvings. Pieces of ebony, teak, tamarind, and sugarfruit wood are chiseled into forms without the use of models. Here live some of Bali's best carvers, and in their workshops little boys take up the chisel and hammer to learn a trade.

Nusa Dua

A new resort in the southern peninsula of Bali has been developed by the government for tourism. The first hotel, Nusa Dua Beach, with 450 luxury rooms, opened in 1982 and is a masterpiece of Balinese art and western comfort.

Another hotel, scheduled to be fully operational by the end of 1985, is the luxurious Hotel Bali Nusa Dua. The Bali Sol with 500 rooms is to open in the second half of 1985. Also in this tourist resort area is a small 50-room hotel. All the hotels have white sandy beach fronts, swimming pools, restaurants, and convention halls. Club Med's Holiday Village, now under construction, is expected to open in 1987.

Watersports

Surfing is becoming the most popular watersport in Bali. Originally started by Australians who brought their boards, the sport has been taken up by Balinese who now compete in international events. Kuta beach is good for surfing almost the whole year-round and an annual festival is held with local and Australian participation. Scuba diving is also being developed and the Gloria Maris Club and Aquanaut have equipment and offer lessons and guided tours to Bali's diving spots.

Cockfighting

The chief diversion of Balinese men is their roosters, which occupy wicker cages in every village on the island. Guides can lead you to cockfighting arenas, where poor men shout their bets in a rising crescendo until the moment the roosters strut out on the floor. They spar briefly before a hushed audience and then, before you're quite aware the fight has begun, one of them fells the other with his metal spur and it's all over. Cockfighting has technically been banned in Bali for several years, but it can still be found in and around the more remote villages.

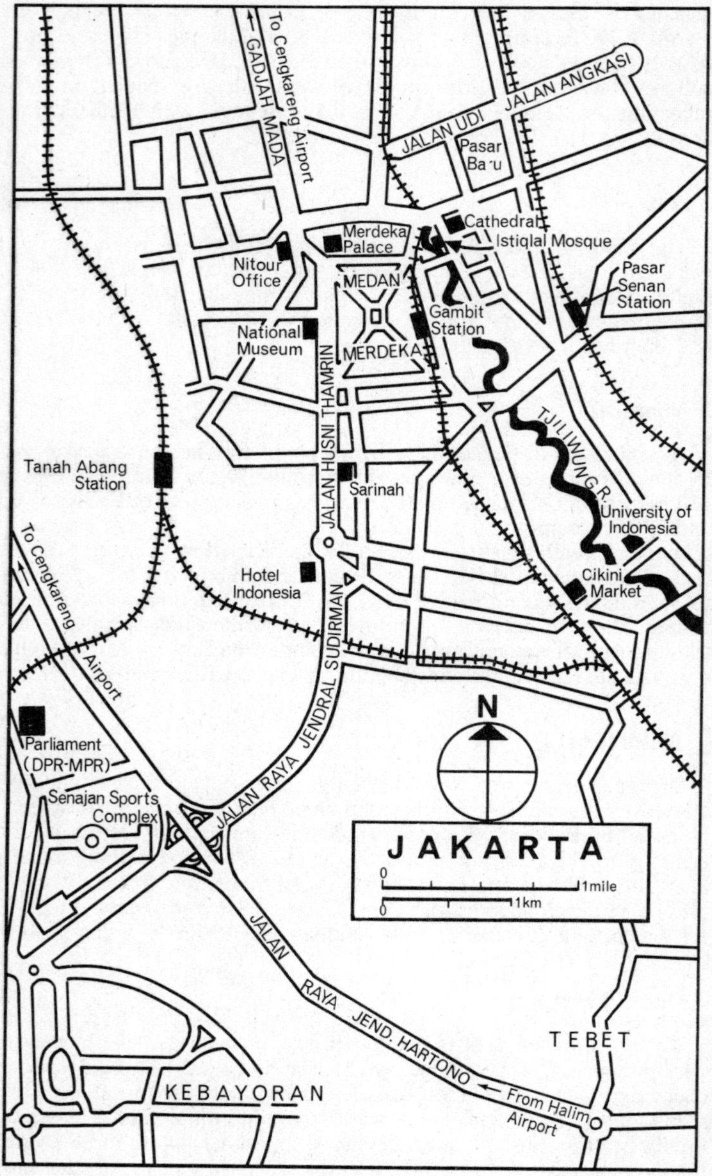
To Cengkareng Airport
GADJAH MADA
JALAN UDI
JALAN ANGKASI
Pasar Ba-u
Cathedral
Istiqlal Mosque
Merdeka Palace
Nitour Office
MEDAN
MERDEKA
National Museum
Gambit Station
Pasar Senan Station
TJILIWUNG R.
JALAN HUSNI THAMRIN
Tanah Abang Station
Sarinah
University of Indonesia
Hotel Indonesia
Cikini Market
To Cengkareng Airport
JALAN RAYA JENDRAL SUDIRMAN
N
Parliament (DPR-MPR)
Senajan Sports Complex
JAKARTA
0
1 mile
0
1 km
JALAN RAYA JEND. HARTONO
TEBET
KEBAYORAN
From Halim Airport

Jakarta

Bali for the Western tourist is a remote never-never land which he will only visit once and then remember in kaleidoscopic detail for the rest of his days. There is a great contrast, however, between Bali and Jakarta, capital of Indonesia. The city has seen a massive influx of rural people over the past decade which has swollen its population to over 6 million and, for a time, threatened to swamp its facilities and utilities.

Under a massive reconstruction program, begun by a former governor of Jakarta, Ali Sadikin, the city has seen fantastic improvements over recent years and it is now much changed from the time when it had the reputation for being one of the region's ugliest cities. New six-lane highways have replaced the old badly kept main arteries. The old system of canals has been somewhat cleaned up and skyscrapers abound.

However, for all its problems, Indonesia's capital reflects its history, which has been stormy. In the center of vast Merdeka Square, rises the 400-foot Freedom Monument, topped by a gold-plated flame and symbolic culmination of the late President Sukarno's "revolution." One of the world's most impressive mosques, the huge, modern Istiqlal Mosque is close to Merdeka Square. A couple of blocks away, in Banteng Square, is a statue of a West Irian man breaking his chains, again symbolic of the final departure of the Dutch from what was formerly Western New Guinea. Jalan Thamrin is a six-laned avenue bordered by multi-storied hotels, banks and embassies.

For a glimpse into Jakarta's earlier history drive down to Sunda Kelapa harbor where, near the end of the 16th century, Dutch and Portuguese traders began to compete for a foothold on Java. One can still find inter-island sailing ships, gabled houses with diamond-paned windows and swinging shutters similar to those found in Dutch cities, ample evidence of the eventual Dutch conquest of what was to become the Netherlands East Indies. Great efforts are being made to preserve and restore particularly fine examples of old architecture such as those buildings near the old Stadhuis (City Hall). Well worth visiting is the "Portuguese" Church, completed by the Dutch in 1695, and housing a magnificent and immense Dutch pump organ, which the church caretaker will unlock if you wish to try playing it. The museum in the Stadhuis should be visited if you are interested in seeing a fine collection of Dutch period antiques. Near Pasir Ikan an old spice godown has been restored and converted into a maritime museum. Entry to the museum is Rp. 200 (closed Mondays). Access to the old harbor area costs Rp. 200.

Back in Menteng, stop by the English Church if you are interested in gleaning some bits of Indonesia's brief English colonial period from the well-inscribed gravestones next to the church.

You may wish to stop by the Cikini Market to look at the remarkable varieties of fruit for sale or browse through the picturesque flower stalls. Nearby on Jalan Surabaya, wander through Jakarta's antique market, where you are sure to find something intriguing to bring home. Not far from Cikini Market is the cultural center, *Taman Ismail Mar-*

suki, which is worth visiting briefly during the day although most of its activities take place in the evening. If you are not visiting Central Java and are interested in seeing how the batik process is done, numerous small batik factories can be visited in the Karet area.

One direct effect of the new outlook in Indonesia is the improvement of all facilities and the general physical appearance of Jakarta. Over recent years a program has been launched to repair roads, complete extensive planting, expand bus services and clean the canals. An annual Jakarta Fair is held in June to promote tourism and commerce. In addition to exhibits by hundreds of private companies and foreign countries, there are numerous pavilions sponsored by the various provincial governments of the outer islands, where you can get some idea of regional commerce and culture. You can also visit two impressive new pleasure domes that have sprung up under the city's development plan. "Indonesia in Miniature" is a sort of open-air museum depicting the various ethnic groups and cultures of Indonesia: a massive project that has taken many years and many millions of dollars to build. Along the beach is the Ancol (pronounced Ann-chol) Dreamland, a complex of hotels, restaurants, aquarium, bowling alley, swimming pool, marina, drive-in theater, and much more.

The latest addition to this recreational area is Fantasy Land, which somewhat resembles Disneyland. Actually this is only the first phase of a huge project which will take ten years to complete and eventually cover 60 hectares of beach front.

A delightful side trip out of Jakarta is to Pulau Putri, a tiny atoll in the "Thousand Islands." A 15-minute flight and a ferryboat ride or, on weekends, a jetfoil ride will take you to this charming island, with bungalows, restaurant, and coral reefs for skin diving.

Sulawesi

The seaport capital of Ujung Pandang (formerly Makassar), on the southwest corner of Sulawesi, formerly called the Celebes, was once famed for the hair oil which Victorian ladies feared might stain the backs of their parlor furniture. Today, the city is still a center for regional commerce and can be reached by daily flights from Jakarta, Denpasar (Bali), or Surabaya. Tourist sites in old Makassar are few, but there are remains of Portuguese and Dutch times, including an old Dutch fort, which has been restored. You will certainly wish to browse through the Central Market where you can see numerous spice stalls selling nutmeg, cloves, cinnamon and other seasonings which drew European traders in the 16th century. The market is also the place to buy the colorful silk cloth woven and worn by the Buginese women who live in the area. On Djalan Somba Opu, you may also wish to look in on some of the goldsmiths who work the filigree jewelry known as Kendari Silver. Or see the orchids and seashells at C.L. Bundt, 15 Jalan Mochtar Lufti.

While it is quite easy to find a boat to take you to Kajangan Island in the harbor for swimming and other entertainment, you might find it more memorable to hire a motor boat and spend a day visiting one of the smaller islands beyond Makassar Bay. Also worth visiting is

Bantimurung, about 30 kms. from Ujung Pandang, famed for rushing waterfalls and butterflies, considered rare by collectors.

From Ujung Pandang, there is a daily flight by Merpati to the mountainous area of Tana Toraja, or you might want to make a tough eight-hour drive through the coastal plains and beautiful mountain scenery. Near the sleepy town of Rantepao, there are still many highlanders who adhere to their animistic beliefs and customs, the most famous of which is the funeral festival. Should you be fortunate enough to visit the area during such an occasion, usually in July or August, you will be invited to join the other guests for the two- to three-week feasting period in a specially constructed village. Up to 100 temporary houses, painted in the bright Toraja style, are constructed for family and friends who in turn bring gifts of water buffalo, pigs, rice, and palm wine to repay favors and other moral debts to the deceased. The atmosphere is gala, climaxed by bullfights and dancing, before the corpse is carried to one of the nearby cliff cemeteries where it is hoisted into a carved-out tomb. Such cemeteries are well worth visiting, whether a burial festival is on or not, in order to see the wooden balconies on which clothed effigies of deceased ancestors stand. Be sure also to visit some of the smaller Toraja villages to see the elaborately carved and painted houses and granaries. Should you arrive in Rantepao on market day, don't fail to wander about the stalls to see what constitutes local commerce, including the huge trade in hogs.

In the far north of Sulawesi a new tourist destination, Manado, can now be reached by air. The area is home of the Minahasas, a group of tribes of Proto-Malays who migrated to the island in megalithic times. Here one can see some grand land- and seascapes, picturesque fishing villages and fine beaches. The ancient stone tombs of the local tribes are also of interest, as are the caves used by Japanese forces during World War II. But above all, Manado has of late become known for the great reefs which surround the islands of Bunaken, Manado Tua, and several others just outside Manado Bay. These reefs with their spectacular dropoffs and teeming marine life are among the most virgin and magnificent of Indonesia and rival, if not equal or excel, some of the world's best-known diving sites. Boats and equipment are available at Malalayang beach and tours can be arranged with diving guides. There are also beautiful reefs within the Tangkoko–Dua Saudara nature reserves.

Komodo and Krakatau

Two other attractions which, as yet, receive very few visitors, are the "dragon" island of Komodo and the volcano island of Krakatau, off the extreme west coast of Java. One can reach Komodo by boat from Bali or from Maumere on Flores Island. The round-trip takes 5–8 days and several leading agents can make the arrangements.

A far easier way of seeing the fearsome lizard known as the Komodo Dragon, however, is by visiting the excellent zoos in Jakarta, Surabaya, or Jogjakarta, where a strong fence is between you and the monsters, which can grow up to 12 ft. in length. Krakatau can be reached by a 4-hour drive from Jakarta to the west, where one can stay at one of the several small but comfortable hotels available and take a 10-hour boat trip onto or close to the volcano island itself. It is, however, advisable to use the services of a tour operator to ensure a safe journey, as the seas can be rough and boats do not always have safety equipment.

Sumatra

You will find the North Sumatran city of Medan a cosmopolitan trading center and convenient jumping-off place to visit Batak highlands including the breathtaking Lake Toba area. Served by daily flights from Jakarta, Singapore, or Penang, you may wish to begin your trip to Indonesia via the north rather than heading directly to Jakarta. The city itself has little of tourist interest, although comfortable hotels are growing in number. You may wish to visit the Great Mosque, built in 1906, or the Sultan's Palace of Deli, dating back to 1888; unfortunately, the Central Market, once the largest and most varied in Indonesia, burned to the ground in 1971, and has been rebuilt in less interesting style. Medan owes its rapid commercial growth to the large tobacco, rubber and palm oil estates which you will pass—and may wish to visit—en route to some of the more picturesque countryside. The Batak people of Tapanuli, in the North Sumatra highlands, are known throughout Indonesia for their forthright approach to life and, unlike the Javanese or Balinese, are quick to show their emotions. En route to Lake Toba, you are likely to drive through three of the five Batak tribal areas which have subtle but distinct cultural and language differences. Head south from Medan via the highland area of Brastagi where you may wish to spend a day playing golf or walking in the forests at the foot of Mount Sibayak and Mount Sinabung, two active volcanoes. The area is a major fruit and vegetable growing center, and you will want to visit the market where the Karo Batak women still wear their wide-brimmed and tasseled headdresses. Take time to visit the villages of Barusjahe and Lingga, where you will see typical Karonese houses, perched on pillars and ornately carved. As you get closer to Prapat, take a side road to visit Pematung Purba to see the royal "palace" compound of a Simalungan Batak tribal chief.

The highlight of your trip around Sumatra will most certainly be Lake Toba. Always a favorite vacation spot for Indonesians, this cool lake resort has recently become a focal point for overseas visitors taking advantage of package tours organized by several airlines.

Lake Toba itself is one of the world's volcanic curiosities. In the center of the lake, created by water cachement of an ancient volcanic crater, is an island. This island also contains a volcanic crater, which has formed a small jewel of a lake. A rough road circles the island but there is little in the way of transportation, so those wishing to view this unusual lake must be prepared for a trek. Trekking enthusiasts, however, will find the trip quite worthwhile as it takes you first up the steep side of the crater edge and then through unspoiled rural countryside and remote Batak villages. (It is advisable to secure the services of a guide through your hotel in Parapat.)

The island, Samosir, provided the last refuge for the fierce Bataks who refused to accept Dutch rule and Protestant missionaries. Today most Bataks in Sumatra are Christians, because the missionaries wisely welded certain aspects of the pagan religion (which included the concept of a single, powerful God) with the tenets of Christianity. On Sundays a visitor should make a point of attending church services to hear the Bataks' magnificent voices. Favorite hymn tunes acquire added color and richness when you hear the soaring rendition of the Batak choirs.

Christianity has also influenced the rolling landscape of the lush Sumatra countryside where tiny, tall-steepled churches perch on nearly every hilltop. At times a visitor may feel he has stepped through a space warp into rural Pennsylvania until suddenly a water buffalo lumbers into view with a small boy riding on its back.

You can get over to the island of Samosir by a variety of boats. The cheapest is the market ferry, which follows no discernibly decipherable schedule. Designed to carry a load of 50 to 80 people, it does not depart until every scrap of space has been filled with men carrying packages and parcels, women shepherding a clutch of children, pigs and chickens —occasionally a cow—baskets heaped with fruit, vegetables, rice, and cargo of every description. The overloaded boat then moves heavily through the water while the unsheltered passengers suffer from either the sun or the rain. It is an unforgettable ride and costs only pennies.

At the other end of the scale you can hire a speedboat which whisks you across the lake in 15 minutes. Also available are excursion launches, which are leased on a group basis. In both cases arrange to have the boat wait while you explore the village of Tomok and perhaps browse among the antiques and souvenirs for sale. Bargaining is definitely in order here—and often is well worth your time and effort.

On Samosir you will have an opportunity to visit Simanindo, a Batak village, and enter the longhouses, which shelter an entire clan. The roofs are shaped like the curved prow of a boat, quite similar to hill tribe dwellings in northern Burma. You will also visit some tomb sites where the Bataks bury royalty in special sarcophagi that are replicas in stone of the wooden houses. You will see the transition from pagan to Christian custom—the oldest tomb (about 300 years) is richly carved with a profusion of figures and ornaments. The more recent, however, are plain and carry only the barest information about the deceased: name, dates and of course a simple cross. Also on Samosir you will find a pavilion with stone tables and chairs designed for royalty.

A pleasant side excursion can be made (arrange with your boatman before you leave Parapat) to the tiny island of Tao, where there are small guest houses, located right on the lane side. Even if you don't stay, you can buy a cold drink and are most certainly welcome to swim and dive from a homemade board, 30 feet up from the cool, inviting waters of Lake Toba.

Another of Sumatra's attractions is the island of Nias. The island is reached by ferry from Sibolga (about 8 hours) or flying to Gunungsitoli from Medan and sailing to the remote villages in the south. This once remote island was the center of a magnificent megalithic culture that lasted well into the 20th century. In their little hilltop villages, with stone-paved streets lined with unique stilted houses, you will see stone obelisks, huge stone benches, tables, chests, and some massive drums.

Although most of the inhabitants of Nias are now Christian, they continue to carve quite well and you can find some exquisite primitive works. If you are lucky you may see some of the "leaping warriors of Nias" performing feats of jumping over the stones as once did their pagan ancestors.

Lombok

A destination of increasing popularity is the island of Lombok, about 20 minutes' flying time from Bali. Though the island is now predominantly Muslim, Balinese influence, emanating from the House of Karangasem of South Bali during the past century, is strong, especially in the western parts around Ampenan, Mataram, and Cakranegara. Here, the Balinese built their temples and pleasure gardens. Orthodox Islam has gained a strong foothold among the local people, the Sasaks, during the past centuries. But a smaller number still adheres to a very peculiar local form of Islam known as Waktu Telu or "Three Times" Muslims. Unlike the orthodox "Waktu Lima," who observe prayers five times a day as prescribed by Islam, the Waktu Telu know only three occasions prescribed for prayer: every Friday, during the end of the holy month of Ramadan and on the birthday of the Prophet Mohammed. Pura Kemalik, at Lingsar, is probably the only Hindu Balinese temple in the world where Hindus and Muslims (of the Waktu Telu sect) meet together once a year, bound by shared traditions which go back for more than a hundred years.

Lombok is known for its beautiful virgin beaches. Cakranegara and a few villages in the surrounding area are excellent places for shopping for traditional handwoven textiles.

East Kalimantan

East Kalimantan is known for its primitive Dayak tribes who live along rivers and keep to ancient beliefs and ancestor worship. While the journey up the Mahakam river may not have modern comforts, the friendliness and hospitality of the people make up for the hardships.

East Kalimantan is easily accessible by air from Jakarta, to Balikpapan, a booming oil and timber center. From here drive to the provincial capital of Samarinda, the old sultanate of Kutai, and the riverfront where boats are available. As the trip can take two to three days, it is better to stock up food and drink and to use a guide. Tour packages are also offered.

On the river is Tenggarong which has a museum where exhibits include heirlooms of the old sultanate and a fine collection of Chinese ceramics. Dance performances are staged in front of the longhouses. The Dayaks do beautiful embroidery work and beading, and make ornaments out of rubber.

The Mahakam River is known for its dolphins which follow boats.

PRACTICAL INFORMATION

FACTS AND FIGURES. Population: 160 million. Birth rate per 1,000: 34. Life expectancy: 47 years. Land area: 1,910,000 sq. kms. Cultivated area: 12% (64% forest). Population engaged in agriculture and fishing: 55%. Average per capita income: US$600 p.a. Number of tourists annually: 630,000.

PLANNING YOUR TRIP. If arranging your own trip, obtain initial information from the Directorate General of Tourism, which has offices abroad, in Los Angeles, Frankfurt, Tokyo, and Singapore. Information is also available from overseas offices of the national airline, Garuda. Plan well in advance and build a time reserve into your schedule. Hold ups can be caused by delayed, overfull or cancelled domestic flights. The hiring of cars, guides, and the organizing of side trips can be arranged more easily on the spot. As you travel reconfirm every next step. Tourism has become better organized in Indonesia over recent years, but there are still many frustrations.

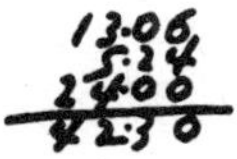

WHAT WILL IT COST? It is almost impossible to give an accurate prior assessment of likely costs in Indonesia; the country, and its tourism facilities, are simply too diverse for the same scale to apply nationwide. Briefly, though, the farther one gets away from large cities and the older the hotels in which one stays, the cheaper will one's expenses be. The following chart will give just an outline of a possible day's budget in a major tourist center, living reasonably well, but by no means at the top of the available scale. Estimating exact costs is currently even more difficult due to the floating rate of the Indonesian rupiah.

A TYPICAL DAY'S COST (IN US$)

Hotel, expensive, half of double, including service & tax	$66.00
Breakfast, Continental, per person	$7.00
Morning city tour	8.00
Light lunch, local café	8.00
Taxi shopping trip, 3 miles	3.00
Dinner at good hotel, no drinks	25.00
Beer in hotel	3.00
Whisky and soda in hotel	5.50
	US$125.50

WHEN TO GO. The best time to visit Indonesia is from May to September when the skies are clear of rain and the festivals are on. Some prefer October and November when the temperature is a few degrees cooler, but in those months the monsoon is starting to drip. It is hard to draw a line between the wet and dry seasons, as there is some rain the year round. Evenings are relatively cool throughout the island republic, and in the hilly hinterland the temperature is pleasant right around the clock.

WHAT TO TAKE. Parts of rural Indonesia are still malarial, so bring along some malaria pills. Insect repellent is useful here, as it is in most tropical regions. Similar sundries, such as suntan lotion, tampons, deodorant, are available at very high prices in hotel drugstores or at much lower prices in supermarkets. Dress is casual unless you are doing business. In that case, you will want to put on a tie or a skirt. Bring along your own disposable light reading: paperbacks are expensive and the selection limited.

Dress Note. Indonesia, being a Muslim country, has strict rules about dress, especially for women. Neither men nor women should wear shorts, other than on the beach, and daring bikinis can cause trouble, except on private hotel beaches where attitudes are rather more tolerant. In temples or mosques, bare shoulders should be covered and shoes always removed.

LOCAL FESTIVALS. May 14. *Waicak Day* is celebrated by Indonesia's Buddhists at the site of former Buddhist glory, Borobudur and Mendut temples. This day commemorates the Lord Buddha's birth, death, and enlightenment.

Variable. *Galungan* in Bali, is the most important holiday of the Balinese year. Galungan celebrates the creation of the world by the Supreme God, and symbolizes the victory of good over evil. The Galungan holidays continue for 10 days.

Kuningan is celebrated 10 days after Galungan. It honors the souls of ancestors and saints.

Variable-early year. *Sekaten,* commemorating the birth of Mohammed, a week-long festival in Yogyakarta. The sultan allows his ancient gamelan musical instruments to be played once in this annual display of these rare musicmakers, and there is a parade from his palace through the streets. Huge mounds of food are carried through the streets to the mosque where it is distributed to the people.

Variable-Spring. *Nyepi* is the Balinese New Year according to the Saka calendar. The holy day is observed with complete stillness. No fires may be lit and no one should be seen on the roads. On the day before, purification ceremonies and offerings are made, and in the evening people bang gongs and pans to arouse evil spirits. On Nyepi all is silent in the hope that the spirits that were aroused the night before will find Bali uninhabited and leave. Nyepi, as of 1983, has been declared a national public holiday. Special passes for flights landing or departing that day. No tours are allowed.

May-October. *Ramayana Ballet Festival,* held in the full moon week each month, features a four-episode dance drama version of the classic Hindu Ramayana epic, by a cast of 500. Setting is the 10th century Roro Jonggrang temple near Yogyakarta.

June. *Idul Fitri* is the most important holiday for Muslims, and everything closes down for two days. It's the end of Ramadhan, the Muslim fasting month. Dates advance 10 days each year. Many festivals in the provinces.

Mid-June. *Jakarta Fair.* Annual seven-week trade and cultural gathering, with colorful shows.

August 17. *Independence Day* is celebrated everywhere in Indonesia with flag-hoisting ceremonies, sports, and cultural performances. The president officiates at a solemn flag-hoisting ceremony at the Merdeka Palace and reviews a parade of floats and march-past by citizens. In the evening, many buildings are illuminated.

Mid-October. *Bull racing* in Madura. Small-scale races are held twice a month with the championship races held in October in the town of Pamekasan. The bulls are heavily decorated and mass dances are performed before the races.

December. *Kesodo Ceremonies,* a midnight offering ceremony, celebrated by the Tenggerese—Hindu devotees—at the still active crater of Mount Bromo, East Java.

HOW TO REACH INDONESIA. A number of major international and regional airlines serve Jakarta with direct flights from America, Australia, and Europe. Jakarta is served by several regional carriers from Asian cities. Bali is served by *Garuda* with direct flights from Tokyo, Hong Kong, Singapore, Jakarta, and other Indonesian cities, and from the Australian cities of Sydney, Melbourne, Perth, Darwin, and Port Hedland. *Qantas* also serves Bali from Sydney, Melbourne, and Perth. There are direct flights from Singapore, Penang, and Kuala Lumpur to Medan and from Singapore to Padang in West Sumatra. Garuda serves all the provincial capitals throughout the archipelago from Jakarta and *Merpati* flies to district centers and airfields in remote areas. Garuda now offers Visit Indonesia Air Passes for travelers from Europe, the US, Australia, and Japan. Travel within Indonesia on any Garuda flights to 5 cities for US$300 for 10 days, 10 cities in 20 days for $400, and 33 cities in 60 days for $500. Tickets must be bought in cities of departure combined with a Garuda international ticket and are restricted to nonresidents of Indonesia.

PASSPORTS AND VISAS. All visitors must be in possession of a passport valid for at least 6 months and have proof of onward passage or a return ticket.

Indonesia offers a tourist visa-free entry for a period of 60 days for nationals of the United States, Canada, the United Kingdom, and most European and Asian countries.

Visa-free entry and departure is only possible through the airports of Polonia (Medan), Batubesar (Batam), Simpang Tiga (Pekanbaru), Tabing (Padang), Cengkareng (Jakarta), Ngurah Rai (Bali), Sam Ratulangi (Manado), Pattimura (Ambon), and Mokmer (Biak); or the seaports of Belawan (Medan), Batu Ampar (Batam), Tanjung Priok (Jakarta), Tanjung Perak (Surabaya), Benoa (Bali), Padang Bai (Bali), Ambon, and Bitung (Mandano).

For other nationals, 30-day tourist visas can be obtained at any Indonesian embassy or consulate upon presentation of return and/or through tickets and confirmed travel reservations to and from Indonesia. There is a small charge for a tourist visa, and 2 passport photos are needed. Business visas for a period of 5 weeks can be required, which can be extended up to six months, but they need supporting documents or letters of recommendation.

You need to have an *International Health Certificate* of inoculation against smallpox, yellow fever, and cholera only if arriving from an infected area. Typhoid and paratyphoid vaccinations are not mandatory but recommended if travel upcountry is intended, and malaria tablets should be taken in advance if visiting the more remote areas.

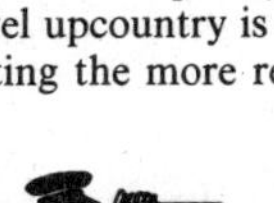

CUSTOMS. Indonesia's customs and immigration officers have recently become more lenient but you should still make sure your papers are in order. Two bottles of liquor and 200 cigarettes permitted. Radios and TV sets are not allowed.

AT THE AIRPORT. The three major gateway airports into Indonesia are Cenkareng, in Jakarta, Medan, in North Sumatra and Denpasar, in Bali. Immigration and customs formalities have eased over recent years. Jakarta's new airport at Cengkareng serves both international and domestic flights. It is about 20km west of the city. Taxi fare is about Rp 6,500 plus toll charges of Rp 2,700 per car. Airport buses charge Rp 1,500 per person to 4 points in the city and to major hotels. Airport tax at Jakarta International Airport Rp 6,000 for international and Rp 2,000 for domestic. In Denpasar most major hotels have meeting services at the airport. If not, taxis are available for about Rp 7,500 to Sanur hotels. Airport departure tax is Rp 6,000 for international flights or Rp 2,000 for domestic.

MONEY. There is no restriction on import or export of foreign currency, in banknotes or travelers' checks. However, there is a limit of Rp 50,000 which can be brought in or taken out of the country. The rupiah exchange rate floats against foreign currencies and in mid-1984 is about Rp 1,000 to a U.S. dollar. Travelers' checks or currency can be changed easily at any of the major banks in Jakarta or with the *Bank Negara Indonesia* facilities in town or at airports. Banks offer a higher rate of exchange in Jakarta than in outlying areas. Hotels do not often give such good rates as banks. Banks open: 8–1 weekdays; 8–12 Saturdays. Credit cards are not widely used in Indonesia, except in major tourist centers such as Jakarta and Bali. It is advisable to use only well-known brands of travelers' checks, as rural banks may refuse those they do not recognize. Small change is in very short supply in rural areas, so take plenty with you from the big towns.

HOW TO GET AROUND. Big distances between tourist spots make air travel the most practical, but much of the country's superb scenery can only be seen by rail or road. Fares are reasonable, but make sure reservations are booked well ahead and always reconfirm.

By air: *Garuda.* Indonesia's national airline has added numerous flights to its inter-island schedule with several flights daily to Bali, Medan, Yogyakarta, Padang, and Ujung Padang. There are shuttle flights between Jakarta-Surabya, Jakarta-Bandung, Jakarta-Semarang, and Jakarta–Pangkal Pinang.

By boat: The national shipping line PELNI operates four large, modern, air-conditioned passenger ships, which have regular sailings between major seaports in Indonesia.

The first class cabins are comfortable with attached bathrooms and fares are quite low.

By train: Rail travel in Indonesia is limited to Java, and local trains in parts of Sumatra. Train travel is generally uncomfortable and not advised except for the air-conditioned overnight sleeper, *Bima* (17 hours Jakarta, Yogyakarta, Surabaya) or the all-coach but air-conditioned *Mutiara* (Jakarta, Cirebon, Semerang, Surabaya). Both trains serve meals and have afternoon departures. There are five services by the *Parahyangan* non air-conditioned fast trains between Jakarta-Bandung (3 hours). Also called *Mutiara* is another overnight express coach serving Bandung-Yogyakarta-Surabaya.

There are an increasing number of overland coach services available in Java from Jakarta to as far away as Bali. Bookings for these can be made through leading travel agents.

By taxi: Taxis, which are generally easy to find, are available at hotels and other central locations and cost Rp 400 for first kilometer, plus Rp 190 for each subsequent km. Taxis are metered only in Jakarta. Seen in a few provincial towns is the *becak,* a bicycle rickshaw, hired either according to distance (you must know exactly where you are going) or by the hour. With luck, you can hire a becak for Rp 1,000 an hour. Three-wheeled *Bajaj* minicars offer cheaper transportation in Jakarta and there are small minibuses in other towns which can be hired. One can hire a jeep and driver on Bali for Rp. 40,000 upwards per day or a motorcycle for about Rp. 12,000.

TIPPING. Compulsory service charge of 10 percent is usually included in leading hotels and restaurants. For airport porters and hotel bell boys Rp 5000. Leave small change for taxi drivers.

TIME. Indonesia has three time zones. The islands of Sumatra, Java and Madura/Bali observe Western Standard Time (GMT plus 7 hours). The islands of Kalimantan, Sulawesi and Nusa Tenggara (except Bali) have Central Standard Time (GMT plus 8 hours). The islands of Maluku and Irian Jaya have Eastern Standard Time (GMT plus 9 hours).

ACCOMMODATIONS. Accommodations in Indonesia are admittedly overpriced, unless you wish to stay at one of the many *losmen,* which are a sort of better-class boardinghouse. One factor that sends your hotel bill soaring is the 10 percent service charge added to your bill, which is then subject to a 5 percent government tax in Jakarta and 10 percent in other areas. In effect you will be charged an extra 15½ or 21 percent for your hotel, restaurant, bar, and laundry bills.

Jakarta hotels are mostly in the *Deluxe* and *First-Class* price ranges. Air conditioning, swimming pool and other recreational facilities, a choice of restaurants and shopping arcades are standard features in these hotels.

In most towns, especially the hill resorts, guesthouse accommodation is inexpensive and comfortable. Information is found from local tourist offices.

Note: The drastic fluctuation of the rupiah makes price estimating difficult. Price categories given here should only be used as general guides. Prices given are for standard double rooms in US dollars.

JAKARTA

Deluxe—US$115 and up

Borobudur Inter-Continental. 866 rooms. On 23 acres of landscaped grounds, with large pools, health club with sauna, six tennis courts. Near shopping and commercial center. Excellent dining. New extension will have 140 suites.

Jakarta Hilton. 664 rooms set in 32 acres, only 45 minutes from the new airport. New luxury Garden Tower.

Mandarin. This 500-room luxury hotel has the same management as the superb Mandarin in Hong Kong and Oriental in Bangkok.

Sari Pacific. Jalan Thamrin. A luxury hotel, with excellent restaurants and disco, and is close to shopping area and department store.

First Class—US$80–110

Aryaduta Hyatt. 235 rooms, all facilities including for conferences.

Horizon. Seaside location in Ancol recreation complex for this first-class 350-room hotel. Outside city, but close to golf, marina, art market.

Indonesia. Centrally located in the main business district; 666 rooms. Large swimming pool, good restaurants and shopping arcade.

Kartika Chandra. 200 rooms located on crosstown highway Jalan. Gatot Subroto. Supper club and movie theater. First class.

President. Associated with JAL, and conveniently located, offers a variety of services and amenities, including three restaurants and a shopping arcade. 354 rooms.

Sahid Jaya. 500-room hotel with full facilities and particularly fine reputation for its restaurants.

Moderate—US$55–70

Jayakarta Tower. 435 rooms, right in Chinatown and business center; 30 minutes from new airport; next to large cinema. 2 restaurants, large shopping area.

Kartika Plaza. Next door, comfortable, has 250 rooms, pool, shopping arcade and all amenities.

Orchid Palace. In a delightful garden setting, 85 rooms with swimming pool, 2 restaurants. Located in outer residential area, 30 minutes from airport, 20 minutes to commercial district.

Inexpensive—US$35–50

Cikini Sofyan. Smaller hotel in business district; restaurant, pub, sauna.

Sabang Metropolitan. 150 comfortable rooms conveniently located in shopping district. Restaurant, pool.

BALI

Deluxe—US$75–90

Bali Hyatt. 400 rooms on the beach. Captures Balinese atmosphere and with excellent facilities, including *Matahari,* the liveliest nightspot on the island. Delightful beachside gardens.

Bali Nusa Dua. Bali's newest hotel. Large, with suites and bungalows available. Balinese decor, pool, tennis court, supper club.

Bali Oberoi. Kuta Beach. Delightful setting. 75 lanai cottages and villas. Superb beach; pool; good restaurant.

Nusa Dua Beach. 450 air-conditioned rooms. Bali's most beautiful hotel, filled with decorative art. Excellent facilities: restaurants, disco, pool, squash, tennis.

Pertamina Cottages. On Kuta Beach near the airport. 178 suites. Good beach. Pool and good restaurant.

First Class—US$60–80

Bali Beach. Modern 8-story tower, garden, 2-story wings and Balinese-style cottages. 600 rooms total, 3 swimming pools and 8 restaurants and bars. Located on Sanur beach, 15 minutes from Denpasar.

Sanur Beach. 244 air-conditioned rooms and 26 private beach bungalows, with swimming pool, restaurants, and white sand beach. Friendly service.

Tandjung Sari. The original Balinese beach-style cottages on Sanur. Relaxed, beautiful and comfortable. 24 cottages.

Moderate—US$40–60

Alit's Beach Bungalows. 98 bungalows. Swimming pool, gardens.

Bali Mandira. Balinese cottages, pool, tennis and squash courts, many tourist facilities. On Kuta beach.

Kuta Beach Club. 89 rooms, swimming pool, restaurants, shopping arcade.

Santrian. On Sanur, 75 beach cottages in a garden setting. Charming bar and restaurant plus pool.

Segara Village. Balinese-style bungalows. 100 rooms with swimming pool, restaurant, pool, beach front.

BALIKPAPAN

Benakutal. 220 air-conditioned rooms with swimming pool, health club, and fine restaurants. Member of the Beaufort hotel chain. First class.

Patra. 24 air-conditioned rooms catering mostly to the oil industry.

BANDUNG

Istana. A delightfully charming garden hotel with good restaurant, bar and 100 comfortable rooms with hot water. First class. Rates include breakfast.

Panghegar. With new extension, a total of 250 rooms, 2 restaurants and bars. Friendly service. In center of town. First class.

Savoy Homann. Favorite with tour groups but tends to be noisy, particularly on the weekends. 120 rooms are fairly comfortable.

BRASTAGI

Bukit Kubu. 15 rooms all with hot and cold water, bar, restaurant. Comfortable hotel in this cool resort setting 40 miles from Medan.

CIREBON

Patrajasa Motel. 55 rooms, air-conditioned. First class.

Grand. An old-style hotel with 82 rooms, some air-conditioned. Centrally located.

LOMBOK

Hotel Melati. Located in the heart of Mataram, West Lombok. The hotel is a Nitour property and has 20 rooms. Clean and comfortable.

Suranadi. A former holiday resort for Dutch colonial functionaries in the foothills of the Punikan range. The swimming pool is spring-fed. There are 11 rooms in the older part of the hotel, but the best are the cottages on the terraced hillside overlooking the pool. Miles away from Cakranegaram it can be lonely at night but the surroundings are beautiful.

MANADO

Kawanua City. 100 rooms. Located in the city center, the hotel offers all the modern comforts expected from a three-star hotel.

Malalayang Beach. Just three guest bungalows, each divided into two sections and each section sleeping two persons. Popular with the international diver crowds although facilities are basic (but clean). Good starting point for boat trips to the reefs.

MEDAN

Danau Toba International. 272 air-conditioned rooms; pool, bowling alley, etc. Bar and restaurant. First class.

Dharma Deli. Older, but clean, with acceptable food. 186 air-conditioned rooms.

Garuda Plaza. 200 rooms, expensive. Centrally located with swimming pool.

Pardede International. Offers 112 air-conditioned rooms, pool and night club. Near airport. Moderate.

Polonia. 200 air-conditioned rooms; swimming pool, health center, good Chinese restaurant. Centrally located.

Tiara Medan. 200 rooms. Two restaurants and bars; pool and health club. Attentive service. Has own taxi service. First class.

MERAK

(West Java)

Anyer Beach Hotel. (Formerly Pertamina Cottages.) Cottages at Anyar are excellent. Just 50 rooms, mostly in luxuriously appointed cottages.

Carita Krakatau. Overlooking famous offshore volcano. Simple style on super beach. 150 cottage-style rooms. Offers inclusive tours, including volcano.

Merak Beach. Visit the Java Straits for swimming or a view of Krakatau Volcano. Cheaper on weekdays.

PELABUHAN RATU

Samudra Beach. More than just exotic. Offers 106 luxurious air-conditioned rooms, large swimming pool, bar and restaurants.

PRAPAT

Danau Toba International. 49 rooms, comfortable.

Natour Prapat. Swimming pool, tennis courts, 75 rooms, comfortable.

Patrajasa. Swimming pool, tennis courts, golf.

Toba Beach. On Samosir island, restaurant, transfer services.

SARANGAN

Sarangan. Located on lake, has mountain resort atmosphere.

Silver Win. Also located on lake. All rooms offering moderate comfort in this Javanese hill setting.

SELECTA

Selecta. 33 rooms and 3 bungalows in this beautiful but chilly hill station. Near fine pool. An ideal place to base yourself for an East Java tour. Good service and food.

SEMARANG

Dibya Puri. 70 rooms, some air-conditioned. First class.

Patra Jasa. 71 rooms, modern and a hotel of international standard, couple minutes' drive from downtown Semarang; complete with swimming pool, bowling alley, restaurants, bars, etc.

SURABAYA

Garden Palace. New hotel with 250 rooms, large dining facilities, Chinese and Japanese. In business district.

Hyatt Bumi Surabaya. Beautiful hotel, 250 rooms. Excellent Chinese restaurant and the only *Hugo's* in Indonesia. Centrally located.

Mirama. 105 rooms. Good facilities in residential area.

Simpang. 128 air-conditioned rooms, swimming pool. In business and entertainment area.

SURAKARTA

(Solo)

Kusuma Sahid Prince. Built around a restored palace, delightful atmosphere. 100 rooms.

Mangkunegaran Palace Hotel. Adjoining the Mangkunegaran Palace. 50 modern rooms; with good pool, but poor dining facilities. Reasonable.

TRETES

Natour Bath. 50 rooms in bungalows; swimming pool, restaurant. Moderately comfortable.

Tandjung. A comfortable hotel in this mountain resort 20 miles south of Surabaya. 51 rooms, clean and moderately comfortable. Tends to be noisy on weekends.

UJUNG PANDANG

(Makassar)

Grand. Centrally located old Dutch-style hotel with 65 rooms, some with air-conditioning.

Makassar Golden. 77 rooms in high rise and cottages. On seafront; best hotel in town; good dining facilities. New.

Marannu. Newest hotel in city center. 206 air-conditioned rooms, pool, disco and restaurants.

Pasanggrahan. 37 rooms overlooking the harbor. Some rooms air-conditioned. Small bar where you can watch the often gorgeous sunsets over Makassar Bay.

RANTEPAO

(Toraja)

Misiliana. 50 rooms, restaurant and bar. Personalized service. Transfers from Ujung Pandang Airport on request. Good food. Toraja décor.

—Toraja Cottages. 63 rooms in hillside cottages. Scenic location. Restaurant and bar.

WONOSOBO

Bima. New hotel with 50 rooms. Not much local color.

P.N.K.A. Wisma. Operated by the state railway system. 5 rooms. Moderately comfortable but best rated for its proximity to the Dieng Plateau temples.

YOGYAKARTA

Ambarrukmo. 250 air-conditioned rooms, all modern facilities including pool. Also good cultural shows and restaurants. First class.

Mutiara. Central location. Stay in new annex. Clean, friendly, moderately priced. 90 rooms.

Puri Artha Cottage. Beautiful Indonesian cottages with reasonable rates and friendly service. Quiet and comfortable. 60 rooms, mostly air-conditioned with private bath.

Sahid Garden. 64 air-conditioned rooms. Full amenities. 5 minutes from airport, 10 to city center. Garden and pool.

Srimanganti. ("Waiting room of the Sultan.") 40 air-conditioned rooms. Traditional-style. Own restaurant but better Chinese one next door.

Sriwedari. 70 rooms. Close to, but much cheaper than the Ambarrukmo. Restaurant and pool.

TOURS. The relative difficulty of organizing itineraries to places other than Jakarta or Bali encourages most foreigners to make use of a local travel agency. Trying to book hotels or domestic flights, for example, can be difficult from abroad as letters of inquiry are often ignored. Leading agents of good repute are *P.T. Vayatour,* 38 Batutulis; *Pacto,* 3rd Floor, Hotel Borobudur Inter-Continental, J1. Lapangan Banteng Selatan; *Satriavi,* Jalan Prapatan 32; *P.T. Tunas Indonesia,* Jalan Abdul Muis 32; and *Panorama,* Jalan Balikpapan 22.

A number of overseas tour agencies, *Neckermann und Reisen, Kuoni,* etc., and airlines such as *Garuda* and *Thai International* operate inclusive tour packages which are the most convenient way of seeing Java, Sumatra and Sulawesi.

WHAT TO SEE. The capital, Jakarta, offers sightseeing from the colonial Dutch and British periods, of which the Fatahillah Square and Pasar Ikan, the old Sunda Kelapa port area are unique. There are several fine museums, old churches, classical and modern civic buildings and an impressive, if stark, modern national mosque. Taman Mini, "Beautiful Indonesia in Miniature," gives an overall view of the architecture and arts of Indonesia in replicas of houses from the 27 provinces of Indonesia. New here is Fantasy Land, reminiscent of Disneyland. Try to see the film at the IMAX theater on Indonesia.

In spite of the many attractions of Jakarta many visitors head straight for fabled Bali when they arrive in Indonesia; however, Central Java, the cradle of Javanese civilization, is equally important with its Hindu-Buddhist monuments, including the fabulous Borobudur, dating back a millennium. The university city of Yogyakarta is the center of the region, and from here you can make side trips to see the ruins and lively culture of the area. Jakarta is a good introduction to the country, and is the jumping-off point for visits to the artistic city of Bandung or the offshore coral island, Pulau Putri. The scenic drive through the mountains and tea plantations will also provide you with an opportunity to visit the world-famous botanical gardens at Bogor. From either Bandung or Bogor, you can head south to the rather isolated coastal town of Pelabuhan Ratu. Surabaya, at the eastern end of Java, is a good base for visits to the temple ruins of the Majapahit Empire and Mount Bromo, one of Indonesia's 128 active volcanoes. The remaining major islands of Indonesia contain a mélange of fascinating cultures and natural beauty but are best visited by those willing to put up with inadequate tourist facilities. Medan is the gateway to North Sumatra with its numerous rubber and palm oil estates, breathtaking Lake Toba and distinctive Batak inhabitants; Tana Toraja in south Sulawesi with its hilly terrain, orange and black carved houses and gala burial festivals; or the primitive cultures of Borneo (now called Kalimantan) and West Papua/New Guinea (now called Irian Jaya), where time has almost stood still since the Stone Age.

ENTERTAINMENT. Indonesia has a rich tradition of ceremonial dances, puppet shows and drama which continue to flourish and grow in spite of the increasing presence of Western-type entertainment. It would therefore be a pity not to make some effort to see some of the traditional cultural forms during your visit. The impressive, new cultural center, *Taman Ismail Marzuki,* at Cikini Raya in Jakarta has a constant and varied schedule featuring dance drama *(wayang orang),* shadow puppet plays *(wayang kulit),* modern Indonesian drama, rotating modern art exhibits and numerous concerts by both the Jakarta symphony as well as visiting performing artists. *Wayang orang* can also be seen nightly at the *Panca Murti* theater near Pasar Senen, but the atmosphere is hot and crowded. You hear gamelan concerts every Sunday morning between 9:30 and 10:30 at the National Museum (the gold exhibit is also open only between those same hours in the museum). The Radio Republic Indonesia studio, Jalan Merdeka Timor, performs and broadcasts a shadow puppet play the last Saturday of each month which visitors may attend. Sunday morning there is a *wayang kulit* play at the puppet museum near the old Stadhuis. Provincial pavilions at Taman Mini take turns in giving performances on Sundays and local dramas are held at the open stage at Pasar Seni in Ancol Dreamland.

In West Java, it is best to ask your hotel or local tourist agency if you wish to see a three dimensional *(wayang golek)* puppet performance, always performed on Saturday nights in Bandung. Such advice also holds true in Central and East Java if you are interested in seeing *ketoprak,* a variation of *wayang orang, ludruk,* low comedy people's theater, or *kuda kepang,* the hobbyhorse trance dance usually performed by wandering street troupes.

The government has opened an impressive outdoor theater at the Prambanan temple complex near Yogyakarta, where the four episode Ramayana in ballet form is performed on the full moon nights between May and October. The same type of Javanese dance performances are also held occasionally in the outdoor theater in Pandaan, East Java.

In Bali, ceremonial dances are performed nearly every day especially for visitors at leading hotels, but it is better to seek out the more genuine and delightful shows in the many village temples.

Outdoor enthusiasts should note that it is easy to rent boats in Ancol at the marina to visit any one of the Thousand Islands which lie beyond the Jakarta harbor. The water is clear and the coral reefs and tropical fish breathtaking. You can even spend the night on a tiny tropic isle, *Pulau Putri,* where modest but comfortable bungalows are available.

MUSEUMS. Jakarta offers several excellent museums. The *Central Museum,* Jalan Merdeka Barat, is one of the finest in Asia with superb collections of ceramic, ethnographic, numismatic and archeological exhibits. Open 8:30 A.M.–2:00 P.M. on Tuesday, Wednesday, Thursday, Sunday; 8:30 to 11:00 on Friday and Saturday. Closed Monday, entrance Rp 100. The *Jakarta Museum* in Fatahillah Square displays a fine collection of colonial Dutch material in the beautifully restored Stadhuis. The *Museum Wayang,* also in Fatahillah Square, houses fascinating collections of puppets from all parts of Indonesia. Open Thursday, Saturday, Sunday 9:00 A.M.–1:00 P.M. Friday till 11:00 A.M. Every Sunday at 10 A.M. a shadow puppet play is performed. Still in Fatahillah

Square, the *Ceramics Museum* has an excellent collection donated by the late Vice President Adam Malik. An adjoining gallery exhibits Indonesian paintings and sculptures. One of the finest ceramic collections in Southeast Asia can be viewed at the *National Museum* at the Merdaka Square. *Museum Indonesia* houses exhibits of contemporary arts and crafts. A museum of textiles, in Jalan Satsuit Tubun, houses displays of batik and weaving from all parts of Indonesia. Open daily except Monday. Entry Rp 100. Down by the old port area of Pasir Ikan, a newly opened *Maritime Museum* is housed in a former spice godown dating from the 17th century.

On Bali: *Bali Museum,* Denpasar (history and culture of Bali), 8 A.M. to 1 P.M., closed Mon.; *Ratna Wartha Museum,* Ubud (painting and sculpture). There are good museums too in Yogyakarta, Solo, Surabaya, and Ujung Pandang.

SHOPPING in Indonesia may be more exciting than you think. *Batik* material with a wide variety of fascinating prints varies from area to area on Java, but cannot be surpassed for craftmanship anywhere in the world. Jakarta still offers the best choice, but if you are going to Cirebon, Pekalongan, Yogya, or Solo, it is best to buy your batiks there. Surabaya also has Madurese batik which is not as fine as the Javanese.

If buying batiks in Jakarta, find the widest variety at the batik cooperative *G.K.B.I.* on Jalan H. A. Salim or *Sarinah Dept. Store,* Jalan Thamrin. For more exclusive batik try *Ramacraft* on 25 Jalan Panarukan or *Danar Hadi* on Jalan Raden Saleh.

Other islands produce other varieties of cloth, some of which make unique wall hangings, particularly Sumba cloths and "ship's cloths" as well as ornate gold embroidered cloths from Sumatra.

Shops line several main "jalans" or streets in Jakarta. Among the best streets for tourist shopping are Haji Agus Salim and Pasar Baru. In Kebayoran, a suburb of Jakarta, the main area is "Blok M." During evenings and weekends there is an art market at Ancol, and for antiques, visit Jalan Surabaya. Several new shopping centers have opened in Jakarta and offer a wide range of quality goods. Try *Aldiron Plaza* and *Sarinah* in Kebayoran Baru, *Ratu Plaza, Duta Merlin,* and *Gajah Mada Plaza.*

In Bali, you will find wood and stone carvings of first quality. Balinese sarongs, masks, paintings, and embroidered, leather, woven ware are also good buys. Your most interesting finds will be in the small shops of Sanur, Kuta, Max, Legion, Ubud, and Klungkung. For finest quality art sculpture in wood visit Ida Bagus Tilem in Mas. In some of the shops on the road between Denpasar and Ubud, you can see stone and wood carvers, as well as silversmiths at work. If you choose to buy at the hotel shops, be prepared by pay a higher price in Indonesia.

In Central Java, silver from Kota Gede (outside of Yogyakarta) and leather shadow puppets are popular purchases, the latter making particularly striking decorative pieces back home. Bandung is home of the *Wayang golek* puppets. Beachwear and modern fashions produced now in Bali are excellent, cheap.

Indonesia is considered one of the last places to find antique Chinese porcelain at reasonable prices. This is particularly so on the outer islands of Kalimantan and Sulawesi, where merchant ships from China touched port three or four centuries ago. On Java, good pieces of porcelain are more difficult to find and you should be wary of imitation except in shops of good reputation. Sumatra offers old coins and Batak tribal goods.

If you are interested in purchasing contemporary Indonesian art, you should make contact with the Taman Ismail Marzuki in Jakarta, the Fine Arts Department of the Bandung Institute of Technology, or the School of Fine Arts in Yogyakarta. Contemporary artists are working in the graphic arts, oil paintings, and modern batik wall hangings. Quality is high, and as time goes on, so are prices.

BARGAINING. Part of the way of life in Indonesia and something every visitor has to get to grips with. An invaluable first step would be to learn to count in Indonesian. Generally, where a price is not displayed, prices are not fixed, and even if the goods do have a price tag, it is usually all right to ask for a "discount," to bargain a little. It is wise to get an Indonesian acquaintance to tell you the general level of prices for the goods or services you might want. Always make sure the price is agreed upon before accepting the article or service, otherwise a captive market is assured for an inflated price. An accepted last gambit in bargaining is to walk away, having made your final offer: you will often find the seller chasing after you to accept it, before you have gone more than a few yards. Beware of strangers offering to help you find what you want. Often they will steer you toward friends of theirs in the hope of getting a commission on goods sold, or they might expect a tip from you for help that was not really necessary.

RESTAURANTS. Indonesia has an abundance of succulent spices, herbs, fresh meats, and vegetables which have created a cuisine of great variation. Hotel coffee shops have a wider choice of Indonesian specialties now; however, the few suitable restaurants in the archipelago concentrate on European food. The Indonesian *Rijstaffel,* made famous by the Dutch, is only a shadow of its former self in Jakarta these days. Visitors might brave the downtown areas and eat in the small Indonesian restaurants for some spicy delights, but this is not recommended for those with tender stomachs. Cheap, varied seafood is a specialty of the many small restaurants in Indonesia's coastal cities.

Visitors must choose between stomach or pocketbook, because Indonesia offers little for unseasoned budget-minded travelers. Hotel coffee shop prices are high: up to US$1.00 for a cup of coffee, US$5.00 for a hamburger. American fast foods are making inroads in Jakarta, but tourist restaurants can be costly: in Bali a pizza costs Rp 2,500. Chinese and *nasi padang* food shops cost much less, but travelers with tight time schedules might consider the expense caused by an upset tummy.

Among other delicacies, many foreign tourists like *sate* (small pieces of grilled meat on a stick served with a tangy sauce), *soto* (a soup), *gado gado* (mixture of vegetables with peanut sauce), and the rice dishes of Yogyakarta and Solo, *nasi opor, nasi rames,* and *nasi gudek.* The Balinese specialty is *babi guling,* a delicious barbecued pig, but many consider it unwise to eat pork dishes on Bali.

JAKARTA

Ramayana Room of Hotel Indonesia serves fine Indonesian and so-so European food, although its noon buffets are delicious.

For a memorable evening, have dinner at the **Oasis,** Jalan. Raden Saleh. While the mixed European and Indonesian menu is good, you will be more impressed by the elegant surroundings and the charming songs of the Toba Batak singers. One of Jakarta's most expensive restaurants.

For lunch, try **Vic's Viking,** Jln. Thamrin, whose 80 varieties of dishes, while good, do not quite live up to their Scandinavian origins. Also for lunch try the **Thistle** in Metropolitan Building, Jalan Sudirman.

For lunch or dinner, the **Swiss Inn,** Arthaloka Building, Jalan Sudirman, and **The Stables,** Hong Kong and Shanghai Bank, Jalan Hayam Wuruk.

Mina's Seafood Restaurant, in the Sahid Jaya Boulevard Hotel offers superb fruits of the sea. Excellent weekday buffet lunches.

Nelayan seafood restaurant at Borobudur Inter-Continental offers steaming baskets of seafood with a variety of sauces. Expensive, but good.

The daily buffet lunches, however, are excellent and very good values.

La Bistro, Jalan Wahid Hasyim, **Pete's Place,** Jalan Gatot Subroto, and the **Jaya Pub,** Jalan Thamkin, belong to the same owners and besides good European food, have music and atmosphere.

Also for seafood, Asian style and delicious, **Yun Njan, Jalan Batu Ceper.**

For good, if expensive, European food try the **Sahid Grill** in the Sahid Jaya Hotel, or the **Toba Rôtisserie** in the Borobodur, Mandarin Hotel **Club Room, Taman Sari** at the Hilton, and Sari Pacific's **Jayakarta Grill.** In the outdoor bazaar section of the Hilton one can get a good pizza. The **Bistro,** in Jalan Wahid Hasyim, is a charmingly converted house with delightful atmosphere and limited menu of good Continental cuisine. Behind Behind Hotel Indonesia, the **George and Dragon** provides a pleasant pub atmosphere with basic meals. Among better places for Indonesian cuisine is the one in the **Hilton Sriwedari Gardens.**

For delicious satay try **Satay House Senayan,** Jalan Kebon Sirih 31. Hot spicy Javanese food at **Jaya,** Jalan Melawai Raya.

Most of the Chinese restaurants have a distressing sameness of décor, which features stainless steel and plastic, but the food is generally excellent.

The **Tjahaja Kota** on Jalan Wahid Hasjim for first choice while the **Sky Room, Hong Kong** and **Paramount** will be good seconds.

More fun, perhaps, will be making the trip down to Chinatown *(glodok)* to sample the food at either the **Kota** or **Sim Jan** restaurant near the Chinese pagoda on Jalan Kemurnian. To reach the latter two places, tell your taxi to turn left on the first street after passing the former Chinese Embassy.

For Japanese dining, try **Kikugawa,** Djl, Kebun Binatang III. Also good but expensive Japanese food in **Hilton, Hyatt, Sari Pacific, President,** and **Borobudur** hotels and **Hama** at Ratu Plaza on Jalan Jendra Sudirman.

The **Omar Khayam** has an excellent Indian buffet lunch on weekdays. Good value for your money.

In the quiet residential suburb of Kebayoran Baru, at Jalan Patiunus I, is **Mira Sari,** which has a menu of authentic Indonesian cuisine. The décor is not exciting but the food has a homemade taste.

Hotel Borobudur's Cultural Night every Friday also offers an authentic Indonesian buffet and performance of traditional dances and music.

Kemang Hill. Beautiful local décor. Indonesian and Continental cuisine. This restaurant is located in the suburb of Kemang, but worth the long ride.

Two new Thai restaurants are the **Sri Thai** on Kuningan and **D'jit Ponchana,** a beautifully decorated restaurant in the new Forestry Building next to the Parliament complex.

OUTSIDE JAKARTA

Bandung: Try *Queen* and *Grand* for Chinese meals. *Istana Hotel* serves reasonable food in pleasant atmosphere.

Yogya: The fried chicken at *Nyonya Suharti* is delicious. Likewise at *Madukoro,* a small roadside restaurant about 9 kilometers outside Solo. If you are not staying at *Wisma L.P.P.* in Yogya, have dinner there primarily to enjoy the spectacular dining room setting. Dining facilities in *Ambarrukmo Palace*

Hotel also good, including the "*Floating*" restaurant, specializing in Indonesian food.

Solo: The *Diamond* and the *Orient* are the best restaurants in Solo, but keep your expectations low. In **Malang,** *Toko Oen,* a long-time restaurant chain which serves fair food in Old World ice-cream parlor surroundings, will be your best bet.

Bali: In addition to the hotels, try the *Rijstaffel* at the Tanjung Sari on Sanur Beach and at Hotel Sanur Beach (especially good for Saturday and Sunday lunch). Among the best places on Sanur are *da Marco* for Italian food, *Swastika, Kul Kul* and *Telaga Naga* for Chinese and Western dishes. *Lenny's* has good Chinese food and *Raouls & Dragon* is excellent for seafood. On Kuta, *Poppies* and *Lennys* have good seafood and *Yasa Samudra* Indonesian, Chinese and Western food. *Pari Selera* is recommended in Denpasar, as is the exquisitely located *Puri Suling,* near Ubud and well worth a lunch-time stop—or for dinner by arrangement. Japanese restaurants are *Bengkay* and *Fujion* on Sanur; and *Pertamina Cottages* has just opened an excellent one.

Ujung Pandang: Try the *Seaview* (restaurant and nightclub) or the *Bamboo Den* if you want a change from the hotel food, but don't expect too much. *Asia Baru* has the best seafood in the city; clean but plain décor. In **Medan,** try *Copacabana* for European food, *Paradise* and *Polonia Hotel* for Chinese or *International* for Indonesian cuisine.

NIGHT LIFE in once dull Jakarta has perked up with nightclubs and other entertainment. However, quality of floor shows does vary and, in general, nightclub prices are high.

The *Tropicana,* Jalan Manila, rivals the *Blue Ocean,* Hajam Wuruk, for the best floor shows in town. Among good discotheques are the *Pitstop* in the Hotel Sari Pacific, *Oriental* at the Hilton, and the *Guwa Rama* in the Hotel Indonesia.

Hotel Indonesia. Dancing every night and floorshows in its top floor *Nirwana* nightclub. Pleasant dining and bar.

You may wish to take your chances on the floorshow fare at the *L.C.C.* in the Jakarta Fair complex.

On Bali, best nightspots are *Matahari,* at the Hyatt, and the *Disco* at Nusa Dua beach.

WATER. Do not drink tap water. All good hotels provide boiled or bottled water. Outside the hotel, ask for tea, which is by necessity made from boiled water, but be sure it is *steaming,* not tepid. Bottled soft drinks are also safe.

MEDICAL SERVICES IN JAKARTA. Most big hotels have English-speaking doctors on call. Christian-operated hospitals are *Rumah Sakit Cikini* (Protestant) and *St. Carolus* (Catholic). There are good pharmacies in big cities, called "Apotiks." There is also the *Pertamina Hospital* which has the most modern facilities. Many foreigners use *The Medical Scheme* in Setia Budi Building on Jalan Rasuna Said, Kuningan, the *Bina Medical Clinic* at Jalan Maluku 8, or the *Metropolitan Medical Centre* at the Wisata International Hotel. In Bali, all hotels retain good medical services.

USEFUL ADDRESSES. Embassies. *American,* Merdeka Selatan 5; *British,* Jalan Thamrin 75; *Canadian,* Jalan Jendral Sudirman 29; *Australian,* Jalan Thamrin 15.

General Information. The Indonesian Directorate General of Tourism strongly advises foreign visitors to make their travel arrangements, including hotel reservations, transportation, guide service, etc., through recognized travel agents or their overseas offices. While the head office is located at 81 Jalan Kramat Raya, Jakarta, there are local tourism offices in provincial capitals.

There are hotel reservation and general information counters at Cengkareng airport in Jakarta and at Ngurah Rai airport in Bali.

Emergencies. Foreign tourists encountering any difficulty during their stay are advised to seek the assistance of the management of major hotels or travel agents. Emergency telephone numbers in Jakarta are 110 (Police) and 118 (Ambulance), but we stress it is wiser to seek action through a major hotel.

LANGUAGE. The language spoken in Indonesia is almost identical with that used in Malaysia. See the Malaysia chapter for phrases that the visitor will find useful in Indonesia.

THE PHILIPPINES

Sunshine, Charm, and Color

"As any intelligent man knows, the Filipino is the most hospitable person in the world," wrote an observer of the Philippines scene some 50 years ago. To cover half a century in three words, we can say simply that things haven't changed. Filipinos are naturally hospitable, and it isn't just Sunday manners. They're courteous and gracious even among themselves. A host will put out all stops to make a guest feel at home even if it breaks him, and it sometimes does.

Despite Bataan, Corregidor, and Magsaysay, the Philippines isn't as well known as it should be in the great outside world. Don't ask us why. It's certainly the loss of the outside world. The Philippines has got everything to become one of the world's sunshine spots for the cold of bone and the depressed of spirit. Statistics tell us that, what with jet travel, the picture is changing and the Philippines is in the process of being discovered. There's plenty of hospitality and sunshine to go around, but our advice is to get here first.

In the Philippines, you'll get all the sunshine, charm, and color of the South Seas, and you won't have to turn beachcomber to do it. You can imbibe all of this in style and comfort. There are plenty of islands to go around, 7,107 in all. Fortunately, you won't have to explore them one by one to learn what makes the Filipinos tick. Most of the population lives on eleven large islands and about 300 in all are inhabited. All of these friendly islands lie south of Taiwan and north of Borneo, a few hundred miles off the Asian mainland. The Philippines is a mountainous country with fertile plains and tropical vegetation and forests. The largest island is Luzon, where Manila is located. Manila has boomed in population right along with the country as a whole. At the latest count, the Filipinos numbered 48 million and were still going upward. The Philippines is old as a country, but young as a nation. It's a developing country, better off than most Asian countries, but there's still the problem of how to feed, clothe, and shelter all those 48 million. Politicians not unnaturally disagree on how it should be done and who can do it best. Nowhere is democratic politics played with such fire and passion. Politics is a national pastime as you'll soon see from the headlines of Manila's lively press. Out of the smoke, fire, and fury, democratic policies are hammered out. Progress has been made; much more remains to be done. The American visitor in particular should be interested in the Philippine political system, for many of the institutions are legacies of almost half a century of American rule.

English-speaking visitors have observed that the Philippines is different, but yet "it's like home." The contrast is because it really is different. The similarity is due partly to the widespread use of English. It's used in the schools, in discussing new laws, in drawing up contracts, writing news stories and, yes, alas, on billboards. This isn't time to go into the pros and cons of English versus Pilipino, the national language, but it's been the subject of many an unsettled debate. The visitor, in any event, will find the popularity of English convenient. It is one of three official languages, Pilipino and Spanish being the other two. English was introduced by the Americans and what with 87 regional dialects and languages in the islands, English has been a great unifier, say its proponents.

Melting Pot of Peoples and Cultures

The Philippines is at the crossroads of Asia. Colonizers and invaders have come and gone. Out of diversity of cultures and blood has come a broad tolerance for other beings and ways. The Philippines is a true melting pot. Its people are somewhat smaller than the Westerner. Their complexion ranges from a light to a dark brown. Their hair is black, their eyes black or brown. The addition of Spanish, Chinese, or European blood to the basic Malay stock is often noticeable. Filipinas, as the women are called, are charming and beautiful. An oft-repeated exclamation of the first-time visitor is: "I didn't know there were so many pretty girls!" Now you know. It's not a case of all beauty either. Filipinas have proven they have a head for business, and are in all the professions and trades. Filipinas have for long been accorded an independence and respect unknown to other Asian women.

The Philippines is old and new, East and West. It's changing by the day, but traditions persist. Relations between the sexes, liberal by Asian standards, are not as formal as before, but it's still not strange for a chaperon to make it a threesome on dates. The menfolk have more freedom and mobility. If old ways prove too confining, a young man, in Manila anyway, can tell his troubles to a professional dancing partner at one of the nightclubs.

Filipino orchestras are the best in Asia and whether in Singapore or Tokyo, you're likely to run across a top Filipino dance band. Filipinos are wonderful dancers, men and women alike. Latin American dances are always in season. The Filipino seems to have an inborn ear for rhythm to the envy of many a foreigner born with two left feet. Young Filipino folk dancers in recent years have been dancing their way through the capitals of the world and leaving everyone breathless with the spontaneous gaiety and amazing variety of their dances. If you can catch one of the frequent folk dancing programs, you'll be treated to a cultural feast of war, religious, courting, and harvest dances.

Whether you're dancing or strolling, you don't have to worry about the heat. For men, bankers and janitors alike, slacks and sport shirts are the order of the day. For party wear, suits are worn, but equally acceptable is the *barong Tagalog,* the most sensible men's wear ever dreamed up by perspiring mankind. The *barong* gives a man a chance to be comfortable and elegant at the same time. It's a loose, almost transparent, shirt with long sleeves and is never tucked into one's trousers. Let it hang out, the better to see the elaborate embroidery which you may choose to wear. Some of the more delicate fibers cost as much as a suit, but simple cotton ones will do, whether at the office or at the swankiest dinner party. By all means, get a *barong,* but wear a T-shirt, not an ordinary undershirt, beneath it.

The accent is more on style for women, but even they normally wear light summer frocks the year around. Filipinas have their traditional clothes, too. Their formal *ternos,* with butterfly sleeves, are often gorgeous creations costing small fortunes. The simpler *balintawaks* have also come down from the past, though you see them worn more in the countryside than in the cities. But in keeping with latest fashion trends, the traditional dresses have been modernized. If you can, see one of Manila's many fashion shows.

In the lowlands, the sun will be your constant companion. Even in the rainy season, the sun competes with the rain and often wins the contest. Make the most of a sun which can get decidedly hot at midday, but which is never really unpleasant provided that you leave your woolens at home. Be like the Filipino farmer. Get up early, enjoy the cool morning air and get your chores out of the way before the heat of the day becomes intense. Rain or shine, however, there are always air-conditioned sanctuaries in Manila and the larger cities where you can duck in for a cool drink.

You don't have to go far for authentic tropical scenery. Manila itself abounds with palm and coconut trees. And only a short distance from Manila, you can find Filipino farmers hard at work in their rice paddies with their ponderous water buffaloes or *carabaos.* Picturesque nipa huts on stilts, surrounded by coconut trees, banana plants, and tropical flowers in pots, are typical rural scenes. Their inhabitants make up a *barrio* or village. So many *barrios* taken together form a municipality with its own administrative organization. The country as a whole is made up of numerous provinces, each with a governor and capital. They may be as small as the tiny rocky islands of Batanes off northern

Luzon or as large as the Empire Province of Cotabato in Mindanao which can swallow up several average-sized provinces.

The Philippines is in the "take-off" stage of industrialization. New plants and buildings are going up all the time. But the population is still largely rural and the wealth still lies primarily in the earth. No one need starve in the Philippines. Nature is bountiful and two crops of rice a year can be grown in many areas. The main exports are sugar, coconuts, abaca or Manila hemp, lumber, tobacco, pineapples, and minerals. The dollars these bring in help finance industrialization.

A Little History: Magellan to Marcos

Filipinos view with wry humor those history books which say their country was "discovered" by Magellan in 1521, when that doughty navigator crossed the Atlantic and then the unknown Pacific to the Philippines where he was killed in a clash with the forces of a native leader. Spanish colonizers, however, did not come until 1565. It was then that Miguel Lopez de Legaspi landed with the cross and the sword. He and his men found a people with a script, laws, and culture of their own. A flourishing trade was carried on with neighboring countries. They lived in tribal units known as *barangays.*

The people were then, as they are today, of predominantly Malay origin. They were part of an adventurous race which had pushed northward from present-day Indonesia in sturdy outrigger boats to settle the islands that constitute the Philippines of today. They subdued or assimilated earlier inhabitants who had reached the islands in other migratory waves thousands of years before. Descendants of these earlier groups are still to be found. They are the primitive Negritos and other tribes bearing a resemblance to the American Indians.

The Philippines, which got its name from King Philip II of Spain, survived some 350 years of Spanish rule and finally overthrew the colonial overlords in 1898. The Spanish influence was a profound one. The culture, architecture, and manners of the country all testify to this. The Roman Catholic religion, introduced by Spanish friars is still the faith of 83 percent of Filipinos. The Philippines is the only Christian nation in Asia. Imposing old churches are to be seen all over the country.

The first Filipino Republic, established in 1898, was the first republic in Asia. It was the culmination of a revolt against Spanish rule started in 1896 and brought to a successful conclusion under the leadership of General Emilio Aguinaldo and with the help of American forces. Commodore George Dewey's naval squadron smashed Spanish naval forces in Manila Bay in 1898. Thus did the Spanish-American War hasten the end of Spanish domination in the Philippines.

Aguinaldo and the Americans had a falling out and the United States acquired possession of the Philippine Islands, as they were then called. The Filipinos never quite forgave President McKinley for his statement that it was the duty of the United States to civilize and Christianize the distant islands. Filipinos, of course, had been Christians for hundreds of years. Almost from the beginning, the United States promised the Filipinos independence and it kept that promise on July 4, 1946, mak-

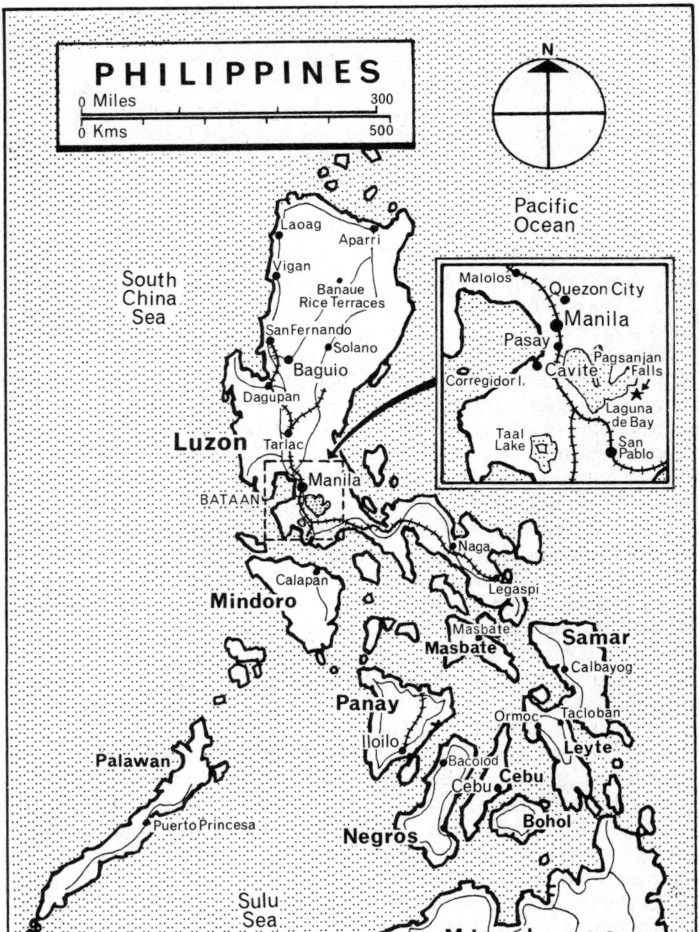
PHILIPPINES
0 Miles 300
0 Kms 500
N
Pacific Ocean
South China Sea
Laoag
Aparri
Vigan
Banaue Rice Terraces
San Fernando
Solano
Baguio
Dagupan
Luzon
Tarlac
Manila
BATAAN
Malolos
Quezon City
Manila
Pasay
Pagsanjan Falls
Cavite
Corregidor I.
Laguna de Bay
Taal Lake
San Pablo
Naga
Legaspi
Calapan
Mindoro
Masbate
Masbate
Samar
Calbayog
Panay
Ormoc
Tacloban
Iloilo
Leyte
Palawan
Bacolod
Cebu
Cebu
Bohol
Puerto Princesa
Negros
Sulu Sea
Mindanao
Davao
Zamboanga
SABAH

ing the Philippines the first of the colonial countries in Asia and Africa to achieve independence. Under American rule, great strides were made in popular government, public education, and public health. All during this period, Filipinos carried on a struggle for independence, not by arms but by the parliamentary route. It was led principally by Manual L. Quezon, the brilliant first president of the Philippine Commonwealth, and Sergio Osmena, Sr., the last president of the Commonwealth. The relations between Filipinos and Americans were remarkably good until the last few years.

The Japanese invaded the country in 1941 and cruelly imposed their will for three years, until American forces liberated the islands in 1944. Filipino and American soldiers fought shoulder to shoulder on Bataan and Corregidor against overwhelming odds and those battles are part of the honored history of both countries. Filipino guerrillas carried on the battle, tying up large contingents of Japanese troops.

The war's end found much of the country in ruins. Manila was said to have suffered more destruction than any city in the world. Buildings, homes, and irreplaceable cultural landmarks were destroyed. Removing the scars of war and building a new nation were complicated by a fierce rebellion by the Communist-led Huks. At one time, the Huks were knocking at the door of Manila itself, but finally they were rolled back and their backbone broken by Defense Secretary Ramon Magsaysay, whose twin measures of force and social justice saved the day. Fantastically popular, Magsaysay became President of the Philippines and served until his tragic death in an airplane crash in 1957. He was succeeded by Carlos P. Garcia, Diosdado Macapagal, and Ferdinand E. Marcos, the first president to be re-elected.

During a period of natural calamity (typhoon), general demoralization and near anarchy, President Marcos placed the country under martial law on Sept. 21, 1972. Local conditions improved; guns were no longer seen in the streets. The crime rate dropped; crimes committed against tourists were severely punished; a general beautification program of cities and towns throughout the country got underway. The president lifted martial law in 1981. Following the tragic assassination of former Senator Benigno Aquino Jr. in late 1983, dramatic developments have taken place in the political scene, and measures have been adopted to normalize the situation, resulting in greater freedom of press, the restoration of the vice-presidency, and new nation-wide voter registration.

EXPLORING THE PHILIPPINES

Manila is a big city but most of the population of the country is still in the rural areas. Manila is the center of commerce, government, education, capital, skilled labor, and about everything else. But the wealth of the land still lies in the rich natural resources and agricultural products in the provinces. Manila is the pacesetter; when it speaks, the whole nation listens. It has beautiful homes and gracious living; it has vast blocks of slums and miserable poverty. Manila is maddening and fascinating, a city in transition, never dull.

To the Spanish, Manila was one of the brightest gems in the Spanish Empire. It was a throbbing cosmopolitan center of trade and commerce when most of the cities of North America were untamed wildernesses. More so than the country at large, Manila is a mixture of contradictory infusions, one whose variegated experiences have given it a composure, if not a sophistication, that has seen it through invasions, wars, occupations, fires, and earthquakes. Indian, Spaniard, Chinese, American, Japanese, have come, stayed, and gone, each leaving his mark.

The dashing Miguel Lopez de Legaspi, a young Spanish officer, founded Manila in 1571 on the ruins of a Mohammedan settlement. The ruins were the handiwork of Spanish invaders the previous year. Within the next 60 years, the Spanish built a huge wall around their Asian outpost. More accurately, Filipino slaves did the work under Spanish direction. In the process, some 3,000 Filipinos died. How durably they built in those days may be judged from the massive walls which can be seen today. In time the city would spill over into the surrounding river plain, but for hundreds of years *Intramuros,* or the Walled City, was the focal point of Spanish rule in the Philippines.

The Walled City

Manila was one of the most romantic ports in the world even then. Ships sailed past Corregidor Island into Manila Bay, boasting a splendid natural harbor of some 800 square miles. Spanish galleons plied between Manila and the Spanish Empire in the New World; fortunes were made and lost in the galleon trade. Chinese junks from proud Cathay sailed in and out of the busy harbor with silk and jade and spices. Sailors from faraway Europe mingled with seafaring men from all over Asia. A prosperous community of Chinese merchants, precursors of the Chinese who play a key role in the business and commercial life throughout Southeast Asia, grew up outside *Intramuros.*

Every night the drawbridges separating *Intramuros* and the world without were hoisted up and the gates closed. Mexican soldiers patrolled the broad walls while the city slept. At dawn the six gates to the city were again opened. The Walled City survived uprisings by the Chinese, invasions by the Dutch and Chinese, and occupation by the British from 1762 to 1764. With the British came *sepoys* from India whose descendants still live in a small town near Manila. Now and again an earthquake would necessitate some repairs, but the old city appeared indestructible. When the Americans took over the country, they drained the moat outside the walls as a health measure. *Intramuros* lost its importance as a governmental center, but it remained the heart of religious activities for the Philippine Islands as the country was then called.

The ancient churches came tumbling down in the Second World War when the Japanese holed up in the city and American GIs with the liberation forces had to blast them out with artillery in 1945 during the savage Battle of Manila. *Intramuros* was in a pathetic condition after the smoke cleared away. The old churches were in ruins. Only St.

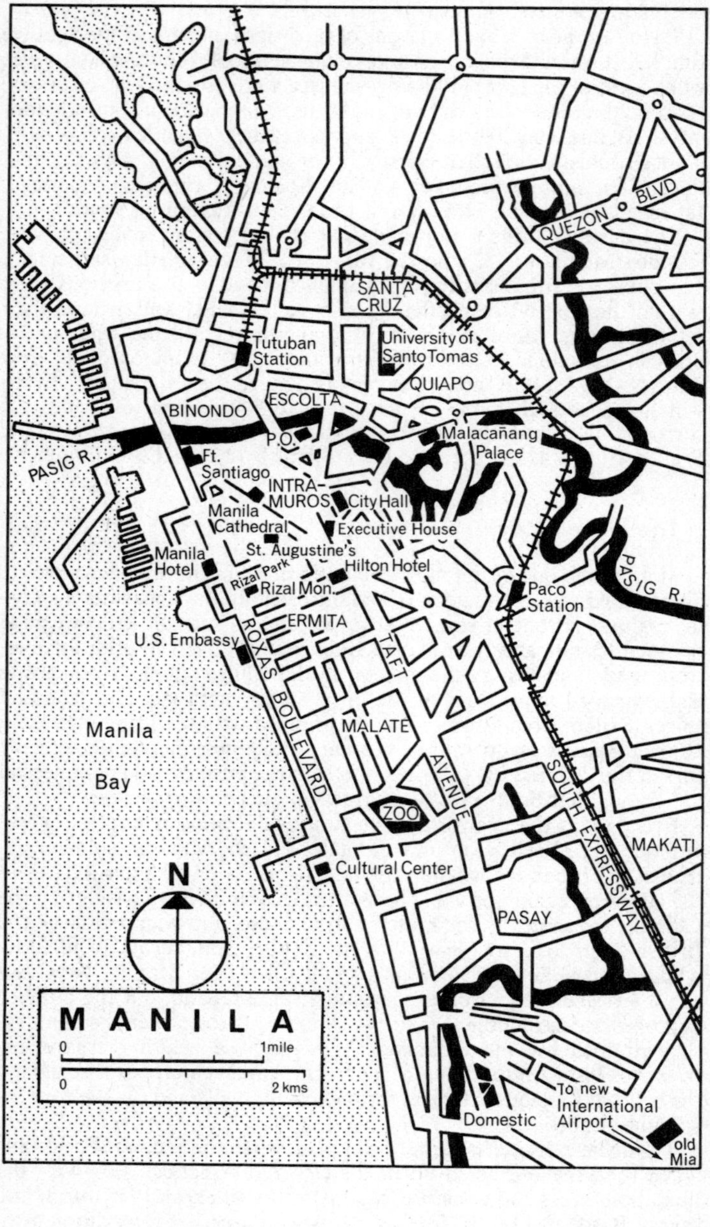

MANILA
0 1mile
0 2 kms
N
Manila Bay
PASIG R.
BINONDO
ESCOLTA
Tutuban Station
SANTA CRUZ
University of Santo Tomas
QUIAPO
QUEZON BLVD
P.O.
Ft. Santiago
Malacañang Palace
INTRAMUROS
City Hall
Manila Cathedral
Executive House
St. Augustine's
Manila Hotel
Rizal Park
Hilton Hotel
Rizal Mon.
Paco Station
PASIG R.
ERMITA
U.S. Embassy
ROXAS BOULEVARD
TAFT AVENUE
MALATE
SOUTH EXPRESSWAY
ZOO
MAKATI
Cultural Center
PASAY
Domestic
To new International Airport
old Mia

Augustine Church, second oldest in the country, remained standing to bear witness to what had been. Built in 1599, St. Augustine's has come through fires, earthquakes and wars; its tranquility belies its past. Celebrated Spanish *conquistadores* were buried here, including the two most fabulous ones, Legaspi, founder of Manila, and Salcedo, who routed early Chinese pirates who had attacked the country with a mighty force. You'll see some remarkable old woodcarvings in the church, which the British made their headquarters when they invaded the Philippines. And in 1898, the Spanish signed the Americans' surrender terms at St. Augustine's.

It was wisely decided to keep intact the sections of the walls that were not demolished. Inside the walls, a new *Intramuros* of modern buildings following Philippine Spanish colonial architecture is going up, along with newly restored Spanish colonial structures.

Plans made by the government to reconstruct the Walled City along its old lines are presently being carried out. Manila Cathedral, destroyed during the Battle of Manila, was rebuilt a few years ago on its former site not far from St. Augustine's. A striking view of the harbor and of the surrounding area may be had from its tall bell tower. Erected originally in 1654, it was destroyed and rebuilt five times. Take note of the Italian mosaic work.

Just outside the walls, on Gen. Luna St., is the newly restored Manila Aquarium, featuring colorful specimens of Philippine marine life and rare shells found only in the Philippines.

Nearby, still in *Intramuros,* are the ruins of Fort Santiago, the mention of which is still enough to send shudders up and down the backs of Filipinos and Americans who were imprisoned there by the Japanese during the war. The Spanish also utilized it as a dungeon in past centuries. Jose Rizal, the national hero of the Philippines, was incarcerated in the fort before he was taken to the Luneta on the other side of the Walled City and shot in 1896. The cell of Rizal is open to visitors. There is also a small museum containing relics of Rizal. The Shrine of the Unknown Soldier is nearby. Fort Santiago, or what is left of it, is a tranquil spot today, but grim memories will forever be associated with it. Here, along the Pasig River, not far from where it flows into Manila Bay, the Japanese massacred a large group of prisoners in the medieval dungeon.

The Philippines may be a republic, but its President lives in a palace —Malacañang Palace. And it really is a palace, a tropical one, along the winding Pasig River. Tourists may visit the gardens of this residence which served as the home of Spanish and American governors-general and then, with the establishment of the commonwealth in 1935, as the home of Filipino presidents. The Palace main building is now closed to tourists. Only the surrounding gardens may be visited, together with the Executive Building, where the office of the Executive Secretary is located. Visiting hours are Mondays, Wednesdays and Thursdays, 9 to 11:30 and 2 to 4. By special arrangement and appointment, visits to the Palace main buildings may still be made. A Japanese cottage, gift of the government in Tokyo, occupies one corner of the grounds.

Any visit to Manila would not be complete without a stop at the Rizal Monument on the Luneta. The Luneta is a large park fronted by the sea and for generations it has been a place where Manilans have gone for a stroll or outing. Here one can go to the Chinese or Japanese garden, or the delightful park for children, with its entertainment and games. Rizal was executed on the Luneta on December 30, 1896. A brilliant 19th-century intellectual, he was physician, poet, writer, linguist, naturalist, educator, scientist—the "Pride of the Malay Race." His writings sparked the first successful revolution in Asia against a Western colonizer. A new Rizal Library has been constructed not far from the Luneta's Rizal Monument.

South of the Rizal Monument, along Roxas Boulevard, is the ultramodern Cultural Center of the Philippines—the forerunner of a new city that is being built on land reclaimed from Manila Bay. Right behind it is the Design Center of the Philippines, the Folk Arts Theater and the Philippine International Convention Center complex.

At the other end of the Luneta, near Taft Avenue, are governmental buildings, like the Ministries of Tourism and Finance and the former Congress building that now houses the Prime Minister's offices, since the National Assembly has transferred to its new building in Quezon City along Mariano Marcos Avenue. If it is in session, one can visit the national assembly, now a unicameral body of representatives from each congressional district, elected by the people from each district, under the new constitution approved in 1973 which provides for a parliamentary form of government. Also in the vicinity is the Manila Post Office, the newly restored Metropolitan Theater and Manila's City Hall, the nerve center of the Philippines' premier city.

Downtown, Chinatown, All Around the Town

Manila proper is divided into districts, each with a character and history of its own. Ermita, for example, was a fancy residential district before the war. Today most of the leading hotels are found here. Shops with the smartest Philippine and foreign products are plentiful. Bars, restaurants and curio shops are likewise numerous. Manila Bay is Ermita's western boundary. Spacious Roxas Boulevard, named for President Manuel Roxas, starts from the Luneta in this part of the city and runs for several miles. Manila Bay is world-famed for its magnificent sunsets.

Downtown Manila, the main commercial and shopping center of the city, lies mainly in the districts of Santa Cruz and Quiapo. Some of the most exclusive shops in town are on Escolta and Dasmarinas streets. On them or nearby are most of the large banks and commercial enterprises. Construction seems to go on all the time.

Chinatown is in the district of Binondo, one of the city's oldest, and is in walking distance from the downtown areas. Its main street, Ongpin, is crowded with small, intriguing restaurants and shops offering products ranging from Chinese pastries to herbs and curios. Signs are mostly in Chinese as are the movies which are from Hong Kong and Taiwan. The Chinese in Manila, as in other places in Southeast Asia, are a hard-working, thrifty class and play a key role in the economy.

In Binondo, you will see small, hole-in-the-wall factories turning out an amazing volume and variety of goods. *Calesas* vie with cars for priority in this district. If you're tired of walking, ride up and down Ongpin in one of these horsedrawn carriages, but come to an agreement first with the *cochero.* Some interesting examples of old-style architecture still exist in Binondo. You may also want to visit the Buddhist temple there.

Virtually all roads in Manila lead to Quiapo, whose denizens boast of traffic jams equal to those of anywhere in the world. In Quiapo, adjacent to the centrally located Quiapo Church, is the plaza where the largest political rallies in the country are held. Manila has many public markets, but perhaps the most convenient to visit is the Quiapo market under Quezon Bridge.

Manila's population of four million people is crowded into less than 15 square miles. Its excess population finds living room in the cities and towns which make up Metro Manila and add another million people to the swelling population. These include the fishing town of Malabon, the industrial suburb of Caloocan, the fast-growing Quezon City, the predominantly residential town of San Juan, the residential and industrial towns of Mandaluyong and Makati.

There is much to interest the tourist or traveler in Quezon City. There is the University of the Philippines, with its modern buildings and sprawling lush green campus, the Parks and Wildlife Center, the Quezon Memorial Circle, with the new government buildings around the rotunda, the Philippine Heart Center for Asia, the Philippine Mint, the new parliament building, the Asian Institute of Tourism nearby, and the Atomic Reactor compound, as well as the Araneta commercial and entertainment center in Cubao.

Cubao has become a bustling social and economic center, with its modern supermarkets, shops, restaurants, hotels, cinemas, and a sports complex which has become highly popular with the suburban community, especially over the weekends.

Excursions from Manila

Corregidor, often called "the Rock," guards the entrance of Manila Bay. Across the way is the peninsula of Bataan. It was on Corregidor and Bataan that American and Filipino forces fought their last, hopeless battle in 1942. A hydrofoil takes sightseers to Corregidor where they can visit the site of the famous battle. You can see Malinta Tunnel, which sheltered General Douglas MacArthur, President Manuel L. Quezon, and General Jonathan Wainwright; the ruins of the mile-long barracks on "Topside"; the now-rusting cannons that were supposed to have made Corregidor impregnable, and the lighthouse at the top of the rugged little island. From the lighthouse, you can have a perfect view of the jungle-covered island, Bataan, Manila Bay, and the China Sea. Corregidor was once a showplace of the U.S. Army; it's a far cry from that now. The jungle has taken over most of the island. A local tour operator now runs the transportation concession on Corregidor Island and a limited number of air-conditioned buses are presently being used to service visitors to the island. The Philippine Navy, in cooperation with the Department of Tourism, operates the daily 44-seater hydrofoil, which makes the trip across Manila Bay in only 50 minutes.

In historic Bataan is Mount Samat, the site of the "Altar of Valor" shrine with its gigantic cross, dedicated to its gallant defenders during the Second World War. Another attraction here is the multimillion dollar Bataan Export Processing Zone in Mariveles, which was the starting-point of the infamous "Death March."

Tagaytay Ridge, about an hour's drive south of Manila, has an elevation of about 2,000 feet and as fine a view as you're apt to see anywhere. Aside from the delightfully cool air, the main attraction is the volcano within a volcano. Taal Volcano rises gracefully from Taal Lake, which is itself the crater of an extinct volcano. *Note:* The last eruption was in 1976.

Pagsanjan Falls, about two hours' drive south of Manila, is known for its rapids, and can guarantee you an exhilarating experience: shooting the rapids in a *banca* or canoe. The scenery is memorable and the boatmen are skillful.

On the edge of Laguna de Bay, the place to go is Hidden Valley in Alaminos, a veritable Eden, with natural pools, waterfalls, tropical flora and fauna. Other places to see in Laguna are the hot springs in Los Baños (The Baths), close to the U.P. College of Forestry and Agriculture; Calamba, the hometown of the National hero, Dr. Jose Rizal; the seven lakes of San Pablo City; the underground cemetery of Nagcarlan; and Lake Caliraya in Lumban.

The *Nayong Pilipino* (or Philippines Village), situated on 54 acres of the Manila International Airport reservation, is Manila's newest and most interesting attraction—a project of Mrs. Imelda Marcos, the First Lady of the Philippines. Designed to give the visitor an idea of the various regions that make up the Philippine Archipelago and featuring their architecture, arts, handicrafts and prominent scenic landmarks, the *Nayong Pilipino* has reproduced the "mosques" and Maranao houses of the Southern Philippines Muslim areas, the mountain huts of the famous Igorot tribes up north, the bamboo houses on stilts of the lowland rural areas, the "Mayon Volcano" of Albay, and the "Chocolate Hills" of Bohol. For shoppers, the best bargains may be had at the various "Village Shops" or at the larger store of the National Cottage Industries Administration (NACIDA) in the *Nayong Pilipino*'s Administration Building.

The Bamboo Organ of Las Pinas, a few miles south of Manila, was built in 1794 by a Spanish friar. The ingenious priest built the organ of bamboo in that early day for want of the usual metal and wire. The 12-foot-wide organ has several hundred bamboo pipes.

The Bat Caves of Montalban, east of Manila, must be visited at dusk if you wish to witness the strange sight of countless bats flying out of the caves in search of food. Antipolo, an hour's ride from Manila, is the object of religious pilgrimages in May in honor of the town's patron saint, The Lady of Peace and Good Voyage, a statue of whom was brought to the Philippines in 1626. The image is reputed to have been responsible for repulsing a Dutch attack during Spanish times.

The North

Baguio is one of the loveliest resorts in Asia. It is located in mountain country, some 5,000 feet above sea level, and is the favorite haven of those who want to escape the summer heat of the lowlands. The invigorating climate, beautiful parks, and hilly drives are a sharp contrast to the flat ricelands you pass over in approaching the mountains in which Baguio is situated. A zigzag road winds upward, passing gorges and waterfalls all along the way. Once in Baguio, you can play golf, hike, ride horses, see the sights, and shop. Some places to see are Camp John Hay Air Base, the Igorot wood-carving villages, the silversmiths of St. Louis University, Brent School campus, Imelda Park, the new international Convention Center, and Mines View Park. Burnham Park, in the center of the city, has recreational facilities for children. Baguio's famous market is crammed with vegetables and fruits, which are shipped all over the island of Luzon. It is one of the few places in the country where you can buy fresh strawberries and blueberries. The brisk mountain air, with the tangy smell of pine trees, is the reason Baguio was proclaimed summer capital of the Philippines. The president of the Philippines has here his official summer home, Mansion House, which is open to visitors.

Handsome mountain people, the Igorots, come to the city in their colorful handwoven dresses and G-strings. They have a culture of their own stretching back thousands of years. Many of them live much as their ancestors did; others are miners in on a holiday from the gold mines in the surrounding mountains. Souvenir shops sell cloth, carvings, and other curios wrought by tribal craftsmen. Years ago these people practiced head-hunting, but, fortunately, they have turned to quieter pursuits.

Baguio may be reached by car, bus, train, or plane. If you take the air-conditioned rail coach from Manila, you will get off at the foot of the mountains at Damortis, where automobiles provided by the railroad company will whisk you up the zigzag road to Baguio.

The manmade rice terraces of Banaue are one of the wonders of the world. About seven hours' ride from Baguio, the Banaue Rice Terraces are a monument to man's ingenuity and will to survive. These terraces cover sides of whole mountains and are said to have been started 2,000 years ago by the ancestors of the present tillers of the plots. Hardy, ruddy-faced mountaineers, taller and heavier than most lowlanders, walk nimbly over the dikes on their way to their fields or terraces. The terraces, with their wonderfully effective irrigation system, are an engineering marvel and a lasting example of cooperative effort. Their size is immense; if put end to end, they would stretch 14,000 miles. The mountain people who reside there subsist mainly on rice, sweet potatoes, and vegetables.

Going or returning from Banaue, you pass through Bontoc, the governmental center of Mountain Province. The people who live in this area are known as the Bontocs. They are a different tribe, though of the same racial stock, as the Ifugaos. Like the other tribesmen, the Bontoc males wear tasseled G-strings and little else. The women wear skirts of material they have woven themselves, and sometimes nothing more. Interesting curios are available in Bontoc.

Be sure to schedule a visit to a Bontoc village. The open-air *ato,* where a fire burns day and night, is headquarters for village elders. A low rock wall circles the *ato* and large rocks worn smooth constitute the flooring. The teenage girls and boys each have their own dormitories, long low huts, where they are initiated into the ways of adulthood. Small gifts of matches or salt are appreciated by the Bontocs. Exhibitions of Bontoc dances can be arranged, or if you arrive during one of the Bontoc festivals, you can visit the outdoor dance site. Sometimes the dances last for several days. Young men beating native gongs dance around a blazing bonfire while the women lined up in rows glide back and forth together on the side, keeping time with the dancing men.

The Sagada Caves near Bontoc are underground caves which also serve as a burial ground. The road to Sagada rises abruptly from Bontoc, taking you by rice terraces, pine forests, unusual rock formations. Don't forget your camera.

Just slightly over an hour's drive from the mountain resort of Baguio are the fine sandy beaches of Bauang, in La Union, facing the South China Sea. Over the past few years, Bauang has developed into the country's premier beach resort area, with a number of comfortable hotels now well established along its scenic coastline. The drive from Baguio through the winding Naguilian Road alone is well worth the trip. All along the road, the panorama is one of sheer cliffs and deep gorges, of rolling hills and the long Ilocos coastline in the distance.

Northern Luzon is the fertile tobaccoland of the nation. The cities in the region, Vigan in particular, are noted for their centuries-old stone churches. The Ilocanos, as the people who inhabit the Ilocos are called, are a hard-working, adventuresome lot.

The South

Man's quest for perfection is realized in the Bicol region, the provinces at the southern end of the island of Luzon. The perfection comes in the almost flawless shape of Mayon volcano which dominates the landscape of Albay Province. The 8,000-foot volcano had a major eruption in July 1979. At present, some minor activity continues to cause occasional mudflows through the surrounding countryside. In 1814 Mayon erupted and buried the town of Cagsawa.

Legazpi is the pleasant, modern capital of Albay Province. You can fly there or take a train from Manila. Stay overnight in one of Legazpi's good hotels, and get an early start for Mayon. You are not expected to scale it hand over hand. Rented cars will take you to the rest house, about 2,500 feet high. You can picnic there but *don't* stay overnight. Bring your own food from Legazpi. Tiwi Hot Springs, near Legazpi, is the most popular resort in the area. You can swim in the hot or cold water pools or take a sulfur health bath. Bulusan Lake is another favorite excursion spot. Bacon, an unspoiled seaside town, has waters so clear that at 30 feet deep you can still see the white sand bottom.

Separating the two largest Philippine islands—Luzon in the north and Mindanao in the south—are the Visayan Islands; the people living there are Visayans. Samar and Leyte, where American liberation forces first landed in strength in 1944, are the main islands in the eastern Visayas. Samar and Leyte were recently linked by the Marcos Bridge, the longest bridge in the country, spanning the San Juanico Strait, a picturesque channel dotted with tiny islets. Panay and Negros are the most prominent in the western Visayas. A little off Panay is Sicogon Island, surrounded with fine beaches and crystalline waters where most tourists and local sightseers engage in waterskiing, sailing, skindiving, squash, pelota, riding and even tennis, bowling, and billiards at the seaside resorts.

On a visit to Bacolod City, the "sugar capital" of the Philippines on the boot-shaped island of Negros, one should not miss seeing the fine homes of the "Sugar Barons," "Hablon" weavers and antique collectors, the rustic chapel of the Hacienda Rosalia in Manapla, the Mambucal Springs Resort, the modern Church of Victorias with a mural by Ossorio, and of course still active Kanlaon volcano.

Bohol Island, where you will find those unique natural formations called the "Chocolate Hills," has its capital in Tagbilaran City. The hemispherical grass-covered hills turn brown during the dry season; hence the name. At Barrio Bo-ol, the local chieftain Sikatuna and the Spanish conquistador Miguel Lopez de Legazpi concluded a treaty of friendship in the early part of the 16th century, called the "Blood Compact," by drinking wine mixed with each other's blood. Old Spanish churches and watchtowers are also worth seeing.

Iloilo is a province of sunlit plains, lovely beaches and beautiful mountains. In the city is the Museo Iloilo, with antique religious images *(santos),* modern art by local artists, religious relics, and artifacts. Other attractions are Baroque and Gothic-inspired churches, shellcraft factories and loom-weaving towns.

North of Iloilo is Kalibo, Aklan, where the Philippines' rowdiest and most colorful folk festival, called "Ati-Atihan," is held. They paint their bodies and faces with soot and, wearing outlandish costumes, parade amid revelry and merrymaking. Aklan also has caves, beach resorts, and the beautiful Jawili Falls.

The crossroads of the islands, Cebu is the heaviest populated island for its size in the Philippines. It's 350 miles south of Manila. Commerce flows in all directions through Cebu City. Ships from all over the islands and from all over the world dock there. In size and importance, it rates second only to Manila. The province has a proud past. It was here that Magellan the navigator was killed by Cebuano chieftain Lapu-Lapu in 1521. Here you will find the oldest city in the country, Cebu City, founded in 1565. The city's plaza contains what is believed to be the cross planted by Magellan when he and his men held mass to celebrate their safe arrival. Cebu City boasts the oldest church in the Philippines, St. Augustine's. Inside the church is the oldest Roman Catholic image in the islands, that of the *Santo Nino* or Holy Child. From Cebu City you can travel by launch to Mactan Island where Magellan was slain. A monument marks the spot. Cebu is noted for its cornfed beauties, for corn is the staple crop on the rocky, mountainous island, not rice, the main diet almost everywhere else in the Philippines.

At the southwestern tip of Mindanao, about 440 miles from Manila, Zamboanga City has long been a favorite of tourists. It's about 2½ hours by plane from Manila, about three days by ship. The weather is surprisingly pleasant, considering that the city lies only a few degrees above the equator. You'll see picturesque fishing villages built on stilts over the sea. There are also the water gypsies who live in their small boats and move to wherever the fishing is the best.

Zamboanga City got its start as a Spanish outpost. The walls of Fort Pilar, built in the 17th century, still stand. Here the Spanish and Christian Filipinos defended themselves against Muslim onslaughts and ventured forth to do battle with fierce Muslim fighters. The Spanish influence is still felt in the local dialect which has a heavy mixture of Spanish in it. Life is leisurely and gracious here. Pasonanca Park is one of the loveliest in the country. If you're a shell collector, Zamboanga is a good place to be. It also has a Barter Trade Market for good buys in Muslim brassware, handwoven fabrics and batik.

If you pull yourself away from Zamboanga, press onward to Jolo in the Sulu Archipelago. Here the Muslims live as they always have, fiercely, proudly, and independently. They have their own *datus* or leaders and their own system of law in addition to the official government one. Annual pilgrimages are still made to Mecca by the faithful. The Sulu Archipelago has been the center of a thriving commerce for centuries. The Spanish were never able to subdue the Muslims in Sulu and their brethren on the island of Mindanao. The Americans fought their share of bloody battles with the Muslims, but finally pacified them through force of arms and fair treatment. The local art is not as distinctive as that of the Muslims in the province of Lanao del Sur, Mindanao, whose brasswork is coveted by collectors. The Muslims who live by the shores of Lake Lanao in Lanao del Sur are known as the Maranaos, generally considered the elite class among the Muslims. Lake Lanao is some 3,000 feet above sea level, and is the source of the swift-flowing Agus River, which plunges some 500 feet at Maria Cristina Falls, and has been harnessed for hydroelectric power. The Mindanao State University occupies a sprawling campus overlooking the lake. Signal Hill and Sacred Mountain are prominent features of the rolling landscape. The native market, the splendid and ancient "Torongan" homes of Maranao Royalty, the Muslim mosques along the lake, and the Tugaya town brassware industry make Marawi City and Lake Lanao fascinating.

Mindanao's industrial center is where the majestic Maria Cristina Falls flows out to the sea. Steel, fertilizer plants, carbon, flour, pulp and paper mills have contributed immensely to the rapid industrialization of the port city of Iligan, which is only a few hours' drive from Marawi City to the south and Cagayan de Oro City to the east.

Cagayan de Oro is strategically located along the central coast of Northern Mindanao, facing Macajalar Bay. As the trade and industrial nucleus of the region, as well as capital to Misamis Oriental, it is famous for the gold found in its mountains, its verdant, lush hills and forests, and its cascading falls and underground caves. Cagayan de Oro City is almost free of typhoons and is blessed with a moderate, pleasant climate, which may be partly the reason that its inhabitants are essentially happy and genteel and warm with their friendship.

Over on the other side of Mindanao, the southeastern coast, lies the city of Davao. It was sometimes called "little Japan" before the war because of the Japanese-developed abaca plantations and the many Japanese merchants. You can make arrangements to visit the Aldevinco Shopping Center, where batik, malongs, Muslim brassware, shells and native bags are sold; the Mascuñana Collection of Muslim antiques; the Menzi Citrus Plantation, the Florendo Abaca and Banana Plantation, the Hijo Banana Plantation, the Adecor Plywood & Marble Factory, the Matti Ceramics and Pottery shop, the San José Muslim Fishing Village, the Mindanao Industrial Confectionary, a Buddhist temple; or do some deep-sea fishing off the Davao Gulf. The famous Aguinaldo Pearl Farm is on nearby Samal Island.

Osmena Park, one of Davao's old landmarks, now features an interesting zoo with some imported and rare native fauna. The strong smell of the "durian" (fruit of the gods), plus other native exotic flora and tropical fruits, together with the sea breeze, permeates the city.

The pearls of the Sulu Archipelago have been famous for centuries. Muslim divers go down fabulous depths in search of the precious pearls or the shells if pearls run short.

And beyond lie the Turtle Islands. It's doubtful whether you'll have the time to go that far, but they're a fascinating place for the insatiably curious. As you might guess, they're the home of turtles, some of them giants. Thousands of the reptiles inhabit the tiny islands which make up the group. Turtle eggs collected here go into turtle soup all over Southeast Asia.

PRACTICAL INFORMATION

FACTS AND FIGURES. Population: 50 million. Birth rate per 1,000 population: 34. Average life expectancy: 61 years. Proportion of population engaged in agriculture and fishing: 53%. Land area: 297,000 sq. kms. Land area cultivated: 38% (43% forest). Average per capita income: US$732 p.a. Number of tourists annually: about one million.

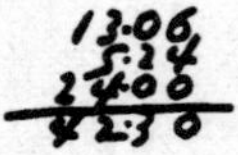

WHAT WILL IT COST? Accommodations will be your biggest expense while in the Philippines and prices vary and may change without prior notice. In a major city such as Manila you may pay as much as US$110 per night for a double room in a deluxe hotel or as little as US$16 for a double in a pension. Likewise, in a provincial capital the deluxe price may be US$40 for a deluxe double and US$7 for a pension. Prices in resort towns also vary greatly: you might pay US$56 for a deluxe double room in Baguio or US$27 for a comparable room in La Union. All rates are subject to 12 percent government tax and the usual 10 percent service charge.

Meals come to between 250 to 500 pesos at the deluxe hotels and restaurants, 150 to 250 pesos at the first-class hotels and restaurants, 90 to 150 pesos at the second-class hotels and restaurants, 80 to 120 pesos at the most moderate hotels and restaurants, and 50 to 80 pesos at the most inexpensive accommodations and restaurants. Some good provincial hotels have lower rates, depending on the season.

Taxis and public transportation facilities in Manila and the provinces are abundant and inexpensive (see *How to Get Around*).

Tonsorial and beauty salon fees are inexpensive. A haircut costs from 30 to 50 pesos depending on where you get it. For the ladies, a manicure costs from 10 to 25 pesos; pedicure: 15 to 30 pesos; shampoo: 10 to 25 pesos; coiffure: 15 to 30 pesos; permanent: 30 to 50 pesos; facial: 25 to 50 pesos; hot oil: 30 to 50 pesos; trimming: 15 to 25 pesos, again depending on where you get it.

Scotch and bourbon cost from 20 to 30 pesos a shot at night spots, though a few good bars charge less. San Miguel (the world famous) beer costs from 6 to 25 pesos, depending on where you drink it. Downtown restaurants usually charge less for food and drinks.

Air-conditioned movies in Manila are first rate and show up-to-date American, English, European, Japanese, Chinese, and Tagalog films. First-run theaters charge 8 pesos for orchestra, 10 pesos for balcony, and 12 pesos for loge.

A box of Manila cigars containing 25 would cost from 75 to 120 pesos. A pack of 30 Manila long and slim black cigarettes would cost from 8 to 12 pesos; the imported blends with 20 to a pack would cost from 15 to 20 pesos depending on the brand.

WHEN TO GO? The climate is tropical, with warm days, cool nights, and pleasant sea breezes. It is fairly humid most of the year. There are two general seasons, though this may vary in different parts of the country. The hot season begins in late March and ends in June. It's followed by the rainy season which lasts up to November. The other four months of the year are the coolest, and the best time of all. Average daily temperature is in the low 80's.

Even in the hot season, a temperature of 100 degrees is rare, April and May, while warm, are popular because of the many fiestas and May flower festivals, as well as perfect sailing weather.

WHERE TO GO. Manila, of course, will be your first destination, and you should spend as much time meeting the people as in sightseeing. An excursion to Taal Lake, a flight to Baguio, and daytime trips out to Bataan and Corregidor are recommended. The more ambitious can take island steamers or Philippine Air Lines flights down to Cebu and Mindanao.

Quezon City is officially the capital city of the country, but most government offices, including the office of the president and the Supreme Court, remain in Manila. Eventually the government will transfer to adjoining Quezon City, named for Manuel L. Quezon, first president of the Philippine Commonwealth.

The major cities are Manila, Baguio, and Legazpi on the island of Luzon; Iloilo, Cebu, Bacolod and Tacloban on the Visayan Islands; and Cagayan de Oro, Davao, Marawi and Zamboanga on the island of Mindanao.

Metro Manila is composed of the cities of Caloocan, Quezon, Manila and Pasay, plus the towns of Makati, Mandaluyong, Parañaque and San Juan.

WHAT TO TAKE. Lightweight informal clothing of washable fabrics is suitable for wear during the day, cotton dresses for women, tropical weight trousers, cotton shirts and light cotton knit sportshirts for men. At night for formal occasions or for visiting nightclubs, the men customarily wear coats or the Filipino native wear for men, the *barong tagalog*, and the women wear cocktail dresses. Lightweight rainwear and umbrella are necessary during the rainy season. Steam laundering and dry cleaning facilities are available at reasonable cost.

ELECTRIC CURRENT. Manila voltage is generally 220, but some hotels have both 110 and 220 facilities. Check at desk first. Alternating and direct current.

LOCAL FESTIVALS. January 1. *New Year's Day.* A noisy, colorful national holiday to welcome the New Year.

January 6. *Feast of the Three Kings* heralds end of the Christmas season. Parades of the Three Kings in full regalia, on horseback, in Cebu and Manila. In Sta. Cruz and Gasan, Marinduque Island, townspeople re-enact the journey of the Three Wise Men in search of the Christ Child.

January 9. *Fiesta of Quiapo District.* Manila's biggest festival, in honor of the Black Nazarene. The faithful gather in Quiapo to help pull a carriage which holds a 200-year-old image of Christ on the way to Calvary. A long procession of people carrying candles circles the district. From Jan. 1 to 9, nightly amateur programs, drama, and band concerts are held in front of the District's baroque church.

Cebu City Fiesta in honor of the Christ child, more popularly known as the Santo Nino. Cebuanos show their devotion by dancing to the patron saint.

(Moveable.) *Hari Raya Hadji* Filipino Muslim festival to commemorate the annual pilgrimage to Mecca.

Appey In Bontoc, Mountain Province. Ritual offerings are held for a bountiful rice harvest, with dances.

Manerway. A dance festival staged by the Bontoc tribes to "awaken the rain gods" to benefit their crops.

Pipigan. In Novaliches, Rizal Province, toasted glutinous rice (*malagkit*) is pounded into *pinipig* (either fried or made into a sweet delicacy) to the accompaniment of a joyful guitar melody.

January (2nd weekend). *Binirayan Festival in San José, Antique.* Colorful pageant to commemorate the "landing of the 10 Bornean *datus* on Panay Island."

January 17. *Constitution Day.* National holiday to commemorate the ratification of the new Philippine Constitution.

(Moveable). *Saranggolahan.* Regional kite-flying contests, with cash awards.

January 23. National celebration held in Malolos, Bulacan Province of the inauguration of the First Philippine Republic in 1899, the first republican form of government in Asia.

January 25. *Vigan Fiesta,* Llocos Sur. (Vigan is one of the few Spanish towns left in the Philippines.) Includes a carnival, cockfights, and native dramas.

January (third weekend). *The "Alti-Atihan" Festival of Kalibo,* Aklan. The Philippines' most colorful and gayest "mardi gras," commemorating the 13th-century peace pact, concluded between the Panay Island aborigines ("aetas") and migrant settlers from Borneo.

(Moveable). *Chinese New Year.* Timed according to the Chinese lunar calendar, it is usually held between January 21 and February 19. The celebration takes place in Manila's Chinatown and, lately, in Makati, with dragon dances and other Chinese festival displays.

February 11. *Lourdes Church Fiesta* in Santa Mesa Heights, Quezon City. A traditional fiesta, featuring a huge procession of penance in the evening.

Easter. *Holy week.* Colorful ceremonies throughout the nation are highlighted by dramatic presentations and elaborate church ceremonies. Holy week in the Philippines is a mixture of Catholic rites and native superstitions. Passion plays are presented in many villages each evening.

Good Friday. Flagellants go about the streets, faces masked, their backs bleeding from numerous beatings. The ritual ends when the flagellant, followed by a huge crowd, walks into the sea. On country roads, the visitor may see a walking figure dressed like Christ, carrying a huge cross.

Easter Sunday. In Cavite, Rizal, and Bulacan. At dawn, two processions issue from separate church doors, one headed by the image of Christ, the other by a veiled image of Mary. The two processions meet in the plaza under a flower decorated arbor. In Boac, Marinduque Island, the *Morian Festival,* a reenactment of the trials and execution of the Roman centurion, Longinus, who pierced the side of Christ on the cross.

(Moveable). *Turrumba Festival.* Observed on the second Tuesday and Wednesday after Holy Week in the lakeshore town of Pakil in Laguna Province. "Turrumba" (a corruption of *Tumumba,* which means to "fall, leap, jump or dance with joy") is exactly what the devotees of Our Lady of Sorrows, Patron Saint of Pakil, do as they follow her image in a massive and joyful procession through the streets.

April 9. *Bataan Day.* A national holiday in commemoration of the Battle of Bataan in 1942. Wreath-laying at the national shrine in Mount Samat, Bataan, attended by the President.

(Moveable). *Mauloddan Nabi.* A Muslim Filipino holiday celebrating the birth of the Prophet Mohammed. Ceremonial readings of the holy Koran are held in all Muslim mosques.

April 28. *Magellan's Landing,* in Cebu City, Cebu. Colorful reenactment of the landing of the Portuguese navigator, Ferdinand Magellan, in Cebu in 1521.

Gaily decorated bancas representing the three ships of Magellan, followed by other watercraft from nearby islands, land on the shore of Cebu Bay after a fluvial procession. Then Magellan's men plant the cross with the assistance of Humabon's men, after which Humabon and his family are baptized as Christians and gifted with the miraculous image of the Holy Child (now in the Cathedral of Cebu) by Magellan.

April 29. *Fiesta,* Hagonoy, Bulacan. Gorgeous street decorations.

April 30–May 2. *Handugan Festival,* San Jose, Antique Province, in Panay Island. A cultural festival centering on "the barter of Panay" in the 13th century. A fluvial pageant and general revelry and merry-making take place after the re-enactment of the barter of the island by the native Chieftain Marikudo to the ten datus of Borneo in exchange for a *golden salakot* (gold hat).

May 1. *Labor Day.* A national holiday observed with an afternoon parade at the Luneta. Many symbolic floats.

May 1–31. *Flores de Mayo,* month-long church festival. Each afternoon small children dressed all in white visit church to offer flowers to the Queen of May.

May 1–31. *Antipolo Pilgrimage.* Devotees of Our Lady of Peace and Good Voyage go on a month-long pilgrimage to the shrine of the miraculous image in Antipolo, Rizal Province, and go picnicking at the Hinulugang Taktak Falls nearby.

May 1–31. *Santa Cruz de Mayo,* the biggest Philippine festival, in commemoration of the finding of the Holy Cross of Jesus by St Helena in 1324 is observed throughout the country. Highlight is a procession of lavishly costumed Filipinos. But the Santacruzan has since turned into a parade of beautiful, elegantly gowned women.

May 14. *Carabao Festival,* celebrated in Pulilan Province. The lowly carabaos (water buffalo) are decorated with flowers and led through the streets to the church.

May 15. *Harvest Festival.* In Sariaya, Quezon Province, streets and houses are decorated with gift-laden bamboo trees and a variety of farm products and native delicacies in honor of San Isidro, the patron saint of farmers. In Lucban, also Quezon Province, multicolored wafers called "kiping" are hung together with native fruits and sweets from windows.

May 17–19. Fertility rites in Obando, Bulacan. Triple religious fête in honor of San Pascual, Santa Clara and the Virgin of Salambao, marked by childless couples dancing in church grounds and main streets, accompanied by brass bands on second day.

May 24–5. *Bale Zamboanga Festival,* staged in Zamboanga City by both Christians and Muslims. Cultural performances, fairs, regattas and religious services.

June 12. *Philippine Independence Day.* Celebrated throughout the country with parades, fireworks, concerts, and the ringing of all the church bells.

June 19. *Birthday of Dr. Jose P. Rizal,* Philippine National Hero. National civic rites and floral offerings.

June 24. *St. John's Day.* Town fiesta in San Juan, Rizal. The baptism of the saint in the river Jordan is observed uniquely by the townspeople of San Juan by dousing passers-by in the town streets with water, from seven in the morning till noontime, after which there is a procession.

June 29. *Apalit River Festival,* Apalit, Pampanga, about 35 miles from Manila. Gaily decorated bancas (native canoes) from the colorful fluvial procession on the Apalit river in honor of the town's patron saint, St. Peter.

July 1 (Sunday). *Bocaue River Festival,* in Bocaue, Bulacan Province, 17 miles from Manila. The "Holy Cross of Wawa" is taken on a fluvial procession aboard an elaborately decorated barge with a pagoda made of bamboo.

July 4. *Philippine-American Friendship Day,* a legal holiday with floral offerings at the American Battle Monuments in Fort Bonifacio and an evening concert at Luneta Grandstand.

July 29. *Pateros Festival and Fair,* in Pateros, Rizal Province, about 20 minutes by car from Manila. The town is noted for its native delicacy, the famous "balut" (partly incubated duck's egg, boiled and always served hot). The town honors its patron saint, Santa Marta, with a river procession.

(Moveable). *Lesles, Tengao and Bagbagto rituals.* Combination of pagan and Christian rites staged by Bontoc tribes in Mountain Province in supplication for a good harvest.

August 1–7. *Dance of the Aetas.* In Bayombong, Nueva Ecija, one of earliest indigenous tribes, "Aetas," come down from their mountain homes and serenade the townspeople.

August 19. *Quezon's Birthday* (the late President Manual Quezon). Civic and military parade in Quezon City and Quezon Province.

August 26. *"Cry of Pugad Lawin" Day,* commemorating the 1896 revolt against Spain. Celebration at monuments in Balintawak, Quezon City, and Caloocan (Pasay), including parades.

August 31. *Magsaysay Day,* in honor of late President Ramon F. Magsaysay. Masses, wreath-offering at his tomb, etc.

September 10. *Sunduan.* Unique folk tradition in La Huerta, Parañaque, Rizal, half hour's drive from Manila. Local belles escorted by young swains holding parasols parade on main streets. Noon reception and luncheon at house of fiesta's senior host (*hermano mayor*).

September (third weekend). *Peñafrancia Festival.* Held in Naga City, Camarines Sur Province, an hour by plane from Manila and six hours by train. The Virgin of Peñafrancia, patron saint of the Bicol region, is honored with a traditional nine-day novena and on the ninth day with a procession down the Naga River.

October 8. *La Naval* procession, Quezon City. Celebrating the Spanish-Filipino victory over the Dutch, who attempted to invade the islands 300 years ago.

November 1. *All Saints' Day.* National holiday commemorating the country's dead.

November 15–30. *Yakan Harvest Festival.* Thanksgiving feast and horse fights (including betting) staged by Yakan Tribe on Basilan Island, Mindanao.

Last Thursday of November. *Thanksgiving Day.* A national holiday.

November 23. *Feast of San Clemente,* held in Angono, a picturesque town 29 km. from Manila, with a socio-religious procession including fisherfolk bearing paddles, bamboo fish-traps and sticks.

November (moveable). *Hari Raya Puasa.* Filipino Muslim holiday commemorating the end of the 30-day fasting period, called *Ramadan.*

November 30. *Bonifacio Day,* in honor of the "Hero of Manila" and "Supremo of the Philippine Revolution" against Spain in 1898. Wreath-laying ceremonies are held before the hero's shrine at Liwasang Bonifacio in front of the Manila Post Office.

December 8. *Feast of Our Lady of the Immaculate Conception,* held in the fishing village of Malabon, Rizal Province, about 20 minutes' ride from Manila.

December 12. *Pagsanjan Town Fiesta.* Famous for its beautiful gorge, falls and rapids, the town of Pagsanjan in Laguna Province celebrates its fiesta in honor of the Nuestra Señora de Guadalupe, its patron saint as well as the Philippines', with a late-afternoon religious procession.

December 24. *Christmas Lantern Festival,* held annually in the evening, in San Fernando, Pampanga Province, 40 miles from Manila. Gigantic lanterns, of bamboo framework and Japanese paper skin, with floral and geometric designs, lighted with from 50 to 100 bulbs and mounted on trucks with their own generators.

December 30. *Rizal Day.* Death anniversary of Dr. Jose P. Rizal, the Philippine National Hero. A national holiday.

December 31. *Bota Flores.* A socio-religious procession is held in the Ermita District in Manila, in which young ladies shower flower petals in a ceremony called "Bota Flores" in honor of Our Lady of Expectation.

HOW TO REACH THE PHILIPPINES. By air: Most of the major airlines and some minor ones visit Manila. *Philippine Air Lines* and *Cathay Pacific* connect with Hong Kong. You can fly *China* from Taiwan and *Thai International* from Bangkok. Manila International Airport, a 15-minute ride by taxi (about P40) from the main hotel section, is one of the finest in the Pacific.

By sea: Manila is served by several international lines, including *APL, RIL Everett, International Harvester Macleod, F.E. Zuellig, Columbian Philippines, Soriamont Steamship, Philippine President Lines, Lloyd Triestino, United States Lines, Mitsui Lines LTD, Smith Bell & Co, Lykes Orient Line, Isthmian Lines,* and *Maritime Company of the Philippines.*

PASSPORTS AND VISAS. Visas not required for visitors staying in the Philippines no longer than 21 days. A valid passport with visa for the next port is required, along with a ticket to that port. Your stay may be extended, under certain conditions, upon application to the Bureau of Immigration in Manila. For longer visits, a passport with a visa issued by a Philippine consular official is required. After 54 days a visitor must register with the Bureau of Immigration. A temporary visitor's visa is good for one year. Citizens from countries with which the Philippines has no diplomatic relations, nationals from restricted countries, and stateless persons are not extended the same privileges granted to foreign tourists from other countries. A regular vaccination certificate is required. A cholera vaccination certificate is required of travelers coming from certain areas.

CUSTOMS. You'll have no trouble with personal belongings. Tourists do not have to file a Customs declaration form and are usually exempted from Customs examination. You can't bring in more than 200 cigarettes or 50 cigars, prohibited drugs, narcotics, explosives and firearms. The liquor limit is one quart.

LANGUAGE. Pilipino is the national language and one of three official languages: English and Spanish are the other two. Spanish is spoken by the old elite. Pilipino is the key language at present. The dialects of the country number 87; the leading languages are these eight: Tagalog, Cebuano, Ilongo, Ilocano, Pampango, Bicol, Samareno, and Pangasinan.

CURRENCY. The Philippine peso is being allowed to seek its own level. The current (mid-1985) floating rate fluctuates from P18.50 to some additional centavos per U.S. dollar, app. P25 per British pound sterling. There are 100 centavos in a peso. The symbol sign for the peso is a capital P with two horizontal lines through the upper part. You can exchange your currency for Philippine currency with Central Bank agents upon arrival or at leading hotels and banks. Currency declaration is not required.

HOW TO GET AROUND. Depending on where you go and how long you stay, you may travel by auto, bus, railroad, airplane, ship, horse, and *carabao.* Taxis and rented cars are plentiful in the larger cities, though the price of the latter can get out of bounds. The main highways are good. The Filipinos drive to the right. A driver's license may be obtained if you present a license issued to you in your own country.

By train. Rail rates on Luzon are reasonable. *The Philippine National Railways* (PNR), with the main terminal at Recto Ave., Manila, dispatches six passenger trains daily to the Northern Lines, passing through the provinces of Rizal, Bulacan, Pampanga, Tarlac, Pangasinan and La Union. First-class passengers bound for the summer capital of Baguio are taken up by cars from the debarkation station at Damortis, La Union, and the third-class passengers by buses. First-class fare in deluxe air-conditioned coaches is approximately P75 one way from Manila to Baguio. To the Southern Lines are dispatched daily the Bicol Day and Night Express trains, the Mayon Ltd. Express Train and two motor car trains, passing through the provinces of Rizal, Laguna, Quezon, Caramarines Sur and Albay. The Manila-Legazpi (Bicol Express) fare one-way is approximately P140, and the Manila-Legazpi tourist class on the Mayon Ltd. fare one way is approximately P120.

By Air: The national carrier PAL (which has absorbed Air Manila and Filipinas Airways) maintains both international and domestic air services from Manila to points throughout the archipelago with daily departures and arrivals at the Manila Domestic Airport. The cost of air travel varies with distance, with economy flights going to some cities. BA6111's, HS748's and DC8's are used by PAL in its domestic services. There are also charter tours in single and twin-engine planes available at the Manila Domestic Airport from *Delta Air, Pacific Airways Corp., Philippine Aviation Corp., Tropical Airways,* and *Universal Air Service.* A DC3 charter service costs approximately US$200 per hour, plus 2 percent tax. Other sample fares are 300 to 600 pesos per hour of flying time in single- and twin-engine Cessnas respectively. PAL one way, Manila-Laoag (up north) is P250; Manila–Zamboanga is P700.

By Boat: Inter-island steamship service is available with domestic shipping terminals (Piers 2, 4, 6, 8, 10, 12, and 14) located at the North Harbor in Tondo, Manila. The following shipping lines have first-class, air-conditioned cabin service: *Aboitiz Shipping Corp.,* at Pier 4 (to Iloilo, Cotabato, Dadiangas, Davao and Cebu); *Carlos Go Thong & Co.,* at Binondo (to Catbalogan, Tacloban and Cebu); *Compania Maritima,* at Juan Luna, Manila (to Cebu, Zamboanga, Cotabato, Dadiangas and Davao); *Negros Navigation,* at Romero Salas, Manila (to Iloilo and Bacolod); *Sweet Line,* at Muelle de Binondo, Manila (to Cebu, Tagbilaran, Iligan, Ozamis, Catbalogan and Tacloban); and *William Lines,* at San Fernando, Manila (to Cebu, Cagayan de Oro, Iligan, Ozamis and Dumaguete). Sample fares from Manila to Bacolod in 19 hours are: 150 pesos per person and 250 pesos round trip cabin class, relaxing, reasonable, and enjoyable if you have the time.

By taxi: Taxis abound in Manila and the suburban area. Regular fare is 350 centavos for the first 250 meters, and P1 every 250 meters thereafter. Buses and jeepneys in Manila and suburbs charge a basic fare of P1, plus 10 to 15 centavos more for trips to more distant suburbs. Jeepneys of which there are 23,000 in Manila alone are ingeniously decorated jeeps converted into small passenger vehicles carrying 10 persons. *Calesas,* horsedrawn rigs, are also used in some areas.

By car: There are also rent-a-car companies like *Avis* or *Hertz* with stations at the Inter-Continental Hotel in Makati, in Ermita, at the Manila International Airport in Cebu City and Davao City. Self-drive rates are from P300 per day for a small sedan car and P570 a day for a larger sedan plus P2.30 per km.; chauffeur-driven and group rates on request.

By bus: Bus lines cover practically the entire Philippine Archipelago. There are some 20 major bus companies employing 100,000 persons. Local bus rates are probably among the lowest in the world (P2 per ride, P6 per mile). There are also air-conditioned buses and cars for hire. Using the latest modern equipment, the sister companies, *Luzon Bus Line* and *Benguet Auto Line* have four daily buses to Baguio. Taking five hours, the trip is P120 round trip. The *Pangasinan Transportation Company* operates four luxury buses daily for Lingayen's famous Blue Beach, a popular swimming spot. The four-hour trip costs P90 round trip. From the Blue Beach town of Dagupan, there are frequent buses to the Hundred Islands National Park, another seaside resort. Ninety minutes trip, P5. The Philippine Navy operates from its station on Roxas Blvd. a daily 50-minute hydrofoil service from Manila to Corregidor and back.

TIPPING. The leading Manila hotels have a 10 percent service charge so tipping isn't a problem. Signs in some hotels make this clear. If you still insist, that's up to you. But it really isn't necessary. Ten percent is adequate for waiters in non-hotel restaurants. If your bill is smaller, then a little more is appreciated. One peso is customary for barbers. Two pesos are about right for porters if you have only two or three bags. Doormen, headwaiters, shoeshine boys, taxi drivers, tour guides, and drivers generally do not expect to be tipped. Washroom attendants get up to two pesos.

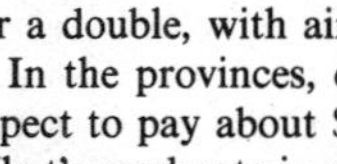

ACCOMMODATIONS. Manila's principal hotels—and those usually recommended for tourists—are all facing or near Manila Bay. The rates are roughly the same for meals and rooms. At the current exchange rate (roughly 18.50 pesos to the American dollar), you can get a comfortable air-conditioned room with bath in Manila for about US$34 (single) or about $39 (double). Some smaller hotels, but definitely nice, may charge $28 or less for a single and $30 for a double, with air-conditioning.

In the provinces, except for first-class hotels, which charge Manila prices, expect to pay about $22 for a single and $26 for a double at moderate hotels. What's moderate in scale may be considered first-class by the local gentry and you will have to pay accordingly. (In-season prices March to May, are comparable to those in Manila's best hotels. Intermediate-season prices, December to February, are down by about one-third, and in the off-season, June to November, they may be only half of what they are in the peak season.) Breakfast, lunch and dinner at hotel dining rooms will total about $20–30 in all. Most hotels offer American, Filipino, and Chinese dishes.

Categories are based on double-occupancy and are in pesos. All of the above rates are subject to a 12 percent government tax and the usual 10 percent service charge.

LUZON ISLAND

Manila

Deluxe—P1,600 and up

Century Park Sheraton. Corner Vito Cruz and M. Adriatico, beside Harrison Plaza shopping center in Malate, Manila. 500 air-conditioned rooms, with 9 restaurants, pool, atrium cocktail lounge, rooftop bar.

Holiday Inn Manila. On Roxas Blvd., 18-story, 314 air-conditioned rooms. French restaurant, nautical bar, sauna, gym, pool.

Hyatt Regency. Located on Roxas Blvd. 265 rooms, pool, 5 restaurants, 2 bars, and a museum annex are featured.

Intercontinental. One of the biggest (420 rooms). 8 miles from center, in Makati. All imaginable luxuries in this 14-story complex.

Manila Garden Hotel. On E. de los Santos Ave., corner Pasay Rd., 525 rooms. Spanish bistro, French-style supper club, 2 Japanese restaurants, 5 bars and cocktail lounges, coffee shop.

Manila Hilton. 416 rooms, plus swimming pool and arcade, heliport and other facilities common to luxury-class establishments. On UN Ave.

Manila Hotel. Katigbak Drive, 548 air-conditioned rooms. Oldest and best known of Philippine hotels. Restored and enlarged with 18-story structure behind old building. Penthouse apartments, fiesta pavilion, 4 specialty restaurants (including barbecue patio facing Manila Bay), 3 bars, tennis, pool, health club, golf course, shopping arcade, disco dancing.

Manila Mandarin. Corner Makati Ave. and Paseo de Roxas with 471 air-conditioned rooms, French restaurant, deluxe coffee shop, pool, and bar, ballroom, circular cocktail lounge.

Manila Peninsula. Corner Ayala Ave. and Makati Ave. 522 air-conditioned rooms, with two 10-story towers joined by a 4-story atrium lobby, with tropical gardens and lawns.

Philippine Plaza. Beside the international Convention Center on Roxas Blvd. The largest of the new hotels, with 676 fully air-conditioned rooms, Manila's largest pool and ballroom, waterfall and reflecting pools on the lower lobby, tennis, discothèque, 3 Continental restaurants.

Regent of Manila. Currently closed for renovation. Corner of Roxas Blvd., and Lovina St., 576 air-conditioned rooms and suites. Specialty restaurant, discothèque, health club.

Silahis International. 1990 Roxas Blvd. 667 rooms. Rooftop cocktail lounge reached by scenic elevator, coffee shop, pool.

First Class—P750–1,400

Admiral. 2138 Roxas Blvd., 110 lavish rooms and suites, air-conditioned. Old World elegance, hospitality and service.

Bayview Plaza. Roxas Blvd. 310 rooms, all air-conditioned with private baths. Cool and intimate cocktail lounge.

Hotel Mirador. On San Marcelino St., just behind Jai Alai Fronton. 340 rooms, supper club, 2 coffee shops, pool and sundeck, sauna.

Manila Midtown, corner M. Adriatico and Pedro Gil Sts. in Malate. 600 rooms, with "biggest ballroom in Asia" (2,000 seating capacity), 3 bars, 5 restaurants, tennis, coffee shop, pool with barbecue terrace.

Philippine Village Hotel. At Nayong Pilipino, near the Manila International Airport, 520 air-conditioned rooms. Shopping arcade, bank-money exchange, free airport transfers, complete hotel services. Deluxe but at rates you can afford.

Tradewinds Hotel. On South Superhighway, corner Gen. Lukban St. 301 rooms. Coffee shop, bar, dining room, cocktail lounge, shops.

Tropical Palace. At BF Homes, Parañaque. 158 air-conditioned rooms in Western- or Oriental-style décor, convention facilities, swimming pool, patisserie, ballroom, beauty and barber shop, sports facilities. First-class accommodations.

Moderate—P400–600

Aloha. 2150 Roxas Blvd. 100 rooms, lounge, night club and coffee shop. Offers massage and Japanese baths.

Ambassador. 2021 A. Mabini St., Malate. 269 rooms with bath. Four restaurants, revolving supper club with a good view of Manila Bay, pool, coffee shop, sauna, basement parking, gift shops.

Aurelio. Roxas Blvd. 132 rooms, restaurant, coffee shop, sauna, medical and dental clinic, gift shops.

Dakota Mansion, 555 Gen. Malvar cor. Adriatico Sts. in Malate, has 145 rooms, restaurants, sauna, shops.

El Grande. Paranaque. 124 fully air-conditioned rooms, with dining-hall, supper club, discothèque and pool. 8 pelota courts, 3 tennis courts, 18-hole golf course, and man-made lagoon for boating and fishing. Luxury-class accommodations.

Enrico. 1324 Leon Guinto St., Ermita, has 231 rooms with bath, radio, and TV; revolving cocktail lounge, tour and travel service, medical and dental clinic, and shops. Deluxe accommodations.

Frederic. Corner of F. B. Harrison and 7th Sts. 128 air-conditioned rooms, with dining room, coffee shop, Japanese restaurant, supper club, sauna, pool, and shopping arcade.

Gilarmi Apartment Hotel. 52 Ayala Ave. 380 rooms with kitchens. Coffee shop, cocktail lounge, pool, sauna. Luxury-class accommodations.

Great Asia. 1243 Soler, in 68 rooms with kitchens; supper club, 2 bars, pool.

Las Palmas. 1616 A. Mabini St., Malate. 100 air-conditioned rooms. Coffee shop, cocktail lounge. Japanese and Korean restaurant. Multilingual staff.

Luneta. T. M. Kalaw St., off Roxas Blvd. facing Luneta Park. 64 rooms, with private baths.

Mabuhay. On A. Mabini, Ermita. 104 rooms, all air conditioned with private baths. Only indoor–outdoor swimming pool in the country. Curio shops.

Manila Royale. 627 Echague St., 208 rooms with baths. Revolving restaurant on top, dining room on 18th floor, coffee shop, cocktail lounge and supper club on 19th, with a full view of Manila and suburbs; heliport, shopping center and basement parking. First-class accommodations.

Otani-Manila. Roxas Blvd. 101 air-conditioned rooms with private baths, including 11 suites. 24-hour snack bar. Chinese restaurant, 11 A.M. to midnight club.

President. 313 Estero Cegado. 130 air-conditioned rooms, dining room which serves international cuisine, coffee shop and bar.

Wonderland Philippines. 1835 Harrison St., Pasay. 30 air-conditioned rooms, with piped-in music, bakeshop, coffee shop, discothèque and convention rooms.

Inexpensive—under P400

Carlston. Roxas Blvd., corner of Airport Rd. 140 air-conditioned rooms, restaurant, and night club.

Charter House. 114 Legaspi Village, Makati. 120 rooms, Has coffee shop, laundry TV, travel service.

Dutch Inn. 1034 Roxas Blvd. 38 rooms, with bar, restaurant, coffee shop.

El Dorado. 100 Roxas Blvd. 168 rooms with kitchens; supper club, 2 bars, pool.

Empire. 2120 A. Mabini. 62 rooms, some with kitchenettes.

Grand. 88C Palanca St., Quiapo. 180 air-conditioned rooms, with restaurant serving European, Chinese, Japanese, and Filipino dishes.

Kamalig Inn. 2160 Taft Ave. Ext. 17 rooms, friendly service. Pool. Good spot for art-lovers.

Merchants Hotel. 711 San Bernardo, corner Soler, in the heart of downtown Manila. 72 rooms with bath, restaurant, bank, barbershop.

Timberland. Ronquillo, Sta. Cruz, has 116 rooms, including 8 suites. Reasonable rates. In the heart of downtown.

Tower. 1313 A. Mabini. 120 rooms, all air-conditioned.

Waldorf Hotel. 1955 A. Mabini St., Malate. 36 rooms, with restaurant, bar.

Baguio

Deluxe—P800 and up

Hyatt Terraces. Luxury hotel with 306 well-furnished rooms in the highland style. Swimming pool, sauna. Swiss restaurant, Japanese and European dining halls.

First Class—P500–700

Pines Hotel. Currently closed for renovation. Has 68 luxurious suites and 156 well-appointed rooms.

Moderate—P350–450

Baguio Park. Harrison Rd. 72 rooms with running water; restaurant, cocktail lounge, and souvenir shop.

Diplomat. Dominican Hill. 40 rooms plus coffee shop and souvenir shops.

Inn Rocio. 68 Kisad Rd. 36 rooms. Restaurant serving Filipino, Spanish, Italian and Indonesian cuisines. Overlooking picture windows offers panoramic view of Baguio.

Montecillo. 23 rooms, dining room, bar, running hot and cold water.

Plaza. Assumption Rd. 26 tastefully appointed rooms and suites. Dining room; efficient service.

Ruff's Inn. 54 rooms. Scenic area, beside the Loakan Airport.

Villa La Maja. Outlook Dr. Native and traditional mountain dances performed on request.

Inexpensive—under P350

Attic Inn. Abanao St. 25 rooms. Iberian-style decor; restaurant.

Munsayac Holiday Inn. 16 rooms, with restaurant, garden, fireplace, car rental, souvenir shop.

Rates are based on double occupancy for the following areas. For a provincial capital such as Cebu, *Deluxe,* P840 and up; *First Class,* P560–800; *Moderate,* P160–240; *Inexpensive,* under P160. For a resort: *Deluxe,* P270 and up; *First Class,* P230–260; *Moderate,* P190–220; *Inexpensive,* under P180. For a small city: *Deluxe,* P370 and up; *First Class,* P250–360; *Moderate,* P160–240; *Inexpensive* under P150.

Banaue

Moderate

Banaue Hotel. Comfortable accommodations for 42. Dining room.

Inexpensive

Roadside Lodge. Banaue, Ifugao. 14 rooms. Dining room, variety store.
Sanafe Lodge. Banaue, Ifugao. 11 rooms. Dining room, lounge room.

Bataan

First Class

Bataan Hilltop. 42 guest rooms, with private balconies, pool, discothèque, pelota and tennis courts, sauna and massage, golf course.

Landoil. Mariveles. 100 rooms, with dining room, meeting rooms, telephone, parking area.

Batangas

Deluxe

Punta Baluarte Inter-Continental Hotel. In Calatagan, Batangas. Luxury resort. 32 rustic cottages with rates similar to luxury hotels in Manila.

First Class

Nasugbu Hotel. In Nasugbu, Batangas. 100 air-conditioned rooms; dining room, cocktail lounge, pool, boating and skindiving, bar and sports club.

Moderate

Alpha, Batangas City. 60 rooms, with bath, dining room, bar, swimming pool.

Volcano Lakeview Resort. Agoncillo, Batangas. 95 rooms, private cottages, rustic atmosphere, dining and swimming facilities.

Bontoc

Moderate

Chico River Inn. 24 rooms with restaurant and curio shop.

Mt. Data Lodge. 7,200 feet above sea level. Located mid-way between the Baguio summer resort and the Banaue Rice Terraces; authentic Igorot dances upon request. 22 rooms, bar, fireplace, dining, curio shop.

Cavite

Deluxe

Puerto Azul Beach Hotel. In Ternate, Cavite. 360 deluxe rooms and suites. Golf, tennis, pelota, scuba-diving, waterskiing, grill room, bar and coffee shop, meeting rooms.

Taal Vista Lodge. Near Taal Lake. 25 rooms. Dining hall, pool.

First Class

Covelandia. In Binakayan, Cavite. 60 air-conditioned rooms. Dining, pool, family cottages; picnic, sports and recreation facilities.

Daet

Moderate

Karilagan. 30 rooms, with a restaurant, barbershop and beauty parlor.

Dagupan City

First Class

McAdore Palace. Galvan Zamora St. 80 rooms. Revolving restaurant, swimming pool, conference room, coffee shop.

Moderate

Hotel Cadena de Amor. 22 rooms, at Calasiao. Restaurant and shuttle bus service.

Urduja. Urdaneta, Pangasinan. 40 rooms. Swimming pool, nightclub/disco, dining room.

Vicar. Torres, Bugallon Ave. 36 rooms. Dining and function rooms.

Victoria. 77 rooms, with restaurant, bar, convention hall, coffee shop, giftshop.

Ilocos Norte

Deluxe

Fort Ilocandia. Laoag City. 250 luxury rooms with private balconies. Restaurant, coffee shop, ballroom, shopping arcade, swimming pool.

Inexpensive

Casa Llanes. Laoag City. 19 air-conditioned rooms, with dining room, parking area.

Texicano Hotel. Laoag City. 47 rooms with restaurant, beach resort, parking area.

YJ Hotel. Laoag City. 20 rooms, air-conditioned, with private or common bath, restaurant.

Ilocos Sur

Moderate

Cordillera. Vigan. 23 rooms, restaurant, movie house, announcement hall.

Suso Beach Resort. Near Vigan. 200 rooms. Cottages, dining pavilion, beach facilities.

Laguna

First Class

Lake Caliraya Country Club. In Lumban, 1,000 feet above sea level, 64 miles from Manila. Ten cabañas, a main pavilion, swimming pool, overlooking a beautiful manmade lake. Motorized bancas, speedboats, horseback riding, pelota court, sauna baths, dining room and cocktail lounge. First-class resort.

Pagsanjan Rapids Hotel. Near the river going to the famous Pagsanjan Falls. Has 32 rooms with bath, 2 restaurants, tour service for shooting the rapids, fishing and hunting, etc.

Moderate

Bato-Bato. In Calamba, about 32 miles from Manila. 16 guest rooms, all with private hot spring baths aside from a main pool also filled with natural hot spring water. Restaurant serving native and Western dishes.

Cuyab Hot Springs. Also in Calamba. Five cottages in sprawling rustic surroundings. Hot spring water in huge swimming pool, six open picnic huts with native dining place. Medicinal waters, highly recommended for soaking rheumatic bones.

Filipinas Golf & Country Club. In San Pedro. Ten air-conditioned cottages. 18-hole golf course, open-air restaurant overlooking the green, and wooded areas for leisurely strolls.

Hidden Valley Springs. Alaminos, 1½ hours by car from Manila. Luxury cottages with private indoor gardens, dancing pavilion and restaurant, located 300 feet deep in a 110-acre crater, surrounded by virgin forests, with a number of natural swimming pools.

Lakeview Resort Hotel. Los Baños, at foot of Mt. Makiling along the shore of Laguna Lake south of Manila. Has 45 rooms with spring baths on the first floor (18 for individuals and 5 for families), pool with running mineral hot spring water, gift shop.

Pagsanjan Tropical Hotel. Near Pagsanjan town, about 2½-hour drive from Manila. Has 55 rooms with bath, restaurant serving Filipino, Chinese, European and American cuisine; pool.

Sierra Lakes Resort. In Lumban, 1,000 feet above sea level and located near the man-made Lake Caliraya. Main rustic resthouse for weekend stays. Cottages for longer stays. Restaurant and watersports facilities.

Villa Pansol. In Calamba, birthplace of the national hero, Dr. Jose P. Rizal. A hot springs resort with 8 guest rooms. Private sunken marble "Roman" baths with natural hot spring water, also four modern swimming pools with the same water. Pavilions, picnic huts, restaurant.

Inexpensive

Nonino. In San Pedro, 12 air-conditioned cottages, with picnic grove, dancing pavilion, adult and children's pool, and restaurant.

Rio Vista. Near the river on the way to Pagsanjan Falls. 20 rooms in well-appointed rustic cottages. Dining pavilion, swimming pool arrangements for boat rides to Pagsanjan Falls.

La Union

First Class

Cresta Ola Beach Resort, Bauang. 20 rooms with kitchenette. Miniature golf course, deep-sea fishing boats, waterskiing, games room.

Moderate

Agoo Playa. In Agoo. 100 rooms. Conference, sports and banquet facilities.

Bay View. San Fernando. 41 rooms. Restaurant, convention hall, bar, sports facilities.

Nalinac Beach Resort. Resort hotel on ocean beach, near town. 100 rooms, 12 cottages. Completely air-conditioned. Swimming pool, waterskiing, scuba diving, boating, fishing, bar, disco.

Sun Valley Resort. Along Bauang beach, with 98 rooms. Pool, beach facilities.

Inexpensive

La Union Country Resort. In Bauang. 34 rooms; beach and swimming facilities.

Legazpi

First Class

Mayon Imperial. On Peñaranda, corner Rizal St. 90 air-conditioned rooms, Japanese restaurant, pool, pelota/squash courts, sauna, shopping arcade.

First Class

La Trinidad. Rizal St. 41 rooms, restaurant, tour service.

Moderate

Albay. Peñaranda St., has 44 rooms, and features penthouse nightclub. Has facilities for swimming, boating, fishing, and tennis.

Xandra. Peñaranda St., offers a panoramic view of Mayon Volcano. 56 rooms, steak house, cocktail lounge and nightclub.

Inexpensive

Rex. Aguinaldo St. 25 rooms. Dining, lounge rooms.

Romacar. Peñaranda St. 42 rooms. Bar, dining room.

Naga City

Inexpensive

Lindez. 46 rooms, some air-conditioned. Restaurant, and excursion boat service.

Plaza Holiday. 55 air-conditioned rooms. Restaurant, steakhouse, coffee shop, bar.

Olongapo

First Class

Marmont Hotel. 83 rooms, with different décor (e.g., the French, Japanese, Chinese, Roman, Maranao Rooms, etc.). Pelota court, swimming pool, sunken Italian garden, honeymoon cottage, Roman ballroom with piped-in music, restaurant and grill rooms, sauna.

Riza. 60 rooms. Bar, curio and souvenir shops, supermart.

Pampanga

Moderate

Maharajah. Angeles City. 87 rooms, with swimming pool, sauna, restaurant, giftshop.

Marisol Manor. Angeles City, fully-equipped resort hotel. 13 rooms.

Marlim Mansions Hotel and Apartments. Angeles City. 97 rooms. Has a shopping mall and restaurant.

Clarktown. Balibago. 75 rooms, with restaurant, nightclub, swimming pool, giftshop.

Jet. 42 rooms, at Angeles City. Swimming pool, restaurant, beauty shop, shopping mall.

Pangasinan

Inexpensive

Maxine By The Sea. Lucap. Alaminos. 21 rooms. Facilites for skin-diving, coral garden exploring, fishing, boats.

Rizal

First Class

Sulo. Matalino St., Quezon City. 60 rooms, air-conditioned. Coffee shop, disco bar, pool, convention facilities.

Moderate

Lynnville By-the-Sea. 20 1st St., Villamar Court, Parañaque. 17 air-conditioned rooms. All modern facilities.

Tagaytay

First Class

Taal Vista Lodge. Located on Tagaytay Ridge, has 50 rooms, cabaña type, with 2 dining rooms serving Continental cuisine.

Moderate

Sierra Grande. Along Tagaytay Ridge, 9 cozy cottages for families and couples, architectured swimming pools, dancing pavilion, panoramic view of countryside.

Inexpensive

Villa Adelaida. Along National Rd. Has 25 rooms. All modern facilities plus croquet lawn.

Tiwi

Inexpensive

Tiwi Hot Springs Resthouse. Located at the spa of the same name, boasts its own thermal baths, and two swimming pools (one cold and one warm). The 15 rooms are inexpensive.

Zambales

Moderate

La Sirena. A beach resort on Subic, with 30 air-conditioned rooms in rustic cottages. Restaurant, cocktail lounge, bar, watersports facilities arranged.

Quality Resort. Subic. 100 rooms plus 5 cottages with kitchenettes; snack bar, nightclub, bowling, boating.

Inexpensive

Sand Valley Beach Resort. Iba. 34 rooms and suites, beach cottages.

BOHOL ISLAND

Tagbilaran

First Class

Gia Gardens. 30 rooms. Restaurant, bar, conference room, sports facilities.

Moderate

La Roca. Seven air-conditioned rooms. Dining room. Native entertainment. Excursion boat service. Swimming pool, conference room, souvenir shop.

Tagbilaran. 15 rooms. Dining, lounge, disco.

CEBU ISLAND

Cebu City

Deluxe

Cebu Plaza. Another addition to Cebu's luxury hotels, with 500 air-conditioned rooms. Pool, restaurant.

First Class

Magellan. Cebu's most luxurious, with 200 air-conditioned rooms, golf course, tennis, bowling alley, and swimming pool. Luxury service will mean luxury prices.

Montebello Resort. 142 air-conditioned rooms. Bar, restaurant, watersports facilities.

Moderate

Cebu Club Pacific. On Sogod St. 62 rooms, restaurant, conference hall, private airport.

Estrella Inn. On Luna St. 36 air-conditioned rooms, with restaurant, bar, shops, bank.

Mercedes. Pelaez St. 57 rooms, with restaurant and conference rooms.

Rajah. 42 rooms. Restaurant and cocktail lounge. Roof garden and giftshop. Fuente Osmeña.

Siesta. D. Jakosalem St., has 24 rooms, with laundry service, giftshop, restaurant.

Triton. M.J. Cuenco Ave. Has 100 rooms, with restaurant, giftshop, conference rooms, barbershop, pelota court, swimming pool.

Skyvue. Plaridel St. has 167 rooms, restaurant, sports and fishing facilities.

Inexpensive

Sta. Rosa by the Sea. In Mactan, has 34 rooms, restaurant, cocktail lounge, laundry service, barbershop.

Tambuli Beach Resort. In Talisay. Has 14 rooms, restaurant, sports facilities.

LEYTE ISLAND

Tacloban City

Deluxe

Leyte Park, 100 luxury rooms, suites. Bar, coffee shop, conference facilities, swimming pool, tennis courts.

MINDANAO ISLAND

Butuan City

Moderate

Butuan Imperial. San Francisco St. 31 rooms. Restaurant, coffee shop.

Elite Tourist Inn. San Jose St. 20 rooms. Restaurant, parking area.

Cagayan de Oro

Moderate

Mindanao. On Chavez corner Corrales Sts. Has 45 rooms, restaurant, conference room, transport service.

Fern's Grand. On Carmen St. 29 rooms, restaurant, bar, pelota court, swimming pool, conference hall.

Ambassador. Don Apolinar Velez St. 77 rooms, dining rooms.

VIP. On G.R. Borja St. 69 rooms, restaurant, bar, swimming pool, coffee shop.

Cotabato City

Inexpensive

Dawns. On Makakua St. 74 rooms, car service, parking area.

Imperial. On Magallanes St. 42 rooms, restaurant, beauty parlor, parking area.

New Grand. On Villamor St. corner Corcuera. 48 rooms, restaurant.

Sultan. On Magallanes St. 50 rooms, parking area.

Davao

First Class

Davao Insular. The last word in modern styling, but won't necessarily make you think you are in Mindanao. Deluxe in service and prices. 160 rooms. The most luxurious hotel in the south.

Maguindanao. On Claro M. Recto Ave. 54 rooms, bar, restaurant, cocktail lounge, supper club.

Moderate

Apo View. On J. Camus St. An old, well-established hostelry with a sound reputation, and if you want atmosphere, this is your place. Good dining room, quiet and efficient service. Swimming pool, 150 rooms.

Fabulous Venees. MacArthur Hwy. 54 rooms. Restaurant, bar, conference hall.

Imperial. On Claro M. Recto Ave. 52 rooms, ballroom, convention room, pelota court, swimming pool, giftshop, supper club.

Inexpensive

New Davao Lodge. San Pedro St. 47 rooms. Dining, lounge room.

Marawi City

Moderate

Marawi Resort. At Marawi. 75 rooms, restaurant, laundry, telephone service, parking area.

Maria Cristina. 37 rooms. Dining room, bar, nightclub, watersports and ocean swimming.

Inexpensive

Al Toro. Cabili Ave. 32 rooms.

Surigao

Moderate

Litang Lodge. Borromeo St. 36 rooms. Restaurant, bar.

New Tavern. On Borromeo St., Surigao City. 25 rooms, restaurant.

Zamboanga

Deluxe

Zamboanga Plaza. On Pasonanca Park. 500 rooms. Offers a panoramic view of the city, the bay and the river valley. Modern business-type establishment.

Moderate

Lantaka. On Valderrosa St., Zamboanga City. A modern hotel by the sea. 96 luxurious rooms with bath. Restaurant, private beach and scuba diving.

New Astoria. On Mayor Taldon St., Zamboanga City, with 52 rooms, souvenir shop, bar, restaurant.

New Sultana. Cor. Pilar & Gov. Lim Ave. 72 rooms. Has convention hall, restaurant, coffee shop, cocktail lounge, shopping center.

Inexpensive

New Imperial. On Brillantes St. 26 rooms. Dining, nightclub, disco.

New Zamboanga. On Magno St. Has 89 rooms, restaurant, meeting rooms and convention hall.

NEGROS ISLAND

Bacolod City

First Class

Bascon II. Gonzaga St., 38 rooms. Air-conditioned.

Seabreeze. San Juan St., 48 rooms. Restaurant, cocktail lounge.

Moderate

Mandarin. On Gov. Gatuslao St. 68 rooms. Cocktail lounge, sauna, conference hall, TV, laundry, and restaurant.

Sugarland. On Singcang St. 89 rooms. Bar cocktail lounge, convention hall, swimming pool, restaurant, service transport.

Inexpensive

Halili. A. Locsin St. 32 rooms. Dining, conference, lounge room.

Vista. A. Locsin St. 36 rooms. Disco, coffee shop.

Dumaguete City

Inexpensive

El Oriente. On Real St. 22 rooms. Cars for hire, parking area.

La Mar. On Rizal Blvd. 19 rooms. Restaurant, parking area.

Insular. On Silliman Ave. 20 rooms. Restaurant.

Three M's Inn. San Jose St. 15 rooms. Dining, bar, function hall.

PALAWAN ISLAND

Puerto Princesa City

Deluxe

Hyatt Rafols Palawan. Luxury hotel with 45 air-conditioned rooms. Coffee shop, seafood grill, cocktail lounge, bar, disco.

PANAY ISLAND

Iloilo City

First Class

Sarabia Manor. 69 rooms. Sauna and massage facilities. Shopping arcade.

Casa Plaza. In residential area. 36 rooms with central air-conditioning. Coffee shop, bar, conference room.

Del Rio. 29 air-conditioned rooms. Nightclub, restaurant with international cuisine. Facilities for skiing, speed-boating.

Moderate

Anhawan. 12 deluxe native-style cottages with restaurant.

Centercon. 20 min. from airport. 57 air-conditioned rooms, with a restaurant serving European, American and Filipino dishes.

River Queen. 50 rooms. Supper club.

Kalibo

Moderate

Aklan Royal. Bankaya St. 17 rooms. Restaurant, reception lounge.

Ati-Atihan. On Bankaya St. 57 rooms. Dining, lounge room.

YOUTH HOSTELS. In recent years youth hostels have sprung up in all parts of the country, mainly through the pioneering work of the Youth Hostels Association of the Philippines, which has chapters all over the archipelago. Mainly designed for student travelers, local as well as foreign, the youth hostels are well managed, their facilities adequate and clean, and their rates within the reach of students. An air-conditioned room generally costs 20 to 25 pesos (about US$3.50) a day, plus 50¢ for the change of linen every three days.

YHAP. *Ystaphil,* Taft Ave., Manila; 1701 San Marcelino, Malate, Manila; *1572 YH,* 1572 Leon Guinto St., Manila; *Quezon City Youth Hostel,* 17 Malinis St. U.P. Village Diliman, Quezon City; *Pagsanjan Youth Hostel,* c/o Pagsanjan Rapids Hotel, Laguna Province; *Sampaloc Lake Youth Hostel,* San Pablo City, Laguna Province; *Villa Milagrosa Youth Hostel,* Dagupan City, Pangasinan Province; *Tiwi Hot Springs Youth Hostel,* Tiwi, Albay; *Igorot Youth Hostel,* Asin Rd., Baguio City; *Banaue Youth Hostel,* Banaue, Mountain Province; *Paracale Youth Hostel,* Tauig Paracale Camarines Norte.

PENSIONS. Pensions, because of their homey and personalized service and their popularity among tourists, have suddenly proliferated in Metro Manila and suburbs. Among these are: *Apartel Mabini,* 1337 Mabini St., Ermita; *Hometown Family Inn,* 3050 F. B. Harrison, Pasay City; *Tropicana Apartel,* 1630 L. Guerrero, Malate; *Rothman,* 1633 Adriatico, Malate; *Dakota Mansions,* M. Adriatico, Malate; *Casa Dalco,* 1318 F. Agoncillo, Ermita; *Yasmin House,* 453 Arquiza St, Ermita; *Casa Olga,* 1406 M. H. del Pilar, Ermita; *Why Not Pension,* 1937 Modesto St., Malate; *Fujiyama Resthouse,* 450 Arquiza St., Ermita; *Casa Unson,* 1525 F. Agoncillo St., Ermita; *Pension Filipina,* Arkansas St., Ermita; *Pelican Pension,* 147 Blumentritt St., San Juan; *Malate Pensione,* 1771 Adriatico St., Malate; *Macopa Pension,* 11 Macopa St., Quezon City; *El Calito Inn,* 804 Pasay Rd., Makati; *Pension Cristo Rey,* 6304 Roxas St., Makati; *Kamalig Inn,* 2160 Taft Ave. Ext., Pasay City; *New Swiss Inn,* Gen. Luna St., Paco; *Dutch Inn,* 1034 Roxas Blvd., *Atami,* 457 P. Faura St.; *Casa Pension,* 1406 M. del Pilar St., Ermita; *Pius XII Catholic Center,* 1175 UN Ave.; *YMCA,* Concepcion St., Ermita; *YWCA,* 880 UN Ave. Rates in most pensions are moderate, and the facilities comparable to the best hotels.

CLOSING DAYS AND HOURS. The popular bazaars and shops generally open between 8 and 9 A.M. and close as late as 9 P.M. except at the Excolta area where closing time is generally at 6. No fixed rule though. Many stores outside of the Escolta area are open Sunday morning. Those in the hotel area are often open seven days a week. Some of the stores take standard two-hour lunch break from noon to 2 P.M., but the majority have no lunch breaks. Government and some private offices are open from 8 A.M. to 5 P.M., Mondays to Fridays.

TOURS. Tours of Manila and outskirts, plus excursions, or longer trips throughout the republic, can be arranged through the following reputable agencies: *American Express Company,* Philamlife Bldg.; *Adkins Travel Agency,* UN Ave.; *Baron Travel Corporation,* 1365 Leon Guinto; *House of Travel,* 1973 A. Mabini; *Pan Asiatic Travel Corp.,* Roxas Blvd.; *Travel Masters,* Pedro Gil; *Everett Travel Service,* 290 Atlanta, Port Area; *Amity Travel Corp.,* 1150 Roxas Blvd.; *Danfil Express,* Magsaysay Center, Roxas Blvd.; *Sharp Travel Service,* Juan Luna, Binondo; *World Tour Operators,* UN Ave., Ermita; *Mantours,* Magsaysay Center, Roxas Blvd.; *Sarkies Tours,* Midland Plaza; *Worldwide Travel Service,* Adriatico, Malate; *Travel-World,* Manila Hilton; *Tours Specialists,* Makati Bel Air Condominium; *Rajah Tours,* UN Ave., Ermita; *Thomas Cook Inc.,* Ayala Ave., Makati; *Tourismo Filipino Inc.,* Mla. Domestic Airport, Pasay; *Jet Travel,* 1556A Mabini St.; *Willines Travel Service,* 1750M Adriatico St.; *Pacific Leisure-Life Travel,* Pasay Rd., Makati; *Baguio City Tours,* Roxas Blvd., Pasay; *Badjao Tours and Travel,* Evangelista Bldg., Zamboanga City; *Carmen Travel Agency,* Gordon Ave., Olongapo City; *David Travel Agency,* Guagua Pamapanga; *Diplomat Travel and Tours,* Session Rd., Baguio City; *Island Tours,* Isabela Bldg., Cebu City; *Sultan Express Tours,* Rajah Hotel, Cebu City; *Tambuli Tours,* Bayot Hotel, Zamboanga City; *Tours Specialist,* Hotel Del Rio, Iloilo City; *Union Tours,* San Fernando, La Union; *Tours Specialist,* Davao Insular Hotel, Davao City; *New City Travel Agency,* Macom Bldg., Olongapo City.

English-, Spanish-, Japanese-, Italian- and French-speaking guides are available.

There are special interest tours, visits and/or stays in Filipino homes throughout the Philippines. Contact city mayors or *Ministry of Tourism,* Agrifina Circle, Rizal Park, Manila.

CHILDREN'S ACTIVITIES. The *Manila Zoological and Botanical Garden,* Dakota and Harrison Blvd., has a wide selection of Philippine and foreign animals, birds, and reptiles. Monkey Island is always a treat, as is the playground. *Manila Aquarium,* in Intramuros, features a variety of Philippine tropical fish. *Nayong Pilipino* (Philippine Village) features the arts and crafts of the Philippines' eight major regions at the Manila International Airport reservation. 54 acres of typical villages and countryside.

PARTICIPANT SPORTS. Golf is popular in the larger cities. The *Muni* (or *Municipal*) *Golf Course and Driving Range,* across from the Manila Hotel, is in the shadows of the southeast wall of Intramuros. Right near by there's a Mini Golf range, where you play miniature golf. If you have friends in Manila, they can perhaps arrange for you to play at country clubs. Some of these clubs are: the *Nichols, Makati, Tagaytay, Calatagan, Tayud, Holiday Hills, Muni, Muntinlupa, Wack Wack, Veterans Memorial, University of the Philippines, Silvertown, Sta. Ana,* and *Valley* golf clubs.

Swimming at *Rizal Memorial pool, Manila Hotel pool,* and three large pools at the *Balara Filter Plant,* located beyond the new Philippine University area, Quezon City, about a 30-minute drive from Manila. This latter public park, with the unglamorous name, also includes picnic grounds, children's playground, and a dance hall. Beaches and pools are plentiful. *Lido Beach* in Cavite is the best beach near Manila.

Tennis courts at the *Manila Hotel* are open to the public, as are those at the *Rizal Memorial stadium.*

Skindivers will be in their element in Philippine waters. Tropical fish, coral, and shells are magnificent. The waters off Corregidor in Manila Bay are frequented by skindiving parties. Batangas and Matabungkay Beach, both only a few hours' drive from Manila, are other favorite skindiving spots as are the Hundred Islands in Pangasinan, about five hours' drive to the north. **Bancas** or canoes may be rented at all beaches, shell-collectors also go on these excursions. Local tour operators in Manila will help with **hunting** and **fishing** excursions. December-August is best for game fishing; September-February for fowl shooting; January-May for wild game.

SPECTATOR SPORTS. Basketball is the rage throughout the year. Fast and able players are the best in Asia. In the countryside, **cockfighting** reigns supreme. Arrangements can be made to see cockfights at one of the pits patronized by Manila cockfighting enthusiasts. Sundays and holidays. *Olympic Stadium* at Grace Park and *La Loma Arena* are the largest cockpits but if you want to watch the blood flow in air-conditioned comfort, you can try to arrange a visit to the *Philippine Cockers Club.* The latter is usually restricted to members and guests, but your travel agent may be able to get you in.

Horseracing in Manila takes place Saturdays and Sundays on either of the city's two tracks, the *Manila Jockey Club,* at San Lazaro and the *Philippine Racing Club* at Sta. Ana. **Bowling** fans can exercise their skill at *Mabini Bowling Lanes* on Mabini St. in Manila, at the *Bowlodrome* on Buendia in Makati, and at the *Coronado Lanes* at the Makati Commercial Center.

Soccer football and American **baseball** are played in Manila, but neither is likely to replace basketball in the public affection. **Boxing** has a large following; glance at the sport pages for matches. *Sipa,* a game which involves the kicking of a small wicker ball back and forth, requires great skill. It is played at the *Rizal Court* on Rizal Ave., Manila, every other day.

Go to *Jay-Alai* on Manila's Taft Ave. for **pelota** matches, which have some ardent win-or-lose-all advocates. The players are from Spain. If you're lucky, a P2 or P5 wager can pay for a big evening on the town. Jai-alai games are held every day, except Sunday, starting at 6 P.M.

POLLUTION REPORT

A National Pollution Control Commission was established by the government with regional offices in the provinces to control and check the pollution of the territorial waters, air and land of the nation. Continuing surveys and research on a nationwide scale are conducted by the Commission. It is now mandatory for all factories and industrial plants to provide their own pollution-control devices, so that their industrial waste products will not pollute the rivers, bays, beaches, etc., as well as the atmosphere in their immediate vicinity. From latest reports from the Commission, the Philippines ranks among the few developing countries that does not suffer from air and water pollution problems. If there has been pollution, it is within tolerable limits, the Commission reports, and so far has not become a hazard to the populace and the environment.

MUSEUMS. *The National Museum,* now housed at the Tourism Building at the Agrifina Circle, has a unique collection of Philippine flora and fauna. New archeological findings and an enviable shell collection as well as a fine arts collection are properly displayed there. There are also cultural and historical museums in San Pablo, Calamba, and Pila, Laguna Province; in Taal, Lipa, and Tanauan, Batangas; in the Taban Caves, Palawan; in Batac, Ilocos Norte; in Baguio City; in Munoz, Nueva Eeija; in Boliuao, Paugasinan; in Naga, Camarinas Sur; in Tacloban, Leyte; in Cebu City, Cebu; in Davao City; in Marawi City; in Cagayan de Oro City; in Dagupan City; in Jolo, Sulir; in Malolos, Bulacan. A *Museum of Traditional Philippine Cultures* was inaugurated at the *Nayong Pilipino* near the Manila International Airport. Not to be missed too are the *Lopez Museum* on 10 Lancaster St., in Pasay City; the *UST Museum* on Espana St. in Manila; the *Ayala Museum* on Makati Ave.; the *CCP Museum* on Roxas Blvd., the *Metropolitan Museum and Museum of Philippine Art* also on Roxas Blvd.; the *Museum of Liturgical Art* at San Agustin Church in Intramuros; and the *Archeological Museum at Sta. Ana Church* in Sta. Ana, Manila.

SHOPPING. In the Philippines, the best buys are handcrafted items and works of art, especially, among the latter, the so-called primitive pieces. Prices and attitudes, as well as quality of service, vary widely, but the English language is official so far as shopkeepers are concerned, so you don't have to worry about being handicapped in the battle of wits you may find yourself waging.

Bargaining or haggling over prices is frowned upon in the smarter stores, but that doesn't mean it isn't done in the others. Over on Rizal Ave., the storekeepers and clerks will be downright surprised if you don't even try to haggle. Sometimes the saving isn't much, but if you're in a haggling mood, a so-called fixed price is not necessarily inflexible. The confirmed bargain hunter should be an early bird. Stores and market vendors sometimes will quote a rock-bottom price to the first customer of the day. The old belief is that if the day starts with a good sale, business for the whole day will prosper.

Woodcarvings, woodenware, a variety of handwoven, richly embroidered fabrics, brassware, pearl and coral products, *abaca, buri* palm and bamboo products, paintings of the Philippine scene, antique Filipino jewelry, Philippine dolls, world-famous cigars, Moro *kris:* these are some of the unique specialties of the Philippines. Tourist duty-free shops may be found at the Manila International Airport; the Makati Commercial Center, at Ayala Ave.; the Manila Garden Hotel Lobby; the Philippine Plaza Hotel; the Manila Hotel shopping arcade; the Manila Hilton lobby; the Hyatt Regency shopping arcade; the Philippine International Convention Center, and at the Zamboanga International Airport.

All of the major hotels have souvenir and handicraft shops or stands. You can find more of them on A. Mabini Street, M. H. Del Pilar, and UN Avenue, all in the hotel area in Manila's Ermita district. Others are in downtown Manila, though they are more scattered. As good a place as any to start a shopping expedition is *Tesoro's* on A. Mabini, *Rustau's* in Makati, and the *Philippine Education Company,* Postal Arcade Bldg., Malcati Shopping Center, has an excellent souvenir department and is worth the short taxi trip. *Lepanto Crafts, Inc.,* 572 A. Mabini, is the sole distributor of colorful and durable Lepanto fabrics, made by mountain weavers north of Baguio on hand looms.

Other handicraft items are available at the *Oriental Handicraft Gift Shop,* 1129 A. Mabini, Ermita; *Philippine Homecrafts,* 494B R. Salas, Ermita; *Leslie's Woodcraft,* 426 M. H. del Pilar, Ermita; *Jim's Merchandising,* 1128 A. Mabini, Ermita; *S. Vizacarra's,* U.N. Ave.; *Tudanca's,* A Mabini; *Edwina Mananzan's,* A. Mabini; *Acacia House,* A. Mabini; *Landichos,* M. H. del Pilar; *Casa Filipina,* 1578 A. Mabini; *Cortes,* A. Mabini; *Galerias Bravo,* Tomas Morato Ave., Q.C.; *Geslani's,* 61 C. Palanca; *Nayong Filipino,* MIA Ave.; *Tesoro's,* A. Mabini; *Silahis,* J. Bocobo, Ermita; *House of Ramie,* 1158 M. H. del Pilar; *Leslie's,* 1760 J. Bocobo; and *Filipiniana,* 1910 A. Mabini.

Ifugao carvings (ash trays, rice bowls, book ends, wooden figures) make interesting and useful souvenirs. Buy them in Baguio if you make the trip north; otherwise, you can find them in almost any souvenir shop. It pays to compare prices before purchasing souvenirs. Prices sometimes vary widely.

Moslem brassware is distinctive. Miniature weapons of Moroland are inexpensive and have an exotic touch.

Numerous art galleries include *Luz Gallery,* 448 E. de Los Santos Ave. (ivory, porcelain, celadon) and *City Gallery,* Rizal Park (Filipino painters). Also: *Solidaridad Galleries* on Padra Faura; *Hidalgo Gallery* at Makati Commercial Center; *Hilton Art Center* at Hilton; *Gallery One* at Greenhills Shopping Center; *Big and Small Gallery* at the Cultural Center; *Metropolitan Museum* and the *Museum of Philippine Art* on Roxas Blvd.; *Museum of Traditional Philippine Cultures* at Nayong Filipino; *National Museum Gallery* at Agrifina Circle, and *Galerie Bleue* at the Rustan Bldg. in Makati; *Milady Art Center* at the Makati Commercial Center, and *The Heritage Art Center* at Lantana St., Quezon City; *ABC Galleries* at A, Mabini, Ermita; the *Hiraya Gallery* on UN Ave., and *Sining Kamalig* on Taft Ave. Ext.

Piña, a pineapple fiber made on hand looms; *jusi,* a sheer handwoven banana fiber; and *ramie,* a weedlike plant which produces material stronger than cotton, offer all sorts of possibilities for men's and women's wear and for home use.

For *real bargains,* there are the Marikina shoes: for men (from P180 to P400) and women (from P150 to P300). Also there are the handcrafted abacca or raffia rugs for the living room (P80), women's bags (P40 up) and dinner sets also of abacca or raffia (from P25 to P35). Other bargains are the embroidered wash-and-wear "barong" shirt materials for men (P120) and embroidered wash-and-wear ramie-tetoron dress materials for women (P120).

Makati, Cubao, Greenhills and Robinson's shopping centers offer the latest in local goods side by side with imported ones.

DINING OUT. You have both the exotic and the familiar to choose from in the Philippines. The various regions of the country all have their own specialties, ranging from the heavy richness of the food in Pampanga Province to the hot spiciness of the dishes in the Bicol region. American, Chinese, and Spanish cuisines are all popular.

The tender suckling pig roasted on a spit is always a favorite. Known as *lechón,* it is served with a thick liver sauce. It's a must at every fiesta and once you've tasted it, you'll understand why. Chicken and pork *adobo* comes in a close second. It consists of pieces of chicken and pork boiled and fried in black pepper, onions, and garlic and has a delicious spicy taste. Then there is *lumpia,* a dish combining shredded coconut pith, shrimps, pork, and vegetables in a tissue-like wrapping, with a special brown sauce.

For breakfast, try scrambled eggs mixed with chopped onions and tomatoes, and *tapa,* dried pork or beef flavored with vinegar, salt, and garlic. Accompany this with thick, aromatic native chocolate and *pan de sal,* the small salted crisp rolls delivered freshly baked to Filipino homes every morning at daybreak. You have an infinite variety of fresh tropical fruits.

The papayas, mangoes, and pineapples are bigger and sweeter than anything you'll encounter this side of the Garden of Eden. Eating and cooking bananas come in many varieties. The small *tondan* type is considered by many to be the sweetest eating banana. *Kalamansi,* a small green citrus fruit similar to a lemon but with more tang, makes a refreshing drink and is also used to bring out the full flavor of other foods including papaya, fish, and *pancit,* a noodlelike dish with chopped shrimps or pork and vegetables. In season, you can try delicately flavored *atis,* small, sweet *lanzones,* large, grapefruit-like *pomelos,* and soft, juicy star apples.

Fish is a staple in the Filipino diet. While Filipinos favor small, tasty fish, you may find some of them too bony. There are others to choose from. One is the *lapu-lapu.* Another is the *bangos;* baked, it is good either hot or cold, with a sauce of onions, vinegar, and whole pepper seeds.

For the adventuresome palate, there's any number of dishes. *Balut,* a boiled duck's eggs with embryo, is considered a delicacy by many. Filipino children love it. The *balut* may be bought in markets or from street vendors who resort to loud, singsong shouts to advertise their product. Ask for *balut sa puti* which is more hard-boiled egg than embryo. Crack the end open, drink the juice, peel and eat. Goes well with a beer.

You may prefer to start on cakes and candies of which there is a delectable variety. Rice, as the staple food of the country, is the basis for a surprising number of delicious sweets. *Bibingka* is one delicacy you shouldn't miss. Made of rice, coconut milk, sugar and eggs, it is native cake baked in a clay oven over charcoal. It may be topped by fresh, grated coconut meat, with salted duck's egg, or native white cheese. *Suman* is a type of cake shaped like a big cigar. Made of glutinous rice and wrapped in coconut leaves, it is especially good with mangoes. For variety, it may be fried and dipped in sugar. *Puto* is a sweet steamed rice cake sold by ambulant vendors, as is corn on the cob or *maize,* which is eaten as a snack.

If you're a beer drinker, ask for a *San Miguel.* It's the only beer produced in the country and very good it is. Philippine rum is vastly underrated.

Filipinos have rather cosmopolitan palates and there are restaurants to suit any taste and pocketbook. Most of the better ones are not far from the major hotels. Meals can be reasonable, but what with food and drinks combined, the price can rise surprisingly. In this list we have broken down the restaurants into the following categories to give you some idea of the price ranges. Prices are for dinner for two, including drinks, tax, and tip: *First Class, P450–P700 and up; Moderate, P350–P450 and up; Inexpensive, P200–P350 and up.*

METRO MANILA

First Class

Au Bon Vivant. 1133 L. Guerrero St., Ermita, also at Makati Shopping Center, offers French-style cooking.

Galing-Galing. On L. Guerrero St., Ermita. Specializes in native Filipino dishes.

Los Hidalgos. Calle Real, Intramuros. Traditional Filipino dishes with Iberian influences, in an Old Manila atmosphere.

L'Hirondelle. At the Manila Mandarin, where the ultimate in Continental cuisine is expertly prepared and courteously served.

Madrid. On E. de los Santos Ave., deluxe, with Spanish specialties and atmosphere.

Maynila. On the ground floor, Manila Hotel. Filipino cuisine with a Continental flair in turn-of-the-century art nouveau setting.

Nielson Tower. On Makati Ave. Serves Continental food, but is better known for its antebellum Philippine cuisine, imaginatively conceived and served. (Open to nonmembers from 5:30 P.M.)

Port Orient. At the Manila Hilton, has gourmet delicacies from Filipino, Chinese, and Japanese cuisines, served in a delightfully typical Polynesian atmosphere.

Prince Albert Rôtisserie. At the Inter-Continental Hotel, serves succulent steaks and the very finest of vintage wines.

La Table du Baron, On 2nd floor, Holiday Inn. Regular French cooking in Louis XIII ambience. Specializes in seafood.

La Tasca. 8426 Mercedes St., Makati. Excellent Spanish dishes in tastefully decorated Iberian dining hall.

Via Mare. At Legaspi Village Makati, has some of the best seafood in town. The atmosphere is casual yet elegant.

Moderate

Adriatico. Corner Remedios and Adriatico, Malate. Features Filipino cuisine and snacks.

Alba's. The best Spanish food in the country. Complete with Moorish décor and Castilian cuisine. At Doña Narcisa Bldg., Paseo de Roxas, Makati.

Alfredo's. T. Morato Ave., Quezon City. Country-style steaks.

Alta Vista. Specializes in Filipino cuisine. Features Filipino dances. Has a glass-paneled cocktail lounge overlooking Roxas Blvd. and the Bay area.

Bistro Burgos. In P. Burgos, Makati. Continental cuisine and ambience.

Casa Guadalupe. At Santa Rita corner E. de Los Santos Ave. Delicious Spanish cooking. Taverna ambience.

El Comedor. 1555 Adriatico St. Authentic Spanish and European cuisine.

Cosa Nostra. Mabini near Remedios, Malate. Small but excellent Italian ambience and cuisine. Plays Caruso records.

Di'Marks. On Tafat Ave. Specializes in pizza and pasta.

Dino's Ristorante. On Makati Ave. Specializes in good Italian food.

L'Eau Vive. 1499 Paz Mendoza Guazon Ave. Excellent French cooking, with banquet rooms, coffee shop.

The Flame. On Roxas Blvd. Features daily fashion shows while you eat. Western and native cuisine. Supper club music.

The Goblet. On Roces Ave., Quezon City. Specializes in quality steaks with personalized service.

Gourmet's Inn. On United Nations Ave., near Roxas Blvd. Some of the best steaks in town.

The Grove. On Makati Ave. A new restaurant offering practically every well-known regional native dish in the Philippines. The cooking is excellent, and a great variety of dishes to choose from. Native décor.

Guernica's. Pasay Rd., cor. EDSA; also on Ermita and Malate. Spanish and continental cuisine, Paella and Leugua are specialties. Spanish music while you dine.

Italian Village. On E. de los Santos Ave. Pizza and spaghetti.

Kasbah. At Greenbelt, Legaspi Village, Makati. Arab cuisine. Elegant middle-eastern ambience.

Luau. South end of Roxas Blvd. Carries South Pacific motif. Excellent music and cuisine.

La Mancha. Magallanes Center, Makati. Good for cocktails, intimate gatherings. Spanish dishes specialty.

Mario's. On Makati Ave. Sizzling steaks. Continental cuisine and cozy atmosphere. Dinner music. Catering services.

Mariposa. On T. M. Kalaw, Ermita, specializes in "aphrodisiac" seafood as well as conventional European and American dishes. Marine décor inside.

Moulin Rouge. At 5347 Gen. Luna, Makati. Open for lunch and supper with a French chef. Perhaps the best French cuisine in town, with typical Parisian appointments and French romantic music while you dine.

Open Steak House. 3 Zamboanga St. "Home-cooked" steaks.

Orfeo Manila. On Gen. Malvar, Malate. Artists' and writers' hangout, serving snacks, wide variety of espresso coffee, and daiquiris; art nouveau ambience in a Filipino setting.

Patio Solana. On Adriatico, Ermita. Continental cuisine. Art and nature combine to create unique, pleasant ambience for dining. Try the roast fillet or beef tenderloin.

Plaza. Makati Commercial center. Filipino, American, and European dishes.

The Pub. 7 Miramar, Magallanes Village, Makati. A cosmopolitan crowd favorite, specializing in European dishes and draught beer.

Pulupandan. 7829 Makati Ave. Traditional native cuisine at its best. Nightly Philippine cultural show. With conference rooms, catering service.

Romulus. On Roxas Blvd. Restaurant and nightclub, with banquet, wedding, party facilities and services, continuous orchestra and combo music. International cuisine.

The Satellite. Another revolving restaurant, on the top floor of Hotel Enrico, 1324 Leon Guinto St. Continental cuisine, also native dishes.

Sid's. On Imelda Ave., Makati. International cuisine, with duck dishes a specialty.

Sulo. Distinctive décor, features Filipino dancing and food. Located in Makati.

Swiss Inn. General Luna St. Good Swiss and European food, informal, pleasant bar, hotel upstairs, opens early and stays open late.

La Taverna. On Adriatico, Ermita. Typical Italian food and wine.

Taxco. 64 South Ave., Quezon City. Mexican food specialties, disco every night. "Mariachi" serenade, catering service.

2001. Revolving restaurant on top floor of the Manila Royal Hotel on C. Palanca St., provides a bird's-eye-view of the city in all directions. Continental cuisine.

Wienerwald. At Greenbelt Park, Makati. Offers Continental dishes cooked with German flair and good blue cheese dressing.

Zamboanga. At Makati Ave. Some of the specialties of the house are the deep-sea crabs caught in the Zamboanga and Sulu sea, seawater catfish from Laguna de Bay, clams steamed and served in bamboo baskets, rice spiced with a mixture of various seafoods.

Inexpensive

Aristocrat. On Roxas Blvd., is open 24 hours a day.

B & B. On M. Adriatico, Malate. Featuring delicious, exotic Singapore dishes, e.g., chicken rice, assorted curries, *gado gado, tauhugoreng,* egg-sambal and *babi-pangang.*

Barrio Fiesta. On Buendia Ave., Makati; also on Cubao, Quezon City. Features native cuisine, with *kari-kari* and crispy *pata* as specialties.

Bronze Pot. At Escolta in downtown Manila. A favorite hangout of businessmen and office workers. Specialties: American, Chinese, and Filipino dishes.

Bulakena. Roxas Blvd. Open-air and air-conditioned, supper club, with combo and vocalist.

Bungalow. 2102 Roxas Blvd., Pasay City. Specializes in native dishes, homemade cakes for all occasions, "takehome" foods, with banquet and catering facilities.

Casa Marcos. Way down at the end of Roxas Blvd., but is worth the trip if you like Spanish cooking.

Cheers. 1230–1240 Gen. Luna St., Ermita. Specializing in native cuisine, but also offers European dishes. Has flower and gift shop, "fruiteria," mini art gallery, catering service, and private rooms for executive meetings and luncheons, as well as dinners.

D & E. At Quezon Blvd. Ext. in Quezon City. Features Filipino food on moving trays led by the waiters and Western cuisine à la carte. Banquet facilities are available.

Fast Food Center. At Makati Commercial Center, Greenhills Commercial Center in San Juan, and Ali Mall in Cubao, where you can find the widest choice of American, European and native, Chinese, Japanese, and other Oriental dishes at moderate prices and need to be served quickly.

Fish Fun. 1799 M. Adriatico St., Ermita. Popular native cuisine.

Jade Vine. On United Nations Ave. Will give you *lechón* if you want it.

Josephine's. At Cubao and Pasay. Popular for its fresh seafoods.

Max's. Manila's well-known fried-chicken house, with branches, one on Roxas Blvd., another in Quezon City, one more in Greenbelt Park in Makati.

Patio Kamalig. 2160 Taft Ave. Ext. Specializes in *Binacol* soup, *lechón kawaili* and *kare-kare,* all favorite Filipino dishes.

Remedios. 462 Remedios, Malate. Offers Pampango dishes and delicacies.

Sinugba. An experience in dining the Filipino traditional way—"Kamayan" or eating with your hands. Native cuisine. At 800 Pasay Rd, Makati.

Taza de Oro. VIP Building, Roxas Blvd. Popular with leading newsmen.

Turo-Turo Sa Nayon. Philippine Cultural Village (Nayong Filipino), Airport Ave. Native dishes from various regions of the Philippines.

Chinese

Manila is full of Chinese restaurants, mainly Cantonese. In downtown Manila, there are large *panciterias* serving hundreds of persons at the same time.

First Class

The Hotel Mabuhay's **Peking House** and Hyatt Regency Manila's **Mandarin Room** specialize in Peking dishes.

Moderate

Eastern House, Montinola Bldg., Ermita, Fookinese food; **Kowloon House** on 1533 Mabini St., Cantonese *dimsum;* **Sze-Chuan House,** at Roxas Blvd., spicy Szechuan dishes; Aristocrat's **Sunya,** on Roxas Blvd., Shanghai food. The **Sulo,** in Makati, has Szechuan cuisine. **See Kee's** on Ongpin, Binondo, Cantonese food; and the **Shantung,** 494 Echaque, serves northern Chinese dishes. Also good: **Dynasty,** on A. Mabini; **Golden Peking,** at 550 Edsa, Quezon City; **New Carvajal** on 636 Carvajal St. **Aberdeen Court** on Makati Ave.; **China Park** on Plaza Ferguson; **Kublai Khan** at Greenhills Com-Center on Ortigas Ave.; **Peony** on P. Faura St.; **Shantung** on C. Palanca St.; **Sing-Ya** on 1064 San Marcelino St.; **Palace** on 1431 A. Mabini; **Moon Palace** on 660 Shaw Blvd., Mandaluyong; **Suntal** at 482 P. Faura St., Ermita; and **Canton House** at 534 Quezon Blvd., Q.C. serve basic Chinese food.

Inexpensive

Hongkong House, 1015 M.H. del Pilar, Ermita, serves proletarian Chinese food. **Mr. Poon's** on Mabini St., Ermita; and **Diamond,** corner UN Ave. and Del Pilai Sts., Ermita.

Japanese

First Class

Aoi at Century Park Sheraton; **Tempura-Misono** at the Hyatt Regency Manila; **Gojinka** at the Manila Garden; **Shiruko** at 500 P. Burgos St. in Makati; **Kuretake** at Manila Midtown Ramada.

Moderate

Kaneko Makati Ave; **Kimpura** Makati Commercial Center; **New Tokyo** on Makati Ave.; **Yamato** at the Philippine Village Hotel; **Kotobuki** at the Bayview Plaza; **Kirishima** at the Tropical Palace in Paranque; **Chinzan-So** at the Makati Rotary Arcade; **Daiichi** at Magallanes Village in Makati; **Hakata,** Ermita; **Golden Kimono** at Hotel Mirador; **Miyako** at Hotel Aurelio; and the **Furusato** on Roxas Blvd.

Inexpensive

Hakata on M.H. del Pilar in Ermita.

Korean

First Class

The Korea Garden on 5051 Burgos St., Makati.

Moderate

Pine Tree on 1933 A. Mabini St., Ermita; the **Chinzan-So** at the Midland Fastfood Center in Makati.

Inexpensive

Fast Food Center in Makati Commercial Center and in the Ali Mall in Cubao, Quezon City.

Indian

Moderate

India House on 1718 M. Adriatico St., Malate; and at **Kashmir Restaurant** on Makati Ave., Makati.

OUTSIDE MANILA

The dining rooms of hotels in this book are, by and large, the best eating places in the respective towns. A few local establishments rate favorable mention, however. Among them are the following:

Baguio

The hotels mentioned are the best food bets, but **Mario's** on Session Rd. is convenient for lunch or a snack, and the **Rice Bowl** at the bottom of Session Rd. offers satisfactory, if standard, Chinese dishes. If you know someone with privileges at the **Baguio Country Club** and **Camp John Hay,** you'll enjoy the best American food in town.

Legazpi City

The city's businessmen gather at the **Mayon Imperial** restaurant, in the deluxe hotel of the same name. It offers native (Bicol), Japanese and international (American and European) cuisine.

Cebu

For the best Chinese food, the **Majestic** on Colon, oldest street in the Philippines, is recommended. **Eddie's Log Cabin,** owned by a former American GI, has thick sizzling steaks. Some say though that the **Beehive** on F. Ramos has even better ones. For Filipino food, drop by **La Suerte.** It has good chicken and pork adobo, *sinigang,* a sour soup with fish in it, and *utap,* a sweet, flaky Cebuano pastry.

Bacolod City

The restaurants at two hotels, the **Bascon** and the **Sea Breeze,** are recommended.

Iloilo City

The food at the **River Queen Hotel** is acknowledged to be the best in this gracious old city of the Ilongos. The sizzling steak is good, but you should try *pancit Molo,* a soup with a spicy type of meatball wrapped in a special dough that originated in the district of Molo and has become a feast-time favorite all over the country. The banana crackers and a variety of Molo cookies are also something. And they're not something you have to write home about; you can buy them in big cans and take them with you. The **The James,** on Basa St. downtown above Bookworld, offers tasty Chinese dishes.

Zamboanga City

Food at the **Lantaka** restaurant is substantial and reasonable, with the usual variety of dishes.

Davao

For Filipino dishes, try the **Bayanihan** on Anda. For American food, the **Family Club** at the Apo View Hotel is popular. The **Insular Hotel** boasts of an outstanding chef and atmosphere.

NIGHT LIFE. Manila: Check the cultural calendar for concerts, ballets, plays, and other performances. Night life in Manila is fun. Not too many clubs have floorshows, but almost all of them have fine vocalists and orchestras. Hostesses (dancing partners) are at many clubs and bars. Unescorted women are not allowed in these places. Only a few clubs have cover charges and often these have them only on Saturdays. Games of chance are not unknown. Even at the 18.50 pesos for a dollar rate, making the rounds can get expensive if you get carried away by the music and the soft lights.

If you're in a luxurious mood, try the *Abelardo's* at the *Philippine Plaza,* the *Champagne Room* of the new *Manila Hotel,* the *Stargazer* at the *Silahis International, L'Hirondelle* of the *Manila Mandarin, La Table Du Baron* at the *Holiday Inn, Quimbaya* at the *Manila Peninsula, Prince Albert* at the *Intercontinental,*

La Concha at the *Hyatt,* or the *Top of the Hilton.* Cozy drinking and dancing at *1571,* down at the *Hilton,* at the *Circuit* of the *Hyatt Regency, Altitude 49* of the *Manila Garden,* the *Playboy Club* at *Silahis, Where Else?* at the *Manila Intercontinental, Alibi Bar,* at the *Regent of Manila;* and the *Jungle Bar* at the *Manila Hotel.*

Spacious nightclubs with hostesses, are lined up in a row in neighboring Pasay City, on Roxas Blvd. The most popular and reputed to have the prettiest girls is the *Bayside.* The night ends at about 3 a.m. The nightclub becomes the *Bayside Day Club* during the day, music and dancing beginning at noon. Similar clubs nearby include *Amihan, Today, Eduardo's, Pepe's Club Gessekai, Lanai* and *Jimmy's.* It's perfectly proper to take wives and dates to these clubs, though not many do. Also in the vicinity, *D'Wave.* Hostess charge is about P180 to P250 an hour.

For smaller, more intimate spots, we suggest *Nina's Papagayo,* on A. Mabini; a stimulating female vocalist and hot chili and other Mexican dishes. The entertainment in the basement of the Manila Hilton Hotel, has a zestful combo and small dance floor. *5 (Cinco) Litros* on Del Pilar, off UN Ave. The owner and chief entertainer is almost legendary guitarist-folk singer, Taboy. *Tropicana Bar* at the Bay View Plaza, *Sultana & Harana* at the Manila Hilton. *Boiler Room Disco* at Hotel Mirador. *Quene* at the Regent of Manila, *Calesa Bar* at the Hyatt Regency Manila, *Le Boulevardier* at Hotel Intercontinental Manila. *Braukeller* at the Holiday Inn, *Taproom* and *Apre's* at the Manila Hotel, *Siete Pecados* and *Lost Horizon* at Philippine Plaza, *Intramuros* and *Sirena* at the Manila Peninsula, *Olé* at the Manila Garden, *The Clipper* and *The Carousel* at the Manila Mandarin, the *Stargazer* and *Capriccio* at Silahis International, and the *Aztec Bar* at Tower Hotel on A. Mabini.

For unattached males only, there are any number of small dancing and drinking spots. Hostesses if you like. The drinks are on you. These bars include the *Kiss,* on 1130 Alhambra St., *Another World* at Greenbelt Park, Makati, *Connie's* on UN Ave., *High Chaparral* on M.H. del Pilar, the *Guadarama,* on UN Ave., the *Chivas Regal,* on A. Mabini, and the *Experanza,* on A. Mabini. Tips to girls up to you. Some of these clubs boast floor shows—strip shows, that is—but have no regular schedule.

Spanish-style bars include *Guernica's* and *El Bodegon,* both on M. H. del Pilar. It's fun if you happen on an impromptu song fest by members of the Spanish community. *Gloria's* on A. Mabini is a good place for a late dinner and Spanish guitars. The *Manila Overseas Press Club,* on Roxas Blvd., has one of the liveliest combos in town. For jazz aficionados there's *Birds of the Same Feather* on T. Morato in Quezon City and the *Vineyard* on Pasay Rd., Makati.

For those who crave more excitement, there is the *Manila Casino,* at the Philippine Village Hotel. There are also casinos in Cebu and Zamboanga.

Outside Manila, night life is not as hectic, but when available can also be enjoyable and interesting.

For those who want to try provincial night life, Cebu City is probably the best place. The *Yarro* in the suburb of Talisay, some eight miles from the city, is one of the best in this area. Hostesses available, and foreigners are welcome as much for their rarity as their pocket-books.

POSTAL SERVICES. Local delivery: P.60 for ordinary and P1.20 airmail. Overseas airmail: (for every 10 grams) United States, P3.60; Canada, P3.60; Australia, P3.00; Great Britain, P3.60. Airletter costs P2.80, but is good only to countries where ordinary air postage costs P2.80. Overseas surface mail: P2 for the first 20 grams or less, and P2 for each additional 20 grams or fraction thereof.

Telegrams can be sent at your General Post Office, from your nearest telegraph office branch, or from your hotel front desk.

CHURCHES. Everywhere you turn, you'll find churches. Manila's Saturday newspapers carry a complete listing of churches and masses for the week. *Catholic* churches within easy reach of the major hotels include the *Ermita Church,* where masses are held on Sundays and holidays at 5:30, 6:30, 7:15, 8, 9, 10, and 11 A.M. and *Manila Cathedral,* where Sunday and Feastday masses are at 6, 7, 8, 9, 10, 11 A.M., 12 noon, and 6 P.M. Many of the churches have sermons in English, including these two. *Protestant* services are held by the English-speaking congregations of practically every sect. The *Church of the Holy Trinity* (Episcopal) is located at 664 San Luis, Ermita, *St. Luke's Pro-cathedral* at 1015 Magdelena St., *Jewish* sabbath services are held at the Temple Emil, 1963 Taft Ave.

MEDICAL SERVICES. Manila's medical facilities are possibly the best in Asia. You can have your choice of Filipino, American, and Chinese physicians, dentists, and hospitals. Many of the big American and European drug concerns have branches here; so the drugs you'll see in the *boticas* (drugstores) will be familiar. A few excellent hospitals are: *Manila Doctors Hospital.* UN Ave.; *Medical Center Manila.* General Luna St.; the *Manila Sanitarium,* on Donada St., operated by Seventh Day Adventists; and the newest, most luxurious hospital, *Makati Medical Center,* off Ayala Ave. in Makati. For information or emergency consultation, refer to the Yellow Pages of the PLDT Telephone Directory.

DRINKING WATER. Absolutely safe in Manila and environs. Generally good elsewhere in population centers.

USEFUL ADDRESSES. Embassies and Consulates. The *Embassy of the United States* is on Manila's Roxas Blvd., within walking distance of all major hotels. The *British Embassy* is at Legaspi Village, Makati; *Canadian Consulate General,* Ayala Ave., Makati; *Australian Embassy,* Paseo Roxas, Makati; *Irish Consulate,* UN Ave., Ermita.

Emergencies. In Manila, should you wish to call the *police,* telephone 59–90–11; a *fire* can be reported at telephone 58–11–76. *Ambulances* may be summoned from the Philippine General Hospital (tel. 59–60–61) or from the North General Hospital (tel. 26–45–11); the Capitol Medical Center (tel. 99–15–71); the Manila Medical Center (tel. 59–16–61); the GSIS General Hospital (tel. 98–66–60); the Makati Medical Center (tel. 815–9911); the Philippine Heart Center for Asia (tel. 98–04–21).

Media Clubs. *Manila Overseas Press Club,* Roxas Blvd., tel. 831–3258 and 831–3321; *National Press Club,* Magallanes Dr., tel. 47–49–14; *Philippine International Friendship Organization,* 1580 Taft Ave., tel. 59–12–96.

General Information. You'll find answers to most of your questions, along with tourist literature in English and ready smiles, at the Ministry of Tourism, MOT Bldg., Agrifina Circle, Manila, tel. 50–17–03 and 50–23–84, or at its overseas offices: at Los Angeles, USA, tel. (213) 487–4525; in Toronto, Canada, tel. (416) 922–8880; in London, tel. (01) 439–348; in Madrid, tel. 410–4419; in

Chicago, USA, tel. (312) 782–1707; in New York, USA, tel. (212) 575–7915; in Frankfurt, West Germany, tel. (0611) 747–725; in Tokyo, Japan, tel. (03) 464–3635 or 464–3690; in Osaka, Japan; tel. (06) 535–5071 or 535–5072; in Sydney, Australia, tel. (02)267–2695 or 267–2756; in Hong Kong, tel. 667–610; and in Singapore, tel. 235–2184/5.

LEAVING THE PHILIPPINES. There is a terminal fee of 200 pesos on departure.

FIVE-MINUTE TAGALOG

Pilipino, based on Tagalog, is the national language. There are more than one hundred linguistic, cultural and racial groups in the Philippines speaking a total of about 87 dialects. English is widely spoken and understood and still remains the basic tool of instruction in schools. It is being used in business, government and in everyday communication.

English	*Tagalog (Phonetic)*
One	Ee-sah
Two	Da-la-wah
Three	Taht-low
Four	Ah-paht
Five	Lee-maw
Six	Ah-neem
Seven	Pee-toe (toe of your foot)
Eight	Wah-low
Nine	See-yahm
Ten	Sam-poo
Eleven-Nineteen	(Prefix the above with "Lah-bing," e.g., 11 is Lah bing-Ee-sah.)
100	Ee-sahng dahn
1,000	Ee-sahng lee-bow (Bow as in archery.)
Yes	Oh-oh
No	Hindi
Left	Kah-lee-wah
Right	Kan-nahm
Stop	Hin-to
Go	Lah-Kahd
Thank you	Sah-lah-maht
Yesterday	Kah-ha-pohn
Today	Nga-yohn
Tomorrow	Boo-Kass
How much	Mahg-kah-no
Toilet	Kah-seal-yahss
Water	Too-big
Good morning	Mah-gahn-dang-umaga poh
Goodbye	Pah-ah-lahm na-poh
Welcome, good luck, goodbye	Mah-boo-high (This is also the Filipino toast, and is written "Mabuhay".)
Hospital	Pah-gahmu-tan
Airport	Pah-li-pah-rahn
Police station	Istah-syon nahng poolish
Bus station	Istah-syon nahng booze

INDEX

In this Index, the following abbreviations have been used:
H: hotels, motels, etc.; R: restaurants

General

BRUNEI
Practical Information

Geographical

BURMA
Practical Information

Geographical

HONG KONG
Practical Information

Geographical

INDONESIA
Practical Information

Geographical

MACAU
Practical Information

Geographical

MALAYSIA

Practical Information

Geographical

PHILIPPINES
Practical Information

Geographical

SINGAPORE
Practical Information

Geographical

TAIWAN
Practical Information

Geographical

THAILAND
Practical Information

Geographical